D1448612

KODANSHA'S **furigana** JAPANESE-ENGLISH DICTIONARY

KODANSHA'S furigana JAPANESE-ENGLISH DICTIONARY

The essential dictionary for all students of Japanese

Based on THE NEW WORLD JAPANESE-ENGLISH DICTIONARY FOR JUNIORS
by Masatoshi Yoshida & Yoshikatsu Nakamura

KODANSHA INTERNATIONAL
Tokyo·New York·London

Note: This dictionary is the full kana version of *Kodansha's Romanized Japanese-English Dictionary* which was adapted for native English language speakers from *The New World Dictionary for Juniors* by Masatoshi Yoshida and Yoshikatsu Nakamura published by Kodansha Ltd.

Distributed in the United States by Kodansha America, Inc., 575 Lexington Avenue, New York, New York 10022, and in the United Kingdom and continental Europe by Kodansha Europe Ltd., 95 Aldwych, London WC2B 4JF.

Published by Kodansha International Ltd., 17-14 Otowa 1-chome, Bunkyo-ku, Tokyo 112-8652 and Kodansha America Inc.

First Edition, 1995

00 01 10 9 8 7 6 5
ISBN 7-7700-1983-1

Designed by Tomoyuki Adachi
Set on a Macintosh in 明朝, *Helvetica*, and Palatino by NAVIX, Tokyo
Printed in Japan by Dai-Nippon Printing Company

Library of Congress Cataloging-in-Publication Data
A catalog record for this book is available from the Library of Congress

Contents

Publisher's Note

KODANSHA'S FURIGANA JAPANESE-ENGLISH DICTIONARY is not the only guide to the Japanese language that has been edited and designed specially for non-native learners. A number of other titles come readily to mind. Indeed, in 1992, we ourselves published our first such dictionary, *Kodansha's Romanized Japanese-English Dictionary,* and then followed with an abridged, pocket-edition of the same work in 1993. The present book has also been edited from the data-base of the original romanized dictionary. It contains almost all the same entry-words, compounds, phrases, and example sentences; very few definitions and translations of example sentences have been changed.

Why then the need for another Japanese-English dictionary for non-native learners? KODANSHA'S FURIGANA JAPANESE-ENGLISH DICTIONARY is different from its predecessor and other similar dictionaries in that it reflects the latest rationale and methodology for teaching Japanese in the United States, Europe, and Australia. Increasingly, influential curriculums in Japanese-as-a-second-language education have emphasized the importance of students mastering the two kana scripts from the outset of their studies. As a result, few Japanese-language programs now use romanization in their instruction. In response to this new trend, Kodansha International decided to publish a basic Japanese-English dictionary for non-native learners already familiar with the hiragana and katakana scripts. To this end, small kana (called **furigana** or **rubi**) have been printed above every kanji appearing in this book, making it possible for the beginner, who has learnt kana, to read even the most difficult and obscure kanji at a glance.

The publisher is heavily indebted to Timothy Vance, editor of *Kodansha's Romanized Japanese-English Dictionary,* who took on the task of completely reworking a Japanese-English dictionary compiled for junior-high-school students and published by Kodansha in 1990 (*The New World Japanese-English Dictionary for Juniors*), and to the editors of this original dictionary, Masatoshi Yoshida and Yoshikatsu Nakamura, for graciously consenting to let their work serve as the basis for this revision. The publisher is also grateful to Tomoyuki Adachi for his timely-assistance in the design of this dictionary and the staff of Navix, whose efforts were indispensable to the completion of the book.

Organization of Entries

1. Entry Words

Each entry word is given first in hiragana and/or katakana, and then where appropriate in kanji. The kanji included in this book are those most likely to be known by educated Japanese and include many that that do not appear on the Ministry of Education's list of 1,945 kanji for general use (常用漢字表(じょうようかんじひょう)).

For some entry words there are alternative Japanese representations involving different kanji but no consistent usage distinction. In such cases, the alternative representations are separated by a comma, as in the following example.

あたたかい 暖(あたた)かい, 温(あたた)かい

When there is a consistently observed distinction in kanji usage, different senses of what is presumably the same word are treated as separate entries. For example, 暑(あつ)い and 熱(あつ)い are listed as separate entry words even though the relationship between the two is obvious. As lexicography, this practice is questionable, but it simplifies cross referencing (see Section 2.j below).

As in all Japanese dictionaries, verbs and adjectives are listed in the informal nonpast affirmative form. If a verb or adjective listed in this dictionary is irregular, it is marked with the notation *{Irreg.}* immediately after the ordinary Japanese writing of the entry word. Unless there is an explicit notation to the contrary, any verb listed in this dictionary with final **-iru** or **-eru** is **ichidan**. If a verb ending in **-iru** or **-eru** is **godan**, its entry in this dictionary contains the notation *{5}* immediately after the ordinary Japanese representation of the entry word. The following entries illustrate how these notations are used.

くる 来(く)る *{Irreg.}*...

はしる 走(はし)る *{5}*...

For details, consult Appendix 1.

2. Definitions

a. Entry Structure

For some entry words only a single definition is provided, but most entries include more than one definition. The following schematic entry shows how definitions are positioned in this dictionary.

エントリー・ワード *1. definition 1ai, definition 1aii; definition 1bi, definition 1bii 2. definition 2ai, definition 2aii; definition 2bi, definition 2bii*

If the definitions can be divided into clearly distinct ranges of meaning, those ranges are numbered. This can be seen in the schematic entry above, where two clearly distinct meaning ranges of the entry word are distinguished. Within each clearly distinct range, closely related meanings are separated by semicolons, and there are two closely related meanings within each clearly distinct meaning range. Commas separate synonymous definitions and each meaning is represented by two synonymous definitions.

There is no clear dividing line between synonymous definitions and closely related definitions, but the distinction between commas and semicolons is useful in the placement of cross-references and notes (see Sections 2.j and 2.k below).

A few definitions include diagonal slashes to separate alternative words and avoid repetition. The following entry illustrates this.

まさる 勝(まさ)る *to be/become better, to be/become superior*

b. Parts of Speech

The entries in this dictionary do not include part-of-speech labels, but the part of speech of any entry word will be clear to users who know basic Japanese grammar.

The definitions for verbs are consistently given in the English infinitive form (that is, containing the word "to"), and this convention serves to distinguish verbs from other parts of speech. For example, the verb 賭(か)ける is defined as *to bet, to wager*, whereas the noun 賭(か)け is defined as *bet*.

The definitions for nouns do not contain articles (*the* or *a/an*) except when the presence of an article can serve to avoid potential confusion with a different part of speech or a different noun meaning. For example, 井戸(いど) is defined as *a well* to make clear that it is not an adverb meaning *well*, and ドレス is defined as *a dress* to make it clear that it does not mean *dress* in the sense of attire.

Part-of-speech labels are used in some explanatory notes (see Section 2.k below).

c. Comparing Alternative Definitions

Needless to say, none of the entries in this dictionary has a perfect set of definitions, but a great deal of effort has gone into making the definition sets as precise as possible within realistic limits. Many potential misunderstandings can easily be avoided simply by looking at all the alternative definitions provided. For example, *to escape* is given as a definition both for 漏れる and for 逃げる, but the basic difference between the meanings of these two Japanese words is clear from the alternative definitions provided in each entry, as shown below.

もれる 漏れる *to leak out, to escape…*

にげる 逃げる *to run away; to escape…*

d. Tildes

In many entries definitions are given not for the entry word alone but for a short phrase containing the entry word. A tilde (～) is used to show the position of the entry word in the phrase. For example, in the entry below, the definition given is not for 圧倒 alone but for 圧倒する.

あっとう 圧倒 ～する *to overwhelm…*

Three types of phrases are especially common in this dictionary. The first is a noun followed by する, the type illustrated in the entry above. An entry of this form indicates that although the entry word is a kind of noun, it does not ordinarily occur as a subject or object in sentences. Instead it combines with する to to serve as a predicate.

The second common type is noun followed by の, as in the entry below.

ちゅうこ 中古 ～の *used, secondhand*

An entry of this form indicates that although the entry word is a kind of noun, it does not ordinarily occur as a subject or object in sentences. Instead, it combines with の to modify a following noun. In most cases, an entry word of this type can also combine with a form of the copula (だ, です, etc.) to serve as a predicate or with に to serve as an adverb.

The third common type is adjectival noun followed by な, as in the entry below.

じゅんしん 純真 ～な *pure-hearted, innocent*

An entry of this form indicates that although the entry word is a kind of noun, it does not ordinarily occur as a subject or object in sentences. Instead, it combines with な to modify a following noun. In most cases, an entry word of this type can also combine with a form of the copula (だ, です, etc.) to serve as a predicate or with に to serve as an adverb.

In some cases, a short phrase containing the entry word has the same meaning as the entry word alone. Parentheses are used to show that the phrase combination is optional. For example, the following entry indicates that the definition applies to はるばる alone as well as to はるばると.

はるばる (〜と) *all the way, covering a great distance...*

There are also cases in which two alternative short phrases have the same meaning. Diagonal slashes are used to show the alternatives, as in the following entry.

じゅんすい 純粋(じゅんすい) 〜な／の *pure...*

In entries which contain numbers indicating clearly distinct ranges of meaning (see Section 2.a above), the placement of phrases with tildes indicates which definitions apply to the phrase. Placement before the first number indicates that all the definitions apply to the phrase. For example, in the entry below, all the definitions apply to 駄目(だめ)な.

だめ 駄目(だめ) 〜な *1....*

Placement after a number, on the other hand, indicates that only the definitions in that particular meaning range apply to the phrase. For example, in the entry below, only the definitions in meaning range *1.* apply to つるつるの.

つるつる *1.* 〜の ...

e. Speech-Level Labels

Some entry words are labeled as belonging to a particular speech level. The following labels are used.

【COL.】Words marked as colloquial are characteristic of casual conversation and are not likely to be used in formal situations.

【CRUDE】Words marked as crude are felt to be inappropriate in polite conversation.

【FORMAL】Words marked as formal are characteristic of formal situations and are not likely to be used in casual conversation. This category includes predicate words that are more polite than semi-formal (see below).

【HON.】This label is used for two types of words. One type is predicate words which express respect for someone by honoring the subject of a sentence. The other type is nouns that express respect for their referents. Especially important among words of the second type are kinship terms which are used to refer to the relatives of someone outside one's own family. Some of these honorific kinship terms can also be used to address one's own relatives who are higher in status. (For example, it is normal to address one's older brother as お兄(にい)さん, but it is not normal to address one's younger brother as 弟(おとうと)さん.)

【HUM.】 This label is used for two types of words. One type is predicate words which express respect for someone else by humbling the subject of a sentence. The other type is nouns that express respect for someone else by humbling their referents.

【SEMI-FORMAL】 This label refers to predicate words in what the Japanese refer to as ですます体(たい). The semi-formal style, in contrast to the informal style, expresses politeness toward the person(s) the speaker is addressing.

In an entry which contains numbers indicating clearly distinct ranges of meaning (see Section 2.a above), the placement of a speech-level label indicates the definitions to which it applies. Placement before the first number indicates that a speech-level label applies to all the definitions of the entry word. For example, in the entry below, the label means that ちんぴら is colloquial in all its definitions.

ちんぴら 【COL.】 *1. young hoodlum, young tough*
2. low-ranking gangster, punk

Placement after a number, on the other hand, indicates that a label applies only to the definitions in that particular meaning range. For example, the label in the entry below means that 平(たい)らげる is colloquial only in meaning range 2.

たいらげる 平(たい)らげる *1. to put down, to suppress; to subjugate*
2. 【COL.】 *to eat up completely*

Many speech-level labels include a cross-reference, as in the entry below.

みょうにち 明日(みょうにち) 【FORMAL for 明日(あした)】 *tomorrow*

To avoid lengthy repetitions, no definitions are provided for some of the entry words which are followed by speech-level labels containing cross-references. The entry below refers the user to まま for definitions.

まんま 【COL. for まま】

f. Parenthesized Material

Many individual definitions in this dictionary contain parenthesized material to specify a meaning precisely. The parenthesized portion of such a definition would not ordinarily be used in a natural English translation of a Japanese sentence containing the entry word, but a definition without the parenthesized portion would be misleadingly broad. The following entry illustrates this.

さくぶん 作文(さくぶん) *(school) composition, (school) essay...*

g. Collocations

Many individual definitions in this dictionary include material in parentheses. Such material is not part of the meaning of the entry word; it simply provides a context that makes the intended meaning of the definition clear. For example, in the entry below, the definition under *2.* means **record** in the sense that record has in the collocation **world record**. (The entry word alone does NOT mean world record.)

レコード ...
2. (world) record...

h. Superordinate Terms

In may cases, the intended meaning of a potentially ambiguous definition is specified by providing a superordinate term in double parentheses following the definition. A superordinate term denotes a broad category within which the definition falls. The two entries below illustrate.

タンク *tank ((container))*

せんしゃ 戦車(せんしゃ) *tank ((vehicle))*

i. American and British Usage

In cases where a difference in usage between American English and British English is common knowledge, the labels (US) and (UK) precede the appropriate definitions. The following entry illustrates.

サッカー *(US) soccer, (UK) football*

There are certainly many additional differences of which the editors are unaware, and no attempt whatever has been made to deal with differences in other English-speaking countries. American spellings are used exclusively throughout, and the English translations of the example sentences (see Section 5 below) are all based on the norms of American English usage.

j. Cross References

Three types of cross-references appear in this dictionary (in addition to the cross-references contained in speech-level labels; see Section 2.e above). A cross-reference to a synonym is marked with a single-pointed arrow (→), and a cross-reference to an antonym is marked with a double-pointed arrow (↔).

When a cross-reference is to a word or phrase that is not itself an entry word, the entry word under which the item referred to appears is given in parentheses and marked with the notation s.v. For example, in the entry below, the cross-reference means that 魅力的(みりょくてき)な is a synonym for チャーミングな and that 魅力的(みりょくてき)な is listed under the entry word 魅力(みりょく).

チャーミング ～な *charming, attractive* [→ 魅力的(みりょくてき)な (s.v. 魅力(みりょく))]

A pointing hand (☞) marks a cross-reference to another location in the dictionary and is used to avoid repeating the same definition in more than one place. The reference may be to an alternative form of the same word (an abbreviation or a longer form), as in the first entry below, or simply to another entry word under which the item in question is defined, as in the second entry below.

トイレット [☞ トイレ]

という [☞ 言(い)う]

When a cross-reference refers to another item within the same entry, the notation (above) or (below) appears at the end of the cross-reference, as in the following entry.

デッキ...
3. [☞ テープデッキ (below)]
テープデッキ tape deck

In entries which contain numbers separating clearly distinct ranges of meaning or semicolons separating closely related meanings (see Section 2.a above), the placement of a cross-reference indicates the definitions to which it applies. Placement before the first number indicates that a cross-reference applies to all the definitions of the entry word. For example, in the entry below, the cross-reference means that 鈍(にぶ)い is an antonym for all the definitions of 鋭(するど)い.

するどい 鋭(するど)い [[↔ 鈍(にぶ)い]] *1. sharp, good for cutting...*
2. keen, acute, sensitive...

Placement at the beginning of a set of closely related meanings separated by semicolons (and directly after a number if there is one) indicates that a cross-reference applies to all the closely related meanings in that particular meaning range. For example, in the entry below, the cross-reference means that 片方(かたほう) is a synonym for all the definitions in meaning range *1.* but not for those in other meaning ranges.

いっぽう 一方(いっぽう) *1.* [[→ 片方(かたほう)]] *one side (of two); one (of two), one (of a pair)...*

Placement at the end of a list of definitions indicates that a cross-reference applies only to the single set of synonymous definitions that immediately precede it. For example, in the entry below, the cross-reference means that 補う is a synonym for 足す in the sense of *to supply, to supplement with* but not in the sense of *to add* in general in meaning range *1.* or in the sense of *to add* in arithmetic in meaning range 2.

たす 足す *1. to add; to supply, to supplement with* [→ 補う 2.]
2. to add (in arithmetic)

Many cross-references include a number to indicate reference to a single meaning range of a specified entry word. The cross-reference to 補う in the entry just above is an example.

All cross-references are enclosed in square brackets, but the brackets are double ([[ ]]) when the cross-reference applies to more than a single set of synonymous definitions. The cross-references to 鈍い and 片方 in the entries above illustrate.

k. Explanatory Notes

Many definitions are accompanied by explanatory notes enclosed in parentheses (...). Some of these notes are as short as a single word, while others are quite lengthy.

In entries which contain numbers separating clearly distinct ranges of meaning or semicolons separating closely related meanings (see Section 2.a above), the placement of a note indicates the definitions to which it applies. The rules for placement are the same as those for cross-references (see Section 2.j above). Placement before the first number indicates that a note applies to all the definitions of the entry word. For example, the note in the following entry means that for all the given definitions of 無くなる, the subject must be inanimate.

なくなる 無くなる *(The subject must be inanimate.) 1. to become lost*
2. to run out, to be used up
3. to disappear, to go away

Placement at the beginning of a set of closely related meanings separated by semicolons (and directly after a number if there is one) indicates that a note applies to all the closely related meanings in that particular meaning range. For example, the note in the entry below means that all the definitions of 裂ける are to be understood as intransitive verbs.

さける 裂ける *(intransitive) to tear, to rip; to split, to crack...*

Placement at the end of a list of definitions indicates that a note applies only to the single set of synonymous definitions that immediately precede it. For example, the note in the following example means that 塔 can refer to a building at a Buddhist temple that is usually called a pagoda in English.

とう 塔 *tower; pagoda (at a Buddhist temple)*

Part-of-speech labels are used in some explanatory notes. The terms noun, verb, adverb, adjective, adjectival noun, and particle refer to the Japanese parts of speech traditionally called 名詞, 動詞, 副詞, 形容詞, 形容動詞, and 助詞, respectively. (The terminology used in textbooks written for English-speaking learners varies, but every good textbook has labels for these six categories.)

In a few cases an explanatory note is given instead of a definition rather than as a supplement to a definition. This practice is resorted to when no appropriate English equivalent is available. The following entries illustrate.

-にん -人 *(counter for people; see Appendix 2)*

はいけい 拝啓【FORMAL】*(a salutation used in formal letters)* [↔ 敬具]

1. Works Consulted

The works listed below were important sources of useful information during the process of revising the definitions in this dictionary for English-speaking users.

文化庁『外国人のための基本語用語辞典』第2版 [Agency for Cultural Affairs, Dictionary of Basic Japanese Usage for Foreigners. 1975.]

Eleanor Harz Jorden & Mari Noda, *Japanese: The Spoken Language*, 3 vols. Yale University Press, 1987-1990.

Samuel E. Martin, *A Reference Grammar of Japanese*, revised ed. Tuttle, 1987.

Akira Miura, *English Loanwords in Japanese*. Tuttle, 1979.

Momoo Yamaguchi & Setsuko Kojima, *A Cultural Dictionary of Japan*. Japan Times, 1979.

3. Phrases

Many entries in this dictionary include as examples short phrases containing the entry word. These phrases are given in the ordinary Japanese writing system. For the most part, the kanji usage in these representations is limited in accordance with Ministry of Education conventions. Consequently, many words are represented in kanji as entry words but in hiragana as elements of phrases.

In some cases, repetition is avoided by combining two or more phrases into a single example by enclosing alternative words in special brackets (〔〕). In the entry below, the combined phrase represents the two phrases 強い皮膚 (defined as *strong skin*) and 弱い皮膚(defined as *delicate skin*).

ひふ 皮膚 *skin(of a person or animal)*
強い〔弱い〕皮膚 strong〔delicate〕skin

In many phrases, the capital letters A and B are used to stand for arbitrary nouns in order to illustrate patterns of usage. The phrase given in the following entry illustrates this.

まちがえる 間違える …
2. to mistake
AをBとまちがえる to mistake A for B

There are also cases in which two alternative phrases have the same meaning. Diagonal slashes are used to show the alternatives (as in phrases marked by tildes; see Section 2.d above). The following entry illustrates.

ふつう 普通 *usually, commonly, ordinarily*
普通の／な usual, common; ordinary, unremarkable…

When a phrase has two or more distinct meanings, the sets of definitions are separated by semicolons, as in the entry below.

ほね 骨 *bone…*
骨を折る to break a bone; to take pains, to make efforts

Even if the definitions of phrases involve clearly distinct ranges of meaning (as in the entry above), semicolons are used; numbers are used only for distinct meaning ranges of entry words (see Section 2.a above). Otherwise, the format conventions for phrase definitions are the same as those for entry-word definitions (see Section 2 above).

4. Compounds and Derivatives

Many entries in this dictionary include compounds and/or derivatives containing the entry word. The compound or derivative is given in the ordinary Japanese writing system. Whenever such representations include kanji, the kanji are used unless they are so obscure that even educated Japanese would be unlikely to know them. (This same practice is followed for entry words.)

The ordinary Japanese representation of a compound or derivative is followed by one or more definitions. When a compound has two or more distinct meanings, the sets of definitions are separated by semicolons. As with phrases (see Section 3 above), even if the definitions involve clearly distinct ranges of meaning, semicolons are used; numbers are used only for distinct meaning ranges of entry words (see Section 2.a above). Otherwise, the format conventions for compound and derivative definitions are the same as those for entry-word definitions (see Section 2 above).

5. Example Sentences

Many entries in this dictionary include one or more sample sentences to illustrate typical usages of an entry word, a phrase, a compound, or a derivative. Each example sentence is given first in the ordinary Japanese writing system and then followed by an English translation. For the most part, the kanji usage in the ordinary Japanese representations is limited in accordance with Ministry of Education conventions. Many words are represented in kanji as entry words or as compounds or derivatives (see Section 4 above) but in hiragana as parts of sample sentences. All kanji appearing in the sample sentences have full furigana readings.

The English translations of sample sentences tend to be literal at the expense of naturalness. For example, the translation of the example sentence in the following entry would be more natural as English with **smells bad** or **stinks** rather than is **bad-smelling**, but these more natural translations would obscure the fact that 臭い is an adjective.

くさい 臭い *bad-smelling, smelly*
この部屋は臭いですね。
This room is bad-smelling, isn't it?

When a fairly literal translation of a sample sentence seems likely to be misleading or difficult to comprehend, two translations are provided. The first is natural enough to be easily understood as English, and the second, appended as a note, is labeled as literal. There is no such thing, of course, as an absolutely literal translation; the label simply means relatively literal. The sample sentence in the following entry illustrates this.

とし 年 *1. year*
よいお年をお迎えください。
Have a happy New Year! (Literally: Please greet a good year.)

A few of the sample sentences in this dictionary are proverbs and are identified as such with a note. Many proverbs include archaisms like the obsolete copula form なり in the proverb given in the entry below.

とき 時 *1. (amount of) time, time span...*
時は金なり。(proverb)
Time is money.

List of Symbols

SYMBOL	USE	SEE
{ }	to enclose a notation about verb or adjective conjugation	1
／	to separate alternative words	2.a, 2.d, 3
~	to indicate the location of an entry word in a phrase	2.d
【】	to enclose a speech-level label	2.e
(( ))	to enclose a superordinate term	2.h
(US)	to mark a definition as American usage	2.i
(UK)	to mark a definition as British usage	2.i
[ ]	to enclose a cross-reference	2.j
[[ ]]	to enclose a cross-reference that applies to more than a single set of definitions	2.j
→	to indicate that a cross-reference is to a synonym	2.j
↔	to indicate that a cross-reference is to an antonym	2.j
☞	to indicate that a cross-reference is to a definition listed elsewhere	2.j
〔〕	to enclose alternative words in a combined phrase	3

The Dictionary

ああ *Oh!, Ah! (an interjection expressing surprise or dismay)*
ああ、どうしよう。
Oh! What shall I do?
ああ、びっくりした！
Oh! What a surprise! (Literally: Oh! I was surprised!)

ああ 【COL. for はい】 *yeah (Generally restricted to male speakers.)*
ああ、わかったよ。
Yeah, I understand!

ああ *like that, in that way*
(Like other Japanese demonstratives beginning with あ, ああ has two uses. One is to refer to something which is in sight and relatively far both from the speaker and from the listener. The other is to refer to something not in sight but which is familiar both to the speaker and to the listener.) [↔ こう; そう]
ああいう that kind of [→あんな]

アーケード *1. arcade, passageway with an arched roof*
2. shopping arcade (i.e., a roofed-over passageway or street with shops on both sides)

アース *(US) (electrical) ground, (UK) (electrical) earth*

アーチ *1. arch ((shape))*
2. archway

アーチェリー *archery*

アーチスト *artist*

アーモンド *almond*

アール *are (unit of area)*
—アール (counter for ares; see Appendix 2)

あい 藍 *1. Japanese indigo plant*
2. indigo dye
藍色 indigo color

あい 愛 *love, affection* [→ 愛情]
子供に対する母の愛はとても深いです。
A mother's love for her child is very deep.

あいかぎ 合鍵 *duplicate key*

あいかわらず 相変わらず *as ever, as before, as usual, still*
道子さんは相変わらず親切です。
Michiko is as kind as ever.
由美さんは相変わらずテニスに夢中です。
Yumi is still crazy about tennis.
木村さんは相変わらず勉強家です。
As before, Ms. Kimura is a studious person.

あいきどう 合気道 *aikido (a Japanese martial art)*

アイキュー IQ [→ 知能指数 (s.v. 知能)]

あいきょう 愛嬌 *charm, amiability*

あいこく 愛国 *love of one's country*
愛国者 patriot
愛国心 patriotic feeling

あいさつ 挨拶 *greeting, courteous expression*
私たちは毎朝あいさつを交わします。
We exchange greetings every morning.
あいさつする to greet
生徒たちは校長先生に「おはようございます」とあいさつします。
The students greet the principal, "Good morning."

あいしょう 愛称 *nickname, pet name*

あいしょう 相性 *compatibility in temperament*
相性がいい to be congenial, to be compatible
あの二人は相性のいいペアです。
Those two are a congenial pair.

あいじょう 愛情 *love, affection*
淳子さんは家族に強い愛情を持っている。
Junko has a strong love for her family.
愛情を込めて with love, with affection

あいじん 愛人 *(illicit) lover*

あいず 合図 *sign, signal*

合図する to make a sign, to signal

準備ができたら、合図します。

When the preparations are done, I'll signal.

アイスクリーム *ice cream*

アイススケート *1. ice skates*

2. ice skating

アイスホッケー *ice hockey*

あいする 愛する *{Irreg.} to love*

美知子さんを愛しているよ。

I love Michiko!

王子はシンデレラを愛するようになった。

The prince fell in love with Cinderella.

あいそ 愛想 *amiability, affability; courtesy, civility*

愛想がいい amiable, affable

あいそう 愛想 [☞ 愛想]

あいだ 間 *1. time during, time while* [→ 内]

夏休みの間に本をたくさん読みます。

I will read a lot of books during the summer vacation.

勉強している間は静かにしてください。

While I am studying, please be quiet.

長い間 for a long time

2. area between; time period between

その島と本州の間には橋が架かっている。

A bridge has been built between that island and Honshu.

7時と8時の間に電話してください。

Please telephone between 7:00 and 8:00.

3. connection between, relationship among

そのゲームは子供たちの間で人気がある。

That game is popular among children.

それは浜田さんと私の間の秘密でした。

That was a secret between Mr. Hamada and me.

あいだがら 間柄 *relationship (between people)*

あいつ 【CRUDE】 *that person*

(Like other Japanese demonstratives beginning with あ, あいつ has two uses. One is to refer to a person who is in sight and relatively far both from the speaker and from the listener. The other is to refer to a person who is not in sight but who is familiar both to the speaker and to the listener.) [↔こいつ; そいつ]

あいついで 相次いで *one after another, in succession*

あいづち 相槌 (This term refers to words or short phrases that are used to assure a person speaking that one is listening. Words for yes (はい, ええ, うん) are the most common, but other typical examples include なるほど, そうですね, etc.)

相づちを打つ to use aizuchi

あいて 相手 *1. partner, companion*

洋子さんを相手に英語の練習をしました。

I practiced English with Yoko as my partner.

酒の相手 drinking partner

2. opponent, rival

テニスの相手 tennis opponent

相手にとって不足はない to be a worthy opponent

遊び相手 playmate

話し相手 person to talk with

相談相手 adviser

アイディア *idea* [→ 考え]

その時いいアイディアが浮かびました。

A good idea occurred to me at that time.

アイドル *1. idol, worshipped object*

2. idol, idolized person, popular famous person

あいにく 生憎 *unfortunately*

あいにくおばあさんは留守でした。

Unfortunately, your grandmother was out.

あいにくの／な unfortunate, inopportune

あいにくの天気ですね。

It's bad weather, isn't it?

アイヌ *Ainu (the aboriginal people of northern Japan)*

アイヌ語 the Ainu language

あいまい 曖昧 ～な *vague, ambiguous, obscure*

洋子さんはよくあいまいな返事をします。
Yoko often gives a vague answer.

アイロン *iron ((appliance))*

Aにアイロンをかける to iron A

あう 合う *1. to fit, to be the right size and shape*

このセーターは私にぴったり合うよ。
This sweater fits me perfectly!

2. to suit; to match

緑が母にとてもよく合います。
Green suits my mother very well.

そのブレザーとシャツはよく合っています。
That blazer and shirt match well.

3. to coincide, to agree [→ 一致する]

私は父と意見が合わないよ。
My opinion and my father's don't agree!

気が合う to get along, to be like-minded

4. to become correct, to become accurate

この時計は合っていますか。
Is this clock correct?

—あう —合う *to do to each other, to do mutually (Added to verb bases.)*

二人は向かい合って立っていました。
The two of them were standing facing each other.

あう 会う *to see, to meet*

Aに／と会う to see A, to meet A

田中さんに会いましたか。
Did you see Mr. Tanaka?

後で会いましょう。
Let's meet later.

どこで中野さんと会う予定ですか。
Where are you planning to meet Mr. Nakano?

帰り道で先生にばったり会いました。
I ran into the teacher on my way home.

あう 遭う *to meet (with an unpleasant experience)*

ひどい目にあう to have a bad experience

アウト ～の *out (in baseball)* [↔ セーフの]

バッターはアウトです。
The batter is out.

アウトプット *(computer) output* [→ 出力] [↔ インプット]

アウトライン *outline, summary* [→ 概略]

あお 青 *1. blue (as a noun)*

濃い〔薄い〕青 dark〔light〕blue

2. green (as a noun) (The range of あお *includes both blue and green, but* みどり *is typically used for green.)* [→ 緑]

信号が青に変わりました。
The traffic light changed to green.

青葉 green leaves

青信号 green (traffic) light

青空 blue sky

あおい 青い *1. blue (as an adjective)*

その人形は青い目をしています。
The doll has blue eyes.

2. green (as an adjective) (The range of あおい *includes both blue and green, but* 緑の *is typically used as a noun modifier for green.)*

青いりんご green apple

3. pale (because of illness or fear)

顔色が青いですよ。どうかしたのですか。
Your face is pale! Is something the matter?

川本さんはそれを見て青くなりました。
Ms. Kawamoto saw that and turned white.

あおぐ 仰ぐ [[→ 見上げる]] *1. to look up at*

私たちは青空を仰ぎました。
We looked up at the blue sky.

2. to look up to, to respect

私は石井さんを指導者として仰いでいる。
I look up to Mr. Ishii as my leader.

あおぐ 扇ぐ *to fan*

母は扇子で顔をあおいでいます。
My mother is fanning her face with a folding fan.

あおじろい 青白い *pale, pallid*

青白い顔 pale face

あおむけ 仰向け ～に *facing upward, on one's back* [↔ うつぶせに]

少年はあお向けに倒れました。
The boy fell over on his back.

あか 赤 *red (as a noun)*

信号が赤になりました。
The traffic light turned red.

濃い〔薄い〕赤 dark〔light〕red

赤電話 red pay telephone (One of several types of public telephone in Japan, red pay telephones accept only ¥10 coins and are found near store and restaurant entrances.)

赤鉛筆 red pencil

赤信号 red (traffic) light

あかい 赤い *red (as an adjective)*

あかくなる 赤くなる *to turn red; to blush*

私は恥ずかしくて顔が赤くなりました。
I was ashamed, and my face turned red.

あかじ 赤字 *deficit, red ink* [↔ 黒字]

アカシア *acacia*

あかちゃん 赤ちゃん *baby*

男〔女〕の赤ちゃん baby boy〔girl〕

あかり 明かり *1. (artificial) light, lamplight*

明かりがついています。
The light is on.

明かりを消してください。
Turn off the light, please.

2. light, illumination [→ 光]

月の明かり the light of the moon

あがる 上がる *1. to go up, to rise* [↔ 下がる]

たこはどんどん高く上がっていきました。
The kite went up higher and higher.

屋上に上がっておしゃべりをしました。
We went up on the roof and had a chat.

気温は36度まで上がりました。
The temperature rose to 36 degrees.

今学期は成績が少し上がるでしょう。
My grades will probably go up a little this term.

2. to end, to be finished

雨が上がりました。
The rain stopped.

3. to get nervous

試験の時上がってしまいます。
I get nervous at exam time.

4. 【HON. for 食べる; 飲む】 [[→ 召し上がる]] *to eat; to drink*

果物を上がってください。
Please have some fruit.

あかるい 明るい [[↔ 暗い]] *1. light, illuminated, bright*

空が明るくなってきました。
The sky has gotten light.

今夜は月がとても明るいね。
Tonight the moon is very bright, isn't it?

明るいうちに帰ってきなさい。
Come back home while it's still light.

明るい色 bright color

2. cheerful

恵子さんはいつも明るいね。
Keiko is always cheerful, isn't she?

少女は明るくほほえみました。
The girl smiled cheerfully.

あかんぼう 赤ん坊 *baby* [→ 赤ちゃん]

あき 秋 *autumn, fall* [↔ 春]

ジムさんはこの秋にアメリカに帰ります。
Jim is going back to the United States this fall.

秋晴れ clear sky typical of autumn

あき 空き *vacancy, opening, space*

空き瓶 empty bottle

空き家 vacant house

あきらか 明らか ～な *clear, plain, obvious*

明らかな証拠はありません。
There is no clear evidence.

明らかにお母さんは疲れているよ。
Clearly mother is tired!

あきらめる 諦める *to give up on, to abandon as hopeless*

友達を探すのをあきらめます。
I will give up searching for my friend.

あきる 飽きる *to get tired of, to get sick of*

私はつまらない映画に飽きてしまった。
I got tired of the boring movie.

アップルパイはもう飽きました。
I'm sick of apple pie already.

アキレスけん アキレス腱 *Achilles tendon*

あきれる 呆れる *to become appalled*

政治家の言葉にはあきれました。
I was appalled at the politician's words.

自分の不注意にあきれてしまいます。
I am appalled at my carelessness.

あく 悪 *badness, wickedness, evil* [↔ 善]

あの人でも善と悪の区別はわかるよ。
Even that person knows the difference between good and evil!

悪影響 bad influence

悪意 ill will

悪事 evil deed

あく 空く *to become vacant, to become empty; to become available for use*

席がやっと１つ空きました。
At last one seat became vacant.

今度の日曜日は空いていますか。
Are you free this coming Sunday?

あく 開く *to open, to become open* [↔ 閉まる]

郵便局は９時に開きます。
The post office opens at 9:00.

この瓶はなかなか開かないね。
This bottle just won't open, will it.

その店は24時間開いています。
The store is open 24 hours a day.

アクアラング *aqualung*

あくしゅ 握手 *handshake, shaking hands*

握手する to shake hands

私は相手と握手しました。
I shook hands with my opponent.

アクション *1. action, act, behavior* [→ 行動]

2. (violent) action (in movies, etc.)

アクション映画 action movie

アクションスター action movie star

アクセサリー *1. fashion accessory (Usually refers to a jewelry item.)*

2. accessory, appurtenance [→ 付属品 (s.v. 付属)]

アクセル *accelerator (pedal)*

アクセント *accent, stress (on a syllable)*

あくび 欠伸 *yawn*

あくびをする to yawn, to give a yawn

山田さんは大きなあくびをしました。
Mr. Yamada gave a big yawn.

あくま 悪魔 *devil, demon* [↔ 天使]

悪魔のような devilish, fiendish

あぐら *sitting cross-legged*

あぐらをかく to sit cross-legged

アクロバット *1. acrobatics* [→ 曲芸]

2. acrobat [→ 曲芸師 (s.v. 曲芸)]

あけがた 明け方 *daybreak, dawn*

明け方に火事が起こりました。
A fire broke out at dawn.

あける 空ける *1. to vacate, to make empty, to make room on/in*

若い女性は老人に席を空けました。
The young woman made room on the seat for an elderly person.

みんな救急車のために道を空けました。

Everyone made way for the ambulance.

2. to empty out (the contents)

花瓶から水を空けてください。

Please empty the water out of the vase.

3.〜穴を〜 *to make a hole*

壁に穴を空けます。

I will make a hole in the wall.

あける 明ける *1.* 夜が〜 *day breaks, night ends*

夜が明ける前に出発します。

We will leave before day breaks.

2. to begin (The subject is a year.)

年が明けました。

The new year began.

3. 〜梅雨が〜 *the rainy season ends*

もうすぐ梅雨が明けます。

The rainy season will end soon.

あける 開ける *to open, to unclose (transitive)* [↔ 閉める]

教科書の50ページを開けなさい。

Open your textbooks to page 50.

ドアを開けておいてはいけないよ。

You mustn't leave the door open!

普通 10時に店を開けます。

We usually open the store at 10:00.

あげる 上げる *to raise, to put higher*

答えのわかる人は手を上げなさい。

People who know the answer, raise your hands.

母が来月小遣いを上げてくれるよ。

My mother will raise my allowance next month!

あげる 揚げる *to fly (a kite); to raise (a flag)*

たこを揚げる to fly a kite

旗を揚げる to raise a flag

あげる 揚げる *to deep-fry*

あげる 挙げる *1. to hold (a ceremony)*

あの二人は教会で結婚式をあげます。

Those two are going to have their wedding at church.

2. to give, to cite (an example)

例をもう１つあげてください。

Please give another example.

あげる 上げる (In either use of this word the recipient must not be the speaker, the speaker's group, or a person or group with whom the speaker is identifying.)

1. to give (to someone)

母の誕生日にセーターを上げます。

We are going to give our mother a sweater for her birthday.

これを友達に上げましょう。

I'll give this to my friend.

2. to do the favor of (following the gerund (-て form) of another verb)

友達の宿題を手伝ってあげます。

I help my friend with her homework.

その人に駅への道順を教えてあげました。

I showed that person the way to the station.

何でも気に入った物を買ってあげるよ。

I will buy you anything you like!

あご 顎 *jaw; chin*

顎髭 beard

アコーディオン *accordion*

アコーディオンカーテン accordion door

あこがれる *to long, to yearn*

山中さんは名声にあこがれています。

Ms. Yamanaka is longing for fame.

弟は歌手になることにあこがれています。

My younger brother is yearning to be a singer.

あさ 麻 *hemp*

あさ 朝 *morning*

私は朝６時に起きます。

I get up at 6:00 in the morning.

日曜日の朝にＵＦＯを見たよ。

I saw a UFO on Sunday morning!

川村君は朝から晩まで勉強します。

Kawamura studies from morning till night.

朝ご飯 breakfast [→ 朝食]

あさい 浅い *shallow* [↔ 深い]

この川はここが浅いです。
This river is shallow here.

母は眠りが浅いです。
My mother's sleep is shallow.

その傷は浅いですね。
That wound is shallow, isn't it?

経験が浅い to have little experience

あさがお 朝顔 *morning-glory ((flower))*

あさって 明後日 *the day after tomorrow*

明明後日 the day after the day after tomorrow

あさばん 朝晩 *morning and night*

あさひ 朝日 *morning sun, rising sun*

あざやか 鮮やか ～な *bright, vivid*

このばらは鮮やかな赤です。
These roses are a bright red.

あざらし *seal ((animal))*

あさり *short-necked clam*

あし 足 *1. foot*

足がしびれています。
My foot is asleep.

足が速い fast at running, fleet-footed

足の裏 sole of the foot

2. leg (including the foot)

父は足が長いです。
My father's legs are long.

足を組んで座るのはきついです。
Sitting with your legs crossed is hard.

足跡 footprint

足取り gait, steps

足元 the area at one's feet

足元にご注意ください。
Please watch your step.

足音 (the sound of) footsteps

あじ 味 *flavor, taste*

このジュースは酸っぱい味がします。
This juice has a sour taste.

味はどうですか。
How does it taste?

このケーキは味が変です。
This cake has a strange flavor.

あじ 鯵 *horse mackerel*

アジア *Asia*

アジア人 an Asian

アジア大陸 the Asian Continent

あしくび 足首 *ankle*

あじさい *hydrangea ((flower))*

アシスタント *assistant*

あした 明日 *tomorrow*

あしたは私の誕生日です。
Tomorrow is my birthday.

あしたの午後にパーティーを開きます。
We'll have a party tomorrow afternoon.

あしたの今ごろまた来ます。
I'll come again at about this time tomorrow.

またあした。
See you tomorrow.

あじわう 味わう *1. to taste, to sample the flavor of*

そのスープを味わってみてください。
Please taste that soup.

2. to experience [→ 経験する]

あす 明日 *tomorrow* [→ 明日]

あずかる 預かる *to keep, to hold, to look after (for someone)*

このお金を預かってください。
Please look after this money.

隣の犬をしばらく預かりました。
We looked after the neighbor's dog for a while.

あずき 小豆 *red bean*

あずける 預ける *to entrust, to leave (in someone's care)*

カメラを先生に預けましょう。
I'll leave my camera with the teacher.
銀行に5000円を預けました。
I put ¥5,000 in the bank.

アスパラガス *asparagus*

アスファルト *asphalt*

あせ 汗 *sweat*

汗をかく to sweat
汗をふく to wipe off sweat
汗びっしょりの sweaty all over, dripping with sweat
冷や汗 cold sweat

あせる 焦る *{5} to become hurried; to get impatient* [→ いらいらする]*; to get excited, to get flustered*

試験がじきに始まるので、焦っています。
The examination starts soon, so I'm flustered.
焦ってはいけません。
You mustn't get flustered.

あそこ *that place (over there), there*

(Like other Japanese demonstratives beginning with あ, あそこ has two uses. One is to refer to a place which is in sight and is relatively far both from the speaker and from the listener. The other is to refer to a place which is not in sight but which is familiar both to the speaker and to the listener.) [↔ ここ; そこ]

あそこに煙突が見えます。
A chimney is visible over there.

あそび 遊び *play, game, recreation, amusement*

大学生はたいてい遊びが大好きです。
College students are almost all very fond of play.
遊びに行く to go and visit
遊びに来る to come and visit
近いうちにうちへ遊びに来てください。
Please come to my house for a visit soon.
遊び相手 playmate
遊び場 playground

あそぶ 遊ぶ *1. to play, to enjoy oneself, to have fun*

子供たちは公園で遊んでいます。
The children are playing in the park.
トランプをして遊びました。
We played cards.
私たちは海岸で楽しく遊びました。
We enjoyed ourselves at the seashore.

2. to be idle

きのうは1日遊んでしまいました。
I was idle all day yesterday.

あたい 値 *value, worth* [→ 価値]

Aに値する to be worth A
この本は一読に値すると思います。
I think this book is worth reading.

あたえる 与える *to give*

その知らせは先生にショックを与えた。
That news gave the teacher a shock.
坂本さんに1等賞を与えましょう。
Let's give the first prize to Ms. Sakamoto.

あたかも *just like, just as if* [→ まるで]

あたし 【COL.】 *I, me*

(There are several Japanese words for **I/me.** The word あたし is ordinarily restricted to female speakers and is less formal than わたし. Other words for **I/me** include 私, 私, 僕, and 俺.)

あたたかい 暖かい, 温かい *1. warm (in temperature)* [↔ 涼しい]

きょうは暖かいですね。
It's warm today, isn't it?
去年の冬は暖かかったです。
Last year's winter was warm.
何か温かい飲み物が欲しいです。
I want something warm to drink.
暖かい日 warm day

2. warm, providing warmth

きょうは暖かいセーターを着ています。
Today I'm wearing a warm sweater.

3. warm (-hearted), kind, kindhearted [→ 親切な] [↔ 冷たい]
竹山さんは暖かい人です。
Mr. Takeyama is a warm person.

あたたまる 暖まる, 温まる *to warm up (intransitive)* [↔ 冷える]
スープがよく温まりましたよ。
The soup has warmed up well!
たき火に当たって暖まりましょう。
Let's warm ourselves at the bonfire.
それは心が温まる話です。
That's a heartwarming story.

あたためる 暖める; 温める *to warm up (transitive)*
洋子さんは牛乳を温めました。
Yoko warmed up the milk.
部屋をすぐに暖めてくれませんか。
Will you warm up the room right away?

アタック *1. attack* [→ 攻撃]
アタックする to make an attack
2. strenuous effort (toward a difficult goal)
アタックする to make a strenuous effort

アタッシュケース attaché case

あだな あだ名 *nickname, sobriquet*
弟のあだ名は「うさぎ」です。
My younger brother's nickname is "Rabbit."
生徒たちは先生に「コアラ」というあだ名をつけました。
The pupils gave the teacher the nickname "Koala."

アダプター *(electrical) adapter*

あたま 頭 *1. head*
父は頭をかくくせがあります。
My father has a habit of scratching his head.
頭が痛い one has a headache
頭を刈る to cut a person's hair
理髪店で頭を刈ってもらいました。
I had my hair cut at the barbershop.
2. head, mind, brains [→ 頭脳]
頭がいい to be smart, to be bright
頭を使う to use one's head
頭が古い to have old-fashioned ideas
頭に来る to get angry
あいつには本当に頭にきたよ。
I really got angry at that guy!

あたまきん 頭金 *down-payment*

あたらしい 新しい *1. new* [↔ 古い]
新しい車が欲しいです。
I want a new car.
新しく開店したデパートに行きましょう。
Let's go to the newly-opened department store.
新しいニュース hot news
2. fresh [→ 新鮮な]
この卵は新しいですか。
Are these eggs fresh?

あたり 辺り *area around, vicinity* [→ 辺]
僕はあたりを見回しました。
I looked around me.
私が戻ってくるまでこのあたりにいなさい。
Stay around here until I return.

あたり 当たり *1. hitting, striking, contact*
2. hit (on a mark, target, etc.)
3. hit, success
その芝居は当たりです。
That play is a hit.
4. correct guess
まぐれ当たり (lucky) fluke
大当たり big hit
当たり前 〜の natural, obvious, unsurprising [→ 当然の]
子供にできないのは当たり前だよ。
It's obvious that a child can't do it!

あたる 当たる *1. to hit, to strike, to make contact*
ボールが息子の頭に当たりました。

A ball hit my son's head.

日が当たる the sun shines (on), sunlight strikes

2. to hit (a mark, target, etc.) [↔ 外れる]

くじに当たる to draw a winning lot, to win a lottery prize

3. to be exposed, to expose oneself (to a natural phenomenon)

私たちは火に当たって暖まりました。
We warmed ourselves at the fire.

4. to prove correct [↔ 外れる]

天気予報は当たりました。
The weather forecast proved correct.

その予想も当たったね。
That prediction also proved correct, didn't it?

5. to be called on, to be assigned

きょうは授業で５回も当たったよ。
I was called on five times in class today!

6. to correspond, to be equivalent

英語の「red」は日本語の「赤」に当たりますね。
English "red" corresponds to Japanese "aka", doesn't it?

今年は子供の日が日曜日に当たります。
This year Children's Day falls on Sunday.

7. to get poisoned, to get ill (from eating or exposure to something)

魚に当たる to get ill from eating fish

あちこち *here and there*

行方不明の子供をあちこち探しています。
We are looking for the lost child here and there.

先月京都中をあちこち訪ねて回りました。
I went around visiting here and there all over Kyoto last month.

あちら 【FORMAL for あっち】

(Like other Japanese demonstratives beginning with あ, あちら has two uses. One is to refer to something which is in sight and relatively far both from the speaker and from the listener. The other is to refer to something which is not in sight but which is familiar both to the speaker and to the listener.)

1. [[↔ こちら; そちら]] that way; over there

東はあちらです。
East is that way.

あちらに着いたら電話をください。
Please give me a phone call when you get there.

青木先生はあちらです。
Mr. Aoki is over there.

2. that person [↔ こちら]

あちらはどなたですか。
Who is that person?

あちら側 the other side, that side over there

川のあちら側は千葉県です。
The other side of the river is Chiba Prefecture.

あっ *Oh!, Ah! (an interjection expressing surprise, alarm, or dismay)*

あっ、危ない！
Oh! Look out! (Literally: Oh! Dangerous!)

あっ、わかった。
Oh! I understand.

あっ、ノートを忘れました。
Ah! I forgot my notebook.

あつい 厚い *1. thick, large from front to back* [↔ 薄い]

ずいぶん厚い本ですね。
It's a really thick book, isn't it?

パンを厚く切ってください。
Please cut the bread thick.

2. warm, friendly, cordial

私たちは厚いもてなしを受けました。
We received a warm welcome.

あつい 熱い *hot (describing something tangible at a high temperature)* [↔ 冷たい]

このみそ汁は熱いよ。
This miso soup is hot!

あつい 暑い *hot (describing a high air temperature or how a person feels when the air temperature is high)* [↔ 寒い]
きょうはとても暑いですね。
Today it's very hot, isn't it?

あっか 悪化 *worsening*
悪化する to worsen (transitive or intransitive)

あつかい 扱い *treatment, handling*
子供扱いする to treat like a child

あつかう 扱う *to treat, to deal with, to handle*
客をていねいに扱いましょう。
Let's treat the customers politely.
その花瓶はていねいに扱ってください。
Please handle the vase carefully.
あの店は漫画は扱っていません。
That store doesn't handle comic books.

あつくるしい 暑苦しい *stuffy, sultry*
暑苦しい部屋から出ました。
I went out of the stuffy room.
暑苦しい夜 sultry night

あつさ 厚さ *thickness*
ここの氷は厚さが30センチです。
The thickness of the ice here is 30 centimeters.

あつさ 熱さ *heat (of something tangible)*

あつさ 暑さ *heat (of the air)* [↔ 寒さ]
きょうの暑さはひどいね。
Today's heat is terrible, isn't it?

あっさり *simply, easily*
田口君は難しい問題をあっさり解くよ。
Taguchi solves the difficult problems easily!

あっさりした *plain, simple*
私はあっさりした食べ物が好きです。
I like plain food.

あったかい 暖かい; 温かい【COL. for 温かい, 暖かい】

あっち【COL. for あちら】

あっとう 圧倒 ～する *to overwhelm*
敵はわれわれを圧倒しました。
The enemy overwhelmed us.
圧倒的な overwhelming

アッピール [☞ アピール]

アップリケ *1. appliqué, sewing on decorative patches*
2. appliqué, decorative patches

あつまる 集まる *1. to gather, to meet, to get together (intransitive)*
生徒たちは先生の周りに集まりました。
The pupils gathered around the teacher.
図書委員は毎週月曜日に集まります。
The library committee members meet every Monday.
お正月には親せきが大勢集まるよ。
A lot of relatives get together at New Year's!
2. to be collected, to be gathered
かなりのお金が集まりました。
Quite a lot of money was collected.
その事件の資料はすぐに集まりました。
Data on that incident were gathered easily.
3. to center, to converge
全員の視線が先生に集まりました。
Everyone's eyes converged on the teacher.

あつめる 集める *to gather, to collect (transitive)*
コーチは周りに選手を集めました。
The coach gathered the players around him.
私の趣味は切手を集めることです。
My hobby is collecting stamps.

あつりょく 圧力 *pressure*
圧力をかける to apply pressure

あて 当て *1. aim, objective* [→ 目的]
当てもなく aimlessly, with no particular objective

2. hope, expectation [→ 期待]

Aを当てにする to count on A, to put one's hopes on A

友達の助けを当てにしてはいけないよ。

You shouldn't count on your friends' help!

－あて －宛 *addressed to, for* (Added to names.)

この手紙は孝子さんあてです。

This letter is addressed to Takako.

あてな 宛名 *addressee's name (on a letter, etc.)*

手紙にあて名を書きなさい。

Write the addressee's name on the letter.

あてはまる 当てはまる *to be applicable, to hold true*

その規則はこの場合にも当てはまります。

That rule applies in this case too.

あてる 当てる *1. to make (something) hit (something else)* [→ ぶつける]

AにBを当てる to make A hit B

ナイフを的に当てるのは難しいです。

It is difficult to make a knife hit the target.

2. to place, to put, to hold (one thing to the appropriate place on another)

祐子さんは目にハンカチを当てました。

Yuko held a handkerchief to her eyes.

3. to guess [→ 推測する]

だれも子供の年を当てられませんでした。

Nobody was able to guess the child's age.

当ててみる to take a guess at

4. to call (on a person by name)

先生は久美ちゃんに当てたよ。

The teacher called on Kumi!

5. to expose, to subject

赤ちゃんを強い日に当ててはいけません。

You mustn't expose a baby to strong sun.

6. to succeed [→ 成功する]

くじで当てる to win a prize in a lottery

小田さんはくじで1000万円当てましたよ。

Ms. Oda won ¥10,000,000 in a lottery!

あと 後 *1. the area behind* [→ 後ろ]

Aの後を追いかける to run after A, to chase after A

犬が子供のあとを追いかけています。

The dog is running after the child.

Aの後に付く to follow along behind A

私たちは先生のあとについていきました。

We followed along behind our teacher.

後を振り返る to look back, to look behind one

後に下がる to step back

後に残る to remain behind

2. time after, time later [↔ 前]

朝食のあとでテニスをします。

After breakfast I play tennis.

宿題をしたあとでテレビを見ます。

I watch TV after I do my homework. (A verb preceding あと is always in the past tense.)

あとで電話をしてください。

Please phone me later.

3. the rest, remainder [→ 残り]

あとはあしたやります。

I will do the rest tomorrow.

4. another, more (preceding a word that specifies a quantity)

学校生活はあと１か月で終わりです。

My school life will be over in a month.

あと５分待ってください。

Please wait five more minutes.

後味 aftertaste

あと 跡 *mark, trace; track, trail*

うさぎの通った跡が見つかりました。

Tracks from a passing rabbit were found.

正雄さんの英語は進歩の跡が見えません。

Masao's English shows no trace of progress.

足跡 footprint

傷跡 scar

後片付け clearing away afterwards; straightening up afterwards

私たちはパーティーの後片づけをした。
We straightened up after the party.

テーブルの後片づけ clearing the table

アドバイス *advice* [→ 助言]

生徒たちは先生のアドバイスに従った。
The pupils followed their teacher's advice.

アドバイスする to advise

先生はベストを尽くすようにと私たちにアドバイスしました。
Our teacher advised us to do our best.

アドバルーン *balloon from which an advertising banner is suspended*

アトラクション *side entertainment (offered to attract customers to the main entertainment)*

アトリエ *atelier, (artist's) studio*

アドリブ *ad-lib*

アドリブでしゃべる to talk ad-lib

アドリブで演奏する to perform ad-lib (on a musical instrument)

アドレス *address* [→ 住所]

あな 穴 *hole*

父は庭に穴を掘りました。
My father dug a hole in the garden.

穴が開く a hole appears (in something)

穴を開ける to make a hole (in something)

アナウンサー *announcer*

アナウンス *announcement (made over a microphone)*

アナウンスする to announce

あなた *1. you*

(There are several Japanese words for **you,** and あなた is the most commonly used in translation from English. In general, however, Japanese speakers prefer to use names or titles rather than words for **you.** It is not appropriate to use あなた to refer to a social superior. Other words for **you** include 君, お前,and 貴様.)

あなたは平均より背が高いね。
You are taller than average, aren't you?

私の髪は黒で、あなたのは金髪です。
My hair is black, and yours is blonde.

あなた自身がそれをやったのです。
You did that yourself.

2. dear, darling (when used by a wife to her husband)

あに 兄 *older brother* [↔ 姉; お兄さん; 弟]

私には兄が３人います。
I have three older brothers.

アニメーション *(movie) animation*

アニメーション映画 animated cartoon

あね 姉 *older sister* [↔ 兄; お姉さん; 妹]

姉はスチュワーデスです。
My older sister is a stewardess.

アネモネ *anemone*

あの *that, those (as a noun modifier)*

(Like other Japanese demonstratives beginning with あ, あの has two uses. One is to refer to something which is in sight and relatively far both from the speaker and from the listener. The other is to refer to something which is not in sight but which is familiar both to the speaker and to the listener.) [↔ この; その]

あの人はだれですか。
Who is that person?

あの時何をしていたのですか。
What were you doing at that time?

あのう *uh, um, er (a pause filler)* [→ ええと]

アパート *1. (US) apartment, (UK) flat*

私たちはアパートに住んでいます。
We live in an apartment.

2. (US) apartment building, (UK) block of flats

このアパートには40世帯が住んでいる。
Forty families live in this apartment building.

あばれる 暴れる *to become violent, to get rowdy, to run amok*
子供たちは家の中で暴れています。
The children are being rowdy in the house.

アピール *1. appeal, attraction*
アピールする to appeal
2. appeal, entreaty
アピールする to appeal [→ 呼びかける]

あびせる 浴びせる *to pour all over, to shower with*

あびる 浴びる *to pour all over oneself; to take (a bath or shower)*
子供たちは川で水を浴びました。
The children poured water all over themselves in the river.
私はいつも寝る前にシャワーを浴びます。
I always take a shower before going to bed.

あぶ 虻 *horsefly*

アフターサービス *after-sales service*

あぶない 危ない *1. dangerous* [→ 危険な] [↔ 安全な]
危ない！
Watch out! (Literally: Dangerous!)
ここでスキーをするのは危ないよ。
It's dangerous to ski here!
2. in danger
その子は命が危ないです。
That child's life is in danger.

あぶら 油 *1. oil*
油を差す to apply oil (to a machine for lubrication)
この自転車に油を差してください。
Please oil this bicycle.
2. grease

あぶら 脂 *(animal) fat* [→ 脂肪]
この肉は脂が多すぎるね。
This meat has too much fat, doesn't it?
脂っこい fatty, greasy

アフリカ *Africa*
アフリカ人 an African
アフリカ大陸 the African Continent

あふれる 溢れる *to overflow*
おふろのお湯があふれているよ。
The hot water in the bath is overflowing!
桂子さんの目には涙があふれていました。
Tears were overflowing in Keiko's eyes.

アプローチ *approach, method*
アプローチする to approach

アベック 【COL.】*couple (man and woman)*

あま 海女 *woman diver*
(A traditional occupation in Japan, 海女 use no breathing equipment and dive for seaweed, shellfish, etc.)

あま 尼 *1. Buddhist nun*
2. Christian nun

アマ [☞ アマチュア]

あまい 甘い *1. sweet (-tasting)*
甘い物が好きです。
I like sweet things.
2. lenient, indulgent
南先生は採点が甘いです。
Mr. Minami's grading is lenient.
3. overly optimistic, naive
ちょっと考えが甘いよ。
Your thinking is a bit overly optimistic!

あまえる 甘える *to presume on the love or kindness (of someone); to act like a baby (toward someone in order to get that person to satisfy one's selfish desires)*
妹は時々母に甘えます。
My younger sister sometimes acts like a baby toward my mother.

アマチュア *an amateur* [↔ プロ]

アマチュアスポーツ amateur sports

あまど 雨戸 *rain door*

(a sliding door or shutter on a Japanese house that is closed to keep out the rain)

あまのがわ 天の川 *the Milky Way*

あまやかす 甘やかす *to indulge, to spoil, to pamper*

お母さんは次郎を甘やかしてしまったね。
Mother spoiled Jiro, didn't she?

あまやどり 雨宿り *taking shelter from the rain*

ここで雨宿りをしましょう。
Let's take shelter here from the rain.

あまり 余り *the rest, remainder, surplus* [→ 残り]

弁当の余りを犬にやったよ。
I gave the rest of my lunch to the dog!

—あまり —余り *over, more than (Added to bases denoting quantities.)*

池田さんたちは１週間あまりハワイにいた。
The Ikeda's were in Hawaii for over a week.

あまり *1. (〜に) too, too much*

あまりに寒いです。
It's too cold.

あまり食べすぎないでね。
Don't eat too much, OK?

あまり暑いので冷たいシャワーを浴びた。
It was too hot, so I took a cold shower.

カレーライスがあまり辛かったので、全部は食べられませんでした。
Since the curry and rice was too (spicy) hot, I couldn't eat it all.

2. (not) very, (not) much, (not) many (in combination with a negative predicate)

ジャズはあまり好きじゃないです。
I don't like jazz very much.

私はあまり映画を見に行きません。
I don't go to see movies very much.

魚はあまりいませんでした。
There weren't very many fish.

正男さんはあまりしゃべりませんね。
Masao doesn't talk very much, does he?

アマリリス *amaryllis* ((plant))

あまる 余る *to remain as surplus, to be left over*

お金はいくら余りましたか。
How much money was left over?

30から13を引くと17余るでしょう？
If you subtract 13 from 30, 17 is left over, right?

あみ 網 *net*

網で捕る to catch with a net

小川で魚を網で捕りました。
I caught a fish with a net in the stream.

網にかかる to become caught in a net

網棚 shelf with a net bottom (typical overhead luggage rack on a Japanese train)

網戸 window screen; screen door

アミノさん アミノ酸 *amino acid*

あみもの 編み物 *knitting*

編み物をする to do knitting

あむ 編む *to knit, to weave; to braid*

父に手袋を編んであげました。
I knitted mittens for my father.

あめ 雨 *rain*

雨は昼ごろにやみました。
The rain stopped around noon.

雨の日は嫌いです。
I dislike rainy days.

雨が降る rain falls

あしたは雨が降るでしょう。
Tomorrow it will probably rain.

日本では６月に雨が多く降ります。
In Japan it rains a lot in June.

雨にあう to get caught in the rain

あめ 飴 *sweetened-starch candy*

アメーバ *amoeba*

アメリカ *1. America, the Americas*

2. the United States [→ 米国]

アメリカ合衆国 United States of America

アメリカインディアン American Indian

アメリカ人 an American

アメリカ人の友達がいますか。
Do you have any American friends?

中央アメリカ Central America

北アメリカ North America [→ 北米]

南アメリカ South America [→ 南米]

ラテンアメリカ Latin America

あやうく 危うく *(in combination with a predicate indicating something undesirable about to happen or likely to happen)*

危うく電車に乗り遅れるところでした。
I nearly missed the train.

あやしい 怪しい *1. suspicion-arousing, suspicious* [→ 疑わしい]

その人が怪しいと思いました。
I thought that person was suspicious.

怪しい人物 suspicious character

ゆうべ怪しい音が聞こえました。
We heard a suspicious sound last night.

2. doubtful, questionable [→ 疑わしい]

田中君の約束は怪しいです。
Tanaka's promises are questionable.

あやしむ 怪しむ *1. to suspect, to become suspicious of* [→ 疑う]

2. to doubt [→ 疑う]

あやとり *cat's cradle*

あやとりをする to play cat's cradle

あやまち 過ち *mistake, error* [→ 間違い]

同じ過ちを二度としてはいけません。
You must not make the same mistake twice.

だれにも過ちはあるもの。 (proverb)
To err is human. (Literally: In everyone there are mistakes.)

あやまり 誤り *mistake, error* [→ 間違い]

あやまる 誤る *to make a mistake in, to do wrongly* [→ 間違える]

方針を誤る to take the wrong course

選択を誤る to make a wrong choice

あやまる 謝る *to apologize for* [→ 詫びる]

菊子さんは自分のまちがいを謝りました。
Kikuko apologized for her own mistakes.

ジョンさんは「遅刻してすみません」と謝りました。
"I'm sorry for being late," apologized John.

あやめ *iris ((flower))*

あゆ 鮎 *ayu (a fresh-water fish commonly eaten in Japan)*

あら *Oh!; Why! (an interjection expressing surprise or dismay; generally restricted to female speakers)*

あらまあ。
Oh, dear!

あら、京子さんもいるわ。
Why, Kyoko's here too!

あらい 荒い *1. rough, violent*

きょうは波が荒いです。
Today the sea is rough.

2. coarse, vulgar

和子さんは言葉づかいが荒いです。
Kazuko's way of speaking is coarse.

あらい 粗い *1. coarse, not fine*

この布は目が粗いですね。
This cloth's weave is coarse, isn't it?

2. rough, not smooth

あらいはだ 粗い肌 *rough skin*

あらう 洗う *to wash*

顔を洗いなさい。
Wash your face.

りんごを水で洗いました。
I washed the apples with water.

手を石けんできれいに洗いましたか。
Did you wash your hands clean with soap?

あらかじめ 予め *in advance* [→ 前もって]
私たちはあらかじめ準備を整えました。
We made preparations in advance.

アラカルト *a la carte item*

あらし 嵐 *storm*
嵐が来そうです。
It looks as if a storm is going to come.
嵐が治まりました。
The storm abated.
男たちは嵐の夜に出ていきました。
The men went out on a stormy night.

あらす 荒らす *to damage, to ruin*
うさぎが畑を荒らしました。
Rabbits damaged the field.

あらすじ 粗筋 *summary, outline, synopsis*

あらそい 争い *1. dispute, quarrel, fight* [→ 喧嘩]; *trouble, conflict, strife*
争いが起こる a dispute arises
2. competition, rivalry [→ 競争]

あらそう 争う *1. to argue, to quarrel, to fight* [→ 喧嘩する]
時々ささいな事で姉と争います。
I sometimes quarrel with my older sister over trivial things.
2. to compete for
私たちはお互いに1等賞を争いました。
We competed with each other for the first prize.

あらたまる 改まる *1. to change, to be replaced by something new*
年が改まる the new year comes
2. to change for the better, to improve (intransitive)
春子ちゃんの性格もだいぶ改まったよ。
Haruko's disposition has also improved a great deal!
3. to become formal, to become ceremonious
そんなに改まる必要はないですよ。
There's no need to become so formal!

あらためて 改めて *again, anew* [→ 再び]
改めて伺います。
I will call on you again.
あとで改めてお電話します。
I will phone again later.

あらためる 改める *1. to change, to replace with something new*
この計画を改めましょうか。
Shall we change this plan?
2. to change for the better, to improve, to correct (transitive) [→ 改善する]
金丸さんは悪い習慣を改めました。
Mr. Kanemaru improved his bad habits.
誤りがあれば改めてください。
If there are errors, please correct them.
3. to examine, to check
お客さんの切符を改めました。
I checked the customers' tickets.

あらゆる *all, every* [→ すべての]
これはあらゆる種類の花に関する本です。
This is a book about all kinds of flowers.
あらゆる努力をしました。
I made every effort.

あられ 霰 *snowy hail*
あられが降る snowy hail falls

あらわす 表す, 現す *1. to show, to make manifest; to express* [→ 表現する]
山田さんは自分の感情を顔に表さない。
Mr. Yamada does not show his feelings on his face.
笑顔で感謝の気持ちを表しました。
I expressed my feeling of gratitude with a smiling face.
姿を現す to appear, to show oneself, to come in sight
2. to stand for, to mean, to represent [→ 意味する]
「ＵＮ」は何を表すのですか。
What does "UN" stand for?

あらわす 著す *to write and publish, to author*

あらわれる 表れる, 現れる *to appear, to come in sight; to be manifested, to show*
映画スターが突然舞台に現れました。
A movie star suddenly appeared on the stage.
太陽が雲の間から現れました。
The sun came out from behind the clouds.
感情が先生の顔に表れています。
Emotion is showing on the teacher's face.

あり 蟻 *ant*
ありの行列 line of ants
ありの巣 ant nest

ありがたい 有り難い *welcome, meriting gratitude*
水を１杯もらえたらありがたいんだけど。
If I could get a glass of water, it would be welcome.
そう言ってくださってとてもありがたいです。
I am very grateful to you for saying so.
ありがたいことに fortunately
ありがたいことに雨がやみました。
Fortunately, the rain stopped.

ありがとう 有難う *Thank you*
ありがとうございます【FORMAL for ありがとう】Thank you very much (for what you are doing or going to do)
ありがとうございました【FORMAL for ありがとう】Thank you very much (for what you have done)
「ご忠告どうもありがとうございました」「どういたしまして」
"Thank you very much for your advice." "You're welcome."

アリバイ *alibi*

ありふれた *commonplace, very common, not at all unusual (Used only as a noun modifier, not as a predicate.)*
太郎はありふれた名前です。
Taro is a very common name.
澄子はありふれたドレスを着ているよ。
Sumiko is wearing a commonplace dress!

ある 或る *certain, unspecified (Used only as a noun modifier, not as a predicate.)*
高木さんはある大学に入りました。
Mr. Takagi entered a certain university.

ある *{Irreg.} 1. (The subject ordinarily must be inanimate.) there is/are; to be (located); to exist* [→ 存在する]
テーブルの上に時計があります。
There is a watch on the table.
私のかばんがいすの下にあります。
My bag is under the chair.
右に曲がると銀行がありますよ。
When you turn right, there is a bank!
このホテルには部屋が60室あります。
There are sixty rooms in this hotel.
2. to have, to possess (What is possessed is treated as a grammatical subject and marked with が *rather than with* を*.)*
兄は車が２台あります。
My older brother has two cars.
3. there is/are, to take place, to happen
何かあったんですか。
Did something happen?
ゆうべ火事がありました。
Last night there was a fire.
きのうパーティーがあったよ。
Yesterday there was a party!
きょう数学の試験もありました。
Today there was also a math exam.

あるいて 歩いて *on foot, by walking*
公園まで歩いて10分です。
It's 10 minutes to the park on foot.
歩いてすぐです。
It's a short walk. (Literally: Walking, it's nearby.)
歩いてずいぶんあります。
It's a long walk. (Literally: Walking, there's quite a lot.)

あるいは 或いは *1. or* [→ または]
里子かあるいは秀子がまちがっている。

Either Satoko or Hideko is wrong.

2. perhaps (This word typically occurs in sentences ending with an expression of possibility (such as かもしれない). Since such a sentence has virtually the same meaning whether or not あるいは is present, あるいは is redundant in a sense, but it serves as a signal of how a sentence will end.)

あるいは母の言うとおりかもしれません。
Perhaps it is as my mother says.

アルカリ *alkali* [↔ 酸]

アルカリの alkaline

アルカリ性 alkalinity

あるく 歩く *to walk*

きょうもずいぶん歩きました。
I walked a great deal today too.

アルコール *alcohol*

アルコール中毒 alcoholism

アルト *1. alto (voice)*

2. alto (singer)

3. alto (part)

アルバイト *part-time job; side job*

姉は英語学校でアルバイトをしています。
My older sister is working part-time at an English school.

アルバイト学生 student with a part-time job

アルバム *1. album (for photographs, stamps, etc.)*

2. (record) album

アルファベット *alphabet*

アルファベット順 alphabetical order

本は著者名のアルファベット順に並べられています。
The books are arranged in alphabetical order according to author.

アルミ *aluminum*

アルミホイル aluminum foil

アルミサッシ aluminum (window) sash

アルミニウム [☞ アルミ]

あれ *that (one)*

(Like other Japanese demonstratives beginning with あ, あれ has two uses. One is to refer to something which is in sight and relatively far both from the speaker and from the listener. The other is to refer to something which is not in sight but which is familiar both to the speaker and to the listener.) [↔ これ; それ]

あれは何ですか。
What is that?

あれは山田君だよ。
That's Yamada! (This use of あれ instead of あの人 to refer to a person is not very polite.)

あれから after that; since then

あれから何をしましたか。
What did you do after that?

あれから父に手紙を書いていません。
I have not written a letter to my father since then.

あれこれ (と) in a manner involving this and that

私たちはあれこれとおしゃべりしました。
We chatted about this and that.

あれ *Dear!; Heavens! (an interjection expressing surprise or dismay)*

あれ、だれもいないよ。
Heavens, there's no one here!

アレグロ *allegro*

あれる 荒れる *1. to become rough (when the subject is the sea, etc.)*

海はきのう荒れていました。
The sea was rough yesterday.

2. to become stormy (when the subject is the weather)

きょうは天気が荒れるそうです。
They say the weather will become stormy today.

3. to become ruined, to become dilapidated

隣の家はすっかり荒れてしまいました。

The house next door became completely dilapidated.

4. to become chapped, to become rough

母の手は台所仕事で荒れています。

My mother's hands are rough from kitchen work.

アレルギー *allergy*

アレルギー体質 allergic constitution

あわ 泡 *bubble; foam*

泡立つ to bubble, to foam

あわせる 合わせる *1. to put together, to unite, to join, to combine*

この２枚の板を合わせてくれる？

Will you put these two boards together?

１等賞を取るために力を合わせましょう。

Let's combine our efforts in order to win first prize.

2. to add up, to total [→ 合計する]

合わせて altogether, in all

合わせて１万円になります。

It comes to ¥10,000 in all.

3. to adjust, to set, to fit, to make match

時計を合わせる to set a clock

美知子さんは音楽に合わせて滑りました。

Michiko skated to the music.

あわただしい 慌ただしい *busy, rushed, hurried*

大阪で慌ただしい１日を過ごしました。

I spent a busy day in Osaka.

弟は慌ただしく下に降りていきました。

My younger brother went downstairs in a hurry.

あわてもの 慌て者 *hasty person; scatter-brain*

あわてる 慌てる *1. to get confused, to get flustered*

運転手は事故で慌てました。

The driver got flustered in the accident.

2. to get in a great hurry

妹は慌てて走っていったよ。

My younger sister ran away in a great hurry!

あわび *abalone ((fish))*

あわれ 哀れ *pity; grief*

哀れな pitiful [→ かわいそうな]

あわれむ 哀れむ *to pity*

あん 案 *1. proposal, suggestion* [→ 提案]

その案は拒否されました。

That proposal was rejected.

2. idea [→ 考え]; *plan* [→ 計画]

何かいい案はありませんか。

Don't you have any good ideas?

あん *sweet bean paste*

あんパン sweet bean-paste bun

アンカー *1. anchor (of a ship or boat)* [→ 錨]

その船は港にアンカーを下ろしました。

The boat dropped anchor in the harbor.

2. anchor (in a relay)

吉田君はリレーでアンカーを務めました。

Yoshida served as anchor in the relay.

あんがい 案外 (〜に) *unexpectedly*

この問題は案外難しいね。

This problem is unexpectedly difficult, isn't it?

案外な unexpected, surprising

あんき 暗記 *memorization, learning by heart*

野木さんは暗記に強いです。

Mr. Nogi is good at memorization.

暗記する to memorize, to learn by heart

この歌詞を暗記しなさい。

Learn these lyrics by heart.

アングル *angle, viewpoint* [→ 角度]

いろいろなアングルで仏像の写真を撮った。

I took photos of the Buddhist image from various angles.

アンケート *questionnaire*

アンケートに記入してください。

Please fill out the questionnaire.

あんこ 【COL. for あん】

あんごう 暗号 *code*

スパイは暗号で通信を送りました。
The spy sent a communication in code.

アンコール *encore*

ドミンゴはアンコールを２曲歌いました。
Domingo sang two encores.

アンコールする to ask for an encore

聴衆はその歌手にアンコールを求めた。
The audience asked that singer for an encore.

あんざん 暗算 *mental calculation, doing arithmetic in one's head*

大村さんは暗算が得意です。
Mr. Omura is good at mental calculation.

あんじ 暗示 *suggestion, hint*

早川さんは暗示にかかりやすいです。
Mr. Hayakawa is easily influenced by suggestion.

暗示する to suggest, to hint at

自己暗示 autosuggestion

あんしつ 暗室 *darkroom*

あんしょう 暗唱 *recitation from memory*

暗唱する to recite from memory

あんしん 安心 [[↔心配]] *relief; peace of mind, ease of mind*

安心する to be relieved; to put one's mind at ease

その知らせを聞いて安心しました。
I was relieved to hear the news.

その事については安心してください。
Please put your mind at ease about that.

あんせい 安静 *rest, peace and quiet*

安静にしている to be resting in bed

2､3日安静にしていなさい。
Rest in bed for two or three days.

絶対安静 complete rest

お父さんは数日絶対安静が必要です。
Your father must have a complete rest for several days.

あんぜん 安全 *safety* [↔危険]

安全な safe [↔ 危ない]

この部屋にいれば安全です。
If you stay in this room you are safe.

「安全第一」 (on a sign)
Safety First

安全弁 safety valve

安全ベルト safety belt

安全地帯 safety zone; refuge

安全保障 security

安全ピン safety pin

安全装置 safety device

安全運転 safe driving

あんだ 安打 *hit (in baseball)*

安打を打つ to get a hit

安打する to hit safely

アンダーシャツ *undershirt*

アンダースロー *underhand throw (in baseball)*

アンダーライン *underline*

アンダーラインを引く to underline A

その単語にアンダーラインを引きました。
I underlined that word.

アンダンテ *andante*

あんてい 安定 *stability*

安定する to become stable, to stabilize

私たちは安定した生活を望んでいます。
We are hoping for a stable life.

このテーブルは安定しています。
This table is stable.

アンテナ *antenna (for electronic signals)*

あんな *that kind of*

(Like other Japanese demonstratives beginning with あ, あんな has two uses. One is to refer to something which is in sight and relatively far both from the speaker and from the listener. The other is to refer to something which is not in sight but which is familiar both to the speaker and to the listener.) [↔こんな; そんな]

あんな人は嫌いですよ。
I dislike that kind of person!

あんな試合を見たことがないです。
I have never seen that kind of game.

あんなに to that extent, that much

あんなに考えなくてもいいですよ。
You don't have to think so hard!

あんない 案内 *1. guiding, going along to show the way*

案内する to guide, to show the way

伯母は京都を案内してくれました。
My aunt showed me around Kyoto.

この人を部屋に案内してください。
Please show this person into the room.

2. information, notification

展覧会の案内が来ました。
Notification of the exhibition came.

案内する to inform, to notify

案内所 information desk; information booth

案内人 guide ((person))

案内書 guidebook

案内図 guide map

アンパイア *umpire*

選手たちはアンパイアに従いました。
The players obeyed the umpires.

アンパイアをする to umpire

アンプ *amplifier*

アンペア *ampere*

ーアンペア (counter for amperes; see Appendix 2)

あんまり 【COL. for あまり】

アンモニア *ammonia*

あんらく 安楽 *comfort, ease*

安楽な comfortable, easy

祖母は安楽に暮らしています。
My grandmother is living comfortably.

安楽椅子 easy chair

安楽死 euthanasia

い 胃 *stomach (the internal organ)*

胃が丈夫です。
My stomach is strong.

父は何か胃の病気です。
My father has some kind of stomach trouble.

いい *{Irreg.} 1. good* [↔ 悪い]

いい知らせがあるよ。
I have good news!

いい天気ですね。
It's good weather, isn't it?

父の体調はとてもいいです。
Father is very fit.

運動は健康にいいです。
Exercise is good for the health.

このカメラはあれよりいいです。
This camera is better than that one.

これは最もいい本です。
This is the best book.

ほうがいい you had better, it would be better to (following a verb) (If the verb is affirmative, it may be in either the past tense or the nonpast tense.)

すぐ行ったほうがいいです。
You had better go right away.

2. all right, OK, appropriate

いいと信じることをやりなさい。
Do what you believe is appropriate.

座ってもいいですか。
May I sit down? (A form of いい following a clause that ends in a gerund (-て form) optionally followed by も is the typical way of expressing permission or

approval in Japanese. Translations into English ordinarily use **may** rather than **all right even if** and **do not have to** rather than **all right even if not.**)

その仕事はやらなくてもいいよ。
You don't have to do that work!

駅へ行くにはこのバスでいいのですか。
Is this bus all right to go to the station?

いいあらわす 言い表す *to express (in words)*

感謝の気持ちを言い表すのは難しいです。
To express a feeling of gratitude is difficult.

いいえ *no (negative response to a question)* [↔ ええ]

「田中さんですか」「いいえ、違います」
"Are you Mr. Tanaka?" "No, I'm not."

「スキーはできないのですね。」「いいえ、できます。」

"You can't ski, can you." "Yes, I can."
(In response to a question that presumes a negative answer, いいえ is used to mean **No, your presumption is incorrect.** A natural English translation will often have **yes** rather than **no.**)

いいかげん いい加減 〜な *1. irresponsible* [→ 無責任な]; *sloppy, haphazard; vague* [→ 曖昧な]

いいかげんな返事をしました。
I made a vague answer.

その人はいいかげんな仕事をしました。
That person did a sloppy job.

2. moderate, appropriate (especially when used in an imperative like the following example)

いいかげんにしなさい。
Start behaving appropriately.

いいかた 言い方 *way of saying, way of speaking*

洋子さんは適切な言い方を知らないね。
Yoko doesn't know the proper way of saying it, does she?

いいすぎ 言い過ぎ *overstatement, exaggeration*

いいすぎる 言い過ぎる *to say too much; to exaggerate, to go too far*

いいだす 言い出す *1. to bring up, to broach (a subject)*

藤田君が最初に言い出したんだよ。
Fujita brought it up first!

2. to propose, to suggest [→ 提案する]

恵子さんはハイキングに行こうと言い出した。
Keiko proposed going on a hike.

いいつける 言いつける *1. to tell to do, to order to do*

父は私にこの仕事を言いつけました。
My father told me to do this work.

2. to tattle about

後藤君のことは先生に言いつけないよ。
I won't tattle to the teacher about Goto!

いいつたえ 言い伝え *tradition, legend* [→ 伝説]

いいはる 言い張る *to keep saying; to insist* [→ 主張する]

弟は映画に行くと言い張った。
My younger brother insisted on going to the movies.

いいわけ 言い訳 *excuse, exculpatory explanation*

それは言い訳にならないよ。
That is no excuse!

言い訳をする to make an excuse

明さんは遅刻の言い訳をしました。
Akira made an excuse for being late.

いいん 委員 *committee member; committee*

委員たちは全員出席しています。
The committee members are all present.

委員長 committee chairperson

委員会 committee; committee meeting

いう 言う *to say; to tell* [→ 告げる]

浅野さんは何と言いましたか。
What did Mr. Asano say?

「のどが渇いた」と洋子さんは言った。
"I'm thirsty," said Yoko.
京子さんはお父さんがパイロットだと先生に言ったよ。
Kyoko told the teacher that her father is a pilot!
言ったとおりにしなさい。
Do as I said.
私の言うことが聞こえますか。
Can you hear what I say?
物を言う to talk, to speak
物が言える to be able to talk
あの赤ちゃんはまだ物が言えません。
That baby cannot speak yet.
寝言を言う to talk in one's sleep
AというB a B called A
小森さんという人も来ました。
A person called Mr. Komori also came.
中尾さんはマウイという美しい島に別荘があります。
Mr. Nakao has a villa on a beautiful island called Maui.

いえ 家 *1. house, home* [→ 家]
伯父は大きな家に住んでいます。
My uncle lives in a large house.
姉の家は公園の近くにあります。
My older sister's home is near the park.
私たちは7時に家を出ます。
We leave home at 7:00.
5時に家に着きました。
I arrived home at 5:00.
6時前には家に戻ります。
I will return home before 6:00.
健さんは家にいますか。
Is Ken at home?
2. household [→ 家庭]; *family* [→ 家族]

いえで 家出 *running away from home*
家出する to run away from home
14歳の時家出しました。
I ran away from home when I was fourteen.
家出人 a runaway

いおう 硫黄 *sulfur*

イオン *ion*

いか *cuttlefish; squid*

いか 以下 *what is below, what follows* [↔ 以上]
データは以下のとおりです。
The data are as follows.

－いか －以下 (Added to noun bases, especially numbers. When -以下 is added to a specific number, the combination is understood to include that number as an upper limit. For example, 五つ以下 means **five or fewer**, not **fewer than five**.) [[↔ －以上]] *less than; or less, or fewer*
このかばんは5000円以下で買えるよ。
You can buy this bag for ¥5,000 or less!
5歳以下の子供は入れません。
Children five or under can't enter.
その生徒の成績は平均以下です。
That student's grades are below average.

いがい 意外 ～な *unexpected*
私たちの劇は意外な成功を収めました。
Our play had unexpected success.
妻の言葉はまったく意外でした。
My wife's words were completely unexpected.
この本は意外に読みやすいね。
This book is unexpectedly easy to read, isn't it?

－いがい －以外 *except, other than (Added to noun bases.)*
父は日曜日以外は毎日仕事に行きます。
My father goes to work every day except Sunday.

いかが 【FORMAL for どう】*how*
西本さん、ご機嫌いかがですか。
How are you, Mr. Nishimoto?
いかがお過ごしですか。
How are you doing?

きょうはご気分はいかがですか。
How do you feel today?

コーヒーをもう１杯いかがですか。
How about another cup of coffee?

いがく 医学 *(the study of) medicine, medical science*

医学部 medical department

医学博士 Doctor of Medicine

いかす 生かす *to make good use of, to make the most of* [→ 活用する]

お金を生かして使うようにしなさい。
Try to make good use of your money.

私たちは時間を生かさなければならない。
We have to make the most of our time.

いかだ 筏 *raft*

いかり 錨 *anchor (of a ship, etc.)*

いかり 怒り *anger*

その男に対して怒りを感じます。
I feel anger at that man.

怒りにわれを忘れました。
I forgot myself in anger.

いかん 遺憾 *regret*

遺憾な regrettable

いき 息 *breath*

驚いて息をのみました。
I caught my breath in surprise.

その女の子はとても速く走ったので、息を切らしています。
That girl ran very fast, so she is out of breath.

息をする to breathe

息を吸う〔吐く〕to breathe in〔out〕

深く息を吸いなさい。
Breathe in deeply.

息を詰める to hold one's breath

いき 行き *going, outbound trip* [↔ 帰り]

行きは電車で、帰りはタクシーです。
We will go by train, and return by taxi.

－いき －行き [☞ 行き]

いきいき 生き生き ～と *animatedly, in a lively manner; vividly*

明夫さんはその試合の様子を生き生きと説明しました。
Akio vividly described the game.

生き生きとする to become lively; to become vivid

京子ちゃんは生き生きとした女の子です。
Kyoko is a lively girl.

いきおい 勢い *1. force, power*

台風の勢いが衰えました。
The force of the typhoon weakened.

2. vigor, spirit

いきがい 生き甲斐 *reason for living, what one lives for*

いきかえる 生き返る *{5} to come back to life; to revive, to return to consciousness*

金魚は水に入れたら生き返ったよ。
The goldfish revived when I put it in water!

いきさき 行き先 [☞ 行き先]

いきさつ *circumstances, details, particulars*

いきなり *suddenly; abruptly* [→ 突然]

いきのこる 生き残る *to survive*

その事故で生き残った人が数人いました。
There were several people who survived the accident.

いきもの 生き物 *1. living thing* [→ 生物]

2. animal, creature [→ 動物]

いきる 生きる *to live, to stay alive*

人間は水がないと生きられません。
A human being cannot live if there is no water.

祖母は80歳まで生きました。
My grandmother lived to eighty.

生きている to be alive

この伊勢海老はまだ生きているよ。
This lobster is still alive!

いく 行く *{Irreg.} to go* [↔ 来る]

このバスは駅へ行きますか。
Does this bus go to the station?

今度の冬休みにスキーに行くつもりです。
During this coming winter vacation I plan to go skiing.

地下鉄で行きましょうよ。
Let's go by subway!

ジェーンさんはカナダに行きました。
Jane went to Canada.

京都には２度行ったことがあります。
I have gone to Kyoto twice.

「健ちゃん、どこにいるの？」「今行くよ」
"Where are you, Ken?" "I'm coming." (In general, Japanese requires 行く rather than 来る for movement away from the speaker's current location.)

遊びに行く to go and visit, to go for a visit

今度の日曜日に遊びに行くよ。
I'll go and visit next Sunday.

うまく行く to go well

すべてうまく行っています。
Everything is going well.

行ってきます。
I'll be back. (Literally: I'll go and come (back).) (This is the standard expression for announcing one's departure and temporary absence from home or a home base of some kind. Typical occasions of calling for its use are leaving the house in the morning, leaving on a trip, and leaving the office on an errand.)

行っていらっしゃい。
See you later. (Literally: Go and come (back).) (This is the standard expression for acknowledging another's departure and temporary absence from home or a home base of some kind.)

いくつ 幾つ *1. how many (for things that are counted using 一つ, 二つ, etc.; see Appendix 2)*

テーブルの上に桃がいくつありますか。
How many peaches are there on the table?

2. how old (because age can be counted using 一つ, 二つ, etc.; see Appendix 2)

妹さんはいくつですか。
How old is your younger sister?

いくつでも any number, as many as you like

いくつでも取っていいよ。
You may take as many as you want!

幾つか some, several

試験でいくつかのまちがいをしました。
I made some mistakes on the examination.

この単語はいくつかの意味があります。
This word has several meanings.

幾つも many

いくら *how much*

この時計はいくらですか。
How much is this watch?

お金はいくら持っていますか
How much money do you have?

いくらでも any amount, as much as you like, a lot

いくらでも食べていいですよ。
You may eat as much as you like!

いくらか some, a little

「牛乳はありますか」「ええ、いくらかあります」
"Do you have any milk?" "Yes, I have some."

叔父はスペイン語がいくらか話せます。
My uncle can speak a little Spanish.

いけ 池 *pond*

いけない (As the regular negative of the potential form of the verb 行く, it has the predictable meanings as well.)

1. bad, unacceptable (This meaning is particularly common in combination with a conditional clause of some kind. Translations of such combinations into English ordinarily use **must not** or **may not** rather than **unacceptable if,** and **must** or **have to** rather than **unacceptable if not**.)

うそをつくことはいけないよ。
You must not tell lies!

この計画のどこがいけないのですか。
What's unacceptable in this plan?

道路でキャッチボールをしてはいけない。
You mustn't play catch in the street.

辞書を見てはいけません。
You may not look at a dictionary.

芝生に入ってはいけない。
Keep off the grass. (Literally: You must not come on the grass.)

すぐそれをしなければいけません。
You must do that at once.

もっと勉強しなければいけないよ。
You have to study harder!

2. unfortunate, too bad

「母は病気で寝ています」「それはいけません」
"My mother is sick in bed." "That's too bad."

いけばな 生け花 *(traditional Japanese) flower arranging*

いけん 意見 *1. opinion* [→ 考え]

松本さんの意見はどうですか。
What is Ms. Matsumoto's opinion?

その問題について意見を述べました。
I expressed my opinion on that subject.

私の意見では矢野さんが正しいです。
In my opinion, Mr. Yano is right.

その事について部長と意見が合いました。
My opinion was the same as the department head on that matter.

2. advice [→ 助言]

私たちは先生の意見に従いました。
We followed our teacher's advice.

少数意見 minority opinion

多数意見 majority opinion

いげん 威厳 *dignity*

威厳のある人 dignified person

いご 囲碁 [☞ 碁]

いご 以後 *from now on* [→ 以前]

以後頑張ります。
I will do my best from now on.

―いご ―以後 *after, since (Added to noun bases referring to points in time.)*

8時以後に電話してください。
Please phone after 8:00.

私もそれ以後和田さんに会っていません。
I haven't seen Mr. Wada since then either.

イコール *equals (Used in giving arithmetic problems or mathematical equations.)*

3＋2＝5
Three plus two equals five.

いごこち 居心地 *feeling about living, feeling about being (that a place gives one)*

居心地がいい comfortable to live in, pleasant to be in

この部屋は居心地がいいですね。
This room is comfortable, isn't it?

居心地よく comfortably

いざ ～となると *when push comes to shove, in a crisis*

いざという時 time of emergency, time of need

いさましい 勇ましい *brave*

いさん 遺産 *inheritance, estate, legacy*

5000万円の遺産を相続しました。
I received an inheritance of fifty million yen.

いし 石 *stone, rock*

この門は石でできています。
This gate is made of stone.

石を投げないでね。
Don't throw stones, OK?

石段 stone steps
石畳 stone pavement

いし 意志 *will, volition*
原口さんは意志が強いです。
Mr. Haraguchi's will is strong.
自分の意志で校長先生に会いに行った。
I went to see the principal of my own volition.

いじ 意地 *1. will power, backbone*
2. stubbornness, obstinacy [→ 意地っ張り]
意地になる to become stubborn
意地を張る to become stubborn

いしき 意識 *consciousness, one's senses; awareness*
その小さい女の子は意識を失いました。
That little girl lost consciousness.
意識して consciously; intentionally [→ わざと]
意識する to become conscious of, to become aware of
意識的な conscious; intentional
由美子さんに意識的に冷たくしました。
I intentionally treated Yumiko coldly.

いじっぱり 意地っ張り *1. stubbornness, obstinacy* [→ 強情]
意地っ張りな stubborn
2. stubborn person

いじめ *bullying, cruel treatment*
いじめっ子 child who bullies others
弱い者いじめ bullying weaker people

いじめる *to bully, to pick on, to treat cruelly*
弟は時々妹をいじめます。
My younger brother sometimes picks on my younger sister.
動物をいじめてはいけないよ。
You mustn't treat animals cruelly.

いしゃ 医者 *doctor, physician*
医者を呼びましょうか。
Shall I summon a doctor?
医者に見てもらったほうがいいですよ。
You'd better have a doctor look at it!
掛かりつけの医者 the doctor one usually sees
歯医者 dentist
目医者 eye doctor

いじゅう 移住 *migration; emigration; immigration*
移住する to migrate; to emigrate; to immigrate
兄は去年カナダへ移住しました。
My older brother emigrated to Canada last year.

いしょ 遺書 *note left behind by a dead person; will* [→ 遺言状 (s.v. 遺言)]

いしょう 衣装 *1. clothes, clothing* [→ 衣服]
馬子にも衣装。 (proverb)
Clothes make the man. (Literally: Even for a horse driver, clothes.)
2. costume (for a play, etc.)
花嫁衣装 wedding dress
民族衣装 national costume

いじょう 異状 *something wrong*
このカメラはどこか異状があります。
There's something wrong with this camera.
エンジンには異状はありません。
There is nothing wrong with the engine.

いじょう 異状 〜な *unusual, abnormal* [↔ 正常な]
この寒さは秋にしては異状です。
This cold is unusual for autumn.

いじょう 以上 *1. what precedes, what is above [↔ 以下]*
2. now that, since
卒業した以上、就職しなければならない。
Now that I've graduated, I have to get a job.

ーいじょう ー以上 (Added to noun bases, especially numbers. When ー以上 is added to a specific number, the combination is understood to include that number as a lower limit. For example, 五つ以上 means **five or more,** not **more than five**.) [[↔ ー以下]] *more than; or more*

部屋には5人以上の生徒がいます。
There are five or more students in the room.

これ以上言う事はありません。
I have nothing more than this to say.

英語の成績は平均以上です。
My English grades are above average.

いじる *{5} to handle; to play with; to fiddle with, to tamper with*

私の机の物をいじらないでください。
Don't fiddle with the things on my desk.

坊やはおもちゃをいじっています。
The little boy is playing with a toy.

いじわる 意地悪 *meanness, spitefulness, ill-naturedness*

意地悪な mean, spiteful, ill-natured

人に意地悪な事をしないで。
Don't do mean things to people.

いす 椅子 *chair; stool*

どうぞいすに腰掛けてください。
Please sit down on the chair.

先生はいすから立ち上がりました。
The teacher rose from the chair.

いずみ 泉 *spring (water source)*

いずれ *1. sometime soon; sooner or later*

2.〜にしても *either way, in any case*

いせい 威勢 [[→ 勢い]] *1. vigor, spirit*

2. force, power

威勢よく in high spirits

いせい 異性 *the opposite sex*

いせき 遺跡 *ruins, remains, relics*

いぜん 以前 *1. before, previously, formerly*

以前その映画を見たことがあります。
I've seen that movie before.

多田さんは以前京都に住んでいました。
Mr. Tada formerly lived in Kyoto.

2. former times, the past

父はずっと以前にローマを訪れました。
My father visited Rome long ago.

以前の previous, former

ーいぜん ー以前 *1. or earlier (Added to a word denoting a point in time.)*

石橋さんは3時以前に着くでしょう。
Mr. Ishibashi will probably arrive at 3:00 or earlier.

2. ago, earlier [→ ー前] (Added to a word denoting a period of time.)

千年以前は砂漠でした。
A thousand years ago it was a desert.

いぜん 依然 〜として *as ever, as before, still* [→ 相変らず]

いそ 磯 *rocky beach, rocky shore*

いそがしい 忙しい *busy* [↔ 暇な]

きょうは忙しいですが、あしたは暇です。
Today I'm busy, but tomorrow I'll be free.

きのうの夜は宿題で忙しかったです。
I was busy with my homework last night.

父はいつも忙しく働いています。
My father is always busy working.

いそぐ 急ぐ *to hurry*

急がないと電車に遅れますよ。
If you don't hurry, you'll be late for the train!

急いで in a hurry, hurriedly (This form is the gerund (-て form) of 急ぐ, and it has the predictable range of meanings as well.)

子供たちは急いで学校に行きました。
The children hurried to school.

急いで家を出ました。
I left the house in a hurry.

いた 板 *board; plate (i.e., a thin, flat sheet of metal, etc.)*

床板 floor board

いたい 痛い *painful, sore, hurting*

痛い！
Ouch!

どこが痛いのですか。
Where does it hurt?

背中が痛くてたまりません。
My back is so painful I can't stand it.

頭が痛い one's head aches

のどが痛い one's throat is sore

おなかが痛い one's stomach aches

いたい 遺体 *corpse, (dead person's) remains*

いだい 偉大 ～な *great, mighty, grand*

ピカソは偉大な芸術家でした。
Picasso was a great artist.

いたす 致す 【HUM. for する】

いたずら *mischief, prank, trick*

いたずらな mischievous, prankish

いたずらをする to do mischief, to play a trick

健ちゃんはよく私にいたずらをするよ。
Ken often plays tricks on me!

いたずらっ子 mischievous child

いたずらに 徒に *in vain, to no purpose*

いただく 頂く *1.*【HUM. for 貰う *1.*】*to receive, to get*

山本さんからこの時計をいただきました。
I got this watch from Mr. Yamamoto.

この本をいただいてもよろしいですか。
May I have this book?

2.【HUM. for 貰う *2.*】*to receive the favor of (following the gerund (-て form) of another verb)*

教授にもう少しゆっくり話していただこう。
Let's have the professor speak a little more slowly.

お名前を教えていただけませんか。
Could you please tell me your name? (Literally: Can't I have you tell me your name?)

3.【HUM. for 食べる*;* 飲む *1.*】*to eat; to drink*

「もっとケーキを召し上がりませんか」
「もう十分いただきました」
"Won't you have some more cake?" "I've already had plenty."

いただきます。
I'm going to begin. (Literally: I will eat/drink) (This expression of deference is required before beginning a meal.)

いただく 頂く *to put on a crown of, to become covered with*

富士山は雪を頂いています。
Mt. Fuji is covered with snow.

いたち *weasel*

いたばさみ 板ばさみ *dilemma*

板ばさみになっている to be in a dilemma

いたまえ 板前 *cook, chef (in a Japanese-style restaurant)*

いたみ 痛み *pain*

背中に激しい痛みを覚えました。
I felt a severe pain in my back.

まったく痛みを感じません。
I don't feel any pain at all.

痛み止め painkiller

いたむ 痛む *to ache, to hurt*

傷がまだ痛みます。
The wound still hurts.

あのかわいそうな子供のことを思うと心が痛みます。
When I think of that poor child, my heart aches.

いたむ 傷む *1. to go bad, to spoil*

この桃は傷んでいます。
This peach is spoiled.

2. to become damaged, to wear out

その自転車はだいぶ傷んでいるね。

That bicycle is badly damaged, isn't it?

いためる 痛める *to injure, to hurt*

転んでひざを痛めました。

I fell down and hurt my knee.

心を痛める to become worried

弟は将来の進路のことで心を痛めている。

My brother is worried about his future course.

いためる 炒める *to fry (in oil in a frying pan)*

いたるところ いたる所 *everywhere*

この本は世界中いたる所で読まれている。

This book is being read everywhere all over the world.

いたわる 労る *to take good care of; to be kind to*

年寄りをいたわるようにしなさい。

Make sure to be kind to old people.

どうぞお体をいたわってください。

Please take care of yourself.

いち 一 *one (see Appendix 2)*

一月 January

いち 市 *market, marketplace*

国際見本市 international trade fair

いち 位置 *position, place, location*

このテーブルの位置を変えてくれる？

Will you change the location of this table?

選手たちはそれぞれの位置につきました。

Each player took her position.

位置について、用意、どん！

On your mark, get set, go!

いちいち 一々 *1. one by one, one after another [→ 一つ一つ (s.v. 一つ)]*

2. all, every single one

私のする事にいちいち文句を言わないで。

Don't complain about every single thing I do.

いちおう 一応 *provisionally, for the time being*

いちご 苺 *strawberry*

いちじ 一時 *1. once, at one time, before*

私たちは一時福島に住んでいました。

We once lived in Fukushima.

2. for a while, for a time, temporarily [→ しばらく]

一時休憩しましょう。

Let's rest for a while.

試合は雨で一時中断されました。

The game was stopped for a while because of rain.

3. one o'clock (see 一時 and Appendix 2)

いちじるしい 著しい *remarkable, notable, striking*

今学期宮本君の勉強の進歩は著しいです。

This term the progress in Miyamoto's studies is remarkable.

事故の数が著しく増えました。

The number of accidents has increased notably.

いちど 一度 *once, one time (see 一度 and Appendix 2)*

もう一度やってみなさい。

Try doing it one more time.

一度に at the same time, at once [→ 同時に]

一度に二つの事はできません。

I can't do two things at once.

一度も ever, even once (in combination with a negative predicate)

一郎は一度も東京に行ったことがない。

Ichiro has never once been to Tokyo.

いちにち 一日 *one day (see 一日 and Appendix 2)*

ローマは１日にして成らず。(proverb)

Rome was not built in a day. (Literally: Rome does not come into existence in one day.)

一日中 all day long

一日一日と day by day; day after day

一日一日と春が近づいています。

Spring is getting closer everyday.

いちにんまえ 一人前 *1. a full-fledged adult*

2. a portion of food for one person (see 人前 and Appendix 2)

いちねん 一年 *one year (see ー年 and Appendix 2)*

一年中 all year round

アラスカは一年中寒いですか。

Is it cold in Alaska all year round?

いちば 市場 *market, marketplace*

買い物に市場へ行きます

I'll go to the marketplace for shopping.

いちばん 一番 *1. (the) number 1 (see ー番 1. and Appendix 2)*

ピッチャーの背番号は１番です。

The pitcher's number is number 1.

2. first place, the first one (see ー番2. and Appendix 2)

娘はコンテストで１番になりました。

My daughter was first in the contest.

一番 the most (indicating a superlative) [→ 最も]

日本でいちばん高い山は富士山です。

The highest mountain in Japan is Mt. Fuji.

文子はクラスでいちばん優秀な生徒です。

Fumiko is the most outstanding student in the class.

平さんはいちばん熱心に勉強しました。

Ms. Taira studied the hardest.

科目の中で歴史がいちばん好きです。

Among school subjects I like history the most.

いちぶ 一部 *1. a part, a portion*

その話はほんの一部だけがほんとうです。

Only a part of that story is true.

一部の人たちはこの案に反対です。

Some of the people are against this plan.

2. one copy (see ー部 and Appendix 2)

一部始終 the whole story, all the details

その事件の一部始終を話してください。

Please tell me all the details of that incident.

いちめん 一面 *1. the whole surface; an unbroken expanse*

野原は一面 の雪でした。

The fields were an unbroken expanse of snow.

一面 に all over (the whole surface)

空は黒い雲で一面 に覆われています。

The sky is covered all over with black clouds.

2. one facet, one side, one aspect (see—面 and Appendix 2)

事件の一面 しか知りません。

I know only one aspect of the incident.

いちょう 胃腸 *stomach and intestines, digestive system*

いちょう *ginkgo*

いちらんひょう 一覧表 *list, listing*

いちりゅう 一流 ～の *first-class, top-rank*

林さんは一流のピアニストです。

Miss Hayashi is a top-rank pianist.

一流ホテル first-class hotel

いちるい 一塁 *first base* [→ ファースト]

一塁手 first baseman [→ ファースト2.] (in baseball)

いつ *when (as a question word)*

お誕生日はいつですか。

When is your birthday?

いつ出発しますか。

When will you depart?

いつから since when, how long, beginning when

いつから待っていますか。

How long have you been waiting?

試験はいつから始まりますか。

When do the examinations begin?

いつまで until when, how long

ここにいつまで滞在しますか。
How long will you stay here?
いつまでに by when
この仕事はいつまでに仕上げられますか。
By when must I finish this work?
いつまでも forever; as long as you like
いつまでも忘れないでしょう。
I will probably never forget.
いつでも any time, no matter when, always
いつでも遊びにいらっしゃい。
Come and visit any time.
「いつお電話しましょうか」「いつでもいいですよ」
"When shall I phone you?" "Any time is all right!"
祖父はいつでもテレビを見ています。
My grandfather is always watching television.

いつか *sometime, some day (i.e., some time in the future); once, before (i.e., some time in the past)*
いつかパリに行きたいよ。
I want to visit Paris some day!
あの人にいつか会ったことがあります。
I have met that person before.

いつか 五日 *(see Appendix 2) 1. five days*
2. the fifth (day of a month)

いっか 一家 *(one entire) family, (one entire) household*
母が一家を支えています。
Mother supports the family.

―いっか ―一家 *and the entire family (Added to bases that refer to persons.)*
土井さん一家は福岡へ引っ越しました。
The Doi family moved to Fukuoka.

いっき 一気 ～に *without pause*
一気に飲む to drink in one gulp

いっけんや 一軒家 *single-family house*

いっこう 一行 *party (i.e., a group of people)*
一行は12名です。
The party is twelve people.

いっさい 一切 *1. everything [→ 全部]*
一切の whole, entire, every
2. completely

いっしゅ 一種 *one kind, one sort*
それはオレンジの一種です。
That's a kind of orange.
これは、まあ、一種のかばんです。
This is, well, a kind of bag.

いっしゅう 一周 *one trip around, one lap (see ―周 and Appendix 2)*
この公園は1周5キロぐらいあります。
This park is about five kilometers once around.
一周する to make one trip around
池の周りを1周しました。
I made one trip around the pond.
世界一周旅行 a trip around the world

いっしゅん 一瞬 *a moment, an instant*
一瞬立ち止まりました。
I stood still for a moment.

いっしょ 一緒 ～の *1. accompanying (as an adjective)*
いっしょに together [→ 共に]
いっしょに散歩に行きますか。
Are you going to go for a walk together?
みんないっしょにやりなさい。
Everyone do it together.
私は浩さんといっしょにテニスをした。
I played tennis with Hiroshi.
みんなハイキングに行きますが、いっしょに行きませんか。
We're all going hiking; won't you go with us?
いっしょになる to join together, to unite (intransitive)
2. simultaneous [→ 同時の]
いっしょに simultaneously, at once
3. same [→ 同じ]
僕たちはクラスがいっしょです。

We're in the same class. (Literally: Our class is the same.)

いっしょう 一生 [[→ 生涯]] *1. throughout one's lifetime, all one's life*

祖母は一生青森で暮らしました。

My grandmother lived in Aomori all her life.

2. lifetime, one's whole life

父は幸福な一生を送りました。

My father lived a happy life.

そのような事件は一生のうちには二度と起こらないでしょう。

That kind of event will probably not happen twice in a lifetime.

いっしょうけんめい 一生懸命（～に） *as hard as one can, with all one's might*

美知子さんは一生懸命勉強しています。

Michiko is studying as hard as she can.

一生懸命に走りなさい。

Run as fast as you can.

いっせい 一斉 ～ *everyone at the same time, all together*

村の人たちは一斉に立ち上がりました。

The people of the village all stood up together.

６人の走者が一斉にスタートしました。

Six runners started off all together.

生徒はみんな一斉に「おはようございます」と言いました。

The pupils said all together, "Good morning."

いっそう 一層 *even more, all the more*

いっそう努力しなければなりません。

You must strive even more.

いったい 一体 *on earth (in combination with a question word)*

いったい何を話しているんですか。

What on earth are you talking about?

いったん 一旦 *once (typically in combination with a conditional)*

いったん約束したら、守るべきです。

Once you make a promise, you must keep it.

いっち 一致 *agreement, match, correspondence*

一致する to come to agree, to come to coincide, to come to match

私は房子さんと意見が一致しています。

My opinion coincides with Fusako's.

いっちょくせん 一直線 ～に *in a straight line, straight*

いつつ 五つ *five (see Appendix 2)*

いつのまにか いつの間にか *before one realizes, before one knows it*

いつの間にか暗くなっていました。

Before I knew it had gotten dark.

いっぱい 一杯 *1. one cupful, one glassful, one bowlful, one spoonful (see* 一杯 *and Appendix 2)*

2.【COL.】*drinking a little (alcohol)*

一杯機嫌 good feeling from being a little drunk

いっぱい 一杯 *1. fully, to full capacity*

かごにはりんごがいっぱい入っています。

The basket is full of apples. (Literally: In the basket there are apples to full capacity.)

いっぱいの full, filled

愛子ちゃんの目は涙でいっぱいです。

Aiko's eyes are filled with tears.

もうおなかがいっぱいです。

My stomach is already full.

2. many, much, lots [→ たくさん]

部屋にはおもちゃがいっぱいあります。

There are lots of toys in that room.

－いっぱい *entire, whole (Most commonly added to bases denoting particular time periods.)*

今週いっぱいはここにいます。

I'll be here the whole week.

いっぱん 一般 ～の *1. general, universal*

2. common, ordinary

一般原則 general principle

一般人 ordinary person; commoner
一般的な [☞ 一般の (above)]

いっぽ 一歩 *one step (see ー歩 and Appendix 2)*
一歩一歩 step by step

いっぽう 一方 *1.[[→ 片方]] one side (of two); one (of two), one (of a pair)*
きょう本を2冊買いました。一方は小説で、もう一方は辞書です。
I bought two books today. One is a novel, and the other is a dictionary.
2. (〜では) on the one hand; on the other hand
肉の好きな人もいますが、一方魚の好きな人もいます。
There are people who like meat, but on the other hand there are people who like fish.
3. to keep on, to do nothing but (in combination with a preceding verb in the non-past tense)
物価は上がる一方です。
Prices keep going up.
一方的な one-sided
社長の意見は一方的です。
The company president's opinion is one-sided.
一方通行 one-way traffic
この通りは一方通行です。
This street is one-way.

いつも *always* [→ 常に]; *usually* [→ 大抵]
兄はいつも忙しいです。
My older brother is always busy.
いつも7時に起きます。
I always get up at 7:00.
いつもより遅く着きました。
I arrived later than usual.

イデオロギー *ideology*

いと 糸 *thread*
針と糸 needle and thread
糸が切れる a thread breaks
釣り糸 fishing line

いど 井戸 *a well*

いど 緯度 *latitude (on the earth's surface)* [↔ 経度]
東京の緯度は北緯35度45分です。
Tokyo's latitude is 35 degrees 45 minutes north latitude.

いどう 移動 *movement (from one place to another)*
移動する to move (transitive or intransitive)
テーブルを右へ移動してくれました。
They moved the table to the right for me.

いとこ *cousin*
おいとこさん【HON. for いとこ (above)】

ーいない ー以内 *within, or less* (Added to bases denoting quantities.) [→ ー以下]
森本さんは1週間以内に帰ってきます。
Mr. Morimoto will come back within a week.
駅は車で5分以内の所にあります。
The station is in a place that's five minutes or less by car.

いなか 田舎 *1. the country, rural area*
2. hometown, birthplace [→ 郷里]
田舎者 country bumpkin
田舎料理 country cooking

いなご *locust*

いなずま 稲妻 *lightning* [→ 稲光]
稲妻が光る lightning flashes

いなびかり 稲光 *lightning* [→ 稲妻]

イニシアチブ *the initiative, leadership role*
イニシアチブを取る to take the initiative
佐野さんは企画のイニシアチブを取った。
Ms. Sano took the planning initiative.

イニシアル *initial (letter)* [→ 頭文字]

イニング *inning* [→ 回] *(in baseball)*

いぬ 犬 *dog*
その犬はわんわんとほえました。
That dog barked bow-wow.
犬小屋 doghouse
犬掻き dog-paddling
子犬 puppy

いね 稲 *rice plant*
稲刈り rice reaping

いねむり 居眠り *dozing off, inadvertently falling asleep*
居眠りする to doze off
居眠り運転 dozing off while driving

いのしし 猪 *wild boar*

いのち 命 *life, animate existence* [→ 生命]
五郎さんはその女の子の命を救ったよ。
Goro saved that girl's life!
命拾い narrow escape from death
命綱 lifeline

いのり 祈り *prayer*
祈りを捧げる to offer a prayer
祈りをする to say a prayer, to say one's prayers
母は食事の前にお祈りをします。
My mother says a prayer before meals.

いのる 祈る *1. to pray; to pray for*
村人は神に祈りました。
The villagers prayed to the god.
2. to wish for, to hope for (for someone else's sake)
ご成功を祈ります。
I wish you success.
幸運を祈るよ。
I wish you good luck!

いばら 茨 *thorn bush, bramble*

いばる 威張る *to become arrogant, to act high and mighty*
あの医者は威張っているよ。
That doctor is arrogant!

違反 violation
Aに違反する to violate A
校則に違反してはいけないよ。
You mustn't violate the school rules!
駐車違反 parking violation
交通違反 traffic violation
選挙違反 election irregularities
スピード違反 speeding violation

いびき *snore, snoring*
いびきをかく to snore

いふく 衣服 *clothing* [→ 服]

イブニングドレス *evening dress*

イベント *1. special event*
2. event (in a competition)

いぼ *wart*

いま 今 *now; just now (in combination with a past-tense verb)*
今とても忙しいです。
I am very busy now.
今の若い人は歩くことを好みません。
Today's young people don't like to walk.
電車は今出ました。
The train left just now.
今まで何をしていましたか。
What have you been doing until now?
今ごろ about now, about this time
来年の今ごろは九州にいるでしょう。
I will be in Kyushu about this time next year.
和子は今ごろはもううちにいるでしょう。
Kazuko is probably already at home about now.

いま 居間 *living room, (UK) sitting room*

いまさら 今更 *at this (belated) point, now (when it's too late)*
いまさら後悔しても遅いよ。
At this point it's too late to be sorry about it!

いまだに 未だに *still, (not) yet* [→ まだ]

いまだに道夫さんは姿を見せません。
Michio has not shown up yet.

いまに 今に *soon, before long, by and by* [→ 間も無く, やがて]

お医者さんは今にここへ来ますよ。
The doctor will come here soon!

今にわかると思います。
I think you'll understand by and by.

今にも at any moment

今にも雨が降りそうです。
It looks as if it's going to rain at any moment.

あの子は今にも泣き出しそうです。
That child looks as if she's going to start crying at any moment.

いみ 意味 *meaning, sense*

この単語はどういう意味ですか。
What is the meaning of this word?

ある意味ではそれは事実です。
In a sense that's true.

母は意味のないことばかり言っています。
My mother is saying nothing but meaningless things.

意味する to mean, to signify

そのマークは危険を意味します。
That mark means danger.

イミテーション *an imitation ((object))*

いみん 移民 *immigrant; emigrant*

移民する to immigrate; to emigrate

イメージ *1. image, conception, mental picture*

2. image, impression on people

白は清潔なイメージを連想させる色だ。
White is a color with a clean image.

イメージアップ improvement in image

イメージダウン deterioration in image

いも 芋 *potato* [→ じゃがいも]; *sweet potato* [→ 薩摩芋]; [→ 里芋]

いもうと 妹 *younger sister* [↔ 姉; 弟]

末の妹 youngest sister

妹さん【HON. for 妹 (above)】

いもり 井守 *newt*

いや 嫌 ～な (This adjectival noun is used to describe both the people who find things distasteful and the people or things that are distasteful.) *distasteful, unpleasant, hateful; unfond, averse, unwilling*

村上は嫌なやつだね。
Murakami is an unpleasant guy, isn't he?

一人で行くのは嫌です。
I don't want to go alone. (Literally: Going alone is distasteful.)

「お野菜も食べなさい」「嫌だ」
"Eat the vegetables too." "No!" (Literally: It's undesirable.)

いやいや 嫌々 *against one's will, unwillingly, grudgingly*

私はいやいやうちに残りました。
I stayed at home unwillingly.

いやいや皿を洗いました。
I washed the dishes grudgingly.

いやがる 嫌がる *to show distaste for, to show aversion to (Used instead of* 嫌だ *when the subject is a third person.)*

洋子ちゃんは薬を飲むのを嫌がるね。
Yoko doesn't like taking medicine, does she?

イヤホーン *earphone*

いやらしい 嫌らしい *1. distasteful, unpleasant* [→ 不快な]

2. indecent, lewd, dirty

嫌らしい言葉を使うのはよくないよ。
It's not good to use dirty words!

あの人はとても嫌らしいです。
That person is very lewd.

イヤリング *earring*

母は真珠のイヤリングをしていました。
My mother was wearing pearl earrings.

いよいよ *1. at last, finally* [→ 遂に]

いよいよ梅雨に入りましたね。
We've entered the rainy season at last, haven't we?

2. more and more [→ 益々]

物語はいよいよおもしろくなりました。
The tale became more and more interesting.

風はいよいよ激しくなっています。
The wind has become more and more intense.

いらい 依頼 *request, favor (to ask)* [→ 頼み]

加藤さんは会社の依頼に応じて参加した。
Ms. Kato participated at the company's request.

依頼する [[→ 頼む]] to request, to ask for; to importune to handle

—いらい —以来 *since (Added to bases denoting past events or past times.)*

私は1978年以来ここに住んでいます。
I have lived here since 1978.

卒業以来10年になります。
It's ten years since graduation.

いらいら ～する *to become irritated, to get impatient*

その騒音にいらいらしていました。
I was irritated by the noise.

イラスト *illustration (in a book, newspaper, etc.)* [→ 挿絵]

この本にはイラストがたくさんあります。
There are a lot of illustrations in this book.

イラストレーター *illustrator*

いらっしゃる *{Irreg.} 1.* 【HON. for 居る】 *to be*

2. 【HON. for 行く】 *to go*

3. 【HON. for 来る *1.*】 *to come*

いらっしゃい。
Welcome! (Literally: Come.) (the imperative form of いらっしゃる)

いらっしゃいませ。
Welcome! (Literally: Come.) (This is a more formal imperative form of いらっしゃる. In Japanese stores, restaurants, etc., it is the standard expression used by employees to greet customers.)

いりぐち 入り口 *entrance, (entry) door-way* [↔ 出口]

正面の入り口から入ってください。
Please come in through the front entrance.

入り口に女の子が立っています。
There is a girl standing at the door.

いりょく 威力 *power, force*

チャンピオンのパンチは威力があるよ。
The champion's punch has power!

いる 居る *1. (The subject ordinarily must be animate.) there is/are; to be (located); to exist* [→ 存在する]

玄関にだれかいます。
There is somebody in the entry.

この学校には生徒が何人いますか。
How many students are there in this school?

あしたはうちにいません。
I will not be home tomorrow.

私はしばらく伯母の所にいます。
I'm going to be at my aunt's place for a while.

2. to have (a person in some relationship to oneself) (A person that someone has in this sense is treated as a grammatical subject and marked with が rather than with を.)

私には兄弟が二人います。
I have two siblings.

3. to be (doing) (in combination with the gerund (-て form) of another verb) (When いる is used as an auxiliary following a gerund, there is no requirement that the subject of the clause be animate.)

英男さんと明美さんは話し合っています。
Hideo and Akemi are talking to each other.

4. to have (done) (in combination with the gerund (-て form) of another verb) (When いる *is used as an auxiliary following a gerund, there is no requirement that the subject of the clause be animate.)*

エレベーターが壊れているよ。
The elevator has broken down!

飛行機はまだ動いていません。
The plane hasn't moved yet.

いる 要る *{5}* (What is needed is treated as a grammatical subject and marked with が rather than with を.) *to need; to be necessary*

お金が要るよ。
I need money!

今何が要りますか。
What do you need now?

このコンマは要りません。
This comma is not necessary.

いるか *dolphin; porpoise*

いれかえる 入れ替える *to replace (one thing with another)*

AをBと入れ替える to replace A with B, to substitute B for A

古い機械を新しいのと入れ替えましょう。
Let's replace the old machines with new ones.

エンジンのオイルを入れ替えました。
I replaced the engine oil.

イレギュラーバウンド *strange bounce, bad hop (in baseball, tennis, etc.)*

いれずみ 入れ墨 *tattoo*

いれば 入れ歯 *false tooth*

いれもの 入れ物 *container, box, case*

いれる 入れる *1. to put into, to insert*

花瓶に水を入れなさい。
Put water into the vase.

コーヒーにクリームを入れますか。
Do you put cream in your coffee?

2. to let in

犬を入れてください。
Please let the dog in.

窓を開けて、きれいな空気を入れました。
I opened the window and let in some clean air.

テニス部に入れてください。
Please let me into the tennis club.

3. to make (tea or coffee)

お客さんにお茶を入れました。
I made tea for the guest.

いろ 色 *color*

上着の色は派手ですね。
The color of the coat is loud, isn't it?

木の葉は秋に色が変わります。
The color of leaves changes in autumn.

明るい〔暗い〕色 bright〔dark〕color

薄い〔濃い〕色 pale〔deep〕color

色鉛筆 colored pencil

いろいろ 色々 (〜と/に) *variously, in various ways, in great variety*

いろいろ話したい事があります。
There is a great variety of things I want to talk about.

いろいろありがとうございました。
Thank you for everything. (Literally: Thank you in various ways.)

いろいろな various [→ 様々の]

いろいろな理由でその会合に出なかった。
For various reasons I was absent from the meeting.

いろは *1. the Japanese kana syllabary* [→ 五十音]

(This name refers to the first three letters in a traditional arrangement of the kana syllabary based on a poem in which each letter occurs once.)

2. rudiments, ABC's [→ 初歩]

いろんな 【COL. for 色々な】

いわ 岩 *(very large) rock*

岩の多い山に登りました。
We climbed a mountain with many rocks.

ボートは岩にぶつかりました。

The boat ran against a rock.

岩登り(いわのぼ) rock-climbing

いわい 祝(いわ)い *1. congratulations; congratulatory celebration*

心(こころ)からお祝(いわ)いを申(もう)し上(あ)げます。

I offer my hearty congratulations. (Literally: From my heart I (humbly) say congratulations.)

新年(しんねん)のお祝(いわ)い New Year's congratulations

2. congratulatory gift

孫(まご)に入学(にゅうがく)のお祝(いわ)いを送(おく)りました。

I sent a congratulatory gift for entering school to my grandchild.

祝(いわ)い事(ごと) happy event; celebration

祝(いわ)い物(もの) [☞ 祝(いわ)い2. (above)]

いわう 祝(いわ)う *1. to celebrate (an event)*

私(わたし)たちはクリスマスを祝(いわ)います。

We celebrate Christmas.

2. to congratulate; to offer congratulations on

人(ひと)を祝(いわ)う to congratulate a person

成功(せいこう)を祝(いわ)う to offer congratulations on a success

いわし 鰯(いわし) *sardine*

いわば 言(い)わば *so to speak, as it were, one might say*

夫(おっと)はいわば大(おお)きな赤(あか)ん坊(ぼう)です。

My husband is, one might say, a big baby.

いわゆる 所謂(いわゆる) *what is called; so-called*

あの方(かた)はいわゆる真(しん)の芸術家(げいじゅつか)です。

That person is what is called a true artist.

いんが 因果(いんが) *cause and effect*

因果関係(いんがかんけい) causal relation

いんかん 印鑑(いんかん) *signature seal* (Documents are ordinarily stamped with a seal rather than signed in Japan.) [→ 判(はん)]

いんき 陰気(いんき) 〜な *gloomy, dreary, melancholy* [↔ 陽気(ようき)な]

その女(おんな)の人(ひと)は陰気(いんき)な顔(かお)をしていました。

That woman had a gloomy face.

インク *ink*

インク消(け)し ink eraser

いんけん 陰険(いんけん) 〜な *cunning, crafty, sly*

あのやくざは陰険(いんけん)です。

That gangster is sly.

いんさつ 印刷(いんさつ) *printing (of books, newspapers, etc.)*

印刷(いんさつ)する to print

印刷物(いんさつぶつ) printed matter

印刷機(いんさつき) printing press

印刷所(いんさつじょ) printing office, print shop

カラー印刷(いんさつ) color printing

いんし 印紙(いんし) *revenue stamp*

いんしょう 印象(いんしょう) *impression (on a person)*

京都(きょうと)の印象(いんしょう)はいかがですか。

What is your impression of Kyoto?

印象(いんしょう)を与(あた)える to make an impression

印象(いんしょう)を受(う)ける to get an impression

印象的(いんしょうてき)な impressive

そのミュージカルはとても印象的(いんしょうてき)でした。

That musical was very impressive.

インスタントー *instant (Added to bases denoting things to eat or drink.)*

インスタントコーヒー instant coffee

インスタントラーメン instant noodles

インスピレーション *inspiration, sudden idea*

突然(とつぜん)インスピレーションがわきました。

Suddenly an inspiration came to me.

インターチェンジ *(highway) interchange*

インターホン *intercom*

いんたい 引退(いんたい) *going into retirement*

引退(いんたい)する to retire, to go into retirement

叔父(おじ)は60歳(さい)で引退(いんたい)しました。

My uncle retired at sixty.

インタビュー *interview (by a reporter)*

インタビューする to do an interview

あの記者は大統領にインタビューした。
That reporter did an interview with the president.

インチ *inch*

ーインチ (counter for inches; see Appendix 2)

インディアン *Native American, Indian* [→ アメリカインディアン (s.v. アメリカ)]

インテリ *an intellectual; the intelligentsia*

インテリアデザイン *interior design*

インテリアデザイナー *interior designer*

イントネーション *intonation*

インフォメーション *information* [→ 情報]

インプット *(computer) input* [→ 入力] [↔ アウトプット]

インフルエンザ *influenza*

先生はインフルエンザにかかったそうだ。
I hear the teacher caught influenza.

インフレ *(monetary) inflation* [↔ デフレ]

インフレで物価が上がっています。
Prices are going up because of inflation.

インフレーション [☞ インフレ]

いんよう 引用 *quotation, citation*

引用する to quote, to cite

「時は金なり」はフランクリンの言葉から引用されています。
"Time is money" is quoted from the words of Franklin.

引用文 quoted passage

引用符 quotation marks

いんりょう 飲料 *beverage, drink*

飲料水 drinking water

いんりょく 引力 *1. gravitational attraction, gravitation*

引力の法則 the law of gravitation

2. magnetic attraction

う

う 鵜 *cormorant*

鵜呑み gulping down; gullibly accepting as true

鵜呑みにする to gulp down; to gullibly accept as true

ウイーク *week* [→ 週]

ウイークデー weekday [→ 平日]

ウイークエンド weekend [→ 週末]

ゴールデンウイーク Golden Week (the period of April 29 through May 5 when three Japanese national holidays fall in close succession: みどりの日 (April 29), 憲法記念日 (May 3), and こどもの日 (May 5))

ウイークポイント *weak point* [→ 弱点]

ウイスキー *whiskey*

ウイルス *virus*

ウインク *wink*

ウインクする to wink

岡田君がきれいな女の子にウインクした。
Okada winked at that pretty girl.

ウインドー *window* [→ 窓]

ウインドーショッピング window shopping

よく恵子と渋谷にウインドーショッピングに行きます。
I often go to Shibuya with Keiko for window-shopping.

ウインドサーフィン *windsurfing*

ウインドサーフィンをする to windsurf

ウール *wool (cloth)* [→ 毛糸]

この靴下はウールです。
These socks are wool.

野口さんはウールのセーターを着ている。
Ms. Noguchi is wearing a woolen sweater.

うえ 上 [[↔ 下]] *1. top; upper part*

丘の上まで登りました。

I climbed to the top of the hill.
上の階に伯父が住んでいます。
My uncle lives on the upper floor.
ピアノの上に人形があります。
There is a doll on top of the piano.
テーブルの上に白いカバーをかけなさい。
Spread a white cover on top of the table.
上の学年 the upper grades (in school)

2. the area above
たこが木の上に上がっています。
A kite is flying above the tree.
田辺さんは驚いて跳び上がりました。
Mr. Tanabe jumped up in surprise.
上に行きなさい。
Go upstairs.

3. the part of a scale or ranking above
テニスの腕は弟のほうが上です。
As for skill at tennis, my younger brother is better.

4.〜の *older*
いちばん上の息子は15歳です。
My oldest son is fifteen.
次郎さんは由美子さんより二つ上です。
Jiro is two years older than Yumiko.

うえ 飢え *hunger*
たくさんの動物が飢えで死にました。
Many animals died of hunger.

ウエーター *waiter*

ウエート *weight ((athletic equipment))*
ウエートリフティング weight lifting [→ 重量挙げ (s.v. 重量)]
ウエートトレーニング weight training

ウエートレス *waitress*

うえき 植木 *garden tree, garden plant; potted plant*
植木鉢 flowerpot
植木屋 gardener

ウエスト *waist*
娘はウエストが細いです。
My daughter's waist is slender.

ウエット 〜な *sentimental, tender-hearted* [↔ ドライな]

うえる 飢える *to get very hungry; to starve*

うえる 植える *to plant*
父は庭にばらを植えました。
My father planted roses in the garden.

うお 魚 *fish* [→ 魚]
飛び魚 flying fish

ウォーミングアップ *warming-up (exercises)*
ウォーミングアップする to warm up

ウォッカ *vodka*

うかい 迂回 *detour; making a detour* [→ 遠回り]
迂回する to make a detour

うがい *gargling*
うがいする to gargle
うがい薬 mouthwash, gargle

うかがう 伺う *1.* 【HUM. for 訪ねる】 *to visit, to pay a call*
あした伺います。
I'll visit you tomorrow.

2. 【HUM. for 尋ねる, 聞く *3.*】 *to ask, to inquire*
伺いたい事があります。
There is something I want to ask you.
ちょっと伺いますが、銀行はどこですか。
Pardon me, but where is the bank? (Literally: I am going to ask you, but where is the bank?)

3. 【HUM. for 聞く *1.*】 *to hear, to be told*

うかぶ 浮かぶ *1. to float (intransitive)* [→ 浮く]
白い雲が青空に浮かんでいる。
White clouds are floating in the blue sky.

2. to occur to one
いい考えが浮かびました。
A good idea occurred to me.

うかべる 浮かべる *1. to float, to sail (transitive)*
私たちは湖にヨットを浮かべました。
We sailed a sailboat on the lake.
2. to show outwardly (on one's face) (transitive)
目に涙を浮かべる to show tears in one's eyes
少女は目に涙を浮かべているよ。
The girl has tears in her eyes!
3. to call, to recall (to mind)
頭に浮かべる to call to mind, to recall
心に浮かべる to call to mind, to recall

うかる 受かる *to pass, to succeed (on a test)* [→ 合格する] [↔ 落ちる2.]
妹は試験に受かったよ。
My younger sister passed the examination!

うきぶくろ 浮き袋 *life preserver* [→ 救命具 (s.v. 救命)]; *life buoy*

うきよえ 浮世絵 *ukiyoe (i.e., a traditional Japanese woodblock print)*

うく 浮く *to float (intransitive)* [→ 浮かぶ 1.]

うぐいす 鶯 *Japanese nightingale*

うけいれる 受け入れる *to accept*
その援助の申し出を受け入れます。
I will accept that offer of help.

うけつぐ 受け継ぐ *to inherit, to succeed to* [→ 継ぐ]

うけつけ 受付 *1. acceptance, receiving, reception*
2. information desk, reception desk
3. receptionist

うけつける 受け付ける *to accept, to receive*
申し込みはあしたから受け付けます。
They will accept applications starting tomorrow.

うけとる 受け取る *to receive, to get, to accept*
鈴木さんはおじいさんから毎週手紙を受け取ります。
Mr. Suzuki receives a letter from his grandfather every week.
先生は生徒たちから贈り物を受け取った。
The teacher accepted a present from the students.

うけみ 受け身 *1. the defensive*
2. the passive (in grammar)

うけもつ 受け持つ *to take charge of, to accept charge of*
加藤先生が私たちのクラスを受け持つよ。
Mr. Kato is in charge of our class!
田中先生は3年生の数学を受け持った。
Ms. Tanaka took charge of third-year math.

うける 受ける *1. to receive*
私たちは大歓迎を受けました。
We received a big welcome.
2. to accept [→ 受け入れる]
その招待を喜んで受けます。
I'll gladly accept that invitation.
3. to take (lessons)
週3時間英語の授業を受けているよ。
I'm taking three hours of English classes a week.
4. to undergo, to experience
この患者はけさ手術を受けました。
This patient underwent surgery this morning.
試験を受ける to take an examination
あしたその試験を受けます。
I will take that examination tomorrow.
損害を受ける to suffer damage
その村は台風で大損害を受けました。
That village suffered great damage in the typhoon.
5. to catch (a ball, etc.)
レフトはボールを両手で受けました。

The left fielder caught the ball with both hands.

6. to become popular

この歌(うた)が若(わか)い人(ひと)に受(う)けています。

This song is popular with young people.

うごかす 動(うご)かす *1. to move (transitive)*

机(つくえ)を動(うご)かしなさい。

Move your desk.

心(こころ)を動(うご)かす to move one's heart, to move one

母(はは)の言葉(ことば)は私(わたし)の心(こころ)を動(うご)かしました。

My mother's words moved me.

手(て)を動(うご)かす to move one's hands

2. to operate, to run (transitive) [→ 操作(そうさ)する]

この機械(きかい)を動(うご)かすことができますか。

Can you operate this machine?

うごき 動(うご)き *movement; action* [→ 行動(こうどう)]

目(め)の動(うご)き eye movement

動(うご)きが取(と)れない to be unable to move, to be stuck

うごく 動(うご)く *1. to move (intransitive)*

もうちょっと左(ひだり)に動(うご)いてください。

Please move a little more to the left.

2. to work, to run, to function

エレベーターは動(うご)いていません。

The elevator is not working.

この機械(きかい)はガソリンで動(うご)きます。

This machine runs on gasoline.

この時計(とけい)は動(うご)いていますか。

Is this clock running?

うさぎ 兎(うさぎ) *rabbit; hare*

うし 牛(うし) *cow; ox; bull*

おじいさんは牛(うし)の乳(ちち)を搾(しぼ)っている。

Grandfather is milking the cows.

子牛(こうし) calf

うしなう 失(うしな)う *to lose, to be deprived of* [→ 無(な)くす]

まったく望(のぞ)みを失(うしな)いました。

I completely lost hope.

チャンスを失(うしな)う to lose a chance

うしろ 後(うし)ろ *the area behind* [↔ 前(まえ)2.]

その家(いえ)の後(うし)ろに大木(たいぼく)がある。

There is a big tree behind that house.

犬(いぬ)は主人(しゅじん)の後(うし)ろをついていきました。

The dog followed behind its master.

この車(くるま)の後(うし)ろの席(せき)は狭(せま)いです。

The back seat of this car is cramped.

後(うし)ろを振(ふ)り返(かえ)る to look back, to look behind one

後(うし)ろ足(あし) hind leg

後(うし)ろ姿(すがた) appearance from behind

うす *mortar (used with a pestle)*

うすい 薄(うす)い *1. thin, small from front to back* [↔ 厚(あつ)い1.]

そのパンを薄(うす)く切(き)ってください。

Please slice that bread thin.

2. [[↔ 濃(こ)い]] *light, pale (describing a color); thin, sparse (describing liquid, hair, etc.); weak (describing coffee, tea, etc.)*

色(いろ)は薄(うす)い青(あお)です。

The color is a light blue.

ここのスープは薄(うす)くてまずいですよ。

The soup here is thin and bad tasting!

うすぐらい 薄暗(うすぐら)い *dim, slightly dark*

薄暗(うすぐら)くなってきました。

It has gotten a little dark.

薄暗(うすぐら)い光(ひかり) dim light

うずまき 渦巻(うずま)き *whirlpool, eddy*

うずら *quail*

うせつ 右折(うせつ) *right turn* [↔ 左折(させつ)]

右折(うせつ)する to turn right

うそ 嘘(うそ) *lie, falsehood (Japanese is not as insulting as English lie.)*

うそ！

You're kidding! (Literally: A lie!)

うそをつく to tell a lie, to stretch the truth

政治家(せいじか)はよくうそをつきます。

Politicians often tell lies.

嘘つき liar (Japanese is not as insulting as English liar.)

うた 歌 *song*

日本の歌を歌いましょう。
Let's sing a Japanese song.

歌声singing voice

うたう 歌う *to sing*

恵子ちゃんは歌を歌うことが好きです。
Keiko likes to sing songs.

私たちはオルガンに合わせて歌います。
We sing along with the organ.

鼻歌を歌う to hum

うたがい 疑い *1. doubt*

あの学生の成功は疑いがないです。
There is no doubt about that student's success.

2. suspicion; mistrust

みんなが私を疑いの目で見ているよ。
Everybody is looking at me suspiciously! (Literally: Everybody is looking at me with eyes of suspicion.)

疑いなく undoubtedly

うたがう 疑う *1. to doubt*

自分の目を疑ったよ。
I doubted my own eyes!

2. to suspect; to mistrust

吉田がやったのではないかと疑いました。
We suspected that Yoshida had done it.

うたがわしい 疑わしい *1. doubtful, questionable* [→ 怪しい2.]

課長がほんとうに出張に行ったかどうか疑わしいです。
It is doubtful whether the section chief really went on the business trip or not.

2. suspicious, suspicion-arousing, suspicious-looking [→ 怪しい1.]

運転手は疑わしい人です。
The driver is a suspicious-looking person.

うち 内 *1. the inside* [→ 内部] [↔ 外]

2. time during, time while, time within [→ 間1.]

冬のうちはずっとここにいます。
We will stay here all winter.

暗くならないうちに帰ります。
I'm going to go home before it gets dark. (Literally: I'm going to go home while it has not gotten dark.)

姉は2、3日のうちに元気になるだろう。
My older sister will probably get well within two or three days.

数日のうちに帰ってきます。
I'll come back within a few days.

鉄は熱いうちに打て。 (proverb)
Strike while the iron is hot.

3. included membership, included range [→ 中2.]

Aのうちでamong A, of A (in combination with a superlative)

太郎は５人のうちでいちばん背が高い。
Taro is the tallest among the five.

うち 家 *1. house* [→ 家1.]

山本さんたちは大きなうちに住んでいる。
The Yamamotos live in a big house.

うちの中で遊ばないで。
Don't play inside the house.

2. my home; my family

時々その子供たちをうちに招きます。
I sometimes invite those children to my home.

もううちに帰ろうよ。
Let's go home now!

うちはみんな早起きです。
My family are all early risers.

うちあける 打ち明ける *to tell, to bring into the open, to reveal*

彼女はその秘密を僕に打ち明けた。
My girlfriend told me that secret.

うちあげる 打ち上げる *1. to launch, to shoot up*

夏には海岸で花火を打ち上げます。
We shoot up fireworks at the seashore in the summer.

来月、ロケットが打ち上げられます。
A rocket will be launched next month.

2. to pop up (in baseball)

センターにフライを打ち上げた。
I popped up to center field.

うちがわ 内側 *the inside, the inner side*
[↔ 外側]

内側は緑色です。
The inside is green.

だれかが門の内側に立っています。
Somebody is standing inside the gate.

うちき 内気 ～な *shy, timid*

その少年は内気です。
That boy is shy.

うちゅう 宇宙 *the universe; (outer) space*

太陽や星は宇宙の一部です。
The sun and stars are part of the universe.

宇宙服 spacesuit
宇宙飛行士 astronaut, cosmonaut
宇宙時代 the Space Age
宇宙人 (space) alien
宇宙旅行 space travel
宇宙船 spaceship, spacecraft
宇宙食 space food
宇宙ステーション space station

うちわ *fan (a round, non-folding fan made of paper on a bamboo frame)*

うちわであおぐ to fan with a fan

うちわ 内輪 ～の *private, internal*

うつ 打つ *to strike, to hit, to beat, to knock*
[→ 叩く]

兄は僕の頭を打ったよ。
My older brother hit me on the head!

選手はバットでボールを打ちました。
The player hit the ball with the bat.

男の子は太鼓を打っています。
The boy is beating a drum.

時計が3時を打ちました。
The clock struck three.

人の心を打つ to move a person, to impress a person

その話は大いに心を打ちました。
That story moved me greatly.

うつ 撃つ *1. to shoot (a person, animal, etc.)*

犯人は警官をけん銃で撃ちました。
The criminal shot the police officer with a pistol.

2. to fire, to shoot (a gun) [→ 発射する]

毎日正午に大砲を撃ちます。
They fire a cannon every day at noon.

撃て！
Fire!

うっかり (～して) *carelessly, absentmindedly*

うっかりして教科書を持ってこなかった。
I carelessly didn't bring my textbook.

うつくしい 美しい *beautiful, lovely*

この花はとても美しいね。
This flower is very beautiful, isn't it?

何と美しい景色でしょう。
What a lovely view!

お姉さんは美しい声をしていますね。
Your older sister has a beautiful voice, doesn't she?

うつす 写す *1. to copy; to trace*

その詩をノートに写します。
I'll copy that poem in my notebook.

2. to take (a photograph) [→ 撮る]

カメラマンは山の写真を写しました。
The photographer took a picture of the mountains.

うつす 映す *1. to reflect (transitive)*

水面が月を映しています。
The water is reflecting the moon.

2. to project, to show (on a screen)

先生はスライドを映しています。
The teacher is showing slides.

うつす 移す *1. to move (from one place to*

another) (transitive)
これらの机を隣の教室に移しなさい。
Move these desks to the next classroom.

2. to give, to transmit (an illness)
友達にかぜをうつしてしまった。
I gave my friend my cold.

うったえる 訴える *1. to appeal for* [→ 呼び掛ける2.]
私たちは世界に平和を訴えています。
We are appealing to the world for peace.

2. to complain of
娘はよく頭痛を訴えます。
My daughter often complains of headaches.

3. to make an accusation
木村はこの男が宝石を盗んだと訴えた。
Ms. Kimura made the accusation that this man stole the jewels.

4. to sue
被害者は社長を訴えました。
The victim sued the company president.

うっとり ～と *with rapture, enchantedly*
妹はオペラをうっとりと聴いているよ。
My younger sister is listening enchantedly to opera!

うっとりする to be captivated

うつぶせ ～に *on one's face, on one's stomach, prone* [↔ 仰向けに]
次郎ちゃんはうつぶせに倒れたよ。
Jiro fell on his face.

うつぶせになる to lie on one's stomach

うつむく 俯く *to look down; to hang one's head*
その子は恥ずかしそうにうつむきました。
That child looked down shyly.

うつる 写る *to be taken, to come out (The subject is a photograph or something photographed.)*
浜野さんの写真はいつもよく写ります。
Ms. Hamano's photographs always come out well.
富士山はこの写真にきれいに写っている。
Mt. Fuji looks beautiful in this picture.

うつる 映る *1. to be reflected*
白い雲が湖に映っていました。
White clouds were reflected on the lake.

2. to be shown, to be projected (on a screen); to come in (on a television, etc.)
このテレビはよく映らないね。
(The picture on) this television doesn't come in well, does it?

うつる 移る *1. to move (from one place to another) (intransitive)* [→ 移動する]
渡辺さんは新しい家に移りました。
Mr. Watanabe moved to a new house.

2. to change, to turn, to shift (from one thing to another) (intransitive)
季節は夏から秋に移りました。
The season changed from summer to fall.
話題はテニスに移りました。
The topic shifted to tennis.

3. to be transmitted (when the subject is an illness)
弟のかぜが母にうつりました。
My younger brother's cold was transmitted to my mother.

うつわ 器 *container, vessel, receptacle*

うで 腕 *1. arm (from shoulder to wrist)*
あの二人は腕を組んで歩いています。
Those two are walking arm in arm.

2. skill, ability [→ 能力]
光子さんのスキーの腕は大したものです。
Mitsuko's skiing ability is really something.

腕時計 wristwatch
腕立て伏せ push-up
腕相撲 arm wrestling

うどん *udon (a kind of wheat noodles popular in Japan)*
うどん屋 udon shop, udon restaurant

うなぎ 鰻 *eel*
うなぎのかば焼き broiled eel

鰻登り steady increase, rapid increase

うなずく 頷く *to nod (in affirmation)*

友子ちゃんはだまって、ただうなずきました。
Tomoko just nodded without speaking.

うなる 唸る *1. to groan, to moan*

2. to growl; to howl

犬が私を見てうなったよ。
A dog looked at me and growled!

うに *1. sea urchin*

2. seasoned sea urchin eggs

うぬぼれ 自惚れ *overconfidence, conceit*

うぬぼれの強い人 very conceited person

うぬぼれる 自惚れる *to become conceited*

うぬぼれた人 conceited person

うばう 奪う *1. to take forcibly*

強盗は老人からお金を奪いました。
The robber took money from an elderly person.

2. to engross, to captivate (a person's mind, attention, etc.)

その劇に心を奪われました。
I was engrossed in that play.

うま 馬 *horse; pony*

馬に乗る to mount a horse; to ride a horse

馬から降りる to dismount from a horse

馬から落ちる to fall from a horse

うまい *1. skillful, good (at) (This adjective is used to describe both people who are skillful and the things they are skillful at.)* [→ 上手な]

弘美さんはテニスがうまいです。
Hiromi is good at tennis.

荒井さんは英語を話すのがとてもうまい。
Mr. Arai is very good at speaking English.

うまく行く to go well

すべてうまく行きました。
Everything went well.

2. good-tasting, delicious [→ 美味しい]

うまれ 生まれ *birth*

生まれはどこですか。
Where were you born?

—うまれ —生まれの *born in/at/on (Added to bases denoting a place or date.)*

ジョンさんは米国生まれの人です。
John is a person born in the United States.

この子は一月一日生まれです。
This child was born on January 1st.

うまれかわる 生まれ変わる *to be reincarnated*

うまれつき 生まれつき *by nature, as an inborn characteristic*

前田さんは生まれつき勤勉です。
Mr. Maeda is diligent by nature.

生まれつきの born, natural

弘さんは生まれつきの詩人です。
Hiroshi is a born poet.

うまれる 生まれる *to be born* [↔ 死ぬ]

川田さんは京都で生まれました。
Ms. Kawada was born in Kyoto.

どこで生まれたんですか。
Where were you born?

生まれてからずっとここに住んでいます。
I have been living here ever since I was born.

ここが私の生まれた町です。
This is the town where I was born.

生まれて初めて for the first time in one's life

生まれて初めて飛行機に乗りました。
I rode on an airplane for the first time in my life.

うみ 海 *1. sea, ocean*

海が荒れています。
The ocean is rough.

その海を船で渡りました。
We crossed that sea by boat.

2. seaside, beach

夏は海へ行きます。
In summer we go to the beach.

うみ 膿 *pus*

うむ 産む, 生む *1. to give birth to*

直美さんは女の子を産みました。
Naomi gave birth to a girl.

ねずみはどんどん子を産む動物です。
Rats are animals that give birth to young in great numbers.

2. to lay (an egg)

この鶏は卵を産まないよ。
This chicken doesn't lay eggs!

3. to produce, to give rise to [→ 生じる1.]

夏目漱石は日本の生んだ偉大な作家です。
Soseki Natsume is a great writer that Japan produced.

うめ 梅 *1. ume, Japanese apricot, plum (The translation plum is traditional, although misleading.)*

2. ume tree

3. ume blossoms

梅干し pickled ume

うめる 埋める *1. to bury*

父はそのつぼを埋めました。
My father buried that pot in the ground.

2. to fill in (transitive)

池を埋める to fill in a pond

空欄を埋める to fill in a blank

うやまう 敬う *1. to respect, to esteem (a person)* [→ 尊敬する]

2. to worship (a deity) [→ 拝む]

うよく 右翼 [[↔ 左翼]] *1. (political) right wing*

2. right field (in baseball) [→ ライト1.]

右翼団体 right-wing group

右翼手 right fielder [→ ライト2.]

うら 裏 *1. back, other side, opposite side* [↔ 表1.]

この名刺の裏に何かが書いてあります。
Something is written on the back of this business card.

裏も見てください。
Please look at the other side, too.

2. the area behind [→ 後ろ1.]

うちの裏に公園があります。
There is a park behind my house.

3. bottom (of an inning) [↔ 表3.]

７回の裏です。
It's the bottom of the seventh inning.

裏番組 program on a different channel

裏通り back street, alley

裏口 back door

裏口入学 gaining admission to a school dishonestly

裏地 lining (of a coat, etc.)

裏門 back gate

うらがえし 裏返し ～の *inside-out; opposite-face-down*

健ちゃんは靴下を裏返しにはいていたよ。
Ken was wearing his socks inside out!

うらがえす 裏返す *1. to turn over, to turn opposite face down (transitive)* [→ ひっくり返す1.]

その２枚のトランプを裏返してください。
Please turn those two cards over.

2. to turn inside out (transitive)

うらぎり 裏切り *betrayal, treachery*

裏切り者 betrayer, traitor

うらぎる 裏切る *{5} to betray*

あの人は友達を裏切るかもしれません。
That person might betray his friends.

結果はわれわれの期待を裏切りました。
The results betrayed our hopes.

うらづける 裏付ける *to provide support for, to back up*

うらない 占い *fortune-telling*

奥さんはトランプで占いをします。

The wife does fortune-telling with cards.

占い師 fortune-teller

うらなう 占う *to foretell, to divine by fortune-telling*

うらみ 恨み *grudge*

あの人に何の恨みもないよ。

I don't have any kind of grudge against that person!

うらむ 恨む *to have a grudge against*

うらやましい 羨ましい *envious*

(This adjective is used to describe both people who are envious and the things they are envious of.)

あの人の成功がうらやましいです。

I am envious of that person's success.

弟もうらやましいようです。

My younger brother also seems to be envious.

うらやむ 羨む *to envy*

ウラン *uranium*

うり 瓜 *melon*

うりきれ 売り切れ *being sold out*

切符は売り切れです。

The tickets are sold out.

うりきれる 売り切れる *to become sold out*

うりだし 売り出し *1. putting on sale, putting on the market*

2. (bargain) sale [→ 特売]

大売り出し big sale

「本日大売り出し」 (on a sign)

Big Sale Today

年末大売り出し big year-end sale

うりだす 売り出す *to put on sale, to put on the market*

その新型カメラは来週売り出します。

They will put that new-model of camera on sale next week.

うりば 売り場 *sales counter; department (of a large store)*

文房具売り場 stationery counter

切符売り場 ticket office; ticket counter

おもちゃ売り場 toy department

うる 売る *to sell (transitive)* [↔ 買う]

あの店では花を売っています。

They're selling flowers at that store.

叔母は田中さんに車を40万円で売った。

My aunt sold a car to Ms. Tanaka for ¥400,000.

うるうどし 閏年 *leap year*

うるさい 煩い *1. noisy* [→ 騒がしい] [↔ 静かな1.]

ラジオがうるさいね。

The radio is noisy, isn't it?

うるさい！

Be quiet! (Literally: You're noisy!)

2. given to nagging, given to complaining

母はいつもうるさいです。

My mother is always given to nagging.

3. particular, fussy

父は食べ物にうるさいです。

My father is particular about food.

4. annoying, bothersome

はえはうるさいね。

The flies are annoying, aren't they?

うれしい 嬉しい *glad, happy* [↔ 悲しい]

(This adjective is ordinarily restricted to describing the speaker's happiness. To describe another person's (apparent) happiness requires a form such as (below).)

合格してたいへんうれしいです。

I am very glad that I passed.

嬉しそうな happy-looking, happy-seeming (This adjective is ordinarily used to describe another person's (apparent) happiness.)

うれる 売れる *1. to sell (intransitive)*

この本はよく売れます。

This book sells well.

その絵は50万円で売れました。

That picture sold for ¥500,000.

2. to become popular, to become well known

アーチャーはよく売れている作家です。
Archer is a very popular writer.

うろこ 鱗 *scale (on the skin of a fish, reptile, etc.)*

うろつく *to loiter, to hang around*

うわぎ 上着 *(suit) coat, (sport) jacket*

うわさ 噂 *rumor; gossip, idle talk*

うわさに耳を貸す to listen to rumors

うわさを立てる to start a rumor

うわさを広める to spread a rumor

人のうわさをする to gossip about a person, to talk about a person

うわさをすれば影。(proverb)
Speak of the devil and he will appear. (Literally: If one talks (about a person), (that person's) shadow (looms).)

噂話 gossip

うわまわる 上回る *to exceed* [→ 越える2., 越す2.]

うん 運 *fortune, luck*

運がいい〔悪い〕to have good〔bad〕luck

運よく luckily

運よく先生に会えました。
Luckily I was able to meet the teacher.

うんが 運河 *canal*

スエズ運河 the Suez Canal

パナマ運河 the Panama Canal

うんざり ～する *to get fed up, to get sick and tired*

太郎は仕事にうんざりしています。
Taro is fed up with his job.

うんざりだ to be fed up, to be sick and tired

そんな自慢話にはもううんざりです。
I'm already sick and tired of that kind of boasting.

うんちん 運賃 *fare*

バスの運賃が来月値上げになるでしょう。
The bus fares will probably be raised next month.

片道運賃 one-way fare

往復運賃 round-trip fare

うんてん 運転 *driving (a vehicle); operating (a machine)*

車の運転ができますか。
Can you drive a car?

この機械の運転の仕方がわかりません。
I don't know how to operate this machine.

運転する to drive; to operate

運転免許証 driver's license

運転者 driver (of a car, etc.)

運転手 driver (of a vehicle as an occupation)

うんどう 運動 *1. (physical) exercise*

水泳はいい運動です。
Swimming is good exercise.

もっと運動をしたほうがいいです。
It would be better to do more exercise.

運動する to exercise, to get exercise

2. campaign, movement (for a political or social cause)

運動する to campaign

3. movement, motion (in physics)

運動の法則 the laws of motion

運動する to move, to go into motion

運動不足 insufficient exercise, lack of exercise

運動具 sporting goods

運動靴 sneakers, athletic shoes

運動場 playground

運動会 athletic meet; field day, sports day (at a school)

交通安全運動 traffic safety campaign

労働運動 labor movement

うんめい 運命 *destiny, fate*

不思議な運命でした。
It was a strange fate.

うんゆ 運輸 *transportation*
運輸省 the Ministry of Transport

え

え 柄 *handle*
この金づちの柄は木でできています。
The handle of this hammer is made of wood.
ほうきの柄 broomstick

え 絵 *picture, painting, drawing (not a photograph)* [↔ 写真]
明子さんは絵が上手です。
Akiko is good at drawing pictures.
これはピカソの絵です。
This is a painting by Picasso.
絵をかく to paint/draw a picture

エアコン *air conditioner*

エアロビクス *aerobics*

えいえん 永遠 ～の *eternal, permanent* [→ 永久の]
永遠に eternally, permanently, forever

えいが 映画 *movie, film*
映画を見に行きましょう。
Let's go and see a movie.
この映画はもう見ましたよ。
I've already seen this movie!
映画ファン movie fan
映画俳優 movie actor, movie actress
映画館 movie theater
映画監督 movie director
映画音楽 movie music
映画祭 film festival
映画スター movie star

えいかいわ 英会話 *English conversation*

えいきゅう 永久 ～の *permanent, eternal* [→ 永遠の]
永久に permanently, eternally, forever
永久歯 permanent tooth

えいきょう 影響 *influence*
影響する to influence
影響を与える to have an influence
テレビは私たちに深い影響を与えます。
Television has a big influence on us.
影響を受ける to receive an influence

えいぎょう 営業 *business (operations)*
営業する to operate a business, to carry on business
営業中の open-for-business
この店は営業中です。
This store is open for business.
営業時間 business hours

えいご 英語 *the English language*
あした英語の試験があるよ。
There's an English test tomorrow!
岡本さんの妹さんは英語の先生です。
Mr. Okamoto's younger sister is an English teacher.

えいさくぶん 英作文 *1. English composition*
2. English composition (course)

えいしゃ 映写 *projection (on a screen)*
映写する to project
映写機 projector

エイズ *AIDS*

えいせい 衛生 *health maintenance, hygiene*
衛生的 sanitary
この流しは衛生的ではありません。
This sink is not sanitary.
公衆衛生 public health
精神衛生 mental health maintenance

えいせい 衛星 *satellite*

衛星中継satellite transmission

その番組は衛星中継で放送されます。
That program will be broadcast by a satellite transmission.

衛星放送satellite broadcasting

衛星通信satellite communication

人工衛星artificial satellite

気象衛星weather satellite

通信衛星communication satellite

えいぞう 映像 *picture, image projected on a screen*

テレビの映像television picture

えいぶん 英文 *1. English text*

2. English sentence

えいやく 英訳 *English translation*

金田さんは漱石の小説を英訳で読んだ。
Mr. Kaneda read Soseki's novel in English translation.

英訳するto translate into English

山村教授はその小説を英訳しました。
Prof. Yamamura translated that novel into English.

えいゆう 英雄 *hero, heroine*

英雄的な heroic

英雄的な行為heroic deed

国民的英雄national hero

えいよう 栄養 *nourishment, nutritiousness*

このサラダは栄養に富んでいます。
This salad is rich in nourishment.

栄養のある食べ物nutritious food

栄養士dietician

えいわじてん 英和辞典 *English-Japanese dictionary*

ええ *yes* [→ はい1.] [↔ いいえ]

「出ますか」「ええ、出ます」
"Are you going to leave?" "Yes, I am."

「ケーキはもうありませんね」「ええ、ありません」
"There's no more cake, is there?" "No, there isn't." (In response to a question that presumes a negative answer, ええ is used to mean **Yes, your presumption is correct.** A natural English translation will often have **no** rather than **yes.**)

エース *1. ace (player)*

中原君はチームのエースです。
Nakahara is the ace of the team.

2. ace ((playing card))

ええと *uh, um, er (a pause filler)* [→ あのう]

「パーティーには何人来ますか」「ええと, 8人です」
"How many people will come to the party?" "Um, eight."

エープリルフール *1. April Fools' Day*

2. an April fool [→ 四月馬鹿 (s.v. 四)]

エール *a cheer (by spectators at a sporting event)*

エールを交すto exchange cheers

えがお 笑顔 *smiling face*

課長は笑顔で入ってきました。
The section chief came in with a smiling face.

えがく 描く *1. to draw, to paint* [→ 描く]

2. to describe, to depict

えき 駅 *(railway) station*

毎日駅まで娘を迎えにいきます。
Every day I go to the station to meet my daughter.

駅弁box lunch sold at a station

駅ビルstation building

駅長stationmaster

駅伝long-distance running relay race

駅員station employee

乗り換え駅 transfer station

始発駅first station (from which a train or bus starts)

終着駅 last station (at which a train or bus stops)

エキサイト ～する *to get excited* [→ 興奮する]

観衆は試合に非常にエキサイトしました。
The spectators get very excited by the game.

エキジビションゲーム *exhibition game*

エキス *extract (solution)*

牛肉のエキス beef extract

エキゾチック ～な *exotic*

えきたい 液体 *liquid* [↔ 気体; 固体]

えくぼ 笑窪 *dimple (which appears in the cheek during a smile)*

恵子ちゃんは笑うとえくぼができるね。
Keiko gets dimples when she smiles, doesn't she?

エゴイスト *egoist*

えさ 餌 *1. (animal) food, feed*

この鳥のえさは何ですか。
What does this bird eat?

Aにえさをやる to feed A

動物にえさをやらないでください。
Please don't feed the animals.

2. bait

えじき 餌食 *prey*

あの小鳥は猫のえじきになったよ
That bird became cat's prey!

えしゃく 会釈 *greeting nod*

会釈する to nod in greeting

エスエフ ＳＦ *(Generally not written out in katakana.) science fiction*

エスカレーター *escalator*

エスカレート ～する *to escalate (intransitive)*

エスキモー *Eskimo*

エスペラント *Esperanto*

えだ 枝 *branch, bough, limb, twig*

枝を折る to break a branch

枝を切る to cut a branch

枝を出す to put out branches, to grow branches

枝豆 green soybean

エチケット *etiquette* [→ 作法]

そうすることはエチケットに反しています。
To do so is against etiquette.

えっ *What?, What! (This exclamatory interjection expresses surprise or doubt. It frequently precedes a question asking for repetition or confirmation of surprising information.)*

えっ、佐藤さんも休むんですか。
What? Sato isn't going to come, either?

エックスせん エックス線 *x-ray (radiation)* [→ レントゲン1.]

エックス線検査 x-ray examination

エッセー *essay*

エッチ ～な *obscene, lewd*

えつらん 閲覧 *perusal, reading*

閲覧する to read, to peruse

閲覧室 reading room

エネルギー *energy*

えのぐ 絵の具 *paints (for pictures)*

絵の具のチューブ tube of paint

絵の具箱 paintbox

絵の具筆 paintbrush

油絵の具 oils, oil paint

水彩絵の具 watercolors

えはがき 絵はがき *picture postcard*

えび 海老 *shrimp, prawn; lobster*

エピソード *1. episode, digression in a longer story*

2. anecdote

エプロン *apron* [→ 前掛け]

えほん 絵本 *picture book*

エメラルド *an emerald*

エラー *error*

エラーをする to make an error

あのショートはよくエラーをするね。
That shortstop often makes errors, doesn't he?

えらい 偉い *1. great, eminent (describing a person or a person's actions)*

キュリー夫人は偉い学者でした。
Madam Curie was a great scholar.

2. important, high-ranking

津田さんは偉い役人です。
Mr. Tsuda is a high-ranking official.

3. terrible, awful [→ ひどい]

えらい雨でしたね。
It was terrible rain, wasn't it?

えらぶ 選ぶ *to choose, to select; to elect*

真理さんはこの辞書を選びました。
Mari chose this dictionary.

欲しい本を選びなさい。
Select the book you want.

僕たちは田中君を委員長に選んだよ。
We elected Tanaka committee chairperson.

えり 襟 *collar (on an article of clothing)*

エリート *the elite; member of the elite*

婚約者は銀行に勤めるエリートです。
Her fiance is a member of the elite who work in banking.

エリート意識elitist attitude

える 得る *to get, to obtain*

林さんは弁論大会で1等賞を得ました。
Mr. Hayashi got first prize in the oratory contest.

エレガント ～な *elegant* [→ 優雅な]

今夜はエレガントなドレスを着ます。
Tonight I will wear an elegant dress.

エレクトロニクス *electronics*

エレベーター *(US) elevator, (UK) lift*

エレベーターで12階まで上がりました。
I went up to the 12th floor on the elevator.

えん 円 *1. circle* [→ 丸]

円をかく to draw a circle

2. yen (the Japanese monetary unit)

—円(counter for yen; see Appendix 2)

定価は1000円です。
The list price is ¥1,000.

円高rise in the value of the yen

円安fall in the value of the yen

えんかい 宴会 *banquet*

えんがわ 縁側 *wooden veranda (projecting outside a ground-floor room under the eaves in traditional Japanese architecture)*

えんがん 沿岸 *coast, shore*

僕の郷里は日本海の沿岸にあります。
My hometown is on the coast of the Japan Sea.

沿岸漁業coastal fishery

沿岸線 coastline, shoreline

えんき 延期 *postponement*

延期する to put off, to postpone

今度の土曜日まで会を延期します。
We will put off the meeting until this coming Saturday.

えんぎ 縁起 *omen, portent*

縁起がいい to be auspicious

縁起が悪い to be inauspicious, to be ominous

えんぎ 演技 *acting, performance*

佐野さんの演技はすばらしかったです。
Ms. Sano's performance was wonderful.

演技する to act, to perform (intransitive)

えんげい 園芸 *gardening, horticulture*

園芸用具gardening tool

エンゲージリング *engagement ring* [→ 婚約指輪 (s.v. 婚約)]

えんげき 演劇 *theatrical performance, drama, play* [→ 劇]

演劇部 drama club

えんし 遠視 *farsightedness, (UK) long-sightedness (i.e., a vision defect)* [↔ 近視]

遠視の far-sighted person, (UK) long-sighted person

エンジニア *engineer, engineering specialist* [→ 技師]

えんしゅう 円周 *circumference*

円周率 pi (π)

えんしゅつ 演出 *production, staging (of a play, movie, etc.)*

演出する to produce, to stage, to put on

次の劇は浅野さんが演出します。

Mr. Asano will stage the next play.

演出家 production director

えんじょ 援助 *help, assistance, aid*

援助する to help, to assist, to aid

えんじる 演じる *to play (a role)*

大川さんはハムレット役を演じました.

Mr. Okawa played the part of Hamlet.

日本はこの問題で重要な役割を演じます。

Japan plays an important role in this problem.

エンジン *engine*

エンジンをかける〔止める〕to start〔stop〕an engine

ディーゼルエンジン diesel engine

ターボエンジン turbocharged engine

えんせい 遠征 *1. (military) expedition, foray*

遠征する to make an expedition, to go on a foray

2. (exploratory) expedition

遠征する to make an expedition

一行は来月エベレストへ遠征します。

The party will make an expedition to Mt. Everest next month.

3. tour (by a sports team)

遠征する to make a tour, to go on the road

遠征チーム visiting team

遠征軍 expeditionary force; visiting team

えんぜつ 演説 *speech, address*

政治家は上手な演説をしました。

The politician made a good speech.

演説する to make a speech, to deliver an address

エンゼル *angel* [→ 天使]

えんせん 沿線 *the area along (a transportation route)*

私たちの学校は鉄道の沿線にあります。

Our school is in the area along the railroad.

えんそ 塩素 *chlorine*

えんそう 演奏 *(musical instrument) performance*

演奏する to perform, to play

あのピアニストの演奏はすばらしいです。

That pianist's performances are wonderful.

野口さんはピアノでソナタを演奏しました。

Ms. Noguchi played a sonata on the piano.

演奏会 concert, recital

演奏者 performer

えんそく 遠足 *one-day outing, (school) field trip*

僕たちは鎌倉へ遠足に行きました。

We went to Kamakura on a field trip.

えんちょう 延長 *1. lengthening, extension (in space)*

延長する to lengthen, to extend

この道路は来年延長されるかもしれない。

This road may be extended next year.

2. prolongation, extension (in time)

延長する to prolong, to extend

阿部さんは滞在をもう１日延長しました。

Ms. Abe extended her stay for another day.

延長戦 overtime game; extra-inning game

えんどう *pea*

えんとつ 煙突 *chimney, smokestack*

エントリー *entry (in a race)*

エントリーする to enter

そのマラソンには70人がエントリーした。
Seventy people entered that marathon.

えんにち 縁日 *day of a fair at a Buddhist temple or Shinto shrine*

えんばん 円盤 *disk; discus*

空飛ぶ円盤 flying saucer

円盤投げ the discus throw

えんぴつ 鉛筆 *pencil*

しんが折れたので、鉛筆を削りました。
The lead broke, so I sharpened the pencil.

鉛筆入れ pencil case

鉛筆削り pencil sharpener

赤鉛筆 red pencil

色鉛筆 colored pencil

えんぶん 塩分 *salt content*

えんりょ 遠慮 *reserve, modesty, (polite) hesitation, diffidence*

遠慮する to be reserved, to hesitate (out of politeness)

遠慮しないで何でも聞いてください。
Please don't hesitate; ask me anything.

遠慮がちな reserved, diffident

遠慮なく without reserve, without hesitating (out of politeness)

遠慮なく話してください。
Please speak without reserve.

遠慮なくサンドイッチを食べてください。
Please eat the sandwiches without hesitating out of politeness.

お一 御一 (This prefix is added to bases that are grammatically nouns, adjectival nouns, or adjectives. The prefix is typically honorific, but in some words it has lost its honorific force. It also appears in some humble forms.)

お書きになる【HON. for 書く】

お金 money

お断りする【HUM. for 断る】

お名前【HON. for 名前】name

お 尾 *tail* [→ 尻尾]

この猿は尾が長いね。
This monkey's tail is long, isn't it?

犬は尾を振りました。
The dog wagged its tail.

オアシス *oasis*

おい *Hey! (an interjection used to get another person's attention)*

おい 甥 *nephew* [↔ 姪]

甥御さん【HON. for (above)】

おいかける 追い掛ける *to pursue, to follow, to go after* [→ 追う1.]

犬はボールを追いかけています。
The dog is going after the ball.

おいこす 追い越す *to pass, to overtake*

バスが私たちの右側を追い越した。
A bus passed us on the right.

「追い越し禁止」(on a sign)
No Passing (Literally: Passing Forbidden)

おいしい 美味しい *good-tasting, delicious (Can be used to describe a restaurant, cafeteria, etc., as well as food itself.)* [↔ まずい1.]

ここのピザはおいしいですね。
The pizza here is delicious, isn't it?

このレストランはあまりおいしくないよ。
This restaurant isn't very good!

美味しそうな delicious-looking
おいしそうだなあ。
Boy, it looks delicious!

おいだす 追い出す *to drive out, to force to go outside*
幸子は猫を追い出したよ。
Sachiko drove the cat out!

おいつく 追いつく *to catch up*
すぐ友達に追いつきます。
I'll catch up my friend right away.

おいで ～になる *1.*【HON. for 行く】*to go*
2.【HON. for 来る *1.*】*to come*

おいはらう 追い払う *to drive away, to make go away, to get rid of* [→ 追う2.]
明夫さんははえを追い払いました。
Akio drove the flies away.

オイル *1. oil* [→ 油]
2. petroleum [→ 石油]
オイルショック oil crisis

おう 王 *king* [↔ 女王]
王がその国を治めています。
A king is ruling that country.
百獣の王 the king of beasts
王冠 crown
王国 kingdom

おう 追う *1. to pursue, to follow, to go after* [→ 追い掛ける]
美知子さんは流行を追っています。
Michiko follows popular trends.
2. to drive away, to make go away, to get rid of [→ 追い払う]

おう 負う *1. to take, to assume (an obligation, responsibility, etc.)*
高野さんはその事故の責任を負いました。
Mr. Takano took responsibility for that accident.
2. to be indebted; to be due, to be attributable
夫の成功は妻の協力に負うところが多い。
There are many ways in which a husband's success is due to his wife's cooperation.
3. to sustain (an injury)
健次さんは事故で重傷を負いました。
Kenji sustained a serious injury in the accident.

おうえん 応援 *1. help, assistance* [→ 援助]
数人の青年が応援に来てくれました。
Several young men came to our assistance.
応援する to help, to assist
2. cheering for, rooting for; (moral) support, backing
応援する to cheer for, to root for; to support, to back
私たちもチームを応援しました。
We also cheered for the team.
応援団 rooter group, cheering section
応援団長 head rooter, cheering section leader
応援演説 campaign speech (for a candidate)

おうごん 黄金 *gold* [→ 金]

おうじ 王子 *prince*

おうし 雄牛 *bull*

おうじて 応じて [☞ に応じて]

おうじょ 王女 *princess*

おうじる 応じる *1. to respond, to reply* [→ 答える]
会社は私の質問に応じてくれました。
The company responded to my question.
2. to consent, to accede, to comply
田中さんの要求に応じるつもりはない。
I have no intention of complying with Mr. Tanaka's demands.
招待に応じる to accept an invitation

おうせつま 応接間 *room in a home where visitors are received*

おうだん 横断 *crossing, going across*

「横断禁止」 (on a sign)
No Crossing (Literally: Crossing Forbidden)
横断する to cross, to go across
ここで道路を横断してはいけません。
You mustn't cross the street here.
横断歩道 pedestrian crosswalk

おうひ 王妃 *king's wife, queen*

おうふく 往復 *round trip, going and returning* [↔ 片道]
往復する to make a round trip, to go and return
湖まで歩いて往復すると、50分かかるよ。
If you go to the lake and back on foot, it takes 50 minutes!
往復葉書 return postcard, postcard with a return card attached
往復切符 round-trip ticket

おうべい 欧米 *Europe and America*
欧米人 Europeans and Americans

おうぼ 応募 *application (for a job, to a school, etc.); positive response to a solicitation for participation*
応募する to apply; to respond positively
姉はその仕事に応募します。
My older sister will apply for that job.
コンクールに応募する to enter a contest
応募者 applicant

おうむ 鸚鵡 *parrot*

おうよう 応用 *application, putting to a particular use*
応用する to apply, to put to use
てこの原理は多くの物に応用されます。
The principle of the lever is applied to many things.
応用範囲 range of application
応用問題 application problem, question posed as an exercise for learners [→ 練習問題 (s.v. 練習)]

おうらい 往来 [[→ 通り]] *1. coming and going, traffic back and forth, traffic in both directions*
この通りは往来が激しいです。
The traffic on this street is heavy.
ここは暗くなると、車の往来が少ない。
When it gets dark, there is little automobile traffic here.
往来する to come and go, to go in both directions
2. road, street [→ 道路]

おうレンズ 凹レンズ *concave lens* [↔ 凸レンズ]

おえる 終える *to finish (transitive)*
その仕事を終えたところです。
I have just finished that work.

おおい 覆い *cover, covering*

おおい 多い *numerous, large in number, large in quantity* [↔ 少ない]
太郎は友達が多いです。
Taro has many friends.
この川には魚がおおいです。
There are many fish in this river.
東京は人口が多いです。
Tokyo's population is large.
この子は学校を休むことが多いです。
This child is often absent from school.
この国は地震が多いです。
This country has many earthquakes.
今年は雨があまり多く降りませんでした。
This year there wasn't much rain.

おおいに 大いに *very, greatly* [→ 非常に]
それはおおいに結構です。
That's very fine.

おおう 覆う *to cover*
テレビをこの布で覆ってください。
Please cover the TV with this cloth.

オーエル ＯＬ *(Generally not written out in katakana.) woman office worker (< office lady)*

おおがた 大型 ～の *extra-large, large-scale, oversized*

その大型の台風は本州に上陸するだろう。
That large-scale typhoon may come ashore on Honshu.

大型バス large bus

おおかみ 狼 *wolf*

おおき 大き ～な (Used only as a modifier, never as a predicate.) [[→ 大きい]] [[↔ 小さな]] *big, large; loud (sound)*

首相の発言は大きな影響力を持つだろう。
The prime minister's declaration will probably have a great influence on us.

そんなに大きな声で歌わないでください。
Please don't sing in such a loud voice.

大きな顔をする to act big, to be haughty

おおきい 大きい [[↔ 小さい]] *big, large; loud (sound)*

姉の旅行かばんは大きいです。
My older sister's travel bag is big.

アメリカは世界で最も大きい国の１つだ。
The United States is one of the largest countries in the world.

その少女は年の割に大きいですね。
That girl is big for her age, isn't she?

体育の先生は声が大きいです。
The physical education teacher has a loud voice.

大きく書いてください。
Please write large.

この写真を大きくしてください。
Please make this photograph bigger.

大きくなったら、劇作家になりたいです。
When I grow up, I want to be a playwright.

その問題は大きくなりました。
That problem got bigger.

ステレオの音を大きくするな。
Don't turn up the volume on the stereo.

口を大きく開ける to open one's mouth wide

おおきさ 大きさ *size*

この箱の大きさは同じです
The size of this box is the same.

この子の靴はどのくらいの大きさですか。
About what size are this child's shoes?

おおく 多く (This word is the adverbial form of 多い and has the predictable meanings as well.)

1. large amount, large quantity

この事件に関して多くを語る必要はない。
It isn't necessary to say very much about this incident.

多くの many, much (as a noun modifier)

この論文には多くの問題点があります。
This thesis has many problems.

2. majority, greater part [→ 大部分2.]

けが人の多くは学生です。
Most of the injured are students.

オークション *auction*

おおくらしょう 大蔵省 *the Ministry of Finance*

オーケー *1. an OK*

僕は父からオーケーをもらったよ。
I got an OK from my father!

オーケーする to okay

2. OK (an interjection expressing agreement)

オーケー、代わりに行ってあげるよ。
OK, I'll go in your place.

おおげさ 大袈裟 *exaggeration* [→ 誇張]

大げさな exaggerated

大げさに言う to exaggerate (what one says)

オーケストラ *1. orchestra* [→ 管弦楽団 (s.v. 管弦楽)]

2. orchestral music [→ 管弦楽]

おおごえ 大声 *loud voice*

兄はいつも大声で話します。
My older brother always speaks in a loud voice.

おおざっぱ 大ざっぱ ～な *rough, sketchy, approximate*

おおぜい 大勢 *a large number (of people)*

大勢の少年少女が歌っています。
A large number of boys and girls are singing.

オーソドックス ～な *orthodox*

おおて 大手 *major corporation*

オーディオ *audio*

オーディション *an audition*

オーディションを受ける to undergo an audition

おおどおり 大通り *main street, major street*

オートバイ *motorcycle*

オートバイに乗る to get on a motorcycle; to ride a motorcycle

オードブル *hors d'oeuvre*

オートマチック *1.* ～な *automatic* [→ 自動の]

2. an automatic (device)

3. automatic transmission

オートマチック車 vehicle with automatic transmission

オートメーション *automation*

オーナー *owner (especially of a professional sports team)* [→ 持ち主, 所有者]

オーバー [☞ オーバーコート]

オーバー 1. ～する *to exceed, to go over (a limit)*

2. ～な *exaggerated, overstated* [→ 大袈裟な]

オーバーコート *overcoat*

オービー OB *(Generally not written out in katakana.) alumnus, old boy*

オーブン *oven*

オーブントースター toaster oven

オープン ～する [[→ 開店する]]

1. to open (said of a store, restaurant, etc., for the business day) (transitive or intransitive)

2. to open (said of a newly established store, restaurant, etc.) (transitive or intransitive)

来月駅前にデパートがオープンします。
Next month a department store will open in front of the station.

オープンせん オープン戦 *preseason professional baseball game*

おおみそか 大晦日 *New Year's Eve*

おおめ 大目 ～に見る *to overlook, to tolerate*

おおもじ 大文字 *capital letter* [↔ 小文字]

おおや 大家 *landlord*

おおやけ 公 ～の *1. public, open*

その知らせを公にしました。
They made that news public.

2. public, official, governmental

オール *oar*

オールスター— *all-star~ (Added to noun bases.)*

オールスターチーム all-star team

オールスター戦 all-star game

オールナイト ～の *all-night*

オールナイト営業 open for business all night

オールナイト営業の薬屋はありますか。
Is there an all-night pharmacy?

オーロラ *aurora (Borealis or Australis)*

おか 丘 *hill*

おかあさん お母さん 【HON. for 母】 *mother* [↔ お父さん]

あの人は義子さんのお母さんです。
That person is Yoshiko's mother.

お母さんはどこにいるの？
Where is Mother?

おかげ お陰, お蔭 *helpful influence*

Aのおかげで thanks to A

部長の援助のおかげで、私は成功した。

Thanks to the department head's help, I succeeded.

君のおかげでバスに乗り遅れたよ。

Thanks to you, I missed the bus!

Aのおかげだ to be thanks to A

私が泳げるのは兄のおかげです。

It's thanks to my older brother that I can swim.

おかげさまで 【HON.】 thanks to you

おかげさまで助かりました。

Thank you for your help.

おがさわらしょとう 小笠原諸島 *the Bonin Islands*

おかしい *1. funny, comical* [→ 滑稽な]

何がおかしいんですか。

What's funny?

2. strange, odd [→ 変な]

佐藤さんが遅れるのはおかしいです。

For Mr. Sato to be late is strange.

機械の調子がおかしいよ。

There's something wrong with the machine! (Literally: The machine's condition is strange!)

おかす 犯す *1. to commit (a crime, sin, error, etc.)*

その人は犯罪を犯しました。

That person committed a crime.

2. to violate, to break

法律を犯してはいけないです。

One must not break the law.

3. to rape

おかす 侵す *to invade, to encroach upon*

人のプライバシーを侵す to invade a person's privacy

おかす 冒す 1. to brave, to face

野崎は生命の危険を冒して実験をした。

Nozaki made the experiment braving the danger to her life.

2. to affect, to attack (when the subject is an illness)

がんが胃を冒しています。

Cancer has affected the stomach.

おかず *supplementary dish in a traditional Japanese meal*

(A Japanese meal is thought of as consisting of a staple food (i.e., rice) and a variety of supplementary dishes. The word refers to the latter.)

夕食のおかずは何がいいですか。

What would be good for okazu at dinner?

おかね お金 *money* [→ 金]

息子は漫画本にお金をたくさん使います。

My son spends a lot of money on comic books.

川口さんはお金をもうけるのが上手です。

Mr. Kawaguchi is good at making money.

その旅行用に少しお金をためました。

I saved some money for that trip.

そのお金はあした払います。

I will pay that money tomorrow.

おがむ 拝む *to pray to (with head bowed and hands together)*

元日にわれわれは日の出を拝みます。

On New Year's Day we pray to the sunrise.

その年寄りは手を合わせて拝みました。

That elderly person put his hands together and prayed.

おかゆ お粥 [☞ 粥]

オカルト *the occult*

オカルト映画 occult movie

おがわ 小川 *stream, creek, brook*

おかわり お代わり *another helping, second helping*

お代わりはいかがですか

How about another helping?

お代わりする to have a second helping

おかわり お変わり [☞ 変わり1.]

おき 沖 *the offshore*

ヨットは沖へ出ました。
The sailboat went out offshore.

ーおき ー置き ～の *at intervals skipping*
(Added to number bases. When the base is three or lower, ー置き denotes intervals skipping that number in between, but there is disagreement among speakers when the base is larger than three. Some speakers interpret ー置き after such larger numbers as meaning each, every.)
1年おきの祭りです。
It's an every-other-year festival.
私たちは1週間おきに映画に行きます。
We go to the movies every other week.

おきあがる 起き上がる *to sit up (from a lying position); to stand up (from a lying position)*

おぎなう 補う *1. to make up for, to compensate for*
人手不足を補う必要があります。
It is necessary to make up for the shortage of help.
2. to supply, to supplement with
空所に適当な単語を補いなさい。
Fill in the blanks with appropriate words.

おきにいり お気に入り *a favorite*
洋子ちゃんは先生のお気に入りだね。
Yoko is the teacher's favorite, isn't she?
お気に入りの favorite
これは私のお気に入りのラケットです。
This is my favorite racket.

おきょう お経 *(Buddhist) sutra*

おぎょうぎ お行儀 [☞ 行儀]

おきる 起きる *1. to get up (out of bed)* [↔ 寝る1.]
きょうは何時に起きましたか。
What time did you get up today?
起きている to be up
2. to wake up (intransitive) [→ 目を覚ます (s.v. 覚ます)] [↔ 寝る2.]
起きている to be awake
父はゆうべ遅くまで起きていました。
My father was awake until late last night.
3. [[→ 起こる]] *to happen, to occur; to break out (when the subject is a fire, war, etc.)*

おきわすれる 置き忘れる *to forget (to take), to leave behind*
[→ 忘れる2.]
バスの中にカメラを置き忘れました。
I left my camera behind in the bus.
父はよくペンを置き忘れます。
My father often forgets to take his pen.

おく 奥 *inner part, recesses*
奥の部屋 inner room, back room
心の奥 the bottom of one's heart
森の奥 the depths of a forest
奥歯 back tooth, molar

ーおく ー億 *hundred million (see Appendix 2)*
1億 one-hundred million
10億 one billion

おく 置く *1. to put, to place, to set*
花瓶を棚の上に置きなさい。
Put the vase on the shelf.
電気スタンドを机の上に置きました。
I set a lamp on the desk.
2. to leave, to let remain [→ 残す]
山本さんは母にメモを置いていきました。
Ms. Yamamoto left a note for my mother and went.
3. to do for some future purpose (following the gerund (-て form) of another verb)
ビールをもう少し買っておいてください。
Please buy a little more beer (for later).
4. to keep, to leave (following the gerund (-て form) of another verb)
部屋のドアを開けておいてください。
Please leave the door of the room open.

おくがい 屋外 *the outdoors, the open air* [↔ 屋内]
会は屋外で開きましょう。
Let's hold the meeting outdoors.
屋外スポーツ outdoor sports

おくさん 奥さん【HON. for 妻】*wife*

おくじょう 屋上 *rooftop*
屋上庭園 roof garden

おくない 屋内 *inside, interior (of a buil-ding)* [↔ 屋外]
梅雨の間は屋内でします。
We do it indoors during the rainy season.
屋内プール indoor pool

おくびょう 臆病 〜な *timid, cowardly*

おくりもの 贈り物 *present, gift*
先生への贈り物です。
It's a present for the teacher.
クリスマスの贈り物 Christmas present

おくる 送る *1. to send (a thing)*
その写真を妹に送ってください。
Please send that photo to my younger sister.
2. to take, to escort (a person to a destination)
英男君は車でうちまで送ってくれたよ。
Hideo took me home in his car!
3. to see off (a departing person) [→ 見送る1.]
4. to spend (a period of time), to live (a life) [→ 過ごす]
祖父は幸福な人生を送りました。
My grandfather lived a happy life.

おくる 贈る *to award, to give (as a gift)*
毎年新入生に辞書を贈ります。
We give dictionaries to the new students every year.

おくれる 遅れる、後れる *1. to be late, to arrive late*
7時の電車に遅れました。
I was late for the 7:00 train.
飛行機は30分ほど遅れるでしょう。
The airplane will probably be about 30 minutes late.
2. to lose time, to become slow (when the subject is a clock) [↔ 進む3.]
私の時計は1週間に1分遅れます。
My watch loses one minute a week.
うちの時計は2分遅れています。
Our clock is two minutes slow.
3. to lag behind
私は友達より英語が遅れています。
I am behind my friends in English.
うちの父は時代に遅れているよ。
My father is behind the times!

おけ 桶 *tub; pail* [→ バケツ]
風呂桶 bathtub [→ 浴槽]

おこす 起こす *1. to wake (transitive)*
6時に森田さんを起こしてください。
Please wake Mr. Morita at 6:00.
2. to set upright, to bring to an upright position
看護婦は老人を起こしました。
The nurse helped the elderly person up.
子供は倒れた自転車を起こしました。
The child set the fallen bicycle upright.
3. to cause [→ 引き起こす]
不注意で運転手は交通事故を起こした。
The driver caused a traffic accident through carelessness.

おこたる 怠る *to neglect (to do), to fail to attend to*
義務を怠る to neglect one's duty

おこない 行い *action* [→ 行動]; *behavior, conduct* [→ 振る舞い]
日ごろの行いに気をつけてください。
Be careful about your everyday behavior.

おこなう 行う [[→ する1.]] *to do, to carry out; to hold (a meeting, ceremony, etc.)*
来週英語の試験を行います。

I will give an English test next week.
会合は1時から会議室で行います。
The meeting will be held in the conference room from 1:00.

おこる 怒る *to get angry*
鈴木さんは課長の言葉に怒っています。
Mr. Suzuki is angry at what the section chief said.

おこる 起こる [[→ 起きる3.]] *to happen, to occur; to break out (when the subject is a fire, war, etc.)*
何も起こらないでしょう。
Nothing will probably happen.
地震が起こって多くの死者が出た。
There was an earthquake and there were many fatalities.
ゆうべ火事が2件起こりました。
Last night two fires broke out.

おごる 奢る *to treat (a person to food and/or drink)* [→ ご馳走する (s.v. ご馳走)]
きょうは僕がおごります。
Today I'll treat.
AにBをおごる to treat A to B

おさえる 押さえる *1. to hold down, to hold steady, to hold tight, to keep from moving*
長田さんは足でドアを押さえました。
Mr. Nagata held the door closed with his foot.
2. to cover (a part of one's body, usually with one or both hands)
真知子さんは口を手で押さえました。
Machiko covered her mouth with her hand.

おさえる 抑える *to control, to restrain, to suppress*
祖父は怒りを抑えることができません。
My grandfather cannot control his anger.

おさがり お下がり【COL.】*hand-me-down clothes*

おさき お先 ～に [☞ 先に3.]

おさげ お下げ *(hair in a) braid, pigtail*

おさない 幼い *1. very young*
原口さんは幼い時から米国に住んでいる。
Ms. Haraguchi has lived in America since she was very young.
2. childish [→ 子供っぽい (s.v. 子供)]
それは幼い考えです。
That's a childish idea.

おさななじみ 幼馴染み *childhood friend*

おさまる 治まる *to subside, to abate, to calm down*
薬を飲んだら、痛みは治まりました。
When I took the medicine, the pain subsided.
風はやっと治まりました。
The wind finally subsided.

おさまる 収まる, 納まる *1. to be settled, to be taken care of*
その事件は収まりました。
That matter was settled.
2. to go, to be put (within a limited space)
お土産は全部その箱に収まりました。
The souvenirs all went into that box.
3. to be paid (when the subject is money owed); to be delivered (when the subject is goods)
注文した部品が期日通りに納まった。
The ordered parts were delivered on time.

おさめる 治める *1. to rule, to govern*
女王があの国を治めています。
A queen rules that country.
2. to quell, to subdue, to settle, to quiet
けんかを治める to settle a quarrel

おさめる 収める, 納める *1. to pay (money owed); to deliver (goods)*
父は税金を納めました。
My father paid the taxes.
2. to accept (something offered)
贈り物を納める to accept a gift

3. to obtain, to secure
勝利を収める to win a victory
利益を収める to make a profit
4. to put away, to store
社長は書類を金庫に収めました。
The company president put the documents away in the safe.

おさん お産 *childbirth, giving birth* [→ 出産]

おじ 伯父, 叔父 *uncle* (Strictly speaking, this word should be written 伯父 if it refers to an uncle who is an older brother of a parent or the husband of an older sister of a parent, and should be written 叔父 if it refers to an uncle who is a younger brother of a parent or the husband of younger sister of a parent.) [↔ 伯母, 叔母]
あさって、叔父に会います。
I will see my uncle the day after tomorrow.

おしい 惜しい *1. unfortunate, regrettable* [→ 残念な]
晴れた日に勉強しているのは惜しいです。
It's unfortunate to be studying on a sunny day.
2. precious, too good to lose or waste
だれでも命は惜しいです。
Life is precious to everyone.
これはまだ捨てるには惜しいよ。
This is still too valuable to throw away!

おじいさん *1.* 【HON. for 祖父】 *grandfather* [↔ おばあさん]
2. old man
ひいおじいさん great grandfather

おしいれ 押し入れ *closet (of the type used for storing bedding in a traditional Japanese-style room)*

おしえ 教え *1. teaching, instruction, lessons*
2. (religious) teachings

おしえる 教える *1. to teach*
吉田先生は音楽を教えています。
Ms. Yoshida teaches music.
英文の手紙の書き方を教えてください。
Please teach me how to write letters in English.
2. to tell, to inform of; to show (how to do something)
駅へ行く道を教えてください。
Please tell me the way to the station.
この道具の使い方を教えてくれませんか。
Will you show me how to use this tool?

おじぎ お辞儀 *bow (i.e., bending forward at the waist to show respect)*
おじぎする to bow
生徒は先生におじぎをしました。
The pupil bowed to the teacher.

おしこむ 押し込む *to cram, to stuff (into a container)*

おじさん 伯父さん, 叔父さん 【HON. for 伯父, 叔父】
—伯父さん, —叔父さん (Added to a given name as a title.)
私は信治叔父さんが大好きです。
I love Uncle Shinji.

おじさん 小父さん *man (This word typically refers to a middle-aged man but a child may use it to refer to a young man.)* [↔ 小母さん]
あのおじさんはだれですか。
Who is that man?

おしつける 押し付ける *1. to push, to press (one thing against another)*
AにBを押しつける to push A against B, to press A against B
高橋さんは机を壁に押しつけました。
Mr. Takahashi pushed the desk against the wall.
2. to force (something on a person) [→ 強制する]
兄はいつも私にその仕事を押しつけるよ。
My older brother always forces that work on me!

おしっこ【COL. for 小便】*pee-pee*

おしつぶす 押しつぶす *to crush, to squash*

帽子の上に腰を下ろして押しつぶしてしまいました。
I sat on top of my hat and crushed it.

おしぼり お絞り *moist hot towel (for cleaning hands before a meal)*

おしまい お仕舞い *end* [→ 終わり]

おしむ 惜しむ *1. to begrudge, to be stingy with*

父は努力を惜しみません。
My father does not begrudge effort.

2. to regret, to lament, to deplore

おしゃべり お喋り *1. chatting, (idle) talking*

授業中のおしゃべりはやめなさい。
Stop that chattering during class.

おしゃべりする to chat

お茶を飲みながらおしゃべりしました。
We chatted while drinking tea.

2. talkative person

おしゃべりな talkative, garrulous [↔ 無口な]

君はおしゃべりだね。
You're talkative, aren't you?

おじゃま お邪魔 [☞ 邪魔]

おしゃれ お洒落 *dressing up, dressing stylishly*

おしゃれな stylish; stylishly dressed

おしゃれな制服ですね。
It's a stylish uniform, isn't it?

真理子さんはいつもおしゃれです。
Mariko is always stylishly dressed.

おしゃれする to dress up, to dress stylishly

そんなにおしゃれしてどこへ行くの？
Where are you going to go so dressed up?

おしょうがつ お正月 [☞ 正月]

おじょうさん お嬢さん【HON. for 娘】*1.daughter*

お嬢さんはおいくつですか。
How old is your daughter?

2. young lady

このお嬢さんは道を教えてくれました。
This young lady told me the way.

おしり お尻 [☞ 尻]

おす 雄 *a male (animal)* [↔ 雌]

この猫は雄ですか、雌ですか。
Is this cat a male or a female?

おす 押す *1. to push* [↔ 引く1.]

安部さんはベルの押しボタンを押しました。
Ms. Abe pushed the doorbell button.

2. to press down to leave a stamped mark

係員は書類に印を押しました。
The clerk-in-charge pressed the seal down on the document.

おすそわけ お裾分け *sharing a gift with another person*

おすそ分けする to share a gift

おせいぼ お歳暮 [☞ 歳暮]

おせじ お世辞 *insincere compliment, flattery*

お世辞がお上手ですね。
You're good at flattery, aren't you?

お世辞を言う to give compliments, to make flattering remarks

おせっかい お節介 *meddling*

おせっかいな meddlesome

Aのおせっかいを焼く to meddle in A's affairs

三田さんはしょっちゅう小野さんのおせっかいを焼いています。
Miss Mita is always meddling in Miss Ono's affairs.

おせん 汚染 *pollution*

環境汚染 environmental pollution [→ 公害]

おそい 遅い *1. late* [↔ 早い]

もう遅いから、帰ります。
It's already late, so I'll go home.

遅い朝食をとりました。
I had a late breakfast.

飛行機は遅く出発しました。
The plane departed late.
遅くまで until late
姉は毎晩遅くまで起きています。
My older sister is up until late every night.
遅くとも at the latest
宮本は遅くとも 6 時までには帰るだろう。
Miyamoto will probably return by 6:00 at the latest.

2. slow [↔ 速い]
津田さんは遅く歩きます。
Mr. Tsuda walks slowly.
電車のスピードが遅くなりました。
The train slowed down.

おそう 襲う *1. to attack, to assault*
くまが村人を襲いました。
A bear attacked a villager.

2. to strike, to hit (when the subject is a natural disaster, an illness, etc.)
台風が九州を襲いました。
A typhoon struck Kyushu.

おぞうに お雑煮 *rice cakes with vegetables boiled in soup (a traditional Japanese New Year's dish)*

おそらく 恐らく [[→ 多分]] *perhaps; probably*
(This word often occurs in sentences ending with an expression of probability. Since such a sentence has virtually the same meaning whether or not is present, is redundant in a sense, but it serves as a signal of how a sentence will end.)
恐らく役に立つでしょう。
Perhaps it will help.
恐らくそれは本当です。
Perhaps that's true.

おそれ 恐れ *1. fear, terror*
恐れを知らない to know no fear

2. fear, danger (that something bad will happen)
その船は沈没の恐れがあります。
That ship is in danger of sinking.
大統領はまた失敗する恐れがあります。
There is fear that the president will fail again.

おそれる 恐れる *to be afraid of, to fear*
動物は火を恐れます。
Animals are afraid of fire.
外国語を話すとき、まちがいを恐れてはいけません。
When speaking a foreign language, one mustn't be afraid of mistakes.

おそろしい 恐ろしい *terrible, frightful, frightening* [→ 怖い1.]
恐ろしい夢を見たよ。
I had a terrible dream!
私は暗やみが恐ろしいよ。
I'm frightened of the dark!
恐ろしい事故 terrible accident

おそわる 教わる *to receive instruction, to be taught*
AにBを教わる to be taught B by A, to learn B from A
私はアメリカ人の女性に英語を教わった。
I learned English from an American woman.

おたがい お互い [☞ 互い]

おたまじゃくし お玉杓子 *tadpole, pollywog*

おだやか 穏やか ～な *peaceful, quiet, calm, gentle*
友子さんは穏やかな海を見ています。
Tomoko is looking at the calm sea.
あの先生は穏やかな人です。
That teacher is a gentle person.
日本の気候は穏やかです。
The climate of Japan is mild.
孝子さんは穏やかな話し方をします。
Takako has a quiet way of speaking.

おちいる 陥る *{5} to fall, to lapse (into a bad condition or situation)*
危険に陥る to fall into danger

おちつき 落ち着き *calmness; composure*
落ち着きがある〔ない〕to be calm〔restless〕
あの子は授業中落ち着きがないです。
That child is restless during class.
落ち着きを失う to lose one's composure

おちつく 落ち着く *1. to calm (oneself) down*
まあ、落ち着きなさい。
Goodness, calm down.
2. to become settled, to become stable
その家族は新しい家に落ち着きました。
That family became settled in their new house.

おちば 落ち葉 *fallen leaf*
落ち葉をかき集める to rake up fallen leaves

おちゃ お茶 *1. tea* [→ 茶]
お茶を１杯いかがですか。
How about a cup of tea?
薄い〔濃い〕お茶 weak〔strong〕tea
お茶を入れる to make tea
お茶が入る tea becomes ready, tea is made
2. green tea [↔ 紅茶]
3. the tea ceremony [→ 茶道]
お茶漬 tea poured over rice (a popular Japanese dish)

おちゅうげん お中元 [☞ 中元]

おちる 落ちる *1. to fall, to drop, to plunge*
バスが川に落ちました。
The bus fell into the river.
パパがはしごから落ちたよ。
Daddy fell from the ladder!
コップが手から落ちました。
The glass dropped from my hand.
学校の成績も落ちました。
My school grades went down too.
2. to fail (on a test, etc.) [↔ 受かる]*; to lose (in an election)*
僕も試験に落ちたよ。
I also failed the examination!
加藤市長は去年の選挙で落ちました。
Mayor Kato lost in last year's election.
3. to come out (when the subject is a stain, etc.)
この汚れは落ちるでしょう。
This dirt will probably come out.

おっかない【COL. for 怖い】

おっしゃる *{Irreg.}*【HON. for 言う】

おっと 夫 *husband* [↔ 妻]

おっとせい *fur seal*

おつまみ *snacks (eaten while drinking beer, etc.)*

おつり お釣り *change (returned in a transaction)*
お釣りは取っておいてください。
Please keep the change.
お釣りを50円もらいました。
I got ¥50 change.

おでこ【COL. for 額】*forehead*

おてんば【COL.】*tomboy*
洋子ちゃんはおてんばだね。
Yoko is a tomboy, isn't she?

おと 音 *sound (i.e., something audible)*
大きい〔小さい〕音 loud〔soft〕sound
大きな音を立てないでください。
Please don't make a loud sound.
テレビの音を小さくしなさい。
Turn the TV volume down.
高い音 high-volume sound; high-pitched sound
低い音 low-volume sound; low-pitched sound

おとうさん お父さん【HON. for 父】*father* [↔ お母さん]
お父さんはどこ？
Where's Father?
お父さんは病院で働いているのですか。
Does your father work at hospital?

おとうと 弟 *younger brother* [↔ 兄; 妹]

いちばん下の弟は7歳です。
My youngest brother is seven years old.

おとうとさん 弟さん【HON. for 弟】

おどかす 脅かす *to threaten, to menace* [→ 脅す]

おとぎばなし おとぎ話 *fairy tale* [→ 童話]
子供たちはおとぎ話を聞いていました。
The children were listening to fairy tales.

おとこ 男 *man, (human) male* [→ 男性] [↔ 女]
ここには男の店員は何人いますか。
How many male salesclerks are there here?
男の人 man
あの男の人はだれですか。
Who is that man?
男の子 boy
男の赤ちゃん baby boy
男物 item intended for men
京子さんは男物のセーターを着ています。
Kyoko is wearing a man's sweater.
男っぽい manly; mannish
男らしい manly
男友達 male friend

おとしだま お年玉 *gift of money given to children at New Year's*
弘叔父さんはお年玉に2000円くれたよ。
Uncle Hiroshi gave me ¥2,000 as a New Year's gift!

おとしもの 落とし物 *thing inadvertently dropped and lost*
石井さんはまだ落とし物を探しています。
Mr. Ishii is still looking for the thing he lost.
落とし物取扱所 lost and found office

おとす 落とす *1. to drop, to let fall, to make fall*
さっき卵を床に落としました。
A little while ago I dropped an egg on the floor.
スピードを落とす to reduce speed
2. to inadvertently drop and lose; to lose
どこかに帽子を落としてしまいました。
I lost my hat somewhere.
命を落とす to lose one's life
人気を落とす to lose one's popularity
気を落とす to lose heart
3. to fail (a student, etc.)
4. to remove (a stain, etc.)

おどす 脅す *to threaten, to menace* [→ 脅かす]
その男は銃で店員を脅しました。
That man threatened the store employees with a gun.

おとずれる 訪れる *to visit, to pay a call on* [→ 訪問する]

おととい 一昨日 *the day before yesterday*
桜井さんはおとといの朝に着きました。
Mr. Sakurai arrived on the morning of the day before yesterday.
一昨昨日 the day before the day before yesterday

おととし 一昨年 *the year before last*

おとな 大人 *adult* [→ 成人]
大人になる to become an adult, to grow up
息子はもう大人になりました。
My son has already become an adult.

おとなしい *1. calm and quiet (describing personality or behavior)*
子供たちはおとなしく本を読んでいます。
The children are reading quietly.
2. well-mannered, well-behaved
次郎ちゃんはおとなしい子です。
Jiro is a well-mannered child.

おとめ 乙女 *1. girl* [→ 少女]
2. virgin, maiden [→ 処女]

おどり 踊り *dance; dancing*

踊り子 dancing girl, female dancer

おとる 劣る *to be/become inferior* [↔ 勝る]

私は英語では妹に劣っています。
I am inferior to my younger sister in English.

この紅茶は前のより品質が劣っています。
The quality of this tea is inferior to the previous one.

おどる 踊る *to dance*

春男は智恵子とタンゴを踊っています。
Haruo is dancing the tango with Chieko.

音楽に合わせて踊る to dance to the music

おとろえる 衰える *to become weak, to decline, to lose vigor*

祖父は足が衰えました。
My grandfather's legs have become weak.

母の健康は衰えました。
My mother's health has declined.

おどろかす 驚かす *to surprise*

その結果は社長を驚かすでしょう。
Those results will probably surprise the company president.

おどろく 驚く *to become surprised* [→ びっくりする]

その知らせを聞いて驚きました。
I was surprised to hear that news.

子供は驚いてお父さんを見上げました。
The child looked up at his father in surprise.

あの人の手際のよさには驚きました。
I was surprised at that person's skill.

おなか お腹 *stomach*

今はおなかがいっぱいです。
My stomach is full now.

父はおなかが出ています。
My father's stomach sticks out.

おなかがすく to get hungry

おなかが痛い one's stomach is aching

おなかを壊す to get an upset stomach

おなじ 同じ *same* (This word modifies a following noun with no intervening particle, but when used as a predicate, it requires a form of だ.)

恵子と私は同じ学校に通っています。
Keiko and I go to the same school.

私は山田さんと同じ仕事をしています。
I do the same work as Ms. Yamada.

林さんと林さんの母親は考え方が同じだ。
Ms. Hayashi and her mother's way of thinking are the same.

おなら *fart* (This Japanese word is not as crude-sounding as the English translation.)

おならをする to fart

おに 鬼 *demon, ogre* (A familiar figure in Japanese fairy tales, an has a human-like body with two horns on its head and fangs. In the game of tag, the person who is "it" is called the おに.)

茂男さんは勉強の鬼です。
Shigeo is a demon for studying.

鬼は外、福は内。
Demons out! Good luck in! (Said as part of the bean throwing ritual traditionally performed on February 3. The beans are thrown to drive demons out of houses.)

鬼のいぬ間に洗濯。(proverb)
When the cat is away, the mice will play. (Literally: While the demon is away, no worries.)

鬼ごっこ (the game of) tag

おにいさん お兄さん【HON. for 兄】*older brother*

おねえさん お姉さん【HON. for 姉】*older sister*

おねがい お願い【HUM. for 頼み*1.*】*request, favor (to ask)*

ちょっとお願いがあるんですが。
I have a favor to ask you. (Literally: I have a little bit of a request, but...)

お願いする【HUM. for 頼む】to request, to ask for
お手伝いをお願いできますか。
Can I ask you for your help?

おの 斧 *ax; hatchet*

おば 伯母, 叔母 *aunt*
(Strictly speaking, this word should be written 伯母 if it refers to an aunt who is an older sister of a parent or the wife of an older brother of a parent, and should be written 叔母 if it refers to an aunt who is a younger sister of a parent or the wife of younger brother of a parent.) [↔ 伯父, 叔父]

おばあさん *1.*【HON. for 祖母】*grandmother* [↔ おじいさん]
おばあさんは足が達者ですね。
Your grandmother's legs are strong, aren't they?
2. old woman
おばあさんに席を譲りました。
I gave up my seat to an elderly woman.
ひいおばあさん great grandmother

おばけ お化け【COL. for 幽霊】*ghost*
お化け屋敷 haunted house

おばさん 伯母さん, 叔母さん【HON. for 伯母, 叔母】
–伯母さん, –叔母さん (Added to a given name as a title.)
広子伯母さんはお父さんのお姉さんです。
Aunt Hiroko is Father's older sister.

おばさん 小母さん *woman (This word typically refers to a middle-aged woman but a child may use it to refer to a young woman.)* [↔ 小父さん]

おはよう *Good morning!*
おはようございます【FORMAL for おはよう (above)】

おび 帯 *kimono sash, obi*

おびえる 怯える *to become frightened*
突然の音におびえました。
I became frightened at the sudden noise.

オフィス *office (where business or government office work is done)* [→ 事務所]

おふろ お風呂 [☞ 風呂]

オペラ *opera*
オペラグラス opera glasses

オペレーター *operator (of a machine); (telephone) operator* [→ 電話交換手 (s.v. 電話)]

おぼうさん お坊さん【HON.】*Buddhist priest, Buddhist monk*

おぼえ 覚え [[→ 記憶]] *1. memory, recollection*
以前上田さんに会った覚えがあります。
I have a recollection of having met Mr. Ueda before.
2. memory, ability to learn
この子は覚えがいいです。
This child has a good memory.

おぼえる 覚える *1. to commit to memory, to learn, to memorize* [→ 記憶する]
毎日単語を五つずつ覚えるつもりです。
I plan to learn five words every day.
あしたまでにこの詩を覚えなさい。
Memorize this poem by tomorrow.
覚えている to remember, to have a memory of
あの人の名前を覚えていますか。
Do you remember that person's name?
2. to feel, to experience
痛みを覚える to feel pain

おぼれる 溺れる *to drown*
二人の男の子が川でおぼれました。
Two little boys drowned in the river.
おぼれる者はわらをつかむ。(proverb)
A drowning man will clutch at a straw.

おぼん お盆 [☞ 盆]

おまえ お前【COL.】*you*
(There are several Japanese words for

you, but in general, Japanese speakers prefer to use names or titles rather than words for **you.** The word is generally used only by male speakers to address intimate social equals or intimate social inferiors. Used in other circumstances, is very insulting. Other words for **you** include あなた, 君, and 貴様.)

おまけ お負け *1. free gift, giveaway, premium (accompanying something one buys)* [→ 景品1.]

この鉛筆はおまけにもらったものだよ。

I got this pencil as a free gift.

おまけする to give as a free gift

2. discount [→ 割引]

あの店では100円おまけしてくれた。

I got a ¥100 discount at that store.

おまけする to discount, to lower in price

おまけに お負けに *in addition; to make matters worse*

おまけに雪も降りはじめました。

To make matters worse, it began to snow too.

おまもり お守り *good-luck charm, talisman (Ordinarily bought at a Shinto shrine or Buddhist temple.)*

神社で交通安全のお守りをもらった。

I got a traffic safety good-luck charm at the shrine.

おまわりさん お巡りさん【COL. for 警官】 *police officer*

おみあい お見合い [☞ 見合い]

おみこし お神輿 [☞ 神輿]

おみやげ お土産 [☞ 土産]

オムレツ *omelet*

おめ お目 ～にかかる【HUM. for 会う】

お目にかける【HUM. for 見せる】

おめでとう *Congratulations!*

合格おめでとう！

Congratulations on passing!

誕生日おめでとう！

Happy birthday!

クリスマスおめでとう！

Merry Christmas!

おめでとうございます【FORMAL for おめでとう (above)】

明けましておめでとうございます。

Happy New Year! (Said only after the new year has arrived.)

おも 主 ～な *main, chief, principal, leading*

今月の主なスポーツ行事は何ですか。

What are this month's main sports events?

利根川は日本の主な川の１つです。

The Tone River is one of Japan's principal rivers.

その国の主な政治家たちが集まりました。

That country's leading politicians gathered.

主に mainly, chiefly, mostly

観客は主に若い女の子です。

The spectators are mainly young girls.

夏休みは主に海岸で過ごします。

I spend the summer vacation mostly at the seashore.

おもい 重い *1. heavy* [↔ 軽い]

この箱は手で運ぶには重いです。

This box is heavy to carry by hand.

気分が重い to feel depressed

2. severe, serious

重い罰 severe punishment

重い病気 serious illness

おもいがけない 思いがけない *unexpected, surprising*

思いがけないお客さんが見えました。

An unexpected visitor came.

それは思いがけないことです。

That's a surprising thing.

おもいきった 思い切った *bold, daring, resolute*

社長は時々思い切ったことをします。

The company president sometimes does daring things.

おもいきって 思い切って *boldly, daringly, resolutely*

由美子は思い切って健に手紙を書いた。
Yumiko boldly wrote a letter to Ken.

おもいきり 思いきり *1. without holding back, to one's heart's content, vigorously, hard*

思いきりボールをけったよ。
I kicked the ball hard!

2. resignation (to fate); decision, resolution

思い切りがいい willing to resign oneself to fate; decisive, resolute

思い切りが悪い indecisive, irresolute

思い切りよく resignedly; decisively, resolutely

おもいこむ 思い込む *to come to a mistaken conclusion*

兄はこれが本物だと思い込んでいます。
My older brother mistakenly believes that this is the real thing.

おもいだす 思い出す *to recall, to recollect, to remember*

あの人の名前を思い出しましたか。
Did you recall that person's name?

雪が降ると、北海道を思い出します。
When it snows, I remember Hokkaido.

おもいつく 思い付く *1. to think of, to come up with (when the subject is a person)*

知事は計画の説明方法を思いつきました。
The governor thought of a way to explain the plan.

2. to occur to one (when the subject is a thought) [→ 浮かぶ2.]

いい案が思いつきません。
A good idea doesn't occur to me.

おもいで 思い出 *reminiscence, memory*

母はよく学生時代の思い出を話します。
My mother often talks about memories of her school days.

楽しい〔悲しい〕思い出 happy〔sad〕memories

おもいやり 思いやり *sympathy, consideration, thoughtfulness*

明美さんは他人に対して思いやりがある。
Akemi has consideration for others.

おもう 思う *to think, to have the idea* [→ 考える1.]

母は電車に間に合わないと思います。
I think that my mother will not make the train.

山田さんは来ると思いますか。
Do you think that Mr. Yamada will come?

犬を飼いたいと思いました。
I thought that I would like to have a dog.

今夜は映画を見に行こうと思っています。
I'm thinking that I'll go to see a movie tonight.

思ったほど難しくないです。
It's not as difficult as I had thought.

AをB (だ)と思う to consider A (to be) B, to think A B

その人をばかだと思います。
I think that person is an idiot.

この計画をどう思いますか。
What do you think of this plan?

おもさ 重さ *weight*

そのスーツケースの重さは10キロです。
The weight of that suitcase is ten kilograms.

おもしろい 面白い *interesting* [→ 興味深い (s.v. 興味)]; amusing, fun [→ 楽しい]

この本は私にはとてもおもしろいです。
This book is very interesting to me.

一人で遊ぶのはおもしろくないよ。
It's not fun playing alone!

大森さんはおもしろい人ですね。
Mr. Omori is an interesting person, isn't he?

スケートボードはとてもおもしろいよ。

Skateboarding is really fun!

おもちゃ *toy*

子供たちはおもちゃで遊ぶのが好きです。
The children like playing with toys.

おもちゃ箱 toy box

おもちゃ屋 toy store; toy-store proprietor

おもて 表 *1. front side, face, obverse* [↔ 裏1.]

封筒の表に名前を書きました。
I wrote the name on the face of the envelope.

2. outdoors, outside [→ 戸外]

子供たちは表で遊んでいます。
The children are playing outdoors.

3. top (of an inning in baseball) [↔ 裏3.]

9回の表です。
It's the top of the ninth inning.

おもむき 趣 *1. gist, purport* [→ 趣旨]

2. appearance, look, air [→ 様子]

おもわず 思わず *unintentionally, involuntarily, in spite of oneself*

私は思わず笑ってしまいました。
I laughed unintentionally.

おもんじる 重んじる *to value, to think highly of*

私の先生は何よりも規則を重んじます。
My teacher values rules more than anything else.

おや 親 *parent*

この親にしてこの子あり。(proverb)
Like father, like son. (Literally: Given this parent there will be this child.)

親御さん【HON. for 親 (above)】

親思い love for one's parents, filial affection

おや *Oh! (an exclamatory interjection expressing surprise or joy)*

おや、小林君も来たよ。
Oh, Kobayashi came too!

おやこ 親子 *parent and child*

親子丼 bowl of rice topped with chicken and egg

おやこうこう 親孝行 *filial piety*

おやすみなさい お休みなさい *Good night.*

お休み (a very informal version of the above)

おやつ【COL.】*mid-afternoon snack*

母は3時におやつを出してくれたよ。
My mother served us a mid-afternoon snack at 3:00!

おやぶん 親分 *boss (of henchmen)* [↔ 子分]

おやゆび 親指 *1. thumb*

2. big toe

およぎ 泳ぎ *swimming* [→ 水泳]

小川さんは泳ぎが上手です。
Ms. Ogawa is good at swimming.

およぐ 泳ぐ *to swim*

兄は海で泳ぐのが好きです。
My older brother likes to swim in the ocean.

およそ *about, approximately* [→ 約]

私は毎日およそ2時間勉強します。
I study about two hours every day.

およぶ 及ぶ *1. to extend, to spread, to amount*

その会合は3時間に及びました。
That meeting extended to three hours.

Aには及ばない to be unnecessary to do A

2. to match, to equal [→ 匹敵する]

英語では小山さんに及ぶ者はいません。
In English there's no one who can match Mr. Koyama.

オランウータン *orangutan*

おり 檻 *cage*

おりの中にライオンがいます。
There's a lion in the cage.

オリーブ *olive*

オリーブ油 olive oil

オリエンテーション *orientation (for people in a new environment)*

新入生はオリエンテーションを受けた。
The new students received orientation.

おりがみ 折り紙 *1. origami, paper folding (the traditional Japanese craft)*

2. folding paper (for doing origami)

折り紙付きの certified, guaranteed, acknowledged

オリジナル *an original (as opposed to a reproduction, copy, translation, etc.)*

オリジナルな original, creative, inventive [→ 独創的な (s.v. 独創)]

おりる 降りる, 下りる *1. to come down, to go down, to descend*

階段を降りる to come/go down the stairs

それから丘を降りました。
After that we went down the hill.

猫が木の上から降りてきました。
The cat came down from the tree.

2. to get off, to get out of (a means of transportation) [↔ 乗る1.]

乗客は電車を降りました。
The passengers got off the train.

文子さんは門の前でタクシーから降りた。
Fumiko got out of the taxi in front of the gate.

3. to quit, to give up in the middle, to drop out of

けがをした選手は試合を降りました。
The injured player dropped out of the game.

オリンピック *the Olympics*

64年のオリンピックは東京で開かれた。
The '64 Olympics were held in Tokyo.

オリンピック記録 Olympic record

オリンピック選手 Olympic athlete

夏季オリンピック the Summer Olympics

冬季オリンピック the Winter Olympics

おる【HUM. for 居る】

おる 折る *1. to break, to snap (transitive) (The direct object must be long and slender.)*

弟は木から落ちて足を折ったよ。
My younger brother fell from a tree and broke his leg!

2. to bend (transitive) [→ 曲げる]

指を折って数える to count by bending one's fingers

3. to fold (transitive) [→ 畳む]

その手紙を四つに折りました。
I folded that letter into four.

おる 織る *to weave*

この村の女達はじゅうたんを織ります。
The women of this village weave carpets.

オルガン *organ ((musical instrument))*

オルガン奏者 organist

オルゴール *music box*

オルゴールが鳴っています。
The music box is playing.

おれ 俺【COL.】*I, me*

(There are several Japanese words for **I/me.** The word is ordinarily restricted to male speakers addressing intimate social equals and intimate social inferiors. Other words for **I/me** include 私, 私, あたし, and 僕.)

おれい お礼 [☞ 礼]

おれる 折れる *1. to break (intransitive) (The subject must be long and slender.)*

この鉛筆はしんがすぐ折れるね。
This pencil lead breaks easily, doesn't it?

2. to fold up (intransitive)

3. to turn (intransitive) [→ 曲がる]

そこで右に折れると、劇場があります。
If you turn to the right there, there is a theater.

オレンジ *1. an orange*

2. (the color) orange

オレンジジュース orange juice

おろか 愚か ～な *foolish* [→ 馬鹿な1.]

愚か者 fool

おろし 卸 *wholesale*

卸売り selling wholesale [↔ 小売り]

卸売りする to sell wholesale

おろす 下ろす *1. to take down, to get down; to lower*

棚から箱を下ろしました。

I took the box down from the shelf.

ブラインドを下ろしてください。

Please lower the blinds.

2. to withdraw (money) [→ 引き出す2.]

おろす 降ろす *to let off, to let out of (a vehicle)* [↔ 乗せる]

次の角で降ろしてください。

Let me off at the next corner, please.

おわり 終わり *end, finish* [↔ 初め]

来月の終わりに出発します。

I will leave at the end of next month.

夏休みも終わりに近づきました。

The summer vacation also has neared its end.

初めから終わりまで黙っていました。

I kept silent from beginning to end.

その本を終わりまで読みましたか。

Did you read that book to the end?

おわる 終わる *to end, to finish (transitive or intransitive)*

試合は９時に終わりました。

The game ended at 9:00.

この仕事を終わったら、帰りましょう。

When we finish this work, let's go home.

学校は３時に終わります。

School ends at 3:00.

おわれる 追われる *to become very busy (with work)* (This word is the passive form of 追う and has the predictable meanings as well.)

私は家事に追われています。

I am very busy with housework.

おん 恩 *kindness, favor; obligation for a favor received, debt of gratitude*

ご恩は決して忘れません。

I'll never forget your kindness.

恩を受ける to receive a favor, to become obligated

原田さんには特別に恩を受けています。

I'm especially obligated to Mr. Harada.

恩になる to become obligated

恩返し repaying a kindness

恩返しする to repay a kindness

おんがく 音楽 *music*

この子は音楽の才能があります。

This child has musical talent.

音楽学校 music school

音楽家 musician

音楽会 concert

おんきょう 音響 *sound, acoustic vibrations*

音響学 (the study of) acoustics

音響効果 acoustics (of a room, etc.)

おんしつ 温室 *greenhouse, hothouse*

温室植物 hothouse plant

おんせん 温泉 *hot spring, spa*

おんだん 温暖 ～な *warm, temperate, mild*

日本は気候が温暖です。

Japan's climate is mild.

温暖前線 warm front

おんち 音痴 *tone-deafness*

音痴の tone-deaf

方向音痴 lack of a sense of direction

おんど 温度 *temperature*

温度は摂氏20度です。

The temperature is 20 degrees centigrade.

温度が上がる〔下がる〕 a temperature rises〔falls〕

高い〔低い〕温度 high〔low〕temperature

温度計 thermometer

おんな 女 *woman, (human) female* [→ 女性] [↔ 男]

女の人 woman

女の赤ちゃん baby girl

女の子 girl

女物 item intended for women

女っぽい womanly, feminine; womanish, effeminate

女らしい womanly, feminine

女友達 female friend

おんぶ【COL.】*carrying a person on one's back*

おんぶする to carry on one's back

おんぷ 音符 *note (in a musical score)*

二分音符 half note

四分音符 quarter note

おんよみ 音読み *Chinese reading (of a kanji)*

か 科 *1. family (in biological taxonomy)*

2. department (of a university, hospital, etc.)

3. course of study

英語科 English department

普通科 the general course of study

ネコ科 the cat family

か 課 *1. lesson (in a textbook)*

第1課 Lesson 1

2. section (of a company, government bureau, etc.)

課長 section chief

販売課 sales section

か 蚊 *mosquito*

赤ん坊が蚊に刺されたよ。
The baby was bitten by a mosquito!

蚊取り線香 mosquito coil

か *1. (As a clause-final particle か marks a clause as a question. The copula form だ is optionally omitted before か in non-final clauses. When か is sentence-final, だ cannot appear before it. Question sentences in the informal style are ordinarily marked only with rising intonation, and using か at the end of such sentences sounds quite rough.)*

これは何ですか。
What is this?

お兄さんはギターが弾けますか。
Can your older brother play the guitar?

キャッチボールをしようか。
Shall we play catch?

あの人はだれ（だ）か知りません。
I don't know who that person is.

2. or (noun-conjoining particle)

父か母がそこへ行かなければなりません。
My father or mother has to go there.

が 蛾 *moth*

が *(noun-following particle marking the subject of a clause)*

猫が魚を食べました。
The cat ate the fish.

僕は数学が好きです。
I like math. (Note that the English translation of a noun marked with が will not necessarily be the subject of the English clause in which it appears.)

が *(clause-conjoining particle) but; and (following a clause providing background information for the following clause)*

姉には欠点がありますが、私は好きです。
My older sister has some faults, but I like her.

父には兄がいますが、とても健康です。
Father has an older brother, and he is in good health.

ガーゼ *gauze*

カーディガン *a cardigan*

カーテン *curtain*

カーテンを開ける〔閉める〕 to open〔close〕a curtain

カード *card (made of thin, stiff material)*

バースデーカード birthday card

クレジットカード credit card

クリスマスカード Christmas card

キャッシュカード automatic teller card

ガード *railroad bridge, railroad overpass*

ガードマン *guard, watchman [→ 警備員 (s.v. 警備)]*

カートリッジ *cartridge*

ガードレール *guardrail*

カーニバル *carnival*

カーネーション *carnation*

カーブ *1. curve, bend*

この道は急なカーブが多いです。
This road has a lot of sharp curves.

2. curve (-ball)

ピッチャーはカーブを投げました。
The pitcher threw a curve.

カーペット *carpet [→ 絨毯]*

カール *(hair) curl*

カールする to curl (transitive or intransitive)

美知子さんは髪をカールしています。
Michiko has curled her hair.

妹の髪は生まれつきカールしています。
My younger sister's hair is naturally curly.

ガールスカウト *1. the Girl Scouts*

2. girl scout

ガールフレンド *casual girlfriend (as opposed to a steady girlfriend or lover) [→ ボーイフレンド]*

かい 会 *1. meeting, gathering [→ 会合]; party*

その会に出席します。
I will attend that meeting.

2. club [→ クラブ]; association, society [→ 協会]

会に入る to join a club; to join an association

会を抜ける to leave a club; to leave an association

歓迎会 welcome party

送別会 farewell party

卒業生の送別会は来週開かれます。
A farewell party for graduates will be held next week.

かい 貝 *shellfish*

貝殻 seashell, (shellfish) shell

かい 回 *1. inning; (boxing) round*

一回 (counter for innings or rounds; see Appendix 2)

2.—回 (counter for number of times; see Appendix 2) [→ —度]

もう1回言ってください。
Please say it one more time.

月に2回、娘から便りがあります。
Twice a month there is a letter from my daughter.

管理人には何回会いましたか。
How many times did you see the manager?

かい 階 *floor, story (of a building)*

上〔下〕の階 the floor above〔below〕

—かい —階 (counter for floor numbers; see Appendix 2); (counter for number of floors; see Appendix 2)

事務所は6階にあります。
The office is on the sixth floor.

A階建ての A-story, having A floors

このビルは60階建てです。
This building has sixty floors.

がい 害 *harm, damage [→ 損害]*

あらしは作物に大きな害を与えました。
The storm did great damage to the crops.

たばこは体に害があります。
Smoking is harmful to one's health. (Literally: Tobacco has harm to the body.)

害する *{Irreg.}* to harm, to damage, to hurt

私は明さんの感情を害しました。
I hurt Akira's feelings.

かいいん 会員 *member (of an association, society, club, etc.)*

会員証 membership card

かいえん 開演 *beginning of a performance*

開演は午後6時です。
The beginning of the performance is 6:00 PM.

かいおうせい 海王星 *(the planet) Neptune*

かいかい 開会 *opening (of a meeting, gathering, conference, etc.) [↔ 閉会]*

開会する to open (transitive)

開会の辞を述べる to give an opening address

開会式 opening ceremony

かいがい 海外 *overseas, foreign countries*

海外ニュース foreign news

海外旅行 overseas travel, traveling abroad

田中さんは毎年海外旅行をします。
Ms. Tanaka takes a trip overseas every year.

かいかく 改革 *reform, improvement*

改革する to reform, to improve (transitive)

かいかつ 快活 〜な *cheerful, jovial* [↔ 憂鬱な]

かいがん 海岸 *seashore, seaside; beach; coast*

毎朝海岸を散歩します。
I walk along the seashore every morning.

海岸はビーチパラソルでいっぱいです。
The beach is full of beach umbrellas.

石井さんは夏休みに海岸へ行きます。
Mr. Ishii goes to the seaside for the summer vacation.

東海岸 east coast

西海岸 west coast

かいぎ 会議 *meeting, conference*

会議中の in conference, in a meeting

戸田さんは今会議中です。
Mr. Toda is in a meeting now.

会議室 conference room

国際会議 international conference

かいきゅう 階級 *1. (social) class 2. rank (in an organization)* [→ 地位]

中流階級 the middle class

上流階級 the upper class

労働者階級 the working class

かいきょう 回教 *Islam*

かいきょう 海峡 *strait, channel*

イギリス海峡 the English Channel

津軽海峡 the Tsugaru Strait

かいぐん 海軍 *navy*

かいけい 会計 *1. accounts, accounting 2. bill, check (to pay)*

会計をお願いします。(in a restaurant)
Check, please.

会計係 accountant, treasurer (in an organization); cashier (in a hotel, restaurant, etc.)

会計年度 fiscal year

会計士 (professional) accountant

かいけつ 解決 *solution (of a problem); settlement (of a dispute)*

解決する to solve, to settle

警察官はその問題を解決しました。
The police officer solved that problem.

がいけん 外見 *outward appearance*

外見で人を判断してはいけません。
You mustn't judge a person by appearance.

かいこ 蚕 *silkworm*

かいごう 会合 *meeting, gathering*

がいこう 外交 *diplomacy*

外交官 diplomat

がいこく 外国 *foreign country*

外国へ行ったことがありますか。

Have you ever been to a foreign country?

外国語 foreign language

外国人 foreigner [→ 外人]

外国製品 foreign manufactured product

外国郵便 foreign mail

かいさい 開催 ～する *to hold (an event)*

72年の冬季オリンピックは札幌で開催されました。

The '72 Winter Olympics were held in Sapporo.

かいさつぐち 改札口 *ticket gate (in a train station)*

かいさん 解散 *break-up, dissolution, dispersing*

解散する to break up, to disperse (transitive or intransitive)

会は午後９時に解散します。

The meeting will break up at 9:00 PM.

かいし 開始 *beginning, start*

開始する to begin, to start (transitive) [→ 始める]

かいしゃ 会社 *company, firm*

どちらの会社に勤めていますか。

Which company do you work for?

父はバスで会社へ行きます。

My father goes to his company by bus.

会社員 office worker, company employee

かいじゅう 怪獣 *monster, monstrous animal*

怪獣映画 monster movie

がいしゅつ 外出 *going out (i.e., temporarily leaving one's home or workplace)*

外出する to go out

午後は外出します。

In the afternoon I'll go out.

兄は今外出しています。

My older brother is out now.

かいしょ 楷書 *block style (of Japanese calligraphy) [↔ 行書; 草書]*

かいじょう 会場 *place where a meeting or gathering takes place, meeting hall*

会場は若い人たちでいっぱいです。

The meeting hall is full of young people.

かいじょう 海上 *the sea (surface)*

救命ボートは海上を５時間も漂っていた。

The lifeboat was floating on the sea for five hours.

海上保険 marine insurance

海上交通 sea traffic

がいしょく 外食 *eating out (at a restaurant, etc.)*

外食する to eat out

がいじん 外人 *foreigner*

かいすい 海水 *seawater*

海水パンツ swimming trunks [→ 水泳パンツ (s.v. 水泳)]

かいすいよく 海水浴 *swimming in the sea*

海水浴は楽しいですね。

Swimming in the sea is fun, isn't it?

海水浴場 swimming beach

かいすう 回数 *the number of times*

横田君の遅刻の回数を数えてください。

Please count the number of times Yokota has been late.

回数券 coupon ticket

かいせい 快晴 *very fine weather*

今日は快晴ですね。

Today it's very fine weather, isn't it?

かいせつ 解説 *explanation, commentary, interpretation*

解説する to explain, to comment on, to interpret
解説者 commentator
ニュース解説 news commentary
野球解説者 baseball commentator

かいぜん 改善 *improvement*
改善する to improve (transitive)
桜井さんは生活を改善しようとしました。
Mr. Sakurai tried to improve his life.

かいそう 海草 *seaweed*

かいそく 快速 *wonderfully high speed*
列車は時速160キロの快速で走っている。
The train is going at a high speed of 160 kilometers an hour.
快速電車 high-speed train

かいぞく 海賊 *pirate*
海賊船 pirate ship

かいたく 開拓 *1. reclamation, bringing under cultivation*
開拓する to reclaim, to bring under cultivation
農村の人たちは荒れ地を開拓しました。
The people of the farming village reclaimed the wasteland.
2. opening up (a new place or a new area of endeavor)
開拓する to open up
開拓者 pioneer, settler

かいだん 会談 *talks, conference*
首脳会談 summit conference

かいだん 階段 *stairs, stairway*
階段を上がる〔降りる〕 to go up〔down〕 the stairs

ガイダンス *guidance counseling (at a school)*

がいちゅう 害虫 *harmful insect*

かいちゅうでんとう 懐中電灯 *(US) flashlight, (UK) torch*

かいちょう 会長 *chairperson, president (of an association, society, club, etc.)*
広瀬君は生徒会の会長です。
Hirose is president of the student council.

かいつう 開通 *opening to traffic*
開通する to be opened to traffic
このトンネルは3月に開通します。
This tunnel will be opened to traffic in March.
開通式 opening ceremony

かいてい 海底 *sea bottom*
海底火山 submarine volcano
海底トンネル undersea tunnel

かいてい 改訂 *revision (of a book, etc.)*
改訂する to revise
改訂版 revised edition

かいてき 快適 ～な *comfortable; pleasant* [→ 愉快な]
ほんとうに快適な旅行でした。
It was a really pleasant trip.

かいてん 回転 *rotation, revolution, turning*
回転する to rotate, to revolve, to turn [→ 回る1.]
回転ドア revolving door
回転競技 slalom
回転木馬 merry-go-round [→ メリーゴーラウンド]

かいてん 開店 [[↔ 閉店]] *1. opening (of a store, restaurant, etc., for the business day)*
開店する to open (transitive or intransitive)
その本屋は午前9時に開店します。
That bookstore opens at 9:00 AM.
2. opening (of a newly established store, restaurant, etc.)
開店する to open (transitive or intransitive)

ガイド *1. guide (person)*

2. [☞ ガイドブック (below)]

ガイドブック guidebook

かいとう 解答 *answer, solution (to a test question or study problem)*

正しい解答 right answer, right solution

まちがった解答 wrong answer, wrong solution

解答する to answer, to solve

かいはつ 開発 *development, exploitation (for human use)*

開発する to develop, to exploit

開発途上国 developing country

かいばつ 海抜 *elevation above sea level*

富士山は海抜3776メートルです。

Mt. Fuji is 3,776 meters above sea level.

かいひ 会費 *membership fee, dues; party participation fee*

きょうのパーティーの会費は2000円です。

The fee for today's party is ¥2,000.

がいぶ 外部 *the outside, outer part* [↔ 内部]

かいふく 回復 *recovery, restoration*

回復する to recover (transitive or intransitive)

福井さんは健康を回復しました。

Mr. Fukui recovered his health.

母は病気から回復しました。

My mother has recovered from her sickness.

天候が回復する the weather improves

かいぶつ 怪物 *1. monster, apparition*

2. enigmatic person

かいほう 開放 ～する *to open, to leave open*

そのプールは一般に開放されています。

That pool is open to the general public.

「開放厳禁」 (sign on a door)

Keep closed (Literally: Leaving Open Forbidden)

かいほう 解放 *liberation*

解放する to liberate, to set free

兵士たちは捕虜を解放しました。

The soldiers set the prisoners free.

やっと宿題から解放されたよ。

Finally I was set free from homework!

かいぼう 解剖 *dissection; autopsy*

解剖する to dissect; to perform an autopsy on

解剖学 (the study of) anatomy

かいもの 買い物 *shopping*

デパートへ買い物に出かけました。

I went out at a department store shopping.

これはいい買い物です。

This is a good buy. (Literally: This is good shopping.)

買い物をする to do shopping, to shop

銀座で少し買い物をしました。

I did a little shopping in Ginza.

買い物袋 shopping bag

買い物客 shopper

がいや 外野 *outfield [↔ 内野] (in baseball)*

外野席 outfield bleachers

外野手 outfielder

がいよう 概要 *outline, summary* [→ 概略]

がいらいご 外来語 *borrowed word, loanword (With respect to Japanese, this term ordinarily refers only to relatively recent loanwords, mostly from European languages, and not to the many loanwords from Chinese.)* [↔ 漢語; 和語]

かいり 海里 *nautical mile*

一海里 (counter for nautical miles; see Appendix 2)

がいりゃく 概略 *outline, summary* [→ 概要]

かいりゅう 海流 *ocean current*

かいりょう 改良 *improvement* [→ 改善]

改良する to improve (transitive)
品種改良 breed improvement

かいわ 会話 *conversation*
会話する to converse, to have a conversation
外人と英語で会話したことがありますか。
Have you ever had a conversation with a foreigner in English?
英会話 English conversation

かいん 下院 [[↔ 上院]] *lower house (of a legislature); the House of Representatives (in the United States Congress); the House of Commons (in the British Parliament)*
下院議員 lower-house member

かう 買う *to buy* [↔ 売る]
自転車を買ってください。
Please buy a bicycle.
そのカメラを5万円で買いました。
I bought that camera for ¥50,000.

かう 飼う *to keep as a pet; to raise (animals)*
僕も犬を飼っているよ。
I also keep a pet dog!
その農場では牛を30頭飼っています。
They're raising thirty cows on that farm.

カウボーイ *cowboy*

ガウン *1. housedress; dressing gown*
2. gown (of the type worn by judges, clergymen, etc.)

カウンセラー *psychological counselor*

カウンター *1. counter (in a store, restaurant, etc.)*
2. counter, counting device

かえす 返す *to give back, to return*
その本を図書館に返しなさい。
Return that book to the library.
そのノートをあした返してね。
Give that notebook back tomorrow, OK?
お金は今度の月曜日に返します。
I will return the money next Monday.

かえで 楓 *maple ((tree))*

かえり 帰り *return (home), returning home*
母親は子供の帰りを待っています。
The mother is waiting for her child's return.
父はいつも帰りが遅いです。
My father's return home is always late.
学校の帰りに友達のお母さんに会った。
I met my friend's mother on my way home from school.
帰り道 way home

かえる 蛙 *frog*

かえる 帰る *{5} to return home*
山本さんはいつ帰りますか
When will Mr. Yamamoto return home?
帰ってくる to come home
友子さんは来週カナダから帰ってきます。
Tomoko will come home from Canada next week.
帰っていく to go home
子供たちは6時ごろ帰っていきました。
The children went home about 6:00.

かえる 返る *{5} 1. to return (to a place of origin) (The subject is inanimate.)*
先週出した手紙が返ってきました。
A letter I mailed last week came back.
2. to return (to an earlier state)
話題に返る to return to a topic
子供に返る to return to childish behavior

かえる 孵る *{5} to hatch (The subject may be either an egg or a baby bird.)*
ひながかえったよ。
The chick hatched!

かえる 変える *to change, to alter (transitive)*
私たちはその計画を変えました。
We changed that plan.

かえる 換える, 替える *to exchange, to convert, to replace* [→ 交換する]

A をB と換えるto exchange A for B

これをLサイズと換えてもいいですか。
May I exchange this for a size L?

A をB に替えるto convert A into B

このお金をドルに替えてください。
Please convert this money into dollars.

かお 顔 *1. face (of a person or animal)*

この子はかわいい顔をしていますね。
This child has a cute face, doesn't she?

顔を見合わせる to look at each other's faces

顔を洗う to wash one's face

2. look (on a face), expression (on a face) [→ 表情]

顔をする to get a look on one's face (Always preceded by a modifier.)

川村さんはそのとき悲しそうな顔をしていました。
Mr. Kawamura had a sad look on his face then.

かおいろ 顔色 *1. color (of a face), complexion*

どうしましたか。顔色が悪いですよ。
What's the matter? Your color is bad!

その知らせに部長は顔色を変えました。
The department head changed color at that news.

2. look (on a face), expression (on a face) [→ 表情]

顔色に出る to appear in one's expression

かおり 香り *fragrance*

この花は香りがいいです。
This flower's fragrance is nice.

かおる 香る *to be fragrant*

がか 画家 *artist who paints or draws*

かかえる 抱える *to hold (under one arm or in both arms)*

小わきに抱えるto hold under one's arm

その学生は辞書を小わきに抱えています。
That student is holding a dictionary under her arm.

かかく 価格 *price* [→ 値段]

価格調整 price adjustment

価格水準 price level

かがく 化学 *chemistry*

化学反応 chemical reaction

化学方程式 chemical equation

化学者 chemist

化学式 chemical formula

化学的な chemical, pertaining to chemistry

かがく 科学 *science*

科学技術 technology

科学博物館 science museum

科学者 scientist

科学的な scientific

人文科学 cultural science

社会科学 social science

自然科学 natural science

かかし 案山子 *scarecrow*

かかと 踵 *1. heel (of a foot)*

2. heel (of a shoe)

林さんはかかとの低い靴をはいています。
Ms. Hayashi is wearing low-heeled shoes.

かがみ 鏡 *mirror*

かがむ 屈む *to bend over, to stoop down*

かがんで、ボールを拾いました。
I bent over and picked up the ball.

かがやかしい 輝かしい *bright, brilliant*

画家はその作品で輝かしい名声を得た。
The artist gained a brilliant reputation because of that work.

輝かしい未来 bright future

かがやく 輝く *to shine (strongly)*

太陽は明るく輝いています。
The sun is shining brightly.

星は夜輝きます。
Stars shine at night.
少年の顔がぱっと輝きました。
The boy's face suddenly brightened.

かかる 掛かる *1. to hang, to be suspended*
壁に絵がかかっています。
A picture is hanging on the wall.
2. to take, to require, to cost
駅まで歩いて10分ぐらいかかります。
It takes about ten minutes to the station on foot.
その旅行はとてもお金がかかるでしょう。
That trip will probably cost a lot of money.
3. to fall on, to be put on (The subject is a liquid or powder.)
いちごにクリームがかかっています。
There's cream on the strawberries.
それに雨がかからないようにしなさい。
Make sure the rain does not fall on that.
4. to come to depend, to become contingent
この仕事は赤塚君の手腕にかかっている。
This job depends on Akatsuka's ability.
5. to start to run (The subject is a machine.)
エンジンがかかる an engine starts
6. 医者に〜 *to consult a doctor*
すぐ医者にかからなければいけません。
You must consult a doctor right away.
7. かぎが〜 *a key is used (on something to lock it)*
ドアにかぎがかかっています。
The door is locked.
8. 電話が〜 *a telephone call arrives*
お留守に恵子さんからの電話がかかってきました。
A telephone call came from Keiko while you were out.

かかる 架かる *to be built (so as to span something from one side to the other)*
ここに橋が架かります。
A bridge is going to be built here.

かかる 罹る *to fall victim (to an illness)*
その赤ちゃんははしかにかかっています。
That baby has caught measles.

かかわらず [☞ にかかわらず; にもかかわらず]

かき 柿 *persimmon*

かき 夏季 *summertime, the summer season* [↔ 冬季]
夏季オリンピック the Summer Olympics

かき 夏期 *summer, the period during summer*
夏期休暇 summer vacation, *(UK)* summer holidays
夏期講習 summer course, summer school

かき 牡蛎 *oyster*
かきフライ deep-fried oysters
生がき raw oyster

かぎ 鍵 *1. key (to a lock)*
これは表のドアのかぎです。
This is the key to the front door.
かぎがかかる a key is used (on something to lock it)
かぎをかける to use a key (on something to lock it)
ドアにかぎをかけてください。
Please lock the door.
2. key, essential means
これが問題を解くかぎです。
This is the key to solving the problem.
3. lock [→ 錠]
鍵穴 keyhole
鍵っ子 latchkey child
合い鍵 duplicate key

かぎって 限って [☞ に限って]

かきとめ 書留 *registered mail*
この手紙を書留で出してください。
Please send this letter by registered mail.
手紙を書留にする to register a letter
書留料 registered mail fee

かきとり 書き取り *writing down (what is said)*

かきとる 書き取る *to write down (what is said)*

かきなおす 書き直す *to rewrite*

かきね 垣根 *fence; hedge*

かきまわす 掻き回す *1. to stir (transitive)*

真紀子さんは紅茶をスプーンでかき回しています。
Makiko is stirring her tea with a spoon.

2. to rummage through (with one's hands)

3. to throw into confusion, to disrupt [→ 乱す]

かきゅう 下級 *low class, low grade* [↔ 上級]

下級生 student in one of the lower grades, (US) underclassman

かぎらない 限らない とは～ *(The word is the negative form of the verb* 限る *and has the predictable meanings as well.) is/are not necessarily (following a noun); it is not necessarily the case that (following a predicate)*

この学校の生徒は優等生とは限りません。
The students at this school are not necessarily honor students.

上田さんは、日曜日にいつもうちにいるとは限りません。
Mr. Ueda is not necessarily always at home on Sunday.

かぎり 限り *1. limit, bound* [→ 限度]

人の力には限りがあります。
There is a limit to a person's power.

2. to the extent that, as far as, as much as (following a predicate)

私の知っている限り道夫さんは勤勉です。
As far as I know, Michio is diligent.

できる限り手伝いましょう。
I'll help you as much as I can.

3. as long as, provided that (following a predicate)

雨が降らない限り大丈夫です。
As long as it doesn't rain, it'll be all right.

かぎる 限る *{5} 1. to limit* [→ 制限する]

スピーチは10分間に限ります。
We will limit the speeches to ten minutes.

2. ～ to be the best (following a noun); it is best to (following a verb in the non-past tense)

旅行は秋に限ります。
For traveling autumn is the best.

こんなときは逃げるに限るよ。
At a time like this it's best to run away!

かく 角 *(geometric) angle*

直角 right angle

鈍角 obtuse angle

鋭角 acute angle

かく 核 *nucleus; kernel; core*

核兵器 nuclear weapon

核保有国 country with nuclear weapons

核実験 nuclear test

核家族 nuclear family

核戦争 nuclear war

かく 欠く *1. to lack*

教授は常識を欠いています。
The professor lacks common sense.

2. to break a piece off, to chip

氷を欠く to chip ice

皿を欠く to chip a dish

歯を欠く to chip a tooth

かく 書く *to write*

答えは鉛筆で書きなさい。
Write your answers with a pencil.

今晩家族に手紙を書きます。
I'm going to write a letter to my family tonight.

かく 描く *to draw; to paint*

地図をかいてあげましょう。
I'll draw you a map.
あの人は油絵をかいています。
That person is painting an oil painting.

かく 掻く *to scratch (The subject is animate.)*
つめで頭をかきました。
I scratched my head with my fingernails.

かくー 各ー *each, every (Added to noun bases.)*
各教室 each classroom

かぐ 家具 *furniture*
家具店 furniture store

かぐ 嗅ぐ *to smell, to sniff*
その花のにおいをかいでください。
Please smell the scent of the flower.

がく 額 *sum (of money)* [→ 金額]
この機械に大きな額を払いました。
I paid a large sum of money for this machine.

がく 額 *picture frame*

かくう 架空 ～の *imaginary*
架空の人物 imaginary character, fictional person

かくえきていしゃ 各駅停車 *train which stops at every station*
この電車は各駅停車ですか。
Is this a train that stops at every station?

かくげん 格言 *proverb, adage, maxim* [→ 諺]

かくご 覚悟 *resignation (to what may happen), preparation (to accept an undesirable outcome)*
覚悟する to resign oneself to, to prepare for
失敗は覚悟しています。
I am resigned to failure.

かくじつ 確実 ～な *sure, certain, beyond doubt* [→ 確かな]
宮本さんが来るのは確実です。
It is certain that Mr. Miyamoto will come.

がくしゃ 学者 *scholar*

がくしゅう 学習 *learning, study* [→ 勉強]
学習する to study [→ 学ぶ]

かくしん 確信 *conviction, certainty, confidence*
確信する to become certain of, to come to really believe
夫が無罪だと確信しています。
I really believe that my husband is innocent.

かくす 隠す *to hide, to conceal*
お金をどこに隠したの？
Where did you hide the money?
この計画は明には隠しておいてください。
Please conceal this plan from Akira.

がくせい 学生 *student (Typically refers to a college student.)* [↔ 先生]
この大学の学生はほとんど東京出身です。
The students at this university are almost all from Tokyo.
学生服 student uniform
学生時代 one's student days
学生生活 student life

かくだい 拡大 *magnification; expansion, extension*
拡大する to magnify; to expand, to extend (transitive or intransitive)
この地図を5倍に拡大してください。
Please magnify this map five times.
拡大鏡 magnifying glass [→ 虫眼鏡]

カクテル *cocktail*

かくど 角度 *1. (the size of an) angle*
角度を測る to measure an angle
90度の角度 90-degree angle
2. angle, viewpoint
私たちはその問題をさまざまな角度から考察しました。
We viewed that problem from different

angles.

かくとく 獲得 *acquisition*

獲得する to acquire, to obtain [→ 得る]

がくねん 学年 *1. school year, academic year*

欧米では新しい学年が9月に始まります。
In Europe and America the new school year begins in September.

2. year in school, (school) grade [→ 学級]

学年末試験 annual examination, (academic year) final examination

がくひ 学費 *school expenses*

がくふ 楽譜 *musical score*

かくめい 革命 *revolution, revolutionary upheaval*

革命家 a revolutionary

フランス革命 the French Revolution

産業革命 the Industrial Revolution

がくもん 学問 *learning, knowledge, scholarship*

学問のある人 a person of learning

がくりょく 学力 *scholarly attainments; scholastic ability*

この生徒は学力があります。
This student does have scholastic ability.

学力テスト scholastic achievement test

がくれき 学歴 *school career, academic background*

かくれる 隠れる *to hide, to conceal oneself*

どこに隠れているの？
Where are you hiding?

押し入れの中に隠れました。
I hid in the closet.

隠れた才能 hidden talent

かくれんぼう *hide-and-seek*

かくれんぼうをする to play hide-and-seek

かけ 賭 *bet*

そのかけに勝つでしょう。
I will probably win that bet.

賭事 wagering, gambling

かげ 陰 *1. shade (i.e., place where light is blocked)*

あの木の陰に座りましょう。
Let's sit in the shade of that tree.

2. the area out of sight behind

壁の陰に隠れました。
We hid behind the wall.

3. the area behind a person's back (figurative)

陰で何をこっそりしているのだ。
What are you doing behind my back?

かげ 影 *1. shadow*

その子は自分の影を怖がっています。
That child is afraid of his own shadow.

2. reflection, reflected image

鏡に顔の影が映っていました。
My face was reflected in the mirror.

影絵 shadow picture

がけ 崖 *cliff*

崖崩れ cliff landslide

かけあし 駆け足 *running (done by a person or animal)*

平野さんは駆け足でやってきました。
Mr. Hirano came running.

かけごえ 掛け声 *shout of encouragement; cheer*

掛け声をかける to shout encouragingly; to cheer

子供たちは「よいしょ」と掛け声をかけました。
The children shouted, "Heave-ho!"

かけざん 掛け算 *multiplication (in arithmetic)* [↔ 割り算]

掛け算をする to multiply [→ 掛ける6.]; to do multiplication

—かげつ —か月 *(counter for number of months; see Appendix 2)*

かけて [☞ にかけて]

かけぶとん 掛け布団 *upper futon, quilt-type futon (The word Futon refers to traditional Japanese bedding, which is folded up an put in closets during the day and laid out on the floor at night.)* [↔ 敷布団]

かけら 欠片 *broken piece, fragment, crumb*

かける 欠ける *1. to become partially broken, to become chipped*

茶わんが欠けているよ。
The teacup is chipped!

2. to become lacking, to become insufficient [→ 不足する]

弟には勇気が欠けている。
Courage is lacking in my younger brother.

3. to wane (when the subject is the moon)

かける 掛ける *1. to hang, to suspend* [→ 吊す]

上着を洋服掛けにかけてください。
Please hang your coat on the hook.

眼鏡をかける to put on glasses (In the -ている form, this expression can mean **be wearing glasses, have glasses on.**)

京子さんは眼鏡をかけています。
Kyoko is wearing glasses.

2. to put as a covering

AにBを掛ける to put B on A as a covering, to cover A with B

テーブルにテーブル掛けをかけなさい。
Put a tablecloth on the table.

3. to sit (Used only for sitting on a chair, etc., not for sitting on the floor.) [→ 腰掛ける]

どうぞかけてください。
Please sit down.

4. to start (a machine)

エンジンをかける to start an engine

5. to spend, to expend [→ 費やす]

姉は着る物にお金をかけます。
My older sister spends money on things to wear.

6. to multiply (in arithmetic)

2に4をかけると、8になるでしょう？
When you multiply 4 times 2, it's 8, right?

3かける5は15。
3 times 5 is 15. (Although odd grammatically, this kind of sentence is a typical way of stating a fact of arithmetic.)

7. to pour, to sprinkle

それにソースをかけてください。
Please pour sauce on that.

8. かぎを～ to use a key (on something to lock it)

ドアにかぎをかけてください。
Please lock the door.

9. 電話を～ to make a telephone call, to telephone

今晩電話をかけてください。
Please telephone tonight.

かける 架ける *to build (so as to span something from one side to the other)*

その川に新しい橋を架けました。
They built a new bridge over that river.

かける 駆ける *to run (The subject is a person or animal.)* [→ 走る1.]

電車に乗るのに急いで駆けました。
I ran hurriedly to board the train.

かける 賭ける *to bet, to wager*

父はそのレースに5000円かけました。
My father bet ¥5,000 yen on that race.

命をかける to stake one's life, to risk one's life

かこ 過去 *1. the past*

過去の悲劇を忘れましょう。
Let's forget the tragedies of the past.

2. for the past, during the past (preceding a word specifying a length of time)

過去3年間欠席したことがないよ。
I have not been absent during the past three years!

過去形 past-tense form

かご 籠 *basket; (bird-) cage*

買い物籠 shopping basket

かこい 囲い *enclosing wall; fence* [→ 柵]

かこう 加工 *manufacturing; processing, treatment*

加工する to manufacture; to process, to treat

加工食品 processed food

かごう 化合 *chemical combination*

化合する to combine chemically (intransitive)

化合物 (chemical) compound

かこむ 囲む *to surround, to encircle, to enclose*

日本は海に囲まれています。
Japan is surrounded by sea.

私たちは火を囲んで座りました。
We sat down around the fire. (Literally: We encircled the fire and sat down.)

かさ 傘 *umbrella; parasol* [→ 日傘 (s.v. 日)]

傘を差す to put an umbrella over one's head

折り畳みの傘 folding umbrella

傘立て umbrella stand, umbrella holder

かさい 火災 *(destructive) fire* [→ 火事]

火災報知器 fire alarm

かさなる 重なる *1. to pile up, to become piled up*

2. to come to overlap; to fall on the same day

今年はクリスマスが日曜日に重なります。
Christmas falls on Sunday this year.

3. to happen one after another, to happen repeatedly

二つの事故が重なりました。
Two accidents happened one after another.

かさねる 重ねる *1. to pile up (transitive)*

そこに本を重ねないでください。
Don't pile up books there.

2. to do repeatedly, to undergo repeatedly

苦労を重ねる to suffer hardships repeatedly

かざり 飾り *decoration, ornament*

クリスマスの飾り Christmas decoration

かざる 飾る *1. to decorate, to adorn*

その部屋を絵で飾りました。
We decorated that room with pictures.

2. to put on display

壁にこのカレンダーを飾りましょう。
Let's display this calendar on the wall.

かざん 火山 *volcano*

火山が噴火する a volcano erupts

火山灰 volcanic ash

火山岩 volcanic rock, igneous rock

火山帯 volcanic zone

活火山 active volcano

休火山 dormant volcano

死火山 extinct volcano

かし 樫 *oak*

かし 菓子 *sweets; cake [→ ケーキ]; candy [→ キャンデー]; cookie [→ クッキー]*

菓子屋 confectionery; confectioner

かし 歌詞 *words of a song, lyrics*

かし 貸し *1. loan ((money)), loaned item*

Aに貸しがある to have a loan to A, to be owed by A

鈴木さんには貸しが5000円あります。
I have a loan to Ms. Suzuki of ¥5,000.

2. lending

3. renting (to someone)

貸しビデオ rental video

貸本 rental book

貸本屋 rental library

貸し自転車 rental bicycle

貸家 rental house

かし カ氏, 華氏 *Fahrenheit* [↔ セ氏]

気温はカ氏60度です。
The temperature is 60 degrees Fahrenheit.

かじ 舵 *rudder*

かじを取る to take the rudder, to steer

かじ 火事 *(destructive) fire*

うちの近くで火事がありました。
There was a fire near my house.

あのビルは火事だよ。
That building is on fire!

火事はまもなく消えました。
The fire soon went out.

かじ 家事 *housework*

かしげる 傾げる *to lean, to tilt (transitive) [→ 傾ける]*

頭を傾げる to tilt one's head to the side (as an expression of doubt)

かしこい 賢い *wise, clever, intelligent* [↔ 馬鹿な]

かしつ 過失 *1. mistake, error (due to negligence)*

2. fault, defect [→ 欠点]

カジノ *casino*

カシミヤ *cashmere fabric*

かしゅ 歌手 *(professional) singer*

流行歌手 pop singer

かしょ 箇所, 個所 *place (within something larger)*

痛みの箇所 place where it hurts

—かしょ —箇所 (counter for places; see Appendix 2)

道路の右側に工事中の場所が3箇所ある。
On the right side of the road there are three places under construction.

かしら *I wonder*

(This sentence-final particle expresses uncertainty and is typically used by female speakers. The word preceding かしら cannot be the copula form だ. When かしら is added to a sentence that would end with だ, the だ does not appear.)

あの人はいったいだれかしら。
I wonder who in the world that person is.

これでいいのかしら。
I wonder if this will do.

早く雨がやまないかしら。
I wonder if the rain won't stop soon.

かしらもじ 頭文字 *1. initial (letter)*

2. capital letter [→ 大文字]

かじる *{5} to bite, to gnaw on, to nibble on*

ねずみが箱をかじって穴をあけた。
The rat gnawed a hole in the box.

かす 貸す [[↔ 借りる]] *1. to lend*

和夫さんにその本を貸しました。
I lent that book to Kazuo.

電話を貸していただけますか。
May I use your telephone? (Literally: Can I have you lend me the telephone?)

2. to rent (to someone)

母はその部屋を学生に貸しています。
My mother is renting that room to a student.

かず 数 *number*

生徒の数は500人です。
The number of students is five hundred.

池のあひるの数を数えなさい。
Count the number of ducks in the pond.

数多く many

広場に数多くの人がいます。
There are a lot of people in the square.

ガス *gas, substance in a gaseous state (This word ordinarily refers to gas used as fuel.)* [→ 気体]

ガスをつける〔消す〕to turn on〔off〕the gas

ガス中毒 gas poisoning

ガスストーブ gas heater

排気ガス exhaust fumes

プロパンガス propane gas

天然ガス natural gas

かすかな 微か ～な *faint, dim, slight*

その女の子のことはかすかに覚えている。
I remember that girl slightly.

かすかな音 faint sound

カスタネット *castanets*

カステラ *sponge cake*

かぜ 風 *wind, breeze*

風が南からそよそよと吹いています。
The wind is blowing gently from the south.

風が出てきたね。
The wind has risen, hasn't it?

気持ちのいい風 pleasant breeze

風の強い日 windy day

風がやむ the wind dies down

北風 north wind

そよ風 gentle breeze

かぜ 風邪 *a cold*

洋子ちゃんはかぜで休んでいるよ。
Yoko is absent because of a cold!

かぜがはやっていますね。
Colds are going around, aren't they?

かぜをひく to catch a cold

先生もひどいかぜをひいています。
The teacher has a terrible cold, too.

風邪気味 feeling of having a slight cold

風邪薬 cold medicine

かせい 火星 *(the planet) Mars*

火星人 a Martian

かせき 化石 *fossil*

かせぐ 稼ぐ *1. to work and earn money*

兄はアルバイトで稼いでいます。
My older brother is earning money with a part-time job.

2. to earn by working (Except in figurative uses, the direct object is a word that refers to money.)

伯母は英語を教えてお金を稼いでいます。
My aunt is earning money by teaching English.

点を稼ぐ to earn a point, to score a point

カセット *cassette*

カセットデッキ cassette deck

カセットテープ cassette tape

かそう 火葬 *cremation* [↔ 土葬, 埋葬]

かぞえる 数える *to count, to reckon the number of*

出席者を数えてください。
Please count the people present.

かそく 加速 *acceleration* [↔ 減速]

加速するto accelerate (transitive or intransitive)

かぞく 家族 *family*

その子の家族は何人ですか。
How many people are there in that child's family?

ご家族【HON. for (above)】

ご家族の皆さんはお元気ですか。
Is everyone in your family well?

大家族 large family

ガソリン *(US)* gasoline, *(UK)* petrol

ガソリンスタンド *(US)* gas station, *(UK)* petrol station

かた 方【HON. for 人】*person*

あの方はどなたですか。
Who is that person over there?

―かた ―方 *way of, how to (Added to verb bases.)*

あの人の考え方はおかしいです。
That person's way of thinking is strange.

コンピューターの使い方を教えてください。
Please teach me how to use a computer.

―かた ―方 *in care of (Added to names and used in addresses.)*

小野様方、山田京子様
Ms. Kyoko Yamada c/o Mr. Ono

かた 肩 *shoulder*

木村さんは私の肩を軽くたたきました。
Mr. Kimura tapped me lightly on the shoulder.

子供たちは肩を並べて歩いています。
The children are walking shoulder to shoulder.

肩をすくめる to shrug one's shoulders

先生は肩をすくめて私の質問を無視した。
The teacher shrugged her shoulders and ignored my question.

肩車 carrying piggyback

肩車に乗る to get on for a piggyback ride

かた 型 *1. type, style, model*

新しい型の車 new model car

2. pattern, model, mold (for making something)

洋服の型 pattern for making clothing

型にはまる to fit a mold, to be stereotypical

3. form, model way of doing something (in a performing art or martial art)

柔道の型 judo forms

型紙 paper pattern (for making clothing)

かたい 固い, 堅い, 硬い 1. [[↔ 柔らかい1.]] *hard, solid, rigid; tough (describing meat)*

この肉は堅いですね。
This meat is tough, isn't it?

堅い木を使ったほうがいいです。
It would be better to use hard wood.

卵を堅くゆでてください。
Please boil the egg hard.

2. firm, strong, tight, unalterable

大統領は意志が固いですね。
The president's will is strong, isn't it?

靴ひもを固く結んだよ。
I tied my shoelaces tightly!

固い友情 firm friendship

Aは頭が固い A is stubborn, A's thinking is rigid

3. sound, solid, reliable

堅い会社 solid company

4. overly serious

堅い話 overly serious talk

5. tense, nervous

そんなに固くならないで。
Don't get so tense.

—がたい —難い *difficult, hard (Added to verb bases.)* [→ —にくい]

信じ難い difficult to believe

かだい 課題 *1. assigned topic, assigned theme*

2. problem, difficult matter [→ 問題2.]

かたおもい 片思い *one-sided love*

かたがき 肩書き *title (of rank); (academic) degree* [→ 学位]

かたかな 片仮名 *katakana (the squarish Japanese syllabary)*

かたこと 片言 *imperfect language, broken language (of children or foreigners)*

片言の日本語 broken Japanese

かたち 形 *shape, form*

それはどんな形ですか。
What kind of shape is that?

そのパンは動物の形をしています。
That bread is in the shape of an animal.

かたづく 片づく *1. to be put in order, to be tidied up*

この部屋はもう片づいています。
The room has already been tidied up.

2. to be finished, to be taken care of, to be settled

宿題は9時までには片づくでしょう。
My homework will probably be finished by 9:00.

かたづける 片づける *1. to put in order, to tidy up, to put in the proper place* [→ 整理する (s.v. 整理)]

まずこの部屋を片づけました。
I tidied up this room first.

茶わんを片づけましょうか。
Shall I clear away the tea cups?

2. to finish, to settle, to take care of [→ 処理する (s.v. 処理)]

山本さんは仕事をてきぱきと片づけました。
Mr. Yamamoto finished his work quickly.

この難問を片づけなくてはなりません。
We must settle this difficult problem.

かたつむり 蝸牛 *snail*

かたな 刀 *sword*

かたほう 片方 *one side (of two); one (of two, of a pair)*

靴のもう片方はどこにあるの？
Where's the other shoe?

道の片方 one side of the street

かたまり 塊; 固まり *lump; mass*

ねん土のかたまり lump of clay

雲のかたまり mass of clouds

かたまる 固まる *to harden (intransitive)*

もうのりが固まったでしょう。
The paste has probably hardened already.

かたみち 片道 *one way (of a trip)* [↔ 往復]

片道切符 (US) one-way ticket, *(UK)* single ticket

片道料金 (US) one-way fare, *(UK)* single fare

かたむく 傾く *to lean, to slant, to tilt (intransitive)*

ピサの斜塔はずいぶん傾いていますね。
The Leaning Tower of Pisa leans a lot, doesn't it?

日が傾く the sun sets

かたむける 傾ける *to lean, to slant, to tilt (transitive)*

愛子さんは首を右に傾けました。
Aiko tilted her head to the right.

おじいさんの話に耳を傾けました。
We listened to grandfather's story. (Literally: We tilted our ears to grandfather's story.)

かためる 固める *to harden (transitive)*

かたる 語る *to talk about, to give a narration of, to tell* [→ 話す2.]

高橋さんは自分の将来の夢を語りました。
Mr. Takahashi talked about his dreams for his own future.

真実を語る to tell the truth

カタログ *catalog*

かだん 花壇 *flower bed*

かち 価値 *value, worth*

この切手は非常に価値があります。
This stamp has great value.

あの家はあまり価値がないです。
That house is not worth very much.

この品物は3,000円の価値があります。
This item has a value of ¥3,000.

この本は読む価値があるそうです。
They say this book is worth reading.

かち 勝ち *victory, win* [↔ 負け]

広島の勝ちです。
It's a win for Hiroshima.

—がち 〜の *having a tendency to, apt to (Added to verb bases.)*

あの生徒は遅刻しがちです。
That student has a tendency to be late.

かちく 家畜 *domestic animal*

がちょう 鵞鳥 *goose*

かつ 勝つ *to win, to be victorious* [↔ 負ける1.]

AがBに勝つ A wins B, A is victorious in B (when B denotes a contest or competition)

僕たちのチームはその試合に５対３で勝ったよ。
Our team won that game 5 to 3!

戦争に勝つ to win a war

AがBに勝つ A is victorious over B, A beats B, A defeats B (when B denotes an opponent.)

レースで平田君に勝ったよ。
I beat Hirata in the race!

かつお 鰹 *bonito ((fish))*

がっか 学科 *(school) subject*

私の好きな学科は音楽です。
The subject I like is music.

がっかり～する *to become disappointed, to become discouraged*

田中さんの返事を聞いてがっかりした。
I was disappointed when I heard Mr. Tanaka's reply.

かっき 活気 *liveliness, vigor, spirit*

この町は活気があります。
This town is lively.

がっき 学期 *(academic) term, (academic) in-session period*

次の学期は9月に始まります。
The next term begins in September.

学期末試験 end-of-term examination, final examination

がっき 楽器 *musical instrument*

打楽器 percussion instrument
弦楽器 string instrument
管楽器 wind instrument
鍵盤楽器 keyboard instrument

かっきてき 画期的～な *epoch-making*

がっきゅう 学級 *(school) class, (school) grade (i.e., students grouped according to year of study)*

学級委員 class officer

かつぐ 担ぐ *1. to carry on one's shoulder* [→ 担う]

和子さんはスキーを担いでいます。
Kazuko is carrying skis on her shoulder.

2. to play a trick on, to deceive [→ 騙す]

加藤君はまたお兄さんを担いだよ。
Kato played a trick on his older brother again!

かっこ 括弧 *parentheses*

その数字をかっこで囲みなさい。
Enclose that number in parentheses.

角括弧 square brackets
二重括弧 double parentheses

かっこ 格好 【COL. for 格好】

格好いい stylish, chic; impressive, attractive, cool

このコートは格好いいね。
This coat is stylish, isn't it?

格好悪い unstylish, not chic; wretched, unattractive, uncool

そんなことをするのは格好悪いよ。
Doing such a thing is uncool!

かっこう 格好 *1. shape, form, appearance* [→ 姿]

2. garb, dress, attire [→ 身なり]

この学校の生徒はみんな変な格好をしています。
The students at this school all wear weird clothes.

3. ～な *suitable, appropriate* [→ 適当な]

格好な値段 reasonable price

かっこう 郭公 *cuckoo*

がっこう 学校 *school*

学校へ行くところです。
I'm about to go to school.

うちの次郎は今年この学校に入りました。
Our Jiro entered this school this year.

京子ちゃんはきのう学校を休んだよ。
Kyoko was absent from school yesterday!

学校は3時に終わります。
School ends at 3:00.

あしたは学校は休みです。
Tomorrow the school has a day off.

学校給食 school lunch
学校生活 school life
学校友達 schoolmate, school friend

がっしょう 合唱 *singing in chorus; choral music, chorus*

合唱する to sing in chorus
生徒たちはその歌を合唱しました。
The students sang that song in chorus.
合唱団 chorus, choral group, choir
合唱曲 choral piece
男声合唱 chorus of male voices
女声合唱 chorus of female voices
混声合唱 mixed chorus
二部合唱 two-part chorus

かっしょく 褐色 *dark brown (as a noun)*

がっそう 合奏 *musical instrument ensemble performance*
合奏する to play in ensemble

かっそうろ 滑走路 *(airport) runway*

ガッツ *guts, pluck, spirit* [→ 根性2.]
健はガッツがあるなあ。
Boy, Ken has guts!
ガッツポーズ holding up both fists in exultation

かって 勝手 *selfishness, doing as one pleases without consideration for others* [→ わがまま]
それは僕の勝手でしょう？
It's up to me to do as I please, right? (Literally: That's my selfishness, right?)
勝手な selfish
そんな勝手なことを言わないでください。
Please don't say such selfish things.
勝手に as one (selfishly) pleases; without permission
勝手にしなさい。
Do as you like. (a rebuke)
これを勝手に使ってはいけないよ。
You shouldn't use this without permission!

カット *cutting away a portion*
賃金のカット cut in wages
カットする to cut away a portion
髪の毛をちょっとカットしましょうか。
Shall I cut my hair a little?
その映画をカットするそうです。
I hear they're going to cut that movie.

カット *cut, illustration (on a printed page)* [→ 挿絵]

かつどう 活動 *activity, activeness*
火山の活動 volcanic activity
活動する to become active
活動的な active, energetic
クラブ活動 club activities

かっぱつ 活発 〜な *active, lively*
英子ちゃんは活発な子供ですね。
Eiko is a lively child, isn't she?
活発な議論 lively discussion

カップ *1. cup ((trophy))*
2. cup with a handle (for drinks)

カップル *couple (man and woman)*

かつやく 活躍 *activity, activeness*
活躍する to become active, to become an active participant (The subject must be human.)
高子さんは音楽部で活躍しているよ。
Takako is active in the music club!

かつよう 活用 *1. practical use*
活用する to put to practical use, to make good use of
このワークブックを大いに活用しなさい。
Make good use of this workbook.
2. inflection (in grammar)
活用する to inflect (intransitive)

かつら 鬘 *wig; hairpiece*

かてい 仮定 *supposition, assumption*
仮定する to suppose, to assume

かてい 家庭 *1. home, household*
2. family (in a household)
森さんは家庭の事情で仕事を辞めました。
Mr. Mori left his job for family reasons.
家庭訪問 home visit (by a child's teacher)

家庭科 homemaking, domestic science (as a school subject)
家庭環境 home environment
家庭教師 home tutor
家庭裁判所 family court
家庭生活 home life, family life
家庭用品 household articles

かど 角 *corner*

(When an enclosed or delimited area has a corner, 角 *refers to the outside of the corner.)*
通りの角に銀行があります。
There is a bank on the street corner.
次の角を左折してください。
Please turn left at the next corner.

かとう 下等 ～な *1. low, inferior*
2. coarse, vulgar, unrefined [→ 下品な]
下等動物 lower animal

カトリック *Catholicism*
カトリック教 [☞カトリック (above)]
カトリック教徒 a Catholic

かなう 敵う *to be a match, to equal* [→ 匹敵する]
水泳では山本さんにかなう者はいません。
In swimming, there's no one who is a match for Yamamoto.

かなう 敵う *to be suitable, to accord, to match*
目的にかなう to suit the purpose

かなう 叶う *to come true, to be fulfilled*
その夢がかなったよ。
That dream came true!

かなしい 悲しい *sad, sorrowful*
(This adjective is ordinarily restricted to describing the speaker's sadness. To describe another person's (apparent) sadness requires a form such as 悲しそう (below).) [↔ 嬉しい]
悲しいことに sadly, unfortunately
悲しいことにその話はほんとうです。
Sadly, that story is true.
悲しそうな sad-looking, sad-seeming
そのとき明子はとても悲しそうでした。
Akiko looked very sad then.

かなしみ 悲しみ *sorrow, sadness*
母の悲しみは深いです。
My mother's sorrow is deep.

かなしむ 悲しむ *to come to feel sad, to become saddened*
その知らせを聞いて悲しみました。
I heard that news and felt sad.
田村さんは深く悲しんでいます。
Ms. Tamura is deeply saddened.

かなづち 金槌 *1. hammer*
2. person who cannot swim
僕は金づちです。
I can't swim.

かならず 必ず *surely, certainly, without fail* [→ きっと]; *always* [→ 常に]
必ず来るよ。
I will certainly come!
池田さんは必ず成功すると信じています。
Mr. Ikeda believes that he will surely succeed.
食事の前にはかならず手を洗います。
I always wash my hands before meals.

かならずしも 必ずしも *(not) necessarily, (not) always (Always occurs in combination with a negative predicate.)*
日本人は必ずしもうなぎが好きなわけではありません。
A Japanese person doesn't necessarily like eel.

かなり *pretty, rather, quite, quite a lot*
亜紀さんは英語をかなりうまく話します。
Aki speaks English fairly well.
気候はかなり暑かったです。
The weather was quite hot.

かなりの considerable, fair

かなりの金額でした。

It was a considerable sum of money.

かに 蟹 *crab ((animal))*

カヌー *canoe*

かね 金 *1. money* [☞ お金]

時は金なり。(proverb)

Time is money.

2. metal [→ 金属]

かね 鐘 *bell (of the type that hangs in a bell tower, etc.)*

鐘を鳴らす to ring a bell

鐘が鳴る a bell rings

かねもち 金持ち *rich person*

金持ちが必ずしも幸福とは限りません。

Rich people are not necessarily happy.

金持ちの rich [↔ 貧乏な]

次郎さんは金持ちの家庭に生まれました。

Jiro was born into a rich family.

かのう 可能 〜な *possible* [↔ 不可能な]

時間までにそこに着くのは可能ですか。

Is it possible to arrive there in time?

可能性 possibility

かのじょ 彼女 *1. she, her*

由美ちゃんは私の友達です。彼女も東中学に通っています。

Yumi is my friend. She also goes to Higashi Junior High School.

2. girlfriend

かば 河馬 *hippopotamus*

カバー *1. cover, covering*

本のカバー book cover (of the type added over the binding or jacket for protection)

ベッドカバー bedspread

枕カバー pillowcase

2. covering (an insufficiency of some kind)

カバーする to cover

かばう 庇う *to protect, to defend, to stick up for (a person)*

その人は娘さんを犬からかばうために前に出ました。

That person stepped in front to protect his daughter from the dog.

森先生は私をかばってくださいました。

Mr. Mori stuck up for me.

かばん 鞄 *satchel, bag; briefcase; suitcase* [→ スーツケース]

旅行鞄 traveling bag

かはんしん 下半身 *lower half of a person's body* [↔ 上半身]

かび 黴 *mold ((organism))*

パンにかびが生えてしまったよ。

Mold appeared on that bread!

がびょう 画鋲 *thumbtack*

かびん 花瓶 *(flower) vase*

かぶ 蕪 *turnip*

かぶ 株 *stock (i.e., shares in a company)*

株券 stock certificate

株主 stockholder

株式 shares

株式会社 joint-stock corporation

―株 (counter for shares of stock; see Appendix 2)

かぶせる 被せる *1. to put on (a hat on someone else's head)*

弟に帽子をかぶせました。

I put a hat on my younger brother's head.

Aに罪をかぶせる to blame a sin/crime on A (A is a person.)

2. to put as a covering, to put to cover up

死んだカナリアに土をかぶせました。

I covered the dead canary with earth.

カプセル *capsule*

カプセルホテル capsule hotel

タイムカプセル time capsule

かぶとむし 甲虫 *beetle*

かぶる 被る *1. to put on*

(The direct object of 被る is generally an article of clothing that goes on the head. Compare 着る and 履く. Like other verbs for putting on clothing, 被る in the -ている form can express the meaning **be wearing, have on.**) [↔ 脱ぐ]

ヘルメットをかぶったほうがいいです。
It would be better to put on a helmet.

ゆかりちゃんは帽子をかぶっていないよ。
Yukari isn't wearing a hat!

2. to become covered with

段ボール箱はほこりをかぶっています。
The cardboard box is covered with dust.

かふん 花粉 *pollen*

花粉症 pollinosis, hay fever

かべ 壁 *wall*

壁に耳あり。(proverb)
The walls have ears.

壁紙 wallpaper

かへい 貨幣 *money, currency*

カボチャ *pumpkin; squash*

かま 釜 *kettle, cauldron*

かま 窯 *kiln; oven; furnace*

かま 鎌 *sickle*

がま 蒲 *cattail ((plant))*

かまう 構う *to mind, to care, to concern oneself*

父は服装には構いません。
My father doesn't care about his attire.

構わない I don't mind, it's all right

(This word is the negative form of 構う and has the predictable meanings as well. Follow-ing a clause that ends in a gerund (-て form) optionally followed by も, a negative form of 構う expresses permission or approval. Translations into English ordinarily use **may** rather than **all right even if** and **do not have to** rather than **all right even if not**.)

ここに座っても構いません
You may sit down here.

がまがえる *toad*

かまきり 蟷螂 *(praying) mantis*

かまぼこ 蒲鉾 *steamed fish paste (a popular Japanese food typically formed into a semicylinder on a small board for sale)*

がまん 我慢 *patience, endurance, forbearance* [→ 辛抱]

我慢する to stand, put up with, to tolerate

それを我慢しなくてもいいですよ。
You don't have to put up with that!

頭が痛くて我慢できないよ。
I have a headache and I can't stand it!

我慢強い patient, forbearing

かみ 神 *god; God*

神を信じますか。
Do you believe in God?

神に祈りましょう。
Let's pray to God.

神棚 household Shinto altar

かみ 紙 *paper*

紙を１枚ください。
Give me one sheet of paper.

紙袋 paper bag

紙屑 wastepaper

紙タオル paper towel

紙やすり sandpaper

かみ 髪 *hair (on a person's head)*

洋子さんは長く美しい髪をしています。
Yoko has long beautiful hair.

髪をセットしてもらいました。
I had my hair set.

かみそり 剃刀 *razor*

かみそりの刃 razor blade

電気剃刀 electric razor

かみなり 雷 *1. thunder*

遠くで雷の音がしました。
In the distance there was the sound of thunder.

雷が鳴る thunder sounds

2. lightning [→ 稲妻]

雷がAに落ちる lightning strikes A

雷がその木に落ちたよ。
Lightning struck that tree!

かみのけ 髪の毛 *hair (on a person's head)* [→ 髪]

かむ 噛む *1. to chew*

食べ物はよくかみなさい。
Chew your food well.

2. to bite

犬は子供の足をかみました。
The dog bit the child's leg.

ガム *(chewing) gum*

風船ガム bubble gum

カムフラージュ *camouflage*

カムフラージュする to camouflage

かめ 亀 *turtle; tortoise*

カメラ *camera*

カメラのシャッターを押す to press a camera's shutter (button), to take a picture with a camera

カメラマン photographer [→写真家 (s.v. 写真)]; camera operator (for television, movies, etc.)

1眼レフカメラsingle-lens reflex camera

カメレオン *chameleon*

かめん 仮面 *mask, false face*

仮面をかぶる to put on a mask

がめん 画面 *1. screen (for movies, etc.)*

2. screen (of a television, computer, etc.)

かも 鴨 *wild duck*

かもく 科目 *(school) subject* [→ 学科]

必修科目 required subject

選択科目 elective subject

かもしか *antelope*

かもしれない かも知れない *it may be that, it might be that*

(This expression generally follows an informal-style predicate, but the word preceding かもしれない cannot be the copula form だ. When かもしれない is added to a clause that would end with だ, the だ does not appear.)

一郎さんはきょうは来ないかもしれません。
Ichiro might not come today.

それはほんとうかもしれない。
That may be true.

かもつ 貨物 *freight, (UK) goods*

貨物列車 freight train, *(UK)* goods train

貨物船 freighter (ship)

かもめ *sea gull*

かやく 火薬 *gunpowder*

かゆ 粥 *rice gruel*

かゆい 痒い *itchy*

背中がかゆいです。
My back is itchy.

かよう 火曜 [☞ 火曜日]

かよう 通う *to commute (back and forth); to attend (school)*

私立高校に通っています。
I'm attending a private high school.

父はバスで会社に通っています。
My father commutes to his office by bus.

弟は歩いて学校に通っています。
My younger brother goes to school on foot.

かようきょく 歌謡曲 *popular song*

がようし 画用紙 *drawing paper*

かようび 火曜日 *Tuesday*

から 空 ～の *empty*

空の箱はもうないです。

There are no more empty boxes.
空にする to make empty, to empty
明ちゃんはグラスを空にしたね。
Akira emptied the glass, didn't he?

から 殻 *shell, husk*
卵の殻 eggshell

から *1. from, out of, off of (noun-following particle)*
大阪から京都まで電車で行きました。
I went from Osaka to Kyoto by train.
太陽は東から昇ります。
The sun rises from the east.
窓から日が差し込んでいます。
The sun is shining in from the window.
バターは牛乳から造られます。
Butter is made from milk.
それは何からできていますか。
What is that made out of?
新しい発明は必要から生まれます。
New inventions come from necessity.
車から降りる to get out of a car
自転車から落ちる to fall off a bicycle
2. from, since, (beginning) at, (beginning) on (noun-following particle)
10ページから始めましょう。
Let's begin at page 10.
学校は月曜日から金曜日まであります。
There is school from Monday through Friday.
けさからずっとここにいます。
I have been here ever since this morning.
夏休みは7月21日から始まります。
Summer vacation begins on July 21.
3. after, since (following the gerund (-て form) of a verb)
ここへ来てから、どのくらいになりますか。
About how long is it since you came here?
シャワーを浴びてから出かけました。
I went out after taking a shower.
4. because, since (clause-conjoining particle)
気分が悪いから、いっしょに行けません。
Since I feel unwell, I can't go with you.
「なぜ来なかったんですか」「忙しかったからです」
"Why didn't you come?" "Because I was busy."

カラー *color* [→ 色]
その映画はカラーではありません。
That movie isn't color.
カラーフィルム color film
カラー写真 color photograph
カラーテレビ color TV

カラー *collar (on an article of clothing)* [→ 襟]

からい 辛い *1. (spicy-) hot*
辛いカレー hot curry
2. salty (In this meaning, normally written in hiragana.) [→ 塩辛い (s.v. 塩)]
このスープはからいですよ。
This soup is salty!
3. severe (describing how a person deals with or evaluates something)
点が辛い one's grading is severe

カラオケ *1. recordings of songs with the vocals left out*
2. singing with such recordings as background

からかう *to tease, to make fun of*

がらくた【COL.】*rubbish, junk*

からし 芥子 *mustard*

からす 烏 *crow*
からすがかあかあ鳴く声が聞こえました。
I heard the voice of a crow calling caw-caw.

ガラス *glass ((substance))*
ガラスを割る to break glass
ガラスの破片 broken piece of glass, glass fragment
ガラス製品 glass manufactured item

窓ガラス window pane

からだ 体 *body (of a living creature)* [→ 身体]

あの人は体が丈夫です。
That person is healthy. (Literally: That person's body is strong.)

次郎ちゃんは体ががっしりしているね。
Jiro's body is sturdily-built, isn't it?

どうぞお体をお大事に。(to a person who is ill)
Please take good care of yourself. (Literally: Please, your body carefully.)

体を洗うto wash oneself (Literally: to wash the body)

体の調子がいい〔悪い〕to be in good〔bad〕health (Literally: the body's condition is good〔bad〕)

体にいい〔悪い〕good〔bad〕for one's health (Literally: good〔bad〕for the body)

カラット *carat*

一カラット (counter for carats; see Appendix 2)

からっぽ 空っぽ ～の【COL. for 空の】

からて 空手 *karate*

からふと 樺太 *Sakhalin*

カラフル ～な *colorful*

かり 仮 ～な *temporary, provisional, tentative*

仮に on the assumption, supposing (a lead-in for a conditional clause)

仮にそんなことが起こったとしたら、どうしますか。
Supposing such a thing happened, what would you do?

仮免許 temporary license

かり 狩り *hunting, hunt*

狩りをする to hunt

狩りに行く to go hunting

かり 借り *1. debt ((money)), borrowed item*

Aに借りがある to have a debt to A, to owe A

岡田さんに5万円の借りがあります。
I have a ¥50,000 debt to Ms. Okada.

2. borrowing

3. renting (from someone)

かりいれる 刈り入れる *to reap, to harvest*

その村の人たちは、今、稲を刈り入れています。
The people of that village are now reaping the rice.

カリウム *potassium*

カリキュラム *curriculum*

カリフラワー *cauliflower*

かりゅう 下流 [[↔ 上流]] *1. the area downriver; the lower part of a river*

その川の下流には魚がいません。
In the lower part of that river there are no fish.

約100メートル下流に橋があります。
About 100 meters down river there is a bridge.

2. lower social stratum

かりる 借りる [[↔ 貸す]] *1. to borrow, to use (temporarily)*

妹は図書館からこの本を借りました。
My younger sister borrowed this book from the library.

電話を借りていいですか。
May I use your telephone?

力を借りる to get assistance

2. to rent (from someone)

伯父は大きな家を借りています。
My uncle is renting a big house.

かる 刈る *to mow, to cut (grass, hair, etc.); to reap* [→ 刈り入れる]

健ちゃんは草を刈っています。
Ken is mowing the grass.

僕も髪を刈ってもらったよ。
I also had my hair cut!

ーがる *to come to show signs of, to come to appear to*

(This suffix is typically added to bases of adjectives expressing internal feelings. Forms with -がる are used to assert that a third person has such feelings.)

山根さんは音楽を習いたがっています。
Mr. Yamane wants to study music.

かるい 軽い *1. light (-weight)* [↔ 重い]

このいすはずいぶん軽いです。
This chair is very light.

2. slight, light, minor

明さんは軽いかぜをひいています。
Akira has a slight cold.

軽い食事 light meal

口が軽い glib; unable to keep a secret

カルシウム *calcium*

カルタ *1. playing cards (ordinarily any of several types used in traditional Japanese card games)*

2. card game

カルテ *medical record, patient's chart*

かれ 彼 *1. he, him*

2. boyfriend

彼によろしく。
My best to your boyfriend.

彼ら they, them

ガレージ *garage*

カレーライス *curry and rice*

かれは 枯れ葉 *dead leaf*

かれる 枯れる *1. to die, to wither (The subject is a plant.)*

この花はじきに枯れるでしょう。
This flower will probably die soon.

枯れている to be dead, to be withered

この木は枯れています。
This tree is dead.

2. to become seasoned, to become mature (The subject is a person's character or art.)

カレンダー *calendar* [→ 暦]

かろう 過労 *overwork*

過労死 death from overwork

かろうじて 辛うじて *just barely*

カロリー *calorie*

ーカロリー (counter for calories; see Appendix 2)

ガロン *gallon*

ーガロン (counter for gallons; see Appendix 2)

かわ 川 *river, stream*

川に沿って歩くのは気持ちがいいです。
Walking along the river is pleasant.

その川を泳いで渡りました。
I swam across that river.

川端 riverside

川岸 riverbank

川口 river mouth

かわ 皮 *skin (of an animal); skin, peel, rind; (tree) bark*

りんごの皮をむいてくれる？
Will you peel the apple for me?

バナナの皮 banana peel

かわ 革 *leather*

このかばんは革ですか。
Is this bag leather?

革靴 leather shoes

革ジャンパー leather jacket

革製品 leather products

がわ 側 *side*

左側 the left side

右側 the right side

向こう側 the other side, the far side

ホテルは郵便局の向こう側にあります。
The hotel is on the other side of the post office.

外側 the outside

その箱の外側は赤く塗ってあります。
The outside of that box has been painted red.
内側 the inside

かわいい 可愛い *cute, darling*
この子はかわいいですね。
This child is cute, isn't he?

かわいがる 可愛がる *to treat with affection, to love*
弟はその犬をとてもかわいがっています。
My younger brother loves that dog very much.

かわいそう ～な *pitiable, unfortunate, pathetic*
忍さんはほんとうにかわいそうな人です。
Shinobu is really an unfortunate person.
その子のかわいそうな話を聞きましたか。
Did you hear that child's pathetic story?
かわいそうに unfortunately (expressing sympathy for a victim)
かわいそうにその小鳥は死にました。
Unfortunately, that bird died.
かわいそうに！
Poor thing! (Literally: Unfortunately!)
かわいそうに思う to feel pity for, to consider pitiable
その野良猫をかわいそうに思いました。
I felt pity for that stray cat.

かわいらしい 可愛らしい *cute, darling* [→ 可愛い]

かわうそ *river otter*

かわかす 乾かす *to dry (transitive)*
シャツを火で乾かしたよ。
I dried my shirt at the fire!

かわく 乾く *to dry (intransitive)*
靴下はまだ乾いていません。
The socks haven't dried yet.

かわく 渇く のどが～ *to get thirsty*
暑いね。のどが渇いたよ。
It's hot, isn't it? I'm thirsty!

かわせ 為替 *1. money order*
2. (monetary) exchange
外国為替 foreign exchange
郵便為替 postal money order

かわせみ *kingfisher*

かわら 瓦 *tile (for exterior use, typically on roofs)*
瓦葺き covering a roof with tiles

かわり 代わり *substitute, replacement*
代わりの人を探しています。
I'm looking for a replacement person.
Aの代わりに instead of A, in place of A
兄の代わりに私が行きます。
I'll go in place of my older brother.
代わりに (following a predicate) instead of; in return for
ジェーンさんに英語を教えてもらう代わりに、日本語を教えます。
In return for having Jane teach me English, I'll teach her Japanese.

かわり 変わり *1. change, alteration* [→ 変化]
お変わりありませんか。
How is everything with you? (Literally: There aren't any changes?)
2. difference, distinction [→ 違い]

かわる 代わる *to trade places, to substitute*
AがBと代わる A trades places with B, A takes the place of B, A substitutes for B
この人と代わってください。
Please take this person's place.
少々お待ちください。今母と代わります。(on the telephone)
Just a moment, please. I'll put my mother on. (Literally: Please wait a little. I'll trade places with mother now.)

かわる 変わる *to change (intransitive)*
雨が雪に変わりました。
The rain changed to snow.
信号が赤に変わりました。

The traffic light turned red.

気が変わる one's mind changes

かわるがわる 代わる代わる *by turns, alternately*

妹と私がかわるがわる部屋の掃除をする。

My younger sister and I take turns cleaning the room.

かん 缶 *(US) can, (UK) tin ((container))*

缶ビール canned beer

缶ジュース canned juice

缶切り (US) can opener, (UK) tin opener

かん 勘 *intuition, perceptiveness*

勘がいい one's intuition is good

かん 管 *pipe, tube* [→ 管]

試験管 test tube

水道管 water pipe

—かん —感 *feeling, sense (Added to noun bases.)*

幸福感 feeling of happiness

責任感 sense of responsibility

かん 巻 *volume (in a set of books)*

一巻 (counter for volumes; see Appendix 2)

第3巻 the third volume, vol. 3

全3巻の three-volume

—かん —間 *1. period, interval (of time) (Added optionally to numbers referring to time spans.)*

雨が3日間降りました。

It rained for three days.

2. the area between (Added to noun bases denoting two or more places. The base often consists of a combination of the names of two places.)

上野—仙台間に駅はいくつありますか。

How many stations are there between Ueno and Sendai?

3. relation between/among (Added to noun bases denoting two or more entities.)

国家間の協定 pact among nations

がん 雁 *wild goose*

がん 癌 *cancer*

かんがえ 考え *1. thought, thinking* [→ 思考]

木村さんは考えにふけっています。

Ms. Kimura is lost in thought.

2. idea

隅田さんはいい考えを思いつく人です。

Mr. Sumida is a person who thinks of good ideas.

3. opinion [→ 意見]

私の考えでは、この人が悪いのではありません。

In my opinion, this man is not to blame.

4. intention [→ 意図]

海外旅行をする考えはありません。

I have no intention of taking a trip abroad.

かんがえなおす 考え直す *to reconsider*

その決心を考え直したほうがいいです。

It would be better to reconsider that resolution.

かんがえる 考える *1. to think, to have the idea* [→ 思う]

私はそうは考えません。

I don't think so.

それについてはどう考えますか。

What do you think about that?

この夏ヨーロッパに行こうと考えています。

I'm thinking of going to Europe this summer.

野村先生はみんなが考えるようないい医者じゃないよ。

Dr. Nomura is not the good doctor everyone thinks he is!

2. to think about, to consider

その問題をよく考えてください。

Please think about that problem carefully.

かんかく 間隔 *interval (or time or space)*

バスは10分間隔で来ます。
The buses come at ten-minute intervals.
机と机の間はいくらか間隔を空けなさい。
Leave some space between the desks.

かんかく 感覚 *1. ability to sense, sensation (involving one of the five senses)*
寒さで指の感覚がなかったです。
Because of the cold I had no sensation in my fingers.
2. sense, sensitivity, capacity for appreciation
感覚が鋭い one's sensitivity is keen
色彩感覚 sense of color

カンガルー *kangaroo*

かんき 換気 *ventilation, ventilating*
換気する to ventilate
換気扇 ventilating fan

かんきゃく 観客 *audience member, spectator*
フットボールの試合は大勢の観客を集めました。
The football game drew many spectators.
観客は少なかったですね。
The audience was small, wasn't it?
観客席 audience seat; stands

かんきょう 環境 *environment, surroundings*
環境に順応する to adapt to an environment
環境破壊 environmental destruction
環境保護 environmental protection
環境汚染 environmental pollution
家庭環境 home environment
社会環境 social environment
自然環境 natural environment

かんけい 関係 *relation, relationship, connection*
私もこの学校と関係があります。
I also have a connection with this school.
父は仕事の関係でニューヨークにいます。
My father is in New York in connection with work.
イギリスと日本との関係は重要です。
Relations between England and Japan are important.
関係する to come to have a relationship
品質管理は利益と密接に関係しています。
Quality control is closely related to profits.
国際関係 international relations
人間関係 human relations

かんげい 歓迎 *a welcome*
歓迎する to welcome
村人は私を歓迎してくれました。
The villagers welcomed me.
歓迎会 welcome party

かんげき 感激 *deep emotion, emotional impression* [→ 感動]
感激する to be deeply moved, to be touched
友達の声援にとても感激しました。
I was deeply moved by the cheers of my friends.

かんけつ 簡潔 〜な *concise, brief*

かんげんがく 管弦楽 *orchestral music*
管弦楽団 orchestra

がんこ 頑固 〜な *stubborn, obstinate*

かんご 漢語 *word of Chinese origin* [↔ 外来語; 和語]

かんこう 観光 *sightseeing*
グアムへ観光に出かけます。
I'm going to go to Guam for sightseeing.
観光案内所 sightseeing information office/booth
観光バス sightseeing bus
観光地 tourist resort, sightseeing spot, place of interest
観光客 sightseer, tourist

観光旅行 sightseeing trip

かんごふ 看護婦 *(female) nurse*

かんこんそうさい 冠婚葬祭 *ceremonial occasions (specifically, coming of age ceremonies, weddings, funerals, and ceremonies venerating ancestors)*

かんさい 関西 *the Kansai (Region of Japan) (Kyoto, Osaka, Shiga, Nara, Mie, Wakayama, and Hyogo Prefectures)* [→ 近畿地方] [↔ 関東]

関西弁 Kansai dialect

かんさつ 観察 *observing, observation*

観察する to observe, to watch

毎晩星を観察しています。

I observe the stars every night.

野鳥を観察するのが私の趣味です。

Watching wild birds is my hobby.

観察者 observer

かんじ 感じ *1. sensation, feeling (ascribed to the perceiver)*

寂しい感じ a lonely feeling

感じがする to have a feeling (Always preceded by a modifier.)

何かが起こりそうな感じがします。

I have a feeling that something is going to happen.

2. impression, feeling (ascribed to what induces the feeling in the perceiver) [→ 印象]

感じがする to give a feeling, to feel (Always preceded by a modifier.)

感じがいい giving a good impression, appealing, pleasant

由美ちゃんはとても感じのいい子ですよ。

Yumi is a very pleasant child!

感じが悪い giving a bad impression, unappealing, unpleasant

かんじ 漢字 *Chinese character, kanji*

がんじつ 元日 *New Year's Day* [→ 元旦]

かんして 関して [☞ に関して]

かんしゃ 感謝 *thanks, gratitude*

感謝する to give one's thanks for, to express gratitude for

ご親切を心から感謝します。

I am very grateful for your kindness. (Literally: I give thanks from the heart for your kindness.)

感謝祭 Thanksgiving Day

かんじゃ 患者 *(medical) patient*

かんしゅう 観衆 *audience, spectators*

観衆は奇術を楽しみました。

The audience enjoyed the magic tricks.

観衆は試合に興奮しました。

The spectators got excited about the game.

がんしょ 願書 *(written) application*

入学願書 application for admission to a school

かんしょう 干渉 *interference, meddling*

干渉する to interfere, to meddle

かんしょう 感傷 *sentimentality*

感傷的な sentimental

かんしょう 観賞 *admiration, enjoyment (of something beautiful)*

観賞する to admire, to enjoy

観賞用植物 decorative plant

かんしょう 鑑賞 *appreciation (of a work of art)*

鑑賞する to appreciate

石川さんは詩を鑑賞します。

Ms. Ishikawa appreciates poetry.

かんじょう 勘定 *1. calculation, computation* [→ 計算]

勘定する to calculate

2. check, bill, account [→ 会計2.]

お勘定をお願いします。 (in a restaurant) Check, please.

勘定は私が払います。

I'll pay the bill.

かんじょう 感情 *feelings, emotion*

父はめったに感情を表しません。
My father seldom shows his feelings.

他人の感情を害さないように気をつけてください。
Please be careful not to hurt the feelings of others.

がんじょう 頑丈 ～な strong, tough, solid

かんじる 感じる *to feel, to sense*

春が近いのを感じます。
I feel that spring is near.

涙がこぼれるのを感じました。
I felt tears overflowing.

痛みは感じません。
I don't feel pain.

疲れを感じる to feel fatigue

かんしん 感心 ～な *admirable, laudable*

感心する to be impressed, to be struck with admiration

明子さんの勇気に感心しました。
I was impressed by Akiko's courage.

かんしん 関心 *(feeling of) interest* [→ 興味]

若者は日本の音楽に関心を示しません。
Young people do not show any interest in Japanese music.

AがBに関心がある A is interested in B

歴史にたいへん関心があります。
I am very interested in history.

かんじん 肝心 ～な *important* [→ 重要な]; *essential* [→ 必要な]

よく眠ることが肝心です。
Sleeping well is essential.

かんする 関する [☞ に関する]

かんせい 完成 *completion (of a tangible object)*

完成する to complete; to be completed

そのビルは来月完成します。
The building will be completed next month.

かんせい 歓声 *shout of joy, cheer*

生徒たちは歓声を上げました。
The students gave shouts of joy.

かんぜい 関税 *customs duty*

かんせつ 間接 ～の *indirect* [↔ 直接の]

間接的な indirect

間接税 indirect tax

かんせつ 関節 *joint (where two bones come together)* [→ 節2.]

関節炎 arthritis

かんぜん 完全 *1. perfection* [→ 完璧]

完全な perfect

2. completeness

完全な complete

完全試合 perfect game (in baseball)

かんそう 乾燥 *dryness, desiccation*

乾燥する to dry (transitive or intransitive)

空気が乾燥してますね。
The air is dry, isn't it?

乾燥機 drying machine, drier

かんそう 感想 *impression(s), thoughts*

この本についての感想を聞かせてください。
Please tell me your thoughts about this book.

かんぞう 肝臓 *liver ((organ))*

肝臓病 liver disease

肝臓癌 liver cancer

かんそく 観測 *observation and measurement (of natural phenomena)*

観測する to observe and measure

観測所 observatory, observation station

気象観測 weather observation

かんたい 寒帯 *frigid zone* [↔ 熱帯]

かんだい 寛大 ～な *generous; magnanimous*

星野さんは友人に寛大です。
Mr. Hoshino is generous to his friends.

かんたん 感嘆 *admiration; wonder*
感嘆するto be struck with admiration; to marvel
感嘆文 exclamatory sentence
感嘆符 exclamation mark

かんたん 簡単 ～な *1. easy, simple* [→ 易しい] [↔ 難しい]
簡単な質問 easy question, simple question
2. simple, uncomplicated [→ 単純な1.] [↔ 複雑な]
簡単な報告を出しました。
I turned in a simple report.
簡単な食事 simple meal

がんたん 元旦 *New Year's Day* [→ 元日]

かんちがい 勘違い *misunderstanding, misapprehension*
勘違いする to misunderstand, to mistake
先生は私を姉と勘違いしました。
The teacher mistook me for my older sister.

かんづめ 缶詰 *(US) canned food, (UK) tinned food*
缶詰の鮭 canned salmon
パイナップルの缶詰 can of pineapple

かんとう 関東 *the Kanto (region of Japan) (Tokyo, Kanagawa, Saitama, Chiba, Ibaraki, Tochigi, and Gunma Prefectures)* [↔ 関西]
関東平野 the Kanto Plain

かんどう 感動 *deep emotion, emotional impression* [→ 感激]
感動する to be moved, to be impressed
その話には深く感動しました。
I was deeply moved by that story.
感動的な moving, impressive

かんとうし 間投詞 *interjection ((part of speech))*

かんとく 監督 *1. superintendent, supervisor; director (in movies, television, etc.); manager (of a baseball team)*
2. supervision, superintendency
監督する to supervise, to superintend

かんな 鉋 *plane ((tool))*
板にかんなをかける to plane a board
鉋屑 plane shavings

カンニング 【COL.】 *cheating, cribbing (on a test)*
カンニングする to cheat
上田君は理科の試験でカンニングしたよ。
Ueda cheated on the science exam!

かんねん 観念 *1. idea, concept* [→ 考え2.]
2. sense, conception
兄は時間の観念がないよ。
My older brother has no sense of time!
経済観念 sense of frugality
固定観念 fixed idea

がんねん 元年 *first year of an imperial reign*
平成元年the first year of the Heisei Era (1989)
明治元年the first year of the Meiji Era (1868)

かんのん 観音 *Kannon (a goddess of mercy)*

かんぱ 寒波 *cold wave ((weather phenomenon))*

カンパ *fund-raising campaign*
カンパする to campaign to raise funds

かんぱい 乾杯 *drinking a toast, ceremonial drink in celebration*
乾杯！
Cheers!
乾杯する to drink a toast
小田先生のために乾杯しましょう。
Let's drink a toast to Dr. Oda.

カンバス *a canvas (for an oil painting)*

がんばる 頑張る *to strive, to persevere*

あの人も一生懸命頑張りました。
That person also strove as hard as she could.

かんばん 看板 *(storefront) sign, signboard*

かんぱん 甲板 *(ship's) deck*

かんびょう 看病 *nursing (a sick person)*

看病する to nurse
幸子さんは病気のお母さんを看病した。
Sachiko nursed her sick mother.

かんぶん 漢文 *classical Chinese writings; writings by Japanese in classical Chinese*

かんぺき 完璧 *perfection, flawlessness* [→ 完全1.]

完ぺきな perfect, flawless
恵子さんの英語はほぼ完ぺきです。
Keiko's English is almost perfect.

かんべん 勘弁 〜する *to forgive, to pardon* [→ 許す2.]

かんり 管理 *management, supervision*

管理する to manage, to supervise
管理人 manager; (US) janitor, (UK) caretaker
管理者 manager

かんりゅう 寒流 *cold (ocean) current* [↔ 暖流]

かんりょう 完了 *completion, finishing*

完了する to complete; to be completed
旅行の準備が完了しました。
The preparations for the trip were completed.

かんれき 還暦 *60th birthday*

(This birth-day is traditionally a special occasion because the ancient Japanese calendar went in sixty-year cycles.)

かんれん 関連 *relation, connection* [→ 関係]

かんろく 貫禄 *dignity, weight of character* [→ 威厳]

祖父は貫禄のある人でした。
My grandfather was a person of dignity.

かんわ 緩和 *mitigation, alleviation*

緩和する to alleviate, to mitigate, to ease

かんわじてん 漢和辞典 *Japanese dictionary for looking up Chinese characters*

き

き 木 *1. tree*

木を植える to plant a tree
木に登る to climb a tree

2. wood

これは木のテーブルです。
This is a wooden table.

き 気 *1. heart, mind, feeling*

気が重い to feel depressed, to feel gloomy
新しい仕事のことを考えると、気が重い。
When I think about my new job, I feel depressed.
気が変わる to have a change of heart, one's mind changes

2. care, concern

Aに気がつく to notice A, to become aware of A
私もその間違いに気がつきました。
I noticed that mistake too.
気をつける to be careful, to take care, to watch out
車に気をつけなさい。
Watch out for cars.
お体に気をつけてください。
Please take care of yourself. (Literally: Please take care of your body.)
気になる to weigh on one's mind, to be troubling
あしたの試験は気になっています。

Tomorrow's exam is weighing on my mind.

気にする to be concerned about, to worry about, to mind

そんなことを気にしないでください。
Please don't worry about such a thing.

3. intention, inclination

気がする to feel like doing (following a verb)

きょうは働く気がしないよ。
Today I don't feel like working!

気に入る to be pleasing, to strike one's fancy

その車が気に入りました。
That car struck my fancy.

4. temper, disposition

気が短い to be short-tempered

気が強い to be strong-minded, to have a strong will

気が小さい to be timid

5. consciousness, one's senses [→ 意識]

気がつく to regain consciousness, to come to one's senses

2、3分してから気がつきました。
I came to my senses after two or three minutes.

気を失う to lose consciousness, to faint [→ 気絶する]

恵子はその知らせを聞いて気を失った。
Keiko heard that news and fainted.

ギア *gear*

きあつ 気圧 *atmospheric pressure; air pressure*

気圧計 barometer

高気圧 high atmospheric pressure

低気圧 low atmospheric pressure

キー *1. key (on a piano, typewriter, etc.)*

2. key (to a lock) [→ 鍵1.]

キーホルダー key ring; key case

キーウィ *kiwi fruit*

キーパー *goalkeeper*

キーボード *keyboard; keyboard (musical) instrument*

きいろ 黄色 *yellow (as a noun)*

信号が黄色に変わりました。
The traffic light turned yellow.

きいろい 黄色い *yellow (as an adjective)*

ぎいん 議員 *member of a legislative assembly*

衆議院議員 member of the House of Representatives (in the Japanese Diet)

参議院議員 member of the House of Councilors (in the Japanese Diet)

きえる 消える *1. to go out (when the subject is something burning or turned on)* [↔ 点く]

電気がぱっと消えました。
The lights suddenly went out.

火事はまもなく消えるでしょう。
The fire will probably go out soon.

2. to disappear [↔ 表れる, 現れる]

その人は人込みの中に消えました。
That person disappeared in the crowd.

きおく 記憶 *memory*

その人には以前会った記憶があります。
I have a memory of having met that person before.

記憶する to commit to memory [→ 覚える 1.]

この事を記憶しておいてください。
Please remember this fact.

記憶力 ability to remember

記憶喪失 amnesia

きおん 気温 *(atmospheric) temperature*

きかい 機会 *chance, opportunity*

娘はロンドンを訪ねる機会がありました。
My daughter had a chance to visit London.

増田さんと会う機会がなかったです。
I didn't have an opportunity to see Mr. Masuda.

今が絶好の機会ですよ。
Now is the best opportunity!

機会を逃す to miss a chance, to let an opportunity get away

きかい 機械 *machine*

この機械はうまく働きません。
This machine doesn't run well.

機械化 mechanization

機械工学 mechanical engineering

機械的な mechanical

ぎかい 議会 *(legislative) assembly, congress, parliament*

議会制度 parliamentary system

議会政治 parliamentary government

県議会 prefectural assembly

市議会 city assembly

きがえ 着替え *1. changing one's clothes*

2. a change of clothes

着替えを持って行きなさい。
Take a change of clothes.

きがえる 着替える *to change one's clothes*

Aに着替える to change into A

次郎さんは学生服に着替えました。
Jiro changed into his school uniform.

きかがく 幾何学 *(the study of) geometry*

きがかり 気掛り *anxiety, concern* [→ 心配]

きかく 企画 *plan (of action)* [→ 計画]; *planning*

企画する to plan

きかざる 着飾る *to get dressed up*

大田さんはパーティーのために着飾った。
Ms. Ota was dressed up for the party.

きかせる 聞かせる *to tell, to tell about*

(This word is the causative form of 聞く and has the predictable range of meanings in addition to the definition given here.)

旅行の話を聞かせてください。
Please tell us about your trip.

きがる 気軽～な *light-hearted, cheerful, unceremonious*

きかん 期間 *(time) period*

長期間 long period

短期間 short period

きかん 器官 *(bodily) organ*

呼吸器官 respiratory organs

消化器官 digestive organs

きかん 機関 *1. engine* [→ エンジン]

2. institution, facility; mechanism, setup, means

機関車 locomotive

蒸気機関 steam engine

交通機関 means of transportation

教育機関 educational institution

きき 危機 *crisis*

危機に直面する to face a crisis

危機を乗り越える to get through a crisis

危機一髪のところで by a hair's breadth, by the skin of one's teeth

石油危機 oil crisis

ききとり 聞き取り *catching (what is said)*

ききとる 聞き取る *to catch (what is said)*

ききめ 効き目 *effect, efficacy* [→ 効果]

父の忠告は弟にはなんの効き目もない。
My father's advice has no effect on my younger brother.

ききゅう 気球 *balloon (i.e., a device designed to rise into the atmosphere)*

きぎょう 企業 *business, company, enterprise*

中小企業 medium- and small-sized enterprises

大企業 large company, large enterprise

公営企業 a public enterprise, a government enterprise

民間企業 a private enterprise, a private company

ききん 飢饉 *famine*

ききん 基金 *fund, endowment*

きく 菊 *chrysanthemum*

きく 効く *to take effect, to work*

この薬は頭痛によく効きます。
This medicine works well for headaches.

きく 利く *1. to work, to function well*

この車はブレーキが利かないよ。
This car's brakes don't work!

鼻が利く to have a keen nose

2. to be possible; to be available for use

洗濯が利く laundering is possible

3. 口を～ *to speak, to say something*

きく 聞く, 聴く *1. to hear*

アリストテレスについて聞いたことあるのか。
Have you ever heard about Aristotle?

2. to listen to

その説明を聞いてください。
Please listen to that explanation.

私たちは日曜日に音楽を聴きます。
We listen to music on Sundays.

ラジオを聞きながら勉強します。
I study while listening to the radio.

その少年は私の言うことを聞いて、帰りました。
That boy listened to what I said and went home.

3. to ask, to inquire [→ 尋ねる]

AにBを聞く to ask A about B

駅への道をその人に聞きました。
I asked that person the way to the station.

「できますか」と金田さんに聞きました。
"Can you do it?" I asked Mr. Kaneda.

きげき 喜劇 *comedy* [↔ 悲劇]

喜劇俳優 comic actor

喜劇的な comic, comical

きけん 危険 *danger*

危険な dangerous [↔ 安全な]

その患者の生命は危険な状態にあります。
That patient's life is in danger.

ここで泳ぐのは危険です。
It is dangerous to swim here.

危険信号 danger signal

きけん 棄権 *abstention (from voting); renunciation (of a right); withdrawal (from a competition)*

棄権する to abstain from; to renounce; to withdraw

投票を棄権する to abstain from voting

競技を棄権する to withdraw from an athletic competition

きげん 紀元 *1. first year of a historical era*

2. the first year of the Christian era (Typically used to mark years as AD *by the Gregorian calendar.)* [→ 西暦]

紀元前 BC.

その哲学者は紀元前60年に生まれました。
That philosopher was born in 60 BC.

新紀元 beginning of a new era

きげん 起源 *origin, genesis*

文明の起源 the origin of civilization

きげん 期限 *time limit*

宿題は期限までに提出しなさい。
Hand in your homework by the time limit.

きげん 機嫌 *1. mood, humor*

父はきょうは機嫌がいいです。
My father's mood is good today.

2. a person's health, a person's welfare

ご機嫌いかがですか。
How are you?

きこう 気候 *climate*

日本は気候が穏やかです。
Japan's climate is mild.

気候の変わり目 change from one season to the next

きごう 記号 *symbol, sign, mark*

発音記号 pronunciation symbol

化学記号 chemical symbol

きこえる 聞こえる *1. to be able to hear; to be audible*

(What is heard is treated as a grammatical subject and marked with が rather than with を.)

もしもし、聞こえますか。
Hello, can you hear me?

鳥が鳴いているのが聞こえます。
I can hear birds singing.

2. to sound, to give an auditory impression

その音楽は耳に快く聞こえますね。
That music sounds pleasant to the ears, doesn't it?

きこく 帰国 *returning home (to one's own country)*

帰国する to return home

その学生は来月アメリカから帰国します。
That student will come home from the United States next month.

ぎこちない *awkward, clumsy*

きさま 貴様【CRUDE】*you*
(There are several Japanese words for **you,** but in general, Japanese speakers prefer to use names or titles instead. The **word** is very insulting. Other words for **you** include あなた, 君, and お前.)

きざむ 刻む *1. to cut, to chop, to slice (into small pieces)*

たまねぎを細かく刻んでください。
Please chop the onion finely.

2. to carve, to engrave [→ 彫る]

AにBを刻む to carve A in/on B, to engrave A on B

牧野君はこの木に名前を刻んだよ。
Makino carved his name on this tree!

きし 岸 *(river) bank; shore; coast* [→ 海岸]

川の岸に歩道があります。
There is a sidewalk on the river bank.

波が岸に打ち寄せています。
Waves are washing against the shore.

きじ 記事 *(news) article*

ぎし 技師 *engineer, engineering specialist*

電気技師 electrical engineer

ぎしき 儀式 *ceremony*

きじつ 期日 *appointed day, date*

その試験の期日を教えてください。
Please tell me the date of that examination.

期日までに支払えますか。
Can you pay by the appointed day?

きしゃ 汽車 *(non-electric) train*

きしゃ 記者 *(press) reporter*

記者会見 press conference, news conference

新聞記者 newspaper reporter

ぎじゅつ 技術 *technique of applying learning, technical skill*

技術者 engineer; technologist

技術的な technical

科学技術 technology

きじゅん 基準 *criterion, standard, basis*

きしょう 気象 *weather, meteorological phenomena*

気象庁 the Meteorological Agency (of the Japanese government)

気象台 weather station

気象衛星 weather satellite

気象観測 weather observation

キス *kiss*

キスする to give a kiss

ジェインさんは次郎さんにキスしました。
Jane gave Jiro a kiss.

きず 傷 *1. wound, visible injury*

その兵士は戦争で頭にひどい傷を受けた。
The soldier received a severe injury to the head in the war.

重い傷 serious wound

2. flaw, defect, blemish

傷つける to wound, to injure, to hurt

人の感情を傷つけないように気をつけろ。
Be careful not to hurt people's feelings.

傷つく to be wounded, to get injured, to get hurt

きすう 奇数 *odd number* [↔ 偶数]

きずく 築く *to build, to construct*

豊臣秀吉が大阪城を築きました。
Hideyoshi Toyotomi built Osaka Castle.

ぎせい 犠牲 *sacrifice*

犠牲を払う to make a sacrifice

犠牲バント sacrifice bunt

犠牲フライ sacrifice fly

犠牲者 casualty

きせき 奇跡 *miracle*

奇跡的な miraculous

きせつ 季節 *season*

どの季節がいちばん好きですか。
Which season do you like best?

毎年この季節には雨が多いです。
Every year in this season there is a lot of rain.

季節外れの out-of-season

かきはもう季節外れです。
Oysters are already out of season.

きぜつ 気絶 *fainting, loss of consciousness*

気絶する to faint, to lose consciousness

少女はその知らせを聞いて気絶しました。
The girl heard that news and fainted.

きせる 着せる *to put on*

(The direct object must be clothing that goes on someone else. Like 着る, this verb is used for articles of clothing that go at least in part on the torso.)

この人形に服を着せてちょうだい。
Please put clothes on this doll.

きそ 基礎 *base, basis, foundation*

建物の基礎 foundation of a building

数学の基礎 the basis of mathematics

基礎工事 foundation work (on a building)

基礎的な basic, fundamental

きそく 規則 *rule, regulation*

規則に従う to follow a rule

規則を破る to break a rule

規則正しい regular, systematic, orderly [↔ 不規則な]

恵さんは規則正しい生活を送っています。
Megumi leads an orderly life.

規則的 regular, systematic, orderly

きた 北 *the north* [↔ 南]

学校は町の北にあります。
The school is in the north of the town.

その湖は町の北の外れにあります。
That lake is on the north edge of the town.

日光は東京の北にあります。
Nikko is north of Tokyo.

うちは奈良の北20キロのところにある。
My house is in a place 20 kilometers north of Nara.

北風 north wind

北向きの north-facing

私の部屋は北向きです。
My room is north-facing.

ギター *guitar*

ギターを弾く to play a guitar

きたい 気体 *gas, substance in a gaseous state* [↔ 液体 固体]

きたい 期待 *hopeful expectation*

期待する to expect, to count on

Aの期待に添う to meet A's expectations

きたえる 鍛える *1. to forge (metal)*

2. to build up through training

体を鍛える to build up one's body

ジョギングは体を鍛えるにはいいよ。
Jogging is good for building up one's body!

きたく 帰宅 *returning home (to one's house)*

帰宅の途中で先生に会いました。
I met the teacher on my way home.

帰宅する to return home

5時に帰宅しました。
I returned home at 5:00.

きたない 汚い *1. dirty, filthy* [↔ 奇麗な2.]

汚い手で触らないで。
Don't touch it with dirty hands.

2. mean, nasty, dirty

相手は汚い手を使ったよ。
My opponent used a dirty trick!

きち 基地 *base (of operations)*

空軍基地 air-force base

きちょう 貴重 〜な *precious, valuable*

貴重な時間 precious time

貴重な体験 valuable experience

貴重品 valuable item

ぎちょう 議長 *chairperson (of a meeting, conference, etc.)*

田口さんが議長に選ばれました。
Mr. Taguchi was elected chairperson.

きちょうめん 几帳面 〜な *punctilious*

Aにきちょうめんな punctilious about A

原田さんは時間にきちょうめんです。
Ms. Harada is punctual.

きちんと *1. neatly*

教室はきちんと片づいています。
The classroom has been neatly tidied up.

きちんとした neat

上田先生はいつもきちんとした服装をしています。
Dr. Ueda always wears neat clothes.

2. regularly; punctually

英語は毎日きちんと勉強しなさい。
Study English regularly every day.

きつい *1. tight-fitting* [→ 窮屈な1.] [↔ 緩い1.]

この靴はきついです。
These shoes are tight.

きついスケジュール tight schedule

2. severe, hard, harsh [→ 厳しい2.]

この仕事は私にはきついです。
This work is hard for me.

3. intense, strong [→ 強烈な]

きつい日差し strong sunshine

4. strong-minded

明ちゃんはきつい子供ですね。
Akira is a strong-minded child, isn't he?

きっかけ *1. opportunity, (favorable) occasion* [→ 機会]

2. motive, motivation [→ 動機]

キック *kick (Ordinarily refers to kicking a ball in sports.)*

キックする to kick

キックオフ kickoff

コーナーキック corner kick

きづく 気付く *to become aware, to notice*

AがBに気づく A becomes aware of B, A notices B

人が入って来るのに気づきました。
I noticed someone coming in.

きっさてん 喫茶店 *tearoom, coffee shop*

キッチン *kitchen* [→ 台所]

ダイニングキッチン combined dining room and kitchen

きつつき 啄木鳥 *woodpecker*

きって 切手 *(postage) stamp*

切手アルバム stamp album

きっと *surely, for sure*

きつね 狐 *fox*

きっぱり (〜と) *flatly, definitely, clearly*
山田君の要求をきっぱり断ったよ。
I flatly refused Yamada's request!

きっぷ 切符 *ticket*
映画の切符を買いましたか。
Did you buy the movie tickets?
京都までの切符を3枚ください。
Three tickets to Kyoto, please.
切符売り場 ticket office, box office, (UK) booking office
片道切符 one-way ticket
往復切符 round-trip ticket

きどう 軌道 *orbit*

きどる 気取る *to put on airs*
ゆかりさんはいつも気取っています。
Yukari is always putting on airs.
気取った人 affected person, conceited person

きにゅう 記入 *1. writing in, filling in, writing as an entry*
記入する to fill in, to write as an entry
このカードにお名前を記入してください。
Please fill in your name on this card.
2. written entry

きぬ 絹 *silk*

きねん 記念 *commemoration, remembrance*
卒業の記念に校庭にタイムカプセルを埋めました。
We buried a time capsule on the school grounds in commemoration our graduation.
記念日 anniversary, day of commemoration
記念碑 monument
記念品 souvenir, memento
記念切手 commemorative stamp
記念写真 souvenir photo

きのう 昨日 *yesterday*
きのうは日曜日でした。
Yesterday was Sunday.
お姉さんはきのうここにいましたか。
Was your older sister here yesterday?

きのう 機能 *function*
心臓の機能は血液を送り出すことです。
The function of the heart is to send out blood.

きのこ 茸 *mushroom*
茸狩り mushroom gathering

きのどく 気の毒 〜な *pitiable, unfortunate* [→ かわいそうな]
その気の毒な人たちを助けましょう。
Let's help those unfortunate people.
友子ちゃんのお兄さんは、気の毒に試験に落ちました。
Tomoko's older brother unfortunately failed the exam.
Aを気の毒に思う to feel sorry for A

きば 牙 *tusk; fang*
1対のきば one pair of tusks

きばらし 気晴らし *recreation, pastime, diversion*
気晴らしに散歩をしましょう。
Let's take a walk for recreation.
父の気晴らしは園芸です。
My father's pastime is gardening.

きびしい 厳しい *1. stern, strict*
私たちの先生はとても厳しいです。
Our teacher is very strict.
2. severe, harsh, bitter
去年の冬は寒さが厳しかったです。
Last winter the cold was severe.

きふ 寄付 *donation*
寄付する to make a donation
寄付金 monetary donation

ぎふ 義父 *father-in-law*

ギプス *cast (for an injury)*

ギフト *gift* [→ 贈り物]

ギフトショップ gift shop

きぶん 気分 *feeling, mood, frame of mind*

今は歌を歌う気分じゃないよ。

I am not in the mood for singing songs now!

気分になる to come to feel like, to get in the mood for (following a verb)

勉強する気分になれません。

I can't get in the mood for studying.

気分転換 something to change one's mood

気分屋 moody person

きぼ 規模 *scale, extent, proportionate size*

伯父は商売の規模を縮小しました。

My uncle reduced the scale of his business.

大規模な／の large-scale

小規模の small-scale

ぎぼ 義母 *mother-in-law*

きぼう 希望 [[→ 望み]] *hope; wish*

医者になるのが僕の希望です。

I hope to become a doctor. (Literally: Becoming a doctor is my wish.)

希望する [[→ 望む]] to hope for; to wish for

希望を失う to lose hope

全世界が平和を希望しています。

The whole world is hoping for peace.

きほん 基本 *basis, foundation (only in an abstract sense, not as a concrete object)*

これが剣道の基本です。

This is the foundation of kendo.

基本的な basic, fundamental

基本的人権 fundamental human rights

きまえ 気前 ～がいい *generous*

気前よく generously

きまぐれ 気まぐれ *caprice, whim*

気まぐれな capricious, changeable

きまって 決まって *regularly, invariably, always*

(This word is the gerund (-て form) of 決まる and has the predictable meanings as well.)

きまり 決まり *1. rule* [→ 規則]

帽子をかぶるのが学校の決まりです。

Wearing a cap is a school rule.

2. settlement, conclusion

Aの決まりが付く A is settled, A is brought to a conclusion

Aの決まりを付ける to settle A, to bring A to a conclusion

3. ～が悪い *to feel awkward, to feel embarrassed*

きまりもんく 決まり文句 *set phrase, stereo-typed expression*

きまる 決まる *to be decided, to be set*

AがBに決まる A is set for B, B is chosen as A

姉の結婚式は１１月１０日に決まった。

My older sister's wedding was set for November 10.

会議の場所が仙台に決まりました。

Sendai was chosen as the conference venue.

Aに決まっている it's certain that it's A (In this pattern, A can be a clause as well as a noun.)

明君は試験に受かるに決まっているよ。

Akira is certain to pass the exam!

きみ 君 *you*

(There are several Japanese words for **you**, but in general, Japanese speakers prefer to use names or titles instead. The use of is typical of a male speaker addressing a younger person or an intimate equal. Female speakers typically use only to address a child. Other words for you include あなた, お前, and 貴様.)

おい、君、窓から入ってはいけないよ。

Hey, you! You mustn't go in through the window!

きみ 黄身 *yolk, yellow (of an egg)* [↔ 白身1.]

きみょう 奇妙 〜な *odd, peculiar, strange* [→ 妙な]
奇妙な風習 odd customs

ぎむ 義務 *duty, obligation*
義務を怠る to neglect one's duty
義務を果たす to carry out one's duty
義務教育 compulsory education

きむずかしい 気難しい *hard to please*

きめる 決める *to decide, to set*
会合の時間と場所を決めましょう。
Let's set the time and place for our meeting.
AをBに決める to decide on B for A, to decide on B as A
新しいデザインをこれに決めました。
I decided on this for the new design.
ことに決める to decide to (following a nonpast-tense verb)
私たちはすぐ行くことに決めました。
We decided to go at once.

きも 肝 *1. liver ((bodily organ))* [→ 肝臓]
2. courage, nerve [→ 度胸]

きもち 気持ち *feeling, how a person feels*
あの人の気持ちがよくわかるよ。
I understand very well how that person feels!
気持ちがいい to feel good (when describing a person); to be pleasant, to be comfortable (when describing a thing)
これは気持ちのいい部屋ですね。
This is a comfortable room, isn't it?
気持ちが悪い to feel bad, to feel sick (when describing a person); to be unpleasant, to be disgusting (when describing a thing)

きもの 着物 *1. kimono*
恵子さんは着物がよく似合います。
Keiko looks nice in a kimono.
2. clothes [→ 服]

ぎもん 疑問 *doubt, uncertainty* [→ 疑い1.]
何か疑問の点がありますか。
Do you have any doubts?
疑問の余地がない there is no doubt
疑問文 interrogative sentence
疑問符 question mark

きゃく 客 *1. visitor; guest*
きのうは客が二人来ました。
I had two visitors yesterday.
2. customer; (paying) passenger [→ 乗客]
今日は客が多いですね。
There are a lot of customers today, aren't there?
お客さん【HON. for (above)】
今晩は食事にお客さんを4人招きました。
Tonight we invited four guests to dinner.

ぎゃく 逆 *the reverse, the opposite* [→ 反対1.]
「高い」は「低い」の逆です。
"High" is the opposite of "low."
逆の reverse, contrary, opposite
子供たちは逆の方向に行きました。
The children went in the opposite direction.
逆効果 opposite effect
逆コース reverse course

ギャグ *gag ((joke))*

ぎゃくたい 虐待 *cruel treatment*
虐待する to treat cruelly
動物を虐待してはいけません。
You must not be cruel to animals.

ぎゃくてん 逆転 *reversal, inversion*
逆転する to become reversed, to become inverted
形勢が逆転する the situation reverses, the tables get turned

きゃくほん 脚本 *script, play (in written form); scenario, screenplay*
脚本家 dramatist, playwright; screenplay writer

きゃくま 客間(きゃくま) *1. room in a home where visitors are received* [→ 応接間(おうせつま)]

2. guest room

キャスト *cast (of a play, movie, etc.)*

きゃっかんてき 客観的(きゃっかんてき) ～な *objective (i.e., not subjective)* [↔ 主観的(しゅかんてき)な]

キャッチ ～する *to catch; to obtain, to pick up*

キャッチボール *playing catch*

キャッチボールをしよう。
Let's play catch.

キャッチャー *(baseball) catcher* [→ 捕手(ほしゅ)]

キャップ *1. cap ((hat))*

2. cap (on a pencil or pen); cap (on a bottle)

ギャップ *gap, difference*

私(わたし)と父(ちち)の考(かんが)え方(かた)には大(おお)きなギャップがあります。
There is a big gap between my way of thinking and my father's.

キャプテン *1. (team) captain* [→ 主将(しゅしょう)]

2. (ship) captain [→ 船長(せんちょう)]

キャベツ *cabbage*

ギャラ *guaranteed payment to a performer for appearing*

キャラクター *1. character, personality* [→ 性格(せいかく)]

2. famous character (in a story, movie, etc.)

キャラクター商品(しょうひん) item of merchandise incorporating a famous character in its design

キャラメル *caramel*

ギャング *1. gangster*

2. mob (of gangsters)

ギャング映画(えいが) gangster movie

キャンセル *cancellation*

キャンセルする to cancel [→ 取(と)り消(け)す]

ホテルの予約(よやく)をキャンセルします。
I will cancel the hotel reservation.

キャンデー *(US) candy, (UK) sweets*

キャンパス *campus*

キャンプ *camping*

山(やま)へキャンプに行(い)こう。
Let's go camping in the mountains.

キャンプする to camp

キャンプファイアー campfire

キャンプファイアーをする to make a campfire

キャンプ場(じょう) campsite, campground

キャンプ村(むら) camping village

キャンペーン *(publicity) campaign*

きゅう 九(きゅう) *nine (see Appendix 2)* [→ 九(く)]

きゅう 急(きゅう) *1. emergency, crisis; urgent need*

急(きゅう)な urgent, pressing

佐藤(さとう)さんは急(きゅう)な用事(ようじ)で出(で)かけました。
Mr. Sato went out on urgent business.

2. ～な *sudden, abrupt* [→ 突然(とつぜん)の]

電車(でんしゃ)が急(きゅう)に止(と)まりました。
The train stopped suddenly.

急(きゅう)に雨(あめ)が降(ふ)りだしました。
Suddenly it began to rain.

3. ～な [[↔ 緩(おだ)やかな1.]] *steep; sharp (describing a curve)*

急(きゅう)な階段(かいだん) steep stairs

急(きゅう)なカーブ sharp curve

4. ～な *swift (describing a flow)* [↔ 緩(ゆる)やかな2.]

この川(かわ)は流(なが)れが急(きゅう)です。
This river's current is swift.

きゅう 級(きゅう) *1. class, grade, rank*

2. (school) class, (school) grade [→ 学級(がっきゅう)]

一級(きゅう) (counter for classes, grades, ranks; see Appendix 2)

明子(あきこ)ちゃんは私(わたし)より1級上(きゅううえ)です。
Akiko is one grade above me.

きゅう－ 旧－ *old, former, ex- (Added to noun bases)* [↔ 新－]
旧制度 old system
旧所有者 former owner

きゅうか 休暇 *time off, (US) vacation, (UK) holidays*
父は１週間の休暇を取りました。
My father took a one-week vacation.
前田さんはあしたは休暇です。
Mr. Maeda will be off tomorrow.
休暇中の on-vacation
ジョンソンさんは今休暇中です。
Ms. Johnson is on vacation now.
夏期休暇 summer vacation

きゅうがく 休学 *absence from school*
休学する to be absent from school
一郎君は長い間休学しています。
Ichiro has been absent from school for a long time.

きゅうきゅう 救急 ～の *for first-aid, for (medical) emergencies*
救急箱 first-aid kit
救急病院 emergency hospital
救急車 ambulance
救急処置 first aid

きゅうぎょう 休業 *temporary closing (of a business)*
休業する to close temporarily (intransitive)
たいていの店が日曜日には休業します。
Most stores are closed on Sundays.
「本日休業」 (on a sign)
Closed Today

きゅうくつ 窮屈 ～な *1. tight-fitting; cramped*
先生は窮屈な上着を着ています。
The teacher is wearing a tight coat.
2. awkward, ill-at-ease, constrained

きゅうけい 休憩 *short rest, break*
休憩する to take a short rest, to take a break
ここでちょっと休憩しよう。
Let's take a break here for a little while.
休憩時間 recess; intermission
休憩室 lounge; lobby

きゅうげき 急激 ～な *rapid, sudden, abrupt*
この国の人口は急激に増加しました。
This country's population increased rapidly.

きゅうこう 休校 *temporary closing of a school*
２日間休校になりました。
School was closed for two days.

きゅうこう 急行 *an express*
この電車は急行ですか。
Is this train an express?
３時20分発の熱海行きの急行に乗ってください。
Please get on the 3:20 express for Atami.
急行券 express ticket
急行料金 express charge

きゅうじつ 休日 *holiday, day off*
きょうは休日ですね。
Today is a holiday, isn't it?
休日はたいていテニスをします。
On holidays I usually play tennis.

きゅうしゅう 吸収 *absorption*
吸収する to absorb

きゅうじょ 救助 *rescue, saving, help*
少年たちは叫んで救助を求めました。
The boys cried out and asked for help.
救助する to rescue, to save [→ 助ける]
救助隊 rescue party, rescue team

きゅうじょう 球場 *ballpark, stadium*
横浜球場 Yokohama Stadium

きゅうしょく 給食 *providing meals; provided meal, school lunch*

給食費 expense for school lunches

きゅうそく 休息 *rest, break* [→ 休憩]

休息する to rest, to take a break

きゅうそく 急速 〜な *rapid, quick, swift*

コンピューター産業は最近急速な進歩を遂げました。

The computer industry has achieved rapid progress recently.

きゅうでん 宮殿 *palace*

ぎゅうにく 牛肉 *beef*

ぎゅうにゅう 牛乳 *(cow's) milk*

牛乳瓶 milk bottle

きゅうびょう 急病 *sudden illness*

妹が急病にかかりました。

My younger sister came down with a sudden illness.

きゅうめい 救命 *lifesaving, saving a person's life*

救命具 life preserver; life jacket, life vest

救命ボート lifeboat

きゅうよう 休養 *rest, respite from work*

休養する to take a rest

きゅうよう 急用 *urgent business*

父は急用で出かけています。

My father is away on urgent business.

きゅうり *cucumber*

きゅうりょう 給料 *pay, salary, wages*

姉の給料は月に16万円です。

My older sister's salary is ¥160,000 a month.

給料日 payday

きよう 器用 〜な *skillful, adroit, dexterous*

母は手先が器用です。

My mother is good with her hands.

きょう 今日 *today*

きょうは何曜日ですか

What day of the week is it today?

中山先生はきょう授業を休みました。

Prof. Nakayama missed class today.

先週のきょう a week ago today

来週のきょう a week from today

ーきょう ー強 *a little more than (Added to number bases.)* [↔ー弱]

あの相撲取りの体重は100キロ強です。

That sumo wrestler's weight is a little more than 100 kilograms.

ぎょう 行 *line (of text)*

ー行 (counter for lines; see Appendix 2)

18ページの3行目を見なさい。

Look at line three on page 18.

1行おきに on every other line

きょうい 胸囲 *chest measurement, circumference of the chest*

きょうい 驚異 *wonder, marvel*

驚異の目をみはる to open one's eyes wide in amazement

驚異的な wonderful, marvelous, amazing

きょういく 教育 *education*

姉はイギリスで教育を受けました。

My older sister was educated in England.

教育する to educate

教育委員会 board of education

教育制度 educational system

教育テレビ educational television

学校教育 school education

きょういん 教員 *teacher, faculty member* [→ 先生1.]

教員室 teachers' room

きょうか 教科 *(school) subject*

きょうかい 教会 *church*

毎週日曜日に教会に行きます。

I go to church every Sunday.

きょうかい 境界 *border, boundary* [→ 境]

その高い山脈が両国の境界です。

That high mountain range is the border between the two countries.

境界線 borderline, boundary line

きょうがく 共学 *coeducation*

共学の大学 coeducational college

男女共学 [☞ 共学 (above)]

きょうかしょ 教科書 *textbook*

きょうぎ 競技 *competition, contest of skill; athletic contest, sporting event*

競技する to compete

競技場 athletic field; stadium

競技会 athletic meet; competition

陸上競技 track and field competition

ぎょうぎ 行儀 *manners*

由美子ちゃんは行儀がいいです。

Yumiko is well mannered.

行儀よく in a well-mannered fashion

行儀よくする to behave oneself

きょうきゅう 供給 *supply (of a commodity, etc.)* [↔ 需要]

供給する to supply

供給者 supplier

きょうくん 教訓 *lesson, teaching, precept*

きょうげん 狂言 *kyogen (a kind of traditional Japanese comic play)*

ぎょうざ 餃子 *jiao-zi (a kind of Chinese stuffed dumpling)*

きょうざい 教材 *teaching materials*

きょうさんしゅぎ 共産主義 *communism*

共産主義者 a communist

きょうさんとう 共産党 *Communist Party*

きょうし 教師 *teacher, instructor* [→ 先生1.]

ぎょうじ 行事 *planned event, function*

学校行事 school event

年中行事 annual event

きょうしつ 教室 *classroom*

きょうじゅ 教授 *professor*

助教授 assistant professor

ぎょうしょ 行書 *running style (of Japanese calligraphy)* [↔ 楷書; 草書]

きょうせい 強制 *force, compulsion, coercion*

強制する to force to do, to compel to accept, to coerce [→ 押しつける2.]

部屋を出るように強制されました。

I was forced to leave the room.

強制的な compulsory, forcible, coercive

きょうそう 競争 *competition, contest*

競争する to compete

競争に勝つ〔負ける〕 to win〔lose〕a competition

競争相手 rival, competitor, opponent

競争意識 competitive consciousness

競争率 degree of competition

競争心 competitive spirit

きょうそう 競走 *(running) race*

競走に勝つ〔負ける〕 to win〔lose〕a race

競走する to run a race

あの丘のふもとまで競走しよう。

Let's race to the foot of that hill.

100メートル競走 100-meter dash

障害物競走 hurdle race

きょうそうきょく 協奏曲 *concerto* [→ コンチェルト]

きょうぞん 共存 *coexistence*

共存する to coexist

きょうだい 兄弟 *siblings, brothers and/or sisters*

兄弟がいますか。

Do you have any brothers or sisters?

健ちゃんと由美ちゃんは兄弟です。

Ken and Yumi are brother and sister.

ー兄弟 group of siblings (Added to bases consisting of a number for counting people.)

私は3人兄弟です。

I am one of three children.

兄弟喧嘩 sibling quarrel

きょうだん 教壇 *teacher's platform (at the front of a classroom)*

きょうちょう 強調 *stress, emphasis*

強調する to stress, to emphasize

きょうつう 共通 ～の *mutual, common, shared*

幸子さんは私たちの共通の友人です。

Sachiko is our mutual friend.

共通点 point in common, something in common

あの二人には共通点があります。

Those two have something in common.

きょうとう 教頭 *head teacher (In a Japanese school this person ranks just below the principal.)*

きょうどう 共同 *cooperation, collaboration*

この部屋は弟と共同で使っています。

I share this room with my younger brother.

共同の joint, united, common

共同する to cooperate, to work together

共同募金 community chest

共同声明 joint statement

きょうどう 協同 *cooperation* [→ 共同, 協力]

協同する to cooperate, to work cooperatively

協同組合 cooperative association

きょうはく 脅迫 *intimidation*

脅迫の threatening, intimidating

脅迫する to threaten, to intimidate

脅迫電話 threatening telephone call

脅迫状 threatening letter

きょうふ 恐怖 *fear, terror, horror*

恐怖映画 horror movie

きょうみ 興味 *(feeling of) interest*

Aに興味を持つ to take an interest in A

Aに興味がある to be interested in A

歴史にたいへん興味があります。

I am very interested in history.

興味深い very interesting

この本は私にはとても興味深いです。

This book is very interesting to me.

きょうよう 教養 *culturedness, educatedness, refinement*

社長は教養のある人です。

The company president is a cultured person.

きょうりゅう 恐竜 *dinosaur*

きょうりょく 協力 *cooperation*

ご協力を感謝します。

I am grateful for your cooperation.

協力する to cooperate

その仕事は友達と協力しなさい。

Cooperate with your friends on that job. (Literally: As for that work, cooperate with friends.)

きょうりょく 強力 *strength, power, might*

強力な strong, powerful, mighty

その政策は強力な支持を受けています。

That policy is receiving strong support.

この機械は強力なモーターで動く。

This machine runs on a powerful motor.

きょうれつ 強烈 ～な *strong, intense, powerful, severe*

ぎょうれつ 行列 *1. (US) line, (UK) queue (i.e., entities arranged in a line)*

劇場の前に長い行列が出来ています。

A long line has formed in front of the theater.

2. (US) lining up, (UK) queueing up

行列する (US) to line up, (UK) to queue

up (intransitive)
人々は切符を買うために行列して待っています。
People are waiting in line to buy tickets. (Literally: People are lining up and waiting to buy tickets.)
仮装行列 fancy-dress parade

きょうわこく 共和国 *republic*

きょか 許可 *permission*
許可なしにその部屋へ入ってはいけません。
You mustn't enter that room without permission.
許可する to permit
父はバイクに乗るのを許可しなかった。
My father didn't permit me to ride a motorbike.
許可を得る to get permission
許可証 permit, license

ぎょぎょう 漁業 *fishery, fishing industry*
沿岸漁業 coastal fishery
遠洋漁業 deep-sea fishery

きょく 曲 *piece (of music)*
この曲はベートーベンが書いたものです。
This piece is one that Beethoven wrote.
洋子さんはその曲をピアノで弾きました。
Yoko played that piece on the piano.
—曲 (counter for musical pieces; see Appendix 2)

きょくげい 曲芸 *acrobatic trick, stunt, feat*
曲芸師 acrobat

きょくせん 曲線 *curve, curved line*

きょくたん 極端 *an extreme, extremity*
極端に走る to go to extremes
極端な extreme
それは極端な例です。
That is an extreme example.

きょくとう 極東 *the Far East*

きょじゅう 居住 *residing, dwelling*
居住する to take up residence [→ 住む]

きょじん 巨人 *giant (person)*

きょぜつ 拒絶 *refusal, rejection*
拒絶する to refuse, to reject [→ 断る1.]

ぎょそん 漁村 *fishing village*

きょだい 巨大 ～な *huge, enormous, gigantic*

きょねん 去年 *last year*
去年の今ごろサイパンにいました。
About this time last year I was in Saipan.
ブラウンさんは去年日本に来ました。
Miss Brown came to Japan last year.

きょひ 拒否 *refusal, rejection, veto*
拒否する to refuse, to turn down, to veto [→ 断る1.]

きょり 距離 *distance*
上野—仙台間の距離は約350キロです。
The distance between Ueno and Sendai is about 350 kilometers.
駅までどのくらいの距離がありますか
About how far is it to the station?

きらい 嫌い ～な (This adjectival noun is used to describe both the people who dislike and the people or things that are disliked.) [[↔ 好きな]] *disliked; unfond*
数学が嫌いなので、エンジニアにはなれません。
Since I dislike math, I can't become an engineer.
私は魚が好きですが、息子は嫌いです。
I like fish, but my son dislikes it.

きらきら *twinklingly, glitteringly, sparklingly*
今夜は星がきらきら輝いています。
Tonight the stars are shining glitteringly.
きらきらする to twinkle, to glitter, to sparkle

きらく 気楽 ～な *easygoing, carefree*
母は今は気楽な暮らしをしています。

My mother now leads a carefree life.

きり 錐 *drill; awl; gimlet*

きり 霧 *1. fog; mist*

まだ早いですが、霧は晴れました。
It's still early, but the fog has cleared up.

けさは霧が深かったです。
This morning the fog was thick.

2. spray, atomized liquid

霧を吹く to spray atomized liquid
霧雨 misty rain, drizzle

きり 切り *end* [→ 終わり]; *limit* [→ 限度]

祖母は話し始めたら、切りがないです。
If my grandmother starts talking, there's no end.

向こうの要求は切りがないです。
The other side's demands have no limits.

きり 桐 *paulownia*

ぎり 義理 *duty, obligation (toward another person as a result of social interaction)*

あの人には義理があります。
I have an obligation to that person.

義理の -in-law; step-
義理の母 mother-in-law; stepmother

ぎりぎり *just barely (within the limit)*

時間ぎりぎりでデートに間に合った。
I just barely made it on time for the date.
ぎりぎりの just-within-the-limit

きりぎりす *katydid ((insect))*

キリスト *(Jesus) Christ*

キリスト教 Christianity
キリスト教徒 a Christian

きりたおす 切り倒す *to cut down, to fell*

大野さんはその木をおので切り倒した。
Mr. Ono cut down that tree with an ax.

きりつ 起立 ～する *to stand up, to rise (to one's feet)*

起立！
Stand up! (This use as a command is typical when ordering an assembled group of people to stand.)

きりつ 規律 *1. order, discipline* [→ 秩序]

2. rules, regulations

きりぬき 切り抜き *(US) (newspaper) clipping, (UK) (newspaper) cutting*

きりぬく 切り抜く *to cut out, to clip (from a newspaper, magazine, etc.)*

兄はその写真を新聞から切り抜きました。
My older brother cut out that picture from the newspaper.

きりゅう 気流 *air current*

上昇気流 ascending air current
下降気流 descending air current
乱気流 turbulent air currents, turbulence

きりょく 気力 *energy, spirit, vigor*

あの人は気力に満ちています。
That person is full of energy.

妹は気力がまったくないです。
My younger sister has absolutely no energy.

きりん 麒麟 *giraffe*

きる 切る {5} *1. to cut (transitive)*

そのケーキを六つに切ってください。
Please cut that cake into six.

パンを切ってくれる？
Will you cut the bread for me?

トランプを切る to shuffle cards; to cut (a deck of) cards
話を切る to stop talking, to break off what one is saying
縁を切る to break off a relationship
電話を切る to cut off a telephone call (ordinarily by hanging up)

電話を切らないでください。
Please don't hang up the phone.

2. to turn off (a device)

寝る前にテレビを切りなさい。
Before you go to bed turn off the TV.

きる 着る *to put on*

(The direct object of is generally an article

of clothing that goes at least in part on the torso. Compare 履く and 被る. Like other verbs for putting on clothing, in the -ている form can express the meaning be **wearing, have on.**) [↔ 脱ぐ]

コートを着なさい。
Put on your coat.

和子さんは新しいセーターを着ています。
Kazuko is wearing a new sweater.

オーバーを着たままで入ってください。
Please come in with your overcoat on.

きれ 切れ *piece of cloth*

ーきれ ー切れ *1. piece, slice (Added to noun bases denoting things that can be sliced or cut)*

紙切れ (cut) piece of paper

パン切れ slice of bread

2. (counter for slices; see Appendix 2)

きれい 奇麗 *1.* ～な *pretty, beautiful* [→ 美しい]

春になると、きれいな花が咲きます。
Beautiful flowers bloom in spring. (Literally: When it becomes spring, beautiful flowers bloom.)

順子ちゃんはきれいな少女ですね。
Junko is a pretty girl, isn't she?

2. ～な *clean* [→ 清潔な] [↔ 汚い]

手をきれいにしておきなさい。
Keep your hands clean.

この湖の水はとてもきれいです。
The water in this lake is very clear.

3. ～に *completely* [→ すっかり]

暗号をきれいに忘れてしまったよ。
I've completely forgotten the code!

きれる 切れる *1. to cut (intransitive) (The subject is a cutting tool.)*

このナイフはよく切れます。
This knife cuts well.

2. to get cut

母の手は寒さでひびが切れていた。
Mother's hands are chapped from the cold.

縁が切れる a relationship is broken off

電話が切れる a phone call is cut off

3. to break (The subject is a string, rope, etc.)

靴のひもが切れた。
My shoe lace broke.

4. to run out, to be used up [→ 尽きる]

砂糖が切れてしまったよ。
The sugar has run out!

報告書の提出期限が切れています。
Time has run out for submitting reports.

5. to be shrewd, to be sharp

正雄さんは切れる人ですね。
Masao is a shrewd person, isn't he?

キロ [☞ キログラム; キロメートル]

ーキロ (counter for kilograms or kilometers; see Appendix 2)

きろく 記録 *1. record, chronicle, document*

記録する to record, to chronicle, to document

2. (world) record

森選手は重量挙げの記録を持っている。
Mori holds the weightlifting record.

記録を破る to break a record

記録映画 documentary film

記録係 recorder; scorer

記録保持者 record holder

世界記録 world record

キログラム *kilogram*

ーキログラム (counter for kilograms; see Appendix 2)

キロメートル *kilometer*

ーキロメートル (counter for kilometers; see Appendix 2)

キロワット *kilowatt*

ーキロワット (counter for kilowatts; see Appendix 2)

ぎろん 議論 *argument, debate; discussion*

議論する to have an argument, to have a debate; to have a discussion

将来の進路について母と議論しました。

I had a discussion about my future course with my mother.

ぎわく 疑惑 *suspicion, misgivings*

きわめて 極めて 【FORMAL for 非常に】 *extremely*

きん 金 *gold*

高山さんは金の指輪をしています。

Ms. Takayama is wearing a gold ring.

金色 gold color

金貨 gold coin

金メダル gold medal

ぎん 銀 *silver*

銀貨 silver coin

銀メダル silver medal

きんえん 禁煙 *1. prohibition of smoking*

2. giving up smoking, abstaining from smoking

禁煙する to give up smoking, to abstain from smoking

伯父は去年から禁煙しています。

My uncle has been abstaining from smoking since last year.

禁煙車 no-smoking car

ぎんが 銀河 *the Milky Way, the Galaxy* [→ 天の川]

きんがく 金額 *amount of money*

その歌手はかなりの金額の宝石を買った。

The singer bought some very expensive jewels.

きんがん 近眼 *nearsightedness* [→ 近視]

きんきちほう 近畿地方 *the Kinki Region of Japan* [→ 関西]

きんきゅう 緊急 *urgency; emergency*

緊急の場合はこの電話を使ってください。

In an emergency, please use this telephone.

緊急な／の urgent, critical

坂本さんは緊急な用事で宮崎に行った。

Mr. Sakamoto went to Miyazaki on urgent business.

きんぎょ 金魚 *goldfish*

金魚鉢 goldfish bowl

きんこ 金庫 *a safe*

きんこう 均衡 *balance, equilibrium* [→ 釣り合い]

ぎんこう 銀行 *bank (i.e., a financial institution)*

銀行からお金を少し引き出します。

I'm going to withdraw a little money from the bank.

兄は銀行に 2 万円預金しました。

My older brother deposited ¥20,000 in the bank.

銀行員 bank clerk; bank employee

銀行家 banker

きんし 近視 *nearsightedness, (UK) shortsightedness* [↔ 遠視]

父も母も近視です。

Both my father and my mother are nearsighted.

きんし 禁止 *prohibition, ban*

禁止する to prohibit, to ban [→ 禁じる]

「駐車禁止」 (on a sign)

No Parking

「立入禁止」 (on a sign)

Keep Out (Literally: Entry prohibited)

きんじょ 近所 *neighborhood, vicinity* [→ 付近]

これは近所の店で買いました。

I bought this in a neighborhood store.

きのう、うちの近所で事故があったよ。

Yesterday, there was an accident in my neighborhood!

この近所に郵便局はありますか。

Is there a post office near here?

近所の人 neighbor

きんじる 禁じる *to forbid, to prohibit*

医者は父に外出を禁じました。
The doctor forbade my father to go out.

この川での水泳は禁じられています。
Swimming in this river is prohibited.

きんせい 金星 *(the planet) Venus*

きんせい 近世 *early modern times*

(In Japanese history, this word is ordinarily used to mean specifically the period from the beginning of the Azuchi-Momoyama period (1568) until the end of the Edo period (1868).)

きんぞく 金属 *metal*

金属バット metal (baseball) bat
金属製品 metal manufactured article

きんだい 近代 *the modern age, modern times*

(In Japanese history, this word is ordinarily used to mean specifically the period from the beginning of the Meiji period (1868) until the end of the Second World War.)

近代史 modern history
近代的な modern, contemporary

きんちょう 緊張 *(mental) tension*

緊張する to become tense

試験の前は緊張します。
I become tense before an exam.

きんとう 近東 *the Near East*

ぎんなん 銀杏 *ginkgo nut*

きんにく 筋肉 *muscle*

きんぱつ 金髪 *blond hair*

金髪の blond, blond-haired

モニカさんは金髪です。
Monica is blond.

きんべん 勤勉 *diligence*

勤勉な diligent, hardworking

弘君は勤勉な生徒です。
Hiroshi is a diligent pupil.

ぎんみ 吟味 *scrutiny*

吟味する to scrutinize

きんむ 勤務 *work, (job) duty (for an organization)*

勤務する to work [→ 働く]
勤務中の on-duty
勤務時間 office hours, working hours
勤務条件 working conditions
勤務先 one's place of employment, one's office

きんよう 金曜 [☞ 金曜日]

きんようび 金曜日 *Friday*

きんろう 勤労 *labor, work, service* [→ 労働]

勤労感謝の日 Labor Thanksgiving Day (a Japanese national holiday on November 23rd)

く 九 *nine (see Appendix 2) [→ 九]*

九月 September

アメリカでは新学年は９月に始まります。
In the United States the new school year begins in September.

く 区 *ward (part of a city)*

私たちの学校は同じ区にあります。
Our school is in the same ward.

ぐあい 具合 *1. condition, state [→ 調子 1.]*

体の具合 state of health, how one feels

2. way (of doing) [→ 調子 2.]

こんな具合にやってください。
Please do it this way.

くい 杭 *stake, post*

くいき 区域 *(delimited) area, zone*

この区域はキャンプに利用されています。

This area is being used for camping.
配達区域 delivery zone, delivery area
危険区域 danger zone, dangerous area

クイズ *quiz*
クイズ番組 quiz program, quiz show

くう 食う *1.* 【CRUDE for 食べる】 *to eat*
2. 【COL.】 *to consume excessively, to use lots of*
この車はガソリンを食うよ。
This car uses lots of gasoline!
3. 【COL.】 *to bite (when the subject is an insect) (Ordinarily used in the passive.) [→ 刺す2.]*
僕も蚊に食われたよ。
I was bitten by a mosquito too!
4. 【COL.】 *to fall for (a trick, etc.)*
その手は食わないよ。
I won't fall for that trick!

くうかん 空間 *space, room*
時間と空間 time and space
宇宙空間 outer space

くうき 空気 *1. air*
自転車のタイヤに空気を入れましょう。
Let's put some air in the bicycle tires.
2. atmosphere, ambience [→ 雰囲気]
息子は新しいクラスの空気になじめない。
My son can't get used to the atmosphere in his new class.
空気銃 air gun

くうぐん 空軍 *air force*

くうこう 空港 *airport*
羽田空港 Haneda Airport
新東京国際空港 the New Tokyo International Airport (located in Narita)

ぐうすう 偶数 *even number [↔ 奇数]*

ぐうぜん 偶然 *1. chance, accident, coincidence*
偶然の accidental, coincidental
2. (〜に) by chance, by accident
きのう偶然友達に会った。
Yesterday I ran into a friend by chance.

くうそう 空想 *fantasy, reverie, daydream*
空想する to fantasize about, to imagine, to daydream about

くうちゅう 空中 *the sky, the air (as a location)*
風船がたくさん空中に浮かんでいます。
Many balloons are floating in the air.
空中ブランコ trapeze

クーデター *coup d'etat*

くうふく 空腹 *hunger, empty stomach*
空腹の hungry
その少年は空腹でした。
That boy was hungry.
空腹にまずいものなし。 (proverb)
Hunger is the best sauce. (Literally: To an empty stomach there is no bad-tasting thing.)

クーラー *1. air conditioner [→ エアコン]*
2. (picnic) cooler

クオーツ *quartz*

くき 茎 *stem, stalk*

くぎ 釘 *nail*
くぎを打つ〔抜く〕to drive〔pull out〕a nail
Aにくぎを刺す to give A a reminder, to give A a warning
釘抜き pincers for pulling out nails

くぎる 区切る *{5} 1. to divide, to partition*
駐車場を白線で五つに区切りましょう。
Let's divide the parking lot into five parts with white lines.
2. to punctuate (a sentence, etc.)

くぐる 潜る *1. to pass through; to pass under*
列車はトンネルをくぐりました。
The train passed through a tunnel.

ボートは橋をくぐりました。
The boat passed under a bridge.

2. to dive (starting in the water) [→ 潜る 1.]

くさ 草 *1. grass*

草の上に寝転ぼう。
Let's lie down on the grass.

草を刈る to cut grass, to mow grass

2. weed [→ 雑草]

草を取る to remove weeds

草花 flower, flowering plant

草刈り機 mower

草取り weeding; person who does weeding

草野球 sandlot baseball

くさい 臭い *bad-smelling, smelly*

この部屋は臭いですね。
This room smells foul, doesn't it?

くさり 鎖 *chain (of metal links)*

くさる 腐る *1. to go bad, to spoil, to rot*

その腐った肉を捨てなさい。
Throw out that rotten meat.

夏は食べ物がすぐ腐ります。
In summer food spoils easily.

2. to become dejected

くし 串 *skewer, (roasting) spit*

くし 櫛 *comb*

髪にくしを入れる to comb one's hair

くじ *1. lot, lottery ticket*

くじを引く to draw a lot

2. lottery [→ 抽選]

くじ引き drawing lots

当たりくじ winning lot, winning ticket

空くじ losing lot, losing ticket

宝くじ public lottery

くじく 挫く *1. to sprain, to strain*

相手は足をくじきました。
My opponent sprained his ankle.

2. to frustrate (a plan, etc.); to disappoint, to dampen (a person's hope, enthusiasm, etc.)

くじける 挫ける *1. to get sprained, to get strained*

2. to be disappointed, to be dampened (The subject is a person's hope, enthusiasm, etc.)

そんなことで勇気がくじけるはずはない。
There's no reason to expect his courage to be dampened by such a thing.

くじゃく 孔雀 *peacock, peahen*

くしゃみ *sneeze*

くしゃみをする to sneeze

くじょう 苦情 *complaint [→ 文句2.]*

苦情を言う to complain, to make a complaint

私たちは隣の人に騒音の苦情を言った。
We complained to our next-door neighbor about the noise.

くじら 鯨 *whale*

くしん 苦心 *effort, pains, hard work [→ 努力]*

医者の苦心はむだでした。
The doctor's efforts were futile.

苦心する to make efforts, to take pains, to work hard

この問題を解くのに苦心しました。
I worked hard to solve this problem.

くず 屑 *1. trash, rubbish [→ ごみ1.]*

2. scrap, crumb

屑籠 wastebasket

紙屑 wastepaper

パン屑 bread crumbs

ぐずぐず *1. ～する to dawdle, to delay, to waste time*

ぐずぐずしてはいけません。
You mustn't delay.

2. ～言う to complain, to grumble

ぐずぐず言わずに、さっさと食器を洗え。
Stop grumbling and wash the dishes quickly.

くすぐったい *affected by a tickling sensation*
足がくすぐったいよ。
My foot tickles!

くすぐる *to tickle (transitive)*

くずす 崩す *1. to demolish, to tear down [→ 壊す2.]*
今年はその建物を崩します。
This year we're going to tear down that building.
2. to break, to change (money from large denominations to small)
このお札を小銭に崩してください。
Please change this bill into small change.

くすり 薬 *medicine, drug*
毎朝この薬を飲んでいます。
I take this medicine every morning.
これはかぜによく効く薬です。
This is a medicine that works well for colds.
薬屋 pharmacy ((store)); druggist

くすりゆび 薬指 *third finger, ring finger*

くずれる 崩れる *to collapse, to disintegrate*
地震で橋が崩れました。
The bridge collapsed because of the earthquake.

くせ 癖 *1. habit*
あの大学生は髪をいじる癖があります。
That college student has a habit of fiddling with her hair.
悪い癖が付く a bad habit develops
悪い癖を直す to break a bad habit
2. peculiarity, idiosyncrasy
それが母の癖です。
That's my mother's peculiarity.

くせに *even though (implying that the speaker regards what follows with disapproval as strange or inappropriate) (This expression follows a predicate, but the word preceding cannot be the copula form だ. When is added to a clause that would end with だ, の (after a noun) or な (after an adjectival noun) appears instead.)*
息子は子供のくせにオペラが好きです。
Even though my son is a child, he likes opera.
知っているくせに教えてくれないよ。
Even though he knows, he won't tell me!

くそ 糞【CRUDE for 大便】*shit*

くだ 管 *tube, pipe*

ぐたいてき 具体的 〜な *concrete (i.e., not abstract) [↔ 抽象的な]*

くだく 砕く *to break, to crush, to smash, to shatter (transitive)*
これでその氷を砕いてください。
Please crush that ice with this.

くだける 砕ける *to break, to smash, to shatter (intransitive)*
波が岩に当たって砕けました。
The waves struck the rocks and broke.
コップが粉々に砕けたよ。
The glass smashed to pieces!

くださる 下さる *{Irreg.}*【HON. for 呉れる】*(In either use of this word the recipient must be the speaker, the speaker's group, or a person or group with whom the speaker is identifying.)*
1. to give
この本は先生がくださいました。
The teacher gave me this book.
何か温かい飲み物をください。
Please give me some kind of warm drink. (Although ください is the imperative form of くださる, ください the use of still conveys an honorific tone that is conventionally reflected in English translations by the use of please.)
2. to do the favor of (following the gerund

(-て form) of another verb)

社長は読んでくださるそうです。
I understand that the company president will read it for me.

ちょっとどいてください。
Please get out of the way. (Literally: Do me the favor of getting out of the way.)

くたびれる *1. to get tired [→ 疲れる]*

運動すると、すぐくたびれる。
When I exercise, I get tired right away.

2. to wear out (when the subject is a thing)

この靴はもうくたびれてしまったね。
These shoes have already worn out, haven't they?

くだもの 果物 *fruit*

新鮮な果物はまったくないです。
There is absolutely no fresh fruit.

トマトは野菜ですか、果物ですか。
Is a tomato a vegetable or a fruit?

果物ナイフ fruit knife

果物屋 fruit store; fruit seller

くだらない *1. worthless, useless, trivial*

こんなくだらない物を贈るのは失礼だ。
It's rude to give such a worthless thing.

2. silly, stupid, foolish

くだらないことを言わないでください。
Please don't say stupid things.

くだり 下り *1. going down, descent [↔ 上り 1.]*

高速道路はここから下りになります。
The expressway is downhill from here on. (Literally: The expressway becomes a descent from here.)

2. going down (a river, etc.) [↔ 上り 2.]

3. going from a capital to a provincial area [↔ 上り 3.]

下り電車 outbound train

下り坂 downward slope

くだる 下る *1. to come down, to go down, to descend [→ 下りる, 降りる 1.]*

2. to go down (a river, etc.) [↔ 上る 2.]

探険家は小船で川を下りました。
The explorer went down the river in a small boat.

3. to go (from a capital to a provincial area) [↔ 上る 3.]

くち 口 *1. mouth*

口を大きく開ける to open one's mouth wide

口に合う to suit one's taste, to have a flavor that one likes

牛肉は娘の口に合わないです。
Beef does not suit my daughter's taste.

口が重い not talkative, uncommunicative

口が軽い talkative; unable to keep secrets

口をきく to talk, to converse

あの選手は大きな口をきくタイプです。
That player is the type that talks big.

口にする to mention, to say; to eat; to drink

友達は大統領の名前をよく口にします。
My friend often mentions the President's name.

2. job, job opening [→ 就職口 (s.v. 就職)]

口下手な poor at talking, clumsy in the use of words

口髭 moustache

口上手な glib, facile-tongued

口数 how much one talks

ぐち 愚痴 *complaining, grumbling*

ぐちを言う to complain, to grumble

くちばし 嘴 *bill, beak (of a bird)*

くちびる 唇 *lip*

(Unlike the English word lip, Japanese is not used to refer to the areas just above and below the actual lips themselves.)

下唇 lower lip

上唇 upper lip

くちぶえ 口笛 *whistling (with one's*

mouth)
口笛を吹く to whistle

くちべに 口紅 *lipstick*

くちょう 口調 *tone (of voice); tone, style (of spoken or written expression)*
警官は怒った口調で話しました。
The police officer spoke in an angry tone.

くつ 靴 *shoe*
この靴をもう１足買ってください。
Please buy one more pair of these shoes.
出かける前に靴を磨きなさい。
Polish your shoes before you go out.
この靴は私には窮屈です。
These shoes are tight for me.
靴を履く〔脱ぐ〕 to put on〔take off〕one's shoes
靴べら shoehorn
靴紐 shoestring, shoelace
靴磨き shoe polishing; shoe polish
靴屋 shoe store; shoe dealer; shoemaker
靴墨 shoe polish

くつう 苦痛 *[[→ 苦しみ]] 1. pain [→ 痛み]*
2. suffering, anguish

クッキー *(US) cookie, (UK) biscuit*

くつした 靴下 *sock; stocking*
寒いから、靴下を履きなさい。
It's cold, so put on your socks.
靴下が裏返しだよ。
Your socks are inside out!

クッション *1. cushion (to sit on)*
2. cushioning, support

ぐっすり ～眠る *to sleep soundly*

くっつく 【COL.】*to stick, to become affixed (intransitive)*
キャラメルが歯にくっついてしまったよ。
The caramel stuck to my teeth!

くつろぐ 寛ぐ *to make oneself at home, to relax*
どうぞ寛いでください。
Please make yourself at home.
父はテレビを見て寛いでいます。
My father is watching television and relaxing.

くとうてん 句読点 *punctuation mark*

くに 国 *1. country, nation*
世界には多くの国があります。
There are many countries in the world.
2. home country, home province, hometown [→ 故郷]
「お国はどちらですか」「カナダです」
"Where is your home country?" "Canada."
高橋さんの国は富山です。
Mr. Takahashi's hometown is Toyama.
国々 countries

くばる 配る *to distribute, to pass out, to deliver*
郵便配達は１日に２回手紙を配ります。
The mail carrier delivers letters twice a day.
先生は試験問題を配りました。
The teacher passed out the test questions.
心を配る to keep watch, to be on guard
トランプを配る to deal cards

くび 首 *1. neck*
あの選手は首が太いですね。
That player's neck is thick, isn't it?
首を長くして expectantly, eagerly
娘は夏休みを首を長くして待っています。
My daughter is waiting eagerly for summer vacation.
2. head (including the neck)
少女は首を横に振りました。
The girl shook her head (no).
首をかしげる to incline one's head to the side (as an expression of doubt)
3. (US) firing, (UK) sacking (of an employee)

君は首だ！
You're fired!
首になる (US) to be fired, (UK) to be sacked
首にする (US) to fire, (UK) to sack

くびかざり 首飾り *necklace [→ネックレス]*

くびわ 首輪 *(animal) collar*

くふう 工夫 *stratagem, device, contrivance, scheme*
何かいい工夫はないですか。
Don't you have any good ideas?
工夫する *to devise, to contrive*

くべつ 区別 *distinction, difference*
惑星と恒星の区別ができますか。
Can you tell the difference between a planet and a fixed star?
AとBを区別する to distinguish A from B

くぼみ 窪み *hollow, depression*

くま 熊 *bear*
白熊 polar bear

くみ 組 *1. class (i.e., one of several groups of pupils in the same year in school) [→ クラス1.]*
美知子ちゃんと次郎ちゃんは同じ組です。
Michiko and Jiro are in the same class.
2. group, party, team, squad
子供たちを三つの組にわけました。
We divided the children into three groups.
一組 (counter for sets, pairs; see Appendix 2)
トランプを一組ください。
Please give me a deck of cards.

くみあい 組合 *union ((organization))*
労働組合 labor union
生活協同組合 cooperative society

くみあわせ 組み合わせ *combination*
色の組み合わせがおかしいです。
The combination of colors is odd.
テニストーナメントの組み合わせが決まった。
The tennis tournament pairings were decided.

くみあわせる 組み合わせる *to combine, to match (transitive)*
三つのグループを組み合わせて、一つにしてください。
Please combine the three groups and make them into one.
バッグと靴の色を上手に組み合わせた。
I matched the color of the bag and shoes well.

くみたてる 組み立てる *to put together, to assemble*
ここで部品を組み立てます。
They put the parts together here.
この工場ではテレビを組み立てます。
In this factory they assemble television sets.

くむ 汲む *to draw (water, etc.)*
少年はバケツで川の水をくみました。
The boy drew water from the river with a bucket.

くむ 組む *1. to put together*
2. to put together (long objects by crossing them over each other), to interlink
腕を組む to fold one's arms; to join arms (with another person)
太郎と由美は腕を組んで歩いていました。
Taro and Yumi were walking arm in arm.
脚を組む to cross one's legs
3. to become partners, to pair up
私はテニスでいつも恵子ちゃんと組むよ。
I always pair up with Keiko in tennis!

くも 雲 *cloud*
空には雲が１つもない。
There isn't a cloud in the sky.
突然雲が出てきました。
All of a sudden clouds began to appear.
厚い〔薄い〕雲 thick〔thin〕clouds

雨雲 rain cloud
茸雲 mushroom cloud
入道雲 thunderhead

くもり 曇り *cloudiness*
曇りの cloudy
曇り、後晴れ。 (a weather forecast)
Cloudy, later fair.
あしたは曇りでしょう。
Tomorrow it will probably be cloudy.
曇りガラス frosted glass
曇り空 cloudy sky

くもる 曇る *1. to become cloudy, to cloud up*
2. to cloud (with anxiety, etc.)
その知らせを聞いて、母の顔が曇りました。
When she heard that news, my mother's face clouded.
3. to fog up
湯気で眼鏡が曇ったよ。
My glasses fogged up with steam!

くやしい 悔しい *vexing, disappointing*
悔しいことに to one's chagrin

くやむ 悔やむ *to be sorry about, to regret*
野球選手はエラーを悔やむね。
Baseball players regret their errors, don't they?

くよくよ ～する *to worry; to brood*
そんなことでくよくよしないで。
Don't worry about such a thing.

くらい 暗い *[[↔ 明るい]] 1. dark (i.e., characterized by an absence of light)*
外は暗くなったよ。
It got dark outside!
コーチはまだ暗いうちに起きます。
The coach gets up while it's still dark.
2. gloomy
将来のことを考えると、暗い気持ちになる。
Thinking about the future makes me gloomy.

くらい 位 *[☞ 位]*

－くらい －位 *[☞－位]*

ぐらい 位 *1. extent, degree (following a predicate in the nonpast tense) [→ 程2.]*
日曜日も休めないぐらい忙しいです。
I'm so busy that I can't even take Sunday off. (Literally: I'm busy to the extent that I cannot take off even Sunday.)
我慢できないぐらいの痛みです。
It's unbearable pain. (Literally: It's pain of a degree that one cannot stand.)
2. approximate amount, approximate extent, approximate degree
駅までどのぐらいありますか。
About how far is it to the station?
友達の身長は僕と同じぐらいです。
My friend is about the same height as I am.

－ぐらい －位 *1. about, (US) around, or so (Added to number bases.)*
月に2度ぐらい両親に手紙を出します。
I send a letter to my parents about twice a month.
2. (Added to noun bases.) about the same extent as; at least the same extent as; at least
手帳ぐらいの大きさがちょうどいい。
A size about the same as a pocket-book is just right.
友子ちゃんに鉛筆ぐらいあげなさい。
Give Tomoko a pencil at least.

グライダー *glider*
ハンググライダー hang glider

クライマックス *climax*
物語はクライマックスに達しました。
The story reached its climax.

グラウンド *playground [→ 運動場 (s.v. 運動)]; playing field [→ 競技場 (s.v. 競技)]*

クラクション *(automobile) horn*

くらげ *jellyfish*

くらし 暮らし *life, livelihood, way of living*

暮らしをする to lead a life
村の人たちは幸福な暮らしをしています。
The people of this village lead happy lives.
暮らしを立てる to make a living, to earn a livelihood

クラシック *1. classical music*
2. a classic [→ 古典]
クラシックな classical

くらす 暮らす *to live, to lead a life, to make a living [→ 生活する]*
祖父は福井で一人で暮らしています。
My grandfather lives alone in Fukui.

クラス *1. class (i.e., one of several groups of pupils in the same year in school) [→ 組 1.]*
太郎はクラスでいちばん足が速いね。
Taro is the fastest in the class, isn't he?
2. class, grade, rank [→ 級 1.]
クラス会 class meeting; class reunion
クラスメート classmate

グラス *(drinking) glass*

グラタン *gratin*
チキングラタン chicken au gratin

クラッカー *cracker*

グラビア *(photo-) gravure*

クラブ *club ((organization))*
クラブに入っていますか。
Are you in a club?
クラブ活動 club activities

クラブ *(golf) club*

クラブ *clubs ((playing-card suit))*

グラフ *graph [→ 図表]*
生徒はこのグラフを書きました。
A student drew this graph.
グラフ用紙 graph paper
棒グラフ bar graph
円グラフ circle graph, pie chart
折れ線グラフ line graph

グラフィックデザイナー *graphic designer*

くらべる 比べる *to compare*
この絵を先生のと比べましょう。
Let's compare this picture with the teacher's.

グラム *gram*
ーグラム (counter for grams; see Appendix 2)

くらやみ 暗闇 *darkness, the dark*
ライオンは暗闇の中を歩きました。
The lion walked through the darkness.

クラリネット *clarinet*

グランプリ *grand prix, grand prize*

くり 栗 *chestnut*

クリーニング *cleaning (of clothing by a professional cleaner)*
クリーニングに出す to take to the cleaner's for cleaning
昨日コートをクリーニングに出した。
Yesterday I took my coat to the cleaner's.
クリーニング屋 cleaner, launderer; cleaner's (shop)
ドライクリーニング dry cleaning

クリーム *1. cream ((dairy product))*
2. cream (food made with milk, eggs, and sugar)
3. cream ((cosmetic))
クリーム色 cream color
コールドクリーム cold cream
生クリーム fresh cream

グリーンピース *green peas*

くりかえす 繰り返す *to do again, to repeat*
間違いを繰り返さないようにしなさい。
Please be careful not to repeat the same mistake.
繰り返して repeatedly, again, over
(This form is the gerund (-て form) of 繰り

返す, and it has the predictable range of meanings as well.)

先生はその単語を何度も繰り返して発音しました。

The teacher pronounced the word over and over many times.

クリスマス *Christmas*

クリスマスおめでとう！

Merry Christmas!

クリスマスイブ Christmas Eve

クリスマスカード Christmas card

クリスマスプレゼント Christmas present

クリスマスツリー Christmas tree

クリップ *1. paper clip*

2. hair curler, curling pin

クリニック *clinic [→ 診療所]*

くる 来る *{Irreg.} 1. to come [↔ 行く]*

バスが来ましたよ。

The bus is coming!

パーティーに来ますか。

Will you come to the party?

手紙がたくさん来ているよ。

Many letters have come.

山田さんはここに２度来たことがあるね。

Mr. Yamada has been here twice, hasn't she?

今度の日曜日遊びに来てください。

Please come and visit this coming Sunday.

「アルバイト」という言葉はドイツ語から来ました。

The word "arubaito" came from German.

2. to begin to, to come to (following the gerund (-て form) of another verb)

日増しに暖かくなってきました。

It has begun getting warmer day by day.

雪が降ってきたよ。

It's started snowing!

くるう 狂う *1. to go crazy, to become insane*

2. to go wrong; to go out of order

計画がすっかり狂ったよ。

The plan went completely wrong!

あの時計は狂っているよ。

That clock is out of order!

グループ *group (of people)*

グループで in a group, in groups

グループ活動 group activities

くるしい 苦しい *1. painful, afflicting, tormenting*

息が苦しい breathing is labored

2. hard, difficult, trying [→ 困難な]

これは苦しい仕事ですよ。

This is a hard job!

苦しい立場 difficult position

3. farfetched, forced

苦しい言い訳 lame excuse

くるしみ 苦しみ *[[→ 苦痛]] 1. pain*

患者はまったく苦しみを感じなかった。

The patient did not feel any pain.

2. suffering, anguish

伯父は苦しみに耐えました。

My uncle bore his suffering.

くるしむ 苦しむ *1. to suffer*

ゆうべはひどい頭痛で苦しみました。

I suffered from a terrible headache last night.

2. to become troubled, to come to have difficulty

くるぶし 踝 *the place on either side of the ankle where the bone protrudes*

くるま 車 *1. [[→ 自動車]] car, (US) automobile, (UK) motorcar; taxi [→ タクシー]; (US) truck, (UK) lorry [→ トラック]*

車は運転できません。

I can't drive a car.

父は車で通勤します。

My father commutes to work by car.

家から駅まで車で10分です。

It's ten minutes by car from my house to the station.

新しい車に乗って、海に行きました。
We got in the new car and went to the ocean.

2. wheel [→ 車輪]

車椅子 wheelchair

くるみ *walnut*

くるみ割り nutcracker

グレー *gray (as a noun) [→ 灰色]*

友達はグレーのジャケットを着ています。
My friend is wearing a gray jacket.

クレーター *crater (on the moon or other planets)*

クレープ *1. crepe (fabric)*

2. (dessert) crepe

グレープジュース *grape juice*

グレープフルーツ *grapefruit*

クレーン *(construction) crane*

クレーン車 crane truck

クレジット *credit (as a purchasing method)*

このバッグはクレジットで買いました。
I bought this bag on credit.

クレジットカード credit card

クレヨン *crayon*

くれる 呉れる *{Irreg.} (In either use of this word the recipient must be the speaker, the speaker's group, or a person or group with whom the speaker is identifying.)*

1. to give

伯父がこの時計をくれたよ。
My uncle gave me this watch!

2. to do the favor of (following the gerund (-て form) of another verb)

学生は親切に荷物を運んでくれました。
The student kindly carried my baggage for me.

窓を開けてくれませんか。
Won't you open the window for me?

くれる 暮れる *1.* 日が〜 *it gets dark (outside), the sun goes down*

もうすぐ日が暮れるよ。
It's going to get dark soon!

2. to end (The subject is a year or season.)

今年も暮れました。
This year, too, has ended.

くろ 黒 black (as a noun) *[↔ 白]*

くろい 黒い *1. black (as an adjective) [↔ 白い]*

平野さんは黒い猫を飼っています。
Mr. Hirano keeps a black cat.

2. dark (describing a person's eyes or skin)

くろう 苦労 *trouble, difficulty, hardship [→ 困難]*

会社設立当初は社長も苦労が多かった。
The company president had many difficulties at the beginning when he set up the firm.

苦労する to have difficulty, to suffer hardship

姉の家を探すのにだいぶ苦労しました。
I had great difficulty in looking for my older sister's house.

ご苦労さま *[☞ ご苦労さま]*

くろうと 玄人 *a professional, an expert [↔ 素人]*

クローバー *clover*

グローブ *(sports) glove*

ボクシング用グローブ boxing gloves

くろじ 黒字 *non-deficit, being in the black [↔ 赤字]*

くろしお 黒潮 *the Black Current, the Japan Current [→ 日本海流 (s.v. 日本)]*

クロスワードパズル *crossword puzzle*

ついにクロスワードパズルが解けました。
At last I was able to solve the crossword puzzle.

クロッカス *crocus ((flower))*

グロテスク ～な *grotesque*

くわ 桑 *mulberry*

くわ 鍬 *hoe*

くわえる 加える *1. to add*

香辛料を少し加えてください。
Add a little spice, please.

4に6を加えなさい。
Add six to four.

2. to let participate, to let join

私も加えてください。
Please let me join in too.

3. to inflict

敵軍に打撃を加えました。
We inflicted a blow on the enemy force.

くわえる 銜える *to take between one's teeth, to take in one's mouth*

猫が魚をくわえて逃げたよ。
The cat ran away with a fish in its mouth!

くわしい 詳しい *1. detailed*

この地図は詳しいね。
This map is detailed, isn't it?

ガイドは歴史を詳しく説明してくれた。
The guide explained the history in detail for us.

2. knowledgeable (about)

お母さんはフランスに詳しいです。
Your mother knows a lot about France.

くわだて 企て *1. attempt, undertaking*

2. plan, scheme, project [→ 計画]

くわだてる 企てる *1. to attempt, to undertake*

2. to plan; to contemplate

くわわる 加わる *1. to be added*

2. to participate, to join

仲間に加わりませんか。
Won't you join our group?

ゲームに加わってもいいですか。
May I join in the game?

ぐん 軍 *1. troops, forces*

2. the military

ぐん 郡 *rural district, rural county (an administrative subdivision of a prefecture in Japan)*

ぐんかん 軍艦 *warship*

ぐんじ 軍事 *military affairs*

ぐんしゅう 群衆 *crowd, multitude (of people or animals)*

公園には大勢の群衆がいました。
There was a large crowd in the park.

くんしょう 勲章 *decoration (conferred as an honor)*

ぐんじん 軍人 *person in the military*

ぐんたい 軍隊 *armed forces, the military*

ぐんとう 群島 *group of islands*

ぐんび 軍備 *armaments, military preparations*

軍備縮小 reduction of armaments

くんよみ 訓読み *Japanese reading (of a kanji)*

くんれん 訓練 training, drill

あの人たちはまだ訓練を受けています。
Those people are still undergoing training.

訓練する to train, to drill (transitive or intransitive)

避難訓練 fire drill, emergency evacuation drill

け 毛 *hair; fur [→ 毛皮]; wool [→ 羊毛]*

この犬は毛が薄くなってきました。
This dog's hair has become thin.

堅い〔柔らかい〕毛 stiff〔soft〕hair

毛深い hairy, shaggy

縮れ毛 curly hair

げい 芸 *1. accomplishment, acquired art or skill*

2. trick, stunt

けいえい 経営 *running, management (of an organization, typically a business)*

経営する to manage, to run

父はレストランを経営しています。
My father is running a restaurant.

経営者 proprietor, manager

けいか 経過 *1. progress, course (of events)*

患者の手術後の経過は良好です。
The patient's post-operation progress is good.

2. passage (of time)

経過する to pass, to elapse *[→ 経つ]*

試合開始後、10分が経過しました。
Ten minutes have passed since the game started.

けいかい 警戒 *1. caution, precaution [→ 用心]*

警戒する to exercise caution against

2. lookout, guarding [→ 見張り]

警戒する to look out for, to watch out for *[→ 見張る]*

警戒信号 warning signal

けいかい 軽快 〜な *1. light, nimble*

その少女は軽快な足どりで踊っています。
That girl is dancing with light steps.

2. light-hearted, cheerful

歌手は軽快なリズムで歌いました。
The singer sang in cheerful rhythm.

けいかく 計画 *plan (of action)*

計画する to plan

計画を実行する to carry out a plan

計画を立てる to make a plan, to make plans

夏休みの計画を立てています。
I am making plans for the summer vacation.

ピクニックに行く計画を立てました。
We planned to go on a picnic.

都市計画 city planning

けいかん 警官 *police officer*

婦人警官 policewoman

けいき 景気 *1. business (conditions); the times, the economy*

景気はどうですか。
How's business?

3年前からずっと景気がいいです。
Business has been good for the past three years.

2. liveliness, vitality [→ 活気]

けいぐ 敬具【FORMAL】*Sincerely yours (Used as a closing phrase in formal letters.) [↔ 拝啓]*

けいけん 経験 *experience*

その人はまったく経験がない。
That person has absolutely no experience.

楽しい〔苦しい〕経験 pleasant〔bitter〕experience

経験する to experience

こんな暑さは経験したことがないです。
I have never experienced such heat.

けいこ 稽古 *practice, training, rehearsal*

毎週日曜日お花のけいこをします。
I take flower arranging lessons every Sunday.

稽古する to practice, to take lessons in

けいご 敬語 *respectful word*

(Japanese respectful vocabulary is usually classified into three types: honorific, humble, and polite.)

けいこう 傾向 *tendency; trend*

ファッションは50年代に戻る傾向にある。
The trend in fashion is a return to the 50's.

けいこうとう 蛍光灯 *fluorescent light*

けいこく 警告 *warning*

警告を受ける to receive a warning
警告する to warn, to give a warning
警官は私たちにその橋を渡らないように警告しました。
The police officer warned us not to cross that bridge.

けいざい 経済 *1. economy (of a country, etc.)*
日本の経済 Japan's economy
経済援助 economic aid
経済学 (the study of) economics
経済学者 economist
2. economy, thrift, frugality
経済的な economical, thrifty, frugal
このストーブはあちらのより経済的です。
This heater is more economical than that one over there.

けいさつ 警察 *police, police force*
警察官 police officer [→ 警官]
警察犬 police dog
警察署 police station

けいさん 計算 *calculation, computation*
妹は計算が速いです。
My younger sister is quick at calculation.
計算する to calculate, to compute
計算器 calculator
計算間違い mistake in calculation
電子計算機 (electronic) computer *[→ コンピューター]*

けいじ 刑事 *(police) detective*

けいじ 掲示 *notice, bulletin*
掲示板 bulletin board, notice board

けいしき 形式 *1. (outward) form [↔ 内容 1.]*
2. a formality
形式的な formal, perfunctory

げいじゅつ 芸術 *an art; art, the arts*
芸術は長く、人生は短い。 *(proverb)*
Art is long; life is short.
芸術家 artist
芸術作品 work of art
芸術的な artistic

けいそつ 軽率 ～な *rash, reckless, careless*

けいたい 携帯 *carrying (along with one)*
携帯する to carry
携帯用の portable
携帯電話 portable telephone
携帯電話を持っていってください。
Please take a portable telephone.

けいてき 警笛 *warning horn, warning whistle*
警笛を鳴らす to sound a warning horn/whistle

けいと 毛糸 *woolen yarn*
毛糸の手袋 woolen gloves; woolen mittens

けいど 経度 *longitude [↔ 緯度]*

げいのうかい 芸能界 *the world of show business*

げいのうじん 芸能人 *entertainer, show business personality*

けいば 競馬 *horse racing*
競馬場 racetrack, (UK) racecourse

けいひ 経費 *expense(s), cost [→ 費用]*
それは経費がかかりすぎます。
That involves too much cost.

けいび 警備 *guarding*
警備する to guard
警備員 guard; watchman

けいひん 景品 *1. free gift, giveaway, premium (accompanying something one buys) [→ お負け]*
2. prize item [→ 賞品]

けいべつ 軽蔑 *contempt, scorn, disdain (for a person)*

軽べつする to look down on, to scorn, to disdain

みんなは幸夫さんを軽べつしています。
Everybody looks down on Yukio.

あんな人は軽べつするわ。
I disdain such a person!

けいほう 警報 *warning, alarm*

警報装置 alarm system
暴風雨警報 storm warning
火災警報 fire alarm

けいむしょ 刑務所 *prison*

けいやく 契約 *contract*

契約する to contract, to enter into a contract
契約期間 contract period
契約書 written contract

—けいゆ —経由 *by way of, via (Added to bases denoting a place where an intermediate stop is made.)*

83便はホノルル経由です。
Flight 83 is via Honolulu.

大阪経由で福岡に行きます。
I'll go to Fukuoka by way of Osaka.

けいようし 形容詞 *adjective*

けいれき 経歴 *educational and employment history, career background*

木村さんはどんな経歴の方ですか。
What is Ms. Kimura's career background? (Literally: Ms. Kimura is a person of what kind of career background?)

けいろうのひ 敬老の日 *Respect for the Aged Day (a Japanese national holiday on September 15)*

ケーキ *cake*

京子さんはケーキを焼いてくれました。
Kyoko baked a cake for me.

ケーキを一切れください。
Please give me one slice of cake.

バースデーケーキ birthday cake
デコレーションケーキ decorated cake
ショートケーキ shortcake

ケース *case ((container))*

ケース *case, instance*

ケースバイケースで case by case, on a case-by-case basis

ゲート *gate, gateway*

空港のゲート airport gate

ゲートボール *gateball (a version of croquet popular among senior citizens in Japan)*

ケーブル *cable*

ケーブルカー cable car

ゲーム *1. game, competitive pastime (This meaning does not include sports.)*

このゲームは子供向きですね。
This game is intended for children, isn't it?

2. game (i.e., a single contest in a game or sport) [→ 試合]

野球のゲーム baseball game
ゲームセンター amusement arcade
ゲームセット end of the game
テレビゲーム video game

けが 怪我 *injury, wound*

けがをする to get hurt, to get injured, to get wounded

ナイフで腕にけがをしました。
I got wounded in the arm with a knife.

その事故でけがをしました。
I got injured in that accident.

けがする to get injured; to injure (a part of one's body)

上田さんは足をけがしました。
Mr. Ueda injured his foot.

怪我人 injured person

げか 外科 *surgery (as a specialty) [↔ 内科]*

外科医 surgeon

けがわ 毛皮 *fur*

毛皮製品 product made of fur

げき 劇 *play, drama [→ 演劇, 芝居]*

劇団dramatic troupe, theatrical company

劇作家dramatist, playwright

劇的な dramatic

げきじょう 劇場 *theater, playhouse*

野外劇場 open-air theater

げきれい 激励 *encouragement*

激励する to encourage, to cheer up [→ 励ます]

けさ 今朝 *this morning*

けさのニュースを見ましたか。
Did you watch this morning's news?

けさ7時に起きました。
I got up at 7:00 this morning.

げし 夏至 *summer solstice [↔ 冬至]*

けしき 景色 *scenery, view*

山の景色が好きです。
I like mountain scenery.

美しい景色ですね。
It's beautiful scenery, isn't it?

丘から見る景色はすばらしいよ。
The view one sees from the hill is wonderful!

けしゴム 消しゴム *(rubber) eraser*

消しゴムでまちがいを消しました。
I erased the error with an eraser.

けじめ *distinction, difference (especially involving morality or social norms)*

けじめを付けるto draw a distinction

げしゃ 下車 *getting off/out of (a train, bus, car, etc.) [↔ 乗車]*

下車する to get (off/out of a train, bus, car, etc.)

げしゅく 下宿 *1. rooming, boarding, lodging (in someone's house)*

下宿する to room, to board, to lodge

2. rented room (in someone's house)

下宿人roomer, boarder

げじゅん 下旬 *last third of a month [↔ 中旬; 上旬]*

首脳会談は6月の下旬に開かれます。
The summit conference will be held in late June.

けしょう 化粧 *make-up*

化粧する to put on make-up

化粧品 cosmetic product

化粧石鹸 toilet soap

化粧室 powder room, bathroom [→ トイレ]

けす 消す *1. to put out (a fire) [↔ 点ける1.]*

水をかけて火を消しなさい。
Pour water on it and put out the fire.

2. to turn off (a device) [↔ 点ける2.]

寝る前にテレビを消してください。
Please turn off the TV before going to bed.

電気を消すのを忘れました。
I forgot to turn off the light.

3. to erase

黒板を消してください。
Please erase the blackboard.

げすい 下水 *1. waste water, sewage*

2. (waste-water) drains, drain system

下水が詰まっています。
The drains are blocked.

下水管 drainpipe, sewer pipe

ゲスト *(television program) guest*

けずる 削る *1. to shave, to scrape*

この板をかんなで削ってくれる？
Will you plane this board for me? (Literally: Will you shave this board for me with a plane?)

鉛筆を削る to sharpen a pencil

2. to cut down, to reduce, to curtail

経費を削る to cut down expenses

3. to delete, to cut out

けた 桁 *1. digit, figure (in a number written in Arabic numerals)*

一桁 (counter for digits; see Appendix 2)

3 けたの数 three-digit number

2. beam, girder; bead rod (on an abacus)

げた 下駄 *geta, Japanese wooden clogs*

下駄履き wearing clogs

下駄箱 footwear cupboard

けだもの 獣 *beast [→ 獣]*

けち *1. 〜な stingy*

2. 【COL.】〜を付ける *to find fault*

Aにけちをつける to find fault with A, to criticize A

けちん坊【COL.】miser, tightwad

けちけち【COL.】 〜する *to be stingy*

ケチャップ *ketchup*

けつ【CRUDE for 尻】 *(US) ass, (UK) arse*

けつい 決意 *determination, resolution [→ 決心]*

決意する *to resolve, to make up one's mind*

けつえき 血液 *blood [→ 血]*

(The ordinary word for blood is 血; 血液 has a scientific or medical nuance.)

血液型 blood type

私の血液型はO型です。
My blood type is type O.

血液銀行 blood bank

けっか 結果 *result, effect [↔ 原因]*

テストの結果はどうでしたか。
How were the test results?

原因と結果 cause and effect

けっかく 結核 *tuberculosis*

けっかん 欠陥 *defect, shortcoming, deficiency (i.e., the lack of something necessary)*

この機械には欠陥があります。
There is a defect in this machine.

欠陥商品 *defective merchandise*

けっかん 血管 *blood vessel*

げっかん 月刊 〜の *(published) monthly*

月刊雑誌 monthly magazine

げっきゅう 月給 *monthly salary*

けっきょく 結局 *after all, in the end*

結局、英子さんは来ませんでした。
In the end, Eiko didn't come.

げっけい 月経 *menstruation [→ 生理2., メンス]*

けっこう 結構 *1. 〜な good, fine, nice [→ 立派な]*

結構な贈り物をどうもありがとう。
Thank you for the nice present.

2. 〜だ all right, fine [→ いい2.]

「すみませんが、ペンはありません」「鉛筆で結構です」
"I'm sorry, but I don't have a pen." "A pencil will be fine."

「コーヒーをもう1杯いかがですか」「いいえ、もう結構です」
"How about another cup of coffee?" "No, thank you." (Literally: No, it's already fine.)

3. quite, rather, considerably [→ かなり]

けっこん 結婚 *marriage*

結婚する to marry, to get married

兄は洋子さんと結婚しました。
My older brother got married to Yoko.

木村さんは結婚しています。
Mr. Kimura is married.

結婚記念日 wedding anniversary

結婚式 wedding

教会で結婚式をあげる予定です。
We plan to hold the wedding ceremony at church.

見合い結婚 marriage resulting from an

arranged meeting
恋愛結婚love marriage

けっさく 傑作 *1. masterpiece*
2. big and humorous blunder

けっして 決して *(not) ever, certainly (not) (Always occurs in combination with a negative predicate.)*
春美さんは決して約束を破りません。
Harumi never breaks a promise.
豊ちゃんは決して学校に遅刻しません。
Yutaka is never late for school.
決して希望は捨てません。
I certainly won't give up hope.

げっしゃ 月謝 *monthly payment for lessons*

けっしょう 決勝 *1. deciding the champion*
2. finals, championship game, title match
決勝戦 [☞ 決勝*2.* (above)]
準決勝semifinals
準々決勝quarterfinals

けっしょう 結晶 *1. a crystal*
雪の結晶snow crystal
努力の結晶result of effort
2. crystallization
結晶する to crystallize

げっしょく 月食 *lunar eclipse*
部分月食 partial lunar eclipse
皆既月食total lunar eclipse

けっしん 決心 *determination, resolution [→ 決意]*
決心する to resolve, to make up one's mind
明さんはパイロットになろうと決心した。
Akira made up his mind to become a pilot.

けっせき 欠席 *absence, nonattendance [↔ 出席]*
欠席する to be absent, to fail to attend
なぜきのう欠席したの？
Why were you absent yesterday?
学校を欠席する to be absent from school
欠席者 absentee, person not in attendance
欠席届 report of absence
長期欠席 long absence

けつだん 決断 *decision, deciding*
あの人は決断が早いです。
That person is quick at deciding.
決断する to decide, to make up one's mind
決断力 decisiveness

けってい 決定 *decision, determination*
決定する to decide, to determine, to set [→ 決める]
決定的な decisive, conclusive

けってん 欠点 *fault, defect, weak point [→ 短所]*
だれにでも欠点があります。
Everyone has weak points.
自分の欠点を直したいです。
I want to correct my own faults.

げっぷ 【COL.】 *burp, belch*
げっぷが出る a burp comes out

げっぷ 月賦 *monthly installment payment*
月賦で買う to buy on monthly installments

けつまくえん 結膜炎 *conjunctivitis, pinkeye*

けつまつ 結末 *ending, conclusion, outcome*
これは悲しい結末の物語です。
This is a story with a sad ending.

げつよう 月曜 [☞ 月曜日]

げつようび 月曜日 *Monday*

けつろん 結論 *conclusion ((idea))*
やっと この結論に達しました。
At last we reached this conclusion.

結論として in conclusion

けど 【COL. for けれども】

けなす 貶す *to speak ill of, to criticize [↔ 褒める]*

秀子さんは時々私の話し方をけなすね。
Hideko sometimes criticizes my way of speaking, doesn't she?

げひん 下品 〜な *coarse, vulgar, unrefined [↔ 上品な]*

けむい 煙い *smoky*

けむし 毛虫 *hairy caterpillar*

けむり 煙 *smoke*

ほら、煙が出ているよ。
Look, smoke is coming out!

火のない所に煙は立たない。(proverb)
Where there's smoke, there's fire. (Literally: In a place where there is no fire, smoke does not rise.)

けもの 獣 *beast*

げり 下痢 *diarrhea*

下痢する to have diarrhea

ゲリラ *guerrilla*

ける 蹴る *{5} to kick*

ボールを思い切りけりなさい。
Kick the ball hard.

けれど *[☞ けれども]*

けれども *but [→ が]; however [→ しかし]*

冬は寒いけれども、私は好きです。
Winter is cold, but I like it.

雪が降っていたけれども、買い物に出た。
It was snowing, but we went out shopping.

けれども、安全は保証できません。
However, I cannot guarantee safety.

ゲレンデ *(ski) slope*

けわしい 険しい *1. steep, precipitous*

日本には険しい山がたくさんあります。
In Japan there are a lot of steep mountains.

2. grim, difficult (describing future conditions)

見通しは険しいですね。
The prospects are grim, aren't they?

3. stern, angry-seeming

険しい声 stern voice

けん 券 *ticket [→ 切符]*

入場券 admission ticket

招待券 invitation ticket

けん 県 *prefecture (Japan has 47 prefectures, and all except Tokyo, Osaka, Kyoto, and Hokkaido are called 県.)*

県知事 prefectural governor

県庁 prefectural office

青森県 Aomori Prefecture

けん 剣 *double-edged sword*

げん 弦 *string (on a musical instrument)*

弦楽器 stringed instrument

けん 件 *matter, incident*

—件 (counter for incidents; see Appendix 2)

—けん —軒 *(counter for houses and small buildings; see Appendix 2)*

けんい 権威 *1. power, authority [→ 権力]*

権威をふるう to exercise authority

2. expert, authority

大野博士は生物学の権威です。
Dr. Ono is an authority on biology.

げんいん 原因 *cause, source, origin [↔ 結果]*

その火事の原因はなんでしたか。
What was the cause of the fire ?

けんか 喧嘩 *quarrel; fight*

けんかする to quarrel; to fight

池上君は中尾君とけんかしたよ。
Ikegami fought with Nakao!

妹と弟はテレビのことでけんかしています。
My younger sister and younger brother

are quarreling about the TV.

げんかい 限界 *limit, limitation [→ 限度]*

けんがく 見学 *study by observation, field trip*

見学する to study by observing, to make a field trip to

私たちは郵便局を見学しました。

We made a field trip to the post office.

げんかん 玄関 *entry, vestibule (the part of a Japanese dwelling, just inside the front door, where shoes are removed)*

どうぞ玄関から入ってください。

Please come in from the entry.

げんき 元気 *1. vigor, liveliness; health*

元気な vigorous, lively; healthy, well *[→ 健康な]*

お元気ですか。

How are you?

祖母はだんだん元気になってきています。

My grandmother has gradually gotten better.

2. good spirits, cheerfulness

元気がいい to be in good spirits, to be cheerful

元気がない to be in low spirits, to be downhearted

元気を出す to cheer up, to become cheerful

元気な spirited, cheerful

弟はとても元気な子です。

My younger brother is a very spirited child.

元気なく spiritlessly, cheerlessly

元気よく spiritedly, cheerfully

けんきゅう 研究 *study; research*

八木先生は日本史の研究を続けている。

Prof. Yagi is continuing research on Japanese history.

研究する to study; to do research on

心理学を研究しています。

I am studying psychology.

研究発表 presentation of research results

研究費 research funds

研究所 laboratory, research institute

げんきん 現金 *cash*

このステレオは現金で買ったよ。

I bought this stereo with cash!

指輪の代金を現金で払いました。

I paid for the ring in cash.

現金書留 cash sent by registered mail

げんきん 厳禁 ～だ *to be strictly prohibited*

厳禁する to prohibit strictly

げんご 言語 *language*

言語学 linguistics

言語障害 speech impediment

けんこう 健康 *health [↔ 病気]*

散歩をするのは健康にいいです。

Taking a walk is good for your health.

健康は富にまさる。 (proverb)

Health is better than wealth. (Literally: Health surpasses wealth.)

健康を害する to injure one's health, to ruin one's health

健康を回復する to recover one's health

健康な healthy, well, fine

家族はみな健康です。

Everyone in my family is healthy.

健康保険 health insurance

健康状態 state of health

健康診断 physical examination, (US) health checkup

げんこう 原稿 *manuscript, (preliminary) draft*

原稿用紙 manuscript paper (divided into small squares, each of which is to be filled by one handwritten character)

げんこく 原告 *plaintiff [↔ 被告]*

けんこくきねんび 建国記念の日 *National*

Founding Day (a Japanese national holiday on February 11th)

げんこつ 拳骨 *fist*

あのやくざは警官をげんこつで殴ったよ。
That gangster hit the police officer with his fist!

けんさ 検査 *inspection, examination*

検査する to inspect, to examine
歯医者が私の歯を検査しました。
The dentist examined my teeth.
母は病院で検査を受けました。
My mother underwent an examination at the hospital.
検査官 (government) inspector
学力検査 scholastic achievement test [→ 学力テスト (s.v. 学力)]
身体検査 physical examination

げんざい 現在 *1. the present (time)*

現在の present, current
これが現在の住所です。
This is my present address.

2. at present, now

大統領は現在入院しています。
The President is in the hospital at present.

げんさく 原作 *the original (written work) (the work on which a movie, translation, etc., is based)*

原作者 author of the original

げんし 原子 *atom*

原子爆弾 atomic bomb

げんし 原始 〜の *primitive, primeval*

原始時代 the primitive ages
原始人 a primitive human

げんじつ 現実 *reality, actuality*

現実の real, actual
現実的な realistic, practical
その考えは現実的ではありません。
That idea is not realistic.

けんじゅう 拳銃 *pistol, handgun*

げんじゅう 厳重 〜な *strict [→ 厳しい 1.]*

厳重な規則 strict rule

けんしょう 懸賞 *1. contest with a prize*

2. contest prize; reward (for finding a criminal)

げんしょう 現象 *phenomenon*

自然現象 natural phenomenon

げんしょう 減少 *decrease [↔ 増加]*

減少する to decrease (intransitive) [→ 減る]
減少率 rate of decrease

げんじょう 現状 *present conditions, present situation*

現状では私はみんなに同意できません。
Under the present conditions I cannot agree with everyone.

けんじょう 謙譲 *humility, modesty [→ 謙遜]*

謙譲語 humble word (one type of respectful vocabulary in Japanese) [↔ 尊敬語 (s.v. 尊敬)]

げんしょく 原色 *primary color*

げんしりょく 原子力 *atomic energy, nuclear power*

原子力発電 nuclear power generation
原子力発電所 nuclear power plant

けんせつ 建設 *construction, erecting, building*

建設する to build, to construct, to erect
宇宙ステーションを建設しました。
They built a space station.
建設中の under-construction
新体育館はまだ建設中です。
The new gym is still under construction.
建設会社 construction company
建設省 the Ministry of Construction

けんぜん 健全 〜な *healthy, sound [→*

健康な]

げんそ 元素 *(chemical) element*

元素記号 symbol for an element

げんそく 原則 *principle, general rule*

原則としてはそれは正しいです。

As a general rule, that is correct.

げんそく 減速 *deceleration [↔ 加速]*

減速する to decelerate (transitive or intransitive)

けんそん 謙遜 *modesty, humility*

けんそんな modest, humble

けんそんな態度 humble attitude

けんそんする to be modest, to be humble

げんだい 現代 *the present age, modern times, today*

現代の若者は歩くことを好みません。

Today's young people don't like walking.

現代はコンピューターの時代です。

The present age is the computer age.

現代の日本 present-day Japan, modern Japan

現代英語 modern English

現代音楽 modern music

現代的な modern, up-to-date

平山さんの家は現代的です。

Mr. Hirayama's house is modern.

けんちく 建築 *1. a building [→ 建物]*

この家はこの町で最も古い建築です。

This house is the oldest building in this town.

2. construction, building [→ 建設]

建築する to build, to construct

私たちは新しい家を建築しています。

We are building a new house.

建築学 the study of architecture

建築家 architect

木造建築 wooden building

げんど 限度 *limit, bound*

それは私の体力の限度を越えています。

That exceeds the limit of my strength.

何事にも限度があります。

There are limits to everything.

限度に達する to reach a limit

けんとう 見当 *1. guess, conjecture, estimate*

私の見当は当たりました。

My guess proved right.

見当を付ける to make a guess, to make an estimate

見当が付く to have some idea, to be able to imagine

それが何だか見当がつかないよ。

I can't imagine what that is!

2. general direction

ーけんとう ー見当 *about, (US) around (Added to number bases.) [→ ーぐらい]*

あの人は50歳見当です。

That person is about 50 years old.

けんとう 検討 *examination, investigation, inquiry*

検討する to examine, to investigate, to inquire into

この問題を検討してみましょう。

Let's examine this problem and see.

けんどう 剣道 *kendo (traditional Japanese fencing)*

毎日剣道のけいこをします。

I do kendo practice every day.

けんびきょう 顕微鏡 *microscope*

けんぶつ 見物 *seeing, watching, visiting (a famous place, an event, etc.)*

見物する to see, to watch, to visit

華厳の滝を見物に行きます。

I'm going to go to see the Kegon Falls.

あしたは美術館を見物する予定です。

Tomorrow I'm planning to visit the art museum.

見物人 sightseer [→ 観光客 *(s.v.* 観光*)*];

spectator [→ 観客]
見物席 (spectator) seat
東京見物 Tokyo sight-seeing

けんぽう 憲法 *constitution (of a country)*
憲法記念日 Constitution Memorial Day (a Japanese national holiday on May 3)
日本国憲法 the Constitution of Japan

げんみつ 厳密 ～な *strict, exact, precise*
厳密に言えば、それは規則違反だ。
Strictly speaking, that's a rule violation.

けんめい 賢明 ～な *wise*
先生に相談したのは賢明でした。
It was wise to consult with the teacher.

けんやく 倹約 *economy, thrift, frugality [→ 節約]*
倹約する to be thrifty, to economize; to save, to avoid using
倹約してお金をためました。
I was thrifty and saved money.
バス代を倹約して歩いて帰りました。
I saved the bus fare and walked home.
倹約家 frugal person
倹約的な frugal, thrifty

けんり 権利 *a right*
あの人に発言する権利はないよ。
That person has no right to speak.
権利と義務 rights and obligations

げんり 原理 *(basic) principle*

けんりつ 県立 ～の *prefectural, administered by a prefecture*
県立高校 prefectural high school

げんりょう 原料 *raw materials*
チーズの原料は何ですか。
What are the raw materials of cheese?

けんりょく 権力 *power, authority [→ 権威, 勢力]*
権力者 person of power

げんろん 言論 *expressing one's ideas*
言論の自由 freedom of speech, freedom of expression

こ 子 *1. child [→ 子供]*
男の子 boy
女の子 girl
2. the young (of an animal)
ライオンの子 lion cub

—こ —個 *(counter for objects, especially spherical or cube-shaped objects; see Appendix 2)*

ご— 御— *(This prefix is typically honorific, but in some words it has lost its honorific force. It also appears in some humble forms.)*

ご 碁 *(the game of) go*
碁石 go stone
碁盤 go board

ご 五 *five (see Appendix 2)*
五月 *May*

ご 語 *word [→ 単語]*
この語はどう発音しますか。
How do you pronounce this word?
—語 (counter for words; see Appendix 2)

—ご —語 *language (Added to bases denoting the names of countries, tribes, etc.)*
メキシコではスペイン語を話しますか。
Do they speak Spanish in Mexico?
中国語 the Chinese language
何語 what language
スワヒリ語 the Swahili language

—ご —後 *after, later, since (Added to noun bases, often numbers denoting* *periods of time.) [↔ ―前]*

その後 after that, since then (In this one combination, 後 behaves like an independent word rather than a suffix.)

その後その人には会っていません。
I haven't seen that person since then.

喜美さんは1時間後に電話しました。
Kimi telephoned one hour later.

二日後に目的地に向けて出発しました。
Two days later I set out for my destination.

帰国後 after returning home (to one's own country)

コアラ *koala*

こい 恋 *(romantic) love [→ 恋愛]*

Aに恋をする to love A; to fall in love with A

王子はその少女に恋をしていました。
The prince was in love with that girl.

恋人 lover

恋する *{Irreg.}* to love; to fall in love with

初恋 first time in love

こい 鯉 *carp*

鯉幟 carp streamer (traditional decorations for Children's Day (May 5))

こいのぼりを立てる to put up carp streamers

こい 濃い *[[↔ 薄い2.]] deep, dark (describing a color); thick, dense, heavy (describing liquid, hair, etc.); strong (describing coffee, tea, etc.)*

文子さんは濃い赤のセーターを着ている。
Fumiko is wearing a deep red sweater.

お茶は濃くしたほうが好きです。
I like strong tea better.

小松先生はひげが濃いですね。
Prof. Komatsu's beard is thick, isn't it?

濃いスープ thick soup

濃い霧 dense fog

濃いコーヒー strong coffee

コイル *(electrical) coil*

コイン *coin [→ 硬貨]*

コインランドリー (US) laundromat, (UK) launderette

コインロッカー coin-operated locker

こう *like this, in this way [↔ そう; ああ]*

加代子さんはこう言って私を見つめたよ。
Kayoko said it in this way and looked at me!

こういう this kind of [→ こんな]

こういうコートが欲しいです。
I want this kind of coat.

―ごう ―号 *(counter for train numbers, issues of magazines, etc.; see Appendix 2)*

こうい 好意 *kindness, goodwill, friendliness*

ご好意に感謝します。
I thank you for your kindness.

好意的な kind, friendly

大家さんは私たちにとても好意的です。
The landlady is very kind to us.

こううん 幸運 *good luck, good fortune*

幸運を祈ります。
I wish you good luck.

幸運な lucky, fortunate

その画家に会えたのは幸運でした。
We were fortunate to be able to meet that painter.

幸運にも fortunately, luckily

幸運にも試合に勝ちました。
Luckily, we won the game.

こうえい 光栄 *honor, glory*

お目にかかれて光栄です。
It is an honor to be able meet you.

こうえん 公園 *park*

国立公園 national park

上野公園 Ueno Park

こうえん 講演 *lecture, talk*

講演する to lecture, to give a lecture

おもちゃの歴史について講演します。
I will give a lecture on the history of toys.
講演会 lecture meeting

こうか 効果 *effectiveness, effect [→ 効き目]*
この薬は頭痛には何の効果もないよ。
This medicine has no effect on headaches!
効果的な effective
英語の効果的な学習法を教えてください。
Please teach me an effective study method for English.
音響効果 sound effect

こうか 高価 *high price*
高価な expensive *[→ 高い3.]*

こうか 校歌 *school song*

こうか 硬貨 *coin*

ごうか 豪華 ～な *luxurious, deluxe, magnificent*
あの豪華な船を見ましたか。
Did you see that luxurious ship?
その歌手は豪華なドレスを着ていました。
The singer was wearing a magnificent dress.

こうかい 公開 *making open to the public; making public*
公開する to open to the public; to make public
そのプールは一般に公開されています。
That pool is open to the general public.
公開の open-to-the-public; in-public
公開講座 open class; extension course
公開討論 public debate

こうかい 後悔 *regret, remorse*
後悔先に立たず。(proverb)
There's no use crying over spilled milk. (Literally: Remorse does not arise beforehand.)
後悔する to come to regret
勤勉でなかったことを後悔しています。
I regret that I was not diligent.
過ちをとても後悔しています。
I very much regret my mistake.

こうかい 航海 *(sea) voyage, (ocean) cruise, (ocean) sailing*
航海する to voyage, to sail
ヨットで太平洋を航海しました。
I sailed the Pacific in a sailboat.
処女航海 maiden voyage

こうがい 公害 *environmental pollution*
われわれは公害に悩んでいます。
We are afflicted by environmental pollution.
公害対策 measures against pollution
騒音公害 noise pollution

こうがい 郊外 *suburbs*
私たちは札幌の郊外に住んでいます。
We live in the suburbs of Sapporo.

こうかいどう 公会堂 *public meeting hall (in a city or town)*

ごうかく 合格 *meeting (a standard), passing (a test) [↔ 不合格]*
合格おめでとう！
Congratulations on passing!
合格する to achieve a passing result, to succeed
Aに合格する to pass A, to succeed on A
佐藤さんも入学試験に合格しました。
Ms. Sato also passed the entrance examination.
合格点 passing mark, passing score

こうかん 交換 *exchange, trade*
交換する to exchange, to trade *[→ 取り替える]*
AをBと交換する to exchange A for B, to trade A for B
この帽子をもっと大きいのと交換したい。
I want to exchange this hat for a bigger one.

洋子さんと切符を交換しました。
I exchanged tickets with Yoko.

交換台 switchboard

交換学生 exchange student

交換手 (telephone) operator

こうぎ 抗議 *protest*

抗議する to make a protest, to protest

選手は審判の判定に抗議しました。
The player protested against the umpire's decision.

私たちはその新しい計画に抗議しました。
We protested against that new plan.

こうぎ 講義 *(academic) lecture*

講義する to lecture

こうきあつ 高気圧 *[[↔ 低気圧]] 1. high (atmospheric) pressure*

2. high pressure (weather) system

こうきしん 好奇心 *curiosity*

好奇心からその箱を開けました。
I opened that box out of curiosity.

信次ちゃんは好奇心の強い少年です。
Shinji is a very curious boy.

こうきゅう 高級 ～の *high-class, high-grade*

高級品 high-quality item

こうきょう 公共 ～の *public, communal*

公共施設 public facilities

こうぎょう 工業 *industry, manufacturing*

工業地帯 industrial district

工業高校 technical high school

工業ロボット industrial robot

工業都市 industrial city

重工業 heavy industry

軽工業 light industry

こうぎょう 鉱業 *mining industry*

こうきょうきょく 交響曲 *symphony ((musical piece)) [→ シンフォニー]*

兄はベートーベンの交響曲が大好きです。
My older brother really likes Beethoven's symphonies.

こうくう 航空 *aviation*

航空便 airmail

航空会社 airline (company)

航空券 airline ticket

こうけい 光景 *sight, spectacle; scene, view [→ 景色]*

私たちはみんなその光景にびっくりしたよ。
We were all surprised at that sight!

ごうけい 合計 *1. sum, total*

合計で in total, all together

合計でいくらですか。
How much is it all together?

合計する to add up, to total

2. [☞ 合計で (above)]

靴と帽子は合計1万円かかりました。
The shoes and the hat cost ¥10,000 all together.

こうげき 攻撃 *attack, assault, offensive*

攻撃する to attack

攻撃的な offensive, attack-like

こうけん 貢献 *contribution*

貢献する to make a contribution, to contribute

首相は世界平和に大いに貢献しました。
The prime minister contributed greatly to world peace.

こうげん 高原 *high plain, plateau*

こうご 口語 *spoken language, colloquial language [↔ 文語]*

口語英語 spoken English

こうご 交互 ～の *mutual, reciprocal [→ 互いの]; alternating [→ 交代の]*

両親は交互に運転しました。
My parents drove alternately.

こうこう 孝行 *filial piety, devotion to one's*

parents [→ 親孝行]
孝行する to be filial, to show devotion to one's parents

こうこう 高校 *high school (an abbreviation of 高等学校 (s.v. 高等))*
高校入試 high-school entrance examination
高校生 high-school student
全国高校野球大会 National Senior High School Baseball Tournament

こうごう 皇后 *the Empress (of Japan)*
皇后陛下 Her Majesty the Empress

こうこく 広告 *1. advertisement*
その会社は新聞に広告を出しています。
The company places advertisements in the newspaper.
広告する to advertise

2. notice, announcement (in the mass media, etc.)
広告する to announce, to make widely known
広告主 sponsoring advertiser, sponsor *[→ スポンサー]*
求人広告 help-wanted ad
死亡広告 obituary notice
テレビ広告 TV commercial *[→ コマーシャル]*

こうさ 交差 *intersecting, crossing*
交差する to intersect, to cross (intransitive)
この通りは鉄道と交差しています。
This street crosses the railroad.
交差点 (point of) intersection

こうざ 講座 *1. (university) chair, professorship*

2. course (of lessons)
英語講座 English course

こうさい 交際 *association, intercourse, companionship*
中村さんは交際が広いです。
Mr. Nakamura has a wide circle of acquaintances. (Literally: Mr. Nakamura's association is wide.)
交際する to associate, to have contact, to keep company
恵子さんと親しく交際しています。
I am very close to Keiko.

こうさく 工作 *1. building, construction work*
工作する to build, to construct

2. handcrafting
工作する to handcraft

3. operations, activities, maneuvering (to achieve some goal)
工作する to operate, to maneuver
工作機械 machine tool
政治工作 political maneuvering

こうさん 降参 *surrender, submission, yielding*
降参する to surrender, to give up, to yield
わかった、わかった、降参するよ。
All right, all right, I give up!

こうざん 高山 *high mountain*
高山病 mountain sickness
高山植物 alpine plant

こうざん 鉱山 *mine (in which something is dug up)*

こうし 講師 *1. (college) lecturer, instructor*

2. speaker, lecturer

こうじ 工事 *construction work; repair work (on major construction projects)*
工事中の under construction; under repair
鉄道はまだ工事中です。
The railroad is still under construction.
道路工事 road building; road repairs

こうしき 公式 *1. (mathematical) formula*

2. 〜の official, formal [→ 正式な]

公式訪問 formal visit, official visit

公式戦 official game, regular-season game

こうじつ 口実 *excuse, pretext*

こうしゃ 校舎 *school building, schoolhouse*

こうしゅう 公衆 *the public*

公衆の面前で in public

公衆便所 public lavatory

公衆電話 public telephone

公衆道徳 public morality

公衆衛生 public health

公衆浴場 public bathhouse

こうしゅう 講習 *course, class*

こうしょう 交渉 *1. negotiation(s)*

交渉する to negotiate; to negotiate about

その事業について市長と交渉しました。
I negotiated with the mayor about that enterprise.

2. connection, dealings (between people)

団体交渉 collective bargaining

こうじょう 工場 *factory, plant, mill*

工場地帯 factory district

工場長 factory manager

ガス工場 gasworks

自動車工場 automobile plant

自動車修理工場 auto repair shop

機械工場 machine shop

製紙工場 paper mill

石油化学工場 petrochemical plant

ごうじょう 強情 *obstinacy, stubbornness*

強情を張る to be obstinate, to be stubborn

強情な obstinate, stubborn *[→ 頑固な]*

こうしん 行進 *march, parade; marching, parading*

行進する to march, to parade

行進曲 march ((musical piece)) *[→ マーチ]*

こうすい 香水 *perfume*

こうずい 洪水 *flood*

この町は昨年洪水にあいました。
This town met with a flood last year.

こうせい 公正 *fairness, impartiality, justice [→ 公平]*

公正な fair, impartial, just

法は何事にも公正でなければなりません。
The law must be fair in everything.

こうせい 厚生 *public welfare*

厚生施設 welfare facilities

厚生省 the Ministry of Health and Welfare

こうせい 恒星 *fixed star*

こうせい 構成 *composition, make-up, organization*

構成する to make up, to compose

アメリカ合衆国は50州で構成されている。
The United states of America is made up of fifty states.

こうせん 光線 *light ray, light beam*

光線銃 ray gun

レーザー光線 laser beam

太陽光線 sunlight, rays of the sun

こうぜん 公然 ～の *open, public*

公然と openly, publicly

それは私たちの間では公然の秘密です。
That is an open secret among us.

こうぞう 構造 *structure, make-up*

こうそうビル 高層ビル *high-rise building*

こうそく 校則 *school regulations, school rules*

校則を守らなければならないよ。
We must obey the school regulations!

こうそく 高速 *high speed*

高速道路 (US) expressway, (UK) motorway

こうたい 交代, 交替 *alternating, taking another's place; (work) shift*
交代の alternating
交代に／で by turns, alternately *[→* 代わる代わる*]*
交代で働く to work in shifts
交代する to alternate, to take another's place
京子さんは妹さんと交代して、壁にペンキを塗りました。
Kyoko took her younger sister's place and painted the walls.

こうだい 広大 ～な *immense, vast*

こうたいし 皇太子 *crown prince*
皇太子妃 *crown prince's wife*

こうちゃ 紅茶 *black tea [↔* お茶*2.]*

こうちょう 好調 ～な *satisfactory, in good condition, favorable*
あの投手は好調です。
That pitcher is in good condition.
すべて好調に進んでいます。
It's all progressing satisfactorily.

こうちょう 校長 *(school) principal, headmaster*

こうつう 交通 *traffic (along a transportation route)*
この道路は交通が激しいです。
On this road the traffic is heavy.
交通違反 traffic violation
交通事故 traffic accident
交通巡査 traffic police officer
交通信号 traffic signal

こうてい 肯定 *affirmation [↔* 否定*]*
肯定する to affirm
大統領は資本主義を全面的に肯定します。
The president fully affirms capitalism.
肯定文 affirmative sentence
肯定的な affirmative

こうてい 皇帝 *emperor*

こうてい 校庭 *school grounds, schoolyard*

こうてつ 鋼鉄 *steel [→* 鉄鋼*]*

こうとう 高等 ～の *high-level, advanced*
高等動物 higher animal
高等学校 high school *[→* 高校*]*
高等専門学校 technical college

こうどう 行動 *act, action; behavior, conduct*
それは軽率な行動です。
That is a careless act.
上村博士の奇妙な行動は理解できません。
We cannot understand Dr. Uemura's strange behavior.
行動する to act; to behave
あの人たちはいつも団体で行動します。
Those people always act in a group.
行動主義 behaviorism

こうどう 講堂 *lecture hall, assembly hall, (US) auditorium*

ごうとう 強盗 *1. robbery*
2. robber

こうねん 光年 *light-year*
－光年 (counter for light years; see Appendix 2)

こうば 工場 *factory, plant [→* 工場*]*

こうはい 後輩 *one's junior (a person who entered the same organization later) [↔* 先輩*]*
上田君は僕の後輩です。
Ueda is my junior.

こうはん 後半 *the second half [↔* 前半*]*

こうばん 交番 *police box, police stand*

こうひょう 好評 *public favor, favorable reception, popularity*
好評の well-received, popular
その映画は若者の間でたいへん好評です。

That movie is very popular among young people.

こうふう 校風 *school traditions (unique to a particular school)*

こうふく 幸福 *[[→ 幸せ]] happiness; good fortune*

幸福な happy; fortunate

こうぶつ 好物 *favorite food/drink; favorite thing to eat/drink*

私の好物はチョコレートです。

My favorite food is chocolate.

こうぶつ 鉱物 *mineral*

鉱物資源 mineral resources

こうふん 興奮 *excitement, excitation, agitation*

興奮する to get excited, to become agitated

興奮して跳び上がった。

I got excited and jumped up.

その演説を聞いて興奮してしまいました。

We heard that speech and got excited.

こうへい 公平 *fairness, impartiality [→ 公正] [↔ 不公平]*

公平な fair, impartial

こうほ 候補 *1. candidacy [→ 立候補]*

候補に立つ to become a candidate, to run

2. candidate

前田さんは会長の候補です。

Ms. Maeda is a candidate for chairperson.

候補者 *[☞ 候補2. (above)]*

優勝候補 one of the favorites for the championship

こうみょう 巧妙 *〜な clever, skillful*

こうみん 公民 *citizen [→ 市民]*

公民館 community center, public hall

こうむいん 公務員 *civil servant, government employee*

こうもり 蝙蝠 *bat ((animal))*

こうもん 校門 *school gate*

こうよう 紅葉 *autumn leaves*

紅葉する to turn color (The subject is leaves.)

木の葉がすっかり紅葉しています。

The leaves of the trees have completely turned color.

こうらくびより 行楽日和 *ideal weather for an outing*

こうり 小売り *retailing, retail [↔ 卸売り (s.v. 卸)]*

小売りする to sell at retail

小売り値 retail price

小売り店 retail store

こうりつ 公立 *〜の public, publicly administered [↔ 私立の]*

公立学校 (US) public school, (UK) state school

こうりつ 効率 *efficiency [→ 能率]*

効率的な efficient

ごうりてき 合理的 *〜な rational, reasonable, logical*

兄はいつも合理的な考え方をします。

My older brother always thinks logically.

こうりゅう 交流 *1. exchange, interchange (between people of different areas, organizations, cultures, etc.)*

交流する to exchange, to interchange (transitive or intransitive)

2. alternating (electrical) current

こうりょ 考慮 *consideration, thought*

考慮に入れる to take into consideration

どうぞその事実を考慮に入れてください。

Please take that fact into consideration.

考慮する to consider, to think over

こうれい 高齢 *advanced age*

高齢者 elderly person

ごうれい 号令 *command, order (spoken to a group)*

号令を掛ける to give a command, to give an order

校長は生徒に「着席」と号令をかけた。
The principal gave the students the command "sit down."
号令する to give a command, to give an order

こうわ 講和 *peace (concluding a war)*
講和する to make peace
講和条約 peace treaty
講和会議 peace conference

こえ 声 *voice*
洋子さんは優しい声をしています。
Yoko has a gentle voice.
田上君は小さな声でしゃべるね。
Tagami talks in a soft voice, doesn't he?
先生の声がよく通ります。
The teacher's voice carries well.
子供たちは声をそろえて叫びました。
The children joined their voices and shouted.
もう少し大きな声で言ってください。
Please say it in a little louder voice.
声を出す to talk aloud
声を出して本を読みました。
I read the book aloud.
声変わり voice change (in an adolescent boy)
うちの太郎は今声変わりの時期です。
Our Taro's voice is changing now.

こえる 越える, 超える *1. to cross over, to go over (a distance or boundary) [→ 越す, 超す 1.]*
自転車でロッキー山脈を越えます。
I will cross the Rocky Mountains by bicycle.
2. to exceed, to go over [→ 越す, 超す2., 上回る]
この子は10歳を越えています。
This child is over ten.

ゴーカート *go-cart*

コース *1. course, itinerary*
2. (race) lane

コーチ *1. (athletic) coach*
青木先生は私たちのチームのコーチです。
Mr. Aoki is the coach of our team.
2. (athletic) coaching
コーチする to coach

コート *court (for tennis, volleyball, etc.)*

コート *coat, overcoat*

コード *(electrical) cord*

コーナー *1. department, counter (in a store) [→ 売り場]*
2. corner (of a boxing ring, playing field, etc.)
3. photo corner (for mounting photographs in an album)

コーヒー *coffee*
朝食はコーヒー１杯で結構です。
A cup of coffee is fine for breakfast.
コーヒーを二つお願いします。
Two coffees, please.
コーヒーを入れる to make coffee, to brew coffee
先生は私たちにコーヒーを入れてくださいました。
Our teacher made coffee for us.
濃い〔薄い〕コーヒー strong〔weak〕coffee

コーラス *1. singing in chorus; choral music, chorus [→ 合唱]*
2. chorus, choral group [→ 合唱団 (s.v. 合唱)]

こおり 氷 *ice*
氷を少しください。
Please give me a little ice.
うちへ帰る途中氷で滑ってしまった。
I slipped on the ice on my way home.
池に氷が張りました。
Ice formed on the pond.
ワインを氷で冷やしました。
I chilled the wine with ice.

こおる 凍る *to freeze (intransitive)*

洗面器の水が凍っています。
The water in the wash basin has frozen.

ゴール *1. (scored) goal (in sports)*
2. finish line
ゴールイン crossing the finish line
ゴールインする to cross the finish line
健ちゃんは1着でゴールインしたよ。
Ken crossed the finish line in first place!
ゴールキーパー goalkeeper *[→ キーパー]*

ゴールデンウィーク *Golden Week (the period of April 29 through May 5 when three Japanese national holidays fall in close succession: みどりの日 (April 29), 憲法記念日 (May 3), and 子供の日 (May 5))*

コールドゲーム *called game*
テニスの試合は、にわか雨でコールドゲームになりました。
The tennis match was a called game because of a rain shower.

こおろぎ *cricket ((insect))*

こがい 戸外 *the outdoors, the open air*
先生は戸外で授業を行ないました。
The teacher held class outside.

ごかい 誤解 *misunderstanding*
それは野崎さんの誤解です。
That is a misunderstanding on Mr. Nozaki's part. (Literally: That is Mr. Nozaki's misunderstanding.)
その話し方は誤解を招くと思います。
I think that way of talking invites misunderstanding.
誤解する to misunderstand
真理子さんは私を誤解しています。
Mariko misunderstands me.

こがす 焦がす *to scorch, to burn (transitive)*
母はアイロンをかけたときに、シャツをちょっと焦がしてしまった。
My mother scorched the shirt a little when she ironed it.

こがた 小型 ～の *miniature, small-sized [↔ 大型の]*
小型の辞書 pocket-sized dictionary

こぎって 小切手 *(bank) check*
ホテル代を小切手で払いました。
I paid my hotel bill by check.
旅行小切手 traveler's check

ごきぶり *cockroach*

こきゅう 呼吸 *1. breathing, respiration*
祖父は呼吸が荒いです。
My grandfather's breathing is hard.
呼吸する to breathe
2. knack, trick [→ こつ]
人工呼吸 artificial respiration
深呼吸 deep breathing, deep breath

こきょう 故郷 *hometown, birthplace*
故郷はどこですか。
Where is your hometown?

こぐ 漕ぐ *to row; to pedal; to pump (a swing)*
湖でボートをこいで遊びました。
We had a good time rowing a boat on the lake.

こくおう 国王 *king of a country*

こくがい 国外 *outside of a country, abroad (as a noun) [↔ 国内]*

こくぎ 国技 *national sport (相撲 in the case of Japan)*

こくご 国語 *1. the language of a country*
2. the Japanese language [→ 日本語 (s.v. 日本)]
国語辞典 Japanese dictionary

こくさい－ 国際－ *international (Added to noun bases.)*
国際電話 international telephone call
国際会議 international conference
国際結婚 marriage between people from different countries

国際空港 international airport

国際連合 the United Nations [→ 国連]

国際親善 international goodwill

こくさいてき 国際的 ～な *international*

こくさん 国産 ～の *1. domestically produced, made in-country*

2. Japanese-made, made in Japan [→ 日本製の (s.v. 日本)]

これは国産の車ですか。
Is this a Japanese-made car?

国産品 domestic product; Japanese-made product

この時計は国産品です。
This watch is a Japanese-made product.

こくじん 黒人 *black person*

こくせき 国籍 *nationality, citizenship*

あの人の国籍はどこですか。
What is that person's nationality?

こくどう 国道 *national highway*

こくない 国内 *inside of a country (as a noun) [↔ 国外]*

そのオペラ歌手は国内でも国外でも人気があります。
The opera singer is popular both at home and abroad.

国内の internal, domestic

国内事情 internal affairs, domestic affairs

国内線 domestic flight

こくはく 告白 *confession*

告白する to confess

こくばん 黒板 *blackboard, chalkboard*

恵子ちゃん、黒板を消してちょうだい。
Keiko, please erase the blackboard.

黒板拭き blackboard eraser

こくほう 国宝 *national treasure*

こくみん 国民 *people (of a country)*

日本人は勤勉な国民だそうです。
I hear that the Japanese are a hardworking people.

国民の祝日 national holiday

国民総生産 gross national product

国民体育大会 the National Athletic Meet

こくもつ 穀物 *(US) grain, (UK) cereal*

こくりつ 国立 ～の *national, nationally administered*

国立大学 national university

国立公園 national park

こくれん 国連 *the United Nations (an abbreviation of 国際連合 (s.v. 国際—))*

国連事務総長 Secretary General of the UN

国連総会 UN General Assembly

国連大使 ambassador to the UN

ごくろうさま ご苦労さま (The addition of でした makes this expression more polite. The less polite form ご苦労さんis sometimes used as well.)

1. Thank you for your trouble. (Used to thank subordinates and people who perform services as an occupation (e.g., a person who makes a delivery).)

2. That was hard work. (Used to comment on how hard another person worked at something. This use is appropriate even toward superiors.)

こけ 苔 *moss*

転がる石にこけは生えない。 (proverb)
A rolling stone gathers no moss. (Literally: No moss grows on a rolling stone.)

こけし *kokeshi (doll) (made of painted wood with a round head and cylindrical body)*

こげる 焦げる *to scorch, to burn (intransitive)*

何か焦げていますよ。
Something's burning!

ここ *this place, here [↔ そこ; あそこ]*

ここに来てください。
Please come here.

ここにニューヨークの地図があります。
There's a map of New York here.

ここからホテルまでどのくらいですか。
About how far is it from here to the hotel?

ここが佐藤さんのお宅です。
This is Mr. Sato's house.

ここはどこですか。
Where am I? (Literally: Where is this place?)

ごご 午後 *[[↔ 午前]] PM; afternoon*

学校は午後3時に終わります。
School ends at 3:00 PM.

土曜日の午後は暇です。
On Saturday afternoon I'm free.

きょうの午後先生を訪ねるつもりです。
I intend to visit the teacher this afternoon.

あしたの午後4時の列車で出発します。
I'm going to leave on the 4:00 PM. train tomorrow.

ココア *cocoa*

熱いココアを1杯飲みました。
I drank one cup of hot cocoa.

こごえる 凍える *to become numb (from the cold)*

けさは寒くて凍えそうです。
This morning it's cold, and it seems likely that I'll get numb.

そのつばめは凍えて死にました。
That swallow became numb from the cold and died.

こごと 小言 *scolding, rebuke*

Aに小言を言う to scold A, to nag A

母はいつも弟に小言を言っています。
My mother is always scolding my younger brother.

ここのか 九日 *(see Appendix 2) 1. nine days*

2. the ninth (day of a month)

ここのつ 九つ *nine (see Appendix 2)*

こころ 心 *1. mind, mentality*

心に掛かる to weigh on one's mind

心に留める to keep in mind

心をこめて with one's whole heart, wholeheartedly

心をこめて仕事をします。
I do my work wholeheartedly.

心が広い〔狭い〕one's mind is broad 〔narrow〕

加藤さんは心の広い人です。
Mr. Kato is a broad-minded person.

2. heart, feelings

洋子さんは心の優しい人です。
Yoko is a kindhearted person.

心から感謝します。
I thank you from my heart.

AがBの心を打つ A touches B's heart

美知子さんの言葉は私の心を打ったよ。
Michiko's words touched my heart!

心を入れ替える to turn over a new leaf, to reform oneself

心からの歓迎 hearty welcome

こころあたり 心当たり *inkling, idea*

だれがこの手紙を送ったか心当たりはないのですか。
Don't you have any idea who sent this letter?

こころがける 心掛ける *1. to keep striving for*

もっと早く起きるように心がけましょう。
Let's keep striving to get up earlier.

2. to keep in mind

こころざす 志す *1. to aspire, to set one's mind*

学問に志す to set one's mind on scholarship

2. to set one's mind on becoming, to aspire to become

本多さんは外交官を志しました。
Mr. Honda has set his mind on becoming

a diplomat.

こころづよい 心強い *[[↔ 心細い]]*

1. reassured, secure, encouraged

2. reassuring, encouraging

こころぼそい 心細い *[[↔ 心強い]]*

1. forlorn, discouraged, helpless-feeling, uneasy

姉がいないと心細いです。

When my older sister isn't here, I feel helpless.

2. discouraging, disheartening

こころみる 試みる *to try, to attempt*

新しい方法を試みましょう。

Let's try a new method.

少年は木に登ろうと試みました。

The boy tried to climb the tree.

こころよい 快い *nice, pleasant*

きょうは快い天気です。

Today it's pleasant weather.

ござ *straw mat*

ございます 【FORMAL for ある】 (more polite than あります)

(This word is a verb with the semi-formal -ます ending. The informal nonpast (the form of a verb that ordinarily appears in a dictionary) is ござる, but such informal forms are not used in modern Japanese.)

でございます *[☞ でございます]*

ござる *{Irreg.} [☞ ございます]*

こし 腰 *lower back (i.e., the back side of the body between the waistline and the widest part of the pelvis)*

きょうは腰が痛いです。

My lower back hurts today.

その女の人は年で腰が曲がっています。

That woman's back is bent with age.

腰を掛ける *[☞ 腰掛ける]*

こじ 孤児 *orphan*

孤児院 orphanage

こしかける 腰掛ける *to sit, to take a seat (Used only for sitting on a chair, etc., not for sitting on the floor.) [→ 座る 1.]*

こじき 乞食 *beggar*

ゴシップ *gossip [→ 噂話 (s.v. 噂)]*

ごじゅうおん 五十音 *the Japanese kana syllabary*

(This word literally means 50 sounds and reflects the traditional arrangement of symbols into a table with 10 columns and 5 rows. There are, however, only 46 distinct basic symbols in modern kana.)

五十音図 table of kana (in the traditional arrangement)

ごしゅじん ご主人 【HON. for 主人】

こしょう 故障 *(mechanical) trouble, breakdown*

故障する to break down

その機械がまた故障しました。

That machine broke down again.

故障中の out-of-order

こしょう *pepper (of the hard, round variety)*

このサラダにこしょうをかけてください。

Please put pepper on this salad.

胡椒入れ pepper shaker, pepper container

ごしょく 誤植 *misprint*

こしらえる 拵える *to make; to prepare; to build*

弁当をこしらえる to pack a lunch

顔をこしらえる to put on one's make-up

お金をこしらえる to raise money, to get money together

こじん 個人 *an individual (person)*

個人教授 private lessons

個人差 difference among individuals

個人主義 individualism

個人的な personal, individual

これは私の個人的な意見です。

This is my personal opinion.

こす 越す, 超す *1. to cross, to go over (a*

distance or boundary) [→ 越える, 超える 1.]
ボールはフェンスを越したよ。
The ball went over the fence!
2. to exceed, to go over [→ 超える, 超える2., 上回る]
値段は5000円を越していました。
The price was over ¥5,000
3. to move (to a new residence) [→ 引っ越す]
私は２年前にこの町に越してきました。
I moved to this city two years ago.
4. to spend (a period of time) [→ 過ごす]
毎年ハワイで冬を越します。
I spend the winter in Hawaii every year.

コスチューム *(stage) costume*

コスト *(monetary) cost*
生産コスト production cost

コスモス *cosmos ((flower))*

こする 擦る *to rub (transitive)*
目をこする to rub one's eyes

こせい 個性 *individual character, individuality*
あの人は個性が強いです。
That person is highly individual.

こせき 戸籍 *family register*
(This word refers to an official document which is kept in a municipal government office and which records the names, birth dates, etc., of a married couple and their unmarried children. Every Japanese citizen is listed on a こせき.)

こぜに 小銭 *small change, coins*
小銭の持ち合せがありません。
I have no small change with me.
小銭入れ coin purse

ごぜん 午前 *[[↔ 午後]] AM; morning*
４月５日の午前に生まれました。
I was born on the morning of April 5.
決勝戦は午前10時に始まります。
The championship game begins at 10:00 AM.
午前中 during the morning, before noon
午前中はずっと雨が降っていました。
It rained all morning.
きのうの午前中はうちにいました。
Yesterday morning I was at home.
午前中に授業があるよ。
In the morning I have class!

こそ *indeed, precisely*
(This particle emphasizes the preceding phrase. The phrase preceding frequently ends in a noun or another particle, but can also appear after a clause ending in から.)
これこそ典型的な例です。
This is indeed a typical example.
できないからこそ練習が必要なのです。
It's precisely because you can't do it that you have to practice.

ごぞんじ ご存じ ～だ【HON. for 知っている *(s.v.* 知る)】

こたい 固体 *a solid (substance) [↔ 液体; 気体]*

こだい 古代 *ancient times, antiquity*
古代史 ancient history

こたえ 答え *answer, reply*
その答えは正しいです。
That answer is correct.

こたえる 応える *1. to respond as hoped, to respond appropriately (to another person's thoughts or actions)*
期待にこたえる to meet expectations
親切にこたえる to repay kindness
2. to affect strongly, to tell on
母の言葉がこたえました。
My mother's words affected me strongly.
身にこたえる to affect one physically, to tell on one physically

こたえる 答える *to give an answer, to reply, to respond*

質問に大きな声で答えました。
I gave an answer to the question in a loud voice.

こだま *echo [→ 山彦]*

こだまする to echo, to reverberate

ごちそう ご馳走 *good food, feast*

姉は私の誕生日のお祝いにごちそうを作ってくれたよ。
My older sister cooked a feast for my birthday.

ごちそうする to treat (a person to food and/or drink) [→ 奢る]

きょうは私がごちそうします。
Today I'll treat.

AにBをごちそうする to treat A to B

先輩の一人が昼食をごちそうしてくれました。
One of my seniors treated me to lunch.

ごちそうになる to be treated to (food and/or drink)

AにBをごちそうになる to be treated by A to B

林さんにおすしをごちそうになりました。
I was treated to sushi by Ms. Hayashi.

ごちそうさま ご馳走さま*(でした) Everything was delicious*

(This is the required expression of thanks after eating. It is typically said to one's host at a meal or to the person who prepared the food, but it can also be addressed to no one in particular as an indication that one has finished eating.)

こちょう 誇張 *exaggeration, over-statement [→ 大袈裟]*

誇張する to exaggerate, to overstate

こちら 【FORMAL for こっち】 *1. [[↔ そちら 1.; あちら 1.]] this way; here*

出口はこちらです。
The exit is this way.

こちらへどうぞ。
This way, please.

こちらへも時々来ます。
We sometimes come here also.

2. this person [↔ あちら 2.]

伊藤先生、こちらが友達の木村君です。
Prof. Ito, this is my friend Kimura.

3. [[↔ そちら 2.]] I, me; my family

もしもし、こちらは加藤です。
Hello, this is Kato.

こつ *knack, trick*

スキーのこつを覚えました。
I learned the skiing knack.

こっか 国家 *nation state, nation, country [→ 国 1.]*

国家試験 state examination

こっか 国歌 *national anthem*

こっかい 国会 *national legislature; the (Japanese) Diet; (United States) Congress; (British) Parliament*

国会議員 member of a national legislature

国会議事堂 the Diet Building

国会図書館 the Diet Library

こづかい 小遣い *pocket money, allowance*

月に3000円の小遣いをもらっています。
I get an allowance of ¥3,000 a month.

小遣いが上がったよ。
My allowance went up!

こっき 国旗 *national flag*

こっきょう 国境 *border between countries, national boundary*

国境線 borderline between countries

コック *cook (in a restaurant serving non-Japanese food)*

こっけい 滑稽 ～な *funny, humorous, comical*

私たちはそのこっけいなできごとに笑ってしまった。
We laughed at that comical happening.

—ごっこ *imitative playing (Added to noun bases.)*

電車ごっこ playing train

学校ごっこ playing school

カウボーイごっこ playing cowboy

鬼ごっこ (the game of) tag

こっこう 国交 *diplomatic relations*

国交断絶 breaking off of diplomatic relations

国交回復 restoration of diplomatic relations

こっせつ 骨折 *(bone) fracture*

骨折する to suffer a fracture, to break a bone

こっそり *(〜と) secretly, in secret*

恵子さんはこっそりと私にそのニュースを話してくれました。

Keiko told me that news secretly.

ごったがえす ごった返す *to become chaotically crowded, to become thronged*

こっち 【COL. for こちら】

こづつみ 小包 *1. (US) small package, (UK) small parcel, small bundle*

2. parcel post

このおもちゃは小包で送りましょう。

I'll send this toy by parcel post.

コップ *(drinking) glass*

毎朝コップ１杯の牛乳を飲みます。

Every morning I drink one glass of milk.

こと 琴 *koto, Japanese harp*

こてい 固定 〜する *to fix, to set, to make stationary*

コテージ *cottage*

こてん 古典 *classic work (of literature, art, etc.)*

古典文学 classical literature

古典的な classical

こと 事 *1. thing, matter, affair*

きょうはする事がたくさんあります。

Today I have a lot of things to do.

その事については何も知りません。

I don't know anything about that matter.

2. to, -ing, that (Makes a preceding clause function as a noun.)

英語を学ぶことはおもしろいです。

It is interesting to study English.

泳ぐことが好きです。

I like swimming.

藤本さんが歌が上手だということは知っています。

I know that Ms. Fujimoto is good at singing.

ことがある it sometimes happens that (following a clause with a predicate in the nonpast tense); it has happened that (following a clause with a predicate in the past tense)

あの火山は噴火することがあります。

That volcano sometimes erupts.

由紀子さんと一度話したことがあります。

I have talked with Yukiko once.

私は鎌倉に行ったことがないです。

I have never been to Kamakura.

ことになる to be decided that (following a verb in the nonpast tense)

兄はあさって出発することになりました。

It has been decided that my elder brother will leave the day after tomorrow.

ことにする to decide to (following a verb in the nonpast tense)

あした帰ることにしました。

I decided to return home tomorrow.

—ごと —毎 *every, each (Added to noun bases, often numbers denoting time periods.)*

日曜日ごとに父と魚釣りに行きます。

Every Sunday I go fishing with my father.

オリンピックは４年ごとに開かれます。

The Olympics are held every four years.

こどう 鼓動 *beat, pulsation*

心臓の鼓動が激しくなりました。

My heart began to beat faster. (Literally: My heartbeat became intense.)

鼓動する to beat, to pulse

こどく 孤独 *loneliness; solitude*

私も孤独は好きではありません。
I don't like solitude either.

東京で孤独を感じています。
I feel lonely in Tokyo.

孤独な lonely; solitary

ことし 今年 *this year*

おじいさんは今年90歳になるね。
Grandfather will be ninety this year, won't he?

今年の夏は英会話の勉強をします。
This summer I'm going to study English conversation.

ことづけ 言付け *[[→ 伝言]] message (that someone asks one person to give to another person); giving a message*

杉山さんへの言づけがあります。
There is a message for Ms. Sugiyama.

言づけをお願いできますか。
Can I leave a message?

ことなる 異なる *to differ [→ 違う]*

ことに 殊に *especially [→ 特に]*

ことば 言葉 *1. language [→ 言語]*

英語は国際的な言葉です。
English is an international language.

2. word [→ 単語]

言葉を換えて言えば in other words

言葉で表す to express in words

言葉遊び word game

ことばづかい 言葉遣い *choice of words, (use of) language*

言葉づかいに気をつけなさい。
Watch your language.

こども 子供 *child*

恵子と明を子供のころから知っているよ。
I have known Keiko and Akira since they were children!

子供の日 Children's Day

子供扱い treating like a child

子供っぽい childish

ことり 小鳥 *small bird (i.e., a bird about the size of a typical songbird)*

ペットとして小鳥を2羽飼っています。
I keep two small birds as pets.

ことわざ 諺 *proverb, adage, maxim*

ことわる 断る *1. to refuse, to decline, to turn down*

山下さんの招待を断りました。
I declined Mr. Yamashita's invitation.

2. to tell in advance, to give prior notice

こな 粉 *1. powder*

2. flour, meal

粉薬 powdered medicine

粉ミルク powdered milk

粉石鹸 soap powder

粉雪 powdery snow

こにもつ 小荷物 *1. small baggage, small luggage*

2. (US) small package, (UK) small parcel (shipped by railway and not sent through the mail)

コネ *connections (with people who can further one's interests)*

父はあの会社に有力なコネがあります。
My father has powerful connections in that company.

この *this, these (as a noun modifier) [↔ その; あの]*

この靴は私のです。
These shoes are mine.

父はこの7月に帰って来ます。
My father will come home this July.

この近くに住んでいるんですか。
Do you live near here?

この辺 the area near here, the area around here

この辺にバス停はありますか。
Is there a bus stop around here?

この辺は初めてです。
It's the first time I've been around here.

この前 previously, last
この前友子さんに会ったのはいつですか。
When did you last see Tomoko?
この前の previous, last
この前の日曜日は23日でした。
Last Sunday was the 23rd.
この前の首相はまだ若いです。
The previous prime minister is still young.
このまま as is, like this
本はこのままにしておきなさい。
Leave the books like this.

このあいだ この間 *1. the other day [→ 先日]*
この間、道で洋子さんに会いました。
The other day I met Yoko on the street.
2. recently [→ 最近]
この間まで九州にいました。
Until recently I was in Kyushu.

このごろ *these days, recently, lately*
このごろ姉はとても忙しいです。
My older sister is very busy these days.
このごろ健さんに会っていません。
I haven't seen Ken lately.

このみ 好み *liking, taste, preference*
この花瓶は私の好みに合いません。
This vase is not to my taste.

このむ 好む *to like, to have a preference for (The direct object cannot be a specific person that one is fond of.)*
ほとんどの大学生はロックを好みます。
Almost all college students like rock.

こばむ 拒む *to refuse, to reject [→ 断る 1.]*
弟は私たちと行くことを拒みました。
Our younger brother refused to go with us.

ごはん ご飯 *1. (cooked) rice [↔ 米]*
けさはご飯を２杯食べました。
This morning I ate two bowls of rice.
ご飯を炊く to cook rice, to boil rice
2. meal [→ 食事]
ご飯の支度をする to prepare a meal

コピー *1. copy, duplicate [→ 複写 1.]*
コピーする to copy
コピーを取る to make a copy
この手紙のコピーを２通取ってください。
Please make two copies of this letter.
2. (advertising) copy
コピーライター copywriter

こぶ 瘤 *swelling, lump, bump (on a person's or animal's body)*
この子は頭に大きなこぶができています。
A large bump has developed on this child's head.
らくだのこぶ camel's hump

ごふく 呉服 *cloth for traditional Japanese clothing*

ごぶさた ご無沙汰【HUM.】 *hiatus in contact (with someone)*
ごぶさたする to fail to get in contact, to fail to get in touch
ごぶさたしております。
I'm sorry for not having been in touch for so long. (Literally: I have failed to get in touch.)

こぶし 拳 *fist [→ 拳骨]*

コブラ *cobra*

こふん 古墳 *ancient burial mound*

こぶん 子分 *henchman, follower [↔ 親分]*

ごぼう *burdock*

こぼす 零す *1. to spill (transitive); to shed (tears)*
ここに牛乳をこぼしたのはだれですか。
Who is the one who spilled milk here?
京子さんは映画を見て涙をこぼしました。
Kyoko saw the movie and shed tears.
2. to complain about, to grumble about
あの人はいつも不運をこぼしています。
That person is always grumbling about his bad luck.

こぼれる 零れる *to spill, to overflow*

母(はは)の目(め)から涙(なみだ)がこぼれました。
Tears spilled from my mother's eyes.
水(みず)がバケツからこぼれました。
Water spilled from the bucket.

こま *top ((toy))*

こまを回(まわ)す to spin a top

ごま 胡麻(ごま) *sesame seed*

胡麻油(ごまあぶら) sesame oil

コマーシャル *a commercial*

コマーシャルソング song used in a commercial

こまかい 細(こま)かい *1. very small, fine (describing a large number of things or something consisting of a large number of pieces)*

細(こま)かい字(じ)を書(か)きますね。
Your writing is very small, isn't it?
この海岸(かいがん)は砂(すな)がとても細(こま)かいです。
The sand on this beach is very fine.
たまねぎを細(こま)かく刻(きざ)みなさい。
Chop the onions fine.
細(こま)かいお金(かね) (small) change *[→ 小銭(こぜに)]*

2. minor, trivial [→ 些細(ささい)な]

細(こま)かい事(こと)でけんかをしないで。
Don't quarrel over trivial things.
細(こま)かい誤(あやま)り minor error

3. detailed, minute

細(こま)かい分析(ぶんせき) detailed analysis
お金(かね)に細(こま)かい stingy; frugal

ごまかす *1. to deceive [→ 騙(だま)す]*

泣(な)いて私(わたし)をごまかさないでください。
Don't deceive me by crying.

2. to cheat out of; to embezzle

支配人(しはいにん)は私(わたし)たちの取(と)り分(ぶん)をごまかしたよ。
The manager cheated us out of our share!

3. to lie about, to misrepresent

年(とし)をごまかす *to lie about one's age*

4. to gloss over, to cover up

過失(かしつ)をごまかす to cover up an error

こまらせる 困(こま)らせる *to annoy, to bother (This word is the regular causative form of 困(こま)る.)*

変(へん)な質問(しつもん)で私(わたし)を困(こま)らせないでください。
Please don't bother me with strange questions.
弟(おとうと)はいたずらをしてよく母(はは)を困(こま)らせるよ。
My younger brother plays pranks and often annoys my mother!

こまる 困(こま)る *to get into difficulty, to get into a quandary, to become troubled*

宿題(しゅくだい)が終(お)わらなくて困(こま)っているよ。
I'm having trouble because I can't finish my homework!
奥田(おくだ)さんは切符(きっぷ)を無(な)くして困(こま)っています。
Mr. Okuda has lost his ticket and is in a quandary.
お金(かね)に困(こま)る to become hard up for money

ごみ *1. trash, garbage; litter*

ごみを捨(す)てる to throw out trash; to litter

2. [[→ 塵(ちり)]] dust; bits of trash

ごみ箱(ばこ) trash can, garbage can

こみち 小道(こみち) *path, lane*

コミック *1. comic (strip), comic (book) [→ 漫画(まんが)]*

2. ～な comical [→ 喜劇的(きげきてき)な (s.v. 喜劇(きげき))]

コミッショナー *commissioner*

コミュニケーション *communication*

こむ 込(こ)む *to become crowded, to become congested*

バスは学生(がくせい)で込(こ)んでいました。
The bus was crowded with students.
道路(どうろ)が込(こ)んでいて遅(おく)れました。
The road was congested, so we were late.

ゴム *rubber*

ゴムの木(き) rubber tree
消(け)しゴム (rubber) eraser
輪(わ)ゴム rubber band

こむぎ 小麦 *wheat*
小麦粉 wheat flour

こめ 米 *(uncooked) rice [↔ ご飯]*
この民族は米を主食にしています。
This ethnic group makes rice their staple food.

こめかみ *temple (i.e., a part of the head)*

コメディー *comedy [→ 喜劇]*

コメディアン *comedian*

ごめん ご免 〜だ *to be something one wants no part of*
海外旅行はご免だよ。
I want no part of traveling abroad!

ごめんください ご免ください *1. Excuse me, is anyone here? (Used upon entering a store or home when no one is in sight.)*
2. Good-by (on the telephone)

ごめんなさい ご免なさい *[[→ すみません]] I'm sorry; Excuse me*
遅れてごめんなさい。
I'm sorry for being late.

こもじ 小文字 *lower-case letter, small letter [↔ 大文字]*

こもり 子守 *1. childcare*
2. person doing childcare
子守歌 lullaby

こもん 顧問 *adviser*

こや 小屋 *hut, cabin*
豚小屋 (US) pigpen, pigsty
犬小屋 doghouse
丸太小屋 log cabin
物置小屋 storage shed
鳥小屋 chicken coop
山小屋 mountain hut

こゆう 固有 〜の *peculiar (to), characteristic*
固有名詞 proper noun

こゆび 小指 *1. little finger*
2. little toe

ごよう ご用【HON. for 用】 *business, matter to attend to*
何かご用ですか。
Is there something I can do for you? (Literally: Is it some kind of business?)

こよみ 暦 *calendar [→ カレンダー]*
暦の上で according to the calendar

こらえる 怺える, 堪える *1. to endure, to bear [→ 我慢する]*
2. to suppress, to control, to refrain from (an expression of one's emotions)
私たちは笑いたいのをこらえました。
We suppressed the urge to laugh.
涙をこらえる to suppress one's tears
怒りをこらえる to control one's anger

ごらく 娯楽 *amusement, entertainment*
娯楽番組 entertainment program
娯楽施設 amusement facilities

コラム *short commentary column (in a newspaper, etc.)*

ごらん ご覧 〜になる【HON. for 見る】
ごらんください。
Please look.

こりつ 孤立 *isolation*
孤立する to become isolated

ごりょうしん ご両親【HON. for 両親】 *parents*

ゴリラ *gorilla*

こりる 懲りる *to learn one's lesson (from a bad experience)*
この失敗で弟も懲りるでしょう。
My younger brother also will probably learn his lesson from this failure.

ごりん 五輪 *the Olympics [→ オリンピック]*

こる 凝る *1. to become ardent, to become absorbed [→ 熱中する]*

息子はスキーに凝っています。
My son is ardent about skiing.

2. to become elaborate

このホテルは凝っていますね。
This hotel is elaborate, isn't it?

3. to get stiff

(The subject is a part of the body in which the muscles become stiff.)

肩が凝って、首が回らないよ。
My shoulders got stiff and my neck won't turn!

コルク *cork*

ゴルフ *golf*

ゴルフ場 golf course

これ *this (one) [↔ それ; あれ]*

これをください。
Please give me this.

これは私の眼鏡です。
These are my glasses.

これから after this, from this point, in the future, from now on *[→ 今後]*

試合はこれから始まります。
The game is going to start from this point.

これほど to this extent, this much *[→ こんなに]*

これまで until now, so far *[→ 今まで]*

これまではすべてうまく行っています。
So far, it's all going well.

これら these (ones)

コレクション *1. collection (of items as a hobby)*

友達の切手のコレクションはすばらしい。
My friend's collection of stamps is wonderful.

2. collection (of a high-fashion clothing designer)

ころ 頃 *[[→ 時2.]] time, occasion; (time) when*

そろそろ勉強を始めてもいいころですよ。
It's almost time for you to start studying!

幼いころはバスの運転手になりたかった。
When I was young I wanted to become a bus driver.

—ごろ *about (Added to bases referring to specific times.)*

洋子ちゃんは5時ごろに帰って来るよ。
Yoko will come home around five.

来年の今ごろまた来ます。
I'll come again about this time next year.

ゴロ *grounder (in baseball)*

ゴロを打つ to hit a grounder

ころがる 転がる *1. to roll (intransitive)*

りんごが袋から転がって出ました。
An apple rolled out of the bag.

2. to fall over, to fall down (The subject is a person.) [→ 転ぶ]

石につまずいて転がりました。
I tripped on a stone and fell down.

3. to lie down [→ 横たわる]

ころす 殺す *1. to kill*

ねずみを殺すつもりですか。
Do you intend to kill the mouse?

2. to suppress, to stifle (one's own breathing, feelings, etc.)

息を殺す to suppress one's breathing

怒りを殺す to suppress one's anger

あくびを殺す to stifle a yawn

3. to let go to waste, to make poor use of

才能を殺す to make poor use of talent

コロッケ *croquette*

ころぶ 転ぶ *to fall over, to fall down (The subject is a person.)*

凍った道で滑って転んでしまったよ。
I slipped and fell down on the frozen road!

こわい 怖い (This adjective is used to describe both the people who are afraid and what they are afraid of. The word is not used to describe the fears of a third person; see 怖がる.)

1. frightening, scary [→ 恐ろしい]
毎晩怖い夢を見るよ。
Every night I have frightening dreams!
2. afraid, frightened
私も怖いです。
I'm afraid too.

こわがる 怖がる *to become afraid of, to get scared of*
(Used instead of 怖い when the subject is a third person.)
子供たちは雷を怖がります。
The children get scared of thunder.
妹はそこへ行くのを怖がっています。
My younger sister is afraid of going there.

こわす 壊す *1. to break, to damage*
その機械を壊してしまいました。
I broke that machine.
お皿を粉々に壊したよ。
I broke the plate into smithereens!
体を壊す to damage one's health
おなかを壊す to get an upset stomach
計画を壊す to frustrate a plan
2. to tear down, to demolish
古い建物を壊したほうがいいです。
It would be better to tear down the old building.

こわれる 壊れる *to break, to get damaged*
そのいすはすぐ壊れるでしょう。
That chair will probably break right away.
この時計は壊れているよ。
This watch is broken!

こん 紺 *dark blue, navy blue*

こんかい 今回 *1. this time [→ 今度 1.]*
2. this coming time, next time [→ 今度 2.]

こんき 根気 *perseverance*
英語の勉強は根気が要ります。
For the study of English one needs perseverance.
根気よく with perseverance

コンクール *contest (in which relative excellence is judged) [→ コンテスト]*
写真コンクール photo contest

コンクリート *concrete*
これはコンクリートの建物です。
This is a concrete building.
鉄筋コンクリート steel-reinforced concrete

こんげつ 今月 *this month*
今月の８日に運動会があります。
There is a field day on the eighth of this month.
今川さんは今月帰ってきます。
Ms. Imagawa will come home this month.

こんご 今後 *after this, from now on, in the future [→ これから]*
今後の予定は何ですか。
What are your plans after this?
今後は宿題を忘れません。
From now on I won't forget my homework.

こんごう 混合 *mixing, blending*
混合する to mix, to blend (transitive or intransitive)
混合物 a mixture
混合ダブルス mixed doubles

コンサート *concert [→ 音楽会 (s.v. 音楽)]*
あしたのコンサートに行こうよ。
Let's go to tomorrow's concert!

こんざつ 混雑 *1. crowding, congestion*
混雑する to become crowded, to become congested [→ 込む]
店は客で混雑していました。
The store was crowded with customers.
2. confusion, disorder [→ 混乱]
混雑する to be thrown into disorder, to become confused

コンサルタント *consultant*

こんしゅう 今週 *this week*
今週の金曜日は休みです。
Friday of this week is a day off.
正子さんは今週ずっと欠席しています。
Masako has been absent all this week.

こんじょう 根性 *1. nature, inborn disposition*
2. willpower, tenacity, spirit
あの人は根性があるね。
That person has tenacity, doesn't she?

コンセント *(electrical) outlet, (electrical) socket*
そのエアコンのプラグをコンセントに差し込んでください。
Please push that air conditioner plug into the outlet.

コンソメ *consomme*

コンタクトレンズ *contact lens*
あの選手はコンタクトレンズをしている。
That player wears contact lenses.

こんだて 献立 *menu [→ メニュー]*

コンチェルト *concerto [→ 協奏曲]*

こんちゅう 昆虫 *insect*
昆虫学 entomology
昆虫採集 insect collecting

コンディション *condition, state of fitness*
コンディションがいい〔悪い〕to be in good〔bad〕condition

コンテスト *contest (in which relative excellence is judged) [→ コンクール]*
姉はそのコンテストで優勝しました。
My older sister was first in that contest.
スピーチコンテスト speech contest

こんど 今度 *1. this time [→ 今回 1.]*
今度はうまくいきました。
This time it went well.
今度は君が歌う番だよ。
This time it's your turn to sing!
2. next time, this coming time [→ 今回2.]
今度はいつ来るのですか。
When are you next coming?
今度の日曜日は遊園地に行きます。
This coming Sunday we're going to go to theme park.
3. sometime soon [→ そのうち]
今度また釣りに行きましょう。
Let's go fishing again sometime soon.

ゴンドラ *1. gondola ((boat))*
2. gondola (on a balloon, aerial cableway, etc.)

コントロール *control, regulating*
そのピッチャーはコントロールがいい。
That pitcher's control is good.
コントロールする to control, to regulate

こんな *this kind of [↔ そんな; あんな]*
こんな天気のいい日に家にいるのはもったいないね。
It's a waste to stay in the house on such a beautiful day, isn't it?
単語はこんなふうに書きなさい。
Write the words this way.
こんなに to this extent, this much
こんなに雪が降るとは思いませんでした。
I didn't think it would snow this much.
こんなに遅くまで何を勉強しているの？
What are you studying until so late?

こんなん 困難 *difficulty, hardship*
多くの困難にあいました。
I met with many difficulties.
あらゆる困難に耐えるつもりです。
I intend to bear every hardship.
困難な difficult, hard *[→ 難しい]*
逆立ちで歩くのは困難なことです。
Walking on your hands is a difficult thing.

こんにち 今日 *today, nowadays*
今日ではだれもそんなことは信じません。
Nowadays nobody believes such things.
今日の日本 Japan today

こんにちは *Good day, Hello*

コンパクトディスク *compact disc*

コンパス *1. compass ((drawing tool))*

敏子さんはコンパスで円をかいています。
Toshiko is drawing a circle with a compass.

2. (ship) compass

3. length of one's stride; length of one's legs

コンパスが長い one's stride is long; one's legs are long

コンパスが短い one's stride is short; one's legs are short

こんばん 今晩 *this evening, tonight [→ 今夜]*

試合は今晩７時に始まります。
The game starts at 7:00 this evening.

こんばんは *Good evening, Hello*

コンビ *1. combination, pair, duo (of people in some activity)*

コンビを組む to form a pair, to become partners

2. article of clothing with a combination of different colors or materials

コンビーフ *corned beef*

コンビニエンスストア *convenience store*

コンピューター *computer*

データをコンピューターに入力しなさい。
Please put the data into the computer.

コンプレックス *(psychological) complex*

こんぽん 根本 *basis, foundation, essence*

根本的な basic, fundamental, essential

その計画を根本的に変更しました。
I changed that plan fundamentally.

コンマ *comma*

こんや 今夜 *tonight, this evening [→ 今晩]*

今夜は月がとてもきれいです。
The moon is very beautiful tonight.

こんやく 婚約 *engagement (to be married)*

婚約する to get engaged

次郎さんと由美さんは婚約しています。
Jiro and Yumi are engaged.

婚約者 fiance, fiancee

婚約指輪 engagement ring *[→ エンゲージリング]*

こんらん 混乱 *confusion, disorder, chaos*

混乱する to be thrown into disorder, to become chaotic

混乱状態 state of confusion, chaotic state

さ 差 *difference, disparity, gap* [→ 違い]

第１位と第２位との差は大きいです。
The difference between the first place and second place is great.

さあ *1. all right now, come on (an interjection expressing encouragement or urging)*

さあ、出かけよう。
All right now, let's go out.

さあ、みんな急いで。校庭に集合しよう。
Come on, hurry everybody. Assemble in the schoolyard!

2. well, gee (an interjection expressing uncertainty)

さあ、知りません。
Gee, I don't know.

さあ、たぶんそれはピカソでしょう。
Well, that's probably a Picasso.

サーカス *circus*

サーキット *1. (electrical) circuit* [→ 回路]

2. auto racing track

サークル *1. circle, ring* [→ 輪]

2. circle, club, group with a common interest

サーチライト *searchlight*

サード *1. third base* [→ 三塁] *(in baseball)*
2. third baseman [→ 三塁手 (s.v. 三塁)] *(in baseball)*

サービス *1. service (to customers)*
この店はサービスがいいです。
This store's service is good.
2. free gift , premium (accompanying something one buys) [→ お負け1.]
サービス料 service charge

サーブ *serve (in tennis, volleyball, etc.)*
サーブする to serve

サーファー *surfer*

サーフィン *surfing*
サーフィンをする to surf

サーフボード *surfboard*

さい *rhinoceros*

―さい ―歳 *(counter for years of age; see appendix 2)*
3歳の女の子もいました。
There was also a three-year-old girl.
何歳ですか。
How old are you?
弟は妹より2歳年下です。
My younger brother is two years younger than my younger sister.

さいあく 最悪 ～の *worst, worst possible* [↔ 最上の1.]
最悪の事態が生じました。
The worst possible situation arose.
最悪の場合には、旅行は中止になります。
In the worst possible case, the trip will be called off.

ざいあく 罪悪 [[→ 罪]] *sin; crime*
罪悪感 sense of guilt

サイエンス *science* [→ 科学]

さいかい 再開 *resumption, beginning again*
再開する to resume, to begin again (transitive or intransitive)

ざいかい 財界 *the financial world, financial circles*

さいがい 災害 *disaster, calamity*

ざいがく 在学 *being enrolled in school*
在学する to become enrolled in school
横溝君は今年は在学しています。
Yokomizo is enrolled in school this year.
在学中の enrolled-in-school
在学証明書 school enrollment certificate

さいきん 細菌 *bacteria, microbe*

さいきん 最近 *recently, lately* [→ このごろ]
最近5年間にこんなインフレはなかった。
There hasn't been this kind of inflation in the last five years.
最近山中さんに会いましたか。
Have you seen Ms. Yamanaka lately?
父は最近まで大阪にいました。
My father was in Osaka until recently.
最近の the latest, recent
最近のニュースを聞きましたか。
Have you heard the latest news?
最近の若者は礼儀正しくないです。
Young people these days are not polite. (Literally: Recent young people are not polite)

さいく 細工 *1. craftsmanship, handicrafting*
2. handcrafted item

サイクリング *cycling, bicycle ride*
あしたサイクリングに行こうよ。
Let's go cycling tomorrow!

サイクル *number of cycles per second*
東京と大阪は電気のサイクルが違います。
The number of cycles per second of electricity differs in Tokyo and Osaka.
―サイクル (counter for cycles per second; see Appendix 2)

さいけん 債券 *bond, debenture*

さいご 最後 *the end, the last* [↔ 最初]

この物語の最後はどうなりますか。
How does the end of this story turn out?

最後の final, last

きょうは1年の最後の日です。
Today is the last day of the year.

最後に at the end, ultimately; last

何回もやってみて、最後に成功しました。
I tried doing it again and again, and ultimately succeeded.

ざいこ 在庫 *stock (of unsold goods)*

さいこう 最高 [[↔ 最低]] *1. maximum, highest point*

最高の highest, maximum

最高に達する to reach the maximum

2. ～の best [→ 最上の1.] [↔ 最悪の]

これは今までに見た最高の映画です。
This is the best film I've seen up to now.

最高気温 highest temperature

最高記録 best record

最高裁判所 the Supreme Court

最高点 highest mark, highest score

さいころ 骰子 *dice*

ざいさん 財産 *fortune, estate, accumulated wealth*

その企業家はばく大な財産を築きました。
That industrialist built up a large fortune.

さいじつ 祭日 *1. national holiday* [→ 祝日]

2. festival day

さいしゅう 採集 *collecting, gathering*

採集する to collect, to gather

さいしゅう 最終 ～の *last, final* [→ 最後の]

最終電車 last train

最終回 last inning; last round

最終決定 final decision

さいしょ 最初 *beginning* [↔ 最後]

映画は最初から最後までおもしろかった。
The movie was interesting from beginning to end.

最初の first, initial

ワシントンはアメリカの最初の大統領だ。
Washington was the first President of the United States.

最初に at the beginning; first

アムンゼンは最初に南極点に到達した人でした。
Amundsen was the person who reached the South Pole first.

最初に飛行機で沖縄に行きます。
First I will go to Okinawa by plane.

最初は at first, initially

最初は僕たちのチームがリードしていた。
At first our team was leading.

さいしょう 最小 ～の *smallest, minimum* [↔ 最大の]

最小限 a minimum

最小量 minimum quantity

さいじょう 最上 ～の *1. best, finest, supreme* [↔ 最悪の]

最上の品物 the finest goods

最上の幸福 supreme happiness

2. top, uppermost

最上階 top floor

さいしん 最新 ～の *latest, newest, up-to-date*

最新のニュース the latest news

最新流行 the latest fashion

サイズ *(clothing) size*

靴のサイズはいくつですか。
What is your shoe size?

これは私のサイズに合いません。
This isn't my size. (Literally: This doesn't match my size.)

さいせい 再生 *1. resuscitation; rebirth, reincarnation*

再生する [[→ 生き返る]] *to be resuscitated; to be reborn*

2. regeneration (of a part of an organism)

再生する to regenerate (intransitive)

このとかげのしっぽは再生しました。
This lizard's tail regenerated.

3. reclamation, recycling

再生する to reclaim, to recycle

4. playback (of a recording)

再生する to play back

ざいせい 財政 *government finances*

さいぜん 最善 *1. 〜の best, most beneficial*

最善の方法 the best method

2. one's best, one's utmost

最善を尽くす to do one's best

さいそく 催促 *pressing, demand*

催促する to press for, to demand

友達は僕に返事を催促しました。
My friend pressed me for an answer.

サイダー *clear soda pop*

さいだい 最大 〜の *largest, maximum* [↔ 最小の]

最大限 a maximum

日本最大の largest in Japan

世界最大の largest in the world

琵琶湖は日本最大の湖です。
Lake Biwa is the largest lake in Japan.

さいちゅう 最中 *midst, middle (of doing something)*

明子さんは今勉強の最中です。
Akiko is in the middle of studying now.

由美は映画を見ている最中に泣き出した。
Yumi began to cry in the middle of watching the movie.

さいてい 最低 [↔ 最高] *1. minimum, lowest point*

給料は最低で50万円です。
The salary is 500,000 yen at minimum.

最低の lowest, minimum

クラスで最低の点をとってしまった。
I got the lowest mark in the class.

2. 〜の worst [→ 最悪の]

私の知る限り、これは最低の小説です。
As for as I know, this is the worst novel.

最低気温 lowest temperature

さいてん 採点 *marking, grading, scoring*

採点する to mark, to grade, to score

先生はまだ答案を採点しています。
The teacher is still grading the examination papers.

サイド *1.* [[→ 横1.]] *side (part); the area beside*

2. side, standpoint

サイドボード sideboard

サイドカー sidecar

サイドスロー sidearm throw

消費者サイド the consumer side

さいなん 災難 *misfortune; calamity, disaster* [→ 災害]

さいのう 才能 *talent, ability*

息子さんには音楽の才能があります。
Your son has musical talent.

隠れた才能 hidden talent

才能のある人 talented person

さいばい 栽培 *growing, cultivation*

栽培する to grow, to cultivate

さいばん 裁判 *(legal) trial*

裁判になる to come to trial, to go to court

裁判を受ける to stand trial

裁判官 judge, magistrate [→ 判事]

裁判所 court; courthouse

地方裁判所 district court

簡易裁判所 summary court

家庭裁判所 family court

高等裁判所 high court
最高裁判所 the Supreme Court

さいふ 財布 *wallet*

さいほう 裁縫 *sewing, needlework*
裁縫する to sew, to do needlework
裁縫道具 sewing implements

さいぼう 細胞 *(organism) cell*
細胞分裂 cell division

さいむ 債務 *debt, liability, repayment obligation*

ざいもく 材木 *(US) lumber, (UK) timber* [→ 木材]

さいよう 採用 *1. adoption, acceptance for use*
採用する to adopt, to accept for use
来年から新しい教科書を採用する予定だ。
From next year they're planning to adopt new textbooks.
この提案が採用されました。
This proposal was adopted.
2. hiring, employment
採用する to hire, to employ
その会社は今年一人だけ採用しました。
That company hired only one person this year.
採用試験 employment examination

ざいりょう 材料 *materials; ingredient*
みそ汁の材料はありますか。
Do you have the ingredients for miso soup?
建築材料 building materials

ザイル *mountain-climbing rope*

サイレン *siren*

サイロ *silo*

さいわい 幸い *1.* [[→ 幸せ]] *happiness; good fortune*
幸いな happy; fortunate
お役に立てば幸いです。
I hope I can be of some help. (Literally: If I can be of help to you, I will be happy.)
2. (〜に) *fortunately*
幸い試験に合格しました。
Fortunately, I passed the examination.

サイン *1. signature* [→ 署名]; *autograph*
サインする to sign
ここに名前をサインしてください。
Please sign your name here.
サインしていただけませんか。
May I have you sign?
2. sign, signal [→ 合図]
捕手は投手にサインを送りました。
The catcher gave a sign to the pitcher.
サイン帳 autograph album
サインペン felt-tip pen; roller-ball pen

サウスポー *a southpaw*

さえ (This word can be used as a noun-following particle or following a gerund (-て form).)
1. even (indicating that what precedes is extreme) (Often followed by も *with no difference in meaning.)*
この子は名前さえ書けません。
This child cannot even write his name.
2. (if) just (in combination with a ーば *conditional)*
これさえ覚えれば、大丈夫ですよ。
If you memorize just this, you'll be fine!

さえぎる 遮る *{5} to interrupt, to obstruct*
お話を遮ってすみません。
I'm sorry to interrupt what you're saying.
このカーテンは光を遮っています。
These curtains are obstructing the light.

さえる 冴える *1. to be clear; to be bright*
さえた頭 clear head
さえた色 bright color
気分がさえない to feel depressed
2. to become honed, to become mature (when the subject is a skill)

典子さんのピアノの腕は冴えてきました。
Noriko's piano skills have matured.

さお 竿 *pole, rod*

釣り竿 fishing pole, fishing rod

さか 坂 *slope, sloping path*

洋子さんの家はこの坂の上にあるね。
Yoko's house is at the top of this slope, isn't it?

急〔緩やか〕な坂 steep〔gentle〕slope

坂を上る〔下る〕to go up〔down〕a slope

下り坂 downward slope, descent

上り坂 upward slope, ascent

さかい 境 *border, boundary*

この公園は東京と埼玉の境にあります。
This park is on the boundary between Tokyo and Saitama.

さかえる 栄える *to prosper, to flourish, to thrive* [→ 繁栄する]

さかさま 逆様 ～の *1. upside down, inverted*

地図をさかさまに見ているよ。
You're looking at the map upside down!

2. backwards, reversed

順序を逆様にする to reverse the order

さがす 捜す, 探す *to look for, to search for*

何をさがしているんですか。
What are you looking for?

さかだち 逆立ち *handstand; headstand*

逆立ちする to do a handstand; to do a headstand

さかな 魚 *fish*

この湖には魚がたくさんいるよ。
There are a lot of fish in this lake!

私は肉より魚のほうが好きです。
I like fish better than meat.

魚を釣る to catch a fish (with hook and line)

魚釣り fishing (with hook and line)

魚屋 fish shop; fish dealer

さかのぼる 遡る *1. to go upstream*

川をさかのぼる to go up a river

2. to go back, to date back (to a time in the past) ; to think back (to a time in the past)

その習慣は17世紀にさかのぼります。
That custom dates back to the 17th century.

さからう 逆らう *1. to act against, to disobey*

親に逆らう to disobey one's parents

2. to move against (a flow or current of some kind)

球は風に逆らって席に飛び込みました。
The ball moved against the wind and flew into the seats.

さがる 下がる *1. to hang down, to be suspended*

天井からランプがたくさん下がっている。
Many lamps are hanging from the ceiling.

2. to go down, to become lower [↔ 上がる1.]

熱がなかなか下がらないね。
The fever just won't go down, will it.

英語の成績が下がってしまいました。
My English grades went down.

3. to step back, to move backward [→ 退く1.]

生徒たちは一斉に後ろへ下がりました。
The students all stepped back together.

さかん 盛ん ～な *vigorous, energetic; thriving; popular*

この町では商業が盛んです。
Business is thriving in this town.

キューバでは野球が盛んですね。
In Cuba baseball is popular, isn't it?

盛んな拍手 thunderous applause

盛んに燃える to burn furiously

さき 先 *1. end, point, tip*

ピッチャーは人さし指の先をけがした。
The pitcher injured the tip of his forefinger.

ひもの先 the end of a rope

鉛筆の先 the point of a pencil

2. the future, later in time [→ 将来]

先の事は心配しないで。

Don't worry about the future. (Literally: Don't worry about future things.)

ー先 from now (Added to bases denoting time periods.)

この学校も５年先にそうなるでしょう。

This school will probably become like that too five years from now.

3. the area ahead; the area beyond

郵便局はスーパーの先にあります。

The post office is beyond the supermarket.

先に立つ to take the lead

ー先 ahead (Added to bases denoting distances.)

小学校は50メートル先です。

The elementary school is 50 meters ahead.

4. ～に beforehand, first; ahead, earlier

どうぞお先に。

Please go ahead of me. (Literally: Please, ahead.)

お先に失礼します。

Excuse me for leaving ahead of you. (Literally: I will be rude earlier.)

先に宿題をやらなければならないよ。

First I have to do my homework!

先程【FORMAL for さっき】a short while ago

さぎ 詐欺 *swindle, fraud*

詐欺にかかる to be swindled

詐欺師 swindler

サキソフォン *saxophone*

さぎょう 作業 *work, working* [→ 仕事]

作業する to work

作業場 workshop

作業中の at-work, working

作業服 work clothes

さく 柵 *fence*

さく 咲く *to bloom, to blossom*

春には花がたくさん咲きます。

In the spring many flowers bloom.

りんごの木にもうすぐ花が咲くでしょう。

The blossoms will probably also bloom on the apple trees soon.

桜が満開に咲いているよ。

The cherry blossoms are in full bloom!

さく 裂く *(transitive) to tear, to rip; to split*

モデルはその写真をずたずたに裂いたよ。

The model tore that photograph to pieces!

さく 割く *to spare, to share*

時間を割く to spare some time

さくいん 索引 *index (of a book, etc.)*

索引カード index card

さくし 作詞 *writing the words to a song, writing lyrics* [↔ 作曲]

だれがこの歌の作詞をしましたか。

Who wrote the words to this song?

作詞する to write the words to a song

作詞家 lyricist

さくじつ 昨日 *yesterday* [→ 昨日]

さくしゃ 作者 *author, writer* [→ 著者]

さくねん 昨年 *last year* [→ 去年]

さくばん 昨晩 *last night* [→ 昨夜]

さくひん 作品 *a work, opus*

文学作品 a literary work

さくぶん 作文 *1. (school) composition, (school) essay*

家族について作文を書きます。

I will write a composition about my family.

2. writing compositions

英作文 English composition

さくもつ 作物 *crops*

作物を育てる to raise crops

さくや 昨夜 *last night*

父は昨夜10時に帰って来ました。
My father came home at 10:00 last night.

さくら 桜 1. *cherry blossom*
桜は今満開です。
The cherry blossoms are now in full bloom.
2. cherry tree
さくらんぼう cherry ((fruit))

さぐる 探る *1. to feel around in, to grope around in*
ポケットを探って、かぎを取り出した。
I felt around in my pocket and took out the key.
2. to spy on, to investigate secretly
兵隊は敵の様子を探ってきました。
The soldier spied on the enemy's situation and came back.
3. to try to find out, to try to discover
原因を探る to try to find out the cause

ざくろ *pomegranate*

さけ 鮭 *salmon*

さけ 酒 *1. sake, Japanese rice wine* [→ 日本酒 (s.v. 日本)]
2. alcoholic beverages, liquor
酒を飲む to drink alcohol

さけぶ 叫ぶ *to shout, to yell* [↔ 囁く]
遭難者は「助けて！」と叫びました。
The accident victim shouted, "Help!"

さける 裂ける *(intransitive) to tear, to rip; to split, to crack*
このカーテンはすぐ裂けるね。
This curtain tears easily, doesn't it?

さける 避ける *to avoid, to keep away from*
松村さんは私に会うのを避けているよ。
Mr. Matsumura is avoiding me!
危険は避ける to avoid danger

さげる 下げる *1. to lower, to bring down*
ラジオの音量を下げてください。
Please turn down the volume on the radio.
Aに頭を下げる to bow to A
2. to hang, to suspend [→ 吊るす]
天井から風鈴を下げましょう。
Let's hang a wind-chime from the ceiling.

ささ 笹 *bamboo grass*

ささい 〜な *trivial, petty*

さざえ 栄螺 *turbo ((shellfish))*

ささえる 支える *to support*
困ったときに希望が支えてくれました。
Hope supported me when I was in trouble.
つえで体を支える to support oneself with a cane

ささげる 捧げる *to offer up, to devote, to dedicate*
キュリー夫人は科学に一生をささげた。
Madame Curie devoted her life to science.
祈りをささげる to offer a prayer

さざなみ さざ波 *ripple, small wave*

ささやく 囁く *to whisper* [↔ 叫ぶ]
Aの耳もとでささやく to whisper in A's ear

さざんか 山茶花 *sasanqua ((flower))*

さじ 匙 *spoon* [→ スプーン]
小匙 teaspoon
大匙 tablespoon

さしあげる 差し上げる【HUM. for 上げる】*to give*

さしえ 挿絵 *illustration (in a book, newspaper, etc.)*

ざしき 座敷 *room with a tatami (mat) floor*

さしこむ 差し込む *1. to thrust into, to insert*
そのかぎを錠に差し込んでください。
Please insert that key into the lock.
2. to shine into (intransitive)
夕日が台所に差し込みます。
The evening sun shines into the kitchen.

さしず 指図 *(verbal) instructions, (verbal) directions; (verbal) orders* [→ 命令]

みんなが主将の指図に従いました。
Everyone followed the captain's instructions.

あいつの指図は受けないよ。
I won't take that guy's orders!

指図する to direct; to give orders to

さしだしにん 差し出し人 *sender (of a letter, etc.)*

さしだす 差し出す *1. to hold out, to present*

明さんは私に手を差し出しました。
Akira held out his hand to me.

2. to hand in, to submit [→ 提出する]

願書を差し出す to submit an application

さしみ 刺身 *sashimi, sliced raw fish*

さす 刺す *1. to prick, to stick, to stab*

母は針で指を刺しました。
My mother pricked her finger with a needle.

2. to bite, to sting (when the subject is an insect, etc.) (Ordinarily used in the passive.)

私たちはひどく蚊に刺されたよ。
We were badly bitten by mosquitoes!

さす 指す *1. to point at, to point to*

ガイドさんは丘の上のお城を指しました。
The guide pointed to a castle on the hill.

2. to designate, to call on

田島先生はよく今井君を指すね。
Ms. Tajima often calls on Imai, doesn't she?

Aの名を指す to call A's name

さす 差す *1. to pour, to let drip, to apply*

目薬を差す to apply eye drops

機械に油を差す to oil a machine

2. (intransitive) to shine into; to shine on

教室に日が差しています。
The sun is shining into the classroom.

3. 傘を〜 *to put an umbrella over one's head*

さすが *1. (〜に) just as one would expect, exactly as one has heard, indeed* [→ やはり]

さすが高橋さんは上手です。
Just as one would expect, Ms. Takahashi is skillful.

2. 〜の *highly-reputed (Used only in the following pattern.)*

さすがのAも even (the highly-reputed) A

さすがの英雄も敗れました。
Even the hero was defeated.

サスペンス *suspense*

ざせき 座席 *seat, place to sit* [→ 席]

座席指定券 reserved-seat ticket

させつ 左折 *left turn* [↔ 右折]

左折する to turn left

させる *(This word is simply the causative form of する.) to make do, to have do; to let do*

東先生は1年生に体育館の掃除をさせた。
Mr. Azuma had the first-year students clean the gymnasium.

ざぜん 座禅 *sitting in Zen meditation*

座禅を組む to sit in Zen meditation

さそう 誘う *1. to invite*

洋子さんがコンサートに誘ってくれた。
Yoko invited me to a concert.

2. to induce, to provoke (a person's response)

涙を誘う to provoke tears

同情を誘う to induce sympathy

さそり 蠍 *scorpion*

ざだんかい 座談会 *round-table discussion, symposium*

さつ 札 *(US) (dollar) bill, (UK) bank note, note*

札入れ wallet, billfold

札束 roll of bills

千円札 thousand-yen bill

—さつ —冊 *(counter for books, magazines, etc.; see Appendix 2)*

その本が2冊必要です。

I need two copies of that book.
兄は本を300冊ぐらい持っているよ。
My older brother has about 300 books!

ざつ 雑 ～な *sloppily done*

さつえい 撮影 *photographing, picture-taking; filming, shooting*
撮影する to take a picture of, to photograph; to film, to shoot
この映画はパリで撮影しましょう。
Let's shoot this movie in Paris.
「撮影禁止」 (on a sign)
No Photographs
撮影所 movie studio

ざつおん 雑音 *noise, static*

さっか 作家 *writer, novelist* [→ 小説家 (s.v. 小説)]

サッカー *(US) soccer, (UK) football*

さっかく 錯覚 *illusion; hallucination*

さっき *a little while ago*
さっき次郎から電話があったよ。
There was a phone call from Jiro a little while ago!

さっきょく 作曲 *composing music* [↔ 作詞]
作曲する to compose music, to write music
作曲家 composer

ざっくばらん 【COL.】～な *frank, open, candid*

さっさと *quickly, promptly*
岡さんはさっさと歩きますね。
Ms. Oka walks quickly, doesn't she?
雨がやんだから、さっさと帰りなさい。
It's stopped raining, so hurry home.

サッシ *(window) sash*

ざっし 雑誌 *magazine, periodical*
この雑誌を取っています。
I subscribe to this magazine.

さつじん 殺人 *murder*
殺人事件 a murder

ざっそう 雑草 *weed*
雑草を取る to pull weeds

さっそく 早速 *at once, right away*
早速悦子さんに会いに行こう。
Let's go to see Etsuko at once.
早速の prompt, immediate

ざつだん 雑談 *small talk, chat*
雑談する to chat

さっちゅうざい 殺虫剤 *insecticide*

ざっと *1. cursorily, briefly, roughly*
課長は計画をざっと説明しました。
The section chief roughly explained the plan.
建築家はざっと家の写生をしました。
The architect roughly sketched the house.
2. approximately, about [→ およそ]
この大学にはざっと2万人の学生がいる。
This college has about 20,000 students.

さっとう 殺到 ～する *to rush, to stampede, to throng, to flood*
その新しい辞書に注文が殺到しています。
Orders for that new dictionary are pouring in.
子供たちは店に殺到しました。
The children rushed into the store.

さっぱり *1.* ～する *to become refreshed; to become relieved*
シャワーを浴びて、さっぱりしました。
I took a shower and felt refreshed.
2. ～した *frank, open-hearted*
兄はさっぱりした性格です。
My older brother has a frank personality.
3. ～した *plain-tasting*
さっぱりした食べ物のほうがいいです。
Plain food would be better.
4. ～した *neat, tidy*
正子さんはさっぱりした服装をしている。
Masako is neatly dressed.

5. (not) at all (in combination with a negative verb)
その説明はさっぱりわからないよ。
I don't understand that explanation at all!

さつまいも 薩摩芋 *sweet potato*

さて *now, well (an interjection indicating a shift in what is being talked about)*
さて、どうしましょう。
Now, what shall we do?
さて、もう帰る時間になりました。
Well, it's already time to leave.

さと 里 *1. village, hamlet* [→ 村]
2. birthplace, hometown [→ 故郷]
3. original family home (of a wife, adopted child, etc.)

さといも 里芋 *taro*

さとう 砂糖 *sugar*
紅茶には砂糖を何杯入れましょうか。
How many spoonfuls of sugar shall I put in your tea?
角砂糖 sugar cube
氷砂糖 sugar candy, rock candy

さどう 茶道 *the tea ceremony*

さなぎ 蛹 *chrysalis, pupa*

さば 鯖 *mackerel*

さばく 砂漠 *desert*

さび 錆 *rust*
錆びる to rust
錆びた釘 rusty nail

さびしい 寂しい *lonely, lonesome*
東京での独り暮らしは寂しいです。
Living alone in Tokyo is lonely.
寂しい場所 lonely place

サファイア *a sapphire*

サファリ *safari*

ざぶとん 座布団 *floor cushion (for a person to sit on)*

さべつ 差別 *discrimination*
差別する to discriminate against
人種差別 racial discrimination

さほう 作法 *manners, etiquette*

サポーター *athletic supporter*

サボテン *cactus*

サボる【COL.】*1. to cut (class), to skip (school)*
2. to do slowly on purpose (when the direct object refers to one's work)

ーさま ー様【HON. for ーさん】
(Roughly equivalent to Mr./Ms. and neutral with respect to sex and marital status, this suffix can be added to a surname alone, to a given name alone, to a full name, and to many occupational titles.)

さまざま 様々 ～な *various* [→ 色々な]
この問題についてさまざまな意見がある。
There are various opinions about this problem.

さます 冷ます *to cool, to lower in temperature*
スープをちょっと冷ましましょう。
Let's cool the soup a bit.

さます 覚ます 目を～ *to wake up (intransitive)*
ラジオの音で目を覚ましました。
I woke up because of the sound of the radio.

さまたげ 妨げ *obstruction, hindrance, obstacle* [→ 邪魔]
違法駐車が交通の妨げになっています。
Illegal parking is an obstruction to traffic.

さまたげる 妨げる *to disturb, to obstruct, to hinder*
叔父のいびきがみんなの睡眠を妨げた。
Uncle's snoring disturbed everyone's sleep.

さまよう 彷徨う *to wander, to roam*

サミット *summit conference* [→ 首脳会談 (s.v. 会談)]

さむい 寒い *cold (describing a low air temperature or how a person feels when the air temperature is low)* [↔ 暑い]

きょうはとても寒いね。
It's very cold today, isn't it?

セーターを着ないと寒くなるよ。
Unless you wear a sweater, you'll get cold!

さむけ 寒け *chill, sensation of cold*

寒けがする to feel a chill

さむさ 寒さ *cold, coldness (i.e., low air temperature)*

寒さで手がかじかんでいるよ。
My hands are numb from the cold!

さむらい 侍 *samurai* [→ 武士]

さめ 鮫 *shark*

さめる 冷める *to get cool, to get cold*

みそ汁が冷めてしまったよ。
The miso soup has gotten cold!

娘の音楽に対する熱は冷めたらしいです。
It seems that my daughter's passion for music has cooled.

さめる 覚める 目が～ *to wake up (intransitive)*

けさの地震で目が覚めました。
I woke up because of this morning's earthquake.

さもないと *otherwise, or else*

急ぎなさい。さもないと電車に遅れるよ。
Hurry up. Otherwise you'll be late for the train!

さゆう 左右 *the right and the left*

左右をよく見てから道路を渡りなさい。
After looking carefully left and right, cross the street.

さよう 作用 *action, effect*

作用する to produce an effect

副作用 side effect

反作用 reaction

さようなら [☞ さよなら]

さよく 左翼 [[↔ 右翼]] *1. (political) left wing*

2. left field (in baseball) [→ レフト1.]

左翼手 left fielder [→ レフト2.]

さよなら *good-by*

さよならを言う to say good-by

あの人はさよならも言わなかった。
That person didn't even saying good-by.

さら 皿 *dish; plate*

京子はテーブルにお皿を並べた。
Kyoko set the plates on the table.

一皿 (counter for helpings, courses; see Appendix 2)

皿洗い dishwashing

サラダ *salad*

サラダ油 salad oil

野菜サラダ vegetable salad

さらに 更に *additionally, still more, further*

私たちは山頂までさらに1時間歩いた。
We walked a further hour to the summit.

その問題をさらに論議しましょう。
Let's discuss that problem further.

サラブレッド *a thoroughbred*

サラリーマン *white-collar worker, salaried worker*

さる 猿 *monkey; ape*

猿も木から落ちる。(proverb)
Everybody makes mistakes. (Literally: Even monkeys fall from trees.)

さる 去る *1. to leave, to go away from*

金子さんは大阪を去ることに決めた。
Ms. Kaneko decided to leave Osaka.

去る者は日々に疎し。(proverb)
Out of sight, out of mind. (Literally: A person who leaves is more unfamiliar day by day.)

2. to pass, to disappear

あらしが去る a storm passes

痛みが去る pain disappears

3. to elapse, to go by

月日が去る the days and months go by

サロン *1. salon, drawing room*

2. art exhibit room

さわ 沢 *1. marsh*

2. stream in mountain ravine

さわがしい 騒がしい *noisy, boisterous*

公園は騒がしい子供たちでいっぱいです。

The park is full of noisy children!

さわぎ 騒ぎ *1. din, racket, noise*

2. clamor, uproar, commotion

騒ぎを起こす to raise a clamor, to cause a commotion

大騒ぎ great racket; great uproar

さわぐ 騒ぐ *1. to make noise, to make a racket*

図書館の中でそんなに騒いではいけない。

You mustn't make so much noise in the library.

2. to make a fuss, to make a clamor

さわやか 爽やか ～な *fresh, refreshing*

朝の空気はさわやかですね。

The morning air is refreshing, isn't it?

泳いだら気分がさわやかになりました。

I felt refreshed after swimming.

さわる 触る *1. to put one's hand, to place one's hand in contact*

恵子ちゃんは私の腕に触った。

Keiko put her hand on my arm.

2. to touch with one's hand, to feel

赤ちゃんはお母さんの鼻を触っています。

The baby is touching her mother's nose.

3. to touch, to come into contact (when the subject is inanimate)

背中に何かが触ったよ。

Something touched my back!

さん 三 *three (see Appendix 2)*

三月 March

三冠王 triple crown winner

さん 酸 *acid* [↔ アルカリ]

酸性 acidity

ーさん *(Roughly equivalent to Mr./Ms. and neutral with respect to sex and marital status, this suffix can be added to a surname alone, to a given name alone, to a full name, and to many occupational titles.)*

さんいんちほう 山陰地方 *The San'in region of Japan (Tottori, Shimane, and northern Yamaguchi Prefectures)*

さんか 参加 *participation, taking part*

参加する to participate, to take part

たくさんの国がオリンピックに参加する。

Many countries take part in the Olympics.

参加者 participant

さんかく 三角 *triangle*

三角定規 drafting triangle

三角形 triangle, triangular figure

三角洲 river delta

さんかん 参観 *observation visit*

参観する to visit and observe

父母はきのう授業を参観しました。

Parents observed yesterday's classes!

参観日 visiting day

さんぎいん 参議院 *the House of Councilors (the upper house in the Japanese Diet)* [↔ 衆議院]

参議院議員 member of the House of Councilors

さんきゃく 三脚 *tripod*

さんぎょう 産業 *industry*

産業革命 the Industrial Revolution

ざんぎょう 残業 *overtime work*

残業する to work overtime

ざんきん 残金 *balance, remaining money* [→ 残高]

サングラス *sunglasses*

さんご 珊瑚 *coral*

さんご礁 coral reef

さんこう 参考 *reference, source of information*
参考のためにその新聞を送ってください。
Please send me that newspaper for reference.
参考にする to refer to, to consult
参考になる to be instructive, to be helpful
兄の意見はいつも参考になるよ。
My older brother's opinions are always helpful!
参考書 reference book

ざんこく 残酷 〜な *cruel*

さんしゅつ 産出 *production, output*
産出する to produce, to yield
あの鉱山はたくさんの石炭を産出します。
That mine produces a lot of coal.

ざんしょ 残暑 *lingering summer heat, late summer heat*

さんしょう 参照 *reference, comparison*
参照する to refer to, to compare
この本を参照してください。
Please refer to this book.

さんしょううお 山椒魚 *salamander*

さんしん 三振 *strikeout (in baseball)*
三振する to strike out (intransitive)
空振り三振 swinging strikeout
見逃し三振 looking strikeout

さんすう 算数 *arithmetic*

さんせい 賛成 *agreement, approval* [↔ 反対]
私もその計画に賛成です。
I am also in favor of that plan.
賛成する to agree, to be in favor
酒井先生には賛成できません。
I cannot agree with Dr. Sakai.

さんそ 酸素 *oxygen*

ざんだか 残高 *balance, remaining money* [→ 残金]

サンタクロース *Santa Claus*

サンダル *sandal*

さんだんとび 三段跳び *triple jump ((athletic event))*

さんち 産地 *producing area*
山梨県はぶどうの産地として有名です。
Yamanashi-ken is famous as a grape-producing area.

さんちょう 山頂 *mountain top, mountain summit*

サンドイッチ *sandwich*

ざんねん 残念 〜な *regrettable, unfortunate, too bad*
佐藤さんが会に参加できないのは残念だ。
It's unfortunate that Ms. Sato can't attend the meeting.
残念ながら unfortunately, regrettably
残念賞 consolation prize

さんば 産婆 *midwife*

さんびか 賛美歌 *hymn*

さんぶつ 産物 *product; result*
努力の産物 the result of one's efforts
副産物 by-product
海産物 marine product
農産物 agricultural product
特産物 special product

サンプル *sample* [→ 見本]

さんぽ 散歩 *walk, stroll*
散歩する to take a walk, to stroll
私たちは朝食を食べて、海岸を散歩した。
We ate breakfast and strolled along the beach.
散歩に行く to go for a walk
犬を散歩させる to walk a dog

さんま 秋刀魚 *mackerel pike*

さんみゃく 山脈 *mountain range*
ヒマラヤ山脈 the Himalayas

さんようちほう 山陽地方 *the San'yo*

region of Japan (Okayama, Hiroshima, and southern Yamaguchi Prefectures)

さんりんしゃ 三輪車 *tricycle*

さんるい 三塁 *third base* [→ サード1.] *(in baseball)*

三塁打 three-base hit, triple

三塁手 third baseman [→ サード2.]

し

し 四 *four (see Appendix 2)* [→ 四]

四月 April

四月馬鹿 an April fool

し 市 *city*

市議会 city council

市立の administered by a city, municipal

市役所 city hall

京都市 Kyoto City

し 死 *death*

事故死 accidental death

急死 sudden death

し 詩 *poem; poetry*

詩人 poet

詩集 collection of poems

詩的な poetic

し *and, and besides that (sentence-conjoining particle)*

この辞書は安いし、とても使いやすい。

This dictionary is cheap, and really simple to use!

ーし ー氏【HON. for ーさん】 *(Roughly equivalent to Mr./Ms.; most commonly used for men.)*

中村氏は会長に任命されました。

Mr. Nakamura was named chairperson.

じ 字 *letter, character (in a writing system)* [→ 文字]

大塚さんは字が上手です。

Ms. Otsuka has nice handwriting. (Literally: Ms. Otsuka's characters are skillful.)

ローマ字 Roman letters

じ 痔 *hemorrhoids*

ーじ ー時 *(counter for o'clock; see Appendix 2)*

私は毎朝6時に起きます。

I get up at 6:00 every morning.

「今何時ですか」「ちょうど3時です」

"What time is it now?" "It's exactly 3:00."

しあい 試合 *competition, game, match, meet*

明日、南高校と野球の試合をします。

Tomorrow we're going to play a baseball game with Minami High School.

しあがる 仕上がる *to be completed* [→ 出来上がる]

レポートがやっと仕上がりました。

The report has finally been completed.

しあげる 仕上げる *to finish, to complete*

夕食前に宿題を仕上げましょう。

Let's finish our homework before dinner!

しあわせ 幸せ [[→ 幸福]] *happiness; good fortune*

幸せな happy; fortunate

秋山さんは結婚して、とても幸せだ。

Mr. Akiyama got married and is very happy.

村の人たちは幸せに暮らしました。

The people of the village lived happily.

シーエム CM *(Generally not written out in katakana.) commercial message* [→ コマーシャル]

シーズン *season (for something)*

ここは秋が観光のシーズンです。

Here autumn is the tourist season.

シーソー *seesaw*

シーソーゲーム seesaw game

シーツ *(bed) sheet*

シート *seat, place to sit* [→ 席]

シート *waterproof canvas covering*

シート *sheet (of paper, etc.)*

その引き出しに切手のシートがあります。
There is a sheet of stamps in that drawer.

ーシート (counter for sheets; see Appendix 2)

シード *seed (in a tennis tournament, etc.)*

第1シード the number one seed

ジーパン *jeans* [→ ジーンズ]

ジープ *jeep*

シール *sticker*

しいん 子音 *a consonant* [↔ 母音]

シーン *scene (in a movie, play, novel, etc.)*

じいん 寺院 *Buddhist temple* [→ 寺]

ジーンズ *jeans* [→ ジーパン]

ブルージーンズ blue jeans

しえい 市営 ～の *operated by a city, municipal*

市営バス city bus

じえい 自衛 *self-defense, self-preservation*

自衛隊 the (Japanese) Self-Defense Forces

自衛隊員 Self-Defense Forces member

ジェスチャー *1. gesture* [→ 身ぶり]

2. charades ((game))

ジェットコースター *roller coaster*

シェパード *German shepherd*

シェルター *a shelter*

しお 塩 *salt*

塩を取ってください。
Please pass the salt.

塩を一つまみ入れます。
I'll put in a pinch of salt.

このスープは塩がききすぎています。
This soup is too salty.

塩辛い salty

塩漬けの salted, preserved with salt

しお 潮 *1. (ocean) tide*

潮の流れが速いね。
The tide's flow is fast, isn't it?

潮が満ちる〔引く〕 the tide rises〔ebbs〕

2. ～を吹く *to spout (The subject is ordinarily a whale.)*

あの鯨は今潮を吹いています。
That whale is spouting now.

潮風 sea breeze

引き潮 low tide

満ち潮 high tide

しおひがり 潮干狩り *gathering seashells, etc., when the tide is out*

江の島に潮干狩りに行きましょう。
Let's go gathering sea shells at Enoshima.

しおみず 塩水 *saltwater, brine* [↔ 真水]

しおり 栞, 枝折り *1. bookmark*

2. guidebook, handbook [→ 案内書 (s.v. 案内)]

しおれる *1. to wither, to wilt (when the subject is a plant)*

2. to become dejected, to become downhearted

しおん 子音 [☞ 子音]

しか 鹿 *deer*

しか *only, nothing but (Always occurs in combination with a negative predicate.)*

今10円しかないです。
I only have ten yen now.

英語は少ししか話せません。
I can only speak a little English.

私にはこれしかできません。
I can only do this.

しかい 司会 *chairmanship, chairing; emceeing*

岩崎さんは会議の司会をします。

Ms. Iwasaki will chair the meeting.

司会する to chair; to emcee

司会者 chairperson; master of ceremonies

しかい 視界 *one's range of sight, one's view*

視界に入る to come into view

視界から消える to disappear from view

しがい 市外 *area surrounding a town, outskirts, suburbs* [→ 郊外]

しがいせん 紫外線 *ultraviolet rays*

しかえし 仕返し *retaliation, getting back*

仕返しする to retaliate, to get back

あの人は私に仕返しするでしょう。

That person will probably get back at me.

しかく 四角 *a square ((shape))*

四角い square (as an adjective)

その四角い箱を使ってください。

Please use that square box.

しかく 資格 *qualifications, eligibility*

姉は中学校の先生の資格があります。

My older sister has the qualifications to be a junior-high-school teacher.

じかく 自覚 *self-awareness, self-knowledge; awakening, realization*

自覚する to become aware of, to realize

自分の弱点を自覚しています。

I am aware of my own weak points.

しかし *however, but*

ゴルフは楽しい。しかし、お金がかかる。

Golf is fun. But, It's expensive.

しかた 仕方 *way of doing, how to do*

この子はまだおじぎの仕方は知らない。

This child doesn't know how to bow yet.

正しいあいさつの仕方を教えてください。

Please teach me the right way to greet people.

しかたがない it can't be helped, there's nothing one can do

もう終わったから、しかたがないね。

It's already ended, so there's nothing we can do, is there?

きょうは蒸し暑くてしかたがないですよ。

Today it's so hot and humid that I can't stand it!

(After a gerund (-て form), しかたがない often has an idiomatic meaning that might be translated as **to such an extent that one can't stand it!**)

じかに 直に *1. directly, with nothing intervening*

2. directly, personally, in person

しがみつく *to clutch, to hold tightly*

しかも *besides, furthermore*

このカメラは小さくて、しかも、安い。

This camera is small. Furthermore, it's inexpensive.

しかる 叱る *to scold*

先生は不注意な生徒をしかりました。

The teacher scolded the careless student.

しがん 志願 *aspiration; applying, requesting; volunteering*

志願する to apply for; to volunteer for

兄はパイロットの職を志願しました。

My older brother applied for a job as a pilot.

志願者 applicant

じかん 時間 *1. (point in) time* [→ 時刻]

寝る時間ですよ。

It's time for bed!

約束の時間に遅れてしまいました。

I was late for the time of my appointment.

時間を守る to be punctual

2. (amount of) time

もう時間があまりないです。

There's not much time left.

3. fixed period of time for a certain activity; class (period)

歴史の時間がいちばん好きです。

I like history class best.

時間通りの on-time

時間表 timetable, (US) schedule
時間割り (US) class schedule, (UK) class timetable
営業時間 business hours
授業時間 time in class
勤務時間 time spent at work, working hours

ーじかん ー時間 *(counter for hours; see Appendix 2)*
友達を2時間待ちました。
I waited for my friend for two hours.
岡山まで電車で何時間かかりますか。
How many hours does it take to Okayama by train?
ここから歩いて2時間ぐらいです。
It's about two hours on foot from here.

しき 式 *1. ceremony* [→ 儀式]
式場 place where a ceremony is held
閉会式 closing ceremony
開会式 opening ceremony
卒業式 graduation ceremony
2. expression, formula (in mathematics, chemistry, etc.) [→ 公式]
化学式 chemical formula

ーしき ー式 *-type, -style (Added to noun bases.)*
アメリカ式の生活に慣れています。
I am used to an American-style way of life.

しき 四季 *the four seasons*
日本の自然は四季を通じて美しいです。
Nature in Japan is beautiful throughout the four seasons.

しき 指揮 *directing, leading, commanding; orders, instructions*
指揮する to direct, to conduct (an orchestra, etc.), to command (an army, etc.)
指揮官 commander
指揮者 conductor, director, leader

じき 時期 *time period, season*
毎年この時期にはよく雨が降ります。
Every year at this time it rains a lot.
今が魚釣りにはいちばんいい時期だよ。
Now is the best season for fishing!

じき 磁気 *magnetism*
磁気テープ magnetic tape

じき 直 1. (〜に) *at once, (US) right away, (UK) straight away* [→ すぐ(に)1.]
2. right, directly [→ すぐ2.]

しきぶとん 敷布団 *lower futon, mattress-type futon*
(The word 布団 refers to traditional Japanese bedding, which is folded up and put in closets during the day and laid out on the floor at night.) [↔ 掛け布団]

しきゅう 子宮 *uterus*

しきゅう 至急 (〜に) *immediately, promptly, as soon as possible*
至急立石さんに連絡してください。
Please get in touch with Mr. Tateishi at once.
至急それを仕上げてください。
Please finish that as soon as possible.
至急の urgent
至急の用事で出かけました。
I went out on urgent business.

しきゅう 四球 *base on balls, walk (in baseball)* [→ フォアボール]
四球で出る to (reach base by a) walk

しきゅう 死球 *pitch that hits the batter* [→ デッドボール]

じぎょう 事業 *work, business, undertaking, enterprise*
父は21歳で事業を起こしました。
My father started a business at the age of twenty-one.
公共事業 public works
教育事業 educational work

しぎょう 始業 [[↔ 終業]] *1. the start of work or school each day*
2. the beginning of a new school term
始業式 start-of-the-term ceremony

しきりに 頻りに *1. frequently, repeatedly, often* [→ 度々]
夕子はしきりに市役所に電話をかけた。
Yuko phones the city hall very often.
2. hard, eagerly, keenly
兄がしきりに愛子に会いたがっている。
My older brother is eager to meet Aiko.

しきん 資金 *funds, capital* [→ 資本]

しく 敷く *to spread out flat, to lay*
床に緑のカーペットを敷きました。
I laid a green carpet on the floor.
砂浜にござを敷いて、日光浴をします。
We'll spread a mat on the beach and sunbathe.
私は毎日父のふとんを敷きます。
I lay out my father's bedding every day.
鉄道を敷く to lay a railroad

じく 軸 *1. axis; axle, shaft*
2. roller (of a scroll)
3. [☞ 掛け軸 *(below)*]
掛け軸 decorative hanging scroll [→ 掛け物]

ジグザグ *a zigzag*

しくじる *{5} to fail at, to fail to do*

ジグソーパズル *jigsaw puzzle*

シグナル [[→ 信号]] *1. signal*
2. traffic signal ((device))

しくみ 仕組み *structure, arrangement, set-up*

シクラメン *cyclamen*

しぐれ 時雨 *late autumn or early winter drizzle*

しけい 死刑 *death penalty*
犯人は死刑の宣告を受けました。
The criminal received the death sentence.

しげき 刺激 *stimulus*
刺激する to stimulate
刺激的な stimulating, exciting
この本は子供には刺激的すぎるだろう。
This book may be too exciting for children.

しける 湿気る *{5} to get soggy, to lose crispness (from absorbing moisture in the air)*

しげる 茂る *{5} to grow thick, to become luxuriant*
庭には雑草がしげっています。
In the garden weeds are growing thick.

しけん 試験 [[→ テスト]] *1. test, examination (to evaluate knowledge or ability)*
きょうは英語の試験があります。
Today there is an English examination.
山田先生は毎日試験をします。
Ms. Yamada gives a test every day.
○×式の試験 true-or-false test
2. test, trial, experiment (to evaluate quality)
試験する to test, to experiment with
試験勉強 studying for a test
試験管 test tube
試験問題 examination question
試験的な experimental, trial
試験用紙 examination paper
中間試験 midterm examination
期末試験 end-of-term examination, final examination
実力試験 achievement test

しげん 資源 *resources*
ロシアは資源が豊かです。
Russia's resources are abundant.
地下資源 underground resources
天然資源 natural resources

じけん 事件 *event, incident* [→ 出来事]
それは恐ろしい事件でした。
That was a frightening incident.
殺人事件 a murder (incident)

じこ 自己 *self, oneself*

自己を知ることが大切です。
It is important to know oneself.
自己紹介 introducing oneself
自己流の in one's own style, of one's own style

じこ 事故 *accident, unfortunate incident*
村田さんはけさの事故でけがをしました。
Mr. Murata was injured in this morning's accident.
交通事故 traffic accident

しこう 思考 *thought, thinking*
思考力 thinking power

じこく 時刻 *(point in) time* [→ 時間1.]
時刻はただいま7時です。
The time is now 7:00.
時刻表 schedule, timetable

じごく 地獄 *hell* [↔ 天国]

しごと 仕事 *work, task; job, employment, business*
しなければならない仕事がたくさんある。
There's a lot of work that I have to do.
姉は仕事を捜しています。
My older sister is looking for a job.
安田さんは仕事で広島にいます。
Ms. Yasuda is in Hiroshima on business.
犬を散歩に連れて行くのは僕の仕事です。
Taking the dog for a walk is my job.
父は朝早く仕事に出かけます。
My father goes to work early in the morning.
仕事をする to work [→ 働く]

じさ 時差 *1. time difference (between different time zones)*
2. time staggering
時差惚け jet lag
時差出勤 staggered work hours

じさつ 自殺 *suicide*
自殺する to commit suicide

じさん 持参 ～する *to bring along, to take along (The direct object must be a thing.)*
水筒を持参しなさい。
Bring along a canteen.
持参金 dowry

しし 獅子 *lion* [→ ライオン]

しじ 支持 *support, backing*
支持する to support, to back
だれもその案を支持しませんでした。
No one supported that plan.
支持者 supporter ((person))

しじ 指示 *1. directions, instructions*
私たちは指導者の指示に従います。
We'll follow the leader's directions.
指示する to direct, to instruct
2. indication, pointing to
指示する to indicate, to point to
この矢印は方向を指示しています。
This arrow indicates the direction.

じじ 時事 *current events, current affairs*

じじつ 事実 *fact, actuality, reality, truth*
そのうわさは事実ですか。
Is that rumor true?
事実は小説よりも奇なり。 (proverb)
Fact is stranger than fiction.
事実の actual, real, true
事実に反する to be contrary to the facts

ししゃ 支社 *branch office*

ししゃ 死者 *dead person, a fatality*
その事故で多くの死者が出ました。
Many fatalities occurred in that accident.

ししゃ 使者 *messenger, envoy*

じしゃく 磁石 *1. magnet*
2. (magnetic) compass

ししゅう 刺繍 *embroidery*
ししゅうをする to do embroidery
刺繍糸 embroidery thread

しじゅう 始終 *always* [→常に]; *often* [→度々]; *constantly, continually* [→絶えず]

じしゅう 自習 *self-study, studying by oneself*

自習する to study by oneself

土曜日の午後は図書館で自習します。

On Saturday afternoons I study by myself in the library.

ししゅつ 支出 *expenditure, disbursement, outgo* [↔収入]

今月は支出が多かったね。

This month there were a lot of expenditures, weren't there?

ししゅんき 思春期 *adolescence*

じしょ 辞書 *dictionary*

その単語を辞書で調べてください。

Please check that word in a dictionary.

辞書を引く to consult a dictionary

じじょ 次女 *second-born daughter*

しじょう 市場 *market*

じじょう 事情 *circumstances, conditions, situation* [→状況]

どんな事情があっても必ず来てください。

You must come no matter what the circumstances!

あの子は家庭の事情で転校しました。

That child changed schools because of family circumstances.

じしょく 辞職 *resignation, quitting one's job*

辞職する to resign

高橋さんは会社に失望して辞職しました。

Mr. Takahashi got discouraged with work and resigned.

じじょでん 自叙伝 *autobiography* [→自伝]

しじん 詩人 *poet*

じしん 自信 *confidence, self-assurance*

数学にはあまり自信がないよ。

I don't have much self-confidence in math!

選手たちは優勝する自信があるようだ。

The players seem to have confidence that they will win the championship.

自信を失う to lose one's confidence

自信満々の very confident, full of confidence

じしん 地震 *earthquake*

ゆうべ強い地震がありました。

There was a strong earthquake last night.

—じしん —自身 *oneself (Added to noun or pronoun bases.)*

自分自身でやりなさい。

Do it yourself.

それは野本さん自身の問題ですよ。

That's Mr. Nomoto's own problem.

しずか 静か ～な *1. quiet, silent* [↔煩い1.]

お宅の明君は静かな子ですね。

Your Akira is a quiet child, isn't he?

校長先生は静かな口調で話します。

The principal talks in a quiet voice.

静かにする to be quiet, to stop making noise

2. calm, still [→穏やかな]

朝の湖はとても静かです。

The lake is very calm in the morning.

3. gentle, slow-moving

静かな流れ gentle current

しずく 滴 *drop (of liquid)*

傘から滴が垂れています。

Drops of water are dripping from the umbrella.

雨の滴 raindrop

しずけさ 静けさ *1. quietness, stillness*

2. tranquility, serenity

システム *system*

しずまりかえる 静まり返る *{5} to become completely silent, to become deathly still*

通りは静まり返っています。

The street has become completely silent.

しずまる 静まる, 鎮まる *become quiet; to*

calm down

やっとあらしが静まりました。
At last the storm calmed down.

しずむ 沈む *1. to sink, to go down*

その船は台風で沈みました。
That ship sank because of a typhoon.

太陽が沈む the sun sets

2. to sink into low spirits, to become depressed

このごろどうして沈んでいるのですか。
Why are you in low spirits lately?

しせい 姿勢 *1. posture*

姿勢がいい one's posture is good

姿勢を正す to straighten up, to stand/sit straight

2. attitude, stance [→ 態度]

しせき 史跡 *historic spot*

しせつ 施設 *institution, facility, installation*

公共施設 public facility

しせん 視線 *one's gaze, one's eyes*

私たちは視線が合いました。
Our eyes met.

視線を注ぐ to fix one's gaze

視線を向ける to direct one's gaze, to turn one's eyes

しぜん 自然 *nature*

日本の自然は美しいです。
Nature in Japan is beautiful.

自然の／な natural [↔ 不自然な]

小林さんの態度はごく自然です。
Ms. Kobayashi's manner is quite natural.

自然に naturally; by itself, without anyone causing it

ドアが自然に閉まったよ。
The door closed by itself!

自然科学 natural science

自然食品 natural food

じぜん 慈善 *charity, benevolence, philanthropy*

慈善事業 charitable work; charities

しそう 思想 *thought, ideas*

思想家 thinker

じぞう 地蔵 *Jizo (the Buddhist guardian deity of children and travelers)*

じそく 時速 *speed per hour*

この特急は時速280キロで走るよ。
This special express runs at a speed of 280 kilometers per hour!

しそん 子孫 *descendant* [↔ 先祖]

じそんしん 自尊心 *self-respect, pride*

社長は自尊心が強いですね。
The company president's self-respect is strong, isn't it?

その言葉で自尊心が傷ついたよ。
My pride was hurt by those words!

した 下 [[↔ 上]] *1. bottom; lower part*

下から２行目を読みなさい。
Read the second line from the bottom.

その本は本棚のいちばん下の段にある。
That book is on the bottom shelf of the bookshelf.

2. the area under, the area below

暑かったから、木の下に座りました。
It was hot, so I sat under a tree.

丘に立つと青い海が下に見えます。
Standing on the hill the blue sea is visible below.

3. the portion of a scale or ranking below

息子はその人の下で働いています。
My son is working under that person.

4. 〜の younger

私は兄より三つ下です。
I am three years younger than my older brother.

した 舌 *tongue*

したい 死体 *dead body, corpse, carcass*

しだい 次第 *circumstances* [→ 事情]

次第によって depending on the circumstances

ーしだい ー次第 *1. as soon as (Added to verb bases.)*
天気になり次第出発しましょう。
Let's start out as soon as it clears up.
2. 〜だ to depend on (Added to noun bases.)
成功は努力次第です。
Success depends on effort.

じたい 事態 *the situation*
事態が好転する the situation takes a favorable turn

じたい 辞退 *modest refusal, nonacceptance*
辞退する to decline, to modestly refuse

じだい 時代 *1. period, era, age*
日本では19世紀は経済成長の時代でした。
In Japan the 19th century was an age of economic growth.
2. the times
時代が変わりました。
Times have changed.
時代劇 samurai drama, historical drama
時代遅れ behind-the-times, out-of-date
学生時代 one's student days
明治時代 the Meiji Period
宇宙時代 the space age

しだいに 次第に *gradually*
天候がしだいに回復してきました。
The weather has gradually improved.

したう 慕う *1. to come to yearn for, to come to long for*
亡命者が故郷を慕うのは当然です。
It is natural for a defector to long for home.
2. to come to adore, to come to idolize
子供たちはあの若い先生を慕っています。
The children adore that young teacher.

したがう 従う *to comply, to go along, to abide, to conform*
兵隊は指揮官の命令に従います。
A soldier complies with his commander's orders.
私たちは先生の忠告に従いました。
We followed our teacher's advice.

したがって 従って (This word is the gerund (-て form) of 従う and has the predictable meanings as well.)
1. therefore, consequently [→ だから]
東京は人口が多く、従って物価が高い。
Tokyo has a large population and consequently, prices are high.
2. [☞ に従って]

したぎ 下着 *underwear, undergarment*

したく 支度, 仕度 *preparations, arrangements* [→ 準備]
母は今朝食の仕度をしています。
My mother is now making the preparations for breakfast.
修学旅行の仕度をしなくてはなりません。
I must make preparations for the school excursion.
支度が出来る readiness is achieved, preparations are made complete
夕食の仕度ができました。
Dinner is ready.
私たちは出かける仕度ができていません。
We aren't ready to go out.
仕度する to prepare, to make ready

じたく 自宅 *one's house, one's home*
浜口さんは自宅にいます。
Ms. Hamaguchi is at home.

したしい 親しい *friendly, intimate, close*
息子には親しい友達はほとんどいません。
My son has almost no close friends.
恵子ちゃんと親しくなったよ。
I've become friendly with Keiko!

したじき 下敷き *underlay (placed under the paper one is writing on)*

したたる 滴る *to drip (intransitive)*

汗がその走者の額から滴っています。
Sweat is dripping from that runner's forehead.

したまち 下町 *traditional shopping and entertainment district of a city, downtown (Typically located in a low-lying area of a Japanese city.)* [↔ 山の手]

しち 七 *seven (see Appendix 2)* [→ 七]

七月 July

じち 自治 *self-government, home rule*

自治会 self-government association; student council

自治省 the Ministry of Home Affairs

自治体 self-governing body

しちごさん 七五三 *the Seven-Five-Three Celebration*

(Boys aged three or five and girls aged three or seven put on their best clothes and visit a neighborhood Shinto shrine on November 15.)

しちふくじん 七福神 *the Seven Gods of Good Fortune*

(These gods are traditionally said to sail into port on a ship filled with treasure on New Year's Eve. The seven are 恵比寿 *(god of fisherman and prosperous commerce),* 毘沙門 *(god of war),* 大黒 *(god of wealth),* 弁天 *(goddess of eloquence and the arts),* 福禄寿 *(god of wealth and longevity),* 寿老人 *(god of longevity), and* 布袋 *(god of happiness).)*

しちめんちょう 七面鳥 turkey

しちや 質屋 *pawn shop*

シチュー *stew*

しちょう 市長 *(city) mayor*

本間さんのお父さんは市長に選ばれた。
Mr. Honma's father was elected mayor.

市長選挙 mayoral election

しちょうりつ 視聴率 *rating (of a TV program)*

このテレビ番組の視聴率は高いです。
This TV program's rating is high.

しつ 質 *quality (i.e., degree of goodness or badness)*

量より質が大切です。
Quality is more important than quantity.

この肉は質が悪いです。
The quality of this meat is bad.

じつ 実 *1. truth, reality* [→ 真実]

実の true, real [→本当の]

実は actually, in fact

実はあの話はうそでした。
In fact, that story was a lie.

実を言うと to tell the truth

実に really, truly, very

2. sincerity [→ 誠意]

野口さんは実のある人です。
Ms. Noguchi is a person of sincerity.

じついん 実印 *registered signature seal (Documents are ordinarily stamped with a seal rather than signed in Japan.)*

しつう 歯痛 *toothache*

じっか 実家 *one's parents' home; family into which one was born*

しっかく 失格 *disqualification*

失格する to be disqualified

矢沢選手は決勝戦で失格になりました。
Yazawa was disqualified from the finals.

しっかり (〜と) *strongly, firmly, tightly, hard*

しっかり勉強しなさい。
Study hard.

生存者はしっかり綱に捕まりました。
The survivors held on to the rope tightly.

しっかりする to become strong, to become dependable

土田さんはしっかりしていますね。
Ms. Tsuchida is dependable, isn't she?

しつぎょう 失業 *unemployment*

失業する to lose one's job

失業中の out-of-work, unemployed

失業率 unemployment rate

失業者 unemployed person

じっきょう 実況 *actual state of affairs; actual scene*

これはニューヨークからの実況です。
This is the actual scene from New York.

実況放送 on-the-scene broadcast

じつぎょう 実業 *business, production and commerce*

実業家 businessman, businesswoman

しつけ 躾 *training in polite behavior, discipline*

両親はしつけが厳しいです。
My parents' discipline is strict.

しつけがいい〔悪い〕well-〔ill-〕bred

しつける 躾ける *to train in polite behavior, to discipline*

しっけ 湿気 *dampness; humidity*

湿気が多い very damp; very humid

じっけん 実験 *experiment, test*

きょうは化学の実験をします。
Today we will do a chemistry experiment.

実験台 experimental subject, guinea pig

実験室 laboratory

核実験 nuclear test

じつげん 実現 *realization, coming true*

実現する to be realized, to come true; to realize, to actualize

大統領は自分の理想を実現しました。
The president realized his own ideals.

その夢は10年後に実現しました。
That dream came true ten years later.

しつこい *1. annoyingly persistent*

会長はその計画をしつこく主張している。
The chairperson is persistently advocating that plan.

2. too strong, too heavy (when describing a flavor, odor, color, etc.)

タイ料理は私にはしつこいです。
Thai cuisine is too strong for me.

じっこう 実行 *putting into practice, carrying out, execution*

実行する to carry out, to put into practice

生徒たちはその計画を実行しました。
The students carried out that plan.

実行委員会 executive committee

実行力 ability to put things into practice

じっさい 実際 *truth, reality, actuality*

この子は実際より年上に見えます。
This child looks older than he really is.

実際の real, actual, true [→ 本当の]

実際に really, actually, truly

これは実際にあった話です。
This is a story that really happened.

しっしん 失神 〜する *to faint* [→ 気絶する]

通行人はその事故を見て失神しました。
A passerby saw that accident and fainted.

しっそ 質素 〜な *simple, plain, unostentatious*

松島さんは質素な暮らしをしています。
Mr. Matsushima is living a simple life.

会長は質素な身なりをしています。
The chairperson is dressed plainly.

しっと 嫉妬 *jealousy*

しっとする to become jealous

僕は兄にしっとしていないよ。
I am not jealous of my older brother!

嫉妬深い jealous

しつど 湿度 *humidity*

湿度計 hydrometer

じっと *1. still, motionlessly; steadily, fixedly*

警官はじっと立っています。
The police officer is standing still.

編集者は写真をじっと見つめていました。
The editor was staring steadily at the

photograph.

2. patiently, without complaint

少年は痛みをじっと我慢しました。

The boy put up with the pain without complaint.

しつない 室内 *interior of a room*

室内の indoor

室内プール indoor swimming pool

室内スポーツ indoor sports

ジッパー *zipper, (UK) zip fastener* [→ ファスナー]

しっぱい 失敗 *failure* [↔ 成功]

失敗は成功の母。 (proverb)

Failure is but a stepping stone to success. (Literally: Failure is the mother of success.)

失敗する to fail (intransitive)

最初の計画は結局失敗しました。

The first plan eventually failed.

じつぶつ 実物 *the real thing* [→ 本物]*; the actual person*

この肖像画は実物にそっくりです。

This portrait looks just like the actual person.

実物大 life size, actual size

しっぽ 尻尾 *tail* [→ 尾]

しつぼう 失望 *disappointment, discouragement*

負けたチームの失望は大きかったです。

The defeated team was extremely disappointed.

失望する to become disappointed, to become discouraged [→ がっかりする]

私たちはその知らせを聞いて失望した。

We heard that news and were disappointed.

その計画に失望しました。

I was disappointed at that plan.

しつもん 質問 *question, inquiry*

何か質問がありますか。

Are there any questions?

報道官はその質問にあっさり答えました。

The press officer easily answered that question.

質問する to ask a question

質問してもよろしいですか。

May I ask a question?

じつよう 実用 *practical use*

実用英語 practical English

実用品 daily necessities, useful articles

実用性 practical usefulness, utility

実用的な practical, of practical use

この新製品はあまり実用的ではない。

This new product is of little practical use.

じつりょく 実力 *real ability, capability, competence*

林先生は実力のある先生です。

Mr. Hayashi is a capable teacher.

菊池さんは英語の実力があります。

Ms. Kikuchi has real ability in English.

実力を付ける to attain competence, to cultivate one's ability

数学の実力をつけたいんです。

I want to improve my competence in math.

実力者 influential person

実力テスト proficiency test

しつれい 失礼 *rudeness, impoliteness*

失礼な rude, impolite

人を指すのは失礼です。

It is rude to point at people.

失礼ですが、どちら様でしょうか。

May I ask who you are? (Literally: This is rude, but who are you?)

失礼する to behave rudely

(This expression is most often used to express politeness by saying that one's own behavior is rude.)

失礼します。

Pardon me (for what I about to do). (Literally: I will behave rudely.)

失礼しました。

Pardon me (for what I did). (Literally: I behaved rudely.)
そろそろ失礼します。
I must be going soon. (Literally: I will soon behave rudely.)

しつれん 失恋 *unrequited love*
失恋する to be disappointed in love

してい 指定 *specification, designation*
指定の specified, designated, set
指定の時間に遅れました。
I was late for the set time.
指定する to specify, to designate, to set
部長は会議の場所を指定しました。
The department head designated the place for the meeting.
指定席 reserved seat [↔ 自由席 (s.v. 自由)]

してき 私的 〜な *private, personal*

してき 指摘 〜する *to point out, to indicate*
父はその誤りを指摘してくれた。
My father pointed out that mistake for me.

してつ 私鉄 *private railroad, non-government railroad*

してん 支店 *branch store, branch office*
支店長 branch manager

しでん 市電 *streetcar*

じてん 辞典 *dictionary* [➞ 辞書]
英和辞典 English-Japanese dictionary
国語辞典 Japanese dictionary
和英辞典 Japanese-English dictionary

じでん 自伝 *autobiography* [➞ 自叙伝]

じてんしゃ 自転車 *bicycle*
駅まで自転車で行きました。
I went as far as the station by bicycle.
順子ちゃんは自転車に乗れる？
Can Junko ride a bicycle?
自転車旅行 bicycle trip, cycling tour

しどう 指導 *direction, guidance, leadership, instruction*
その研究は落合教授の指導で進められた。
That research progressed under Prof. Ochiai's leadership.
指導する to direct, to guide, to lead, to instruct
上岡さんはサッカーを指導しています。
Mr. Ueoka is teaching soccer.
指導員 instructor
指導力 leadership ability
指導者 leader

じどう 自動 〜の *automatic*
自動ドア automatic door
自動販売機 vending machine
自動的な [☞ 自動の (above)]

じどう 児童 *1. child* [➞ 子供]
2. elementary-school pupil [➞ 小学生]
児童文学 children's literature

じどうし 自動詞 *intransitive verb* [↔ 他動詞]

じどうしゃ 自動車 [[➞ 車1.]] *(US) automobile, (UK) motorcar; (US) truck, (UK) lorry* [➞トラック]
自動車事故 automobile accident
自動車教習所 driving school
自動車レース auto race
自動車ショー auto show

しな 品 [[➞ 品物]] *useful article; item of merchandise*
その店にいろいろな品があります。
There is a variety of merchandise in that store.
品切れの out-of-stock, sold-out

しなもの 品物 [[➞ 品]] *useful article; item of merchandise*

シナリオ *scenario, screenplay*
シナリオライター scenario writer

じなん 次男 *second-born son*

じにん 辞任 *resignation (from a job)*

辞任する to resign from

しぬ 死ぬ *to die (The subject must be a person or animal.)* [↔ 生まれる]

祖父は53歳で死にました。
My grandfather died at 53.

首相は病気で死にました。
The prime minister died of an illness.

自動車事故で死ぬ人が多いです。
There are many people who die in automobile accidents.

姉は死んだ祖母のことをよく覚えている。
My older sister remembers our dead grandmother very well.

死んでいる to be dead

しのぐ 凌ぐ *1. to endure, to bear, to stand* [→ 忍耐する]

2. to exceed, to surpass, to outstrip

3. to avoid, to take shelter from

しのぶ 忍ぶ *1. to bear, to endure, to stand* [→忍耐する]

2. to conceal oneself from

人目を忍ぶ to avoid being seen

しはい 支配 *rule, governing, control*

支配する to rule, to govern, to control

その国は王様が支配しています。
A king rules over that country.

支配人 manager

支配者 ruler

しばい 芝居 *1. play, drama, theatrical presentation*

芝居をする to put on a play

2. an act, faking

芝居をする to put on an act

しばしば【FORMAL for 度々】 *often*

しばしば父と釣りに行きます。
I often go fishing with my father.

しはつ 始発 *1. the first train or bus departure of the day*

2. the first train or bus of the day

けさは京都行きの始発に間に合いました。
This morning I was in time for the first Kyoto-bound train.

3. starting point, origin (of a train or bus)

始発駅 starting station

じはつてき 自発的 〜な *spontaneous, voluntary*

しばふ 芝生 *lawn, grass*

男の子が芝生に寝転んでいます。
The boy is lying on the grass.

「芝生に入らないでください」(on a sign)
Keep off the grass. (Literally: Please do not come on the grass.)

しはらい 支払い *payment*

支払い日 date of payment

しはらう 支払う *to pay (The direct object is the money, charge, expense, etc.)* [→ 払う1.]

しばらく 暫く *1. for a while*

私たちはしばらく待っていました。
We were waiting for a while.

2. for quite a while, for a long time

しばらくですね。
It's been a long time (since I saw you last), hasn't it?

しばる 縛る *to bind, to tie, to fasten*

その包みをひもで縛ってください。
Please tie that package with string.

少女は髪をリボンで縛りました。
The girl tied her hair with a ribbon.

じひ 慈悲 *mercy*

慈悲深い merciful

じびき 字引き *dictionary* [→ 辞書]

生き字引き walking dictionary, walking encyclopedia

しびれる 痺れる *to become numb, to fall asleep*

寒さで指がしびれてしまった。

My fingers became numb with cold.
足がしびれたよ。
My legs have fallen asleep!

しぶい 渋い *1. astringent-tasting*
この柿は味が渋いです。
This persimmon is astringent.
2. subdued, tasteful, refined
先生は渋いネクタイをしています。
The teacher is wearing a tasteful tie.
渋い色 subdued color

しぶき 飛沫 *spray from splashing water*

ジプシー *Gypsy*

じぶん 自分 *oneself*
初めて自分をテレビで見ました。
I saw myself for the first time on TV.
自分で by oneself, on one's own
その宿題を自分でやりなさい。
Do that homework yourself.
自分の one's own
自分の消しゴムを使いなさい。
Use your own eraser.
私は自分の家を持っています。
I have my own house.
自分自身 oneself (emphatic)
自分勝手な selfish

しへい 紙幣 *paper money, (US) bill, (UK) note*

しほう 四方 *every side, all sides; every direction, all directions*
見張りは四方を見回しました。
The guard looked around in every direction.
子供たちは四方に逃げました。
The children ran away in all directions.

しぼう 死亡 *death*
死亡する to die, to pass away [→ 死ぬ]
死亡率 death rate

しぼう 志望 *aspiration, desire, hope*
志望する to aspire to be
洋子さんは看護婦を志望しています。
Yoko is aspiring to be a nurse.
志望学校 school one hopes to enter
第1志望 one's first choice

しぼう 脂肪 *fat; grease*
この肉は脂肪が多すぎるよ。
This meat has too much fat!

しぼむ *1. to wither, to wilt (when the subject is a plant)*
その花は1日だけでしぼんでしまった。
Those flowers wilted in just one day.
2. to become deflated
その風船がしぼんだよ。
That balloon deflated!

しぼる 絞る *to wring liquid out of, to squeeze liquid out of*
そのぬれたタオルを絞ってください。
Please wring out that wet towel.
姉はレモンを絞ってジュースにしました。
My older sister squeezed a lemon and made some lemon juice.

しほん 資本 *capital, funds* [→ 資金]
資本家 capitalist, financier
資本金 operating capital, capitalization
その大企業の資本金は20億円です。
That big company's capitalization is two billion yen.
資本主義 capitalism
資本主義国家 capitalist country

しま 縞 *stripe*
この赤いしまのセーターが大好きです。
I love this sweater with the red stripes.

しま 島 *island*
島国 island nation
離れ島 remote island

しまい 姉妹 *sisters*
姉妹校 sister school
姉妹都市 sister city

しまう 仕舞う *1. to put away*

このケーキを冷蔵庫にしまってください。
Please put this cake away in the refrigerator.

店をしまう to close a store; to go out of business

2. to do/happen to completion, to do/happen beyond the point of no return (following the gerund (-て form) of another verb)

弟はケーキを全部食べてしまいました。
My younger brother ate up all the cake.

しまうま *zebra*

しまつ 始末 *1. disposal, disposition, settling* [→ 処分1.]

始末する to dispose of, to take care of, to settle

2. circumstances, state of things

しまる 閉まる *to close, to shut (intransitive)* [↔ 開く]

ドアは自動的に閉まります。
The door closes automatically.

窓がどうしても閉まらないよ。
The window won't shut no matter what I do!

しまる 締まる *to become tight; to become firm*

じまん 自慢 *showing pride; boasting*

自慢する to show pride in; to boast about

宮村さんは娘さんを自慢しています。
Ms. Miyamura is showing pride in her daughter.

八木さんは歌がうまいことを自慢します。
Mr. Yagi boasts that he is good at singing.

しみ 染み *stain, spot*

このシャツに染みがついています。
There is a stain on this shirt.

染み抜き stain removal

じみ 地味 ～な *plain, quiet, not flashy, not gaudy* [↔派手な]

このドレスは子供にはちょっと地味です。
This dress is a little plain for a child.

シミュレーター *simulator*

しみる 染みる *1. to soak(into), to penetrate(into), to permeate(into)*

インクが服にしみました。
Ink soaked into the clothes.

雨が降っても、すぐ地面にしみるだろう。
Even if it rains, it will probably soak into the ground right away.

身にしみる to touch one's heart; to feel piercing

その親切が身にしみました。
That kindness touched my heart.

寒さが身にしみるよ。
The cold is piercing!

2. to come into contact with and cause to hurt

煙が目にしみました。
Smoke got in my eyes and made them hurt.

しみん 市民 *citizen*

市民権 citizenship

じむ 事務 *office work, clerical work*

事務員 clerical worker

事務室 office (single room)

事務所 office (more than one room)

事務総長 secretary-general

しめい 氏名 *full name, surname and given name*

しめい 使命 *mission, appointed task*

使命を果たす to carry out one's mission

しめい 指名 *nomination, naming, designation*

指名する to nominate, to name, to designate (The direct object must be a person.)

谷本さんは議長に指名されました。
Ms. Tanimoto was nominated as chairperson.

指名打者 designated hitter (in baseball)

しめきり 締め切り *deadline*

きょうが申し込みの締め切りです。

Today is the deadline for applications.
締め切りは午後５時です。
The deadline is 5:00 PM.

しめきる 閉め切る *{5} 1. to close completely*

2. to keep closed
部屋の戸を閉め切ってはいけないよ。
You mustn't keep the door of the room closed!

しめきる 締め切る *{5} to stop accepting (something that must be submitted)*
入学願書の受け付けを締め切ります。
We will stop accepting applications for admission.

しめす 示す *to show, to indicate, to point out*
平さんはこの本に興味を示しました。
Mr. Taira showed interest in this book.
実例をいくつか示してください。
Please show me a few actual examples.
矢印が頂上への道を示しています。
The arrow indicates the way to the top.
温度計は20度を示しています。
The thermometer is showing 20 degrees.

しめる 湿る *{5} to get damp*
雨で洗濯物が湿ってしまいました。
The laundry got damp with rain.

しめる 占める *to occupy, to get, to take (a place, position, or proportion)*
水田が村の半分を占めています。
Rice fields occupy half the village.
日本はオリンピックで第１位を占めた。
Japan took first place in the Olympics.

しめる 閉める *to shut, to close (transitive)* [↔ 開ける]
窓を閉めてください。
Please close the window.
門は６時に閉めるそうです。
I hear they shut the gate at 6:00.

しめる 締める *1. to fasten, to tie securely (The direct object is often an article of clothing that is tied on. Like other verbs for putting on clothing, in the -ている form can express the meaning be wearing, have on.)*
シートベルトを締めてください。
Please fasten your seat belt.
兄はネクタイを締めています。
My older brother is wearing a tie.

2. to tighten (transitive) [↔ 緩める]
ねじを締める to tighten a screw

じめん 地面 *ground, surface of the ground*

しも 霜 *frost*
霜柱 frost needles on the ground
霜焼け frostbite
初霜 first frost of the year

じもと 地元 *local area, area directly involved*

しもん 指紋 *fingerprint*

しや 視野 *1. one's range of sight, one's field of view* [→ 視界]
視野に入る to come into view

2. view of things, vision, way of looking at things
加藤さんは視野が狭いです。
Mr. Kato's view of things is narrow.

ジャー *thermos bottle* [→ 魔法瓶 (s.v. 魔法)]

ジャージー *1. jersey cloth*

2. a jersey ((shirt))

ジャーナリスト *journalist*

シャープ *(musical) sharp* [↔ フラット]

シャーベット *sherbet*

しゃいん 社員 *company staff member, company employee*

しゃかい 社会 *society, the world*
息子は来年社会に出ます。
My son will go out into the world next year.
社会のために働きたいです。
I want to work for the good of society.

社会奉仕 social service
社会人 full-fledged member of society
社会科学 social science
社会問題 social problem, social issue
社会主義 socialism
社会生活 social life
社会党 the Socialist Party

じゃがいも *potato*

しゃがむ *to crouch, to squat*

しゃく 癪 ～にさわる *to be provoking, to be offensive, to get on one's nerves*
小松さんはしゃくにさわる人ですね。
Mr. Komatsu is a person who gets on one's nerves, isn't he?

－じゃく －弱 *a little less than (Added to number bases.)* [↔－強]
それは50年弱かかりました。
That took a little less than 50 years.

しゃくし 杓子 *1. ladle*
2. rice paddle

しやくしょ 市役所 *city hall, town hall*

じゃぐち 蛇口 *(US) faucet, (water) tap*
蛇口を開ける〔閉める〕 to turn on〔off〕a faucet

じゃくてん 弱点 *weak point, shortcoming* [→弱み]
自分の弱点を克服しようと努力します。
I will work hard to overcome my own weak points.

しゃくはち 尺八 *shakuhachi (a kind of bamboo flute)*

しゃげき 射撃 *shooting, firing a gun*
射撃を始める〔やめる〕to open〔cease〕fire
射撃する to shoot, to fire a gun

ジャケット *1. jacket ((article of clothing))*
2. (record) jacket

しゃこ 車庫 *garage; carport*

しゃこう 社交 *social interaction, socializing*
社交ダンス social dancing
社交性 sociability
社交的な sociable

しゃしょう 車掌 *conductor (on a train or bus)*

しゃしん 写真 *photograph*
写真はピンぼけでした。
The photograph was out of focus.
写真を現像して、焼いてもらいました。
I had my photographs developed and printed.
この写真を引き伸ばしてください。
Please enlarge this photograph.
写真を撮る to take a photograph
友達の写真を撮りました。
I took a photograph of my friend.
写真が撮れる a photograph is taken
この写真はよく撮れていますね。
This is a good photograph, isn't it? (Literally: This photograph is well taken, isn't it?)
写真を焼き増す to make a reprint of a photograph
写真家 photographer
写真機 camera [→カメラ]
写真うつり the way one looks in photographs
妹さんは写真うつりがいいです。
Your younger sister looks good in photographs.
写真屋 camera store, photography shop
カラー写真 color photograph
記念写真 souvenir photo
白黒写真 black-and-white photograph
スピード写真 fast photo

ジャズ *jazz*

しゃせい 写生 *1. drawing/painting without embellishment, drawing/painting from life*

写生する to draw/paint without embellishment, to draw/paint from life

校舎を2、3枚写生しました。
I drew two or three pictures of the school building.

2. sketching

写生する to sketch, to make a sketch of

写生画 a drawing/painting from life; sketch

しゃちょう 社長 *company president*

副社長 vice-president

シャツ *shirt*

半袖シャツ short-sleeved shirt

ランニングシャツ sleeveless T-shirt

ティーシャツ, Tシャツ T-shirt

じゃっかん 若干 *a small amount, some* [→ 少し]

しゃっきん 借金 *debt, borrowed money*

5000円の借金を返しました。
I paid back a debt of ¥5,000

太郎は淳に10万円の借金があるよ。
Taro has a debt of ¥100,000 to Jun!

借金する to borrow money, to get a loan

しゃっくり *hiccup, the hiccups*

しゃっくりが止まりません。
My hiccups won't stop.

しゃっくりが出る a hiccup comes out

ジャッジ *1. judge (for a competition)*

2. judgment (given by a judge for a competition)

ジャッジする to judge

シャッター *1. (camera) shutter*

すみませんが、シャッターを押してくださいませんか。
Excuse me, won't you please press the shutter for us?

2. roll-up metal shutter (Used to secure an entry or window.)

シャットアウト *1.* 〜する *to shut out, to exclude*

2. shutout (in baseball) [→ 完封]

しゃぶる *to suck on*

しゃべる 喋る *{5} to talk, to chat* [→ 話す]

京子さんはよくしゃべるね。
Kyoko talks a lot, doesn't she?

学生たちはお茶を飲みながらしゃべった。
The students chatted while drinking tea.

シャベル *shovel*

シャボンだま シャボン玉 *soap bubble*

じゃま 邪魔 *obstruction, hindrance, obstacle*

邪魔な burdensome, obstructive, in-the-way

邪魔する to disturb, to interrupt, to obstruct, to hinder

Aの邪魔をする to disturb A, to obstruct A, to hinder A

勉強の邪魔をしないでください。
Please don't disturb my studying.

Aの邪魔になる to interfere with A, to get in the way of A

ギターの音が読書の邪魔になります。
The sound of the guitar interferes with my reading.

お邪魔する 【HUM.】to intrude

(This expression is used as a polite way of describing a visit by labeling it an intrusion.)

お邪魔します。(when entering another person's home, office, etc.)
Pardon me for intruding. (Literally: I will intrude.)

では、来週の水曜日にお邪魔します。
Well then, I'll visit you on Wednesday of next week.

お邪魔しました。(when leaving another person's home, office, etc.)
Sorry to have intruded. (Literally: I have intruded.)

しゃみせん 三味線 *shamisen (a three-stringed, banjo-like musical instrument)*

ジャム *jam ((food))*

パンにジャムを塗りました。
I spread jam on the bread.

苺ジャム strawberry jam

しゃめん 斜面 *slope, hillside; sloping surface*

これからは急な斜面を登ります。
From here on we're going to climb a steep slope.

しゃもじ *rice paddle*

じゃり 砂利 *gravel, small pebbles*

砂利道 gravel road

しゃりん 車輪 *vehicle wheel*

しゃれ 洒落 *pun, play on words*

しゃれを言う to pun, to make a play on words

しゃれた *fashionable, stylish (This word is the past-tense form of 洒落る and has the predictable range of meanings as well.)* [→ お洒落な]

しゃれる 洒落る *to get dressed up, to dress stylishly*

シャワー *shower (bath)*

シャワーを浴びる to take a shower

ジャングル *jungle*

ジャングルジム jungle gym

じゃんけん じゃん拳 *"scissors-paper-rock" game (Used to determine the order of turn-taking, etc.)*

じゃんけんする to do "scissors-paper-rock"

じゃんけんで決める to decide by doing "scissors- paper-rock"

シャンソン *chanson, French-style popular song*

シャンデリア *chandelier*

ジャンパー *windbreaker*

シャンパン [☞ シャンペン]

ジャンプ *(upward) jump* [→ 跳躍]

ジャンプする to jump [→ 跳ぶ]

シャンプー *shampoo*

シャンプーする to shampoo

ゆうべ髪をシャンプーしました。
I shampooed my hair last night.

シャンペン *champagne*

ジャンボ *jumbo jet*

しゅう 州 *state, province*

オーストラリアにはいくつの州がありますか。
How many states are there in Australia?

州議会 state/provincial legislature

ニューヨーク州 New York State

オンタリオ州 Ontario Province

しゅう 週 *week*

週に3回英語の授業があります。
There are English classes three times a week.

今週 this week

毎週 every week

毎週テストがあるよ。
There's a test every week!

来週 next week

さ来週 the week after next

先週 last week

先々週 the week before last

じゆう 自由 *freedom, liberty*

個人の自由を尊重しなくてはなりません。
We must respect individual liberty.

言論の自由 freedom of speech

自由な free, unrestrained

自由な時間がほとんどないです。
I have almost no free time.

この辞書を自由に使ってください。
Please use this dictionary freely.

大石さんは英語を自由に話します。
Mr. Oishi speaks English fluently.

自由民主党 the Liberal Democratic Party

[→ 自民党]
自由席 unreserved seat [↔ 指定席 (s.v. 指定)]
自由市場 free market
自由主義 liberalism
自由主義国 free nation
自由主義者 liberalist
自由の女神像 the Statue of Liberty

じゅう 十 *ten (see Appendix 2)*
十月 October

じゅう 銃 *gun (of a type small enough to carry)*
拳銃 pistol
機関銃 machine gun
ライフル銃 rifle

-じゅう -中 *1. throughout, all through (Added to bases denoting time periods.)*
私は夏休み中親せきの別荘にいました。
I was at my relatives' villa all through the summer vacation.
2. all over, throughout (Added to bases denoting places.)
あの人は日本中に知られています。
That person is known all over Japan.
町中が大騒ぎになっていました。
The whole town was in a great uproar.
一晩中 throughout the night, all night long
一年中 throughout the year, all year round
一日中 throughout the day, all day long
きのうは一日中模型を作っていました。
I was making a model all day yesterday.
世界中 all over the world

しゅうい 周囲 [[→ 周り]] *1. circumference, distance around*
この池は周囲が２キロあります。
This pond is two kilometers around.
2. surroundings, environment, area around
ガードマンは周囲を見回しました。
The guard looked around at the surroundings.
家の周囲は木で囲まれています。
The area around the house is surrounded by trees.

じゅうい 獣医 *veterinarian*

じゅういち 十一 *eleven (see Appendix 2)*
十一月 November

しゅうかい 集会 *meeting, gathering, assembly*
集会の自由 freedom of assembly

しゅうかく 収穫 *harvest, crop, yield*
今年は米の収穫が多かったです。
This year the rice crop was large.
収穫する to harvest, to gather in

しゅうがくりょこう 修学旅行 *school excursion, educational trip (with one's teacher and fellow students)*
３年生は修学旅行で東京に行きます。
The third-year students will go to Tokyo on a school excursion.

しゅうかん 習慣 *habit, custom*
習慣が付く a habit forms
誕生日に赤飯を炊くのは日本の習慣です。
Cooking rice with red beans on birthdays is a Japanese custom.

しゅうかん 週刊 ～の *published weekly*
週刊誌 weekly magazine

-しゅうかん -週間 *1. week (Added to bases denoting an activity or purpose.)*
交通安全週間 Traffic Safety Week
2. (counter for weeks; see Appendix 2)
太郎ちゃんは２週間学校を休んでいます。
Taro has been absent from school for two weeks.

しゅうぎいん 衆議院 *the House of Representatives (the lower house in the Japanese Diet)* [↔ 衆議院]

衆議院議員 member of the House of Representatives

しゅうきょう 宗教 *religion*

しゅうぎょう 終業 [[↔ 始業]] *1. the end of work or school each day*

2. the end of a school term

終業式 end-of-the-term ceremony

じゅうぎょういん 従業員 *employee*

シュークリーム *cream puff*

しゅうごう 集合 *gathering, meeting, assembling*

集合する to gather, to meet (intransitive) [→ 集まる1.]

生徒は運動場に集合しました。

The students gathered on the playground.

集合場所 meeting place

集合時刻 meeting time

じゅうこうぎょう 重工業 *heavy industry*

じゅうごや 十五夜 *full-moon night*

しゅうさい 秀才 *brilliant person; talented person*

しゅうし 修士 *master's degree holder*

修士号 master's degree

修士論文 master's thesis

しゅうじ 習字 *learning calligraphy; learning penmanship*

じゅうじ 十字 *cross shape, the shape of the character for "ten" (十)*

十字架 cross for crucifixion

じゅうじつ 充実 *substantialness, repleteness; enrichment*

充実する to become more substantial, to become replete; to become enriched

しゅうしふ 終止符 *period ((punctuation mark))*

終止符を打つ to put a period; to put an end

じゅうじゅん 従順 〜な *obedient; docile*

花子ちゃんはおじいさんにとても従順だ。

Hanako is very obedient to her grandfather.

じゅうしょ 住所 *address*

名前と住所を記入しました。

I filled in my name and address.

住所録 address book, list of addresses

じゅうしょう 重傷 *serious injury*

運転手は事故で重傷を負いました。

The driver suffered a serious injury in the accident.

しゅうしょく 就職 *getting a job, being hired*

就職する to get a job, to find a job

姉は銀行に就職しました。

My older sister got a job at a bank.

就職を申し込む to apply for a job

就職口 job, job opening

就職試験 employment examination

しゅうしんけい 終身刑 *life sentence*

ジュース *1. juice*

2. fruit-flavored soft drink

しゅうぜん 修繕 *repair, fixing* [→ 修理]

修繕する to repair, to fix

じゅうたい 重態, 重体 *serious condition (due to illness)*

患者さんは重態です。

The patient is in a serious condition.

じゅうたい 渋滞 *delay, lack of progress, bogging down (most commonly used in reference to traffic)*

渋滞する to become delayed, to bog down

じゅうだい 十代 *the 10-19 age range, the teen years*

学生たちはまだ全員十代です。

The students are all still in their teens.

十代の少年〔少女〕 teenage boy〔girl〕

じゅうだい 重大 〜な *1. important* [→ 重要な]

2. serious, critical [→深刻な]

これは重大な問題です。
This is a serious problem.

じゅうたく 住宅 *house, dwelling, residence*
住宅地 residential area
住宅問題 housing problem
公団住宅 Japan Housing Corporation apartment
木造住宅 wooden house

しゅうだん 集団 *group, mass*
日本人はよく集団で行動するそうです。
They say that Japanese people often act in groups.
集団生活 group living
集団的な collective, group-oriented

じゅうたん 絨毯 *carpet; rug*
この部屋にじゅうたんを敷くつもりです。
I plan to lay a carpet in this room.
ペルシャじゅうたん Persian rug

しゅうちゅう 集中 *concentration, convergence*
集中する to concentrate, to focus (transitive or intransitive)
自分の仕事に集中してください。
Please concentrate on your own work.
選手たちはきょうの試合に注意を集中しています。
The players are focusing their attention on today's game.
集中力 ability to concentrate

しゅうてん 終点 *last stop, terminal, (UK) terminus*
私たちは終点でバスを降りました。
We got off the bus at the last stop.

じゅうてん 重点 *importance, emphasis, stress*
Aに重点を置く to put emphasis on A
この学校は音楽教育に重点を置いている。
This school is putting emphasis on music education.
重点的な high-priority

シュート *shot (in soccer, basketball, etc.)*
シュートする to shoot

シュート *screwball (pitch) (in baseball)*
シュートを投げる to throw a screwball

しゅうと 舅 *father-in-law* [→ 義父] [↔ 姑]

じゅうどう 柔道 *judo*
柔道部 judo club, judo team

しゅうとく 習得, 修得 *mastery, thorough learning*
習得する to master
あの天才は8歳で代数を習得しました。
That genius mastered algebra at the age of eight.

しゅうとめ 姑 *mother-in-law* [→ 義母] [↔ 舅]

じゅうなん 柔軟 ～な *flexible, pliant, supple*
大統領の考え方は柔軟です。
The president's way of thinking is flexible.

じゅうに 十二 *twelve (see Appendix 2)*
十二月 December
十二支 the twelve signs of the Chinese zodiac

じゅうにぶん 十二分（～に） *more than fully, to the fullest*

しゅうにゅう 収入 *income* [↔ 支出]
学校の先生の収入は少ないです。
A schoolteacher's income is small.

じゅうばこ 重箱 *stacked square lacquered boxes (for carrying food)*

しゅうばん 週番 *1. week-long duty*
2. person on duty for the week
私は今週の週番です。
I am the person on duty this week.

じゅうびょう 重病 *serious illness*
石山さんのお父さんは重病です。
Ms. Ishiyama's father is seriously ill.

しゅうぶん 秋分 *autumnal equinox* [↔ 春分]
秋分の日 Autumnal Equinox Day (a national holiday in Japan)

じゅうぶん 十分（～に） *enough, sufficiently; plenty, fully*
切符を買うお金は十分に持っています。
I have plenty of money to buy the ticket.
箱は十分に大きいです。
The box is large enough.
もう十分いただきました。
I've already had plenty.
この仕事は10日は十分にかかるでしょう。
This work will probably take a full ten days.
十分な sufficient, ample
30分あれば十分です。
Thirty minutes will be enough.

しゅうまつ 週末 *weekend*
週末に長崎へ旅行しました。
We made a trip to Nagasaki on the weekend.

じゅうみん 住民 *resident, inhabitant*
住民登録 resident registration
原住民 original inhabitant

じゅうやく 重役 *company executive, company director*

しゅうよう 収容 *accommodating, admitting, taking in*
収容する to accommodate, to admit, to take in
この会館は1000人収容できます。
This public hall can accommodate 1,000 people.
収容所 asylum; internment camp, concentration camp

じゅうよう 重要 ～な *important* [→大切な]
重要文化財 important cultural property
重要人物 very important person

じゅうらい 従来 *until now, heretofore*

しゅうり 修理 *repair, fixing*
この時計は修理が必要です。
This watch needs repair.
修理する to repair, to fix
父は壊れたドアを修理しました。
My father repaired the broken door.
この自転車を修理してもらいました。
I had this bicycle fixed.

しゅうりょう 終了 *end, conclusion* [→ 終わり]
終了する to end, to conclude (transitive or intransitive) [→ 終わる]

じゅうりょう 重量 *weight (of an object)*
重量挙げ weight lifting
重量挙げ選手 weightlifter

じゅうりょく 重力 *gravity (in physics)*
先生は重力の法則を説明してくださった。
The teacher explained the law of gravity to us.
無重力状態 weightlessness

しゅえい 守衛 *security guard for a building*

しゅえん 主演 *leading role, starring role*
主演する to play the leading role, to star
三船敏郎はあの映画で主演しました。
Toshiro Mifune starred in that movie.

しゅかんてき 主観的 ～な *subjective* [↔ 客観的な]
これは私の主観的な印象にすぎません。
This is nothing more than my subjective impression.

しゅぎ 主義 *principle, doctrine*
主義を守る to stick to one's principles
－主義 -ism (Added to noun bases.)
社会主義 socialism
資本主義 capitalism

じゅきょう 儒教 *Confucianism*

じゅぎょう 授業 *class, lessons at school*
1週間に34時間の授業があります。

There are 34 hours of classes a week.
1時間目に英語の授業があります。
We have an English class first period.
授業は3時に終わります。
Class ends at 3:00.
授業料 school fee, tuition
授業参観 class visit, parent's day

じゅく 塾 *after-school tutoring school*

じゅくご 熟語 *1. compound word written with two or more Chinese characters*
2. compound word [→ 複合語]

しゅくじつ 祝日 *national holiday*

しゅくしょう 縮小 *reduction, cutback*
縮小する to reduce, to cut back

じゅくする 熟する *{Irreg.} to ripen*
ぶどうは秋に熟します。
Grapes ripen in fall.
トマトはまだ熟していないね。
The tomatoes are not ripe yet, are they.
機が熟する the time becomes ripe

しゅくだい 宿題 *homework*
夏休みにも宿題がありますか。
Is there homework for the summer vacation too?
妹の宿題を手伝ってやった。
I helped my younger sister with her homework.

しゅくはく 宿泊 *lodging, staying (in a hotel, etc.)*
宿泊する to lodge, to stay
私たちは毎年このホテルに宿泊します。
We stay at this hotel every year.
宿泊料 room charge

しゅくふく 祝福 *blessing*
祝福する to bless
神父さんは赤ちゃんを祝福しました。
The priest blessed the child.

じゅくれん 熟練 *expert skill*
熟練する to become skilled
熟練工 skilled worker

しゅげい 手芸 *handicraft*

しゅけん 主権 *sovereignty*

じゅけん 受験 *taking an entrance examination*
受験する to take the entrance examination for
私も南高校を受験するつもりです。
I, too, intend to take the entrance examination for Minami High School.
受験番号 examinee's number
受験勉強 studying for an entrance examination
受験票 admission ticket for an examination
受験科目 entrance examination subjects
受験生 student preparing for an entrance examination

しゅご 主語 *subject (of a sentence)* [↔ 述語]

しゅさい 主催 *sponsorship, auspices*
花の展示会はテレビ局の主催です。
The flower show is sponsored by a TV station.
主催する to sponsor
主催者 sponsor, promoter

しゅざい 取材 *gathering information (for a book, news report, etc.)*
取材する to gather information for
AにBを取材する to gather information from A for B

しゅし 趣旨, 主旨 *1. main idea, point, purport*
その政治家の演説の趣旨がわかりません。
I don't understand the point of that politician's speech.
2. aim, objective, purpose [→ 目的]
議員は法案の趣旨を説明しました。

The Diet member explained the aim of the bill.

しゅじゅつ 手術 *surgery, operation*

手術を受ける to undergo an operation

しゅしょう 主将 *(team) captain*

早見君は野球部の主将です。

Hayami is captain of the baseball team.

しゅしょう 首相 *prime minister*

首相官邸 the Official Residence of the Prime Minister (of Japan)

じゅしょう 受賞 ～する *to win a prize*

青山さんは弁論大会で１等賞を受賞した。

Ms. Aoyama won first prize in the debating contest.

受賞者 prize winner

しゅしょく 主食 *principal food, staple food*

日本では米が主食です。

In Japan rice is the staple food.

しゅじん 主人 *1. husband* [→ 夫]

2. master; employer

3. proprietor, shop owner; head of the household

主人公 hero, heroine, protagonist (of a story)

ご主人【HON. for (above)】

じゅしん 受信 [[↔ 発信]] *receipt of a message; reception of a broadcast*

受信する to receive

受信機 receiver ((machine))

じゅず 数珠 *rosary, string of rosary beads*

しゅだい 主題 *main subject, theme*

主題歌 theme song

しゅだん 手段 *means, way* [→ 方法]

医者は赤ちゃんを救うために、あらゆる手段を尽くしました。

The doctor exhausted every means to save the baby.

その問題を解決する手段はないです。

There is no way to settle that problem.

手段を取る to take measures

しゅちょう 主張 *assertion, insistence*

主張する to insist on, to assert

被告は自分が正しいと主張しました。

The defendant insisted that he was right.

市民は権利を主張しました。

The citizens asserted their rights.

しゅつえん 出演 *appearance as a performer*

出演する to appear as a performer, to perform

あの歌手はあしたテレビに出演します。

That singer will appear on TV tomorrow.

娘は学校の劇に出演します。

My daughter will perform in a school play.

出演料 performance fee, appearance fee

出演者 performer, player

しゅっきん 出勤 *going to work, presence at work*

出勤する to go to work, to appear at work

父は土曜日も出勤します。

My father goes to work on Saturday too.

しゅっけつ 出血 *bleeding, hemorrhage*

出血する to bleed, to hemorrhage

じゅつご 述語 *predicate* [↔ 主語]

しゅっこく 出国 *departure from a country* [↔ 入国]

出国する to depart (from a country)

しゅっさん 出産 *giving birth*

出産する to give birth to [→ 産む]

しゅつじょう 出場 *taking part, participation (in a performance or contest)*

出場する to take part, to participate

マラソンに出場しようよ。

Let's participate in the marathon!

しゅっしん 出身 *1. origin, being born*

ご出身はどちらですか。

Where are you from?

2. being a graduate
父は京都大学の出身です。
My father is a graduate of Kyoto University.
出身地 home town, birthplace
出身校 alma mater

しゅっせき 出席 *presence, attendance* [↔ 欠席]
出席する to be present, to attend
全員が出席しています。
All the members are present.
そのパーティーに出席するつもりです。
I plan to attend that party.
出席を取る to call the roll, to take attendance
出席簿 roll, attendance book
出席者 person who is present

しゅっちょう 出張 *business trip*
出張する to make a business trip
父はあした福岡へ出張します。
My father is going to make a business trip to Fukuoka tomorrow.

しゅっぱつ 出発 *departure, starting out* [↔ 到着]
エンジン故障のため出発が1時間延びた。
Because of engine trouble, the departure was delayed for an hour.
出発する to depart, to leave, to start out
私たちは日の出前に出発しました。
We started out before sunrise.
出発時刻 departure time
出発点 starting point

しゅっぱん 出版 *publishing, publication*
出版する to publish
この絵本は去年出版されました。
This picture book was published last year.
出版物 a publication
出版社 publishing company

しゅっぴ 出費 *expenditure, outlay, expense*
出費を切り詰める to cut down on one's expenses

しゅつりょく 出力 *output* [→ アウトプット] [↔ 入力]

しゅと 首都 *capital*
日本の首都は東京です。
The capital of Japan is Tokyo.
首都圏 the Tokyo metropolitan area
首都高速道路 the (Tokyo) Metropolitan Expressway

しゅとく 取得 *acquisition*
取得する to acquire, to obtain

しゅにく 朱肉 *vermilion inkpad (used to ink signature seals)*

しゅのう 首脳 *head, leader*
首脳会談 summit meeting

しゅび 守備 *1. defense against attack*
守備する to defend, to guard
2. defense (in sports), fielding (in baseball)
守備に就く to go on defense, to take the field

しゅふ 主婦 *housewife, homemaker*

しゅみ 趣味 *1. hobby, pastime*
私の趣味は切手収集です。
My hobby is stamp collecting.
2. taste, preference, liking [→ 好み]
松波さんは服の趣味がいいです。
Ms. Matsunami's taste in clothes is good.

じゅみょう 寿命 *life span*
象は寿命が長いですね。
An elephant's life span is long, isn't it?
平均寿命 average life span
日本人女性の平均寿命は80歳を越えた。
The average life span of Japanese women has exceeded 80 years.

しゅもく 種目 *item of a particular type;*

event (in a competition)
フィールド種目 field events
トラック種目 track events

しゅやく 主役 *leading part, starring role*
恵子さんは劇で主役を演じます。
Keiko will play the leading part in the play.

しゅよう 主要 ～な *main, chief, principal, major* [→ 主な]
主要産業 principal industries
主要都市 major cities

じゅよう 需要 *demand, desire to obtain* [↔ 供給]
需要供給 supply and demand

しゅりょう 狩猟 *hunting*
狩猟に行く to go hunting
狩猟家 hunter

しゅるい 種類 *kind, sort, type*
この種類の本を買いました。
I bought a book of this kind.
この二つは種類が同じです。
These two are the same kind.
あらゆる種類 all kinds
一種類 (counter for kinds; see Appendix 2)
何種類のりんごがありますか。
How many kinds of apples are there?

じゅわき 受話器 *receiver (i.e., the part of a telephone or other device held to the ear to hear a transmission)*

じゅん— 準— *semi-, quasi- (Added to noun bases.)*
準決勝 championship semifinal
準々決勝 championship quarter final

じゅん 順 *order, sequence* [→ 順序]
順に in order, in sequence, by turns
背の順に並んでください。
Please line up in order of height.
子供たちは順にバスに乗りました。
The children got on the bus in order.
順々に one by one, each in turn; one step at a time
生徒たちは順々に歌を歌いました。
The students each sang a song in turn.
番号順 numerical order
ABC順 alphabetical order
先着順 order of arrival

じゅんい 順位 *order, ranking*
順位を決めるのに時間がかかりました。
It took time to decide the ranking.

しゅんかん 瞬間 *1. moment, instant*
瞬間に instantaneously, in an instant
2. (～に) the moment, the instant (following a past-tense verb)
蛇を見た瞬間、弟は泣き出したよ。
The moment he saw the snake, my younger brother started crying!

じゅんかん 循環 *circulation; rotation; cycle*
循環する to circulate; to rotate; to move in a circular path

じゅんさ 巡査 *police patrol officer*
交通巡査 traffic police officer

じゅんじょ 順序 *order, sequence* [→ 順]
ページの順序が違うよ。
The page order is wrong!
順序正しい orderly, systematic
順序よく in appropriate sequence, in orderly fashion

じゅんしん 純真 ～な *pure-hearted, innocent*

じゅんすい 純粋 ～な／の *pure*
純粋な心 pure heart

じゅんちょう 順調 ～な *smooth, free from difficulties*
手術後の経過は順調です。
My progress has been smooth since the operation.
すべて順調に進行しました。

Everything went smoothly.

しゅんとう 春闘 *spring labor offensive (when Japanese labor unions traditionally demand wage increases and threaten strikes)*

じゅんばん 順番 *1. order, sequence* [→ 順序]

順番に in order, in sequence, by turns

2. one's turn [→ 番1.]

ここで順番を待ってください。

Please wait for your turn here.

じゅんび 準備 *preparations* [→ 用意]

父は出張の準備で忙しいです。

My father is busy with preparations for a business trip.

私たちは修学旅行の準備をしています。

We are making preparations for the school excursion.

準備する to prepare, to make ready

準備運動 warm-up exercise

しゅんぶん 春分 *vernal equinox* [↔ 秋分]

春分の日 Vernal Equinox Day (a national holiday in Japan)

しよう 私用 *1. private use, personal use*

2. private business, personal business

父は私用で京都に行きます。

My father will go to Kyoto on personal business.

しよう 使用 *use*

使用する to use [→ 使う]

この計算機を使用してもいいですか。

May I use this calculator?

使用中の in-use

使用法 way of using

使用者 user

しょう 省 *(government) ministry; department (in the U.S. federal government)*

しょう 章 *chapter*

—章 (counter for chapters; see Appendix 2)

しょう 賞 *prize, award*

娘は書道展で賞を取りました。

My daughter won a prize in the calligraphy exhibition.

アカデミー賞 Academy Award

一等賞 first prize

ノーベル賞 Nobel Prize

—じょう —畳 *(counter for mats (i.e.,), the traditional units of measure for room size; see Appendix 2)*

じょう 錠 *lock*

かぎでドアの錠を開けました。

I opened the lock on the door with the key.

錠が掛かる a lock becomes locked

このスーツケースは錠がかかっています。

This suitcase's lock is locked.

錠を掛ける to lock a lock

じょういん 上院 [[↔ 下院]] *upper house (of a legislature); the Senate (in the United States Congress); the House of Lords (in the British Parliament)*

上院議員 upper-house member

じょうえん 上演 *staging, performance*

上演する to stage, to put on

来月その劇を上演します。

They will stage that play next month.

しょうか 消化 *digestion*

消化する to digest

生野菜は消化するまでに時間がかかる。

Raw vegetables take time to digest.

消化器官 digestive organs

消化不良 indigestion

しょうか 消火 *fire extinguishing*

消火する to put out (The direct object must be a dangerous fire.)

消火に当たる to fight a fire

消火器 fire extinguisher

消火栓 fire hydrant

しょうが 生姜 *ginger ((spice))*

しょうかい 紹介 *introduction, presentation*

紹介する to introduce, to present

由美ちゃんを両親に紹介しました。

I introduced Yumi to my parents.

この記事は今月の新刊を紹介しています。

This article introduces this month's new books.

紹介状 letter of introduction

自己紹介 introducing oneself

しょうがい 生涯 *one's lifetime, one's whole life* [→ 一生]

しょうがい 障害 *obstacle, impediment*

障害物競走 obstacle race

言語障害 speech impediment

しょうがくきん 奨学金 *a scholarship*

しょうがくせい 小学生 *(US) elementary school pupil, (UK) primary school pupil*

妹はまだ小学生です。

My younger sister is still an elementary-school pupil.

しょうがつ 正月 *1. the New Year season (the first several days of the new year)*

お正月を楽しみにしています。

I'm looking forward to the New Year season.

2. New Year's Day [→ 元日]

お正月にはお雑煮を食べます。

On New Year's Day we eat ozoni.

しょうがっこう 小学校 *(US) elementary school, (UK) primary school*

弟が小学校に入学しました。

My younger brother entered elementary school.

妹は小学校の５年生です。

My younger sister is a fifth-year pupil in elementary school.

しょうがない 【COL. for 仕方がない *(s.v.* 仕方*)*】 *it can't be helped, there's nothing one can do*

じょうき 蒸気 *steam, vapor*

蒸気機関車 steam locomotive

じょうぎ 定規 *drafting tool; ruler*

三角定規 drafting triangle

T定規 T-square

じょうきゃく 乗客 *(paying) passenger*

電車にはたくさんの乗客が乗っていました。

A lot of passengers were riding on the train.

じょうきゅう 上級 *high rank, upper class* [↔ 下級; 初級]

上級の high-ranking, advanced

上級コース advanced course

上級生 student in one of the upper grades, (US) upperclassman

しょうぎょう 商業 *commerce, business*

商業英語 business English

商業高校 commercial high school

じょうきょう 状況 *circumstances, state of affairs*

状況を説明してください。

Please explain the circumstances.

じょうきょう 上京 *going to Tokyo (from elsewhere in Japan)*

上京する to go to Tokyo

しょうきょくてき 消極的 〜な *passive, not actively involved, lacking an active interest* [↔ 積極的な]

村山さんは消極的な性格です。

Mr. Murayama has a passive personality.

その作家の人生観は消極的です。

That writer's view of life lacks an active interest.

しょうきん 賞金 *prize money; reward money*

Aに賞金を出す to offer prize/reward money for A

忍は迷子になった犬に賞金を出した。

Shinobu offered reward money for her lost dog.

じょうげ 上下 *top and bottom; high and low*
ゴンドラは上下に動きます。
The gondolas move up and down.
上下する to go up and down, to rise and fall

しょうげき 衝撃 *1. shock, impact*
衝撃を受ける to receive a shock, to receive an impact
衝撃を与える to give a shock, to make an impact
2. (emotional) shock, trauma [→ ショック]

しょうけん 証券 *securities, stocks and bonds*
証券会社 securities company

じょうけん 条件 *condition, prerequisite*
一生懸命勉強することが合格の条件です。
Studying hard is a condition of success.
飛行機に乗らないという条件で行きます。
I will go on condition that we will not board a plane.
条件付きの conditional

しょうこ 証拠 *evidence, proof*
この人が犯人だという証拠があるのか。
Is there any evidence that this person is a criminal?
それはだれでもできるという証拠です。
That's proof that anyone can do it.
証拠を集める to gather evidence

しょうご 正午 *noon*
正午のニュースは放送されませんでした。
The noon news was not broadcast.

じょうざい 錠剤 *tablet ((medicine))*

しょうじ 障子 *shoji (a sliding door or sliding screen made of translucent paper glued to a wooden lattice)*

しょうじき 正直 *honesty, truthfulness, frankness*
正直な honest, frank
太郎ちゃんは正直な少年です。
Taro is an honest boy.
正直に言って、上田さんは嫌いです。
Frankly speaking, I dislike Mr. Ueda.
三度目の正直。(proverb)
Third time lucky. (Literally: Honesty of the third time.)

じょうしき 常識 *common sense, common knowledge*
あの人は常識がないね。
That person has no common sense, does he?

じょうしゃ 乗車 *boarding, getting on/in (a train, bus, car, etc.)* [↔ 下車]
乗車する to get (on/in a train, bus, car, etc.)
乗車券 ticket (for a ride)

じょうじゅん 上旬 *the first third of a month* [→ 初旬] [↔ 中旬; 下旬]
4月の上旬には桜が満開でしょう。
In early April the cherry trees will probably be in full bloom.

しょうしょ 証書 *deed; bond; certificate*
卒業証書 diploma

しょうじょ 少女 *girl* [↔ 少年]
少女雑誌 girls' magazine

しょうしょう 少々 *a little, a bit, slightly* [→ やや]

しょうじょう 賞状 *certificate of merit, certificate of commendation*

しょうじょう 症状 *symptoms, condition (of illness)*

しょうじる 生じる *1. to give rise to, to bring about*
2. to arise, to come about, to occur

じょうず 上手 〜な *skillful, good (at)*
(This adjectival noun is used to describe both the people who are skillful and the things they are skillful at.) [↔ 下手な]
京子さんは英語が上手です。
Kyoko is good at English.
母は父よりテニスが上手です。
My mother is better at tennis than my father.

特別に話し上手な人はいません。
There is nobody especially good at talking.

しょうすう 小数 *decimal fraction*

小数点 decimal point

しょうすう 少数 [[↔ 多数]] *1. ～の few, a small number of*

ごく少数の学生がその事を知っています。
A very small number of students know that fact.

2. minority

少数意見 minority opinion

しょうせつ 小説 *novel, story, work of fiction*

この小説はベストセラーになるでしょう。
This novel will probably become a best seller.

小説家 novelist

歴史小説 historical novel

推理小説 mystery novel, detective story

しょうぞう 肖像 *portrait, likeness (of a person)*

しょうそく 消息 *news, tidings, word*

古川さんからは何も消息がありません。
There is no word from Ms. Furukawa.

しょうたい 招待 *invitation*

招待する to invite [→ 招く1.]

誕生日会に花子ちゃんを招待します。
I'll invite Hanako to my birthday party.

招待状 invitation, letter of invitation

招待券 invitation ticket

じょうたい 状態 *condition, state*

現在の状態では、出発できません。
We cannot leave under present conditions.

健康状態 state of health

精神状態 mental state

しょうだく 承諾 consent, assent [→ 承知1.]

承諾する to consent to

じょうたつ 上達 *improvement, progress*

上達する to improve, to make progress

洋子さんはスケートが大いに上達した。
Yoko's skating greatly improved.

じょうだん 冗談 *joke, jest*

その冗談がわからなかった。
I didn't understand that joke.

冗談じゃないよ。
Get serious! (Literally: It's not a joke!)

冗談に jokingly, in jest

冗談を言う to joke, to tell a joke, to make a joke

あの先生は授業中によく冗談を言います。
That teacher often tells jokes during class.

冗談半分に half in jest

しょうち 承知 *1. consent, assent* [→ 承諾]

承知する to consent to

若杉さんは転勤することを承知しました。
Mr. Wakasugi consented to being transferred.

承知しました。
All right. (Literally: I have consented.)

2. knowing, being aware

承知の上で knowingly, intentionally

承知する to come to know, to become aware of

ご承知のように 【HON.】 as you know

しょうちょう 象徴 *symbol, emblem*

はとは平和の象徴です。
The dove is the symbol of peace.

象徴する to symbolize

しょうてん 商店 *(US) store, shop* [→ 店]

商店街 shop-lined street; shopping center

商店主 storekeeper

しょうてん 焦点 *focus, focal point*

Aの焦点を合わせる to focus A

カメラの焦点を鳥に合わせました。
I focused my camera on the bird.

焦点が合っている to be in focus
焦点が外れている to be out of focus

じょうとう 上等 〜の *first-class, excellent, high-quality*
お土産に上等のワインをもらいました。
I received first-class wine as a gift.
上等品 high-quality item

しょうどく 消毒 *disinfection, sterilization*
消毒する to disinfect, to sterilize

しょうとつ 衝突 *1. collision*
衝突する to collide
車が木に衝突しました。
The car collided into a tree.
2. clash, conflict
兄は母とよく意見が衝突します。
My older brother's opinion often clashes with my mother's.
衝突事故 collision accident
正面衝突 head-on collision

しょうにか 小児科 *pediatrics*

しょうにん 商人 *merchant; (US) storekeeper, shopkeeper*

しょうにん 証人 *witness, person who gives testimony*

じょうねつ 情熱 *passion, enthusiasm*
情熱的な passionate, enthusiastic

しょうねん 少年 *boy* [↔ 少女]
一郎君は利口な少年です。
Ichiro is a bright boy.
少年時代 one's boyhood years
少年雑誌 boys' magazine

じょうば 乗馬 *1. horse riding*
2. riding horse
乗馬クラブ horse-riding club

しょうばい 商売 *1. business, buying and selling*
祖父は15歳で商売を始めました。
My grandfather started a business at the age of fifteen.
うちの商売は八百屋です。
My family's business is a vegetable store.
2. occupation, profession, trade [→ 職業]
商売道具 tools of one's trade

じょうはつ 蒸発 *evaporation, vaporization*
蒸発する to evaporate, to become vaporized
水は熱すると、蒸発します。
Water evaporates when it heats up.

じょうはんしん 上半身 *upper half of the body* [↔ 下半身]

しょうひ 消費 *consumption, expending* [↔ 生産]
消費する to consume, to use up
このストーブは石油を大量に消費します。
This heater consumes a lot of oil.
消費者 consumer
消費税 consumption tax, sales tax

しょうひん 商品 *item for sale, item of merchandise*
商品券 gift certificate

しょうひん 賞品 *prize item*
運動会で賞品をたくさんもらったよ。
I got a lot of prizes in the athletic meet!

じょうひん 上品 〜な *genteel, elegant, refined* [↔下品な]
次郎さんのお母さんは上品な方です。
Jiro's mother is a refined person.
高内さんは上品なドレスを着ています。
Ms. Takauchi is wearing an elegant dress.

しょうぶ 勝負 *game, match, contest* [→ 試合]
ついに勝負に勝った。
At last we won the game
勝負する to play a game, to have a match, to compete
勝負に勝つ〔負ける〕 to win〔lose〕a game
いい勝負 evenly-matched contest

勝負事 gambling

じょうぶ 丈夫 ～な *1. strong, healthy, robust*

祖父は80歳ですが、とても丈夫です。
My grandfather is 80, but he's very healthy.

2. solid, strong, durable

丈夫な縄を使ってください。
Please use a strong rope.

しょうべん 小便 *urine*

小便をする to urinate

寝小便 bed wetting

じょうほ 譲歩 *concession, yielding*

譲歩する to make a concession, to yield

しょうぼう 消防 *fire fighting*

消防自動車 fire engine

消防士 fireman, (US) fire fighter

消防署 fire station, fire house

じょうほう 情報 *information, piece of information*

その情報は今入りました。
That information came in just now.

情報を得る to obtain information

情報化社会 information-oriented society

情報産業 information industry

最新情報 the latest information

じょうみゃく 静脈 *vein ((blood vessel))* [↔ 動脈]

しょうめい 証明 *proof, verification*

証明する to prove, to verify

弁護士は私がそこにいたことを証明した。
The lawyer proved that I was there?

証明書 certificate

しょうめい 照明 *(artificial) lighting, (artificial) illumination*

舞台照明 stage lighting

しょうめん 正面 *1. front side, front surface*

そのビルの正面は大理石でできています。
The front of that building is marble.

2. the area straight in front, the area facing

駅の正面に花屋があります。
There is a flower shop opposite the station.

正面玄関 front vestibule

正面衝突 head-on collision

じょうやく 条約 *treaty*

首相はその条約に調印しました。
The prime minister signed the treaty.

平和条約 peace treaty

日米安全保障条約 the Japan-US Security Treaty

しょうゆ 醤油 *soy sauce*

じょうよう 常用 *common use, general use, everyday use*

常用する to use commonly, to use regularly, to use generally

常用漢字 Characters for General Use

(the 1,945 (Chinese characters) designated by the Japanese Ministry of Education in 1981 to be taught in the first nine years of schooling)

しょうらい 将来 *1. the future* [→ 未来]

将来の夢は何ですか。
What are your dreams for the future?

近い将来に宇宙旅行ができるでしょう。
We will probably be able to travel into space in the near future.

2. in the future

将来デザイナーになりたいと思います。
In the future I think I'd like to be a designer.

しょうり 勝利 *victory* [→ 勝ち] [↔ 敗北]

勝利を得る to win a victory

勝利者 victor, winner

勝利投手 winning pitcher

じょうりく 上陸 *coming ashore, landing*

上陸する to come ashore, to land

避難民はサンフランシスコに上陸した。

The refugees landed at San Francisco.

しょうりゃく 省略 *1. omission, leaving out*

省略する to omit, to leave out

この文の「that」は省略してもいいです。
You may omit "that" in this sentence.

2. abbreviation; abridgement

省略する to abbreviate; to abridge

ロサンゼルスを省略してロスと呼びます。
One abbreviates Los Angeles as Los.

じょうりゅう 上流[[↔ 下流]] *1. the area upriver; upper portion of a river*

この橋の上流にダムがあります。
There is a dam upriver from this bridge.

2. upper social stratum

上流階級upper class [↔ 中流階級]

じょうりゅう 蒸留 *distillation*

蒸留する to distill

蒸留水 distilled water

しょうりょう 小量 ～の *a little, a small amount of* [↔ 多量の]

しょうわ 昭和 *(Japanese imperial era name for the period 1926-1989)*

昭和時代 the Showa Era

昭和天皇 the Showa Emperor

ショー *a show*

ショーウインドー *display window*

じょおう 女王 *queen* [↔ 王]

女王蜂 queen bee

エリザベス女王Queen Elizabeth

ジョーカー *joker ((playing card))*

ジョーク *joke* [→ 冗談]

ショート *shortstop* [→ 遊撃手]

ショート *short (circuit)*

ショートする to short-circuit (intransitive)

ショール *shawl*

ショールーム *showroom*

しょき 初期 *beginning period, early stage*

この作品は江戸の初期の物です。
This work is from the beginning of the Edo period.

しょき 書記 *secretary, clerk*

書記長 chief secretary

しょきゅう 初級 *beginning rank, beginning class* [↔ 上級]

ジョギング *jogging*

ジョギングする to jog

しょく 職 *job, position, employment*

兄は今年の 4 月にこの職に就きました。
My older brother took this job in April of this year.

しょくいん 職員 *staff member*

治さんのお父さんはこの病院の職員です。
Osamu's father is a staff member of this hospital.

職員会議 staff meeting

職員室 staff room

しょくえん 食塩 *table salt*

食塩水 salt-water solution

しょくぎょう 職業 *occupation, profession, vocation*

お父さんの職業は何ですか。
What is your father's occupation?

職業安定所 employment security office

職業学校 vocational school

職業教育 vocational education; professional education

しょくじ 食事 *meal, repast*

来る前に軽く食事をとりました。
I had a light meal before I came.

小西さんは私たちを食事に招いてくれた。
Ms. Konishi invited us over for a meal.

食事をする to have a meal, to eat

私たちは一日に三度食事をします。
We eat three times a day.

今晩は外で食事をします。
I will eat out tonight.
食事中の in the middle of having a meal

しょくたく 食卓 *dining table*
どうぞ食卓に着いてください。
Please sit at the dining table.
食卓を用意する to set the table
食卓を片付ける to clear the table

しょくどう 食堂 *1. dining room*
2. restaurant; cafeteria
食堂車 dining car

しょくにん 職人 *craftsman, artisan*
職人芸 craftsmanship, skillful work

しょくひん 食品 *food item, grocery item*
インスタント食品 instant food
加工食品 processed food
健康食品 health food
冷凍食品 frozen food
自然食品 natural food

しょくぶつ 植物 *plant, vegetation*
母は室内で植物をたくさん育てています。
My mother grows a lot of plants indoors.
野生の植物 wild plant
植物園 botanical garden
植物学 botany
植物学者 botanist
植物人間 vegetable ((person))
高山植物 alpine plant
熱帯植物 tropical plant

しょくみん 植民 *1. colonization*
植民する to start a colony, to settle
2. colonist, settler
植民地 colony

しょくもつ 食物 *food* [→ 食べ物]

しょくよう 食用 *use as food, using for food*
食用の edible
食用油 cooking oil

しょくよく 食欲 *appetite*
きょうは食欲があまりないです。
I don't have much appetite today.
おう盛な食欲 hearty appetite, good appetite

しょくりょう 食料 *food* [→ 食べ物]
食料になる to be edible
食料品 food item, grocery item [→ 食品]
食料品店 grocery store

しょくりょう 食糧 *food, foodstuff*
キャンプの間の食糧は十分あります。
We have plenty of food for camping.
食糧危機 food crisis
食糧問題 food problem

じょげん 助言 *advice, helpful suggestion*
医者の助言に従いました。
I followed the doctor's advice.
助言する to advise
私は由美に早めに出るよう助言しました。
I advised Yumi to leave early.

じょこう 徐行 ~する *to go slow*
工事のため電車は徐行しています。
The train is going slow because of construction work.

しょさい 書斎 *study ((room))*

じょし 女子 [[↔ 男子]] *girl; woman* [→ 女性]
女子大学 women's college
女子大生 woman college student
女子高校 girls' high school
女子生徒 girl pupil

じょし 助詞 *particle (a part of speech in traditional Japanese grammar)*

じょしゅ 助手 *assistant, helper*
運転助手 assistant driver

しょじゅん 初旬 *the first third of a month*

[→ 上旬]

しょじょ 処女 *virgin, maiden*

処女作 maiden work, first work

じょじょに 徐々に *gradually, slowly, little by little* [→ 段々]

手島さんの健康は徐々に回復しています。
Mr. Teshima's health is gradually improving.

しょしんしゃ 初心者 *beginner, novice*

じょせい 女性 *woman* [↔ 男性]

女性解放 women's liberation

しょぞく 所属 *affiliation, membership*

所属する to become affiliated, to become a member

私は美術部に所属しています。
I belong to the art club.

しょたい 所帯 *(independent) household*

しょたいめん 初対面 *first meeting (between people)*

池口さんとはきょうが初対面です。
Today will be the first time for me to meet Mr. Ikeguchi.

しょち 処置 *measure, step, action*

処置する to deal with, to take care of

しょっき 食器 *tableware, dish*

食器棚 dish cupboard

ジョッキ *beer mug, stein*

ジョッキー *jockey*

ショック *(emotional) shock, trauma* [→ 衝撃2.]

かわいがっていた猫が死んで、梅木さんはショックでした。
The cat she loved died, and Ms. Umeki was shocked.

ショック死 death from shock

しょっちゅう【COL. for 始終】 *always; often; constantly*

ショッピング *shopping* [→ 買い物]

けさ銀座へショッピングに行きました。
This morning I went shopping in Ginza.

しょてん 書店 *(US) bookstore, (UK) bookshop*

じょどうし 助動詞 *inflected auxiliary suffix (a part of speech in some versions of Japanese grammar)*

しょとく 所得 *income* [→ 収入]

所得税 income tax

しょひょう 書評 *book review*

しょぶん 処分 *1. disposal, disposition, settling* [→ 始末1.]

処分する to dispose of, to take care of, to settle

この空き箱をどう処分しましょうか。
How shall we dispose of these empty boxes?

2. punishment [→ 罰]

処分する to punish [→ 罰する]

しょほ 初歩 *rudiments, basics*

私はイタリア語の初歩を復習しています。
I'm reviewing the rudiments of Italian.

妹は初歩からピアノを習います。
My younger sister is going to study piano from the basics.

しょみん 庶民 *ordinary people, the general public, the masses*

庶民的な popular among the masses

しょめい 署名 *signature*

署名する to sign one's name

お客さんは小切手に署名しました。
The customer signed his name on the check.

署名運動 signature-collecting campaign

しょゆう 所有 *possession, ownership*

所有する to come to possess, to come to own

池田さんがこの建物を所有しています。
Mr. Ikeda owns this building.

所有物 belongings, possessions

所有者 owner

じょゆう 女優 *actress*

しょり 処理 *management, treatment, disposal* [→ 処分1.]

処理する to manage, to treat, to deal with, to take care of

その問題は処理できません。
I cannot deal with that problem.

しょるい 書類 *documents, papers*

重要書類 important documents

ショルダーバッグ *shoulder bag*

しょんべん【CRUDE for 小便】 *piss*

しらが 白髪 *gray hair; white hair*

あの白髪の男性はだれですか。
Who is that gray-haired man?

白髪になる to become gray-haired

しらかば 白樺 *white birch*

しらける 白ける *to become uninteresting, to lose it's pleasant atmosphere*

しらせ 知らせ *notification, news*

その知らせを聞いて驚きました。
I heard that news and was surprised.

しらせる 知らせる *to tell, to report, to let know*

AにBを知らせる to tell A B, to report B to A, to let A know B

新しい住所を知らせてください。
Please let me know your new address.

しらべる 調べる *1. to examine, to investigate, to look into, to look up*

歴史家は昔の記録を調べました。
The historian examined the old records.

その場所を地図で調べなさい。
Look up the place on the map.

2. to search, to consult

図書館で百科事典を調べました。
I consulted an encyclopedia in the library.

しらみ 虱 *louse*

しらんかお 知らん顔 *acting as if one doesn't know, attitude of indifference*

知らん顔をする to act as if one doesn't know, to show indifference

しり 尻 *buttocks, bottom*

尻取り word-chain game

(A game in which each player must say a word beginning with the last letter in the previous player's word. For example, if one player says (さかな), the next player might say (なつ).)

尻餅 slipping and falling on one's bottom

尻餅をつく to slip and fall on one's bottom

しりあい 知り合い *an acquaintance*

宮下さんは私の知り合いです。
Ms. Miyashita is an acquaintance of mine.

シリーズ *1. series (of games between the same opponents)*

2. series (of books, movies, etc.)

日本シリーズ the Japan Series (the championship series in Japanese professional baseball)

シャーロック・ホームズのシリーズ the Sherlock Holmes series

しりぞく 退く *1. to move back, to step back*

2. to retire from, to resign from

しりぞける 退ける *1. to repulse, to turn away*

2. to keep away, to prevent from approaching [→ 遠ざける1.]

3. to refuse, to reject [→ 断る1.]

しりつ 市立 ～の *municipal, administered by a city*

市立高校 municipal high school

市立図書館 municipal library

しりつ 私立 ～の *private, privately administered* [↔ 公立の]

娘は私立の女子中学校に通っています。
My daughter is going to a private junior high school for girls.

私立高校 private high school

私立探偵 private detective

しりょう 資料 *materials, data*

資料を集める to collect data

しりょく 視力 *eyesight, vision, ability to see*

倉田さんは交通事故で視力を失いました。
Mr. Kurata lost his eyesight in a traffic accident.

視力がいい〔悪い〕 one's eyesight is good〔bad〕

視力検査 eye test

しる 汁 *1. juice; sap*

レモンの汁 lemon juice

2. soup; broth

味噌汁 miso soup

しる 知る *{5} to come to know, to find out*

テレビでそれを知りました。
I found that out from TV.

知っている to know, to know about

(The corresponding negative, however, is 知らない; the expected form 知っていない is not used.)

明子さんは歌をたくさん知っているよ。
Akiko knows a lot of songs!

ずっと前から坂田さんを知っています。
I've known Ms. Sakata since long ago.

日本のことはあまりよく知りません。
I don't know very much about Japan.

純がどこに住んでいるか知っていますか。
Do you know where Jun lives?

シルエット *silhouette*

シルクハット *silk hat, top hat*

しるし 印 *1. identifying mark*

印をつける to put a mark

新しい単語に赤鉛筆で印をつけました。
I put marks on the new words with a red pencil.

2. sign, symbol, token

課長は同意の印にうなずきました。
The section chief nodded as a sign of agreement.

シルバーシート *"silver" seat, priority seat (Provided for elderly and handicapped passengers on public transportation in Japan.)*

しろ 白 *white (as a noun)*

白地 white background

しろ 城 *castle*

しろうと 素人 *an amateur, a non-expert* [↔ 玄人]

しろい 白い *1. white (as an adjective)*

会長は白い服を着ています。
The chairperson is wearing white clothes.

2. fair, light (describing a person's skin)

正子さんは肌が白いです。
Masako's skin is fair.

シロップ *syrup*

しろみ 白身 *1. white (of an egg)* [↔ 黄身]

2. white meat (of a fish)

白身の魚 fish with white meat

しわ 皺 *wrinkle*

しわざ 仕業 *act, deed, (a person's) doing*

これは弟の仕業に違いないよ。
This must be my younger brother's doing!

しん 芯 *core, pith, heart*

このりんごはしんまで腐っているよ。
This apple is rotten to the core!

ろうそくのしん candle wick

鉛筆のしん pencil lead

しん－ 新－ *new (Added to noun bases.)* [↔ 旧－]

新記録 new record

新体操 rhythmic gymnastics

しんか 進化 *evolution*

進化する to evolve

進化論 the theory of evolution

シンガー *singer*

シンガーソングライター singer-songwriter

しんがく 進学 *advancement, going on (to a higher-level school)*

進学する to advance, to go on

工業高校に進学したいです。

I want to go on to a technical high school.

じんかく 人格 *personal character, personality*

人格者 person of fine character

二重人格 dual personality

しんがた 新型 *new model, new type*

これは新型の車です。

This is a new-model car.

しんかんせん 新幹線 the Shinkansen, the Bullet Train

新幹線で名古屋へ行きました。

We went to Nagoya on the Shinkansen.

東海道新幹線 the Tokaido Shinkansen

しんきゅう 進級 *promotion (to a higher grade in school or to a higher rank)*

進級する to be promoted, to move up

しんくう 真空 *vacuum*

真空管 vacuum tube

ジンクス *jinx*

シングルス *singles (in sports)* [↔ ダブルス]

シンクロナイズドスイミング *synchronized swimming*

しんけい 神経 *a nerve*

神経が太い to have a lot of nerve, to be daring

神経が鋭い〔鈍い〕to be sensitive〔insensitive〕(describing a person)

神経学 neurology

神経質な nervous by temperament, high-strung

神経症 neurosis [→ ノイローゼ]

神経痛 neuralgia

しんげつ 新月 *new moon* [↔ 満月]

しんけん 真剣 ～な *serious, earnest* [→ 本気の]

警官は真剣な顔をしています。

The police officer has a serious look on his face.

真剣にそう言いましたよ。

I said so seriously!

じんけん 人権 *human rights*

人権問題 human rights question

人権宣言 the Declaration of Human Rights

基本的人権 fundamental human rights

しんこう 信仰 *religious faith, religious belief*

信仰する to come to believe in, to come to have faith in

おばあさんは仏教を信仰しています。

Grandmother believes in Buddhism.

しんこう 進行 *progress, advance, forward movement*

進行する to make progress, to proceed, to move forward

計画は順調に進行しています。

The plan is proceeding smoothly.

しんごう 信号 *1. signal; signaling*

信号する to send a signal

2. railroad signal; traffic light

信号が青になってから道を渡ります。

We cross the street after the traffic light turns green.

信号を守る〔無視する〕to obey〔disregard〕a traffic light

信号機 signal ((device))

赤信号 red light

青信号 green light

じんこう 人口 *population*

東京の人口はどれぐらいですか。

About how much is the population of Tokyo?
日本は世界で7番目に人口が多いです。
Japan has the seventh largest population in the world.
人口密度 population density

じんこう 人工 *human skill, human work*
人工の artificial
人工衛星 artificial satellite
人工呼吸 artificial respiration
人工芝 artificial grass

しんこく 深刻 〜な *serious, grave, severe*
それは深刻な問題ですね。
That's a serious problem, isn't it?
首相はその事件を深刻に受けとめている。
The prime minister faced the incident seriously.

しんこん 新婚 〜の *newly-married*
新婚夫婦 newly-married couple
新婚旅行 honeymoon
あの二人はハワイに新婚旅行に行きます。
Those two will go to Hawaii on their honeymoon.

しんさつ 診察 *medical examination*
診察する to examine
田島先生に診察していただきました。
I had Dr. Tajima examine me.

しんし 紳士 *gentleman*
紳士服 men's wear

しんしつ 寝室 *bedroom*

しんじつ 真実 *truth*
先生に真実を話しました。
We told the truth to the teacher.
真実の true, real [→ 本当の]

しんじゃ 信者 *religious believer*

じんじゃ 神社 *Shinto shrine*

しんじゅ 真珠 *pearl*
上野さんは真珠の首飾りをしています。
Ms. Ueno is wearing a pearl necklace.

じんしゅ 人種 *race (of people)*
人種問題 race problem
人種差別 racial discrimination

しんじる 信じる *to believe, to be sure of*
花岡さんの言う事を信じます。
I believe what Ms. Hanaoka says.
チャンピオンの勝利を信じています。
I am sure of the champion's victory.

しんじん 新人 *newcomer (in a given field of endeavor); rookie*
新人歌手 new singer

しんせい 申請 *application (to the authorities)*
申請する to apply for

しんせい 神聖 *sacredness, holiness*
神聖な sacred, holy

じんせい 人生 *(a person's) life, human existence*
夢のない人生は惨めです。
A life without dreams is pitiful.
人生は一度しかないですよ。
One has only one life!
人生を楽観〔悲観〕的に見る to look on the bright〔dark〕side of life
人生観 view of life

しんせき 親せき *a relative* [→ 親類]
大学総長は私の遠い親せきに当たります。
The university president is my distant relative.

シンセサイザー *(musical) synthesizer*

しんせつ 親切 *kindness*
親切な kind, nice [↔ 不親切な]
洋子さんはだれにでも親切です。
Yoko is kind to everyone.
正男君は親切にノートを見せてくれた。
Masao kindly showed me his notebook.

しんぜん 親善 *friendship, amity, goodwill*

親善試合 goodwill game, goodwill match
親善使節 goodwill mission
国際親善 international friendship

しんせん 新鮮 〜な *fresh*
新鮮な空気をちょっと入れてください。
Please let in a little fresh air.

このいちごは新鮮です。
These strawberries are fresh.

しんぞう 心臓 *heart ((bodily organ))*
その手紙を受け取ったとき、心臓がどきどきしました。
My heart beat fast when I received that letter.
心臓が強い to have a strong heart; to be brazen
心臓が弱い to have a weak heart; to be timid
心臓病 heart disease
心臓移植 heart transplant
心臓麻痺 heart failure, heart attack

じんぞう 人造 〜の *man-made, artificial, synthetic*
人造湖 artificial lake
人造人間 android, cyborg

じんぞう 腎臓 *kidney*

しんたい 身体 *body (of a living creature)* [→ 体]
身体検査 medical checkup, physical examination
身体障害者 physically handicapped person

しんだい 寝台 *bed* [→ ベッド]; *(sleeping) berth*
寝台車 sleeping car

しんだん 診断 *1. medical examination* [→ 診察]
診断を受ける to undergo a medical examination
2. diagnosis
診断する to diagnose
診断書 medical certificate
健康診断 medical checkup

しんちゅう 真鍮 *brass ((metal))*

しんちょう 身長 *stature, height*
身長はどのぐらいですか。
About how tall are you?

しんちょう 慎重 *caution, prudence*
慎重な careful, cautious, prudent [→ 注意深い (s.v. 注意)]
父はとても慎重に運転します。
My father drives very carefully.

しんとう 神道 *Shinto, Shintoism (the indigenous Japanese religion)*

しんどう 振動 *vibration; oscillation*
振動する to vibrate; to oscillate

しんにゅう 侵入 *invasion, intrusion, break-in*
侵入する to invade, to intrude, to break in
ゆうべ会社に泥棒が侵入しました。
A thief broke into the company last night.
侵入者 invader, intruder

しんにゅうせい 新入生 *new student, student in the lowest class*

しんねん 信念 *belief, faith, conviction*

しんねん 新年 *new year*
新年おめでとう！
Happy New Year!
新年会 New Year's party (Held after the new year has begun.)

しんぱい 心配 *anxiety, worry, concern* [↔ 安心]
母の病気が心配です。
My mother's illness is a worry.
心配する to become anxious about, to get worried about
由美さんはそれを心配していたよ。
Yumi was worried about that!

心配の種 source of worry, cause of anxiety

Aに心配をかける to cause A anxiety

シンバル *cymbals*

しんぱん 審判 *1. umpire* [→ アンパイア]; *referee* [→ レフェリー]; judge (for a competition) [→ ジャッジ]

2. umpiring; refereeing; judging (for a competition); decision, judgment

審判する to umpire; to referee; to judge

しんぴ 神秘 *mystery, something unexplained*

神秘的な mysterious

しんぷ 神父 *(Catholic) priest*

ー神父 Father (Added to a priest's name as a title.)

ラサール神父は来月お帰りになります。

Father La Salle will go home next month.

しんぷ 新婦 *bride (at a wedding)* [↔ 新郎]

シンフォニー *symphony ((musical piece))* [→ 交響曲]

じんぶつ 人物 *person, character, figure*

家康は歴史上の偉大な人物です。

Ieyasu is a great figure in history.

危険人物 dangerous character

シンプル 〜な *simple, not ornate*

しんぶん 新聞 *newspaper*

新聞をもう読みましたか。

Have you already read the newspaper?

新聞によると、梅雨が明けたそうです。

According to the newspaper, the rainy season has ended.

新聞配達 newspaper delivery; person who delivers newspapers

新聞記事 newspaper article

新聞記者 newspaper reporter

新聞社 newspaper company

しんぽ 進歩 *progress, improvement*

進歩する to make progress, to improve

沢田さんの英語力はずいぶん進歩したね。

Mr. Sawada's English has improved a lot, hasn't it?

科学技術が急速に進歩しました。

Technology progressed rapidly.

進歩的な progressive

しんぼう 辛抱 *patience, endurance* [→ 我慢]

辛抱する to put up with, to endure

辛抱強い patient

子供たちは辛抱強くバスを待ちました。

The children waited patiently for the bus.

シンポジウム *symposium*

シンボル *symbol* [→ 象徴]

シンボルマーク symbol, logo

じんみん 人民 *people (of a country)* [→ 国民]

人民共和国 people's republic

しんや 深夜 *the middle of the night, the late night* [→ 真夜中]

林さんは毎晩深夜まで勉強します。

Ms. Hayashi studies until the middle of the night every night.

深夜放送 late-night broadcasting; late-night program

しんゆう 親友 *close friend, good friend*

名取君は僕の親友の一人です。

Natori is one of my close friends.

しんよう 信用 *1. trust, confidence* [→ 信頼]

信用する to put confidence in, to put trust in

2. reputability

あれは信用のあるメーカーです。

That's a reputable manufacturer.

しんらい 信頼 *trust, confidence, reliance*

信頼する to put trust in, to rely on

みんながコーチを信頼しています。

Everyone has trust in the coach.

その人は信頼できる友達です。

That person is a friend I can rely on.

しんり 心理 *psychology, mentality*
心理学 (the study of) psychology
心理学者 psychologist

しんり 真理 *a truth, indisputable fact*

じんりきしゃ 人力車 *rickshaw*

しんりゃく 侵略 *invasion (of another country)*
侵略する to invade
侵略者 invader

しんりょうじょ 診療所 *clinic*

しんりん 森林 *forest, woods* [→ 森]

しんるい 親類 *a relative* [→ 親せき]
先週四国の親類を訪ねました。
I visited a Shikoku relative last week.
あの人は近い親類です。
That person is a close relative.

じんるい 人類 *humankind*
人類学 anthropology

しんれき 新暦 *the new (solar) calendar* [→ 太陽暦 (s.v. 太陽)]

しんろ 進路 *course, way, path*
まだ将来の進路を決めていません。
I haven't yet decided on my future course.

しんろう 新郎 *groom (at a wedding)* [↔ 新婦]
新郎新婦 the bride and groom

しんわ 神話 *myth*
ギリシャ神話 Greek myth

す 巣 *nest; web; hive*
巣箱 birdhouse

す 酢 *vinegar*
酢の物 side dish with vinegar as the seasoning

ず 図 *figure, diagram, illustration*
第1図 figure 1

ずい 髄 *marrow*

スイートピー *sweet pea*

すいえい 水泳 *swimming*
由美子さんは水泳が上手です。
Yumiko is good at swimming.
水泳をする to swim
水泳教室 swimming class
水泳パンツ swimming trunks
水泳大会 swimming meet

すいか 西瓜 *watermelon*

すいがい 水害 *flood damage, flooding*
この町は去年水害を受けました。
This town suffered flood damage last year.

すいがら 吸殻 *cigarette butt*

すいきゅう 水球 *water polo*

すいぎゅう 水牛 *water buffalo*

すいぎん 水銀 *mercury, quicksilver*

すいこむ 吸い込む *to suck in; to inhale, to breathe in (transitive)*
新鮮な空気を胸いっぱい吸い込んだ。
I took a deep breath of fresh air. (Literally: I breathed in a chestful of fresh air.)

すいさいが 水彩画 *watercolor painting*

すいじ 炊事 *cooking, kitchen work* [→ 料理1.]
炊事する to cook, to do the cooking

すいしゃ 水車 *waterwheel*
水車小屋 waterwheel-powered mill

すいじゅん 水準 *level, position on a scale*
文化水準 cultural level

すいしょう 水晶 *quartz crystal*

すいじょうき 水蒸気 *steam; water vapor*

すいしん 推進 *1. propulsion*

推進する to propel

2. promotion, furthering

推進する to promote, to further

すいせい 水星 *(the planet) Mercury*

すいせい 彗星 *comet*

彗星の尾〔核〕 the tail〔nucleus〕of a comet

ハレー彗星 Halley's comet

すいせん 水仙 *narcissus*

らっぱ水仙 daffodil

すいせん 推薦 *recommendation*

推薦する to recommend

先生がこの本を推薦してくださいました。
The teacher recommended this book to us.

推薦状 letter of recommendation

すいそ 水素 *hydrogen*

水素爆弾 hydrogen bomb

すいそう 水槽 *water tank, cistern*

すいそく 推測 *guess, conjecture*

これは推測にすぎないよ。
This is no more than conjecture!

推測が当たる〔外れる〕 a guess proves right〔wrong〕

推測する to guess, to conjecture

すいぞくかん 水族館 *aquarium ((institution))*

すいちょく 垂直 ～な／の *1. perpendicular*

2. vertical

垂直線 vertical line; perpendicular line

スイッチ *(electrical) switch*

電気のスイッチを入れる〔切る〕 to switch on〔off〕the lights

すいとう 水筒 *canteen, flask*

すいどう 水道 *water service, public water-supply facilities*

水道の水 tap water, city water

水道を引く to connect the water service

水道管 water pipe

水道料金 water charges

ずいひつ 随筆 *essay (consisting of the writer's random thoughts)*

随筆家 essayist

すいぶん 水分 *water content, moisture content*

水分の多い果物 very juicy fruit

ずいぶん 随分 *very, a lot* [→ 非常に]

けさはずいぶん寒かったよ。
It was very cold this morning!

相撲の事をずいぶん知っているね。
You know a lot about sumo, don't you?

すいへい 水平 ～な／の *level, horizontal*

水平線 the horizon (between sky and sea) [↔ 地平線]; horizontal line

水平線上に above the horizon

すいへい 水兵 *(navy) sailor*

すいみん 睡眠 *sleep, slumber*

ゆうべは十分に睡眠をとりました。
I got plenty of sleep last night.

睡眠不足 lack of sleep, insufficient sleep

すいもの 吸い物 *clear soup*

(This is one kind of soup commonly served with traditional Japanese meals, and it typically consists of vegetables with fish or chicken in a fish broth flavored with salt and a small amount of soy sauce.)

すいよう 水曜 [☞ 水曜日]

すいようび 水曜日 *Wednesday*

すいり 推理 *reasoning, inference*

その推理はまちがっています。
That reasoning is mistaken.

推理する to infer

推理小説 mystery novel, detective story

すいりょく 水力 *waterpower*

水力発電 hydroelectricity generation

水力発電所 hydroelectric power plant

すいれん 水蓮 *water lily*

スイング *1. swing (of an athlete)*

そのバッターのスイングはすばらしいね。
That batter's swing is wonderful, isn't it?

2. swing (music)

すう 数 *number* [→ 数]

偶数 even number

奇数 odd number

すう 吸う *1. to suck in; to inhale*

新鮮な空気を深く吸いました。
I deeply inhaled the fresh air.

息を吸う to take in a breath

2. to suck on (in order to draw out a liquid or gas)

赤ちゃんがお母さんの乳を吸っています。
The baby is sucking on her mother's breast.

たばこを吸う to smoke (cigarettes)

3. to absorb [→ 吸収する]

このスポンジはあまり水を吸いません。
This sponge doesn't absorb very much water.

すう― 数― *several (Generally added to a counter; see Appendix 2.)*

数日 several days (This word is exceptional because is not the counter for days.)

数年 several years

数人 several (when counting people)

―すう ―数 *number, quantity (Added to the counter appropriate for what is being counted; see Appendix 2.)*

鉛筆の本数を確かめてください。
Please check the number of pencils.

車の台数はここに書いてあります。
The number of cars is written here.

すうがく 数学 *mathematics*

きょうは数学の授業があるよ。
We have math class today!

数学者 mathematician

すうじ 数字 *numeral, figure*

ローマ数字 Roman numerals

ずうずうしい *impudent, shameless, brazen*

スーツ *suit ((clothing))*

森さんはきょう新しいスーツを着ている。
Ms. Mori is wearing a new suit today.

スーツケース *suitcase*

スーパー [☞ スーパーマーケット]

スーパーマーケット *supermarket*

スーパーマン *superman*

スープ *soup*

スープを飲む to eat soup (Literally: to drink soup)

野菜スープ vegetable soup

すえ 末 *1. end, close* [→ 終わり]

祖母は先月の末に退院しました。
My grandmother was discharged from the hospital at the end of last month.

2. after, as a result

数年の努力の末、金メダルを獲得しました。
As a result of many years of effort, she won the gold medal.

よく考えた末、行くことにしました。
After thinking about it a lot, I decided to go.

3. the future

Aの行く末 A's future, how A's future will go

すえっこ 末っ子 *the youngest child in a family*

僕は4人兄弟の末っ子です。
I'm the youngest of four children.

すえる 据える *1. to place, to set, to lay* [→ 置く1.]

2. to appoint, to place (a person in a job

or position)

ずが 図画 (This word is ordinarily used when the drawing or painting is done in school.)

1. drawing (pictures), painting (pictures)

2. picture, drawing, painting

スカート *skirt*

スカーフ *scarf*

ずかい 図解 *explanation by diagram*

図解する to explain by a diagram

ずがいこつ 頭蓋骨 *skull*

スカウト *1. (personnel) scout*

2. scouting for personnel

スカウトする to scout for personnel

すがお 素顔 *face without make-up, true face*

すがすがしい 清々しい *refreshing, fresh* [→ 爽やかな]

夕立の後は空気がすがすがしいです。
The air is refreshing after a late afternoon shower.

すがた 姿 *form, appearance, figure*

その馬はほんとうに美しい姿をしている。
That horse really has a fine figure.

俳優は鏡に自分の姿を映しました。
The actor looked at his appearance in the mirror.

姿を現わす to appear, to come in sight

姿を消す to disappear

ずかん 図鑑 *illustrated book*

スカンク *skunk*

すき 好き 〜な *(This adjectival noun is used to describe both the people who like and the people or things that are liked.) liked; fond* [↔ 嫌いな]

肉はあまり好きじゃないです。
I don't like meat very much.

八木さんは冬より夏のほうが好きです。
Mr. Yagi likes summer better than winter.

いちばん好きな果物はバナナだよ。
The fruit I like best is the banana!

好きなだけ食べてください。
Please eat as much as you like.

好きなようにしなさい。
Do as you like.

納豆が好きな人はいますか。
Is there anyone who like natto?

弟はテレビを見るのが好きです。
My younger brother likes watching TV.

すき 隙 *1. opening, gap* [→ 透き間]

2. chance, opportunity [→ 機会]

逃げるすきがなかったよ。
I had no chance to escape!

3. unguarded point, weak point; unguarded moment

柔道の選手は相手のすきをねらいます。
Judo contestants aim for their opponent's unguarded point.

すぎ 杉 *Japanese cedar*

—すぎ —過ぎ *1. past, after (Added to bases denoting times or ages.)*

10時15分過ぎです。
It's 10:15.

真夜中過ぎまで起きていました。
I was up until after midnight.

おじいさんは70過ぎだよ。
Grandfather is past 70!

2. excess, too much (Added to verb bases.)

飲みすぎ excessive drinking

スキー *1. skiing*

僕は友達と蔵王にスキーに行きました。
I went skiing at Zao with my friend.

スキーをする to ski

2. ski

スキー靴 ski boot

スキー場 ski resort

スキーヤー skier

すききらい 好き嫌い *likes and dislikes*

この子は好き嫌いがはげしいです。
This child's likes and dislikes are intense.

スキップ skipping (gait)
スキップする to skip

すきとおる 透き通る *to be transparent*

すきま 透き間 *opening, gap, crack*
塀の透き間から猫が入ってきました。
A cat came in through an opening in the fence.
透き間風 draft, wind coming in through a crack

スキャンダル *scandal*

すぎる 過ぎる *1. to pass by, to pass through* [→ 通過する]
飛行機が頭上を過ぎていきました。
A plane passed overhead.
2. to exceed, to pass (a time or age)
もうお昼を過ぎたよ。
It's already past noon!
に過ぎない to be nothing more than, to be merely (following a noun or a clause)
それは著者の意見に過ぎないです。
That's nothing more than the author's opinion.
社長は判を押したに過ぎません。
The company president did nothing more than stamp it with his seal.
3. to elapse, to pass [→ 経つ]
この学校に入学してから2年が過ぎた。
Two years have passed since we entered this school.
冬が過ぎて、春になりました。
Winter passed, and it became spring.

―すぎる ―過ぎる *to excess, over- (Added to verb, adjective, and adjectival noun bases.)*
働きすぎるのは健康に悪いです。
Overworking is bad for one's health.
この試験は簡単すぎるでしょう。
This examination is probably too simple.
そのパソコンは高すぎて、とても買えない。
That personal computer is too expensive and I can't possibly buy it.

すく 空く *to become empty; to become uncrowded* [↔ 込む]
このバスはすいています。
This bus is uncrowded.
おなかがすく to get hungry (Literally: one's stomach becomes empty)

すぐ 直ぐ *1. (～に) at once, (US) right away, (UK) straight away*
すぐ出発しましょう。
Let's start out at once.
もうすぐ(に) soon, any time now
とすぐ(に) as soon as (following a non-past-tense verb)
弟は帰って来るとすぐにテレビをつけました。
As soon as my younger brother came home, he switched on the TV.
2. right, directly
すぐ前の人に聞きました。
I asked the person right in front of me.
すぐの nearby, close
その工場は港からすぐです。
That factory is close to the port.
3. (～に) easily, readily
この子はすぐ泣くよ。
This child cries easily!

すくい 救い *help, rescue*
坊やは救いを求めて叫びました。
The little boy yelled for help.

スクイズ *squeeze (play) (in baseball)*

すくう 救う *to help, to rescue, to save*
困っていたが、友達が救ってくれた。
I was having trouble, but my friend helped me.
先生はおぼれている子供を救いました。
The teacher saved the drowning child.

すくう 掬う *to scoop up*
子供たちは網で金魚をすくいました。

The children scooped up goldfish with nets.

Aの足をすくう to trip A up

スクーター *motor scooter*

スクープ *(news) scoop* [→ 特種]

スクープする to get a scoop about

スクールバス *school bus*

すくない 少ない *small in number, small in quantity* [↔ 多い]

この町には木がとても少ないです。
There are very few trees in this town.

去年は雪が少なかったです。
There was little snow last year.

成功する望みは少ないです。
There is little hope of succeeding.

父が日曜日にうちにいることは少ない。
There are few times when my father is at home on Sunday.

すくなくとも 少なくとも *at least* [→ せめて]

少なくとも1年に1回は旅行します。
I take a trip at least once a year.

スクラップ *1. scrap (metal)*

2. (US) (newspaper) clipping, (UK) (newspaper) cutting [→ 切り抜き]

スクラップブック *scrapbook*

スクラム *scrum*

スクラムを組む to form a scrum

スクリーン *(movie) screen*

スクリュー *screw, propeller (of a ship)*

すぐれた 優れた *excellent, superior (when modifying a following noun)*

若松さんは優れた作曲家です。
Ms. Wakamatsu is an excellent composer.

すぐれる 優れる *to become superior*

この作品は前のより優れています。
This work is superior to the previous one.

スケート *1. skating*

スケートをする to skate

2. skate

スケート場 skating rink

スケール *scale, extent, proportionate size* [→ 規模]

スケジュール *schedule*

あしたはスケジュールが詰まっています。
Tomorrow my schedule is crowded.

スケッチ *1. sketching*

スケッチする to sketch, to make a sketch of

私はパンダをスケッチしました。
I sketched the panda.

2. sketch, rough drawing

スケッチブック *sketchbook*

スコア *score (of a contest)*

僕のチームは5対1のスコアで勝ったよ。
Our team won by a score of 5 to 1!

スコアボード *scoreboard*

すごい 凄い *amazing, tremendous, astounding, startling*

すごい！
Wow!

スポーツカーがすごい速度で走っている。
The sports car is moving at a tremendous speed.

スコール *squall*

すこし 少し *a few, a little, a small amount* [↔ たくさん]

りんごも少し買ってください。
Please buy a few apples too.

体育館には生徒が少ししかいません。
In the gym there are only a few students.

このスープに塩を少し入れてください。
Please put a little salt in this soup.

英語が少し話せます。
I can speak a little English.

すこしずつ 少しずつ *little by little*

患者は少しずつ治ってきました。
The patient got better little by little.

すこしも 少しも *(not) at all, (not) even a little, (not) even a few (Always occurs in*

combination with a negative predicate.)
少しも疲れていないよ。
I am not tired at all!

すごす 過ごす *to spend, to pass (a period of time)*
今年は冬休みを京都で過ごします。
This year I will spend the winter vacation in Kyoto.
パーティーで楽しく過ごしましたか。
Did you have a good time at the party?

スコップ *shovel* [→ シャベル]

すし 寿司, 鮨 *sushi*
寿司屋 sushi shop; sushi restaurant

すじ 筋 *1. muscle* [→ 筋肉]; *tendon, sinew*
筋を違える to pull a muscle, to strain a muscle
2. line (mark on a surface) [→ 線1.]; *stripe* [→ 縞]
3. plot (of a story)
この小説の筋は単純すぎます。
The plot of this novel is too simple.
4. 〜が通っている *to make sense, to be coherent*
この説明は筋が通っていると思います。
I think that this explanation makes sense.

すす 煤 *soot*
消防士の顔はすすで真っ黒です。
The fire fighter's face is completely black with soot.
煤ける to become sooty

すず 鈴 *bell (usually the type consisting of a small bead inside a metal shell)*

すず 錫 *tin ((metal))*

すすぐ 濯ぐ *to rinse*
シャンプーの後はよく髪をすすぎなさい。
Rinse your hair well after the shampoo.
口をすすぐ to rinse out one's mouth

すずしい 涼しい *cool* [↔ 暖かい, 温かい]
丘の上には涼しい風が吹いています。
A cool wind is blowing on top of the hill.
フィルムは涼しい場所に保管しなさい。
Keep the film in a cool place.

すすむ 進む *1. to go forward, to move ahead* [→ 前進する]
止まらないで、進んでください。
Don't stop, please move ahead.
私たちはゆっくり進みました。
We went forward slowly.
もう少し前へ進んでください。
Please move forward a little more.
2. to progress, to advance [→ 進歩する]
建設作業は順調に進んでいます。
Construction is making smooth progress.
それは進んだ考えです。
That's an advanced idea.
3. to gain, to become fast (when the subject is a clock) [↔ 遅れる2.]
この時計は１日に１秒進むそうです。
I hear that this clock gains one second a day.

すずめ 雀 *sparrow*

すすめる 進める *1. to make go forward, to send forward*
軍を進める to send troops forward
2. to go ahead with, to cause to progress
私たちはさまざまな困難を乗り越えて、その計画を進めました。
We overcame various difficulties and went ahead with that plan.
3. to set forward (a clock)
時計を５分進めました。
I set the clock forward five minutes.

すすめる 勧める *1. to advise, to encourage, to suggest*
教授は学生たちにこの本を読むよう勧めました。
The professor advised the students to read this book.
2. to offer
友達のお母さんが紅茶を勧めてくれました。

My friend's mother offered me some tea.

すすめる 薦める *to recommend* [→ 推薦する]

すずらん 鈴蘭 *lily of the valley*

すそ 裾 *portion at the lower hem (of a kimono, skirt, pants leg, etc.)*

山のすそ the foot of a mountain

裾分け [☞ お裾分け]

スター *star (performer)*

映画スター movie star

大スター big star

スタート *start, start-off*

スタートする to start, to make a start

スタートの合図 start signal

スタートを切る to make a start

そのランナーはいいスタートを切りました。
That runner made a good start.

スタート係 starter ((person))

スタートライン starting line

スタイリスト *1. hair stylist; wardrobe stylist*

2. person who dresses stylishly

スタイル *1. style, fashion*

水沢さんはいつも最新のスタイルの服を着ています。
Mr. Mizusawa always wears the latest style of clothes.

2. personal appearance

友子さんはスタイルがいいですね。
Tomoko's appearance is nice, isn't it?

スタジアム *stadium*

スタジオ *(movie) studio*

スタッフ *staff; staff member*

スタミナ *stamina*

あのピッチャーはスタミナがないよ。
That pitcher has no stamina!

すたれる 廃れる *to go out of use; to go out of fashion*

スタンダード ～な *standard, typical*

スタンド *stands (in a stadium, etc.)*

スタンド *electric lamp* [→ 電気スタンド (s.v. 電気)]

スタンプ *1. stamp (for making an ink impression)*

スタンプを押す to apply a stamp

2. stamp (i.e., an ink impression)

スチーム *1. steam* [→ 蒸気]

2. steam heat; steam heating

その部屋はスチームが通っています。
That room is steam-heated. (Literally: As for that room, steam heat passes through.)

スチュワーデス *stewardess*

－ずつ *in amounts of (Added to bases denoting quantities.)*

一人ずつ教室に入りなさい。
Enter the classroom one by one.

鉛筆を２本ずつ取ってください。
Please take two pencils each.

少しずつ運びましょう。
Let's carry it little by little.

ずつう 頭痛 *headache*

頭痛がする to have a headache

スツール *stool ((seat))*

すっかり *completely, entirely, utterly*

父はもうすっかり元気になりました。
My father has already gotten completely better.

この靴はすっかりぬれてしまいました。
These shoes got completely wet.

すっかり忘れる to forget completely

ズック *canvas ((cloth))*

ずっと *1. all along, all the way, the whole time*

一晩中ずっと雪が降っていました。
It was snowing all through the night.

ずっと岡崎さんといっしょでした。

I was with Ms. Okazaki the whole time.
今までずっとどこにいたのですか。
Where were you all this time until now?
太郎はこの前の金曜日からずっと休みだ。
Taro has been off since last Friday.

2. far, extremely (preceding a word denoting a separation in space or time)

ずっと前に a long time ago

3. by far, much

中国は日本よりずっと広いです。
China is much larger than Japan.

すっぱい 酸っぱい *sour*

この青いりんごは酸っぱいよ。
This green apple is sour!

ステーキ *steak*

ビーフステーキ beefsteak

サーロインステーキ sirloin steak

ステージ *(theater) stage* [→ 舞台]

すてき 素敵 ～な *splendid, wonderful, nice*

先生はすてきなセーターを着ていますね。
The teacher is wearing a nice sweater, isn't she?

ステッカー *sticker, adhesive label*

ステッキ *walking stick, cane* [→ 杖]

ステップ *1. (dance) step*

2. step (in a process)

3. steps (on a bus, train, etc.)

すでに 既に *1. already* [→ もう1.]

健に電話したときには、すでに出ていた。
When I telephoned Ken, he had already left.

2. (no) longer, (not) any more (in combination with a negative predicate) [→ もう2.]

恵はすでにそのアパートに住んでいない。
Megumi was no longer living in that apartment.

すてる 捨てる *1. to throw away, to discard*

この古雑誌を捨てましょう。
Let's throw away these old magazines.
それをくず入れに捨てないでください。
Don't throw that away in the wastebasket.

2. to abandon, to desert, to give up on

家族を捨てる to abandon one's family

ステレオ *1. a stereo*

ステレオでこのレコードをかけてくれ。
Play this record on the stereo.

2. stereo, stereophonic sound reproduction

ステレオ放送 stereo broadcasting

ステンドグラス *stained glass*

ステンレス *stainless steel*

スト 【COL. for ストライキ】

ストーブ *room heater*

電気ストーブ electric heater

ガスストーブ gas heater

石油ストーブ oil heater

ストッキング *stocking*

ストック *stock (of unsold goods)* [→ 在庫]

ストック *ski pole*

ストップウォッチ *stopwatch*

ストライキ *(labor) strike*

ストライキをする to go on strike

賃上げストライキ strike for higher wages

ストライク *strike (in baseball)*

ストライプ *stripe* [→ 縞]

ストライプのネクタイ striped necktie

ストレート *1. fastball (in baseball)*

2. ～な straight, consecutive, uninterrupted

ストレートで勝つ to win in straight games, sets, etc.

ストレス *stress, strain*

ストロー *(drinking) straw*

子供はストローでミルクを飲みました。
The child drank milk through a straw.

ストローク *stroke (in sports)*

ストロボ *1. strobe light*

2. electric flash ((camera attachment))

すな 砂 *sand*

靴に砂が入ったよ。
Sand got in my shoes!

砂場 sandbox, (UK) sandpit

砂浜 sandy beach

すなお 素直 〜な *gentle, meek; obedient, unresisting*

明ちゃんは素直な少年です。
Akira is an obedient boy.

祖父の言うことを素直に聞きました。
I listened meekly to what my grandfather said.

弟は素直な性格です。
My younger brother has a gentle nature.

スナック *1. snack food*

2. (A kind of bar where the bill includes a nominal table charge for a small appetizer which is automatically served to all customers.)

スナップ *1. snap (fastener)*

2. snap of the wrist (in throwing or hitting a ball)

3. snapshot

すなわち 即ち *that is (to say)*

山本博士は先週の金曜日、すなわち12月10日に出発しました。
Dr. Yamamoto started out last Friday, that is, on December 10.

スニーカー *sneakers*

すね 脛 *lower leg (below the knee and above the ankle)*

妹は私のすねをけったよ。
My younger sister kicked my lower leg!

ずのう 頭脳 *brains, thinking ability*

スパート *spurt (in a race)*

スパートする to spurt

スパートをかける to put on a spurt

スパイ *spy*

スパイク *1. (athletic-shoe) spike*

スパイクする to spike (a player)

2. spiked shoe

スパイク *spike, spiking (in volleyball)*

スパイクする to spike

スパゲッティ *spaghetti*

スパナ *(US) wrench, (UK) spanner*

すばやい 素早い *quick-moving, quick-acting, agile, nimble*

すばらしい 素晴らしい *wonderful, splendid, magnificent*

ゆうべはすばらしく楽しかったよ。
Last night was wonderfully enjoyable!

すばらしい映画でしたね。
It was a wonderful movie, wasn't it?

ずばり (〜と) *frankly, unreservedly*

スピーカー *speaker, loudspeaker*

スピード *(rate of) speed* [→ 速度]

その車はスピードが出ません。
That car cannot produce speed.

スピードを出す to increase speed, to speed up

スピードを落とす to reduce speed, to slow down

スピード違反 speeding violation

ずひょう 図表 *chart, graph*

スフィンクス *sphinx*

スプーン *spoon*

カレーライスはスプーンで食べます。
One eats curry and rice with a spoon.

紅茶にスプーン一杯の砂糖を入れました。
I put a spoonful of sugar in my tea.

ずぶぬれ ずぶ濡れ 〜の *soaked-to-the-skin*

夕立でずぶぬれになったよ。
I got soaked to the skin in the afternoon shower!

スプリング *(metal) spring* [→ ばね]

スプリンクラー *sprinkler*

スプレー *1. spray, atomized liquid* [→ 霧2.]; *spraying*

スプレーする to spray (transitive)

2. sprayer, atomizer

スペア *a spare (item)*

スペアキー spare key

スペアタイヤ spare tire

スペース *space, room*

スペースシャトル *space shuttle*

スペード *spades ((playing-card suit))*

スペクタクル *spectacle, spectacular show*

スペクタクル映画 movie spectacular

すべて *all, everything* [→ 全部]

これが入手できた情報のすべてです。
This is all of the information that I could get hold of.

アメリカ人がすべて英語を話すというわけではない。
It is not the case that Americans all speak English.

すべての all, every

すべての生徒が体育館に集合しました。
All the students gathered in the gym.

すべりこむ 滑り込む *to slide into*

ランナーは二塁に滑り込みました。
The runner slid into second base.

すべりだい 滑り台 *(playground) slide*

すべる 滑る *{5} 1. to slide (intransitive); to skate, to ski*

花子とスキー場に行って、一日中滑った。
I went to a ski resort with Hanako and skied all day long.

2. to slip (intransitive)

凍った道で滑らないように気をつけてね。
Take care not to slip on the frozen road.

口が滑る the tongue slips, something unintended is said

3. to be slippery (when the subject is a surface)

雪が降って、道が滑るよ。
It snowed and the road is slippery!

すべりやすい 滑りやすい *slippery, easy to slip on*

この床は滑りやすいよ。
This floor is slippery!

スポイト *(medicine) dropper*

スポークスマン *spokesperson*

スポーツ *sport, sports*

太郎君はどんなスポーツが好きですか。
What kind of sports does Taro like?

順子さんはスポーツが得意です。
Junko is good at sports.

スポーツ番組 sports program

スポーツジャケット sport jacket

スポーツカー sports car

スポーツニュース sports news

スポーツシャツ sport shirt

スポーツウエア sportswear

スポーツ用品 sporting goods

スポーツマン person who participates in sports, athlete

スポーツマンシップ sportsmanship

スポットライト spotlight

ズボン *pants, trousers, slacks*

ズボンを１本買いました。
I bought a pair of pants.

ズボンをはく〔脱ぐ〕to put on 〔take off〕 one's pants

ズボン吊り (US) suspenders, (UK) braces

半ズボン short pants, shorts

スポンサー *sponsor*

スポンジ *sponge*

スポンジケーキ sponge cake

スマート ～な *1. slim, slender*

英子さんはとてもスマートになりました。
Eiko has gotten very slim.

2. smart, stylish

すまい 住まい *residence, dwelling*

すます 済ます *1. to finish, to complete* [→ 終える]

私たちはもう昼食を済ませました。
We have already finished our lunch.

2. to make do, to get by [→ 済む2.]

夕食はラーメンで済ませましょう。
Let's make do with noodles for dinner.

スマッシュ *smash (in tennis, etc.)*

スマッシュする to hit a smash

すみ 炭 *charcoal*

炭火 charcoal fire

すみ 隅 *corner (within an enclosed or delimited area), nook*

部屋の隅にいすがあります。
There is a chair in the corner of the room.

隅に立つ to stand in the corner

すみ 墨 *(US) India ink, (UK) Indian ink, Chinese ink; ink stick*

祖母は墨で手紙を書いています。
My grandmother is writing a letter in India ink.

墨絵 traditional India-ink painting

すみません *1. I'm sorry; Excuse me* [→ ご免なさい]

「ほんとうにすみません」「どういたしまして」
"I'm very sorry." "Not at all."

遅刻してすみません。
I'm sorry I'm late.

すみませんが、両替をお願いできますか。
Excuse me, but can you exchange some money?

2. Thank you (In this use, the speaker expresses thanks by apologizing for putting the listener to trouble.)

「どうぞご遠慮なく召し上がってください」「すみません」
"Help yourself, please." "Thank you."

すみれ 菫 *violet ((flower))*

さんしょくすみれ pansy

すむ 住む *to reside, to live*

どこに住んでいますか。
Where are you living?

妹は今伯母といっしょに住んでいます。
My younger sister is now living with my aunt.

北海道に住んでみたいです。
I want to try living in Hokkaido.

すむ 済む *1. to become finished, to become over*

部屋の掃除は7時までには済むでしょう。
Room cleaning will probably be finished by 7:00.

英語の試験は済みました。
The English examination is over.

2. to make do, to get by [→ 済ます2.]

何も買わないで済みました。
I got by without buying anything.

すむ 澄む *to become clear, to become transparent*

山の澄んだ空気は気持ちがいいです。
The fresh mountain air feels good.

スムーズ ~な *smooth, free from difficulty* [→ 滑らかな2.]

万事がスムーズに運びました。
Everything progressed smoothly.

すもう 相撲 *sumo (wrestling)*

相撲を取る to do sumo

相撲取り sumo wrestler

スモッグ *smog*

光化学スモッグ photochemical smog

スライス *1. slicing, cutting in slices*

スライスする to slice

2. slice

スライスチーズ sliced cheese

スライス *(in tennis, golf, etc.) hitting a slice; slice*

スライスする to hit a slice

スライディング *sliding (in baseball)*

スライド *(photographic) slide*

ロンドンのスライドを見(み)せてください。
Please show us the slides of London.

スライド映写機(えいしゃき) slide projector

ずらす *1. to shift, to move slightly by sliding (transitive)*

2. to shift out of overlap (in space or time) (transitive)

すらすら (〜と) *smoothly, easily, fluently*

春男(はるお)はその難(むずか)しい質問(しつもん)にすらすら答(こた)えた。
Haruo answered that difficult question easily.

スラックス *slacks*

スランプ *1. (emotional) slump*

村上投手(むらかみとうしゅ)はスランプで悩(なや)んでいるそうだ。
Murakami, the pitcher seems to be worried about his slump.

スランプに陥(おちい)る to fall into a slump

2. (economic) slump [→ 不景気(ふけいき)]

スリ *1. pickpocketing*

2. pickpocket

「スリにご用心(ようじん)」 (on a sign)
Beware of Pickpockets

すりきず 擦(す)り傷(きず) *scratch, abrasion ((injury))*

すりきれる 擦(す)り切(き)れる *to become worn out (from abrasion)*

この生地(きじ)はすぐに擦(す)り切(き)れます。
This cloth wears out easily.

その人(ひと)は擦(す)り切(き)れたコートを着(き)ていた。
That person was wearing a worn-out coat.

すりこぎ *wooden pestle* [↔ すりばち]

スリップ *slip ((underwear))*

スリップ *slip, skid*

スリップする to slip, to skid [→ 滑(すべ)る2.]

すりばち *earthenware mortar* [↔ すりこぎ]

スリラー *thriller*

スリル *thrill*

きのうスリルに満(み)ちた映画(えいが)を見(み)ました。
Yesterday I saw a movie full of thrills.

スリルがある to be thrilling

する 擦(す)る *to rub, to chafe, to abrade (transitive)*

マッチをする to strike a match

する *{Irreg.} 1. to do, to engage in* [→ 行(おこな)う]

何(なに)をしているんですか。
What are you doing?

きょうはする事(こと)がたくさんあります。
I have a lot of things to do today.

会社(かいしゃ)のためなら、何(なん)でもします。
I'll do anything if it's for the company.

政治家(せいじか)は演説(えんぜつ)をしました。
The politician made a speech.

父(ちち)は散歩(さんぽ)をしています。
My father is taking a walk.

さあ、トランプをしましょう。
Well, let's play cards.

2. AをBに〜 *to make A into B*

委員(いいん)たちは中山(なかやま)さんを委員長(いいんちょう)にしました。
The committee members made Mr. Nakayama the chairperson.

3. to come to have (when the direct object is a feature)

あの子(こ)はかわいい顔(かお)をしています。
That child has a cute face.

この家(いえ)はピラミッドの形(かたち)をしています。
This house has a pyramid shape.

4. to be noticeable, to be felt

ひどい頭痛(ずつう)がします。
I have a bad headache.

変(へん)な音(おと)がしました。
There was a strange sound.

5. to cost

この時計(とけい)は8000円(えん)しました。
This watch cost ¥8,000.

6. time passes

あと10分(ぷん)したら大丈夫(だいじょうぶ)だよ。
After another ten minutes, it'll be fine!

ずるい 狡い *sly, tricky; unfair*

ずるい事をする to do something unfair, to cheat

するどい 鋭い [[↔ 鈍い]] *1. sharp, good for cutting*

もっと鋭いナイフを使いなさい。
Use a sharper knife.

鋭い言葉 sharp words, scathing words
鋭い批評 sharp criticism
鋭い痛み sharp pain
鋭い目 piercing look

2. keen, acute, sensitive

犬は鼻が鋭いです。
Dogs' noses are keen.

すれちがう 擦れ違う *to pass by each other going in opposite directions*

通りで杉山さんとすれ違ったでしょう。
I probably passed by Mr. Sugiyama on the street.

この狭い道路で車がすれ違うのは困難だ。
It's dangerous for cars to pass each other on this narrow road.

ずれる *1. to shift out of overlap (in space or time) (intransitive)*

2. to shift out of proper position (in space or time) (intransitive)

スリッパ *(house) slippers (backless slippers worn in rooms without (floor mats))*

スローガン *slogan*

スロープ *slope, hillside* [→ 斜面]

スローモーション *slow motion*

すわる 座る *1. to sit, to take a seat* [→ 腰掛ける]

三上さんはベンチに座っています。
Ms. Mikami is sitting on a bench.

ガイドはいちばん前の席に座った。
The guide sat in the frontmost seat.

2. to sit on one's knees

(This way of sitting, with the buttocks resting on the heels, is the formal posture for sitting on the floor in Japan.)

畳にきちんと座ってください。
Please sit straight on the tatami.

スワン *swan* [→ 白鳥]

すんぽう 寸法 *measurements (for clothing)*

洋服屋さんは上着の寸法を取りました。
The tailor took the measurements for a jacket.

せ

せ 背 *1. back (of the body)* [→ 背中]

恵子さんはあの人に背を向けました。
Keiko turned her back on that person.

いすの背 chair back
山の背 mountain ridge

2. height, stature [→ 身長]

背はどのくらいですか。
About how tall are you? (Literally: About what is your height?)

妹はずいぶん背が伸びましたよ。
My younger sister has grown quite tall!

背が高い〔低い〕 to be tall〔short〕
背番号 number on the back of a player's shirt

せい 姓 *surname* [→ 名字]

せい 性 *1. sexuality*

2. sex (ie, male or female) [→ 性別]

性的な sexual
性教育 sex education

せい 背 *height, stature* [→ 背2.]

せい 所為 *fault, cause for blame*

それは私のせいじゃないよ。
That's not my fault!

AをBのせいにする to blame B for A

弟は自分の誤りを私のせいにしました。
My younger brother blamed me for his own mistake.

Aのせいで because of A (when A is blamed)

雪のせいで列車のダイヤが乱れました。
Because of the snow, the train schedule became disrupted.

—せい —製 *1. made in (Added to noun bases denoting places.)*

ドイツ製の車は人気があります。
German cars are popular.

このカメラは日本製です。
This camera is Japanese-made.

2. made of (Added to noun bases denoting materials.)

鋼鉄製の made of steel

—せい —生 *student, pupil (Added to noun bases.)*

私は公立中学の2年生です。
I am a second-year student at a public junior high school.

大学生 college student

大学院生 graduate student

1年生 first-year student

高校生 high-school student

ぜい 税 *tax* [→ 税金]

地方税 local tax

消費税 consumption tax, sales tax

所得税 income tax

せいい 誠意 *sincerity*

大統領の誠意を信じます。
I believe in the president's sincerity.

誠意のある人 sincere person

誠意をもって sincerely, with sincerity

医者は誠意をもって患者に話しました。
The doctor spoke sincerely to the patient.

せいいっぱい 精一杯 *as hard as one can, as best one can*

精いっぱい勉強します。
I study as hard as I can.

精いっぱいやりなさい。
Do it as best you can.

せいえん 声援 *cheering, shout of encouragement*

声援する to cheer on, to shout encouragement to

地元の野球チームを声援します。
We cheer on the local baseball team.

せいおう 西欧 *Western Europe* [↔ 東欧]

せいかい 正解 *correct answer*

塚本さんの答えが正解ですよ。
Mr. Tsukamoto's reply is the correct answer!

せいかい 政界 *the political world, political circles*

せいかく 正確 〜な *correct, exact, accurate*

正確な時間を教えてくれませんか。
Will you tell me the correct time?

この報告書は正確です。
This report is accurate.

せいかく 性格 *character, personality, disposition*

その兄弟は性格が全然違うね。
The personalities of those brothers are entirely different, aren't they?

兄は明るい性格です。
My older brother has a cheerful disposition.

せいかつ 生活 *life, living, livelihood*

あの留学生は質素な生活を送っています。
That foreign student is leading a simple life.

生活する to live, to lead a life, to make a living [→ 暮らす]

叔母は英語を教えて生活しています。
My aunt makes her living by teaching English.

生活費 cost of living, living expenses

生活水準 standard of living

学校生活 school life

家庭生活 home life

日常生活 everyday life, daily life

都会生活 city life

ぜいかん 税関 *customs (where import duties are collected)*

一行は成田空港で税関を通過しました。
The party went through customs at Narita Airport.

せいき 世紀 *century*

一世紀 (counter for centuries; see Appendix 2)
21世紀は何年から始まりますか。
From what year does the twenty-first century begin?

せいぎ 正義 *justice, righteousness*

あの運動家は正義のために戦っています。
That activist is fighting for justice.
正義感 sense of justice

せいきゅう 請求 *request; demand*

請求する to ask for, to request; to demand
テープの代金として1000円を請求します。
We request 1,000 yen as the tape fee.
請求書 bill (to pay)

ぜいきん 税金 *tax*

父はたくさんのお金を税金に払いました。
My father paid a lot of money in taxes.
このカメラは税金がかかりません。
Tax does not apply to this camera.

せいけいげか 整形外科 *plastic surgery*

せいけつ 清潔 ～な *clean, pure* [↔ 不潔な]

清潔なタオルを使ってください。
Please use a clean towel.
手を清潔にしておかなければいけません。
You must keep your hands clean.

せいげん 制限 *limit, restriction*

制限する to limit, to restrict
答えは100語に制限されています。
The answer is restricted to 100 words.
制限時間 restricted hours; time limit
制限速度 speed limit
重量制限 weight limit
年齢制限 age limit

せいこう 成功 *success* [↔ 失敗]

ご成功をお祈りします。
I wish you success.
失敗は成功のもと。 (proverb)
Failure is but a stepping stone to success. (Literally: Failure is the basis of success.)
成功する to succeed
兄はついに仕事を見つけるのに成功した。
At last my older brother has succeeded in finding a job.
大成功 great success
そのコンサートは大成功だったよ。
That concert was a great success!

せいざ 星座 *constellation*

せいざ 正座 *to sit ceremonially on one's knees*

(This way of sitting, with the buttocks resting on the heels, is the formal posture for sitting on the floor in Japan.)
正座する to sit ceremonially

せいさく 政策 *(government) policy*

せいさく 制作 *(artistic) production*

制作する to make, to produce
多くのテレビドラマを制作していますよ。
We produce many TV dramas!
制作者 (movie) producer [→ プロデューサー]

せいさく 制作 *manufacturing, production* [→ 製造]

制作する to make, to manufacture
この機械はアメリカで制作されました。
This machine was manufactured in America.
製作者 manufacturer [→ メーカー]; (movie) producer [→ プロデューサー]
製作所 factory, manufacturing plant

せいさん 生産 *production, producing* [↔

消費]

カメラの生産は伸びています。

The production of cameras is increasing.

生産する to make, to produce

この工場は何を生産しているのですか。

What does this factory produce?

生産物 product

生産高 output

生産者 producer

国民総生産 gross national product

大量生産 mass production

せいじ 政治 *politics, government*

伯父は政治に興味があります。

My uncle is interested in politics.

政治学 political science

政治家 statesman, politician

民主政治 democratic government

せいしき 正式 ～な／の *formal, official*

由美に正式に結婚を申し込んだよ。

I formally proposed marriage to Yumi.

せいしつ 性質 *nature, character, quality, property*

ゴムのもつ性質のひとつは弾性です。

One of the properties of rubber is elasticity.

性質のよい人 good-natured person

せいじつ 誠実 ～な *sincere, faithful, honest*

京子さんは誠実な人です。

Kyoko is a sincere person.

せいしゅん 青春 *youth, adolescence*

青春は二度と来ないよ。

Youth will never come again!

青春時代 one's youth

父は青春時代を京都で過ごしました。

My father spent his youth in Kyoto.

せいしょ 聖書 *the Bible*

旧約聖書 the Old Testament

新約聖書 the New Testament

せいじょう 正常 ～な *normal* [↔ 異常な]

息子の体温はやっと正常に戻りました。

My son's temperature finally returned to normal.

せいじょうき 星条旗 *the Stars and Stripes, the American flag*

せいしん 精神 [[↔ 肉体]] *spirit, soul; mind*

福本さんは科学的な精神の持ち主です。

Ms. Fukumoto has a scientific mind.

精神一到何事か成らざらん。(proverb)

Where there is a will, there is a way. (Literally: With the spirit concentrated, something is bound to come of it.)

精神病 mental illness

精神年齢 mental age

精神力 mental power

精神的な spiritual [↔ 物質的な]; mental

せいじん 成人 *adult (person)* [→ 大人]

成人する to grow up, to reach adulthood

上原さんは成人した娘さんもいます。

Mr. Uehara also has a grown-up daughter.

成人の日 Coming-of-Age Day (a Japanese national holiday on January 15)

成人向きの intended for adults

成人式 coming-of-age ceremony (Held on January 15th for people who have turned 20 during the preceding year.)

せいじん 聖人 *saint*

せいず 製図 *drafting, mechanical drawing*

せいぜい 精々 *1. at most, at best* [→ 高々]

2. as hard as one can, as best one can [→ 精一杯]

せいせいどうどう 正々堂々（～と） *fairly, in aboveboard fashion*

正々堂々と勝負しましょう。

Let's compete fairly.

せいせき 成績 *(achieved) result, showing, performance; (school) mark, (US) (school) grade*

今月の営業の成績はよくありません。

This month's sales figures are not good.

長田君は英語でいい成績をとったよ。

Nagata got a good grade in English!

友子ちゃんの音楽の成績は５だよ。

Tomoko's grade in music is an A!

(Many Japanese schools use a 1-5 grading scale with 5 being the highest.)

成績表 report card

せいぞう 製造 *manufacturing, production* [→ 製作]

製造する to manufacture, to make

せいぞん 生存 *being alive, existence*

水は生存のために必要です。

Water is necessary for existence.

生存する to exist, to live; to survive [→ 生き残る]

生存競争 the struggle for existence

生存者 survivor

せいたい 声帯 *vocal cords*

せいだい 盛大 〜な *grand, splendid*

盛大な歓迎会を開きました。

We held a grand welcome party.

ぜいたく 贅沢 *extravagance*

ぜいたくな extravagant

その金持ちはぜいたくに暮らしていた。

That rich person was living extravagantly.

せいちょう 生長 *growth (especially of plants)*

雑草は生長が早いですね。

Weeds grow quickly, don't they? (Literally: As for weeds, growth is fast, isn't it?)

生長する to grow

せいちょう 成長 *growth (especially of animals)*

成長する to grow

栗山さんは知的な女性に成長しました。

Ms. Kuriyama has grown into an intellectual woman.

経済成長 economic growth

せいてき 静的 〜な *static, stationary* [↔ 動的な]

せいてん 晴天 *fair weather*

本日は晴天なり。

Today is fair weather.

(This archaic sentence is used to test whether a microphone is turned on.)

せいでんき 静電気 *static electricity*

せいと 生徒 *student, pupil* [↔ 先生]

そのクラスには何人の生徒がいますか。

How many students are there in that class?

生徒会 student council, students' association

生徒大会 students' meeting

せいど 制度 *system*

この学校には奨学金の制度があります。

At this school there is a scholarship system.

社会制度 social system

せいとう 正当 〜な *just, right, fair*

正当防衛 self-defense

正当化 justification

正当化する to justify

せいとう 政党 *political party*

米国には大きな政党が二つあります。

In the United States there are two major political parties.

政党内閣 party cabinet

政党政治 party government

保守政党 a conservative party

革新政党 a progressive party

せいどう 青銅 *bronze*

青銅器時代 the Bronze Age

せいとん 整頓 *putting in order* [→ 整理]

整とんする to put in order
部屋を整とんしておきなさい。
Keep your room in order.

せいなん 西南 *the southwest* [→ 南西]

せいねん 青年 *young adult, a youth*
(Typically used to refer to a young man.)
明さんは前途有望な青年です。
Akira is a promising young man.
青年時代 one's youth, one's young days
その画家は青年時代をパリで過ごした。
That painter spent his youth in Paris.

せいねんがっぴ 生年月日 *date of birth*

せいのう 性能 *capacity, ability*
性能のいい機械 efficient machine

せいはんたい 正反対 *the exact opposite*

せいび 整備 *repair, maintenance*
兄のバイクは整備が行き届いています。
My older brother's motorcycle is in good repair.
整備する to repair, to put in good condition
父は車を整備してもらいました。
My father had his car repaired.
整備士 repairman; mechanic

せいびょう 性病 *venereal disease*

せいひん 製品 *(manufactured) product*
この会社の製品は評判がいいです。
This company's products have a good reputation.
外国製品 foreign products
工業製品 industrial products
新製品 new product

せいふ 政府 *the government*
日本政府 the Japanese Government

せいぶ 西部 *the western part* [↔ 東部]
西部劇 a Western (drama)

せいふく 制服 *a uniform*
(This word is typically used for school or company uniforms, but not for athletic uniforms.)
郵便集配人は濃紺の制服を着ています。
Mail carriers wear dark blue uniforms.
あの制服を着た警官に尋ねましょう。
Let's ask that uniformed police officer.
この学校の制服は格好が悪いね。
This school uniform is ugly, isn't it?

せいふく 征服 *conquest*
征服する to conquer
征服者 conqueror

せいぶつ 生物 *living thing*
月には生物がいますか。
Are there living things on the moon?
生物学 (the study of) biology
生物学者 biologist

せいべつ 性別 *sex (i.e, male or female)*

せいぼ 歳暮 *1. end of the year* [→ 年末 (s.v. 年)]
2. year-end gift

せいぼう 制帽 *regulation cap; school cap*

せいほうけい 正方形 *a square ((geometrical shape))*
これは1辺が5センチの正方形です。
This is a square with sides of 5 centimeters.

せいほく 西北 *the northwest* [→ 北西]

せいみつ 精密 〜な *precise, detailed, minute*
運転手は精密な地図を必要としています。
The driver needs a detailed map.
精密検査 close medical examination
精密機械 precision machine

ぜいむ 税務 *taxation work, tax collection*
税務署 taxation office

せいめい 生命 *life, animate existence* [→ 命]
父親は生命の危険を冒して娘を救った。
The father braved the danger to his life and saved his daughter.

患者の生命は危険な状態にあります。
The patient's life is in a critical condition.
生命保険 life insurance

せいめい 声明 *public statement*
声明を出す to make a public statement
共同声明joint statement

せいめい 姓名 *full name* [→ 名前]

せいよう 西洋 *the West* [↔ 東洋]; *Europe* [→ ヨーロッパ]
西洋文明 Western civilization; European civilization
西洋人a Westerner; a European

せいよう 静養 *rest; recuperation*
静養する to rest quietly; to recuperate
医者は患者に一週間静養するよう勧めた。
The doctor advised the patient to rest quietly for a week.

せいり 整理 *putting in order, arranging; adjustment*
整理する to put in order, to arrange; to rearrange, to adjust
棚の上の本を整理しましょう。
Let's rearrange the books that are on the shelf.
身の回りの物を整理してください。
Please put your belongings in order.
整理番号reference number
整理券numbered ticket
交通整理 traffic control

せいり 生理 *1. physiology (of an organism) 2. menstruation* [→ 月経, メンス]
生理学(the study of) physiology

せいりつ 成立 *coming into existence, formation, completion*
成立する to come into existence, to be formed, to be completed

せいりょういんりょう 清涼飲料 *soft drink*

せいりょく 勢力 *power, influence*
台風の勢力は明朝少し弱まるでしょう。
The power of the typhoon will probably weaken a little tomorrow morning.
勢力のある人 influential person
勢力争い power struggle

せいりょく 精力 *energy, vigor, vitality*
候補者は選挙に精力を傾けました。
The candidate applied his energy to the election.
精力的な energetic, vigorous

せいれき 西暦 *the Western calendar*
(Typically used to mark years as AD. by the Gregorian calendar.) [→ 紀元]
この城は西暦850年に建てられました。
This castle was built in 850AD.

せいれつ 整列 ～する *to line up in orderly fashion, to form an orderly line*
私たちは4列に整列しました。
We lined up in four lines.

セーター *sweater*

セーフ ～の *safe (in baseball)* [↔ アウトの]
ランナーは三塁でセーフになった。
The runner was safe at third.

セーラーふく セーラー服 *sailor suit*
(Typically worn as a uniform by girls in Japanese secondary schools.)

セール *(bargain) sale* [→ 安売り]
バーゲンセールbargain sale

セールスポイント *selling point*
この商品のセールスポイントは何ですか。
What is the selling point of this article?

セールスマン *(traveling) salesperson*

せおう 背負う *to carry on one's back*
青年はバックパックを背負っていました。
The young man was carrying a backpack on his back.

せおよぎ 背泳ぎ *the backstroke* [→ 背泳]

せかい 世界 *world*
パリは世界で最も美しい都市の一つです。

Paris is one of the world's most beautiful cities.

湯浅さんはすぐれたピアニストとして世界に知られています。

Ms. Yuasa is known to the world as a great pianist.

子供の世界 the world of children

夢の世界 the world of dreams

世界銀行 The World Bank

世界平和 world peace

世界一の the best in the world

世界一周旅行 round-the-world trip

世界記録 world record

世界選手大会 world championship (athletic event)

世界史 world history

世界大戦 world war

セカンド *1. second base* [→ 二塁]

2. second baseman [→ 二塁手 (s.v. 二塁)] *(in baseball)*

せき 咳 *cough*

先生のせきがひどいですね。

The teacher's cough is terrible, isn't it?

せきをする to cough

咳払い clearing one's throat

せきばらいをする to clear one's throat

咳止め cough suppresant

せき 席 *seat, place to sit*

この席に座ってもよろしいですか。

May I sit in this seat?

席は全部ふさがっています。

The seats are all occupied.

お年寄りに席を譲るようにしなさい。

Make sure to give your seat to elderly people.

山本さんは席をまちがえたようです。

It appears that Mr. Yamamoto took the wrong seat.

席に着く to take one's seat

席を立つ to leave one's seat

指定席 reserved seat

せきがいせん 赤外線 *infrared rays*

せきじゅうじ 赤十字 *the Red Cross*

赤十字病院 Red Cross hospital

せきたん 石炭 *coal*

ここでは石炭をたいて部屋を暖めます。

Here they burn coal and warm the rooms.

せきどう 赤道 *the equator*

せきにん 責任 *responsibility*

社長がその失敗の責任を取りました。

The company president took responsibility for that failure.

責任のある地位 a position with responsibility

責任感 sense of responsibility

島崎さんは責任感が強いです。

Ms. Shimazaki's sense of responsibility is strong.

責任者 person in charge

せきはん 赤飯 *rice with red beans*

(Traditionally made to celebrate a happy occasion.)

せきゆ 石油 *petroleum, oil; kerosene* [→ 灯油]

石油会社 oil company

石油ストーブ kerosene heater

せけん 世間 *the world, the way the world is, society, people*

妹は世間をあまり知りません。

My younger sister doesn't know much about the world.

あの青年は世間に通じています。

That young man knows a lot about the world.

太郎は世間が何を言っても気にしない。

Taro isn't bothered by anything people say.

世間話 gossip; small talk

世間知らず knowing little of the ways of the world; person who knows little of the ways of the world

世間体 appearances, one's public reputation

セコンド *a second (in boxing)*

せし セ氏 [☞ 摂氏]

ゼスチュア [☞ ジェスチャー]

せだい 世代 *a generation*

世代の断絶 generation gap

若い世代 the younger generation

せつ 説 *1. theory; doctrine*

学者は新しい説を立てました。
The scholar advanced a new theory.

2. opinion, view [→ 意見]

それについてはさまざまな説があります。
There are various opinions about that.

ぜつえん 絶縁 *1. breaking the connection, disconnection*

絶縁する to break the connection

2. (electrical) insulation

絶縁する to insulate

絶縁体 (electrical) insulator

せっかい 石灰 *lime ((substance))*

せっかく 折角 *fruitlessly taking special trouble*

母がせっかく作った料理も無駄になった。
The food that mother prepared was in vain.

せっかくの precious but not taken advantage of

せっかくのお招きですが、今回はお受けできません。
It's a kind invitation, but I can't accept this time.

せっきょう 説教 *1. sermon, preaching*

説教する to preach, to give a sermon

2. admonition, scolding [→ 小言]

説教する to admonish, to scold, to lecture

遅く帰って母に説教されました。
I came home late and was scolded by my mother.

せっきょくてき 積極的〜な *positive, active, actively involved* [↔ 消極的な]

兄は何事にも積極的です。
My older brother is actively involved in everything.

先生は積極的に援助してくださいました。
The teacher helped us actively.

せっきん 接近 *approach, nearing*

接近する to approach, to get near

この大型台風は九州に接近しています。
This large-scale typhoon is approaching Kyushu.

セックス *sex, sexual intercourse*

セックスする to have sex

せっけい 設計 *plan, design*

設計する to plan, to design

有名な建築家がこの校舎を設計しました。
A famous architect designed this school building.

このホテルはうまく設計されています。
This hotel is well designed.

設計者 designer

設計図 plan, blueprint

せっけん 石鹸 *soap*

石けんで手を洗いなさい。
Wash your hands with soap.

石鹸箱 soapbox

石鹸水 soapy water

洗顔石鹸 facial soap

洗濯石鹸 laundry soap

浴用石鹸 bath soap

ゼッケン *racing number (attached to the front or back of an athlete's shirt)*

ぜっこう 絶好 〜の *best, ideal, excellent*

絶好のチャンスを逃してしまいました。
I missed the best chance.

絶好調 best condition, top form

せっし 摂氏 *centigrade, Celsius* [↔ カ氏]

最高気温は摂氏30度でした。
The high temperature was 30 degrees Celsius.

せっしょく 接触 *1. (physical) contact*

接触する to come into contact [→ 接する1.]

外れた電線が屋根に接触しました。
The loose electric wire came into contact with the roof.

2. (social) contact, touch

接触するto come into contact, to get in touch

接触を保つ to keep in touch

せっする 接する *{Irreg.} 1. to come into (physical) contact*

2. to border, to be adjacent, to touch

直線はここで円に接するでしょう？
The straight line touches the circle here, right?

3. to come into (social) contact, to meet [→ 会う]

外国人と接する機会がありませんでした。
I had no chance to come into contact with foreigners.

せっせと *hard, diligently* [→ 一生懸命]

せっせん 接戦 *close game, close race*

接戦の末チャンピオンが勝ちました。
At the end of a close game the champion won.

せつぞく 接続 *1. connection, joining*

接続する to connect, to join, to link

2. (transportation) connection [→ 連絡2.]

接続する to connect

この電車は京都で新幹線に接続します。
This train connects with the Shinkansen at Kyoto.

接続詞 conjunction ((part of speech))

ぜったい 絶対（～に） *absolutely, unconditionally, positively*

この計り方は絶対にまちがっているよ。
This way of measuring is positively wrong!

私たちは戦争には絶対反対です。
We are absolutely against war.

数日は絶対に安静にしたほうがいいです。
You should get absolute rest for a few days.

絶対の absolute, unconditional

絶対多数 absolute majority

せっちゃくざい 接着剤 *bonding agent, glue, adhesive*

この部品を接着剤でつけました。
I attached this part with glue.

瞬間接着剤 quick drying glue

せってい 設定 *establishing, setting up, instituting*

設定する to establish, to set up, to institute

セット *1. set (of things that go together)*

コーヒーセット coffee set (ice., coffee and accompanying extras treated as a single menu item)

2. (movie) set

3. set (in sports such as tennis)

ーセット (counter for sets; see Appendix 2)

優勝は５セットの試合で決まりました。
The championship was decided in a five-set match.

セット ～する *1. to set (hair)*

髪をセットしてもらいました。
I had my hair set.

2. to set (a device)

せっとうご 接頭語 *prefix* [↔ 接尾語]

せっとく 説得 ～する *to persuade*

父を説得して自転車を買ってもらったよ。
I persuaded my father to buy me a bicycle!

説得力 persuasiveness

せつない 切ない *trying, distressing* [→ 辛い]

せつび 設備 *equipment; facilities*

あのホテルは設備が非常にいいです。

That hotel's facilities are extremely good.
この学校は暖房の設備があります。
This school has heating facilities.
設備する to install, to provide

せつびご 接尾語 *suffix* [↔ 接頭語]

せっぷく 切腹 *harakiri*
切腹する to commit harakiri

せつぶん 節分 *(This name refers to the last day of winter according to the old lunar calendar. It now refers to February 3, the day on which the bean throwing ritual is performed. The beans are thrown to drive demons out of houses.)*

ぜつぼう 絶望 *despair, hopelessness*
絶望する to despair, to give up hope
弟は絶望して帰宅しました。
My younger brother came home in despair.
決して絶望してはいけないよ。
You must never give up hope!
絶望的な hopeless
この試合は絶望的だと感じました。
I felt that this game was hopeless.

せつめい 説明 *explanation*
この問題は説明が必要ありません。
This problem needs no explanation.
説明する to explain
私は遅刻した理由を説明しました。
I explained the reason I was late.
図書館の利用方法を説明してください。
Please explain the method of using the library.
説明書 (written) instructions

ぜつめつ 絶滅 *extinction, dying out*
絶滅する to become extinct, to die out
日本ではこの鳥は絶滅しました。
This bird died out in Japan.

せつやく 節約 *economy, saving, conservation*
節約する to save, to economize on, to conserve
/ お金を節約するのは難しいです。
Saving money is difficult.
節約家 frugal person

せつりつ 設立 *establishing, founding, setting up*
設立する to establish, to found, to set up
この学校は50年前に設立されました。
This school was founded fifty years ago.
設立者 founder

せとないかい 瀬戸内海 *the Seto Inland Sea (surrounded by Honshu, Shikoku, and Kyushu)*

せともの 瀬戸物 *china, earthenware, pottery* [→ 陶器, 焼き物]

せなか 背中 *back (of the body)* [→ 背1.]
背中がまだ痛いよ。
My back still hurts!
僕は時々おふろで弟の背中を流します。
I sometimes wash my younger brother's back in the bath.
背中合わせに back to back

せのび 背伸び ～する *to stand on tiptoe*

セパレーツ *separates ((women's clothing))*

ぜひ 是非 *by all means, at any cost, without fail*
あしたの試合にはぜひ勝ちたいよ。
I want to win the tomorrow's game without fail!

セピア *sepia (as a noun)*

せびろ 背広 *(business) suit*

せぼね 背骨 *backbone*

せまい 狭い [[↔ 広い]] *1. narrow*
大型バスもこの狭い道路を走ります。
Big buses also run along this narrow road.
2. small (in area), cramped
この部屋は狭いですね。
This room is small, isn't it?

せまる 迫る *1. to approach, to draw near, to close in* [→ 近づく]

出発の時刻が迫っています。
The departure time is approaching.

2. to press for, to urge to give

記者はスポークスマンに回答を迫った。
The reporter pressed the spokesperson for an answer.

せみ 蝉 *cicada*

せみが鳴き始めました。
The cicadas have begun to sing.

ゼミ *seminar*

セミナー *seminar* [→ ゼミ]

ゼミナール [☞ ゼミ]

せめて *at least* [→ 少なくとも]

せめて靴を磨いたほうがいいです。
You should at least shine your shoes.

せめる 攻める *to attack* [↔ 守る2.]

陸軍は敵を攻めました。
The army attacked the enemy.

せめる 責める *to reproach, to censure; to say in reproach*

乗客は事故が運転手のせいだと責めた。
The passengers said in reproach that the accident was the driver's fault.

セメント *cement*

父はセメントで石のブロックを接合した。
Father joined the stone blocks with cement.

セメント工場 cement factory

ゼラチン *gelatin*

ゼリー *jelly*

せりふ 台詞 *(actor's) lines*

女優はせりふを忘れました。
The actress forgot her lines.

セルフサービス *self-service*

この店はセルフサービスです。
This store is self-service.

セルロイド *celluloid*

セレナーデ *serenade*

ゼロ *zero* [→ 零]

セロテープ *cellophane tape*

せろん 世論 *public opinion* [→ 世論]

世論はその計画に反対です。
Public opinion is against that plan.

世論調査 public opinion poll

せわ 世話 *1. taking care, looking after*

Aの世話をする to take care of A, to look after A

父は庭の植木の世話をしています。
My father is taking care of the garden shrubs.

妹は子供たちの世話をするのが好きです。
My younger sister likes to look after children.

2. help, aid, assistance

世話になる to become obliged for having received help

お世話になりました。
I am much obliged to you.

世話人 caretaker; sponsor

せん 千 *thousand (see Appendix 2)*

千円札 thousand-yen bill

せん 栓 *stopper, plug, (wine) cork, (bottle) cap*

ワインの栓を抜いてくれましたか。
Did you pull out the wine cork for me?

栓抜き bottle opener; corkscrew

せん 線 *1. line (mark on a surface)*

細い〔太い〕線 fine〔bold〕line

線を引く to draw a line

2. (transportation) line, route

3. (electrical) line, wire

電話線 telephone wire

平行線 parallel lines

国際線 international route

曲線 curved line

点線 dotted line

ぜん 善 *goodness* [↔ 悪]
善は急げ。(proverb)
Don't hesitate to do good. (Literally: As for goodness, hurry.)
善悪 good and evil

ぜん 禅 *Zen (Buddhism)*
禅宗 the Zen sect

ーぜん ー膳 *1. (counter for pairs of chopsticks; see Appendix 2)*
2. (counter for bowlfuls of rice; see Appendix 2)

ぜんあく 善悪 *good and evil, right and wrong*

せんい 繊維 *fiber*
これらは羊毛の繊維です。
These are wool fibers.
繊維工業 textile industry
繊維製品 textile goods
合成繊維 synthetic fiber
化学繊維 chemical fiber
天然繊維 natural fiber

ぜんい 善意 *good will, good intentions*
善意で out of good will, with good intentions
善意であの人に手紙を書きました。
I wrote a letter to that person out of good will.

ぜんいん 全員 *everyone involved, all*
代表は全員その案に賛成しました。
The representatives all agreed to the proposal.

せんきょ 選挙 *election*
来年は選挙が行われます。
The election will be held next year.
田島君が選挙で生徒会の会長に選ばれた。
Tajima was elected president of the student council in the election.
選挙する to elect
選挙演説 campaign speech
選挙権 the right to vote
選挙運動 election campaign
総選挙 general election

せんきょうし 宣教師 *missionary*

せんげつ 先月 *last month*
先月は雨が多かったです。
Last month there was a lot of rain.

せんげん 宣言 *declaration, proclamation*
宣言する to declare, to proclaim
アメリカは何年に独立を宣言しましたか。
In what year did the United States declare independence?

せんご 戦後 *postwar period* [↔ 戦前]

ぜんご 前後 *1. the time periods before and after*
夕食の前後に英語を勉強しました。
I studied English before and after supper.
2. the areas in front and behind
足を前後に動かしましょう。
Let's move our legs back and forth.

ーぜんご ー前後 *1. about, approximately (Added to bases denoting points in time.)* [→ーごろ]
面接は10時前後に終わるでしょう。
The interview will probably end at about 10:00.
2. about, approximately (Added to bases denoting specific quantities.) [→ーぐらい]
その人の体重は60キロ前後です。
That person's weight is about 60 kilograms.

せんこう 専攻 *major (field of study at a college)*
専攻する to major in

せんこう 線香 *incense stick*

ぜんこく 全国 *the whole country*
選手たちは全国から集まりました。
The athletes gathered from all over the country.
全国大会 national convention; national meet
全国的な nationwide

村上は作家として全国的に知られている。
Murakami is known as a writer nationwide.

センサー *sensor*

せんざい 洗剤 *detergent, cleanser*

合成洗剤synthetic detergent

せんし 戦死 *death in battle*

戦死する to die in battle

祖父は第二次世界大戦で戦死しました。
My grandfather died in World War II.

戦死者 person killed in battle

せんしつ 船室 *ship cabin*

せんじつ 先日 *the other day*

先日辻村さんのお宅を訪ねました。
I visited Ms. Tsujimura's house the other day.

ぜんじつ 前日 *the preceding day*

試験の前日はテレビを見なかったよ。
I didn't watch television the day before the examination!

せんしゃ 戦車 *tank ((vehicle))*

せんしゅ 選手 *player, athlete*

野球の選手 baseball player

—選手 (Added to an athlete's surname as an alternative to —さん; roughly equivalent to Mr./Ms.)

選手権 championship, title

森川選手はスキーの選手権を取りました。
Ms. Morikawa took the skiing championship.

選手権大会 championship competition

代表選手 representative player

最優秀選手 most valuable player

せんしゅう 先週 *last week*

先週雪が少し降りました。
It snowed a little last week.

先週の木曜日に図書館に行きました。
I went to the library last Thursday.

先々週 the week before last

ぜんしゅう 全集 *the complete works*

シェークスピア全集 the complete works of Shakespeare

せんじゅつ 戦術 *tactics*

戦術家 tactician

せんじょう 戦場 *battlefield*

ぜんしん 全身 *whole body*

真紀子は全身ずぶぬれで震えていたよ。
Makiko got soaked, and her whole body was shivering!

全身像 full-length portrait

ぜんしん 前進 *advance, going forward*

前進する to advance, to go forward

せんしんこく 先進国 *advanced country* [↔ 発展途上国 (s.v. 発展)]

せんす 扇子 *folding fan*

センス *sense, sensitivity, judgment* [→ 感覚2.]

岸さんには色のセンスがあります。
Ms. Kishi has a sense of color.

伯母は服装のセンスがいいよ。
My aunt's judgment in clothing is good!

せんすい 潜水 ~する *to dive, to become submerged (from a starting point in the water)* [→ 潜る1.]

潜水夫 diver, frogman

潜水服 diving suit

潜水艦 a submarine

せんせい 先生 *1. teacher* [↔ 生徒; 学生]

両親は二人とも高校の先生です。
My parents are both high school teachers.

あの方は日本語の先生です。
That person is a teacher of Japanese.

—先生 (Added to the surname of a teacher instead of —さん as a title of respect roughly equivalent to Mr., Ms., or Dr.)

林先生は音楽を教えていらっしゃいます。
Ms. Hayashi teaches music.

2. Sir, Ma'am; the respected person

(Used to address or refer to a person who is not a teacher but is accorded a similar kind of special respect, typically a doctor, lawyer, or elected official.)

ー先生 (Added to the surname of such a person instead of ーさん as a title of respect.)

せんせい 宣誓 *oath*

宣誓する to take an oath, to swear

せんせい 専制 *despotism, autocracy*

センセーション *sensation, uproar*

この小説は世界中にセンセーションを巻き起こしました。

This novel created a sensation all over the world.

ぜんぜん 全然 *(not) at all, completely* [→ 全く]

きょうは全然仕事をする気になりません。

I don't feel like doing any work at all today.

私はそれについて全然知りません。

I don't know anything at all about that.

それは全然別の事ですよ。

That's a completely different matter!

ぜんせん 前線 *1. (weather) front*

2. front line (in a battle)

せんぞ 先祖 *ancestor* [→ 祖先] [↔ 子孫]

先祖伝来の ancestral, handed down from one's ancestors

せんそう 戦争 *war* [↔ 平和]

戦争は3週間で終わりました。

The war ended in three weeks.

父は戦争で負傷しました。

My father was wounded in the war.

その戦争は1939年に始まりました。

That war began in 1939.

私たちは戦争に反対です。

We are against war.

戦争に勝つ〔負ける〕 to win〔lose〕a war

戦争映画 war movie

核戦争 nuclear war

ぜんそく 喘息 *asthma*

センター *center ((institution))*

研究センター research center

旅行センター tourist center

センター *1. center field (in baseball)*

2. center fielder (in baseball)

センターフライ fly ball to center

ぜんたい 全体 *the whole, entire thing* [↔ 部分]

全体として as a whole, on the whole

この計画は全体としてうまくいっている。

This plan is going well as a whole.

ー全体 the whole (Added to noun bases.)

町全体が穏やかです。

The whole town is quiet.

全体的な overall (as a noun modifier)

この作文は全体的に上手に書けています。

This composition is well written overall.

せんたく 洗濯 *washing clothes, doing laundry*

洗濯する to wash clothes, to do the laundry; to launder, to wash

汚れたTシャツを洗濯しました。

I washed the dirty T-shirts.

私も日曜日に洗濯します。

I also do the laundry on Sundays.

このドレスは洗濯できますか。

Can this dress be laundered?

洗濯鋏み clothespin, (UK) clothes peg

洗濯機 washing machine

洗濯物 clothes to wash, laundry

せんたく 選択 *choice, selection*

もう選択の余地はないと思います。

I think that there is no longer any room for choice.

選択する to choose [→ 選ぶ]

選択科目 elective subject

センチ *centimeter*

ーセンチ (counter for centimeters; see Appendix 2)

センチメートル [☞ センチ]

センチメンタル ～な *sentimental* [→ 感傷的な]

せんちょう 船長 *ship captain*

ぜんてい 前提 *premise*

せんでん 宣伝 *1. advertising, publicity*

宣伝する to advertise, to publicize

この薬はテレビで宣伝されています。
This medicine is being advertised on TV.

2. propaganda

宣伝する to propagandize

宣伝ビラ advertising leaflet; propaganda leaflet

宣伝ポスター advertising poster

セント *cent*

ーセント (counter for cents; see Appendix 2)

ぜんと 前途 *one's future, one's prospects*

有望な前途 a promising future

前途有望な promising

お嬢さんは前途有望なピアニストです。
Their daughter is a promising pianist.

せんとう 銭湯 *public bathhouse* [→ 風呂屋 (s.v. 風呂)]

せんとう 先頭 *the head, the lead*

モロッコの選手がレースの先頭を切った。
The Moroccan athlete took the lead in the race.

先頭に立つ to lead, to go first

主将が選手たちの先頭に立って行進した。
The captain is marching at the head of the players.

チアガールがパレードの先頭に立ちます。
Cheerleaders will lead the parade.

先頭打者 lead-off hitter

セントラルヒーティング *central heating*

ぜんにん 善人 *good person, virtuous person* [↔ 悪人]

せんねん 専念 ～する *to devote oneself*

梨田先生は植物の研究に専念しています。
Dr. Nashida is devoting himself to the study of botany.

せんぱい 先輩 *one's senior (i.e., a person who entered the same organization earlier)* [↔ 後輩]

中井さんは美術部の先輩です。
Mr. Nakai is my senior in the art club.

せんばつ 選抜 *selection, picking out (from a large pool of candidates)*

選抜する to select, to pick out

選抜に漏れる to be left out of those selected

選抜チーム all-star team

ぜんはん 前半 *the first half* [↔ 後半]

試合の選抜が見られませんでした。
I could not watch the first half of the game.

ぜんぶ 全部 *all, the whole, the total* [→ 全て]

コップは全部割れてしまいました。
All the glasses broke.

この切手は全部私のです。
These stamps are all mine.

父はその魚を全部食べました。
My father ate that whole fish.

この本を全部読んだわけではありません。
I haven't read all these books.

全部で in all, all together

全部で3000円持っています。
I have ¥3,000 in all.

せんぷうき 扇風機 *(electric) fan*

扇風機をかける〔止める〕to turn on〔off〕a fan

せんべい 煎餅 *Japanese rice cracker*

ぜんぽう 前方 *the area ahead*

前方に島が見えます。
We can see an island ahead.

50メートル前方にバス停があります。
There is a bus stop 50 meters ahead.

ぜんまい *(metal) spring* [→ ばね]

オルゴールのぜんまいを巻いてください。
Please wind the spring of the music box.

ぜんめつ 全滅 *complete destruction, annihilation*

全滅する to be completely destroyed

その村は山崩れで全滅しました。
That village was completely destroyed by a landslide.

せんめん 洗面 ～する *wash one's face*

洗面台 sink

洗面道具 toilet articles

洗面所 place for washing-up; bathroom [→ トイレ]

洗面器 washbowl, portable washbasin

せんもん 専門 *specialty, area of expertise, field of specialization*

隣の店はコーヒーが専門です。
At the shop next-door coffee is the specialty.

ご専門は何ですか。
What is your field of specialization?

その問題は清原先生の専門です。
That problem is in Dr. Kiyohara's area of expertise.

Aを専門にする to specialize in A; to major in A

専門外の outside one's field of specialization

専門学校 vocational school

専門家 specialist, expert

ぜんや 前夜 *preceding night, eve*

期末試験の前夜にかぜをひきました。
I caught a cold the night before the final examinations.

クリスマス前夜 Christmas Eve

せんよう 専用 ～する *to use exclusively*

－専用の for the exclusive use of (Added to noun bases.)

ここは従業員専用の食堂です。
This is a cafeteria for the exclusive use of employees.

この部屋は女性専用です。
This room is for women only.

専用車 car for personal use

せんりゃく 戦略 *strategy*

戦略家 strategist

せんりゅう 川柳 *satirical poem about people and daily life (with the same 5-7-5 format as a haiku)*

せんりょう 占領 *(military) occupation*

占領する to occupy

この都市はドイツ軍に占領されました。
This city was occupied by the German army.

ぜんりょく 全力 *all one's strength, all one's might*

全力で with all one's might

全力を尽くす to do one's utmost

全力を尽くして試験を終えました。
I did my utmost and finished the exam.

せんれい 洗礼 *baptism*

洗礼を受ける to receive baptism, to be baptized

せんろ 線路 *(railroad) track*

線路に入らないでください。
Please do not go on the tracks.

線路伝いに along the tracks

ぞ *(This sentence-final particle expresses strong exclamation and is generally used only by male speakers.)*

だめだぞ。
It's no good!

―ぞい ―沿い ～の *alongside, on (Added to noun bases denoting roads, rivers, etc.)*
国道沿いの店で食事しました。
They ate at a shop alongside the national highway.
川沿いに歩きましょう。
Let's walk along the river.

そいつ【CRUDE】*that person*
(Like other Japanese demonstratives beginning with そ-, そいつ has two uses. One is to refer to a person who is in sight and is relatively far from the speaker but relatively close to the listener. The other is to refer to a person not in sight who is familiar only to the speaker or only to the listener.) [↔ こいつ; あいつ]

そう 沿う *(used in connection with roads, rivers, etc.) to be alongside; to follow*
私たちは川に沿って走っていました。
We were running along the river.

そう *like that, in that way, so*
(Like other Japanese demonstratives beginning with そ-, そう has two uses. One is to refer to something which is in sight and is relatively far from the speaker but relatively close to the listener. The other is to refer to something not in sight which is familiar only to the speaker or only to the listener.) [↔ こう; ああ]
先生にそう言いましょう。
Let's say so to the teacher.
私もそう思います。
I think so too.
一生懸命勉強しなさい。そうすれば試験に受かるでしょう。
Study hard. If you do so, you'll probably pass the examination.
そういう such, that kind of [→ そんな]

そう ～だ *1. to be that way; that's right, that's so (as an affirmative response to a question)*
「今夜雪になるでしょうか」「そうかもしれません」
"I wonder if it's going to snow tonight." "Maybe so."
「恵子さんはとても親切ですね」「そうですね」
"Keiko is very kind, isn't she?" "Yes, she is, isn't she?"
「太郎は明るいね」「次郎もそうだよ」
"Taro is cheerful, isn't he?" "So is Jiro!"
「これは君の帽子ですか」「そうです」
"Is this your hat?" "Yes, it is."
2. I hear that, they say that (following a clause)
横山さんはフランス語が話せるそうです。
I hear that Ms. Yokoyama can speak French.
洋子のお父さんはパイロットだそうだよ。
I hear that Yoko's father is a pilot!
ゆうべ大阪で大火事があったそうです。
They say that there was a big fire in Osaka last night.

―そう ～な *seeming to be, looking, appearing likely to (Added to verb, adjective, and adjectival noun bases.)*
姉はとても幸せそうです。
My older sister looks very happy.
この質問は難しそうですね。
This question seems difficult, doesn't it?
雪が降りそうだよ。
It looks like it's going to snow!

ぞう 象 *elephant*

ぞう 像 *image; portrait; statue*
彫刻家は木で像を彫っていました。
The sculptor was carving an image out of wood.
大理石の像 marble statue
自由の女神像 the Statue of Liberty
石像 stone image

そうい 相違 *difference* [→ 違い]
母と私の間では意見の相違があります。

There is a difference of opinion between my mother and me.

そうおん 騒音 *noise, annoying sound*
騒音公害 noise pollution

そうか 増加 *increase* [↔ 減少]
増加する to increase (intransitive) [→ 増える]
大学生の数が増加しています。
The number of college students has increased.

そうかい 総会 *general meeting*
生徒総会 general meeting of the students' association

そうがく 総額 *total amount of money, sum*
費用の総額は 3 万円になりました。
The total expenditure came to ¥30,000.

そうがんきょう 双眼鏡 *binoculars*

そうきん 送金 *remittance; sending money*
送金する to remit

ぞうきん 雑巾 *dusting cloth; floor-wiping cloth*
雑巾掛け cleaning with a cloth
雑巾掛けする to clean with a cloth

ぞうげ 象牙 *ivory*
象牙細工 ivory (craft) work

そうこ 倉庫 *warehouse, storehouse*

そうご 相互 〜の *mutual, reciprocal* [→ 互いの]
相互理解 mutual understanding

そうごう 総合 〜する *to consolidate, to synthesize*
さあ、みんなの考えを総合してみよう。
Now, let's try consolidating everyone's ideas.
総合病院 general hospital
総合計画 overall plan
総合点 total points

そうさ 捜査 *criminal investigation*
捜査する to investigate
捜査本部 investigation headquarters

そうさ 操作 *operation, manipulation, running*
操作する to operate, to manipulate, to run
この機械を操作するのは難しい。
Operating this machine is difficult.

そうさく 創作 *1. creation, origination*
創作する to create, to originate
2. creative writing, original writing
創作する to write (as an original work)
3. an original written work, a work of creative writing
創作活動 creative activity

そうさく 捜索 *search, searching*
捜索する to search (a place)
数人の警官がその家を捜索しました。
Several police officers searched that house.
捜索隊 search party

そうじ 掃除 *cleaning (by sweeping, wiping, etc.)*
掃除する to clean
私は毎日部屋を掃除します。
I clean my room every day.
掃除機 vacuum cleaner

そうしき 葬式 *funeral*
葬式に参列する to attend a funeral
葬式を営む to hold a funeral

そうして [☞ そして]

そうしゃ 走者 *runner*
最終走者 anchor runner

そうじゅう 操縦 *operation, flying (a plane), driving (a vehicle)*
操縦する to operate, to fly, to drive
操縦席 pilot seat, cockpit
操縦士 pilot
操縦装置 controls

そうじゅく 早熟 ～な *precocious, early-maturing*

そうしょ 草書 *grass style (of Japanese calligraphy)* [↔ 行書; 楷書]

そうしょく 装飾 *decoration, adornment*
装飾する to decorate, to adorn [→ 飾る1.]
この絵は私の部屋のいい装飾になります。
This picture will be a nice decoration for my room.
装飾品 decoration, ornament
室内装飾 interior decoration

そうせいじ 双生児 *twins* [→ 双子]
一卵性双生児 identical twins
シャム双生児 Siamese twins

ぞうせん 造船 *shipbuilding*
造船所 shipbuilding yard

そうせんきょ 総選挙 *general election*

そうぞう 創造 *creation*
創造する to create
創造者 the Creator
創造的な creative
天地創造 the Creation

そうぞう 想像 *imagination, imagining; surmise, guess* [→ 推測]
それは読者の想像に任かせます。
I will leave that to the reader's imagination.
想像する to imagine; to surmise
昔の人々の生活を想像してみましょう。
Let's try imagining the life of people long ago.
想像がつく one can imagine
想像力 imagination, imaginativeness
洋子ちゃんは想像力が豊かです。
Yoko's imagination is rich.
想像力を働かせる to use one's imag-ination
想像上の imaginary

そうぞうしい 騒々しい *noisy, boisterous* [→ 騒がしい]
あの男の子たちはいつも騒々しいよ。
Those boys are always noisy!

そうぞく 相続 *inheritance, succession*
相続する to inherit, to succeed to
父は祖父からその財産を相続しました。
My father inherited that fortune from my grandfather.
相続人 heir
相続財産 inherited fortune

そうたいてき 相対的 ～な *relative, comparative*

そうだん 相談 *consultation, talking over*
相談する to consult, to talk over, to have a talk
将来の進路について両親と相談しました。
I had a talk with my parents about my future course.
野口さんはその問題で弁護士に相談した。
Mr. Noguchi consulted with a lawyer about that matter.
相談に乗る to give advice
相談相手 person to consult with

そうち 装置 *device, apparatus, equipment*
安全装置 safety device
舞台装置 stage setting
暖房装置 heating apparatus

そうとう 相当 *1. (～に) considerably, fairly, quite* [→ かなり]
兄はギターが相当うまいです。
My older brother is quite good at the guitar.
けさは相当寒いね。
It's quite cold this morning, isn't it?
相当な／の considerable, fair
月に1万円は相当なお小遣いだよ。
¥10,000 a month is considerable pocket money!
2. ～する to be equivalent, to correspond [→ 当たる6.]

1ドルは日本円でいくらに相当しますか。
How many Japanese yen are there to the dollar?
「花」に相当する英語は何ですか。
What is the English that corresponds to "hana"?
ー相当の worth (Added to bases denoting amounts of money.)
これは10万円相当の花瓶です。
This is a vase worth 100,000 yen.
3. 〜な／の appropriate, suitable, befitting [→ 適当な]
相当する to be appropriate, to suit, to befit
それは学生に相当な仕事です。
That's work appropriate for a student.

そうどう 騒動 *commotion, trouble, confusion; riot* [→ 暴動]
騒動を起こす to cause a commotion; to start a riot
学園騒動 campus riot

そうなん 遭難 *life-threatening accident*
遭難する to meet with an accident; to be wrecked (when the subject is a ship)
日本の登山隊がエベレスト山で遭難した。
A Japanese mountain-climbing team met with an accident on Mt. Everest.
その船は台風で遭難しました。
That ship was wrecked in a typhoon.
遭難者 accident victim
遭難信号 distress signal

そうにゅう 挿入 *insertion*
挿入する to insert

そうば 相場 *1. market price, quotation*
2. market speculation, playing the market

そうび 装備 *1. (installed) equipment*
2. equipment installation
装備する to install as equipment
その船は核兵器を装備していない。
That ship has not been equipped with nuclear weapons.

そうべつ 送別 *farewell, send-off*
送別会 farewell party

そうめん *very thin wheat noodles, Japanese vermicelli*

そうり 総理 [☞ 総理大臣]
総理府 the Prime Minister's Office

ぞうり 草履 *Japanese sandals (with a flat sole and a thong fitting between the big toe and the second toe)*

そうりだいじん 総理大臣 *the Prime Minister (of Japan)*

そうりつ 創立 *founding, establishment* [→ 設立]
創立する to found, to establish
この学校は1950年に創立されました。
This school was founded in 1950.
創立記念日 anniversary of the founding
創立者 founder

そうりょう 送料 *freight charge; postage*
この小包の送料はいくらですか。
How much is the postage for this package?
この荷物の送料は受け取り人が支払う。
The freight charge for baggage will be paid by the receiver.

そうりょうじ 総領事 *consul general*
総領事館 consulate general [→ 領事館]

そえる 添える *to attach, to add*
その贈り物に手紙を添えますか。
Are you going to enclose a letter with that present?
写真を添えて願書を提出します。
I will attach a photograph and turn in my application.

ソース *sauce*
ステーキにソースをかけますか。
Shall I put sauce on your steak?
ホワイトソース white sauce
ウスターソース Worcestershire sauce

ソーセージ *sausage*

ソーダ *1. soda, sodium carbonate 2. soda (pop)*

ソーダ水 [☞ ソーダ2. (above)]

ーそく ー足 *(counter for pairs of footwear; see Appendix 2)*

ぞくご 俗語 *slang*

そくし 即死 *instant death, death on the spot*

即死する to die instantly, to be killed on the spot

そくしん 促進 *promotion, encouragement*

促進する to promote, to encourage

ぞくする 属する *{Irreg.} to belong, to be affiliated*

うちの明は野球部に属しています。
Our Akira belongs to the baseball club.

そくせき 即席 ～の *impromptu; instant* [→ インスタントー]

ぞくぞく ～する *to shiver*

外は寒くてぞくぞくしました。
I was shivering because it was cold outside.

ぞくぞく 続々 (～と) *one after another, in succession* [→ 相次いで]

そくたつ 速達 *(US) special delivery, (UK) express delivery*

この手紙を速達で送ってください。
Please send this letter by special delivery.

速達料金 special delivery charge

そくど 速度 *speed, velocity*

この列車の速度は時速約200キロです。
The speed of this train is approximately 200 kilometers an hour.

速度を上げる to speed up

速度を落とす to slow down

速度計 speedometer

最高速度 maximum speed, speed limit

そくばく 束縛 *restriction, constraint*

束縛する to restrict, to constrain

そくりょう 測量 *(land) survey, surveying*

測量する to survey

測量技師 surveyor

そくりょく 速力 *speed* [→ 速度]

ソケット *electrical socket*

そこ 底 *bottom, lowermost part*

かごの底がぬけてしまいました。
The bottom of this basket has fallen out.

靴の底 sole of a shoe

そこ *that place, there*

(Like other Japanese demonstratives beginning with そ-, そこ has two uses. One is to refer to a place which is in sight and is relatively far from the speaker but relatively close to the listener. The other is to refer to a place not in sight which is familiar only to the speaker or only to the listener.) [↔ ここ; あそこ]

そこで何をしているの？
What are you doing there?

そこの生徒に聞きなさい。
Ask the student there.

そこに郵便ポストがあるでしょう？
There's a mailbox there, right?

そこからバス停まで何分ぐらいですか。
About how many minutes is it from there to the bus stop?

母はそこまでは知っています。
My mother knows that much. (Literally: My mother knows up to there.)

そこで thus, thereupon, accordingly (The literal meaning at that place is also possible.)

田中さんは会社を辞めました。そこでお金に困っています。
Mr. Tanaka quit his company. So, he's having money problems.

そこなう 損なう *to harm, to damage*

Aの感情を損なう to hurt A's feelings

ーそこなう ー損なう *to miss doing, to fail*

to do (Added to verb bases.)
けさ父はいつも乗る電車に乗り損なった。
This morning my father missed the train he usually takes.
大好きなテレビ番組を見損なったよ。
I missed my favorite TV program!

そしき 組織 *organization*
組織する to organize
メンバーは委員会を組織しました。
The members organized a committee.

そしつ 素質 *the makings, aptitude*
お嬢さんは大歌手になる素質があります。
Your daughter has the makings of a great singer.

そして *1. and then, after that*
兄は京都、大阪、そして神戸に出張した。
My older brother went on business to Kyoto, Osaka, and then Kobe.
2. and, and also
バンコクは暑く、そして湿度も高い。
Bangkok is hot and also humid.

そしょう 訴訟 *lawsuit*
訴訟を起こす to file suit

そせん 祖先 *ancestor* [→ 先祖] [↔ 子孫]

そそぐ 注ぐ *1. to pour (transitive) (The direct object must be a liquid.)*
姉はコップにコーラを注いでくれた。
My older sister poured some cola into a glass for me.
2. to flow, to empty (into a lake)
利根川は太平洋に注ぎます。
The Tone River flows into the Pacific Ocean.
3. to concentrate, to focus, to devote
注意を注ぐ to focus one's attention
全力を注ぐ to devote all one's energy

そそっかしい *careless*

そそのかす 唆す *to tempt, to entice*
やくざは少年を唆して、すりをさせた。
The gangster enticed the boy and made him pick pockets.

そだつ 育つ *1. to grow (intransitive)*
みかんは温暖な地方に育ちます。
Mandarin oranges grow in warm regions.
2. to grow up, to reach maturity, to be brought up
いとこは京都で生まれ、京都で育ちました。
My cousin was born and brought up in Kyoto.

そだてる 育てる *1. to grow (transitive)*
母の趣味はばらを育てることです。
My mother's hobby is growing roses.
2. to bring up, to raise
池森さんは３人の子供を育てました。
Ms. Ikemori raised three children.

そち 措置 *step, measure, action* [→ 処置]
措置をとる to take measures, to take action

そちら 【FORMAL】
(Like other Japanese demonstratives beginning with そ-, そちら has two uses. One is to refer to something which is in sight and is relatively far from the speaker but relatively close to the listener. The other is to refer to something not in sight which is familiar only to the speaker or only to the listener.)
1. [[↔ こちら1.; あちら1.]] *that way; there*
森先生はそちらにいらっしゃいますか。
Is Ms. Mori there?
2. [[↔ こちら3.]] *you; your family*
そちらのご意見はいかがでしょうか。
What is your opinion?

そっき 速記 *shorthand, stenography*
姉は速記を習っています。
My older sister is learning shorthand.

そつぎょう 卒業 *graduation (i.e., successful completion of a course of study)*
卒業する to graduate from
美知子の兄は来年大学を卒業する。
Michiko's older brother will graduate from college next year.

卒業式 graduation ceremony
卒業証書 diploma
卒業生 graduate

ソックス *sock*

そっくり *1.* ～の *just like*
息子さんはお父さんにそっくりです。
The son looks just like his father.
2. all, entirely
宝石を空き巣にそっくり盗まれました。
The jewels were all stolen by a sneak thief.

そっち 【COL. for そちら】

そっちょく 率直 ～な *frank, candid, outspoken*
首相は率直な意見を述べました。
The prime minister stated his candid opinion.

そっと *1. quietly, softly, gently, lightly*
そっとする to leave undisturbed, to leave alone
直子ちゃんをそっとしておきましょう。
Let's leave Naoko alone.
2. secretly, stealthily [→ こっそり]
岡さんはそっと太郎に目くばせしました。
Mr. Oka secretly signaled Taro with his eyes.

ぞっと ～する *to shudder (The subject is a person.)*
蛇を見てぞっとしたよ。
I saw a snake and shuddered!

そで 袖 *sleeve*
そでをまくる to roll up one's sleeves

そと 外 *1. the outside* [↔ 内1.]
だれかが外からドアを開けました。
Somebody opened the door from the outside.
2. outside, outdoors
洋子ちゃんは外にいるよ。
Yoko's outside!
少女は窓から外を眺めています。
The girl is looking out of the window.
外へ遊びに行こう。
Let's go outside to play.

そとがわ 外側 *the outside, the outer side* [↔ 内側]
箱の外側を白く塗るつもりです。
I intend to paint the outside of the box white.

そなえる 備える *1. to provide, to furnish, to install*
事務所にコンピューターを備えました。
We installed a computer in the office.
2. to prepare oneself, to make provisions [→ 準備する]
吉野さんは将来に備えて貯金しています。
Ms. Yoshino is saving to make provisions for the future.
生徒はみんな入試に備えて勉強している。
The students are all studying in preparation for the entrance examination.

ソナタ *sonata*

その *that (as a noun modifier)*
(Like other Japanese demonstratives beginning with そ-, そ has two uses. One is to refer to something which is in sight and is relatively far from the speaker but relatively close to the listener. The other is to refer to something not in sight which is familiar only to the speaker or only to the listener.) [↔ この; あの]
その窓を開けてください。
Please open that window.
その日はとても風が強かったよ。
That day the wind was very strong!
そのとおりです。
That's right. (Literally: It is that way.)
その上 besides that, moreover
由美はとてもやさしく、そのうえ利口だ。
Yumi is very kind. Besides that, she is bright.
そのうち sometime soon, before long, by and by
そのうちハワイに行こうと思っています。

I'm thinking of going to Hawaii sometime soon.

その後 after that, since then

その後松川さんからは便りがありません。
Since then there haven't been any letters from Ms. Matsukawa.

その後また事故を起こしてしまいました。
After that I caused another accident again.

そのころ in those days, at that time

そのころ関さんは京都に住んでいました。
In those days Ms. Seki was living in Kyoto.

その時 then, at that time

その時おふろに入っていました。
I was in the bath at that time.

その場で on the spot

すりはその場で捕まったよ。
The pickpocket was caught on the spot!

そのまま as is, as things are

すべてそのままにしておきなさい。
Leave everything as it is.

そのままお待ちください。(on the telephone)
Hold the line, please. (Literally: Please wait as is.)

そば 傍, 側 *the area nearby, the area beside*

図書館のそばに公園があります。
There is a park by the library.

猫は私のそばに座りました。
The cat sat beside me.

立松さんはうちのそばに住んでいます。
Mr. Tatematsu lives near my house.

もっとそばに来なさい。
Come closer beside me.

あの男の子はいつも母親のそばにいます。
That boy is always near his mother.

そば *1. buckwheat*

2. soba, buckwheat noodles

そば屋 soba shop; soba shop proprietor

そばかす *freckle*

そびえる 聳える *to rise, to tower*

お寺の塔が高くそびえています。
The temple tower rises high.

そふ 祖父 *grandfather* [↔ 祖母; おじいさん 1.]

ソファー *sofa*

お客さんはソファーに座っています。
The guest is sitting on the sofa.

ソフトウエア *software* [↔ ハードウエア]

ソフトクリーム *soft ice cream*

ソフトボール *1. (the game of) softball*

2. a softball

ソプラノ *1. soprano (voice)*

2. soprano (singer)

3. soprano (part)

そぼ 祖母 *grandmother* [↔ 祖父; おばあさん1.]

そぼく 素朴 ～な *simple, unpretentious, artless*

花村さんの素朴な話し方が好きです。
I like Mr. Hanamura's simple way of talking.

そまつ 粗末 *1.* ～な *low-quality, crude*

この店では粗末な物を売ります。
They sell low-quality things in this store.

2. ～にする *to treat carelessly, to use carelessly*

お金を粗末にしてはいけないよ。
You mustn't use your money carelessly!

そむく 背く *to act contrary, to disobey*

あの二人は校則に背いてたばこを吸った。
Those two disobey school regulations and smoke cigarettes.

伝統に背く to act contrary to tradition

そめる 染める *to dye*

母は髪の毛を黒く染めました。
My mother dyed her hair black.

そもそも *in the first place, to begin with*

そもそもの original, initial

そら 空 *sky*

空はすぐに晴れるでしょう。
The sky will probably clear up soon.
空には雲が一つもないね。
There's not a cloud in the sky, is there?
空の旅はやはりまだ高価ですね。
As you'd expect, air travel is still expensive, isn't it?
空色 sky blue (as a noun)
空模様 the look of the sky, the weather
空高く high up in the sky; high into the sky
ジェット機が空高く飛んでいます。
A jet is flying high up in the sky.

そらまめ 空豆 *broad bean*

そり *sled; sleigh*

そる 反る *to warp, to bend (intransitive)*

その板は熱で反ってしまいました。
That board warped in the heat.

そる 剃る *to shave (The direct object can be a part of the body or a kind of hair.)*

あの人は１日に２回ひげをそります。
That person shaves twice a day.
顔をそる to shave one's face
頭をそる to shave one's head

それ *that (one)*

(Like other Japanese demonstratives beginning with それ-, それ has two uses. One is to refer to something which is in sight and is relatively far from the speaker but relatively close to the listener. The other is to refer to something not in sight which is familiar only to the speaker or only to the listener.) [↔ これ; あれ]
叔父がそれをくれたよ。
My uncle gave that to me!
いつそれを捨てましたか。
When did you throw that away?
それはだれの靴ですか。
Whose shoes are those?
それから (The literal meaning from that is also possible.) [[→ そして]] after that, since then; and, and also
父は大阪に行き、それから福岡へ向います。
Father will go to in Osaka, and after that he will head for Fukuoka.
私たちはそれから話し合っていません。
We haven't talked to each other since then.
それで (The literal meaning by that, using that is also possible.) for that reason, so; and then, and so (Used in questions.)
熱がありました。それで欠席したんです。
I had a fever. For that reason, I was absent
「ゆうべ映画を見に行きましたよ」「それで何時に終わりましたか」
"I went to see a movie last night!" "And so what time did it end?"
それに besides that, moreover (The literal meanings to that, on that, etc., are also possible.)
暑いですね。それに風もないですね。
It's hot, isn't it? Besides that, there's no wind, is there?
それどころか on the contrary, quite the opposite of that
「谷森さんはそれを聞いて悲しみましたか」
「それどころか喜びましたよ」
"Was Ms. Tanimori sad to hear that?"
"On the contrary, she was glad!"
それほど that much, to that extent, so
問題はそれほど難しくないです。
The problem is not so difficult.
それまで until then
それまで待たなければなりませんよ。
You'll have to wait until then!
それまでに by then
それまでに宿題を仕上げます。
I will finish my homework by then.

それぞれ *each, each respectively*

参加者はそれぞれ自分の意見があります。
The participants each have their own opinion.

先生は生徒たちにそれぞれノートを1冊ずつあげました。
The teacher gave the students one notebook each.

それぞれの each, each respective

それぞれの国には独特の習慣があります。
Each country has its own unique customs.

それでは *well then, in that case*

それでは、お休みなさい。
Well then, good night.

それでは、小野さんに会う必要はない。
In that case, there's no need to see Mr. Ono.

それとも *or (connecting alternative questions)*

このペンは先生のですか、それとも小倉さんのですか。
Is this pen yours, or is it Mr. Ogura's?

ソロ *a solo* [→ 独唱; 独奏]

ピアノソロ piano solo

そろう 揃う *1. to gather, to come to the same place* [→ 集まる]

みんなそろいましたか。
Is everybody here? (Literally: Has everybody gathered?)

2. to become the same, to become uniform

このクラスの生徒は英語の力がほとんどそろっています。
The English ability of the students in this class is almost uniform.

3. to be gathered into a complete set, to be gathered into a wide assortment

図書館には言語学の本がそろっています。
There is a wide selection of linguistics books in the library.

そろえる 揃える *1. to arrange, to place in orderly fashion*

テーブルの上の新聞をそろえてください。
Please arrange the newspapers on the table.

机をきちんとそろえました。
We arranged the desks neatly.

2. to make the same, to make uniform

足並みをそろえる to get in step

3. to get a complete set of, to get a wide assortment of

材料をそろえる to get all the ingredients

そろそろ (〜と) *1. soon* [→ 間も無く]

そろそろガードマンが現れるでしょう。
The guard will probably appear soon.

そろそろ7時になります。
It will soon be 7:00.

2. slowly, little by little

登山隊はそろそろ頂点に登りました。
The mountain-climbing party climbed slowly to the summit.

そろばん 算盤 *abacus*

そわそわ 〜する *to become restless; to become nervous*

息子はそわそわした子供です。
My son is a restless child.

京子さんはそわそわした様子でしたね。
Kyoko looked nervous, didn't she?

そん 損 *loss, disadvantageous outcome* [↔ 得]

それを買うのは損です。
Buying that would be disadvantageous.

損をする to incur a loss, to suffer a loss

結局5000円の損をしたよ。
In the end I suffered ¥5,000 loss!

その会社はひどく損をしました。
The company incurred terrible losses.

損をして売る to sell at a loss

損する [☞ 損をする(above)]

そんがい 損害 *damage, harm, loss*

その損害は500万円に上りました。
That loss amounted to 5 million yen.

損害を受ける to be damaged, to suffer a loss

損害を与える to cause damage, to cause a loss

そんけい 尊敬 *respect, esteem (for a person)* [↔ 軽蔑]

尊敬する to come to respect, to come to revere

私は父を尊敬しているよ。
I respect my father!

選手たちは浩を監督として尊敬している。
The players respect Hiroshi as their coach.

尊敬語 honorific word (one type of respectful vocabulary in Japanese) [↔ 謙譲語]

そんざい 存在 *existence, being*

前山さんは神の存在を信じています。
Mr. Maeyama believes in the existence of God.

存在する to exist

その少女は幽霊が存在すると信じている。
That girl believes that ghosts exist.

そのような物はこの世に存在しないよ。
That kind of thing does not exist in this world!

ぞんじあげる 存じ上げる 【HUM. for 知る *when the direct object is a person*】

そんしつ 損失 *loss, detrimental occurrence*

社長の急死は会社にとって大きな損失だ。
The president's sudden death was a great loss to the company.

ぞんじる 存じる *1.* 【HUM. for 知る *when the direct object is not a person*】

2. 【HUM. for 思う】

そんちょう 村長 *village head*

そんちょう 尊重 *respect, esteem (for a thing)*

尊重する to respect, to have a high regard for

しかし、裁判官の意見を尊重します。
However, I respect the judge's opinion.

そんな *that kind of*

(Like other Japanese demonstratives beginning with そ-, そんな has two uses. One is to refer to something which is in sight and is relatively far from the speaker but relatively close to the listener. The other is to refer to something not in sight which is familiar only to the speaker or only to the listener.) [↔ こんな; あんな]

そんなことは言わなかったよ。
I didn't say such a thing!

そんな動物はいますか。
Is there such an animal?

そんなに to that extent, that much

そんなに速く走らないで。
Don't run so fast.

た 田 *rice field, rice paddy*

田植え rice planting

た 他 ～の *other, another* [→ 外の, 他の]

だ *to be*

(This word is the informal nonpast form of the copula, which follows nouns and nominal adjectives and expresses meanings roughly equivalent to be identical to or be characterized by. For details, see Appendix 1.)

僕も学生だよ。
I'm a student too!

生徒たちはとても静かだね。
The students are very quiet, aren't they?

娘はあしたで14歳だよ。
My daughter will be fourteen years old tomorrow!

ダース *dozen*

一ダース (counter for dozens; see Appendix 2)

鉛筆を1ダース買いました。
I bought a dozen pencils.

タートルネック *turtleneck (sweater)*

ターミナル *(transportation) terminal*

たい 鯛 *sea bream*

たい 対 *1. versus*

日本対中国の試合はあしたです。
The Japan vs. China game is tomorrow.

2. to (Typically used in giving scores.)

私たちのチームは３対１で勝ったよ。
Our team won by 3-to-1!

その試合は３対３の同点で終わりました。
The game ended in a 3-to-3 tie.

ーたい *to want to*

(Added to verb bases to form words that are grammatically adjectives. To express the desire of a third person, ーがる is added to the base of an adjective formed with -たい. When -たい is added to a verb with a direct object, the object can be marked either with を or with が.)

あしたもテニスをしたい。
I want to play tennis tomorrow too.

何も飲みたくない。
I don't want to drink anything.

ヨーロッパに行きたいなあ。
Boy, I want to go to Europe.

兄に手伝ってもらいたいのです。
I want my older brother to help me.

社長と話したいと思います。
I'd like to talk with the company president. (Adding と after softens the assertion of desire, but the literal translation **I think I want to** usually sounds rather unnatural. In most cases, the less literal **I'd like to** is preferable.)

弟はこのケーキを食べたがるでしょう。
My younger brother will probably want to eat this cake.

だい 代 *a person's time (as head of a family, company, country, etc.)*

この家は祖父の代に建てられました。
This house was built in my grandfather's time.

ー代 (counter for number of people in succession to a headship; see Appendix 2)

この人は20代目の大統領でした。
This person was the 20th president.

ーだい ー代 *decade of a person's life (Added to numerals that are multiples of 10.)*

20代 one's twenties

40代 one's forties

だい 代 *charges, fare, fee*

バス代 bus fare

電話代 telephone charges

だいー 大ー *big, great (Added to noun and adjectival noun bases.)*

大洪水 great flood

大成功 great success

大好きな greatly liked; greatly fond

だいー 第ー *-th (Added to number bases to make ordinal numbers.)*

これは成功への第一歩です。
This is the first step to success.

ーだい ー台 *(counter for vehicles, machines; see Appendix 2)*

だい 台 *stand, rest, platform, pedestal*

踏み台 footstool

洗面台 washstand

だい 題 *title (of a book, etc.)*

たいあたり 体当たり *1. throwing oneself (against something)*

体当たりする to throw oneself

男の人はドアに体当たりしました。
The man threw himself against the door.

2. devoting all one's energy, throwing oneself (into something)

体当たりでやる to do with all one's energy

たいい 大意 *gist, general idea*

たいいく 体育 *physical training; physical education*

体育の日 Health-Sports Day (a Japanese

national holiday on October 10)
体育館 gymnasium

だいいち 第一 ～の *first, foremost*
第一に first, first of all
まず第一に宿題をしなければならない。
First of all I have to do my homework.
「安全第一」 (on a sign)
Safety First
第一印象 first impression

たいいん 退院 *leaving the hospital, being discharged from the hospital* [↔ 入院]
退院する to leave the hospital, to be discharged from the hospital
この患者はあした退院できるでしょう。
This patient will probably be able to leave the hospital tomorrow.

たいおん 体温 *(body) temperature*
体温を計る to take a temperature
体温計 (clinical) thermometer

たいかい 大会 *1. mass meeting; general meeting [→ 総会]; convention*
2. tournament, meet, competition
弁論大会 speech contest
陸上大会 track meet
マラソン大会 large marathon race
生徒大会 students' meeting
水泳大会 swim meet

たいがい 大概 *1. generally, usually* [→ 普通1.]
大概の general, usual
2. for the most part, almost completely [→ 殆ど1.]
大概の most, almost all
3. [[→ 多分]] perhaps; probably
4. ～の moderate, reasonable

たいかく 体格 *build, physique*
田坂先生はがっしりした体格の人です。
Mr. Tasaka is a person of strong build.
体格がいい one's build is good

だいがく 大学 *university; college*
兄は今年大学に入りました。
My older brother entered college this year.
姉は来年大学に行きます。
My older sister will go to college next year.
大学院 graduate school
大学入試 college entrance examination
大学生 college student
大学卒 college graduate
短期大学 junior college

たいき 大気 *atmosphere, the air*
大気圏 atmosphere, atmospheric zone
大気汚染 air pollution

だいきん 代金 *price, cost, charge*
このラケットの代金はいくらですか。
What is the cost of this racket?

たいきん 大金 *large amount of money*

だいく 大工 *carpenter*
大工道具 carpenter's tools

たいくつ 退屈 ～な *boring, dull*
これは退屈なテレビ番組です。
This is a boring TV program.
退屈する to get bored
会長の長いスピーチに退屈しました。
We got bored with the chairperson's long speech.

たいけん 体験 *an experience*
友達はローマでの体験を話してくれた。
My friend told me about her experiences in Rome.
体験する to experience

たいこ 太鼓 *drum ((musical instrument))*
小太鼓 snare drum
大太鼓 bass drum

たいこう 対抗 *opposition; rivalry*

対抗する to match, to rival [→ 匹敵する]; to oppose [→ 反対する]
空手では斉藤君にだれも対抗できないよ。
Nobody can match Saito in karate!

たいこく 大国 *great country, powerful country*

だいこん 大根 *daikon, Japanese radish*

たいざい 滞在 *stay (away from home), sojourn*
滞在する to stay
パリにはいつまで滞在するつもりですか。
Until when are you planning to stay in Paris?

たいさく 対策 *countermeasure*

だいさんしゃ 第三者 *third party, disinterested person*

たいし 大使 *ambassador*
大使館 embassy
駐米日本大使 Japanese ambassador to the United States
駐日アメリカ大使 American ambassador to Japan

たいじ 退治 *extermination (of a pest)*
退治する to exterminate, to get rid of
まずねずみを退治しましょう。
First let's get rid of the rats.

だいじ 大事 *1. ～な [[→ 大切な]] important [→ 重要な]; precious [→ 貴重な]*
大事にする to take good care of; to value
どうぞこの本を大事にしてください。
Please take good care of this book.
2. very important matter, serious matter

ダイジェスト *digest, summary*

たいした 大した *great, outstanding; serious, important*
あの方は大した芸術家です。
That person is a great artist.
大したけがではないです。
It's not a serious injury.

たいして 大して *(not) very, (not) especially (Always occurs in combination with a negative predicate.)*
きょうは大して暑くない。
It is not especially hot today.

たいして 対して [☞ に対して]

たいしゅう 大衆 *the general public, the masses*
大衆向きの popular, of wide appeal
大衆作家 popular writer
大衆小説 popular novel

たいじゅう 体重 *(body) weight*
体重はどのぐらいありますか。
About how much do you weigh?
体重が2キロ増えました。
I've gained two kilograms.
体重計 (body-weight) scale

たいしょう 大将 *(army) general; admiral*

たいしょう 大正 *(Japanese imperial era name for the period 1912- 1926)*
大正時代 the Taisho Era
大正天皇 the Taisho Emperor

たいしょう 対象 *object, target*
村井先生の研究の対象は昆虫です。
The object of Dr. Murai's research is insects.

たいしょう 対照 *contrast*
対照する to contrast (transitive)
AをBと対照する to contrast A with B

たいじょう 退場 *leaving (a sporting event, concert, etc.)* [↔ 入場]
退場する to leave

だいじょうぶ 大丈夫 ～な *all right, OK, safe*
薬を飲んだから、大丈夫です。
I took the medicine, so I'm all right.
この池でスケートしても大丈夫ですか。
Is it safe to skate on this pond? (Literally:

Even if one skates on this pond is it safe?)

たいしょく 退職 *leaving one's job*

退職する to retire; to resign

叔父は65歳で退職します。

My uncle will retire at sixty-five.

退職金 retirement allowance

だいじん 大臣 *(government) minister*

外務大臣 Foreign Minister

文部大臣 Education Minister

だいず 大豆 *soybean*

だいすう 代数 *algebra*

たいする 対する [☞ に対する]

たいせい 体制 *organization, system, structure (ordinarily of a society or country)*

経済体制 economic structure

政治体制 political system

たいせいよう 大西洋 *the Atlantic Ocean [↔ 太平洋]*

たいせき 体積 *(cubic) volume*

たいせつ 大切 〜な *[[→ 大事な]] important [→ 重要な]; precious [→ 貴重な]*

読書をすることは大切です。

Reading books is important.

これは大切な学校行事です。

This is an important school event.

健康はとても大切です。

Good health is precious.

大切に carefully, with care

大切に扱ってください。

Handle with care.

大切にする to value; to take good care of

たいそう 体操 *1. gymnastics*

2. calisthenics

体操部 gymnastics club; gymnastics team

美容体操 shape-up calisthenics

器械体操 apparatus gymnastics

だいたい 大体 *1. approximately, about [→ およそ]*

私は大体11時ごろ寝ます。

I go to bed at about 11:00.

大体の rough, approximate

2. in general, for the most part, almost completely

この作文は大体よくできています。

This composition is good for the most part.

第5課は大体済せました。

I've almost finished Lesson 5.

3. gist, substance, main points

大体の general, rough

4. originally, to begin with [→ 元々]

だいだい 橙 *bitter orange ((fruit))*

橙色 (the color) orange [→ オレンジ2.]

だいたすう 大多数 *the great majority*

生徒の大多数は泳げます。

The great majority of the students can swim.

だいたん 大胆 〜な *bold, daring*

だいちょう 大腸 *large intestine, colon*

タイツ *tights*

たいてい 大抵 *1. usually, generally* [→ 普通]

私はたいてい6時に起きます。

I usually get up at 6:00.

母は午前中はたいていうちにいます。

My mother is usually at home in the morning.

2. for the most part, almost completely [→ 殆ど1.]

大抵の most, almost all

3. [[→ 多分]] probably; perhaps

4. 〜の (no) ordinary (in combination with a negative predicate)

それはたいていの能力ではありません。

That's no ordinary ability.

たいど 態度 *attitude, manner, bearing, deportment*

私たちに対する態度は好意的です。

Their attitude toward us is friendly.

弘美ちゃんは授業中の態度が非常によい。
Hiromi's class manner is very good.

だいとうりょう 大統領 *president (of a country)*
一大統領 (Added to a surname as a title.)
リンカーン大統領は暗殺されました。
President Lincoln was assassinated.
大統領選挙 presidential election
アメリカ合衆国大統領 the President of the United States of America
副大統領 vice-president

だいどころ 台所 *kitchen*
台所仕事 kitchen work

タイトル *1. title (of a book, etc.) [→ 題]*
2. (championship) title [→ 選手権 (s.v. 選手)]
タイトルマッチ title match

だいなし 台無し *ruination*
台なしにする to ruin, to spoil
台なしになる to be ruined, to be spoiled
ピクニックは雨で台無しになったよ。
The picnic was spoiled by the rain!

ダイナマイト *dynamite*

ダイナミック ～な *dynamic*

ダイニングキッチン *a room used as both a dining room and a kitchen* [→ D K]

たいばつ 体罰 *corporal punishment*

タイピスト *typist*

だいひょう 代表 *1. representing, representation*
代表する *to represent*
2. a representative
明子ちゃんは私たちのクラスの代表です。
Akiko is our class representative.
代表団 delegation

ダイビング *1. (competitive) diving (into a pool, etc.)*
2. (underwater) diving
スカイダイビング skydiving
スキンダイビング skin diving

タイプ *1. type, style, model* [→ 型1.]
息子はこのタイプの自転車が好きです。
My son likes this type of bicycle.
2. type (of person)
上村さんは僕の好きなタイプです。
Ms. Uemura is the type I like.

タイプ [☞ タイプライター]

だいぶ 大分 *very, much [→ 随分]; rather, pretty [→ かなり]*
だいぶ暗くなってきたね。
It's gotten very dark, hasn't it?
気分はだいぶよくなりました。
I feel much better.
きょうはだいぶ暑いですね。
Today is rather hot, isn't it?

たいふう 台風 *typhoon*
九州はよく台風に襲われます。
Kyushu is often hit by typhoons.
台風の目 eye of a typhoon
台風５号 Typhoon No. 5
(Typhoons are given numbers rather than names in Japan.)

だいぶつ 大仏 *great statue of Buddha*
奈良の大仏 the Great Buddha at Nara

だいぶぶん 大部分 [[→ 殆ど]] *1. mostly, almost completely*
桜の花は大部分散ってしまいました。
The cherry blossoms have almost completely fallen.
きょうの仕事は大部分終わっています。
Today's work is almost over.
2. majority, greater part [→ 多く2.]
大部分の学生がその提案に賛成です。
Most of the students are in agreement with that proposal.
この家は大部分が木でできています。
Most of this house is made of wood.

タイプライター *typewriter*

タイプライターを打つ to do typing, to type

たいへいよう 太平洋 *the Pacific Ocean* [↔ 大西洋]

太平洋戦争 the Pacific War

(Refers to the part of World War II between Japan and the Allies in 1941-45.)

南太平洋 the South Pacific

たいへん 大変 *1. very, extremely* [→ 非常に]

その知らせにたいへん驚きました。
I was very surprised at that news.

2. 〜な terrible; terribly difficult

それはたいへんな問題ですね。
That's a terribly difficult problem, isn't it?

指導者はたいへんな誤りをしました。
The leader made a terrible mistake.

たいへんだ！
Good Heavens! (Literally: It's terrible!)

だいべん 大便 *feces*

たいほ 逮捕 *arrest*

逮捕する to arrest

逮捕状 arrest warrant

たいほう 大砲 *artillery gun, cannon*

だいほん 台本 *script, scenario [→ 脚本]*

だいみょう 大名 *daimyo, Japanese feudal lord*

タイミング *timing (with which something is done)*

実にいいタイミングで関口さんが部屋に入ってきた。
Mr. Sekiguchi came into the room with truly good timing.

タイムリー *〜な timely, well-timed*

タイムリーヒット timely hit (in baseball)

だいめいし 代名詞 *pronoun*

タイヤ *tire*

このタイヤがパンクしたよ。
This tire went flat!

スノータイヤ snow tire

スペアタイヤ spare tire

ダイヤ *(written) train schedule*

事故でダイヤが乱れています。
The schedule has been disrupted by an accident.

ダイヤ *1. [☞ ダイヤモンド]*

2. diamonds ((playing-card suit))

ダイヤモンド *diamond*

ダイヤル *dial*

ダイヤルを回す to turn a dial

父は運転しながらラジオのダイヤルを回していました。
My father was turning the radio dial while he was driving.

私は番号をまちがえてダイヤルを回した。
I dialed the wrong number. (Literally: I made a mistake on the number and turned the dial.)

たいよう 太陽 *sun*

太陽は西に沈むでしょう？
The sun sets in the west, right?

太陽電池 solar battery

太陽エネルギー solar energy

太陽系 solar system

太陽暦 solar calendar

たいら 平ら *〜な flat, level* [→ 平たい]

労働者は運動場を平らにしました。
The workers made the playground level.

平らな土地 flat land

たいらげる 平らげる *1. to put down, to suppress; to subjugate*

2. 【COL.】 *to eat up completely*

だいり 代理 *1. acting on another's behalf, acting in another's place, acting by proxy*

小野先生が杉先生の代理をしました。
Mr. Ono acted on Mr. Sugi's behalf.

私の代理で園田さんがその会に出席した。
Mr. Sonoda attended the meeting in my place.

2. person acting on another's behalf, proxy

代理人 [☞ 代理2. (above)]
代理店 agency (for business transactions)
部長代理 acting department head

たいりく 大陸 *continent*
アジア大陸 the Asian Continent

だいりせき 大理石 *marble ((stone))*

たいりつ 対立 *mutual opposition, mutual antagonism* [↔ 一致]
対立する to be opposed (to each other)
二人の意見は対立しています。
The opinions of the two are opposed.

たいりょう 大量 *large quantity*
日本は大量の石油を輸入しています。
Japan imports large quantities of oil.
大量に in large quantities
大量生産 mass production

たいりょく 体力 *physical strength, stamina*
おばあさんの体力は衰えたね。
Grandmother's stamina has weakened, hasn't it?
体力テスト physical strength test

タイル *tile (of the type used on floors and walls)*
タイルを張る to lay tiles
タイルの浴室 tiled bathroom

ダイレクトメール *direct mail*

たいわ 対話 *conversation [→ 会話]; dialog*
この教授は学生との対話が好きだ。
This professor likes to have conversations with his students.
対話する to have a conversation; to have a dialog

たえず 絶えず *continually, incessantly*

たえる 耐える, 堪える *1. to stand, to endure, to bear, to put up*
Aに耐える to stand A, to endure A, to bear A, to put up with A
私は一晩中歯の痛みに耐えました。
I put up with a toothache all night long.
この暑さには耐えられないよ。
I can't stand this heat!
2. to withstand
Aに耐える to withstand A
この家は大きな地震にも耐えます。
This house will withstand even a big earthquake.

たえる 絶える *1. to come to an end, to end*
母親の心配事は絶えません。
A mother's worries never end.
2. to die out [→ 絶滅する]

だえんけい 楕円形 *ellipse, oval*

たおす 倒す *1. to make fall over*
子供が花瓶を倒しました。
The child knocked over a vase.
2. to defeat [→ 負かす]

タオル *towel*
バスタオル bath towel

たおれる 倒れる *1. to fall over, to topple over*
その少年はあおむけに地面に倒れました。
That boy fell over on the ground backwards.
2. to fall ill, to collapse

たか 鷹 *hawk*

たかい 高い *1. [[↔ 低い1.]] high; tall*
K 2は世界で2番目に高い山です。
K2 is the second highest mountain in the world.
兄は父より3センチ背が高いです。
My older brother is three centimeters taller than my father.
ジェット機が高く飛んでいるよ。
A jet is flying high!
チアガールはとても高くジャンプした。
The cheerleader jumped very high.
高い鼻 prominent nose

2. loud [↔ 低い2.]

3. expensive [↔ 安い]

この本は高いですね。
This book is expensive, isn't it?

その自転車は高くて買えないよ。
That bicycle is expensive, so I can't buy it!

このような古い切手は高く売れます。
This kind of old stamp sells at a high price.

たがい 互い 〜の *mutual*

互いに each other, mutually

兄弟は互いに助け合わなければならない。
Brothers and sisters must help each other.

あの二人は互いに贈り物を交換しました。
Those two exchanged gifts.

だかい 打開 *breakthrough to a solution, overcoming (of a difficult situation)*

打開する to make a breakthrough in, to overcome

たかさ 高さ *1. height*

このビルの高さは約50メートルです。
The height of this building is approximately 50 meters.

2. loudness

3. expensiveness

たかだか 高々 *at most, at best [→ 精々1.]*

だがっき 打楽器 *percussion instrument*

たかまる 高まる *to rise, to increase*

たかめる 高める *to raise, to increase*

たがやす 耕す *to plow, to till*

畑を耕す to plow a field

たから 宝 *treasure, precious thing*

宝くじ public lottery; lottery ticket

宝物 precious thing

宝捜し treasure hunt

だから *that's why, for that reason*

(This word is simply a combination of the copula だ and the clause-conjoining particle から, but the combination can be used initially in a sentence. The combination ですから, with the semi-formal copula form, can also be used sentence-initially in the same way.)

雨が降りだした。だから外出をやめたよ。
It started to rain. That's why we gave up on going out!

ーたがる [☞ ーがる]

たき 滝 *waterfall*

その滝は高さが30メートルあります。
The height of that waterfall is 30 meters.

ナイアガラの滝 Niagara Falls

たきぎ 薪 *firewood [→ 薪]*

だきしめる 抱き締める *to hug tightly*

たきび 焚き火 *fire (built on the ground); bonfire*

野原でたき火をしました。
We built a fire in the field.

だきょう 妥協 *compromise*

妥協する to compromise

たく 焚く *1. to make, to build (The direct object is a fire.)*

火をたく to make a fire

2. to burn (as fuel)

この船は石炭をたいて走ります。
This ship runs by burning coal.

3. to heat (a bath to the appropriate temperature) [→ 沸かす2.]

ふろをたく to heat a bath

たく 炊く *to cook (by boiling until the liquid is absorbed)*

妹がご飯をたきました。
My younger sister cooked rice.

だく 抱く *to hold in one's arms, to embrace*

母は赤ちゃんを優しく抱きました。
The mother held her baby gently.

たぐい 類い *sort, type, kind [→ 種類]*

たくさん *many, much, a lot* [↔ 少し]

たくさんの学生がテニス部に入ります。
Many students join the tennis club.

箱の中にオレンジがたくさんあります。
There are a lot of oranges in the box.

きょうは宿題がたくさんあります。
Today I have a lot of homework.

6月には雨がたくさん降ります。
In June it rains a lot.

タクシー *taxi*

タクシーに乗りましょう。
Let's take a taxi.

駅までタクシーで行きました。
I went to the station by taxi.

タクシーを呼んでください。
Please call a taxi.

タクシー代 taxi fare

タクシー乗り場 taxi stand (UK) taxi rank

タクシー運転手 taxi driver

たくましい 逞しい *1. robust, sturdy, powerfully built*

2. strong-minded, resolute

たくみ 巧み ～な *skillful, clever, ingenious*

たくわえ 蓄え *1. savings, money put away [→ 貯金2.]*

2. store, stock, supply

たくわえる 蓄える *to store, to save [→ 貯める]*

たけ 竹 *bamboo*

竹の子 bamboo shoot

竹藪 bamboo grove

竹竿 bamboo pole

だけ *1. only, just*

信子さんだけがわかります。
Only Nobuko understands.

それを母だけに話しました。
I told that only to my mother.

失敗したのは私だけではありません。
I am not the only one who failed.

少しだけ食べてちょうだい。
Eat just a little.

テレビで見ただけです。
I only saw it on television.

2. extent [→ 程度]

できるだけ飲んでください。
Please drink as much as you can.

たけうま 竹馬 *bamboo stilts (on which a person walks)*

次郎は竹馬に乗るのがうまいよ。
Jiro is good at walking on stilts!

だげき 打撃 *1. (physical) blow, hit*

あらしは米の収穫に打撃を与えました。
The storm dealt a blow to the rice crop.

2. (psychological) blow, shock [→ ショック]

3. batting, hitting

金山選手の打撃はすばらしいよ。
Kaneyama's batting is wonderful!

たこ 凧 *kite ((toy))*

凧揚げ kite flying

たこ 蛸 *octopus*

たこ *callus*

ださんてき 打算的 ～な *calculating, mercenary*

だし 出し *broth, (soup) stock*

たしか 確か *if I remember correctly*

結婚式は確か来週の土曜日です。
The wedding is definitely next Saturday.

確かな sure, certain, beyond doubt

宮城さんの成功は確かだと思います。
I think Ms. Miyagi's success is beyond doubt.

確かに surely, certainly, definitely

確かに友美ちゃんにかぎを渡したよ。
I definitely handed the key to Yumi!

たしかめる 確かめる *to make sure of, to confirm, to verify*

会合の日時を確かめてください。
Please verify the date of the meeting.

戸締まりを確かめましたか。
Did you make sure the doors were locked? (Literally: Did you make sure of the door locking?)

たしざん 足し算 *addition (in arithmetic)* [↔ 引き算]
足し算する to add [→ 足す2.]
この表の数字を足し算しなさい。
Add up the figures on this chart.

だしゃ 打者 *batter, hitter (in baseball)*
1番打者 leadoff hitter
強打者 slugger

たしょう 多少 *to some extent, somewhat*
久保田君の答案には多少誤りがあります。
There are some mistakes on Kubota's examination paper.
これからは多少楽になります。
It will get somewhat easier from now on.

たす 足す *1. to add; to supply, to supplement with [→ 補う2.]*
2. to add (in arithmetic) [↔ 引く4.]
2足す3は5。
Two plus three is five.
(Although odd grammatically, this kind of sentence is a typical way of stating a fact of arithmetic.)

だす 出す *1. [[↔ 入れる1.]] to take out; to put out*
乗客はポケットから切符を出しました。
The passenger took the ticket out of her pocket.
窓から顔を出すのは危ないです。
Putting your head out of the window is dangerous.
2. to let out [↔ 入れる2.]
子供が猿をおりから出してしまいました。
A child let the monkey out of the cage.
3. to hold out, to present [→ 差し出す1.]
あの人が犯人だという証拠を出しなさい。
Present evidence that this person is a crook.
4. to show, to expose, to exhibit
元気を出す to cheer up
口に出す to voice, to put into spoken words
スピードを出す to speed up
5. to hand in, to turn in, to submit [→ 提出する]
さあ、答案を出しなさい。
OK, hand in your test papers.
6. to send, to mail [→ 送る1.]
返事を出す to send a reply
7. to publish, to put out
本を出す to publish a book
8. to serve, to offer
母はお客さんに紅茶とケーキを出した。
My mother served the guest tea and cake.

ーだす ー出す *to begin to (Added to verb bases.)*
雪が降りだしました。
It began to snow.
生徒たちは教室を掃除しだしました。
The students began to clean the classroom.

たすう 多数 [[↔ 小数]] *1. 〜の many, a large number of*
2. majority
多数決 decision by majority

たすかる 助かる *1. to be rescued, to be saved*
患者は手術を受けて助かりました。
The patient had an operation and was saved.
2. to be helped
それで家計が大いに助かったよ。
The family budget was greatly helped by that!
おかげ様で助かりました。
Thank you for your help.

たすけ 助け *help, assistance*
被害者は助けを求めましたが、だれも応じ

ませんでした。
The victim asked for help, but no one responded.
先生の忠告は大きな助けになるでしょう。
The teacher's advice will probably be a big help.

たすける 助ける *1. to help, to lend a helping hand to*
中野さんはいつも困った人を助けます。
Mr. Nakano always helps people in trouble.
2. to help with
宿題を助けてくれる？
Will you help me with my homework?
3. to rescue, to save
消防士は赤ちゃんを火の中から助けた。
The fire fighter rescued the baby from the fire.

たずねる 訪ねる *to visit, to call on*
先週伯父を訪ねました。
I visited my uncle last week.
あした福地さんの所を訪ねるつもりです。
I intend to visit Mr. Fukuchi's place tomorrow.

たずねる 尋ねる *to ask, to inquire* [→ 聞く3.]
AにBを尋ねる to ask A about B
駅へ行く道を警官に尋ねました。
I asked a police officer the way to the station.

たそがれ 黄昏 *dusk, twilight*

ただ 唯, 只 *1. only, just, merely* [→ 単に]
兄はただ恋人に会うためにやってきた。
My older brother only came to see his girlfriend.
ただの mere; ordinary, run-of-the-mill [→ 普通の]
2. however [→ しかし]
3. 〜の free (of charge) [→ 無料の]
ただで for free, without charge
このノートをただでもらったよ。
I got this notebook for free!

ただいま 只今 [[→ 今]] *now; just now (in combination with a past-tense verb)*
父はただいま入浴中です。
My father is taking a bath right now.
母はただいま戻ったところです。
My mother has just now returned.

ただいま *I'm home, I'm back*
(Japanese etiquette requires this announcement upon one's return.)
お母さん、ただいま。
Mom, I'm home.

たたかい 戦い *fight, battle*
戦いに〔勝つ〕負ける to win〔lose〕a battle

たたかう 戦う *to fight, to battle, to struggle*
通行人は強盗と勇敢に戦いました。
A passerby fought bravely with the robber.
参加者は平和のために戦っています。
The participants are fighting for peace.

たたく 叩く *to strike, to hit* [→ 打つ]*; to pat; to knock on*
友達は私の頭をたたいたよ。
My friend hit me on the head!
ファンは選手の背中をたたきました。
The fan patted the player on the back.
だれかがドアをたたいています。
Someone is knocking on the door.

ただし 但し *however* [→ しかし]

ただしい 正しい *right, correct*
小田さんの言うことはいつも正しい。
What Ms. Oda says is always right.
正しい時間を教えてください。
Please tell me the correct time.
次郎は私の言葉を正しく理解してくれた。
Jiro understood my words correctly.
その単語を正しく発音しなさい。
Pronounce that word correctly.

ただす 正す *to correct, to rectify*
誤りがあれば、正してください。
If there are errors, please correct them.

たたみ 畳 *tatami, straw floor mat*

たたむ 畳む *to fold (over onto itself), to fold up (transitive)*

メイドはテーブルクロスを畳みました。
The maid folded up the tablecloth.

ハンカチを四つに畳んでください。
Please fold the handkerchief in four.

傘を畳む to close an umbrella

ただよう 漂う *to drift*

ボートが海上に漂っています。
A rowboat is drifting on the sea.

ーたち ー達 *(This suffix indicates the plural and is added to noun bases referring to people or to personified animals.)*

私たち we, us

たちあがる 立ち上がる *to stand up, to rise to one's feet*

みんなすぐに立ち上がりました。
They all stood up immediately.

たちいり 立ち入り *entering, setting foot in*

「立入禁止」 (on a sign)
Keep Out (Literally: Entering prohibited)

たちぎき 立ち聞き *eavesdropping*

立ち聞きする to eavesdrop on

他人の話を立ち聞きしてはいけないよ。
You mustn't eavesdrop on other people's conversations!

たちぐい 立ち食い【COL.】 *eating while standing up*

立ち食いする to eat standing up

たちさる 立ち去る *to leave, to go away from*

報道陣は9時ごろに現場を立ち去った。
The press left the scene at about 9:00.

たちどまる 立ち止まる *to stop walking*

お父さんは立ち止まって、地図を見ました。
Dad stopped walking and looked at the map.

たちば 立場 *standpoint, place, position*

Aの立場になる to put oneself in A's position

校長先生の立場になって考えてください。
Please put yourself in the principal's place and think about it.

だちょう 駝鳥 *ostrich*

たちよみ 立ち読み *reading while standing up*
(This word typically refers to reading at a bookstore without buying anything.)

立ち読みする to read standing up

たちよる 立ち寄る *to drop in, to stop by*

時々学校の帰りに本屋に立ち寄ります。
I sometimes drop in at a bookstore on my way home from school.

たつ 立つ *1. to stand; to stand up, to rise to one's feet* [→ 立ち上がる]

奥さんは門の所に立っています。
A lady is standing at the gate.

窓のそばに立っている女性が中尾さんだ。
The woman standing by the window is Ms. Nakao.

丘の上に小さな家が立っています。
A little house stands on the hill.

2. to leave, to depart from [↔ 着く1.]

その電車は8時に東京を立ちます。
That train leaves Tokyo at 8:00.

たつ 建つ *to be built, to be erected*

高いビルが駅前に建つそうです。
I hear that a tall building is going to be built in front of the station.

たつ 経つ *to elapse, to pass*

私が東京に来てから5年がたちました。
Five years have passed since I came to Tokyo.

たっきゅう 卓球 *table tennis, Ping-Pong*

卓球をする to play table tennis

卓球台 Ping-Pong table

タックル *tackle, tackling*

タックルする to tackle

だっこ【COL.】 *picking up and holding in one's arms (The direct object is a child, pet, etc.)*

だっこする to pick up and hold in one's

arms

ダッシュ *(running) dash*
ダッシュする to dash

ダッシュ *dash ((punctuation mark))*

たっする 達(たっ)する *{Irreg.} 1. to reach, to arrive*
あしたの朝山頂(あささんちょう)に達(たっ)するでしょう。
They will probably reach the summit tomorrow morning.
探検家(たんけんか)は1か月(げつ)で南極点(なんきょくてん)に達(たっ)しました。
The explorer reached the South Pole in one month.
2. to attain, to accomplish, to achieve
首相(しゅしょう)はついに目的(もくてき)を達(たっ)しました。
The prime minister finally achieved his aim.

だつぜい 脱税(だつぜい) *tax evasion*
脱税(だつぜい)する to evade paying taxes

だっせん 脱線(だっせん) *derailment*
脱線(だっせん)する to jump the rails, to become derailed
列車(れっしゃ)がトンネルの中(なか)で脱線(だっせん)した。
The train was derailed inside the tunnel.

たった【COL. for 唯(ただ), 只(ただ)*1.*】 *only, just, merely*
私(わたし)はたった200円(えん)しか持(も)っていないよ。
I only have ¥200!
職員室(しょくいんしつ)には先生(せんせい)がたった二人(ふたり)しかいない。
There were only two teachers in the staff room.
たった一人(ひとり)で all by oneself, all alone
たったの mere; ordinary, run-of-the-mill

たったいま たった今(いま)【COL.】 *just now (always in combination with a past-tense verb)*
市川君(いちかわくん)はたった今出(いまで)かけたよ。
Ichikawa just went out!

タッチ *1. tag (in baseball)*
タッチする to make the tag
二塁手(にるいしゅ)はランナーにタッチできなかった。
The second baseman couldn't make the tag on the runner.
2. (artistic) touch, manner of execution
3. ～する to touch upon, to have to do with

だって *1.*【COL. for でも*1.*】*even, even if it is*
2.【COL. for でも*2.*】*no matter (following a phrase beginning with a question word)*
3.【COL. for でも*4.*】*however, but (at the beginning of a sentence)*
4.【COL.】*the reason is (at the beginning of a sentence)*
もう食(た)べられない。だってまずいんだよ。
I can't eat any more. The reason is, it's foul!

たづな 手綱(たづな) *reins*

たつのおとしご 竜(たつ)の落(お)とし子(ご) *sea horse*

たっぷり *1. (～と) plentifully, plenty*
たっぷり時間(じかん)があるよ。
There's plenty of time!
ペンキをたっぷり塗(ぬ)ってください。
Please apply plenty of paint.
2. fully, a full
海岸(かいがん)へ行(い)くのにたっぷり3時間(じかん)はかかる。
It takes a full three hours to go to the beach.
自信(じしん)たっぷりの self-assured, very confident

たつまき 竜巻(たつまき) *whirlwind, tornado*

たて 縦(たて) *1. [[↔ 横(よこ)2.]] length (as opposed to width); height (as opposed to width)*
このテーブルは縦(たて)が3メートルで、横(よこ)が1メートルです。
This table is three meters long and one meter wide.
2. ～の [[↔ 横(よこ)の3.]] vertical; end-to-end
縦(たて)の線(せん) vertical line

たて 盾(たて) *(hand-held) shield*

－たて －建(た)て *～no -story, -floor (Added to bases consisting of a number containing the counter －階(かい).)*
20階建(かいだ)てのマンションが建(た)ちました。

A twenty-story condominium was built.
川村さんの家は2階建てです。
Ms. Kawamura's house is two stories.
2階建てバス double-decker bus

たてふだ 立て札 *(freestanding) signboard*
管理人は「禁煙」の立て札を立てました。
The manager set up a "No smoking" signboard.

たてまえ 建て前, 立て前 *outwardly expressed feelings, stated motivation* [↔ 本音]

たてもの 建物 *a building*

たてる 立てる *to stand, to set up*
その本を本棚に立てなさい。
Stand those books on the bookshelf.
コーチは高いさおを地面に立てました。
The coach stood a tall pole in the ground.

たてる 建てる *to build, to erect*
兄は大きな家を建てました。
My older brother built a large house.
持ち主はガレージを建てました。
The owner built a garage.

たどうし 他動詞 *transitive verb* [↔ 自動詞]

たとえ *even if*
(This word introduces a clause ending in a gerund (-て form) plus も. Since the clause has the same meaning whether or not たとえ is present, たとえ is redundant in a sense, but it serves as a signal that the clause will end this way.)
たとえあした雨が降っても出発します。
Even if it rains tomorrow, I will start out.
たとえあの人が何を言っても信じないよ。
I wouldn't believe anything that person says!

たとえば 例えば *for example, for instance*

たとえる 例える *to liken, to compare*
この作家はよく人生を航海に例えます。
This writer often compares life to a voyage.

たな 棚 *shelf*
本棚 bookshelf

たなばた 七夕 *Tanabata Festival, the Star Festival (July 7)*

たに 谷 *valley*
谷川 mountain stream

ダニ *tick ((insect))*

たにん 他人 *1. other person*
他人に頼るのはよくないよ。
It's not good to depend on others!
2. unrelated person, non-relative
3. outsider, third party, person not involved
4. stranger, person one does not know
他人扱い treating as a stranger
他人扱いする to treat as a stranger

たぬき 狸 *raccoon dog*

たね 種 *1. seed; stone (of a cherry, etc.); pit (of a peach, etc.)*
種から芽が出てきました。
The seeds have started sprouting.
種をまく to sow seeds, to plant seeds
母は庭に朝顔の種をまきました。
My mother planted morning-glory seeds in the garden.
2. cause, source [→ 原因]
心配の種 source of anxiety
3. material (to talk or write about)
話の種 topic of conversation
4. the secret (of a magic trick, etc.)

たのしい 楽しい *pleasant, fun, delightful*
みんな楽しい時を過ごしました。
Everyone had a pleasant time.
遠足は楽しかったですか。
Was the excursion fun?

たのしみ 楽しみ *pleasure, enjoyment*
水泳は祖父の楽しみの一つです。
Swimming is one of my grandfather's pleasures.
楽しみにする to look forward to

僕たちは夏休みを楽しみにしています。
We are looking forward to the summer vacation.

たのしむ 楽しむ *to enjoy, to take pleasure in*

娘さんは旅行を楽しんだそうですね。
I hear your daughter enjoyed her trip.

子供たちは野球の試合を見て楽しんだ。
The children enjoyed watching the baseball game.

たのみ 頼み *1. request, favor (to ask)* [→ 依頼]

杉本さんの頼みでここへ来ました。
I came here at Ms. Sugimoto's request.

君に頼みがあるよ。
I have a favor to ask you!

2. reliance, trust [→ 信頼]

頼みになる to be reliable

頼みにする to rely on, to put one's trust in

頼みの綱 one's only hope

たのむ 頼む [[→ 依頼する]] *1. to request, to ask for*

僕は姉にケーキのお代わりを頼んだよ。
I asked my older sister for another piece of cake!

警官は被害者にテープを聴くよう頼んだ。
The police officer asked the victim to listen to a tape.

そんなに速く走らないでと友達に頼んだ。
I asked my friend not to run so fast.

2. to importune to handle, to ask to take care of

課長は加藤さんにその仕事を頼みました。
The section chief asked Ms. Kato to handle that job.

たのもしい 頼もしい *1. reliable, dependable, trustworthy*

健さんは頼もしい人です。
Ken is a reliable person.

2. promising (describing a person)

たば 束 *bundle; bunch*

一束 (counter for bundles, bunches; see Appendix 2)

おばあちゃんは一束の古い手紙を焼いた。
Grandma burned a bundle of old letters.

束ねる to bundle together

古雑誌を束ねてくれませんか。
Won't you bundle together the old magazines for me?

たばこ *cigarette; cigar; tobacco*

父はたばこをやめました。
My father gave up smoking.

たばこを吸う to smoke (cigarettes)

大滝教授はたばこを吸いすぎますね。
Professor Otaki smokes too much, doesn't she?

たばこ屋 tobacconist's; tobacconist

たび 旅 *trip, journey, travel* [→ 旅行]

たび 足袋 *tabi, Japanese split-toed sock*

地下足袋 worker's tabi (long with rubber soles typically worn by construction workers and other laborers)

たびたび 度々 *often*

英雄はたびたび学校に遅れるよ。
Hideo is often late for school!

兄はたびたび図書館に行きます。
My older brother often goes to the library.

たびに 度に *every time (Always follows a verb in the nonpast tense.)*

姉は帰郷するたびにその丘に登ります。
My elder sister climbs that hill every time she goes back home.

タフ ～な *tough, hardy*

正男はタフなやつだ。
Masao is a tough guy.

タブー *a taboo*

ダブルス *doubles (in sports)* [↔ シングルス]

男子ダブルス men's doubles

女子ダブルス women's doubles

混合ダブルス mixed doubles

たぶん 多分 *perhaps; probably*

(This word typically occurs in sentences ending with an expression of possibility (such as と思う) or probability (such as だろう). Since such a sentence has virtually the same meaning whether or not たぶん is present, is redundant in a sense, but it serves as a signal of how a sentence will end.)

たぶんあしたは晴れるでしょう。
It will probably clear up tomorrow.
北川さんはたぶん来ると思います。
I think perhaps Ms. Kitagawa will come.

たべすぎ 食べ過ぎ *eating too much*

たべほうだい 食べ放題 *as much as one wants to eat*

食べ放題のバイキング all-you-can-eat smorgasbord

たべもの 食べ物 *food*

どんな食べ物がいちばん好きですか。
What kind of food do you like best?
刺身は私の好きな食べ物の一つです。
Sashimi is one of my favorite foods.
何か食べ物を持ってきましたか。
Did you bring some food?

たべる 食べる *to eat*

お昼には何を食べましたか。
What did you eat for lunch?
ケーキを食べませんか。
Won't you have some cake?

たま 玉 *1. spherical object, ball (-shaped object); bead*

毛糸の玉 ball of yarn

2. lens [→ レンズ]

眼鏡の玉 glasses lens

たま 球 *1. ball (used in a game)*

球を投げる to throw a ball

2. light bulb [→ 電球]

たま 弾 *bullet; cannonball*

たま 〜の *occasional, infrequent*

たまに occasionally, infrequently
竹川さんはたまにバイオリンを弾きます。
Ms. Takekawa occasionally plays the violin.

たまご 卵 *egg*

卵の白身〔黄身〕 egg white〔yolk〕
生卵 raw egg

たましい 魂 *soul*

だます 騙す *to cheat, to deceive*

監督は俳優をだましました。
The director deceived the actor.

たまたま *1. by chance, unexpectedly, coincidentally [→ 偶然2.]*

2. occasionally, infrequently [→ たまに]

たまねぎ *onion*

たまむし 玉虫 *jewel beetle*

たまらない 堪らない *to be unable to stand, to be unable to bear*

(This word is grammatically a negative verb form and it ordinarily follows a clause ending in a gerund (-て form) of an adjective.)

堀部君はそのボクシングの試合を見たくてたまらない。
Horibe wants to see that boxing match so much he can't stand it.
寒くてたまりません。
I'm so cold I can't stand it.

たまる 溜まる, 貯まる *to collect, to accumulate (intransitive)*

テーブルの上にほこりがたまっています。
Dust has settled on the table.
貯金が200万円たまったよ。
I've saved up ¥2,000,000! (Literally: Savings of ¥2,000,000 have accumulated!)

だまる 黙る *to stop talking, to become silent*

先生が来たので、私たちは黙りました。
We stopped taking, when the teacher

came in.

浜野さんは午前中ずっと黙っていました。

Mr. Hamano kept quiet all morning.

ダム *dam*

ため 為 *1. (〜に) in order to (following a verb in the nonpast tense)* [→ のに2.]

写真を撮るために公園に行きます。

I'm going to go to the park to take pictures.

2. (〜に) because, since (following a clause) [→ ので]

雨が降ったために涼しくなりました。

Because it rained, it got cool.

3. の〜(に) because of, due to (following a noun)

雨のために野球の試合は中止になった。

The baseball game was called off due to the rain.

4. benefit, sake

明は私のためにピアノを弾いてくれた。

Akira played the piano for me.

ためになる to be beneficial

だめ 駄目 〜な *1. no good, useless; futile* [→ 無駄な]

この電池はだめですよ。

This battery is no good!

浜中さんは努力しましたが、だめでした。

Ms. Hamanaka made efforts, but they were futile.

2. impermissible, unacceptable

(This meaning is particularly common in combination with a conditional clause of some kind. Translations of such combinations into English ordinarily use **must not** or **may not** rather than **unacceptable if** and **must** or **have to** rather than **unacceptable if not**.) [→ いけない1.]

この川で泳いではだめです。

You must not swim in this river.

「外出してもいい？」「だめだよ」

"May I go out?" "You may not!"

もっと勉強しないとだめだよ。

You must study more!

ためいき 溜息 *sigh*

ため息をつく to sigh, to heave a sigh

ためす 試す *to try out, to sample, to test*

この新しい冷凍食品を試してみましょう。

Let's try this new frozen food.

ためらい *hesitation, wavering*

ためらいもなく without hesitation

ためらう *to hesitate about, to waver about*

質問をするのをためらっていました。

I hesitated to ask a question.

ためる 貯める *to save, to store* [→ 蓄える]

ワープロを買うためにお金をためます。

I am saving up to buy a word processor.

たもつ 保つ *to keep, to maintain, to preserve*

健康を保つために何をしていますか。

What are you doing to maintain your health?

電車はずっと同じスピードを保っている。

The train is maintaining a constant speed.

たより 便り *news, word, tidings, correspondence*

長い間幸子さんから便りがありません。

There hasn't been any word from Sachiko for a long time.

たより 頼り *thing/person to rely on*

頼りになる to be reliable

その医者は頼りになります。

That doctor is reliable.

頼りにする to rely on, to depend on

他人の助けを頼りにしないで。

Don't rely on the help of others.

Aを頼りに with the help of A, relying on A

地図を頼りにその病院を探しました。

With the aid of a map, I looked for that hospital.

たよる 頼る *to rely, to depend*

水谷さんはお兄さんに頼っています。

Mr. Mizutani is depending on his older brother.

たら 鱈 *cod*

たらい 盥 *washtub*

ーだらけ【COL.】～の *full of; covered with (Added to noun bases denoting something viewed with disfavor.)*

この日本語の手紙はまちがいだらけだよ。
This Japanese letter is full of mistakes!

この人形はほこりだらけです。
This doll is covered with dust.

だらしない *1. slipshod, careless, sloppy*

あの人は服装がだらしないね。
That person's attire is sloppy, isn't it?

2. (morally) loose

だらしない生活をしてはいけないよ。
You mustn't lead a loose life!

ーたらず ー足らず *less than (Added to bases denoting specific quantities.)*

10分足らずでバス停に着きます。
You will arrive at the bus stop in less than ten minutes.

タラップ *gangway*

だりつ 打率 *batting average (in baseball)*

ダリヤ *dahlia*

たりょう 多量 ～の *much, large quantity of* [↔ 少量の]

多量に in great quantity

たりる 足りる *to be enough, to suffice*

生徒が５人いれば、足ります。
If there are five students, that's enough.

1000円で足りるでしょう。
¥1,000 will probably be enough.

その国は食糧が足りないそうです。
I hear there is not enough food in that country.

たる 樽 *barrel, cask, keg*

だるい *languid, heavy-feeling, listless*

全身がだるいです。
My whole body is listless.

だるま 達磨 *1. Bodhidharma (the monk who introduced Zen from India into China)*

2. a doll portraying Bodhidharma sitting in Zen meditation

(The most common type of Daruma doll is made of plaster and sold with no pupils painted in the eyes. Such a doll is used as a good-luck charm by painting in one pupil when a wish is made and painting in the other pupil when the wish comes true.)

たるむ 弛む *1. to become loose, to slacken*

ロープが少したるんでいます。
The rope is a little slack.

2. to become indolent

息子はこのごろたるんでいます。
My son is indolent recently.

だれ 誰 *who (as a question word)*

あの女の人はだれですか。
Who is that woman?

だれが歌を歌っているの？
Who is singing?

これはだれのペンですか。
Whose pen is this?

だれに会いたいのですか。
Who do you want to see?

だれを捜しているのですか。
Who are you looking for?

だれでも everyone, anyone, no matter who it is

だれでもその単語を知っているよ。
Everyone knows that word!

だれでも私たちのクラブに入れます。
Anyone can join our club.

だれか someone, somebody

だれかがやってくれるよ。
Someone will do it for us!

だれか手伝ってくれませんか。
Won't somebody help me?

だれも nobody, no one, *(not)* anyone

(Always occurs in combination with a negative predicate.)

だれも遅刻しませんでした。
Nobody was late.

だれもけがをした人はいませんでした。
Nobody was injured.

たれる 垂れる *1. to hang down, to droop, to dangle*

少女の髪は背中に垂れていました。
The girl's hair was hanging down her back.

2. to drip [→ 滴る]

天井から水が垂れています。
Water is dripping from the ceiling.

タレント *1. talent* [→ 才能]

2. star, show-business personality (who appears on television or radio)

テレビタレント TV star

だろう *1. probably is/are*

(When it follows a noun or a nominal adjective, this word is the informal tentative form of the copula だ. For details, see Appendix 1. With falling intonation, it simply makes an assertion tentative.)

ここは静かだろう。
This place is probably quiet.

2. probably

(With falling intonation following a predicate, marks a sentence as tentative.)

その列車は時間どおりに着くだろう。
That train will probably arrive on time.

上山さんがこの絵をかいただろう。
Mr. Kamiyama probably drew this picture.

3. right?, don't you think?

(With rising intonation, urges the listener to agree with the speaker. Rising intonation can be used on either 1. or 2. (above).)

コンサートは楽しかっただろう？
The concert was fun, right?

タワー *tower*

東京タワー Tokyo Tower

たん 痰 *phlegm*

だん 段 *(stair-) step; rung*

石段 stone steps

たんい 単位 *1. unit (of calculation)*

2. unit, (US) credit (of academic work)

－単位 (counter for units of academic work; see Appendix 2)

たんか 担架 *stretcher*

タンカー *tanker*

だんかい 段階 *1. grade, rank*

2. step, stage, phase

たんき 短期 *short period of time [↔ 長期]*

たんき 短気 *short temper*

短気な short-tempered

短気を起こす to lose one's temper

たんきょり 短距離 *short distance* [↔ 中距離 長距離]

短距離競走 short-distance race, sprint

タンク *tank ((container))*

タンクローリー (US) tank truck

だんけつ 団結 *unity, solidarity*

団結する to unite, to band together

地元の人たちと団結して働きましょう。
Let's work united with the local people.

たんけん 探検 *exploration, expedition*

探検する to explore

探検家 explorer

探検隊 expedition team

だんげん 断言 *unequivocal assertion*

断言する to assert unequivocally

たんご 単語 *word, vocabulary item*

単語表 vocabulary list

英単語 English word

基本単語 basic word

だんご 団子 round flour dumpling

たんこう 炭鉱 *coal mine*

ダンサー *(professional) dancer*

たんさん 炭酸 *carbonic acid*

炭酸ガス carbon dioxide (gas)
炭酸水 soda water

だんし 男子 [[↔ 女子]] *boy; man* [→ 男性]

男子中学校 boys' junior high school
男子高校 boys' high school
男子生徒 schoolboy
男子チーム men's team

たんしゅく 短縮 *shortening, reduction*

短縮する to shorten, to reduce
授業が10分ずつ短縮されました。
Each class was reduced by ten minutes.

たんじゅん 単純 ～な *1. simple, uncomplicated* [↔ 複雑な]

それはごく単純な事です。
That's a very simple matter.

2. simple-minded, simple-hearted

上田さんは子供のように単純です。
Mr. Ueda is simple-minded like a child.

たんしょ 短所 *fault, weak point* [↔ 長所]

高木さんには短所がありません。
Ms. Takagi has no faults.

だんじょ 男女 *man and woman, men and women; boy and girl*

男女平等 sexual equality
男女同権 equal rights for men and women
男女共学 coeducation

たんじょう 誕生 *birth*

誕生する to be born [→ 生まれる]
誕生パーティー birthday party
誕生石 birthstone

たんじょうび 誕生日 *birthday*

誕生日はいつ？
When's your birthday?
きょうは私の14歳の誕生日です。
Today is my fourteenth birthday.
お誕生日おめでとう。
Happy birthday.
父は誕生日のプレゼントに時計をくれた。
My father gave me a watch as a birthday present.

たんす 箪笥 *chest of drawers; wardrobe; cupboard*

茶箪笥 cupboard, sideboard
洋服箪笥 dresser

ダンス *dance; dancing*

ダンスをする to dance
ダンスパーティー party with dancing
フォークダンス folk dance
社交ダンス social dance

たんすい 淡水 *fresh water* [→ 真水] [↔ 塩水 (s.v. 塩)]

たんすいかぶつ 炭水化物 *carbohydrate*

たんすう 単数 *the singular [↔ 複数]*

だんせい 男性 *a man* [↔ 女性]

男性的な manly

だんぜん 断然 *1. resolutely, decisively*

社長は従業員の提案には断然反対です。
The company president was resolutely against his employees' proposal.

2. absolutely, decidedly

この映画のほうが断然おもしろいよ。
This movie is decidedly more interesting!

たんそ 炭素 *carbon*

だんたい 団体 *group (of people)*

団体で行動するのは好きじゃないよ。
I don't like to act in a group!
団体競技 team sport
団体旅行 group tour
団体生活 living in a group
団体割引 group discount

だんだん 段々 *gradually, little by little* [→

次第に]

試合はだんだんおもしろくなりました。
The game gradually became interesting.

だんだん暗くなってきました。
It has gradually gotten darker.

だんち 団地 *(apartment) housing development*

いとこは団地に住んでいます。
My cousin lives in a housing development.

たんちょう 単調 〜な *monotonous, dull*

たんてい 探偵 *(private) detective*

探偵小説 detective story

たんとう 担当 *charge, being in charge*

担当する to take charge of [→ 受け持つ]

担当者 person in charge

だんな 旦那 *1. husband [→ 夫]*
2. patron (of a woman)

旦那さん【HON. for (above)】

たんに 単に *only, merely* [→ 唯, 只1.]

たんにん 担任 *1. charge, responsibility*
2. teacher in charge, homeroom teacher

私たちの担任は加藤先生です。
Our homeroom teacher is Mr. Kato.

たんぱ 短波 *a shortwave*

短波放送 shortwave broadcasting

たんぱくしつ 蛋白質 *protein*

タンバリン *tambourine*

ダンピング *dumping (on the market)*

ダンピングする to dump

ダンプカー *dump truck*

たんぺん 短編 *a short work (story or movie)*

短編映画 short film

短編小説 short story

たんぼ 田んぼ *rice field, rice paddy [→ 田]*

たんぽ 担保 *collateral, security (for a loan)*

だんぼう 暖房 *(indoor) heating* [↔ 冷房]

この部屋は暖房が利きすぎています。
The heating in this room is turned up too high.

暖房装置 heating equipment

だんボール 段ボール *corrugated cardboard*

段ボール箱 corrugated cardboard box

たんぽぽ *dandelion*

たんまつ 端末 *(computer) terminal*

端末装置 [☞ 端末 (above)]

だんらく 段落 *paragraph*

だんりゅう 暖流 *warm (ocean) current*
[↔ 寒流]

だんりょく 弾力 *elasticity; flexibility*

だんろ 暖炉 *fireplace; heating stove*

だんわ 談話 *talk, casual conversation, chat*

談話する to have a talk, to have a casual conversation

ち

ち 血 *blood* [→ 血液]

血が出る blood comes out

血の染み blood stain

血だらけの blood-covered

けが人の顔は血だらけだよ。
The injured person's face is covered with blood!

チアガール *(girl) cheerleader*

ちあん 治安 *public peace, public order*

ちい 地位 *position, post, rank*

地位の高い人 person of high position

社会的地位 social position

ちいき 地域 *area, district*
工業地域 industrial area

ちいさ 小さ ～な *(Used only as a modifier, never as a predicate.) [[→ 小さい]] [[↔ 大きな]] small, little; soft (sound)*
小さな声で言うと、聞こえないよ。
I can't hear you when you speak softly!

ちいさい 小さい [[↔ 大きい]] *small, little; soft (sound)*
このシャツは僕には小さいと思います。
I think this shirt is small for me.
小さいとき、パイロットになりたかった。
When I was a little, I wanted to become a pilot.
この人形はとても小さいね。
This doll is very small, isn't it?
小さい声 soft voice, low voice

チーズ *cheese*
チーズケーキ cheesecake
粉チーズ powdered cheese

チーフ *a chief, a head*

チーム *team*
そのチームに入りたいです。
I want to join that team.
チームワーク teamwork

ちえ 知恵 *wisdom*

チェーン *chain* [→ 鎖]
チェーンストア chain store
タイヤチェーン tire chain

チェス *chess*

チェック *1. check, verification*
チェックする to check
2. check (mark)
チェックアウト *(*hotel*)* check-out
チェックイン *(*hotel*)* check-in

チェック *check (pattern)*
友美はチェックのスカートをはいている。
Tomomi is wearing a checked skirt.

チェック *(bank) check [→ 小切手]*

チェロ *cello*
チェロ奏者 cellist

ちか 地下 *(the area) underground* [↔ 地上]
新しい駅が地下50メートルに建設された。
The new station was built 50 meters underground.
地下道 (US) underpass, (UK) subway
地下街 underground shopping center
地下2階 second floor underground
地下室 basement room
地下水 underground water
地下鉄 (US) subway, (UK) underground

ちかい 地階 *basement*

ちかい 近い *near, close* [↔ 遠い]
いちばん近い郵便局はどこですか。
Where is the nearest post office?
クリスマスが近いですね。
Christmas is near, isn't it?
祖父は70に近いです。
My grandfather is nearly seventy.
近いうちに soon, in the near future
近いうちにまたその人に会います。
I will see that person again soon.

ちかく 近く *the area nearby*
(This word is the adverbial form of 近い and has the predictable meanings as well.)
祖母は毎日近くの公園に散歩に行きます。
My grandmother goes for a walk in a nearby park every day.
私は学校の近くに住んでいます。
I live near the school.

ーちかく ー近く *nearly (Added to bases denoting specific quantities.)*
飛行機は30分近く遅れました。
The plane was nearly thirty minutes late.

ちがい 違い *difference, distinction*
柔道と空手の違いは何ですか。
What is the difference between judo and

karate?

ちがいない 違いない [☞ に違いない]

ちかう 誓う *to swear, to pledge*

新入社員は最善を尽くすことを誓った。

The new employee promised to do his best.

ちがう 違う *1. to be different, to differ* [→ 異なる]

お嬢さんの性格はお母さんとは違います。

The daughter's character is different from her mother's.

2. to be wrong, to be incorrect

その答えは違うと思うよ。

I think that answer is wrong!

「これですか」「いいえ、違います」

"Is this it?" "No, it isn't." (Using as in this example is a relatively gentle way of contradicting someone. It is not nearly as abrupt as saying **You're wrong** in English.)

ちかごろ 近ごろ *recently, lately* [→ このごろ]

ちかづく 近づく *to get near, to approach*

バスは終点に近づきました。

The bus approached the last stop.

外国人が私のほうへ近づいてきました。

A foreigner approached me.

ちかづける 近づける [[↔ 遠ざける]]

1. [[→ 寄せる]] to bring near, to put close; to let approach

2. to begin to associate with, to become friendly with

ちかてつ 地下鉄 *(US) subway, (UK) underground*

東京から後楽園まで地下鉄で行きました。

I went from Tokyo to Korakuen by subway.

ちかみち 近道 *shortcut*

それは図書館への近道です。

That's a shortcut to the library.

近道をする to take a shortcut

高畑さんは近道をして公園へ行きました。

Mr. Takabatake took a shortcut to the park.

ちかよる 近寄る *to get near, to approach* [→ 近づく]

その猿に近寄らないで。

Don't go near that monkey.

ちから 力 *1. power, strength*

力が強い〔弱い〕 to be strong〔weak〕

その選手はとても力の強い人です。

That athlete is a very strong person.

法律の力 the power of the law

2. ability [→ 能力]

村上さんにはその仕事を一人でやり遂げる力があると思います。

I think Ms. Murakami has the ability to do that work by herself.

3. effort, exertion [→ 努力]

力を合わせる to combine efforts

力一杯(に) with all one's strength

浩は力いっぱい自転車のペダルをこいだ。

Hiroshi is pumping the bicycle pedals with all his strength!

ちきゅう 地球 *the (planet) earth*

地球は太陽の周りを回っています。

The earth revolves around the sun.

地球儀 globe ((map))

ちぎる 千切る *{5} 1. to tear into pieces*

真紀子ちゃんはその紙を二つにちぎった。

Makiko tore that paper in two.

2. to pluck off, to tear off

花をちぎる to pick a flower

チキン *chicken (meat)*

ちく 地区 *district, region, area [→ 地域]; zone* [→ 地帯]

この学校は地区の代表でした。

This school was the district representative.

住宅地区 residential area

商業地区 business district

ちくしょう 畜生 【CRUDE】*Damn it!*

ちくび 乳首 *nipple*

チケット *ticket* [→ 切符]

ちこく 遅刻 *arriving after the starting time, being late*
遅刻する to be late
池上君はけさ学校に10分遅刻したよ。
Ikegami was ten minutes late for school this morning!

ちじ 知事 *governor (of a prefecture, state, etc.)*
千葉県知事 the Governor of Chiba Prefecture

ちしき 知識 *knowledge*
森先生はかなり歌舞伎の知識があります。
Mr. Mori has quite a knowledge of kabuki.
知識人 an intellectual
基礎知識 basic knowledge

ちしつがく 地質学 *(the study of) geology*

ちしまれっとう 千島列島 *the Kurile Islands*

ちじょう 地上 *(the area) above ground* [↔ 地下]
そのビルは地上50階、地下3階です。
That building is fifty stories above ground and three stories underground.

ちじん 知人 *an acquaintance* [→ 知り合い]

ちず 地図 *map*
世界の地図を見てみよう。
Let's have a look at a map of the world.
ロンドンを地図で捜しなさい。
Look for London on the map.
地図帳 atlas
道路地図 road map
日本地図 map of Japan

ちせい 知性 *intellect*
知性的な intellectual

ちたい 地帯 *zone; region* [→ 地域]
安全地帯 safety zone; safety island, refuge
森林地帯 forest region

ちち 父 *father* [↔ 母; お父さん]
父は釣りが大好きです。
My father loves fishing.
父の日 Father's Day
父親 father, male parent [↔ 母親 (s.v. 母)]

ちち 乳 *1. mother's milk*
2. breast; teat
牛の乳を搾る to milk a cow

ちぢまる 縮まる *to shrink, to contract, to shorten (intransitive)*

ちぢむ 縮む *to shrink (intransitive)*
このセーターは洗濯で縮んでしまったね。
This sweater shrank in the laundry, didn't it?

ちぢめる 縮める *to shorten, to reduce (transitive)* [→ 短縮する]
スカートを少し縮めたほうがいいだろう。
It would probably be better to shorten the skirt a little.
首を縮める to duck one's head

ちぢれる 縮れる *to become curly*
縮れた髪 curly hair

ちつじょ 秩序 *order, discipline*
法と秩序を保つ to preserve law and order
社会秩序 public order

ちっそ 窒素 *nitrogen*

ちっそく 窒息 *suffocation, asphyxiation*
窒息する to suffocate, to be asphyxiated

ちっちゃい【COL. for 小さい】

ちっとも【COL.】 *(not) at all (Always occurs in combination with a negative predicate.)*
僕はちっとも疲れていないよ。
I'm not tired at all!

チップ *tip, gratuity*
父はホテルのボーイにチップを渡した。

My father handed a tip to the hotel bellboy.

ちてき 知的 ～な *intellectual, mental*

ちどり 千鳥 *plover*

ちのう 知能 *intelligence, mental powers*

犬はうさぎより知能が高い。
A dog is more intelligent than a rabbit. (Literally: A dog's intelligence is higher than a rabbits)

知能指数 intelligence quotient [→ アイキュー]

知能テスト intelligence test

ちび【COL.】*short person, shrimp [↔ のっぽ]*

ちぶさ 乳房 *(woman's) breast*

チフス *typhus*

ちへいせん 地平線 *horizon (between sky and land)* [↔ 水平線 (s.v. 水平)]

太陽が地平線に近づきました。
The sun approached the horizon.

地平線上に above the horizon

地平線下に below the horizon

ちほう 地方 *1. area, region [→ 地域]*

2. the parts of a country away from the capital, the provinces

いとこは地方に住んでいます。
My cousin lives in the provinces.

地方公務員 provincial civil servant

地方新聞 local newspaper, provincial newspaper

地方色 local color

関東地方 the Kanto region

ちめい 地名 *place name*

ちめいしょう 致命傷 *fatal wound*

ちめいてき 致命的 ～な *fatal*

ちゃ 茶 *tea* [→ お茶1.]

茶匙 teaspoon

茶の湯 the tea ceremony [→ 茶道]

チャーター *(vehicle) charter*

チャーターする to charter

チャーター機 chartered plane

チャーハン *fried rice*

チャーミング ～な *charming, attractive [→ 魅力的な (s.v. 魅力)]*

チャイム *chime*

ほら、チャイムが鳴っているよ。
Listen, the chimes are ringing!

ちゃいろ 茶色 *brown (as a noun)*

薄い茶色 light brown

焦げ茶色 dark brown

－ちゃく －着 *1. (counter for suits, dresses, etc.; see Appendix 2)*

2. (counter for places in the order of finish in a race; see Appendix 2)

ちゃくじつ 着実 ～な *1. steady (-going), constant*

姉の料理の腕は着実に上がっています。
My older sister's cooking skill is steadily improving.

計画は着実に進んでいます。
The plan is progressing steadily.

2. sound, trustworthy

着実な営業 sound management

ちゃくせき 着席 *taking a seat*

着席する to take a seat

代表全員が着席しました。
The representatives all took their seats.

ちゃくりく 着陸 *landing (of an airplane, etc.)* [↔ 離陸]

着陸する to land

飛行機は無事に成田空港に着陸しました。
The plane landed safely at Narita Airport.

ちゃのま 茶の間 *(a room in a traditional Japanese house where the family has meals and relaxes)*

チャリティー *charity* [→ 慈善]

チャリティーショー charity show

チャレンジ [[→ 挑戦]] *1. challenge, invitation to combat*
チャレンジする to challenge (to combat)
2. taking on a challenge
チャレンジする to make a challenge
Aにチャレンジする to make a challenge at A

チャレンジャー *challenger (in sports)*

ちゃわん 茶碗 *1. rice bowl*
2. teacup
茶碗蒸し thick steamed custard soup served in a teacup with a lid

チャンス *chance, opportunity* [→ 機会]
絶好のチャンス best chance
チャンスを逃す to miss a chance

ちゃんと *neatly, precisely; properly, in accordance with accepted standards*
少女はちゃんと服を着ました。
The little girl put on her clothes properly.
ちゃんとした neat, precise; proper, up-to-standard

チャンネル *(television) channel*
チャンネルを切り替える to change the channel
ーチャンネル (counter for channels; see Appendix 2)
4チャンネルで野球を見よう。
Let's watch baseball on Channel 4.
チャンネル争い dispute over which channel to watch

ちゃんばら 【COL.】 *sword battle*
ちゃんばら映画 sword battle movie

チャンピオン *champion*

ちゅう 注 *annotation, note*
脚注 footnote

ちゅう 中 *mediocrity, the average*
中以上 above average
この学生の会話力は中以上です。
This student's speaking ability is above average.

ーちゅう ー中 *(Added to noun bases.)*
1. (〜に) during
授業中おしゃべりをしてはいけないよ。
You mustn't talk during class!
ローマ滞在中に絵を勉強しました。
During my stay in Rome, I studied painting.
2. 〜の in the midst of, under
父の車は修理中です。
My father's car is being repaired.
先生方は今、会議中です。
The teachers are in a meeting now.
工事中 under-construction

ちゅうい 注意 *1. attention, notice* [→ 注目]
指導者の説明に注意を払いなさい。
Pay attention to the leader's explanation.
注意する to pay attention, to give heed
2. care, caution [→ 用心]
注意する to take care, to be careful
お体に十分注意してください。
Please take good care of yourself.
「取り扱い注意」 (on a sign)
Handle With Care
「足元注意」 (on a sign)
Watch Your Step
「頭上注意」 (on a sign)
Watch Your Head
3. warning, admonition
注意する to warn, to admonish, to caution
お医者さんの注意に従ったほうがいいよ。
You had better follow the doctor's warning!
注意深い careful, cautious

チューインガム *chewing gum* [→ ガム]

ちゅうおう 中央 *the center, the middle* [→ 真ん中]
市役所は市の中央にあります。
The city hall is in the center of the city.
中央アジア Central Asia
中央部 central part

ちゅうがく 中学 *junior high school*
私は中学の１年生です。
I am a first-year student in junior high school.
中学生 junior-high-school student

ちゅうがっこう 中学校 [☞ 中学]

ちゅうかりょうり 中華料理 *Chinese cuisine, Chinese food*

ちゅうかん 中間 *the area about halfway between; the area between*
浜松は大阪と東京の中間にあります。
Hamamatsu is about halfway between Osaka and Tokyo.
中間報告 interim report
中間試験 midterm examination

ちゅうきょり 中距離 *middle distance, intermediate distance* [↔ 長距離; 短距離]
中距離競走 middle-distance (running) race

ちゅうけい 中継 *relay broadcast*
中継する to broadcast by relay
中継放送 relay broadcast
舞台中継 relay broadcast of a play from the stage
衛星中継 satellite relay broadcast
野球中継 relay broadcast of a baseball game

ちゅうげん 中元 *midsummer gift*

ちゅうこ 中古 ～の *used, secondhand*
中古車 used car

ちゅうこく 忠告 *advice*
私は父の忠告に従います。
I will follow my father's advice.
忠告する to advise
父親は息子にもっと勉強しろと忠告した。
The father advised his son to study more.

ちゅうごく 中国 *China*

ちゅうごくちほう 中国地方 *The Chugoku region of Japan (Okayama, Hiroshima, Yamaguchi, Shimane, and Tottori Prefectures)*

ちゅうし 中止 *suspension, calling off*
中止になる to be suspended, to be called off
その試合は大雨のため中止になりました。
That game was called off because of heavy rain.
中止する to suspend, to call off
ボーイスカウトはキャンプを中止した。
The boy scouts called off their camp.

ちゅうじつ 忠実 ～な *faithful, loyal*
この犬は主人に忠実です。
This dog is faithful to its master.

ちゅうしゃ 注射 *injection, shot*
注射する to inject
注射を受ける to get a shot
医者は赤ちゃんにペニシリンを注射した。
The doctor injected penicillin into the baby.
注射器 syringe
予防注射 preventive injection, inoculation

ちゅうしゃ 駐車 *parking*
駐車する to park
花屋さんは車を店の前に駐車しました。
The florist parked his car in front of his shop.
「駐車禁止」 (on a sign)
No Parking
駐車違反 parking violation
駐車場 (US) parking lot, (UK) car park

ちゅうじゅん 中旬 *the middle third of a month* [↔ 上旬, 初旬; 下旬]
10月の中旬に検査があります。
There's an inspection in the middle of October.

ちゅうしょうてき 抽象的 ～な *abstract, not concrete* [↔ 具体的な]

ちゅうしょく 昼食 *lunch* [→ 昼ご飯 (s.v. 昼)]
昼食は済せましたか。
Did you have lunch?
僕たちは昼食を食べて、テニスをした。
We ate lunch and then played tennis.
昼食にスパゲッティを食べました。
I had spaghetti for lunch.
昼食時間 lunchtime

ちゅうしん 中心 *the center, the middle [→ 真ん中]; core, heart*
東京は日本の商業の中心です。
Tokyo is the business center of Japan.
中心部 central part
駅は町の中心部にあります。
The station is in the central part of the town.
中心点 central point

ちゅうせい 中世 *the Middle Ages*
(the Kamakura and Muromachi Periods in Japanese history)
中世の medieval

ちゅうせいし 中性子 *neutron* [↔ 陽子; 電子]

ちゅうせん 抽選 *lottery, drawing [→ くじ 2.]; drawing lots* [→ くじ引き (s.v. くじ)]
抽選で当たったよ。
I won the lottery!
抽選で順番を決めよう。
Let's decide the order by drawing lots.
抽選する to draw lots
抽選券 lottery ticket

ちゅうだん 中断 *interruption, stoppage*
中断する to interrupt, to stop in progress
学生は勉強を中断して、公園に出かけた。
The student stopped studying and went out to the park.

ちゅうと 中途 ～で *halfway, in the middle* [→ 途中で]
中途で引き返す to turn back on the way
中途半端な half-done, incomplete
宿題を中途半端にしてはいけないよ。
You mustn't leave your homework half-done!

ちゅうとう 中東 *the Middle East*

ちゅうどく 中毒 *1. poisoning, toxic effects*
中毒する to get poisoned, to suffer toxic effects
中毒を起こす to get poisoned, to suffer toxic effects
父は生がきを食べて中毒を起こしました。
My father ate raw oysters and got poisoned.
2. addiction
アルコール中毒 alcoholism
ガス中毒 gas poisoning
食中毒 food poisoning

ちゅうねん 中年 *middle age, one's middle years*
中年の middle-aged

チューブ *1. tube, pipe [→ 管]*
2. inner tube
3. squeeze-tube container

ちゅうぶちほう 中部地方 *the Chubu area of Japan (Niigata, Toyama, Ishikawa, Fukui, Nagano, Yamanashi, Shizuoka, Aichi, and Gifu Prefectures)*

ちゅうもく 注目 *attention, notice*
注目する to pay attention, to take notice
政治家はみんなこの問題に注目しました。
The politicians all paid attention to this problem.
注目を引く to attract attention
注目に値する to be noteworthy
注目の的 the center of attention

ちゅうもん 注文 *order, requisition*
注文する to order

本屋に本を2冊注文しました。
I ordered two books from the bookstore.

ちゅうりつ 中立 *neutrality*
中立を守る to maintain neutrality
中立の立場 neutral standpoint
中立地帯 neutral zone
中立国 neutral country
中立的な neutral
中立的な態度 neutral attitude

チューリップ *tulip*

ちゅうりゅうかいきゅう 中流階級 *the middle class*

ちょう 腸 *intestines*
大腸 large intestine
小腸 small intestine

ちょう 蝶 *butterfly*

ーちょう ー兆 *trillion (see Appendix 2)*
1兆円 one trillion yen

ちょうえき 懲役 *penal servitude*

ちょうおんそく 超音速 *supersonic speed*

ちょうおんぱ 超音波 *ultrasonic waves*

ちょうかく 聴覚 *hearing, auditory sense*

ちょうかん 朝刊 *morning edition of a newspaper [↔ 夕刊]*

ちょうかん 長官 *chief, director (of a government agency); cabinet secretary (in the United States government)*
国務長官 the Secretary of State

ちょうき 長期 *long period of time* [↔ 短期]
長期計画 long-range plan

ちょうきょり 長距離 *long distance* [↔ 短距離; 中距離]
長距離競走 long-distance (running) race
長距離電話 long-distance telephone call

ちょうこう 聴講 *auditing (of classes)*
聴講する to audit
聴講生 auditor ((student))

ちょうこく 彫刻 *sculpture, engraving*
彫刻する to sculpt, to engrave
先生は大理石で像を彫刻しました。
The teacher sculpted an image in marble.
彫刻家 sculptor

ちょうさ 調査 *investigation, survey*
その事故の調査は進んでいます。
The investigation of that accident is progressing.
調査する to investigate, to do a survey on

ちょうし 調子 *1. condition, state* [→ 具合1.]
調子がいい to be in good condition; to be operating well; to be feeling well
あのピッチャーはきょうは調子がいいね。
That pitcher is in good condition today, isn't he?
調子が悪い to be in bad condition; to be operating badly; to be feeling unwell
文子さんは体の調子が悪かったよ。
Fumiko wasn't feeling well!
調子はどうですか。
How are you feeling?

2. way (of doing) [→ 方法, 具合2.]
その調子で続けてください。
Please continue it in that way.

3. tune, tone; pitch, key
歌手は低い調子で歌を歌いました。
The singer sang low key.
調子が合っている to be in tune
このピアノは調子が合っています。
This piano is in tune.
調子が狂っている to be out of tune

4. rhythm, tempo [→ 拍子]

5. [[→ 口調]] tone (of voice); tone, style (of expression)

6. spirit, impetus
調子に乗る to get carried away, to be-

come elated

調子外れの out of tune; off-key

ちょうしゅう 聴衆 *audience*

ホールは大勢の聴衆で満員でした。

The hall was filled with a large audience.

ちょうしょ 長所 *strong point* [↔ 短所]

由美さんの長所は忍耐です。

Yumi's strong point is patience.

だれでも長所を持っているよ。

Everyone has strong points!

ちょうじょ 長女 *oldest daughter* [↔ 長男]

洋子さんは長女です。

Yoko is the oldest daughter.

ちょうじょう 頂上 *summit, top (of a mountain)* [↔ ふもと]

私たちは山の頂上まで登りました。

We climbed to the top of the mountain.

ちょうしょく 朝食 *breakfast* [→ 朝ご飯 (s.v. 朝)]

毎朝７時に朝食を食べます。

I eat breakfast at 7:00 every morning.

父の朝食は牛乳１杯とトースト２枚です。

My father's breakfast is a glass of milk and two slices of toast.

ちょうせい 調整 *regulation, adjustment*

調整する to regulate, to adjust

ちょうせつ 調節 *adjustment, regulation*

調節する to adjust, to regulate

ちょうせん 挑戦 *1. challenge, invitation to combat*

挑戦する to challenge (to combat)

相手はその挑戦に応じるでしょう。

The opponent will probably accept that challenge.

2. taking on a challenge

挑戦する to make a challenge

Aに挑戦する to challenge A, to take on A

チャンピオンに挑戦したらどうですか。

How about taking on the champion?

挑戦者 challenger

ちょうだい 頂戴 *1.* ～する【HUM. for 貰う *1.*】*[→ 頂く 1.]*

2. ～する【HUM. for 食べる; 飲む】*[→ 頂く 3.]*

3. please give me

そのチョコレートをちょうだい。

Please give me that chocolate.

4. please (be good enough to) (following the gerund (-て form) of a verb)

これを使ってちょうだい。

Please use this.

ちょうちょう 蝶々 [☞ 蝶]

ちょうちょう 町長 *town mayor*

友達のお父さんは町長に選ばれたよ。

My friend's father was elected town mayor!

ちょうちん 提灯 *paper lantern*

ちょうつがい *metal hinge*

ちょうてん 頂点 *top, zenith, peak*

ちょうど 丁度 *just, exactly*

バスはちょうど２時に出発します。

The bus will leave at exactly 2:00.

西沢さんはちょうど電車に間に合った。

Mr. Nishizawa was just in time for the train.

姉はちょうど宿題を終ったところです。

My older sister has just finished her homework.

ちょうどその時、会長が部屋に入ってきた。

Just then, the chairperson came into the room.

ちょうなん 長男 *oldest son* [↔ 長女]

あの子がうちの長男です。

That child is our oldest son.

ちょうのうりょく 超能力 *supernatural power*

ちょうへい 徴兵 *conscription, (military) draft*

ちょうほうけい 長方形 *rectangle*

ちょうまんいん 超満員 *crowded beyond capacity (with people)*

ちょうみりょう 調味料 *(food) seasoning*

ちょうやく 跳躍 *(upward) jump*

跳躍する to jump (upward) [→ 跳び上がる]

ちょうれい 朝礼 *morning assembly (at a school, factory, etc.)*

ちょうわ 調和 *harmony, accord*

調和する to harmonize, to become in harmony

この家具は絨毯の色と調和している。
This furniture goes well with the color of the carpet.

チョーク *chalk*

黒板にチョークで名前を書きなさい。
Write your name with chalk on the blackboard.

ちょきん 貯金 *1. saving money; depositing money (in a bank, etc.)*

貯金する to save money; to save (money); to deposit money; to deposit (money)

伯父は郵便局に貯金しています。
My uncle saves money at the post office.

2. savings, money on deposit

奥さんは銀行から貯金を下ろしました。
His wife withdrew her savings from the bank.

貯金箱 savings box, piggy bank

貯金通帳 passbook, bankbook

郵便貯金 postal savings

ちょくせつ 直接 (〜に) *directly* [↔ 間接に]

社長と直接連絡を取ります。
I will get in touch directly with the company president.

その質問は直接先生にしてください。
Please ask the teacher that question directly.

直接の direct

直接目的語 direct object

直接税 direct tax

ちょくせん 直線 *straight line*

直線を引く to draw a straight line

ちょくつう 直通 〜の *direct (flight), through (train); nonstop*

直通する to go straight through, to go directly

直通列車 through train; nonstop train

チョコレート *chocolate*

ちょしゃ 著者 *writer, author*

ちょすいち 貯水池 *reservoir (i.e., an artificial water-storage pond)*

ちょぞう 貯蔵 *storing*

貯蔵する to store

ちょちく 貯蓄 [[→ 貯金]] *saving money; savings*

貯蓄する to save money

ちょっかく 直角 *right angle*

直角三角形 right triangle

ちょっかん 直感 *intuition*

直感で by intuition

チョッキ *(US) vest, (UK) waistcoat*

ちょっけい 直径 *diameter*

この円の直径は2メートルです。
The diameter of this circle is two meters.

ちょっと *1. a little while, a moment*

ちょっと待ってください。
Wait a moment, please.

ちょっと電話を使っていいですか。
May I use the phone for a while?

2. a little, a few [→ 少し]

この問題は3年生にはちょっと難しい。
This problem is a little difficult for third-year students.

トマトもちょっともらおうかな。
May I take a few tomatoes too.

3. Frequently used simply to make a request sound less demanding. In such cases, a literal translation such as a little while or a little will be inappropriate.)

ちょっとこの写真を見て。
Look at this picture.

ちょっと通してください。
Please let me through.

4. Say, I say (Used to get a person's attention.)

ちょっと京子ちゃん、これはどう？
Say, Kyoko, how about this?

ちょんまげ *samurai topknot*

ちらし 散らし *handbill*

ちり 塵 *dust [→ 埃]; bits of trash*

塵取り dustpan

ちり 地理 *geography*

ちりがみ 塵紙 *kleenex, tissue [→ ティッシュペーパー]; toilet paper [→ トイレットペーパー (s.v. トイレット)]*

ちりょう 治療 *(medical) treatment*

その人はまだ治療を受けています。
That person is still undergoing treatment.

治療する to treat

ちる 散る *{5} 1. to fall and be scattered on the ground (when the subject is blossoms, leaves, etc.)*

木の葉が散っています。
Leaves are falling.

さくらがすっかり散ってしまいました。
The cherry blossoms have all fallen.

2. to scatter, to disperse (intransitive) [↔ 集まる]

群衆が散る a crowd disperses

気が散る to become distracted

ちんぎん 賃金 *wages*

チンパンジー *chimpanzee*

ちんぴら 【COL.】 *1. young hoodlum, young tough*

2. low-ranking gangster, punk

ちんぼつ 沈没 *sinking (in water)*

沈没する to sink

船はしばらくして沈没しました。
The ship sank after a while.

ちんもく 沈黙 *silence, not talking*

沈黙する to become silent, to stop talking [→ 黙る]

警官はその間ずっと沈黙を守っていた。
The police officer maintained his silence the whole time.

ついに大統領は沈黙を破りました。
At last the president broke his silence.

ちんれつ 陳列 *exhibiting, display*

陳列する to exhibit, to put on display

たくさんの絵がここに陳列されています。
Many pictures are being exhibited here.

陳列品 item on exhibit

陳列窓 display window

陳列室 showroom

ツアー *group tour*

兄は２週間のツアーに行きます。
My older brother will go on a two-week group tour.

つい 対 *pair*

これらのペンダントは対になっています。
These pendants make a pair.

一対 (counter for pairs; see Appendix 2)

母は一対のこけし人形を買いました。
My mother bought a pair of kokeshi dolls.

つい *1. just, only (modifying a time or distance)*

ついきのう長田さんに会いました。
I saw Mr. Nagata just yesterday.

2. carelessly [→ うっかりして]; uninten-

tionally, inadvertently [→ 思わず]

ついか 追加 *addition, supplement, addendum*

追加の additional, supplementary

追加する to add, to append

追加料金 additional charge

ついきゅう 追及 *pursuit, search*

追及する to pursue, to seek after

ついせき 追跡 *chase, pursuit*

追跡する to chase, to pursue

数台のパトカーが赤い車を追跡している。

Several patrol cars are chasing a red car.

ついたち 一日 *the first (day of a month) (see Appendix 2)*

津田さんは五月一日に京都へ行きます。

Mr. Tsuda will go to Kyoto on the first of May.

ついて [☞ について]

ついで 序で ～に *while one is at it; (since it's convenient) in addition to (following a clause)*

ついでにオイルもチェックしてください。

While you're at it, please have them check the oil too.

駅へ行くついでにこの手紙を出すよ。

I'll mail this letter on my way to the station!

ついていく 付いて行く [☞ 付く]

ついてくる 付いて来る [☞ 付く]

ついとつ 追突 *rear-end collision*

追突する to collide from behind

オートバイが車に追突しました。

A motorcycle crashed into the back of a car.

ついに 遂に *1. at last, finally [→ やっと 1.]*

ついにその夢は実現しました。

At last that dream became true.

2. after all, in the end [→ 結局]

ついに前の走者には追いつけなかった。

In the end I wasn't able to catch up with the runner ahead.

ついほう 追放 *expulsion, banishment, exile, deportation*

追放する to expel, to banish, to exile, to deport

ついやす 費やす *to spend, to expend [→ 使う 2.]*

毎日宿題に2時間を費やします。

I spend two hours every day on homework.

ついらく 墜落 *fall, drop (from a high place); crash (of an airplane, etc.)*

墜落する to fall, to drop; to crash

－つう －通 *(counter for letters, documents; see Appendix 2)*

つうか 通貨 *currency, money in circulation*

つうか 通過 *passing by; passing through*

通過する to pass by; to pass through

もう京都を通過しましたか。

Have we already passed through Kyoto?

その法案は国会を通過するでしょう。

That bill will probably pass the Diet.

つうがく 通学 *commuting (back and forth) to school, attending school*

通学する to go to school, to commute to school

娘はバスで通学しています。

My daughter commutes to school by bus.

私は去年から歩いて通学しています。

Since last year I've been going to school on foot.

つうきん 通勤 *commuting (back and forth) to work*

通勤する to commute to work

父は地下鉄で通勤しています。

My father commutes to work by subway.

つうこう 通行 *passing along, going along; traffic*

通行する to pass along, to go along

通行を妨げる to obstruct traffic

「通行禁止」 (on a sign)
No Passage (Literally: Passing along prohibited)

通行止めの closed-to-traffic

通行権 right of way

通行人 passerby

通行料金 road toll

左側通行 left-side traffic (Typically used on signs to mean Keep left.)

一方通行 one-way traffic

つうさんしょう 通産省 [☞ 通商産業省]

つうじょう 通常 *usually, ordinarily, generally* [→ 普通]

通常の usual, ordinary, regular

つうしょうさんぎょうしょう 通商産業省 *the Ministry of International Trade and Industry (MITI)*

つうじる 通じる *1. to lead (when the subject is a path, etc.)*

この道は公園に通じています。
This road leads to the park.

2. to run, to provide transportation (when the subject is a vehicle)

バスはここから東京駅に通じています。
The buses run from here to Tokyo Station.

3. 電話が〜 *a telephone call goes through*

4. to be understood, to be intelligible

その国で英語は通じますか。
Is English understood in that country?

つうしん 通信 *(long-distance) communication, correspondence*

通信する to communicate

通信簿 report card [→ 通知表 (s.v. 通知)]

通信衛星 communications satellite

通信販売 mail-order selling

通信教育 correspondence course

通信社 news agency

つうち 通知 *notification, report*

通知する to notify of, to report

通知表 report card [→ 通信簿 (s.v. 通信)]

つうちょう 通帳 *passbook*

ツーピース *woman's suit consisting of a jacket and skirt*

つうやく 通訳 *1. (language-to-language) interpretation*

通訳する to interpret

戸田さんが通訳してくれるでしょう。
Ms. Toda will probably interpret for us.

2. interpreter

同時通訳 simultaneous interpretation; simultaneous interpreter

つうよう 通用 *current use; current usability*

通用する to be in current use; to be usable at present

オーストラリアでは英語が通用します。
English is used in Australia.

この硬貨はもう通用しないよ。
This coin is no longer in use!

つうろ 通路 *passageway; aisle*

この荷物が通路をふさいでいます。
This luggage is blocking the aisle.

通路側 side by the aisle

通路側の席 aisle seat

つえ 杖 *walking stick, cane*

つか 塚 *mound*

つかい 使い *1. errand for another person*

使いに行ってくれる？
Will you go on an errand for me?

2. person who does an errand for another person

つかう 使う *to use*

この傘を使ってもいいですか。
May I use this umbrella?

この箱は何に使うのですか。
What are you going to use this box for?

ワープロを使うのは難しいですか。
Is it difficult to use a word processor?

つかう 遣う *to spend* [→ 費やす]

友達はお小遣い全部を本に遣ってしまう。
My friend will spend all of her allowance on books.

つかまえる 捕まえる *1. to take hold of, to grab onto with one's hand*

弟の手を捕まえて、道路を渡りました。
I took hold of my younger brother's hand and crossed the road.

2. to capture, to catch; to arrest [→ 逮捕する]

猫がねずみを捕まえたよ。
The cat caught a mouse!

警官がすりを捕まえました。
The police officer arrested a pickpocket.

つかまる 捕まる *1. to be captured, to be caught; to be arrested*

森本さんはスピード違反で捕まったよ。
Mr. Morimoto was caught for a speeding violation!

2. to take hold, to grab

Aに捕まる to take hold of A, to grab onto A

そのロープに捕まりなさい。
Take hold of that rope.

つかむ *1. to grasp, to grip with one's hand*

松野さんは突然私の手をつかみました。
Mr. Matsuno suddenly grasped my hand.

2. to grasp, to understand

つかれ 疲れ *fatigue, weariness*

つかれる 疲れる *to get tired, to get fatigued*

歩いてとても疲れたよ。
I got tired from walking!

疲れて動けないよ。
I'm so tired I can't move!

つき 月 *1. the moon*

飛行士たちは月に着陸しました。
The astronauts landed on the moon.

明るい月が出ました。
A bright moon came out.

2. month

月に1度母に手紙を出します。
I send a letter to my mother once a month.

月の初め〔半ば, 終わり〕 the beginning 〔middle, end〕 of the month

月明かり moonlight

月夜moonlit night

毎月every month

つぎ 次 *the next one*

次はだれですか。
Who's next?

次の next (in order), following

次の電車に乗りましょう。
Let's take the next train.

次のページを見なさい。
Look at the next page.

次に next (as an adverb)

いちばん早い行き方は地下鉄で、次に早いのはバスです。
The fastest way of going is the subway, and the next fastest is the bus.

次に何をしましょうか。
What shall we do next?

つぎ 継ぎ *patch (for repairing clothes)*

母はズボンに継ぎを当ててくれました。
My mother put a patch on my pants.

つきあい 付き合い *personal association, social contact*

付き合いがいいsociable

付き合いが広いcircle of friends is wide

つきあう 付き合う *1. to associate, to carry on social contact, to keep company*

課長は天野さんと付き合っているよ。
The section chief is going out with Ms. Amano!

2. to go along, to do together (to keep a

person company)
買い物に付き合ってくれる？
Will you come shopping with me?
食事を付き合ってください。
Please dine with me.

つきあたり 突き当たり *end (of a path, etc., so that one cannot continue going straight ahead)*
通りの突き当たりに教会があります。
There is a church at the end of the street.

つきあたる 突き当たる *1. to run into, to bump into [→ ぶつかる]*
おもちゃの自動車は壁に突き当たった。
The toy car ran into the wall.
2. to come to an end (when the subject is a path, etc.)
この道は駐車場に突き当たります。
This street ends at a parking lot.
3. to go along to the end (of a path)
この廊下を突き当たって、左へ曲がると校長室があります。
If you go to the end of this hall and turn left, there is the principal's office.

つきさす 突き刺す *1. to stick, to stab, to poke (one thing into another)*
兄は肉にナイフを突き刺しました。
My older brother stabbed a knife into the meat.
2. to stab, to pierce (one thing with another)
パブロフさんはフォークでじゃがいもを突き刺して食べました。
Mr. Pavlov stabbed a potato with his fork and ate it.

つきそい 付き添い *1. attending (to be of service), accompanying (to be of service); escorting*
付き添いの看護婦さんもいました。
There was also an attending nurse.
2. attendant; escort

つきそう 付き添う *to attend (to take care of); to escort*
姉は病気の子供に付き添っています。
My older sister is attending a sick child.

つきだす 突き出す *1. to thrust out*
2. to turn over (a person to the police)

つぎつぎ 次々 ～に／と *one after another, in close succession*
私たちは次々に先生と握手しました。
We shook hands with the teacher one after another.

つきでる 突き出る *to protrude, to stick out*

つきひ 月日 *time, the days and months*
月日がたつ time passes

つぎめ 継ぎ目 *joint, juncture, seam*

つきる 尽きる *to run out, to be used up, to be exhausted [→ 無くなる2.]*

つく 付く *to become attached, to become affixed; to become part of, to be added*
このシャツに染みが付きました。
This shirt got stained. (Literally: A stain attached itself to this shirt)
その机には引き出しが五つ付いています。
That desk has five drawers.
付いて行く to go along, to follow, to accompany
先に行ってください。私は後から付いていきます。
Please go ahead. I'll follow after you.
付いて来るto come along, to follow, to accompany
私に付いてきてください。
Please follow me.

つく 点く *[[↔ 消える1.]] to start burning (when the subject is a fire); to catch on fire, to light; to go on (when the subject is an electric light, appliance, etc.)*
隣の家に火がつきました。
The house next-door caught on fire.
テレビはまだついているよ。
The television is still turned on!
電気がつく lights go on
マッチがつく a match lights

つく 着く *1. to arrive [→ 到着する] [↔ 立つ2.]*
大島さんはきのう博多に着きました。
Mr. Oshima arrived in Hakata yesterday.
さあ、着いたよ。
Well, we've arrived!
2. to sit down, to take one's place
どうぞ席に着いてください。
Please take a seat.
食卓に着く to sit down at the dining table

つく 就く *to take up, to go into (The direct object is a job.)*
職業に就く to take up an occupation

つく 突く *1. to prick, to stab (one thing with another) [→ 突き刺す2.]*
ピンで指を突きました。
I pricked my finger with a pin.
2. to poke, to jab, to prod
伊藤さんは指でその人の胸を突きました。
Mr. Ito poked that person in the chest with his finger.
3. to use as a support
つえを突く to use a cane
ひじを突く to prop one's elbows

つぐ 注ぐ *to pour (into a container) (transitive)*
もう1杯コーヒーをついでください。
Please pour me another cup of coffee.

つぐ 継ぐ *to succeed to, to inherit*
長男がお父さんの仕事を継ぐでしょう。
The oldest son will probably inherit his father's business.
Aの後を継ぐ to succeed A
太郎が父親の後を継いで社長になった。
Taro succeeded his father and became the company president.

つくえ 机 *desk*
塩田さんは机に向かって勉強しています。
Ms. Shioda is studying at her desk.

つくす 尽くす *1. to use up, to exhaust*
ベストを尽くす to do one's best
全力を尽くす to do everything in one's power
2. to make great efforts, to persevere tirelessly
小田先生は科学のために尽くしました。
Dr. Oda persevered for the sake of science.

つぐなう 償う *to make up for, to make amends for*
君はもうその失敗を償ったよ。
You already made up for that mistake!

つくりばなし 作り話 *made-up story*

つくる 作る *1. to make, to create*
恵美ちゃんはきのう夕食を作ったよ。
Emi made dinner yesterday!
母はこのドレスを作ってくれました。
My mother made me this dress.
ワインはぶどうから作ります。
They make wine from grapes.
音楽を作る to write music
2. to form, to organize
3年生は読書クラブを作るそうです。
I hear the third-year students are going to form a reading club.
3. to grow, to raise [→ 栽培する]
母は野菜を作るのが趣味です。
My mother's hobby is growing vegetables.

つくる 造る *1. to manufacture, to produce* [→ 製造する]
この工場でワインを造ります。
They produce wine at this factory.
2. to build, to construct
この下請け業者は橋を造っています。
This subcontractor is building a bridge.

つくろう 繕う *to mend, to fix*

つげぐち 告げ口 *tattling*
告げ口する to tattle about

真里は私たちのことを先生に告げ口した。
Mari tattled about us to the teacher.

ーづけ ー付け *dated (Added to bases denoting dates.)*

12月25日付けの手紙が届きました。
A letter dated December 25 was delivered.

つけもの 漬け物 *pickle*

つける 付ける *1. to attach, to affix; to make part of, to add*

自転車に錠を付けてください。
Please attach a lock to the bicycle.

名前を付ける to give a name

味を付ける to add flavoring

人の後を付ける to follow a person, to tail a person

2. to write, to enter

合計を付ける to enter the total

3. to make regular entries in, to keep

日記を付ける to keep a diary

つける 点ける *1. to light (a fire) [↔ 消す1.]*

たばこに火をつける to light a cigarette

2. to turn on (a device) [↔ 消す2.]

ラジオをつける to turn on the radio

つける 着ける *to put on*

(The direct object is ordinarily an incidental item or accessory that a person wears. Like other verbs for putting on clothing, in the -ている form 着ける can express the meaning **be wearing, have on**.)

女優はネックレスを着けました。
The actress put on a necklace.

つげる 告げる *to tell, to announce*

その秘密はだれにも告げないでね。
Don't tell anybody that secret, OK?

つごう 都合 *1. circumstances, conditions* [→ 事情]

仕事の都合で出席できませんでした。
Because of circumstances at work, I was unable to attend.

都合がいい〔悪い〕circumstances are favorable〔unfavorable〕

2. (one's) convenience

都合がいい〔悪い〕to be convenient〔inconvenient〕for one

都合のいいときに電話してください。
Please phone at your convenience.

私たちはあしたが都合がいいです。
Tomorrow is convenient for us.

つた 蔦 *ivy*

つたえる 伝える *1. to tell, to report, to communicate* [→ 知らせる]

その知らせをみんなに伝えましょう。
Let's tell that news to everybody.

私に電話するように小池さんに伝えていただけますか。
Will you tell Mr. Koike to phone me?

2. to transmit, to hand down, to impart, to teach; to introduce (from abroad)

伝説を伝える to hand down a legend

知識を伝える to impart knowledge

3. to transmit (vibrations), to conduct (electricity)

空気は音波を伝えます。
Air transmits sound waves.

つたわる 伝わる *1. to be widely communicated, to spread*

そのうわさは学校中に伝わりました。
That rumor has spread all over the school.

2. to be transmitted, to be handed down, to be imparted; to be introduced (from abroad)

禅は12世紀に中国から日本に伝わった。
In the 12th century Zen was introduced into Japan from China.

3. to be transmitted, to be conveyed, to travel (when the subject is sound, electricity, etc.)

電気はこの線を伝わります。
The electricity is transmitted through this line.

つち 土 *earth, soil; the ground*

土でその穴を埋めなさい。
Fill that hole with earth.

海賊はその宝物を土の中に埋めました。
The pirates buried that treasure in the ground.

土が肥えて〔やせて〕いる the soil is rich 〔poor〕

つちかう 培う *to cultivate, to foster*

つつ 筒 *tube, empty cylinder*

つつく 突く *1. to poke (one thing with another)*

2. to peck

つづく 続く *to continue, to last, to go on*

あらしは1日中続きました。
The storm continued all day.

つづける 続ける *to continue, to keep doing*

その仕事を続けてください。
Please continue that work.

—つづける —続ける *to continue to (Added to both transitive and intransitive verb bases.)*

息子は何時間も勉強し続けました。
My son continued studying for many hours.

あと30分ぐらい歩き続けてください。
Please continue walking for about thirty minutes.

つっこむ 突っ込む *1. to thrust into, to stuff into*

検査官はかばんの中に手を突っ込んだ。
The inspector thrust her hand into the bag.

2. to plunge into (intransitive)

その車は池に突っ込みました。
That car plunged into the pond.

つつじ *azalea ((flower))*

つつしむ 慎む *1. to be careful about, to be prudent about*

言葉を慎む to be careful about one's words

2. to refrain from, to abstain from

たばこを慎む to refrain from smoking

つつみ 堤 *dike, embankment, levee* [→ 堤防]

つつみ 包み *(US) package, (UK) parcel, bundle*

本の包みを受け取りました。
I received a package of books.

包み紙 wrapping paper

つつむ 包む *to wrap (in a covering)*

これをきれいな紙に包んでください。
Please wrap this in pretty paper.

つづり 綴り *1. spelling (in an alphabet)*

2. binding together (typically said of papers)

3. bound pad, bound of sheaf (typically said of papers)

つづる 綴る *1. to spell (in an alphabet)*

その単語はどうつづりますか。
How do you spell that word?

2. to write, to compose (a text)

作文をつづる to write a composition

3. to bind together (The direct object is typically papers.)

その書類はつづって提出してください。
Bind and submit those documents please.

つとめ 勤め *(white-collar) job*

兄はその会社に勤めが見つかりました。
My older brother found a job at that company.

勤め人 salaried worker, white-collar worker

勤め先 one's workplace

つとめ 務め *duty (to be performed)*

務めを果たす to fulfill one's duties

つとめる 勤める *to work (in a white-collar job)*

石川さんは銀行に勤めています。
Ms. Ishikawa works at a bank.

つとめる 務める *to serve in the role of, to serve in the post of*

井上さんは今会長を務めています。
Ms. Inoue is now serving as chairperson.

つとめる 努める *to exert oneself, to make efforts, to work hard [→ 努力する]*

毎日運動するように努めています。
I am making efforts to do exercise every day.

つな 綱 *rope, cord; cable*

明さんは2本の木の間に綱を張りました。
Akira stretched a rope between the two trees.

綱引き tug of war

綱渡り tightrope walking; tightrope walker

つなぐ 繋ぐ *1. to tie, to fasten, to tether*

カウボーイは馬を木につなぎました。
The cowboy tied his horse to a tree.

2. to tie together, to connect, to join

手をつなぐ to join hands

3. to connect (a phone call)

鈴木先生につないでください。
Please connect me with Dr. Suzuki.

つなみ 津波 *tsunami, tidal wave*

つね 常 *the usual, the ordinary course of things*

世の常 the way of the world

常の usual, ordinary, common

常に [[→ いつも (s.v. いつ)]] always; usually

つの 角 *horn, antler*

角笛 horn (i.e., an animal's horn made into a musical instrument)

つば 唾 *spittle, saliva*

つばを吐く to spit

つばき 椿 *camellia ((flower))*

つばさ 翼 *wing [→ 羽2.]*

つばめ *swallow ((bird))*

つぶ 粒 *grain (of rice, etc.); drop (of liquid) [→ 滴]*

—粒 (counter for grains, drops; see Appendix 2)

この薬を朝夕2粒ずつ飲んでください。
Take two drops of this medicine morning and evening.

大粒 large drops

つぶす 潰す *to crush, to smash, to squash*

ワインを作るためにぶどうをつぶします。
To make wine you crush grapes.

卵をつぶす to smash an egg

時間をつぶす to kill time

つぶやく 呟く *to mutter, to murmur*

母は「つかれたわ」とつぶやきました。
My mother muttered, "I'm tired!"

つぶれる 潰れる *1. to get crushed, to get smashed, to get squashed*

段ボール箱がつぶれました。
The cardboard box got crushed.

卵が全部つぶれたよ。
All the eggs got smashed!

2. to go bankrupt, to go out of business [→ 破産する]

駅前のパン屋がつぶれたそうです。
They say the bakery in front of the station went out of business.

つぼ 壺 *pot; jar*

つぼ 坪 *(a unit of area (= approx. 3.3 m^2))*

—坪 (counter for; see Appendix 2)

つぼみ *(flower) bud*

桃のつぼみが膨らんでいるよ。
The peach blossom buds are swelling!

つま 妻 *wife [↔ 夫; 奥さん]*

つまさき 爪先 *toe tip*

つま先で歩く to walk on tiptoe

つまずく *to stumble*

少女は石につまずいて転びました。

The girl stumbled on a stone and fell down.

つまむ 摘む *to take hold of with the fingertips*

ポテトチップスをつまんで食べました。
I ate potato chips with my fingers.

ひどいにおいに鼻をつまみました。
I held my nose at the terrible smell.

つまようじ 爪楊枝 *toothpick* [→ 楊枝]

つまらない *1. dull, boring* [→ 退屈な]

このパーティーはつまらないなあ。
Boy, this party is dull.

まったくつまらない映画だったよ。
It was a really boring movie!

2. trifling, trivial [→ 些細な]

妹たちはつまらない事でけんかする。
My younger sisters quarrel about trivial things.

3. worthless, good-for-nothing

つまらない物にお金を遣わないで。
Don't spend money on worthless things.

つまらない物ですが、どうぞ。

This is for you; I hope you like it. (Literally: It's a worthless thing, but please.)

(Japanese etiquette calls for denigrating a gift one gives as a way of showing respect for the recipient. The implication is that the recipient deserves better.)

つまり *1. in other words, that is (to say)* [→ 即ち]

元旦、つまり一月一日は私の誕生日です。
New Year's Day, that is, January 1st, is my birthday.

2. in short, to sum up [→ 要するに]

つまり、その男にだまされたわけです。
In short, the fact is that we were deceived by that man.

つまる 詰まる *1. to become stopped up, to become clogged, to become blocked* [→ 塞がる *1.*]

また下水が詰まっているよ。
The drain is blocked up again.

2. to be packed, to be crammed (into a container)

その鞄にはお土産がいっぱい詰まっている。
That bag is packed full of souvenirs.

3. to become full, to become jam-packed

この本箱は漫画本で詰まっています。
This bookcase is full of comic books.

4. to become shorter, to shrink [→ 縮まる*]*

日が詰まる the days become shorter

つみ 罪 *crime, offense; sin*

人をだますのは罪です。
To deceive people is a sin.

罪な cruel, heartless

罪のある〔ない〕人 guilty〔innocent〕person

罪を犯す to commit a crime

つみき 積み木 *(toy) building block*

つむ 摘む *to pick, to pluck*

家族で畑でいちごを摘みました。
They picked strawberries in the field as a family.

つむ 積む *1. to load (as freight)*

このトラックに米を積みましょう。
Let's load the rice onto this truck.

2. to pile up, to stack; to amass, to accumulate

先生は机の上に本を積みました。
The teacher piled up books on her desk.

お金を積む to accumulate money

つめ 爪 *(finger-) nail; claw*

つめを切る to cut nails

爪切り nail clipper

つめこむ 詰め込む *to cram, to pack (into a container)*

この車に牛10頭を詰め込むのは無理だ。
It's impossible to cram ten cows into this truck.

つめたい 冷たい *1. cold (describing an*

object or tangible substance at a low temperature) [↔ 熱い]

外は冷たい風が吹いているよ。
A cold wind is blowing outside!

何か冷たい飲み物をください。
Please give me something cold to drink.

2. cold (-hearted), unfriendly [→ 冷淡な] [↔ 温かい3.]

湯沢はその手紙に冷たい返事を出した。
Yuzawa sent a cold answer to that letter.

美幸さんは僕には冷たいよ。
Miyuki is cold to me!

つめる 詰める *1. to pack, to put (into a container)*

この箱にオレンジを詰めました。
They packed oranges in this box.

2. to move closer, to move closer together (transitive)

席をちょっと詰めてください。
Please move your seats a little closer together.

3. to make shorter, to shrink [→ 短縮する]

洋服を詰める to shorten clothes

つもり *1. intention*

つもりだ to intend to, to be planning to (following a clause ending in a nonpast-tense verb)

あしたはテニスをするつもりです。
Tomorrow I intend to play tennis.

将来何になるつもりですか。
What do you plan to become in the future?

つもりがない to have no intention of, not to be planning to (following a clause ending in a nonpast-tense verb)

その保険に加入するつもりはありません。
I have no intention of subscribing to that insurance policy.

2. (possibly mistaken) belief

つもりだ to think (perhaps mistakenly) (following a clause ending in a past-tense verb)

電気を消したつもりですが、確かめます。
I think I turned out the lights, but I'll make sure.

つもる 積もる *to accumulate, to pile up (intransitive)*

この雪はあまり積もらないでしょう。
This snow will probably not accumulate very much.

つや 艶 *gloss, shine, luster*

つゆ 露 *dew*

露が降りる dew settles, dew forms

つゆ 梅雨 *the Japanese rainy season (typically mid-June through mid-July)*

梅雨に入る to enter the rainy season

梅雨が明ける the rainy season ends

つよい 強い *strong* [↔ 弱い]

強い風が吹いているよ。
A strong wind is blowing!

ドアを強く押して開けてください。
Please push the door strongly and open it.

雨が強く降っています。
It's raining hard.

Aに強い strong in A, good at A; not easily affected adversely by A

山根さんは科学に強いね。
Ms. Yamane is good at science, isn't she?

つよさ 強さ *strength*

つよまる 強まる *to become stronger [↔ 弱まる]*

つよめる 強める *to make stronger [↔ 弱める]*

つらい 辛い *hard, trying, bitter*

毎朝5時に起きるのはつらいよ。
It is hard to get up at 5:00 every morning!

つらい目にあう to have a trying experience

つらぬく 貫く *1. to pierce through, to penetrate through; to pass through*

この矢は的を貫きました。

This arrow penetrated the target.
川は町を貫いて流れています。
The river flows through the city.
2. to carry through, to accomplish [→ やり遂げる]
目的を貫く to accomplish an objective

つらら *icicle*

つり 釣り *fishing (with hook and line), angling*
釣りをする to fish
兄は釣りが大好きです。
My older brother loves fishing.
あしたは川へ釣りに行くつもりです。
Tomorrow I'm planning to go to the river for fishing.
釣り針 fish hook
釣り堀 fishing pond
釣り糸 fishing line
釣り竿 fishing rod, fishing pole

つり 釣り [☞ お釣り]

つりあい 釣り合い *balance, equilibrium*
釣り合いを取る to attain balance
平均台の上で釣り合いを取って歩いた。
I attained balance and walked along the beam.
釣り合いを保つ to maintain balance

つりあう 釣り合う *to balance, to become in balance*

つりかわ 吊り革 *hanging strap (for standing passengers on a bus or train)*
電車に乗ったら、つり革につかまってね。
When you get on the train, hold on to a hanging strap, OK?

つる 蔓 *vine*

つる 鶴 *crane ((bird))*

つる 釣る *to catch (with a hook and line)*
この川で魚を釣ります。
I catch fish in this river.
きのうますを5匹釣ったよ。
I caught five trout yesterday!

つる 吊る [☞ 吊るす]

つるす 吊るす *to hang, to suspend*
軒下に風鈴をつるしました。
I hung a wind chime under the eave.

つるつる *1. 〜の smooth (-surfaced) [→ 滑らかな 1.]*
つるつるする to become smooth
つるつるにはげている to be completely bald
2. slippingly, slidingly
つるつるの slippery
つるつるする to become slippery
つるつる滑る to slide slippingly

つるはし *pick, pickax*

つれて [☞ につれて]

つれていく 連れて行く [☞ 連れる]

つれてくる 連れて来る [☞ 連れる]

つれる 連れる *to travel with as one's companion (Ordinarily occurs as a gerund (-て form) followed by a verb of motion.)*
連れて行く to take (an animate being along)
いとこは私を公園に連れていってくれた。
My cousin took me to the park.
いとこは京都のいろいろな所へ連れていってくれました。
My cousin took me to a lot of places in Kyoto.
連れて来る to bring (an animate being along)
妹さんを連れてきてください。
Please bring your younger sister with you.

ツンドラ *tundra*

て

て 手 *1. hand*
明さんにも手を振ったよ。

I waved my hand to Akira too!
子供たちは手をつないで歩きました。
The children walked hand in hand.
手を上げる to raise one's hand
手を貸す to lend a hand
手に入れる to come into one's possession
手が掛かる to require a lot of work, to be laborious

2. arm (including the hand)

3. means, method [→ 手段]

ほかの手を使ってみましょう。
Let's try using another method.

4. kind, sort [→ 種類]

その手の物は輸出できないでしょう。
One probably cannot export that kind of thing.
手首 wrist
手の平 palm of the hand
手の甲 back of the hand

で *(noun-following particle) 1. in, at, on (indicating a place which is the site of some activity)*

母は大阪で生まれました。
My mother was born in Osaka.
空港で友達を出迎えました。
I met a friend at the airport.
野木さんは農場で働いているね。
Mr. Nogi is working on a farm, isn't he?

2. by means of, with, using

電話で話すのは嫌いです。
I don't like talking on the telephone.
鉛筆で書いてください。
Please write with a pencil.
ここまではバスで来ました。
I came this far by bus.
英語でスピーチをしました。
I made a speech in English.

3. of, from (indicating materials or ingredients)

この橋は石でできています。
This bridge is made of stone.
チーズは牛乳で作ります。
Cheese is made from milk.

4. because of, on account of, from

雨で試合は中止になりました。
The game was called off because of rain.
うちの犬は頭のけがで死にました。
Our dog died from a head injury.

5. in (indicating a period of time)

上原さんは30分で戻ります。
Ms. Uehara will be back in 30 minutes.

6. at, for (indicating a point on a scale)

このカメラを8000円で買いました。
I bought this camera for ¥8,000.
あの電車はすごい速力で走っているよ。
That train is running at incredible speed!
姉は18歳で留学しました。
My older sister studied abroad at eighteen.

7. by, according to (indicating an information source or criterion)

私の時計でちょうど２時です。
It's exactly 2:00 by my watch.
鉛筆はダースで売るでしょう？
Pencils are sold by the dozen, right?

であう 出会う *to happen to meet, to come across, to run into*

市場で偶然洋子さんに出会ったよ。
I happened to run into Yoko at the market!

てあし 手足 *1. arms and legs*

2. hands and feet

てあたりしだい 手当たり次第（〜に） *at random*

夏休みの間は手当たり次第に本を読んだ。
During the summer vacation I read books at random.

てあつい 手厚い *warm, solicitous*

てあて 手当 *1. medical treatment* [→ 治療]

少女は病院で手当を受けました。
The girl was treated at the hospital.
手当する to treat

2. salary supplement, allowance

家族手当 family allowance

応急手当 first-aid

てあらい 手洗い *washroom, bathroom, restroom*

(Toilets and bathtubs are traditionally in separate rooms in Japan. This word refers to a room containing a toilet.) [→トイレ]

ていあん 提案 *proposal, suggestion*

理事会は私の提案に賛成しました。
The board of directors agreed to my proposal.

提案する to propose, to suggest

市川さんはいい計画を提案しました。
Ms. Ichikawa proposed a good plan.

ディーケー ＤＫ *(Generally not written out in katakana.)* [☞ ダイニングキッチン]

ティーシャツ Ｔシャツ *T-shirt*

ディーゼルエンジン *diesel engine*

ていいん 定員 *number of persons set by rule; maximum number of persons allowed, capacity*

このバスの定員は60名です。
The capacity of this bus is 60 people.

ティーンエージャー *teenager*

ていえん 庭園 *(spacious and decorative) garden*

ていか 定価 *list price, regular price*

この時計の定価は5000円ですが、特売で買いました。
The list price of this watch is ¥5,000, but I bought it on sale.

この自転車を定価で買いましたか。
Did you buy this bicycle at list price?

ていき 定期 *1. fixed time period*

定期の regular, regularly scheduled

組合員は定期の会合を開きます。
The union members will hold their regular meeting.

2. [☞ 定期券 *(below)*]

定期入れ commuter-pass holder

定期券 (US) commuter pass, (UK) season ticket

定期試験 regular examination

定期的な regular, occurring at regular intervals

豊は月に２回定期的に親に手紙を書く。
Yutaka writes a letter to his parents regularly twice a month.

定期預金 time deposit

不定期の irregular, not regularly scheduled

ていぎ 定義 *a definition*

定義する to define

ていきあつ 低気圧 [[↔ 高気圧]] *1. low atmospheric pressure*

2. low pressure (weather) system

ていきゅうび 定休日 *regular day to be closed for business*

ていきょう 提供 *providing, furnishing; offer*

提供する to provide, to furnish; to offer

奥村さんも資料を提供してくれました。
Mr. Okumura also provided data for me.

ていこう 抵抗 *resistance, opposition*

敵軍は何の抵抗もしませんでした。
The enemy forces put up no resistance.

抵抗する to resist, to oppose

学生たちは警官隊に抵抗しました。
The students resisted the police force.

ていこく 帝国 *empire*

ていし 停止 *1. stopping, cessation of movement*

停止する to come to a stop

バスは停止しました。
The bus came to a stop.

2. suspension, interruption

停止する to suspend, to interrupt

この会社はきのう営業を停止しました。
This company suspended operations yesterday.

ていじ 定時 *fixed time, set time*

学校は定時に始まります。
School starts at a set time.

定時制高校 part-time high school (Japanese schools of this type are ordinarily in session from 6:00 to 10:00 PM.)

ていしゃ 停車 *stop, stopping (by a train, bus, car, etc.)*

停車する to come to a stop, to make a stop

この電車は各駅に停車します。
This train stops at every station.

急停車 sudden stop

ていしゅ 亭主 【COL. for 夫】 *husband* [↔ 女房]

ていしゅつ 提出 *handing in, turning in (of documents, etc.)*

提出する to hand in, to turn in

では、答案を提出しなさい。
All right, hand in your examination papers.

ていしょく 定食 *set restaurant meal*

ディスカウント *discount* [→ 割引]

ディスカウントストア discount store

ディスカッション *discussion* [→ 討論]

ディスカッションする to have a discussion

ディスクジョッキー *disk jockey*

ディスコ *disco*

ていせい 訂正 *correction, rectification*

訂正する to correct, to rectify

資料の誤りを訂正します。
I will correct the mistakes in the data.

ていせつ 定説 *generally accepted theory*

ティッシュ [☞ ティッシュペーパー]

ティッシュペーパー *tissue, kleenex*

ていでん 停電 *electrical outage, power failure*

ゆうべ20分間の停電がありました。
There was a twenty-minute power failure last night.

ていど 程度 *degree, extent; level* [→ 水準]

会長の言う事はある程度までわかります。
I understand what the chairperson says to some extent.

この練習問題は私には程度が高すぎるよ。
The level of this exercise is too high for me!

ていねい 丁寧 ～な *1. polite* [→ 礼儀正しい (s.v. 礼儀)]

長尾さんはだれに対してもていねいです。
Mr. Nagao is polite to everybody.

ていねいな返事を受け取りました。
I received a polite reply.

スポークスマンはていねいに答えました。
The spokesperson answered politely.

2. careful, attentive to details

もっとていねいに書きなさい。
Write more carefully.

丁寧語 polite word (one type of respectful vocabulary in Japanese)

ていねん 定年 *mandatory retirement age*

ていぼう 堤防 *embankment, dike, levee* [→ 堤]

でいり 出入り *going in and out*

出入りする to go in and out

その犬は窓から出入りします。
The dog goes in and out through the window.

出入り口 combined entry and exit

ていりゅうじょ 停留所 *stop (where a bus or streetcar stops)*

バスの停留所 bus stop

ていれ 手入れ *1. taking care, maintenance*

手入れが行き届く maintenance is scrupulous

手入れする to take care of, to maintain

運動場はよく手入れしてあります。
The playground has been well taken care of.

2. police raid

ゆうべそのバーに手入れがありました。
There was a police raid on that bar last night.

ディレクター *director (of movies, television shows, etc.)*

データ *data*

デート *date (with a person)*

デートする to go on a date
弘はきょう夏子とデートするんだよ。
Hiroshi is going to go on a date with Natsuko today!

テープ *1. magnetic tape, recording tape*
歌手はその歌をテープに録音しました。
The singer recorded that song on tape.
テープにとる to get on tape
2. finish-line tape
テープを切る to break the tape
3. adhesive tape
4. paper streamer
テープレコーダー tape recorder

テーブル *table*
テーブルの上を片づけてください。
Please clear the table. (Literally: Please tidy the top of the table.)
テーブルに着く to take a seat at a table
テーブルチャージ cover charge
テーブルクロス table cloth
テーブルマナー table manners
テーブルスピーチ after-dinner speech

テーマ *theme, subject matter* [→ 主題]
テーマソング theme song

ておくれ 手遅れ ～の *too late (to do any good)*
今から始めても手遅れだよ。
Even if you start now it's too late!

でかい 【COL. for 大きい】 *big*

てがかり 手掛かり *clue, trace*

でかける 出掛ける *to go out (to do something); to set out, to leave* [→ 出発する]
散歩に出かけましょうか。
Shall we go out for a walk?
母は今出かけています。
My mother is out now.
父はあした神戸へ出かけます。
My father will leave for Kobe tomorrow.

てがみ 手紙 *letter ((message))*
洋子ちゃんから手紙をもらったよ。
I got a letter from Yoko!
お手紙をどうもありがとうございました。
Thank you very much for your letter.

てがる 手軽 ～な [[→ 簡単な]] *simple; easy*
けさは手軽な朝食を食べました。
I ate a simple breakfast this morning.
それは手軽な仕事です。
That's an easy task.

てき 敵 *enemy [↔ 味方]; adversary, opponent*
敵軍 enemy military force, enemy troops
敵味方 friends and enemies
敵無しの unrivaled

－てき －的 *-like, -ish, -ic, -al (Added to noun bases to form adjectival nouns.)*
科学的な scientific
音楽的な musical
天才的な genius-like

できあがる 出来上がる *to be completed*

てきい 敵意 *hostility*

てきおう 適応 *1. adaptation*
適応する to adapt oneself
その留学生は日本の生活様式にすぐ適応しました。
That foreign student soon adapted herself to the Japanese life-style.
2. suitability
適応する to become suitable, to become suited

できごと 出来事 *occurrence, event*

これは日常のできごとです。
This is an everyday occurrence.
ラジオはきのうの珍しいできごとを報道した。
The radio reported yesterday's unusual events.
今年の大きなできごとについて話します。
We will talk about the major events of this year.

テキスト *textbook* [→ 教科書]
これは英語のテキストです。
This is an English textbook.

てきする 適する *{Irreg.} to be fit, to be appropriate*
この水は飲むのに適するそうです。
They say this water is fit to drink.
塚本さんはその仕事に適しています。
Ms. Tsukamoto is right for that job.
この場所は釣りに適していると思います。
I think this place is suitable for fishing.

てきせつ 適切 ～な *appropriate, proper, apt* [→ 相応しい]
適切な処置を取ってください。
Please take appropriate measures.

できたて 出来立て ～の *freshly made, just finished*
このクッキーはできたてです。
These cookies are freshly baked.

てきど 適度 ～の *moderate*

てきとう 適当 ～な *appropriate, suitable* [→ 相応しい]
これは中学生に適当な本です。
This is an appropriate book for junior high school students.
その服は運動するのに適当じゃないよ。
Those clothes aren't appropriate for doing exercise!

てきぱき (～と) *quickly, promptly, with dispatch*

できる *1. to be able to do, can do*
(This is the potential form of する. What a person is able to do is treated as a grammatical subject and marked with が rather than with を.)
スケートができますか。
Can you skate?
三田さんは英語がよくできるそうです。
They say that Ms. Mita can speak English well.
できれば、電話をください。
If you can, please give me a telephone call.
できるだけ to the extent one can, to the extent possible
あしたはできるだけ早く出発しましょう。
Tomorrow let's start out as early as possible.
できるだけ本を読みなさい。
Read as many books as you can.
2. ことが～ to be able to (following a nonpast-tense verb)
私たちは試合に勝つことができました。
We were able to win the game.
いつか火星へ行くことができるでしょう。
Someday one will probably be able to go to Mars.
3. to be completed, to get finished
朝食の用意ができましたよ。
Breakfast is ready! (Literally: The breakfast preparations are finished!)

てぎわ 手際 ～がいい *to be skillful*
手際が悪い to be unskillful
手際よく skillfully

でぐち 出口 *exit, exit doorway* [↔ 入り口]

テクニック *technique*
そのレーサーはすぐれた運転のテクニックを持っています。
The racer has excellent driving technique.

てくび 手首 *wrist*

でございます 【FORMAL for だ】
(The word is a verb with the semi-formal ending. The informal nonpast (the form of a verb that ordinarily appears in a dic-

tionary) is ござる, but such informal forms are not used in modern Japanese.)

でこぼこ 凸凹 *unevenness, bumpiness*

凸凹な uneven, bumpy

てごろ 手頃〜な *1. handy, easy to handle*

この辞書は手ごろな大きさです。
This dictionary is a handy size.

2. reasonable, inexpensive

このグローブは手ごろな値段です。
This glove is reasonably priced. (Literally: As for this glove, it's a reasonable price.)

デザート *dessert*

デザートにはアイスクリームを食べた。
I had ice cream for dessert.

デザイナー *designer*

デザイン *1. design, plan*

2. designing

デザインする to design

グラフィックデザイン graphic design

てざわり 手触り *feel, perception triggered by touching*

これは毛皮のような手触りです。
This feels like fur. (Literally: As for this, it's a feel like fur)

でし 弟子 *pupil, disciple; apprentice*

てした 手下 *follower, underling, subordinate*

デジタル 〜の *digital*

デジタル時計 digital watch; digital clock

てじな 手品 *magic trick*

森先生はトランプの手品が上手です。
Mr. Mori is good at card tricks.

手品師 magician

でしゃばる 出しゃばる *to meddle, to act obtrusively*

川合さんは決して出しゃばらない人です。
Mr. Kawai is the type that never meddles.

でしょう 【SEMI-FORMAL for だろう】

です *1.* 【SEMI-FORMAL for だ】

2. 【SEMI-FORMAL for だ】 *(This word is used to mark the semi-formal style of adjectives in both the nonpast and past tenses.)*

この本は高いです。
This book is expensive.

試験は非常に難しかったです。
The exam was extremely difficult.

てすう 手数 *time and effort, trouble, bother* [→ 手間]

お手数ですが、この手紙を速達で出してくださいませんか。
I'm sorry to trouble you, but will you mail this letter by special delivery for me? (Literally: It's a bother, but will you mail this letter by special delivery for me?)

Aに手数をかける to trouble A, to impose on A

手数がかかる to be a lot of trouble

手数料 handling charge, commission fee

テスト [[→ 試験]] *1. test (to evaluate knowledge or ability)*

きのう英語のテストがあったよ。
There was an English test yesterday!

2. test, trial (to evaluate quality)

新しい飛行機のテストは1か月続きます。
The tests of the new plane will continue for a month.

テストする to test

学力テスト scholastic achievement test

てすり 手すり *handrail*

てそう 手相 *the pattern of lines on the palm of the hand*

手相を見る to read a person's palm

でたらめ 【COL.】 *nonsense, bunk; random talk, haphazard talk; nonsensical behavior, haphazard behavior*

でたらめな nonsensical, absurd; random, haphazard

あの人はいつもでたらめを言っているね。
That person is always talking nonsense, isn't he?

てちょう 手帳 *small notebook for reminders, (UK) pocketbook*

てつ 鉄 *iron ((metal))*

鉄は熱いうちに打て。(proverb)
Strike while the iron is hot.

鉄屑 scrap iron

てつがく 哲学 *(the study of) philosophy*

哲学者 philosopher

デッキ *1. deck (of a boat) [→ 甲板]*

2. railroad car vestibule

3. [☞ テープデッキ (below)]

テープデッキ tape deck

てっきょう 鉄橋 *iron bridge, (US) railroad bridge, (UK) railway bridge*

てづくり 手作り〜の *handmade; homemade*

この手作りの人形は南米で買いました。
I bought this handmade doll in South America.

手作りのアイスクリームはおいしいね。
Homemade ice cream is delicious, isn't it?

てっこう 鉄鋼 *steel* [→ 鋼鉄]

デッサン *rough sketch* [→ スケッチ2.]

てつだい 手伝い *1. help, assistance (with a task)*

2. helper, assistant

てつだう 手伝う *1. to help, to assist*

きょうはうちで母を手伝います。
I'll help my mother at home today.

2. to help with, to assist with

兄は宿題を手伝ってくれました。
My older brother helped me with my homework.

てつづき 手続き *procedure, course of action*

てってい 徹底 〜する *to be thorough, to be exhaustive*

徹底的な thorough, exhaustive

てつどう 鉄道 *railroad, railway*

鉄道事故 railroad accident

デッドヒート *dead heat*

デッドヒートを演じる to run a dead heat

デッドボール *pitch that hits a batter (in baseball)*

デッドボールを食らう to be hit by a pitch

てつぼう 鉄棒 *1. iron bar*

2. horizontal bar (in gymnastics)

てっぽう 鉄砲 *gun*

てつや 徹夜 *staying up all night*

徹夜する to stay up all night

あしたが締め切りだから今晩は徹夜する。
Tomorrow is the deadline, so I'll stay up all night tonight.

徹夜の all-night

徹夜で all night long

ゆうべは徹夜で勉強しました。
Last night I studied all night long.

テナー [☞ テノール]

テナーサックス tenor saxophone

テニス *tennis*

テニスをする to play tennis

日曜日は友達とテニスをします。
On Sundays I play tennis with a friend.

テニスボール tennis ball

テニスコート tennis court

テニスラケット tennis racket

テニスシューズ tennis shoes

軟式テニス rubber-ball tennis

てにもつ 手荷物 *hand-baggage, luggage*

まず手荷物を預けたいのです。
First I want to check my luggage.

手荷物一時預かり所 baggage room, (US) checkroom, (UK) cloakroom

てぬぐい 手拭い *hand towel*

手拭い掛け hand-towel hanger

テノール *1. tenor (voice)*

2. tenor (singer)

3. tenor (part)

テノール歌手 [☞ テノール2. (above)]

てのこう 手の甲 *back of the hand*

てのひら 手のひら *palm of the hand*

では *well then, in that case [→ それでは]*

デパート *department store*

お母さんはデパートへ買物に行ったよ。
Mother went shopping at the department store.

てばなす 手放す *to part with, to let someone else have*

このレコードは絶対に手放さないよ。
I absolutely will not part with this record!

てびき 手引き *1. guidance, guiding*

2. guide ((person))

3. primer, manual, guide

デビュー *debut*

デビューする to debut, to make one's debut

正は14歳で歌手としてデビューした。
Tadashi made his debut as a singer at the age of fourteen.

てぶくろ 手袋 *gloves; mittens*

右の手袋を無くしてしまいました。
I lost my right glove.

デフレ *(monetary) deflation* [↔ インフレ]

デフレーション [☞ デフレ]

てほん 手本 *1. example, model*

あの人を手本にしましょう。
Let's make that person our example.

2. copybook, book of model characters (for Japanese calligraphy)

手本を見ながらこの字を書きました。
I wrote this character while looking at the copybook.

てま 手間 *time and effort, trouble, labor* [→ 手数]

この仕事は手間がかかるね。
This work takes time and effort, doesn't it?

デマ *false rumor*

てまえ 手前 *1. the area on this side, the area nearer*

公園の手前に駐車場があります。
There is a parking lot on this side of the park.

林さんは名古屋の一つ手前の駅で降りた。
Mr. Hayashi got off one station this side of Nagoya.

2. consideration of decorum (in front of other people); out of consideration for decorum (in front of other people)

お客さんの手前怒るわけには行きません。
Out of consideration for decorum in front of guests, I can't very well get angry.

でまえ 出前 *delivery of ordered meals*

でまど 出窓 *bay window*

てまね 手真似 *hand gesture*

課長は手まねで私を呼びました。
The section chief beckoned me with a gesture.

手まねで話す to talk by gestures

でむかえる 出迎える *to go out and meet (an arriving person)*

駅までいとこを出迎えました。
I went to meet my cousin at the station.

でも *(The examples of でも given here can all be analyzed as a combination of the gerund (-て form) of the copula だ with the particle も. Other examples are combinations of the particle で with the particle も.)*

1. even, even if it is

小さな子供でもそんなことはできるよ。
Even little children can do such a thing!

ここは冬でも雪がほとんど降りません。
Even in winter it hardly snows here.

AでもBでも either A or B, whether it's A or B

きょうでもあしたでもいいです。
Either today or tomorrow is all right.

2. no matter (following a question word or

a phrase beginning with a question word)
このトランプの中からどれでも1枚引いてください。
Please pull out any one from these cards.

3. or something
新聞でも読んで待ちましょう。
Let's read a newspaper or something and wait.

4. however, but (at the beginning of a sentence) [→ しかし]

デモ *demonstration (i.e., a public exhibition of protest, etc.)*
デモをする to demonstrate
デモ行進 demonstration march
デモ隊 demonstrator group

デモクラシー *democracy* [→ 民主主義]

てもと 手元 *the area near at hand, the area within reach*
手もとに at hand, within reach
いつもノートを手もとに置いています。
I always keep a notebook at hand.

デュエット *duet*

てら 寺 *(Buddhist) temple*

てらす 照らす *to illuminate, to shine on*
シャンデリアがホールを照らしています。
Chandeliers are illuminating the hall.
月が野原を照らしています。
The moon is shining on the field.

テラス *terrace (adjoining a building)*

デラックス 〜な *deluxe*

デリケート 〜な *delicate*

てる 照る *{5} to shine (The subject must be the sun or the moon.)*
今夜は満月が明るく照っています。
The full moon is shining brightly tonight.

でる 出る *1. to go out, to come out, to exit, to leave*
Aから／を出る to exit (from) A, to leave A
学生たちはやっと教室から出ました。
The students finally came out of the classroom.

2. to leave, to start off, to depart [→ 出発する]
バスが出るところだよ。
The bus is about to leave!

3. to appear, to emerge, to come out [→ 現われる]
芽がそろそろ出るでしょう。
The buds will probably appear soon.
その本は来月出ます。
That book will come out next month.

4. to attend, to take part
大森さんもこの会に出ます。
Mr. Omori will also attend this meeting.
サントスさんは弁論大会に出るつもりだ。
Ms. Santos is planning to take part in the speech contest.

5. to graduate from [→ 卒業する]
息子は立教大学を出ました。
My son graduated from Rikkyo University.

テレックス *telex*
兄は事務所に報告をテレックスで送った。
My older brother sent his report to the office by telex.

テレパシー *telepathy*

テレビ *1. television (broadcasting)*
学生たちはいつも夕食後にテレビを見る。
The students always watch television after supper.

2. television (set)
父はテレビで野球を見ています。
My father is watching baseball on television.
太郎ちゃん、テレビの音を小さくしてね。
Taro, turn down the volume on the TV.
テレビをつける〔消す〕 to turn on〔off〕 the television
テレビ番組 television program
テレビ電話 videophone
テレビゲーム video game

テレビ局 television station
テレビカメラ television camera
カラーテレビ color TV

テレホンカード *telephone card (a debit card for use in public telephones in Japan)*

てれや 照れ屋 *shy person*

てれる 照れる *to come to feel shy, to get embarrassed*
先生の前でピアノを弾いて、照れました。
I played the piano in front of the teacher and got embarrassed.

テロ *terrorism*

テロリスト *terrorist*

てわたす 手渡す *to hand, to pass* [→ 渡す 1.]

てん 天 *1. the sky, the heavens* [→ 空]
負けた選手は天を仰ぎ、ため息をついた。
The defeated athlete looked up at the sky and sighed.
2. heaven, God, the gods; fate, destiny
天と地 heaven and earth
天に任せる to leave up to God; to leave up to fate

てん 点 *1. point, dot*
点を打つ to make a dot, to write a point
先生は地図に点を打ちました。
The teacher made a dot on the map.
2. spot, speck, blot
うちの猫のタマには白地に黒い点がまだらについています。
Our cat, Tama, is white with black spots.
3. (scored) point; mark, (US) grade (expressed as a number)
細川君は英語でいい点を取ったよ。
Hosokawa got a good grade in English!
一点 (counter for points; see Appendix 2)
このクラスの平均は80点です。
This class's average is 80 points.
4. point, respect; viewpoint
その点では社長も同じ意見です。
On that point the company president also has the same opinion.
満点 perfect score, (UK) full marks
小数点 decimal point
一点 (counter for items; see Appendix 2)

でんあつ 電圧 *voltage*

てんいん 店員 *(US) salesclerk, (UK) shop assistant*
姉はデパートの店員をしています。
My older sister is working as a salesclerk in a department store.

でんえん 田園 *the country, rural area; suburban area with greenery*
田園の rural, pastoral
田園都市 garden city

てんか 点火 *ignition, lighting*
点火する to provide ignition, to set fire
Aに点火する to ignite A, to light A

てんか 天下 *1. the whole world, everything under heaven*
2. the whole country, the realm
天下を取る to take power, to bring the whole country under one's rule
3. having one's own way, being in one's element

てんかい 展開 *development; expansion, spread*
展開する (transitive or intransitive) to develop; to expand, to spread

てんき 天気 *1. the weather*
きょうの天気はどうですか。
How is today's weather?
天気はよくなりそうです。
It looks as if the weather will improve.
山の天気は変わりやすいです。
Mountain weather is easily changeable.
2. fair weather
天気になる to become fair, to clear up

天気予報 weather forecast

天気予報ではあしたは雪だそうです。

According to the weather forecast, it will snow tomorrow.

天気予報が当たりました。

The weather forecast proved correct.

天気図 weather map, weather chart

でんき 伝記 *biography*

明治天皇の伝記を読んだことがあります。

I have read a biography of the Meiji Emperor.

でんき 電気 *1. electricity*

この機械は電気で動きます。

This machine works by electricity.

2. electric light [→ 電灯]

電気をつける〔消す〕 to turn on〔off〕a light

電気釜 electric rice cooker

電気器具 electrical appliance

電気毛布 electric blanket

電気スタンド electric lamp

でんきゅう 電球 *light bulb*

60ワットの電球はもうないです。

There are no more 60-watt light bulbs.

電球が切れる a light bulb burns out

てんきん 転勤 *changing jobs, taking a different job*

転勤する to change jobs, to be transferred (to a different job)

父は高崎支店に転勤しました。

My father was transferred to the Takasaki branch.

てんぐ 天狗 *long-nosed goblin*

(A familiar character in folk tales, a is human in form with a red face and wings and is said to live deep in mountains.)

てんけん 点検 *inspection, examination, check*

点検する to inspect, to examine, to check

うちを出る前に買物のリストを点検した。

I checked my shopping list before leaving home.

でんげん 電源 *electric power supply*

電源を切る to shut off the power

てんこう 天候 *(short-term) weather pattern*

てんこう 転校 *changing schools, moving to a different school*

転校する to change schools, to transfer (to a different school)

去年この学校に転校しました。

I transferred to this school last year.

転校生 transfer student

てんごく 天国 *heaven, paradise* [↔ 地獄]

でんごん 伝言 [[→ 言付け]] *message (that someone asks one person to give to another person); giving a message*

これは大竹さんへの伝言です。

This is a message for Ms. Otake.

伝言する to give a message, to send word

お兄さんに伝言してください。

Please give your older brother the message.

伝言板 message board

てんさい 天才 *1. genius, great talent ((attribute))*

2. genius ((person))

モーツァルトは音楽の天才でした。

Mozart was a musical genius.

天才的な highly gifted

岡田さんは天才的なピアニストです。

Ms. Okada is a highly gifted pianist.

てんさい 天災 *natural calamity, natural disaster*

てんさく 添削 *correction (of a text)*

添削する to correct

てんし 天使 *angel* [↔ 悪魔]

てんじ 点字 *braille*

てんじ 展示 *exhibiting, display* [→ 陳列]
展示する to put on display, to exhibit
新しい車がたくさん展示されているよ。
A lot of new cars are being exhibited!
展示会 show, exhibition [→ 展覧会]

でんし 電子 *electron* [↔ 陽子; 中性子]
電子計算機 (electronic) computer [→ コンピューター]
電子顕微鏡 electronic microscope
電子音楽 electronic music
電子オルガン electronic organ
電子レンジ microwave oven

でんしゃ 電車 *(electric) train; streetcar*
この電車は奈良に行きますか。
Does this train go to Nara?
娘は電車で通学しています。
My daughter commutes to school by train.
電車賃 train fare
通勤電車 commuter train

てんじょう 天井 *ceiling*
天井に美しいシャンデリアがついています。
A beautiful chandelier is attached to the ceiling.
この部屋は天井が低いですね。
This room's ceiling is low, isn't it?

でんせつ 伝説 *legend*
伝説上の legendary

てんせん 点線 *dotted line*

でんせん 伝染 *contagion*
伝染する to spread (by contagion); to be contagious
インフルエンザは伝染するね。
Influenza is contagious, isn't it?
伝染病 contagious disease

でんせん 電線 *electric wire, electrical cable*

てんたい 天体 *heavenly body*
天体望遠鏡 astronomical telescope
天体観測 astronomical observation

でんち 電池 *battery*
電池が切れる a battery goes dead
乾電池 dry battery
太陽電池 solar battery

でんちゅう 電柱 *utility pole, telephone pole*

テント *tent*
テントを張る to put up a tent, to pitch a tent
テントを畳む to fold up a tent, to strike a tent

でんとう 伝統 *tradition*
その学校は70年の伝統があります。
That school has a 70-year tradition.
伝統的な traditional
相撲は日本の伝統的なスポーツです。
Sumo is a traditional sport of Japan.

でんとう 電灯 *electric light*
懐中電灯 (US) flashlight, (UK) torch

てんねん 天然 ～の *natural*
天然ガス natural gas
天然記念物 natural monument
天然資源 natural resources

てんのう 天皇 *the Emperor (of Japan)*
天皇杯 the Emperor's Trophy (Presented to the winner of each Grand Sumo tournament.)
天皇陛下 His Majesty the Emperor
天皇誕生日 the Emperor's Birthday (a Japanese national holiday (on December 23 in the Heisei Era))
昭和天皇 the Showa Emperor

てんのうせい 天王星 *(the planet) Uranus*

でんぱ 電波 *electric wave, radio wave*

てんぴ 天火 *oven [→ オーブン]*

てんぷく 転覆 *overturning, capsizing*

転覆する to overturn, to capsize (intransitive)

風でヨットが転覆しました。

The sailboat capsized in the wind.

てんぷら 天麩羅 *tempura*

(a dish consisting of relatively small pieces of food (typically seafood and vegetables) dipped in a flour-and-egg batter and deep fried in vegetable oil)

でんぷん 澱粉 *starch (in or extracted from food)*

テンポ *tempo*

でんぽう 電報 *telegram, cablegram*

電報で結果を知らせてください。

Please let me know the result by telegram.

けさおじいさんから電報が届いたよ。

This morning a telegram arrived from grandfather!

電報を打つ to send a telegram

電報料金 telegram fee

至急電報 urgent telegram

てんもん 天文 *astronomical phenomena*

天文台 astronomical observatory

天文学 astronomy

天文学者 astronomer

てんらんかい 展覧会 *exhibition, show*

きょうモネの絵の展覧会を見に行きます。

Today I'm going to go to see an exhibition of Monet's pictures.

でんりゅう 電流 *electric current*

でんりょく 電力 *electric power*

電力会社 electric power company

でんわ 電話 *1. telephone*

電話が鳴っているよ。

The telephone is ringing!

ゆうべ洋子さんと電話で話しました。

Last night I talked with Yoko on the telephone.

電話を借りてもいいですか。

May I use your telephone?

電話に出る to answer the phone; to come to the phone

2. telephone call

近藤さん、電話ですよ。

Mr. Kondo, there's a telephone call for you! (Literally: Mr. Kondo, it's a telephone call!)

お電話をありがとうございました。

Thank you for your telephone call.

電話する to telephone, to call

電話を切る to cut off a phone call (ordinarily by hanging up)

Aに電話をかける to make a telephone call to A

Aから電話がかかる a telephone call comes from A

電話番号 telephone number

電話帳 telephone directory

電話中の (in the midst of talking) on the phone

電話口 the area at the telephone

電話交換手 telephone operator

と 戸 *door*

だれかが戸をたたいているよ。

Someone is knocking on the door!

戸を開ける〔閉める〕to open〔close〕a door

戸口 doorway

と 都 [☞ 東京都 (below)]

都知事 Governor of Tokyo

都民 citizen of Tokyo

東京都 Tokyo (Metropolitan) Prefecture

と (noun-following particle) *1. and*
(Connects nouns but not clauses; optional after the last item mentioned.)
私は英語と歴史と音楽が好きです。
I like English and history and music.
美紀ちゃんと祐子ちゃんは仲よしです。
Miki and Yuko are good friends.
2. (indicating a partner, opponent, etc.) with; against
敏子さんは先生とテニスをしています。
Toshiko is playing tennis with the teacher.
いつも弟とけんかします。
I always quarrel with my younger brother.
3. with (when a comparison is involved); from (when a difference is involved)
今年の赤字を去年のと比べましょう。
Let's compare this year's deficit with last year's.
これは古いのと違います。
This differs from the old one.

と (This clause-conjoining particle always follows a predicate in the nonpast tense.) *when, whenever; if*
雨が降ると、うちの猫は外に出ません。
My cat doesn't go outside, when it rains.
急がないと、列車に間に合わないよ。
If you don't hurry, you'll miss the train!

と *that*
(This quotative particle follows what is said or thought and precedes a verb of saying or thinking.)
西山さんは来ると言いました。
Ms. Nishiyama said that she would come.
ジャイアンツは負けたと思います。
I think that the Giants lost.

－ど －度 1. *(counter for number of times; see Appendix 2)* [→－回2.]
月に一度洋子さんに手紙を書きます。
I write a letter to Yoko once a month.
2. (counter for degrees (of arc or of temperature); see Appendix 2)
気温は今10度です。
The temperature is now ten degrees.
直角は90度です。
A right angle is 90 degrees.

ドア *door* [→ 戸]

とい 問い *question, inquiry* [→ 質問]

といあわせる 問い合わせる *to inquire about, to ask about*
AにBを問い合わせる to ask A about B
出発時刻を野崎さんに問い合わせよう。
Let's ask Ms. Nozaki about the departure time.

という [☞ 言う]

どいつ 【CRUDE】 *which person*

トイレ *bathroom, restroom, lavatory*
(Toilets and bathtubs are traditionally in separate rooms in Japan. This word refers to a room containing a toilet.) [→ 手洗い]
トイレを借りていいですか。
May I use your bathroom?

トイレット [☞ トイレ]
トイレットペーパー toilet paper

とう 党 *(political) party* [→ 政党]*; clique*
党員 party member
野党 opposition party
与党 government party, party in power

とう 塔 *tower; pagoda (at a Buddhist temple)*
五重の塔 five-storied pagoda
管制塔 control tower
ロンドン塔 The Tower of London
テレビ塔 television tower

とう 等 *and so on, etcetera (noun-following particle)* [→ など1.]

－とう －等 *(counter for classes, rankings, etc.; see Appendix 2)*
土田君は競走で１等になりました。

Tsuchida was first in the race.

一等賞 first prize

ーとう ー頭 *(counter for large animals; see Appendix 2)*

どう 胴 *torso, trunk*

船の胴 ship's hull

どう 銅 *copper; bronze*

銅貨 copper coin

銅メダル bronze medal

銅像 bronze statue

どう *how (as a question word)*

(In many uses, natural English translations have **what** rather than **how**.)

コンサートはどうでしたか。
How was the concert?

「文化」は英語でどう言いますか。
How do you say "bunka" in English?

コーヒーをもう1杯どうですか。
How about another cup of coffee?

どうしたんですか。
What's the matter?

この本をどう思いますか。
What do you think of this book?

どういう what kind of, what [→ どんな]

この単語はここではどういう意味ですか。
What meaning does this word have here?

かどうか whether or not (This expression generally follows an informal-style predicate, but the word preceding cannot be the copula form だ. When added to a clause that would end with だ, the だ does not appear.)

それは本物かどうかわかりません。
I don't know whether or not that's the real thing.

あした来るかどうか山下さんに尋ねた。
I asked Mr. Yamashita whether or not he will come tomorrow.

どうか somehow (Often used in requests.)

どうか9時までに済せてください。
Please finish it somehow by 9:00.

どうかする to have something go wrong

この機械はどうかしているよ。
There's something wrong with this machine!

とうあん 答案 *examination paper*

どうい 同意 *agreement, approval* [→ 賛成]

同意する to agree, to give one's approval

私は中津さんに同意します。
I agree with Ms. Nakatsu.

課長はその計画に同意しました。
The section chief agreed to that plan.

どういたしまして *not at all*

(Used as a response to a thank-you (= you're welcome), an apology, or a compliment.)

「どうもありがとうございました」「どういたしまして」
"Thank you very much." "Not at all."

とういつ 統一 *unity; uniformity; unification*

このチームは統一を欠いています。
This team lacks unity.

統一する to unify

とうおう 東欧 *Eastern Europe* [↔ 西欧]

とうがらし 唐辛子 *red pepper, cayenne pepper*

どうかん 同感 *agreement, shared opinion, shared feeling*

とうき 陶器 *china, earthenware, pottery* [→ 瀬戸物, 焼き物]

とうき 冬季 *wintertime, the winter season* [↔ 夏季]

冬季オリンピック the Winter Olympics

とうぎ 討議 *discussion*

討議する to discuss; to have a discussion

先生方は校則について長い間討議した。
The teachers discussed the school rules for a long time.

この問題を校長先生と討議しました。
We discussed this problem with the principal.

どうき 動機 *motive, motivation*

ジョギングを始めた動機は何ですか。
What was your motivation to start jogging?

とうぎゅう 闘牛 *bullfight; bullfighting*

闘牛士 bullfighter

どうきゅう 同級 *the same grade in school*

弘美ちゃんと洋子ちゃんは同級です。
Hiromi and Yoko are in the same grade.

同級生 student in the same grade

どうきょ 同居 *living together (in the same household)*

同居する to live together

どうぐ 道具 *tool, utensil*

道具箱 toolbox

台所道具 kitchen utensils

大工道具 carpenter's tools

どうくつ 洞窟 *cave* [→ 洞穴]

とうげ 峠 *mountain pass*

とうけい 統計 *statistics*

統計によると according to statistics

とうこう 登校 *going to school, attending school*

登校する to go to school, to attend school

毎日自転車で登校します。
I go to school by bicycle every day.

登校拒否 refusal to attend school

とうごう 統合 *synthesis, unification, unity* [→ 統一]

統合する to synthesize, to unify, to combine

どうさ 動作 *(bodily) movement, (bodily) action*

その少年は動作が早いです。
That boy's movements are fast.

とうざい 東西 *east and west* [↔ 南北]

古今東西 all times and places

とうし 凍死 *death from freezing*

凍死する to freeze to death

とうし 闘志 *fight, fighting spirit*

あの相撲取りは闘志を失ったようです。
It seems as if that sumo wrestler has lost his fighting spirit.

闘志満々の full of fighting spirit

とうし 投資 *investment*

投資する to invest

とうじ 冬至 *winter solstice* [↔ 夏至]

とうじ 当時 *the time in question, that time, then, those days*

当時の総理大臣は福田さんでした。
The Prime Minister at that time was Mr. Fukuda.

どうし 動詞 *verb*

どうじ 同時 〜の *simultaneous, concurrent*

その二人は同時に出発しました。
Those two started out simultaneously.

同時通訳 simultaneous interpretation

とうじつ 当日 *the day in question, that day*

当日はすばらしい天気でした。
It was wonderful weather that day.

どうして *1. why* [→ なぜ]

どうしてそんなに疲れているの？
Why are you so tired?

どうして英語を勉強しているんですか。
Why are you studying English?

2. how, in what way [→ どう]

この機械はどうして動かすんですか。
How does one operate this machine?

どうしても *no matter what (one does)*

どうしてもアメリカに行きます。
I will go to the United States no matter what.

このドアはどうしても開かないよ。
This door won't open no matter what!

どうしてもあの人の名前が思い出せない。
No matter what I do, I can't remember that person's name.

とうしゅ 投手 *(baseball) pitcher* [→ ピッチャー]

とうしょ 投書 *letter to the editor; written suggestion to an institution*

投書する to send a letter to the editor; to send in a suggestion

父はよく新聞に投書します。
My father often sends letters to the newspaper editor.

投書箱 suggestion box

投書欄 readers' column, letters-to-the-editor column

とうじょう 搭乗 *boarding, getting on/in (a vehicle, especially an airplane)*

搭乗する to get (on/in a vehicle)

搭乗券 boarding pass

とうじょう 登場 *1. appearance (as a character in a play, novel, etc.)*

登場する to appear, to make one's appearance

あの俳優はよくテレビに登場します。
That actor often appears on TV.

2. appearance (of a new public figure or product)

登場する to appear

登場人物 character

どうじょう 同情 *sympathy, compassion*

Aの同情を得る〔失う〕to gain〔lose〕A's sympathy

同情する to feel sympathy, to feel compassion

被害者に同情します。
I feel sympathy for the victim.

どうせ *in any case, anyway*

(Used to express the feeling that something unpleasant is unavoidable.)

どうせあの人は失敗するでしょう。
In any case, that person will probably fail.

どうせやるなら、最善を尽くしましょう。
If we're going to do it anyway, let's do our best.

どうせい 同棲 *living together, cohabitation (especially by an unmarried couple)*

同せいする to live together

どうせい 同性 *the same sex*

同性愛 homosexuality

とうせん 当選 *1. being elected*

当選する to be elected

山田さんが生徒会長に当選しました。
Ms. Yamada was elected student council president.

2. winning a prize

当選する to win a prize

当選番号 winning number

当選者 winning candidate; prize winner

とうぜん 当然 *as a matter of course, naturally, not surprisingly*

当然の natural, obvious, unsurprising [→ 当たり前の]

課長は計算ミスを見つけ、当然怒った。
The section chief found a miscalculation, and naturally he got angry.

国民がそう考えるのは当然です。
It's natural for the people to think so.

どうぞ *please, if you please*

(Used both in requests and in offers. In offers, phrases such as **here you are** or **go ahead** are often used as natural English translations.)

どうぞお入りください。
Please come in.

どうぞこちらへ。
This way, please.

「塩を取ってください」「はい、どうぞ」
"Please pass me the salt." "Here you are."

とうそう 闘争 *struggle, conflict*

闘争する to struggle, to fight [→ 戦う]

どうぞう 銅像 *bronze statue*

どうそうかい 同窓会 *1. alumni association*

2. alumni meeting

とうだい 灯台 *lighthouse*

どうたい 胴体 *torso, trunk* [→ 胴]

飛行機の胴体 airplane fuselage

とうちゃく 到着 *arrival* [↔ 出発]

到着する to arrive

電車は時間どおりに博多駅に到着した。
The train arrived at Hakata Station on time.

1時間で神戸に到着しました。
We arrived in Kobe in an hour.

到着ホーム arrival platform

到着時刻 arrival time

とうてい 到底 *(not) possibly, absolutely*
(Always occurs in combination with a negative predicate or a predicate with a negative meaning.)

山根さんには到底そんなことはできない。
Mr. Yamane cannot possibly do such a thing.

それは到底無理だと思います。
I think that's absolutely impossible.

どうてき 動的 ～な *dynamic* [↔ 静的な]

どうてん 同点 *tie score*

同点になる to become tied

とうとう 到頭 [[→ 遂に]] *1. at last, finally*

2. in the end, after all

どうとく 道徳 *morals, morality*

道徳的な moral

公衆道徳 public morality

交通道徳 standards of behavior for drivers

とうなん 東南 *the southeast* [→ 南東]

東南アジア Southeast Asia

とうなん 盗難 *robbery*

盗難品 stolen item

どうにゅう 導入 *introduction (of one thing into another)*

導入する to introduce

とうにょうびょう 糖尿病 *diabetes*

とうばん 当番 *1. one's turn on duty*

2. person whose turn on duty it is

きょうはだれが当番ですか。
Who is on duty today?

掃除当番 cleaning duty

とうひょう 投票 *voting, casting a vote*

投票で委員長を選びましょう。
Let's choose the committee chairperson by voting.

その計画に賛成の投票をします。
I'm going to vote for that plan. (Literally: I will cast a vote of agreement for that plan.)

投票する to vote

私も伊藤さんに投票しました。
I also voted for Mr. Ito.

投票日 election day

投票所 polling place

投票用紙 ballot

とうふ 豆腐 *tofu, bean curd*

豆腐を1丁買ってきました。
I went and bought one block of tofu.

とうぶ 東部 *eastern part* [↔ 西部]

どうふう 同封 ～の *enclosed in the same envelope*

同封する to enclose in the same envelope

最近の写真を同封します。
I enclose a recent photograph.

どうぶつ 動物 *animal*

鳥も魚も人間も動物です。
Birds, fish, and human beings are all animals.

動物園 zoo

動物学 zoology
動物学者 zoologist
動物界 the animal kingdom, the animal world

とうぶん 糖分 *sugar content*

とうぶん 当分 *for a while; for the present, for the time being*

どうほう 同胞 *fellow countryman, compatriot*

とうほく 東北 *the northeast* [→ 北東]

とうほくちほう 東北地方 *the Tohoku region (of Japan) (Aomori, Akita, Iwate, Yamagata, Miyagi, and Fukushima Prefectures)*

どうみゃく 動脈 *artery (blood vessel)* [↔ 静脈]

とうみん 冬眠 *hibernation*

冬眠に入る to go into hibernation
冬眠から覚めるto come out of hibernation

とうめい 透明 ～な *transparent, clear*

どうめい 同盟 *alliance, union, league*

同盟する to ally, to form an alliance
同盟国 allied country

どうも *1. very, quite* [→ とても]

どうもありがとう。
Thank you very much.
どうもすみません。
I'm very sorry.

2. somehow, for some reason [→ 何だか]

どうも猫が嫌いです。
I don't like cats for some reason.

とうもろこし *(US) corn, (UK) maize*

とうもろこしを３本食べました。
I ate three ears of corn.

どうやら *1. perhaps (in combination with a word indicating likelihood, such as* らしい *1. or a word ending in* ーそう*.)*

どうやら雪が降りそうですね。
It looks as if perhaps it's going to snow, doesn't it?

2. somehow or other, barely, with difficulty

どうやら学校に間に合いました。
I was barely in time for school.

とうゆ 灯油 *kersosene; lamp oil*

とうよう 東洋 *the East, the Orient* [↔ 西洋]

東洋美術 Oriental art
東洋文明 Oriental civilization
東洋人 an Oriental

どうよう 動揺 *1. trembling, swaying, jolting*

動揺するto tremble, to sway, to jolt

2. agitation, unrest, disturbance

動揺する to become agitated, to become disturbed

その知らせにみんなが動揺しました。
Everyone became agitated at that news.

どうよう 同様 ～の *same, similar* [→ 同じ]

新品同様の as good as new, just like new

どうり 道理 *reason, logic, rationality (of something)*

道理にかなう to become reasonable, to become rational

その要求は道理にかなっています。
That request is reasonable.

どうりょう 同僚 *colleague, fellow worker*

とうるい 盗塁 *stealing a base (in baseball)*

盗塁する to advance by stealing a base

ランナーは二塁に盗塁しました。
The runner advanced to second base by stealing.

盗塁王 base-stealing champion

どうろ 道路 *road, street* [→ 通り]

道路地図 road map
道路標識 road sign
道路工事 road repair; road construction

高速道路 superhighway, (US) expressway, (UK) motorway
有料道路 toll road

とうろう 灯籠 *Japanese garden lantern*

とうろく 登録 *registration*
登録する register (transitive)
登録商標 registered trademark

とうろん 討論 *discussion, debate*
討論する to discuss, to debate about
討論会 debate contest

どうわ 童話 *fairy tale* [→ おとぎ話]

とお 十 *ten (See Appendix 2.)*

とおい 遠い *far, distant* [↔ 近い]
小学校はここから遠いですか。
Is the elementary school far from here?
洋子ちゃんは私の遠い親せきです。
Yoko is my distant relative.
耳が遠い to be hard of hearing
遠い昔 the distant past

とおか 十日 *(see Appendix 2) 1. ten days*
2. the tenth (day of a month)

とおく 遠く *an area far away, the distance*
富士山が遠くに見えます。
Mt. Fuji is visible in the distance.

とおざかる 遠ざかる *1. to move away, to recede into the distance*
飛行機はだんだん遠ざかって行きました。
The airplane gradually receded into the distance.
2. to stay away, to distance oneself
それ以後小泉さんから遠ざかっています。
Since then I've been staying away from Mr. Koizumi.

とおざける 遠ざける [[↔ 近付ける]] *1. to keep away, to prevent from approaching*
2. to keep at arm's length, to refrain from associating with
今川さんは杉江さんを遠ざけています。
Ms. Imagawa is keeping Mr. Sugie at arm's length.

－とおし －通し ～の *continually (Added to verb bases.)*
夜通し運転してスキー場に着きました。
I drove all through the night and arrived at the ski resort.

とおす 通す *1. to make pass by, to make pass through; to let pass by, to let pass through*
ちょっと通してください。
Please let me pass.
針に糸を通す to thread a needle
法案を通す to pass a bill
2. to show in, to usher in
お客さんを部屋に通しました。
I showed the guest into the room.

トースター *toaster*

トースト *toast*

ドーナツ *doughnut*

トーナメント *tournament*

とおまわし 遠回し ～な／の *indirect, roundabout*
遠回しに言う to say in a roundabout way

とおまわり 遠回り *making a detour, taking the long way*
遠回りする to make a detour, to take the long way
その道は通行止めだったので、遠回りしなければなりませんでした。
The road was blocked, so we had to make a detour.

ドーム *dome*

とおり 通り [[→ 往来]] *1. street, road* [→道路]
通りで友人に会いました。
I met a friend on the street.
この教室は通りに面しています。
This classroom faces the street.
通りを横切る to cross the street

2. coming and going, traffic in both directions

この交差点は車の通りが多いです。

This intersection has a lot of automobile traffic.

とおり 通り *(～に) as, like, in accordance (modifying a predicate)*

弟はいつものとおり10時に寝ました。

My younger brother went to bed at 10:00 as usual.

医者の言うとおりにしなさい。

Do as the doctor says.

そのとおりです。

It's as you say.

とおりの as, like (modifying a noun)

－とおり －通り *～の according to, in keeping with (Added to noun bases.)*

バスは時間どおりに着きました。

The bus arrived on time.

計画どおりの according-to-plan

文字どおりの literal

とおりすぎる 通り過ぎる *to go past, to pass beyond*

うっかりして神田駅を通り過ぎました。

I carelessly went past Kanda Station.

とおりぬける 通り抜ける *to pass through and emerge from*

遭難者は森を通り抜けました。

The accident victims passed through the woods.

とおる 通る *1. to pass by, to pass through*

きのうこの店の前を通りました。

I passed by this store yesterday.

法案が通る a bill passes

声が通る a voice carries

2. to pass (on a test, etc.) [→ 合格する]

Aに通る to pass A

入学試験に通りましたか。

Did you pass the entrance examination?

3. to pass, to be accepted (as adequate)

そんな言い訳は通らないでしょう。

That kind of excuse will probably not be accepted.

4. to be known (as); to go (by a name)

Aで通る to be known as A; to go by A

犯人はジミーという名前で通っていた。

The criminal went by the name of Jimmy.

とかい 都会 *city* [→ 都市]

娘は都会に住んでいます。

My daughter lives in a city.

都会化 urbanization

都会生活 city life

とかげ *lizard*

とかす 溶かす *1. to melt (transitive)*

高熱は鉄を溶かします。

High heat melts iron.

2. to dissolve (transitive)

薬を水に溶かして飲みました。

I dissolved the medicine in water and drank it.

とがった 尖った *pointed, sharp*

とき 時 *1. (amount of) time, time span* [→ 時間2.]

時がたつにつれて、その記憶も薄れた。

As time passes, that memory also faded.

ゆうべは楽しい時を過ごしました。

I had a pleasant time last night.

時は金なり。(proverb)

Time is money.

2. time, occasion; (time) when

そのとき私は勉強中でした。

At that time I was studying.

健さんは５歳のときに神戸に来ました。

Ken came to Kobe when he was five years old.

気分が悪いときは、病院に行きなさい。

When you feel sick, go to the hospital.

あした出かけるときに電話してください。

Please telephone me when you go out tomorrow.

時には sometimes, occasionally [→ 時々]

とき 鴇 *Japanese crested ibis*

ときどき 時々 *sometimes, now and then*

時々黒崎さんに電話します。
I sometimes telephone Ms. Kurosaki.

海は時々荒れます。
The sea sometimes gets rough.

時々その人に会います。
I sometimes see that person.

どきどき 〜する *to throb with a fast heart-beat*

ドキュメンタリー *a documentary*

どきょう 度胸 *courage, nerve* [→ 勇気]

とく 得 *profit, gain, benefit* [↔ 損]

これを勉強しても得になりません。
Even if you study this, it won't be any benefit.

得をする to profit, to benefit

得する [☞ 得をする (above)]

とく 解く *1. to solve, to resolve, to clear up* [→ 解決する]

誤解を解く to clear up a misunderstanding

2. to solve (a puzzle, arithmetic problem, etc.)

淳子ちゃんは黒板の問題を全部解いたよ。
Atsuko solved all the problems on the blackboard!

3. to untie, to unfasten, to undo [→ 解く]

4. to cancel, to remove

禁止を解く to remove a prohibition

とぐ 研ぐ *to whet, to hone, to sharpen by grinding*

どく 毒 *a poison*

たばこの吸いすぎは体に毒だよ。
Smoking too much is bad for your health!

毒ガス poison gas

毒蛇 poisonous snake

毒茸 poisonous mushroom

どく *to get out of the way (intransitive)*

とくい 得意 *1. 〜の／な good at (This noun modifier is used to describe both the people who are skillful and the things they are skillful at.)* [→ 上手な]

大石さんは英語が得意です。
Ms. Oishi is good at English.

2. 〜の proud, triumphant, elated

あの人を褒めると、得意になるよ。
When you praise that person, she becomes elated!

3. customer who buys regularly

とくぎ 特技 *one's special ability*

どくさい 独裁 *dictatorship, despotism, autocracy*

独裁する to rule dictatorially

独裁政治 dictatorial government

どくじ 独自 〜の *original, one's own*

独自の発明 original invention

どくしゃ 読者 *reader*

読者欄 readers' column

とくしゅ 特殊 〜な *special, particular* [→ 特別の]

とくしゅう 特集 *1. special edition focusing on a particular topic*

8月号はオリンピックの特集です。
The August issue is a special edition on the Olympics.

2. compiling a special edition focusing on a particular topic

特集する to compile a special edition

特集号 special issue

特集記事 feature article

どくしょ 読書 *reading a book, reading books*

読書する to read a book, to read books

娘は読書が好きです。
My daughter likes reading books.

読書室 reading room

どくしょう 独唱 *vocal solo*

独唱する to sing a solo

独唱会 solo recital

とくしょく 特色 *distinctive characteristic, special feature* [→ 特徴]

どくしん 独身 ～の *unmarried, single*

兄はまだ独身です。

My older brother is still single.

どくせん 独占 *exclusive possession; monopoly*

独占する to get for oneself alone; to monopolize

姉は２階を独占しているよ。

My older sister has the second floor all to herself!

どくそう 独奏 *instrumental solo*

独奏する to play a solo

独奏会 solo recital

どくそう 独創 *originality, inventiveness*

独創的な original, creative, inventive

とくだね 特種 *exclusive news story, scoop*

とくちょう 特長 *strong point, merit* [→ 長所]

とくちょう 特徴 *distinctive characteristic, special feature* [→ 特色]

鈍い動作はパンダの特徴の一つです。

Clumsy movement is one of the panda's distinctive characteristics.

とくてん 得点 *scored point; score*

得点する to score, to score a point

得点掲示板 scoreboard

どくとく 独特 ～の *unique, special*

あの哲学者には独特の考え方があります。

That philosopher has a unique way of thinking.

－独特の unique to, peculiar to (Added to noun bases.)

日本独特の unique to Japan

とくに 特に *especially, particularly*

きょうは特に暑いね。

It's especially hot today, isn't it?

兄は音楽、特にジャズが大好きです。

My older brother loves music, particularly jazz.

とくばい 特売 *selling at a bargain; bargain sale*

特売で買う to buy on sale

特売品 bargain, item on sale

とくはいん 特派員 *correspondent (for a newspaper, etc.)*

とくべつ 特別 ～の／な *special, particular*

特別の理由はありませんでした。

There was no special reason.

特別に especially, particularly

今日は特別にあつらえた服を着ます。

Today I will wear specially-ordered clothes.

特別番組 special program

特別号 special issue

特別急行 a special express

特別席 special seat

とくめい 匿名 ～の *anonymous*

匿名の手紙 anonymous letter

とくゆう 特有 ～の *unique, special* [→ 独特の]

－特有の unique to, peculiar to (Added to noun bases.)

日本特有の unique to Japan

どくりつ 独立 *independence*

アメリカは1776年に独立を宣言しました。

The United States declared its independence in 1776.

独立の independent

独立する to become independent

独立記念日 Independence Day
独立国 independent country
独立心 independent spirit

とげ 棘 *thorn; splinter*

Aにとげが刺さる a thorn/splinter gets stuck in A
指にとげが刺さったよ。
I got a splinter in my finger! (Literally: A splinter got stuck in my finger.)

とげを抜く to remove a thorn/splinter

とけい 時計 *clock; watch*

時計が3時を打ちました。
The clock struck three.

その時計では今何時ですか。
What time is it now by that clock?

この時計は合っていますか。
Is this clock correct?

時計が進む a clock/watch becomes fast, a watch/clock gains time
私の時計は2分進んでいます。
My watch is two minutes fast.
時計が遅れる a clock/watch becomes slow, a watch/clock loses time

この時計は1日に3秒遅れます。
This clock loses three seconds a day.
時計の長針〔短針〕 minute hand 〔hour hand〕 of a clock
時計台 clock tower
時計店 watch store, clock store
デジタル時計 digital watch, digital clock
鳩時計 cuckoo clock
目覚まし時計 alarm clock

とけこむ 溶け込む *to blend (into), to mix (with) (intransitive)*

とける 溶ける *1. to melt (intransitive)*

雪だるまは少しずつ溶けています。
The snowman is melting little by little.

2. to dissolve (intransitive)

その薬は水に溶けるでしょう？
That medicine dissolves in water, right?

とげる 遂げる *to achieve, to attain, to accomplish*

望みを遂げる to attain one's desire

どける *to remove, to get out of the way*

その箱をテーブルからどけてください。
Please remove that box from the table.

とこ 床 *bed*

床につく to go to bed; to become confined to bed
父は病気で1週間床についています。
My father has been confined to bed for a week because of illness.

どこ *what place, where*

私のバッグはどこですか。
Where is my bag?
佐々木さんはどこに住んでいますか。
Where does Ms. Sasaki live?

どこへ行きましょうか。
Where shall we go?
どこか somewhere
週末にどこかに行きますか。
Will you go somewhere on the weekend?

とこのま 床の間 *alcove (in a traditional Japanese-style room)*

とこや 床屋 *1. barber*

2. barbershop

ところ 所 *1. place, location* [→ 場所]

ここは漱石が生まれた所です。
This is the place where Soseki was born.
安藤さんの住んでいる所がわかりますか。
Do you know where Mr. Ando lives?
洋子さんはドアの所にいます。
Yoko is by the door. (Literally: Yoko is at the place of the door.)

2. point in time

(In this meaning ところ follows a verb. When the action is referred to by the verb is already completed, ところ is typically translated as **having just**. When the action has not yet begun, ところ is typically translated as **being about to**. When the action is in progress, ところ is typically translated as **being in the middle of**.)

恵に手紙を書こうとしているところです。
I'm about to write a letter to Megumi.

父はその仕事をちょうど終えたところだ。
My father has just finished that job.

きょうの復習をしているところです。
I'm in the middle of reviewing today's lesson.

どころか *far from, quite the opposite of, to say nothing of*

(This expression generally follows an informal-style predicate in the nonpast tense, but the word preceding どころか cannot be the copula form だ. When どころか is added to a clause that would end with だ, the だ does not appear.)

春江さんは笑うどころか怒ってしまった。
Far from laughing, Harue got angry.

パソコンどころかワープロも買えないよ。
I cannot even buy a word processor, to say nothing of a computer!

それは有益どころか害になるよ。
Far from beneficial, that'll be harmful!

ところで *1. well, now (indicating a shift in what is being talked about)* [→ さて]

ところで、そろそろ出かけましょうか。
Well, shall we start out soon?

2. by the way

ところで、あしたの午後は忙しいですか。
By the way, are you busy tomorrow afternoon?

ところどころ 所々 *here and there, various places* [→ あちこち]

とざん 登山 *mountain climbing*

父は登山が好きです。
My father likes mountain climbing.

登山する to climb a mountain

登山家 mountaineer, alpinist

とし 年 *1. year*

よいお年をお迎えください。
Have a happy New Year! (Literally: Please greet a good year.)

年の始め〔暮れ〕 beginning〔end〕of the year

2. age (of a person or animal) [→ 年齢]

お年はいくつですか。
How old are you?

お母さんは年の割に若く見えますね。
Your mother looks young for her age, doesn't she?

春子さんと京子さんの年は同じ25歳です。
Haruko and Kyoko are the same age of 25 years.

年を取る to get older

年取った old, elderly [↔ 若い]

とし 都市 *city* [→ 都会]

パリはフランスでいちばん大きな都市だ。
Paris is the largest city in France.

都市ガス city gas

都市計画 city planning

工業都市 industrial city

どじ【COL.】*goof, blunder* [→ へま]

どじを踏む to blunder, to make a goof

どじな goof-prone, blundering

としうえ 年上 ～の *older (when describing a person or animal)* [↔ 年下の]

姉は兄より5歳年上です。
My older sister is five years older than my older brother.

秀子と幸子とどちらが年上ですか。
Who is older, Hideko or Sachiko?

3人のうちで弘がいちばん年上です。
Hiroshi is the oldest of the three.

とじこめる 閉じ込める *to shut up, to confine (The direct object must be a person or animal.)*

テロリストは人質を小屋に閉じ込めた。
The terrorist shut the hostage up in a hut.

とじこもる 閉じ籠る *to shut oneself up, to confine oneself*

息子は部屋に閉じこもりました。
My son shut himself up in his room.
かぜで三日間家に閉じこもっていました。
I stayed in the house for three days because of a cold.

としごろ 年ごろ *1. (approximate) age (of a person or animal)*
その二人の少女はほぼ同じ年ごろです。
Those two girls are about the same age.
2. marriageable age (of a woman)
田中さんには年ごろの娘さんがいます。
Mr. Tanaka has a daughter of marriageable age.

としした 年下 ～の *younger* [↔ 年上の]
弘子さんは桂子さんより３歳年下です。
Hiroko is three years younger than Keiko.

として *as, in the capacity of; for, with respect to being*
ルノワールは画家として有名です。
Renoir is famous as a painter.
風間さんはガイドとして同行しました。
Ms. Kazama went along as a guide.
私としては何も言うことはありません。
As for me, I have nothing to say.

とじまり 戸締まり *closing and locking the doors*
戸締まりする to close and lock the doors, to lock up
出かける前に戸締まりしなさい。
Lock up before you go out.

どしゃぶり 土砂降り *heavy rain, downpour*

としょ 図書 *books*
図書館 library ((building))
図書館員 librarian
図書目録 catalog of books
図書室 reading room, library ((room))

としより 年寄り *elderly person*
年寄りに親切にしなさい。
Be kind to elderly people.

とじる 閉じる *to close, to shut (transitive or intransitive)* [↔ 開く1.]
さあ、本を閉じましょう。
All right, let's close our books.
目を閉じる to close one's eyes
門が閉じる a gate closes

とじる 綴じる *to bind together (The direct object must be sheets of paper, etc., or something containing such sheets.)*
その新聞をとじておいてください。
Please bind those newspapers together.
本をとじる to bind a book

トス *1. toss, light throw*
トスする to toss
2. coin toss, coin flip

どせい 土星 *(the planet) Saturn*

とそう 塗装 *coating with paint*
塗装する to paint, to coat with paint

どそう 土葬 *burial, interment (of a dead body)* [↔ 火葬]
土葬する to bury, to inter

どそく 土足 *having one's shoes on*
土足で with one's shoes on
校舎に土足で入ってはいけないよ。
You mustn't enter the school building with your shoes on!
「土足厳禁」(on a sign)
Remove your shoes (Literally: Shoes are prohibited.)

どだい 土台 *foundation, base* [→ 基礎]

とだな 戸棚 *cupboard*

とたん 途端 ～に *just as, as soon as (following a past-tense verb)*
エレベーターに乗ったとたんに停電した。
Just as I got on the elevator, there was a power failure.

トタン *galvanized sheet iron*
トタン屋根 tin roof

とち 土地 *1. land, ground, lot; soil* [→ 土]
伯父は神戸に土地を買うつもりです。
My uncle intends to buy land in Kobe.
2. region, locality [→ 地方1.]
土地付きの including land, with a lot

とちゅう 途中 *the way between departure point and destination; the time between start and finish*
うちへ帰る途中です。
I'm on my way home.
途中で on the way; in the middle
学校へ行く途中で友達に出会いました。
On the way to school, I ran into a friend.
勉強を途中でやめてはいけないよ。
You mustn't give up studying in the middle!

どちら【FORMAL】*1. which one (Used when there are only two alternatives.)* [↔ どれ]
明子さんのラケットはどちらですか。
Which one is Akiko's racket?
太陽と地球とどちらが大きいですか。
Which is larger, the sun or the earth?
牛肉と豚肉のどちらが好きですか。
Which do you like better, beef or pork?
2. which way; where
どちらへお出かけですか？
Where are you going?
どちらか one or the other
あの二人のどちらかがこの仕事をあしたまでに終えなければなりません。
One or the other of those two has to finish this work by tomorrow.
どちらかがまちがっています。
One or the other is wrong.
どちらも both (in combination with an affirmative predicate); neither one (in combination with a negative predicate)
私たちはどちらも音楽に興味があります。
Both of us have an interest in music.
父は英語もフランス語もどちらもできる。
Father can speak both English and French.
その学生たちはどちらも知らなかったよ。
I didn't know either one of those students!
どちら様【HON. for 誰】who (as a question word) [→ どなた]

とっか 特価 *special price*
特価品 bargain item

とっきゅう 特急 *a limited express, a special express*

とっきょ 特許 *patent*

ドッキング *docking (of spacecraft)*
ドッキングする to dock

とっくに【COL.】*long ago, long since*

とっくり 徳利 *ceramic bottle for heating and pouring sake*

とっしん 突進 *rush, dash, charge*
突進する to rush, to dash, to charge
選手たちはゴールに向かって突進した。
The players charged toward the goal.

とつぜん 突然 *suddenly*
バスは突然止まりました。
The bus stopped suddenly.
突然天気が変わったよ。
Suddenly the weather changed!
突然の sudden

どっち【COL. for どちら】

どっちみち【COL.】*either way, in any case, anyway*
どっちみち堀田さんに会うつもりだった。
I was planning to see Mr. Horita anyway.

とって 取っ手 *handle, knob*

とって [☞ にとって]

とっておく 取っておく [☞ 取る2.]

とっても【COL. for とても】

とっぱ 突破 ～する *1. to break through; to surmount, to overcome*
難関を突破する to overcome a difficulty

2. to exceed, to go over [→ 上回る]
この国の人口は１億人を突破しました。
The population of this country exceeded one hundred million.

トップ *top, head, lead*
知恵美ちゃんはいつもクラスのトップだ。
Chiemi is always top of the class.

とつレンズ 凸レンズ *convex lens* [↔ 凹レンズ]

どて 土手 *earth embankment, earth levee*

とても *1. very* [→ 非常に]
2. (not) possibly (in combination with a negative predicate)
そんなことはとてもできないよ。
I can't possibly do such a thing!

とどく 届く *1. to be delivered, to arrive*
私の手紙は届きましたか。
Did my letter arrive?
2. to reach, to extend
手が届く one's hand reaches, one is able to reach
子供はこのベルに手が届かないでしょう。
A child probably cannot reach this bell.

とどけ 届け *notification, notice, report*
欠席届け notification of absence

とどける 届ける *1. to send, to have delivered* [→ 送る1.]
この島には食料を船で届けます。
They send food to this island by boat.
2. to deliver, to take
太郎ちゃんはその財布を交番に届けたよ。
Taro took that wallet to the police box!
3. to report, to give notice of
もう郵便局に住所の変更を届けましたか。
Have you already notified the post office of your change of address?

ととのえる 整える, 調える *1. to prepare, to ready* [→ 用意する]*; to supply oneself with, to provide oneself with*
夕食を整えるのは時間がかかります。
Preparing supper takes time.
2. to put in order, to adjust
Aの調子を整える to tune A
体調を整える to get oneself in good physical condition

となえる 唱える *1. to advocate; to advance, to voice*
2. to recite, to chant

どなた 【HON. for 誰】 *who (as a question word)*
どなたですか。
Who is it?

となり 隣 *the area directly beside; the area next door*
隣の家はとても古いです。
The house next door is very old.
スーツケースは隣の部屋にあるよ。
The suitcase is in the next room!
本屋は花屋の隣にあります。
The bookstore is next to the flower shop.
隣に座っていいですか。
May I sit next to you?
小池さんは岸さんの隣に住んでいます。
Mr. Koike lives next door to Mr. Kishi.
隣近所 the neighborhood; the neighbors

どなる 怒鳴る *to shout at, to yell at*
先生は怒って、生徒たちをどなりました。
The teacher got angry and shouted at the students.

とにかく *anyway, anyhow, in any case*
とにかくもう一度やってみましょう。
Anyway, let's try doing it one more time.

どの *which (as a noun-modifying question word)*
どの本が先生のですか。
Which book is the teacher's?
どのスポーツがいちばん好きですか。
Which sport do you like best?
どの席に座ってもいいですよ。
Sit in whichever seat you like!

どのA…も every A (in combination with an affirmative predicate); (not) any A (in combination with a negative predicate)

どの候補者もそんなことをしました。
Every candidate did that kind of thing.

どの生徒もその問題を解けなかった。
No student could solve that problem.

どの質問にもすぐには答えられません。
I can not answer any of the questions right away.

どのくらい [☞ どのぐらい (below)]

どのぐらい about how many, about how much, about to what extent

かごの中に栗はどのぐらいありますか。
About how many chestnuts are there in the basket?

駅までバスでどのぐらいかかりますか。
About how long does it take to go to the station by bus?

どのように how, in what way [→ どう]

とのさま 殿様 *1. Japanese feudal lord*

2. liege lord; nobleman

3. generous and unworldly person of leisure

とばす 飛ばす *1. to let fly, to make fly, to fly; to throw* [→ 投げる]*; to send flying*

子供たちが紙飛行機を飛ばしています。
Children are flying paper planes.

強い風が看板を飛ばしました。
The strong wind sent the signboard flying.

2. to make go very fast

車を飛ばす to drive a car very fast

3. to skip, to pass over

できない問題を飛ばすことにしました。
I decided to skip the problems I couldn't do.

とび 鳶 *kite ((bird))*

とびあがる 跳び上がる *to jump up*

晃は跳び上がって、ボールを受けました。
Akira jumped up and caught the ball.

とびうお 飛び魚 *flying fish*

とびおきる 飛び起きる *to jump out of bed*

とびおりる 飛び降りる *to jump down*

泥棒は窓から飛び降りました。
The burglar jumped down from the window.

とびこむ 飛び込む *to jump (into), to dive (into)*

小泉さんはプールに飛び込みました。
Ms. Koizumi dived into the pool.

犯人は橋から川に飛び込みました。
The criminal jumped from the bridge into the river.

とびだす 飛び出す *to rush out, to run out, to jump out*

ベルが鳴ると、私は教室から飛び出した。
When the bell rang, I ran out of the classroom.

とびつく 飛び付く *to jump (at/on) (in an attempt to catch)*

猫はすずめに飛びつきました。
The cat jumped on the sparrow.

トピック *topic, subject* [→ 話題]

とびのる 飛び乗る *to jump, to jump (into/onto a vehicle)*

広川君は自転車に飛び乗って逃げたよ。
Hirokawa jumped on his bicycle and escaped!

とびばこ 跳び箱 *vaulting horse*

とび箱を跳ぶ to vault over a vaulting horse

とびら 扉 *door* [→ 戸]

とぶ 飛ぶ *to fly (intransitive)*

末永さんはあしたハワイに飛びます。
Mr. Suenaga will fly to Hawaii tomorrow.

この鳥はシベリアから飛んできました。
This bird flew from Siberia.

とぶ 跳ぶ *to jump, to leap*

浩は走り幅跳びで6メートル以上跳んだ。
Hiroshi jumped over six meters in the long jump.

とほ 徒歩 〜で *on foot* [→ 歩いて(s.v. 歩く)]

そこまで徒歩で15分かかります。
It takes fifteen minutes to there on foot.

徒歩旅行 walking tour, hike

とほう 途方 *1.* 〜に暮れる *to be left at a loss, to become perplexed*

森永さんは失業して途方に暮れています。
Mr. Morinaga became unemployed and is at a loss.

2. 〜もない *absurd, ludicrous, outrageous* [→ とんでもない]

米田さんは途方もない値段で家を買った。
Mr. Yoneda bought a house at an outrageous price.

とぼける 【COL.】 *to pretend ignorance*

とぼしい 乏しい *scanty, meager, scarce* [↔ 豊かな1.]

この国は天然資源が乏しい。
This country's natural resources are meager.

AがBに乏しい A is lacking in B, A has meager B

田口さんは医者としての経験に乏しい。
Mr. Taguchi is lacking in experience as a doctor.

トマト *tomato*

とまる 止まる *1. to stop (moving), to halt (intransitive)*

そのパトカーは銀行の前で急に止まった。
That patrol car stopped suddenly in front of the bank.

この時計は止まっていますね。
This watch has stopped, hasn't it?

2. to stop, to cease (intransitive)

患者の脈が止りました。
The patient's pulse stopped.

3. to alight, to perch

電線に鳥が止っています。
A bird is perched on the power line.

とまる 泊まる *to lodge, to stay (over)*

一行はパリのホテルに泊まっています。
The party is staying at a hotel in Paris.

あしたは親せきの家に泊まります。
Tomorrow I'm going to stay at a relative's house.

とみ 富 *riches*

とむ 富む *to become rich, to come to abound*

その国は天然資源に富んでいます。
That country is rich in natural resources.

とめる 止める *1. to stop (the motion of), to halt (transitive); to stop the flow of, to turn off*

父は学校の前に車を止めました。
My father stopped the car in front of the school.

ガスを止めるのを忘れないでください。
Please don't forget to turn off the gas.

2. to stop, to bring to an end (intransitive)

けんかを止める to break up a fight

とめる 泊める *to provide lodging for, to let stay over, to put up*

今夜だけ泊めてくださいね。
Please let me stay over just tonight, OK?

とめる 留める *to affix, to fasten; to fasten together; to fix in place*

息子は歌手の写真を壁に留めました。
My son stuck a singer's photo to the wall.

とも 友 *friend* [→ 友達]

—とも *both, all (Added to bases denoting more than one entity.)*

私たちは二人とも英語が話せます。
Both of us can speak English.

弟はドーナツを5個とも食べたよ。
My younger brother ate all five doughnuts!

ともかく *anyway, anyhow, in any case* [→ とにかく]

ともだち 友達 *friend*
(Unless otherwise specified, this word is ordinarily understood to mean the speak-

er's friend, i.e., my friend.)
こちらは友達の洋子さんです。
This is my friend Yoko.
岡さんは母の昔からの友達です。
Ms. Oka is a friend of my mother's from long ago.
私たちはポールさんと友達になりました。
We became friends with Paul.
親しい友達 close friend

ともなう 伴う *1. to involve, to have as a concomitant*
その実験は危険を伴います。
That experiment involves danger.
2. to travel with as one's companion
(Ordinarily occurs as a gerund (-て form) followed by a verb of motion.) [→ 連れる]
友達を伴って九州に行きました。
I went to Kyushu with a friend.
3. to go along, to be concomitant, to accompany
台風には大雨が伴います。
Heavy rain accompanies a typhoon.

ともに 共に *together, collectively* [→ 一緒に]

どもる 吃る *to stutter, to stammer*

どようび 土曜日 *Saturday*

とら 虎 *tiger*

トライ *try (in rugby)*
トライする to score a try

ドライ ～な *unsentimental, pragmatic-minded* [↔ ウェットな]

ドライアイス *dry ice*

トライアングル *triangle ((musical instrument))*

ドライバー *screwdriver* [→ ねじ回し (s.v. ねじ)]

ドライバー *driver (of a car, etc.)* [→ 運転者 (s.v. 運転)]

ドライブ *drive, automobile trip*
ドライブイン drive-in

ドライヤー *drier ((machine))*

トラクター *tractor*

トラック *truck*
私の兄はトラックの運転手です。
My older brother is a truck driver.

トラック *(running) track*
トラック競技 track events

とらのまき 虎の巻 【COL.】*book explaining the content of a textbook in simplified terms*

トラブル *trouble, discord*
トラブルを起こす to cause trouble

ドラマ *a drama, a play* [→ 劇]

ドラマチック ～な *dramatic*

ドラム *drum ((musical instrument))* [→ 太鼓]
ドラムを演奏する to play the drums

トランク *trunk, suitcase*

トランシーバー *transceiver*

トランジスター *transistor*

トランプ *playing card*
トランプをする to play cards

トランペット *trumpet*

トランポリン *trampoline*

とり 鳥 *bird*
鳥が枝に止まりました。
A bird alighted on a branch.
鳥籠 bird cage
鳥肉 chicken (meat)

とりあえず *1. for the time being, for the present* [→ 当分]
2. immediately, at once [→ 早速]

とりあげる 取り上げる *1. to pick up with one's hand*
母が受話器を取り上げて、渡してくれた。
Mother picked up the receiver and handed it to me.
2. to take away, to confiscate

先生はぼくが読んでいた本を取り上げた。
The teacher took away the book I was reading.

3. to take up, to consider

問題を取り上げる to take up a problem

とりあつかい 取り扱い *handling, treatment* [→ 扱い]

「取扱注意」(on a label)
Handle With Care

とりい 鳥居 *(Shinto shrine) gateway*

とりいれ 取り入れ *harvesting, harvest*

とりいれる 取り入れる *1. to harvest, to gather in*

8月にはとうもろこしを取り入れます。
In August we harvest the corn.

2. to gather and take inside

雨が降ってきたので洗濯物を取り入れた。
Since it started raining, I took the laundry inside.

3. to adopt, to accept

この提案を取り入れましょうか。
Shall we adopt this proposal?

とりえ 取り柄 *merit, good point* [→ 長所]

トリオ *trio*

とりかえす 取り返す *to get back, to take back, to regain* [→ 取り戻す]

友達に貸したお金を取り返してください。
Get back the money you lent to your friend.

とりかえる 取り替える *to exchange, to trade* [→ 交換する]

AをBと取り替える to exchange A for B, to trade A for B

光一は自転車を新しい時計と取り替えた。
Koichi exchanged the bike for a new watch.

とりかかる 取り掛かる *to start in, to set about*

父はすぐに仕事に取りかかった。
My father started in on the work right away.

夕食を食べてから宿題に取りかかった。
After eating dinner I started in on my homework.

とりかこむ 取り囲む *to surround, to gather around*

ファンが歌手の車を取り囲みました。
The fans surrounded the singer's car.

とりくむ 取り組む *to grapple, to wrestle*

とりけす 取り消す *to cancel, to call off, to revoke*

電話で約束を取り消しました。
I canceled the appointment by telephone.

とりしらべ 取り調べ *examination, investigation, inquiry*

とりしらべる 取り調べる *to examine, to investigate, to inquire into*

とりだす 取り出す *to take out with one's hand*

学生はポケットから単語帳を取り出した。
The student took a vocabulary notebook out of his pocket.

とりつ 都立 ～の *administered by Tokyo Prefecture, Tokyo metropolitan*

都立高校 a Tokyo metropolitan high school

トリック *trick, deception*

トリック撮影 trick photography

とりのぞく 取り除く *to remove, to take away*

生徒たちはグラウンドの石を取り除いた。
The students removed the playground stones.

とりはだ 鳥肌 *goose-flesh*

鳥肌が立つ one gets goose-flesh

とりひき 取り引き *transaction, buying and selling, business*

取り引きする to transact business, to do business

ドリブル *dribbling (in sports)*

ドリブルする to dribble

とりぶん 取り分 *share, portion (that one is entitled to take)*

とりもどす 取り戻す *to get back, to take back, to regain* [→ 取り返す]

やっとそのお金を取り戻しました。
I finally got that money back.

どりょく 努力 *effort, exertion*

これからも努力が必要です。
From now on, too, effort will be necessary.

努力する to make efforts, to strive, to exert oneself

英語の力を伸ばそうと努力しています。
I am making efforts to improve my English.

努力家 hard worker

とりよせる 取り寄せる *to have sent, to have brought*

父はこの雑誌をアメリカから取り寄せた。
My father had this magazine sent from the United States.

ドリル *1. drill ((tool))*

2. drill, study by repetitive practice

とる 取る *1. to take hold of; to pick up*

弟の手を取って、道を渡りました。
I took my younger brother's hand and crossed the street.

受話器を取る to pick up the receiver

2. to obtain, to get

母は朝早く並んで、いい席を取りました。
My mother lined up early in the morning and got a good seat.

取って来る to go and get

辞書を取ってきてもいいですか。
May I go and get my dictionary?

学位を取る to get an academic degree

取っておく to keep, to set aside

3. to steal, to take away

犯人は財布を取って逃げました。
The culprit stole the wallet and ran away.

4. to take, to choose, to pick

全部好きでしたが、小さいのを取った。
I liked them all, but I took the small one.

5. to pass, to hand [→ 手渡す]

こしょうを取ってください。
Please pass the pepper.

その金づちを取ってくれる？
Will you hand me that hammer?

6. to take down, to write down

その説明のメモを取りましたか。
Did you take notes on that explanation?

7. to eat, to have (a meal)

きょうは２時過ぎに昼食をとりました。
Today I had lunch after 2:00.

8. to take off, to remove; to take out, to delete

部屋の中では帽子を取りなさい。
Take off your hat inside the room.

9. to take, to subscribe to

どの新聞を取っていますか。
Which newspaper do you take?

とる 捕る *to catch, to capture*

うちの猫はねずみを捕りません。
Our cat does not catch mice.

とる 採る *1. to gather, to search for and collect*

花を採る to gather flowers

2. to employ, to hire [→ 雇う]

あの会社は大卒しか採りません。
That company only hires college graduates.

ドル *dollar*

—ドル (counter for dollars; see Appendix 2)

どれ *which one (Used when there are more than two alternatives.)* [↔ どちら1.]

この３台のスポーツカーのうちでどれがいちばん好きですか。
Out of these three sports cars which do you like best?

どれでも any one

どれでも選んでください。
Please choose any one.

どれか one of them

どれかを安子ちゃんにあげなさい。
Give one of them to Yasuko.

どれも every one, all of them (in combination with an affirmative predicate); none of them (in combination with a negative predicate)

このレコードはどれも好きです。
I like every one of these records.

どれも買いませんでした。
I didn't buy any of them.

どれくらい [☞ どれぐらい (below)]

どれぐらい about how many, about how much, about to what extent [→ どのぐらい (s.v. どの)]

どれい 奴隷 *slave*

トレーナー *1. sweat shirt*

2. trainer (in sports)

トレーニング *training (in sports)*

試合に備えてトレーニングに励んでいる。
We are training hard in preparation for the match.

トレーニングする to train

トレーニングキャンプ training camp

トレーニングパンツ sweat pants

トレーニングシャツ sweat shirt [→ トレーナー1.]

トレーラー *trailer ((vehicle))*

ドレス *a dress*

ドレッシング *(salad) dressing*

とれる 取れる *1. to come off, to come loose*

コートのボタンが一つ取れたよ。
One of my coat buttons came off!

2. to be produced, to be obtained

この地方ではりんごがたくさん取れます。
Many apples are produced in this area.

3. to disappear, to go away

肩の痛みは取れましたか。
Has the pain in your shoulder gone away?

とれる 撮れる *to be taken, to be captured on film*

この写真はよく撮れていますね。
This is a good photograph, isn't it? (Literally: This photograph is well taken, isn't it?)

どろ 泥 *mud*

バスが私のドレスに泥を跳ねました。
A bus splashed mud on my dress.

泥だらけの mud-covered

泥道 muddy road, muddy path

泥水 muddy water

ドロップ *candy drop*

どろぼう 泥棒 *thief; burglar; robber* [→ 強盗2.]

ゆうべその店に泥棒が入りました。
A thief broke into that store last night.

トロリーバス *trolleybus*

トロンボーン *trombone*

どわすれ 度忘れ 〜する *to have slipped one's mind*

あの人の名前を度忘れしました。
That person's name has slipped my mind.

トン *(metric) ton (=1,000 kilograms)*

—トン (counter for (metric) tons; see Appendix 2)

どん 丼 *1. large ceramic bowl (used to serve food)*

2. [☞ 丼物 (below)]

丼物 meal served in a large ceramic bowl

どん 〜と *with a banging noise, with a bang*

銃がどんと鳴りました。
A gun sounded with a bang.

用意、どん。
Ready, go! (when starting a race)

とんかつ *pork cutlet*

どんかん 鈍感 〜な *insensitive, unfeeling* [↔ 敏感な]

どんぐり 団栗 *acorn*

とんちんかん 頓珍漢 【COL.】〜な *incoherent, illogical; irrelevant*

とんでもない *absurd, preposterous, outrageous*

とんでもないことがあったよ。
A preposterous thing happened!

「真二と結婚するの？」「とんでもない！」
"Are you going to marry Shinji?" "Of course not."
(In this use, labeling a suggestion preposterous serves as an emphatic denial.)

「どうもありがとうございました」「とんでもありません」
"Thank you very much for your kindness." "Not at all."
(In this use, labeling a thank-you preposterous serves as a polite denial that one deserves any thanks. English Don't be silly has a similar use but is not as polite.)

とんとん *(〜と) with a tap-tap*

だれかが戸をとんとんとたたきました。
Someone tapped on the door.

どんどん *1. (〜と) with a bam-bam, poundingly*

警官は戸をどんどんたたきました。
The police officer banged on the door.

2. rapidly; more and more; on and on

私たちはどんどん歩きました。
We walked on and on.

どんな *what kind of*

京都ではどんな所を訪ねましょうか。
What kind of places shall we visit in Kyoto?

どんな音楽に興味がありますか。
What kind of music are you interested in?

どんな服装でも結構です。
It doesn't matter what you wear.

家族のためなら、どんなことでもします。
I will do anything for my family.

どんなに to what extent, how much

どんなに高いですか。
How expensive is it?

トンネル *tunnel*

とんぼ 蜻蛉 *dragonfly*

とんや 問屋 *1. wholesale store*

2. wholesaler

どんより 〜する *to become cloudy, to become gray*

きょうは空がどんよりしていますね。
Today the sky is gray, isn't it?

な 名 *name* [→ 名前]

なあ *Oh!, Boy!, Man! (sentence-final particle expressing emotional involvement)*

金持ちだったらいいなあ。
Oh, it would be nice to be rich!

妹が欲しいなあ。
Boy, I want a little sister!

かわいい女の子だなあ。
Boy, that's a cute girl!

ない *(the irregular informal negative form of ある; see Appendix 1.) 1. there is/are no*

バケツには水がないよ。
There's no water in the bucket!

花瓶はあったけど、花はなかったね。
There was a vase, but there were no flowers, were there?

2. not to have, to have no

あのこじきには食べる物がないね。
That beggar doesn't have anything to eat, does he?

ない *(negative marker for adjectives and for the copula だ; see Appendix 1.)*

この店はそれほど安くないよ。
This shop isn't that cheap!

あの人は森さんではないね。
That person isn't Ms. Mori, is she?

—ない *(negative marker for verbs; see Appendix 1.)*
池田さんも知らないでしょう。
Ms. Ikeda probably doesn't know either.

ないか 内科 *internal medicine (as a specialty)* [↔ 外科]
内科医 internist

ないかく 内閣 *(government) cabinet*
内閣総理大臣 the Prime Minister (of Japan) [→ 総理大臣]

ないしょ 内緒 *a secret* [→ 秘密]
この案を社長には内緒にしておこう。
Let's keep this plan a secret from the company president.
内緒話 confidential talk

ないしょく 内職 *side job*

ないしん 内心 *1. one's mind, one's heart, one inner thoughts*
2. in one's heart, inwardly
父は内心私のことを心配してくれている。
In his heart my father is worried about me.

ないしんしょ 内申書 *confidential report of one's record at a school*

ないせん 内戦 *civil war*

ないぞう 内臓 *internal organ*

ナイター *night game (in sports)*

ナイフ *knife*

ないぶ 内部 *the inside, inner part* [↔ 外部]

ないや 内野 *infield* [↔ 外野]
内野手 infielder

ないよう 内容 *1. content, substance* [↔ 形式1.]
会長の演説の内容はすばらしかったです。
The content of the chairperson's speech was excellent.
2. contents [→ 中身]

ナイロン *nylon*

なえ 苗 *young plant, seedling*

なお 尚 *1. still, (not) yet* [→ まだ1.]
2. still more, even more [→ 一層]
きのうも暑かったが、きょうはなお暑い。
It was hot yesterday too, but today it's even hotter.

なおす 直す *1. to repair, to mend, to fix* [→ 修理する]
父は壊れたいすを直してくれた。
My father mended the broken chair for me.
2. to correct, to rectify [→ 訂正する]
この文章の誤りを直してください。
Please correct the errors in this passage.
3. to translate [→ 翻訳する]
この文を日本語に直してください。
Please translate this sentence into Japanese.

なおす 治す *to cure, to heal*
平田先生はその患者を治してくれた。
Dr. Hirata cured that patient.
歯医者は私のひどい歯痛を治してくれた。
The dentist cured my terrible toothache.

なおる 直る *to get repaired, to get mended, to get fixed*
私の自転車は直りましたか。
Is my bicycle fixed?

なおる 治る *to be cured, to heal, to get well, to recover*
母はもうすっかり治りました。
My mother has already completely recovered.

なか 中 *1. the inside, the area inside*
その箱の中を見たいです。
I want to see inside that box.
外は暑いですが、中は涼しいです。
It's hot outside, but it's cool inside.
犬は犬小屋の中で眠っています。
The dog is asleep in the doghouse.
鉛筆を筆入れの中にしまいなさい。

Put the pencils into the pencil case.
弟が家の中から出てきました。
My younger brother came out from inside the house.
私たちは公園の中を通りました。
We passed through the park.
2. included membership, included range [→ 内3.]
Aの中で among A, of A (in combination with a superlative)
明は3年生の中で走るのがいちばん速い。
Akira is the fastest runner among the third graders. (Literally: As for Akira, among the third graders, his running is fastest.
京子さんは3人の中でいちばん背が高い。
Kyoko is the tallest of the three.

なか 仲 *terms, relationship (with someone)*
AがBと仲がいい〔悪い〕 A is on good〔bad〕terms with B
洋子ちゃんは京子ちゃんと仲がいいです。
Yoko is on good terms with Kyoko.
鈴木さんと課長は仲が悪いなあ。
Mr. Suzuki and the section chief are on bad terms, right?

ながい 長い *long* [↔ 短い]
父に長い手紙を書きました。
I wrote my father a long letter.
北海道の冬は長くて寒いです。
The Hokkaido winter is long and cold.
残念ながら長くはいられません。
I'm sorry I can't stay long.
長い間 for a long time
由美さんは長い間黙っていました。
Yumi was silent for a long time.

ながいき 長生き *long life, living long*
長生きする to live long
私も長生きしたいと思います。
I think I'd like to live long too.

ながぐつ 長靴 *knee-length boot*

ながさ 長さ *length*
この川の長さはどのぐらいですか。
About how long is this river? (Literally: As for the length of this river, about how much is it?)

ながし 流し *sink ((plumbing fixture))*

ながす 流す *1. to let flow; to shed (tears); to pour out*
市長はその知らせを聞いて涙を流した。
The mayor heard the news and shed tears.
2. to float, to set adrift, to let the current take
兄はそのボートを川に流しました。
My older brother set that boat adrift on the river.
3. to wash away (transitive)
4. to wash (a part of the body with water)
父の背中を流しました。
I washed my father's back.

なかなおり 仲直り *reconciliation, making up*
仲直りする to reconcile, to make up
緑と口げんかをしたが、すぐ仲直りした。
I had an argument with Midori, but I soon made up with her.

なかなか *1. rather, quite, pretty* [→ かなり]
このテレビ番組はなかなかおもしろい。
This TV program is pretty interesting.
この質問はなかなか答えにくいよ。
This question is quite hard to answer!
2. just, readily (in combination with a negative predicate)
春がなかなか来ないね。
Spring just won't come, will it.

なかば 半ば *1. half (as an adverb)*
作文は半ばできています。
The composition is half finished.
2. approximate middle (of a time span)
黒田さんは4月の半ばに来ます。
Mr. Kuroda will come in the middle of

April.
父は50代の半ばです。
My father is in his mid-fifties.

ながびく 長引く *to be prolonged, to run overtime*
会議が長引いて、約束の時間に遅れた。
The meeting ran overtime and I was late for an appointment.

なかま 仲間 *companion, colleague, fellow*
いい〔悪い〕仲間と付き合う to keep good 〔bad〕 company
仲間に入る to join in

なかみ 中身 *contents*
箱の中身はだれも知らないよ。
Nobody knows the contents of the box!

ながめ 眺め *view, vista*
山頂からの眺めはすばらしいものでした。
The view from the mountaintop was wonderful.

ながめる 眺める *to gaze at, to look at, to view*
吉田さんは窓の外を眺めています。
Ms. Yoshida is gazing at the area outside the window.
女の子が踊っているのを眺めました。
I watched the girl dancing.

ながもち 長持ち *lasting a long time, durability*
長持ちする to last a long time
この晴天は長持ちするでしょう。
This nice weather will probably last a long time.
その万年筆は長持ちしました。
That fountain pen lasted a long time.

なかゆび 中指 *middle finger*

なかよし 仲良し *1. person one is friends with, close friend*
2. friendly terms

ーながら *while, as (Added to verb bases to join two clauses. The subject of both clauses must be the same.)*
弟はテレビを見ながら眠ってしまった。
My younger brother fell asleep while watching TV.
私たちはコーラを飲みながら話しました。
We chatted while drinking cola.

ながれ 流れ *stream, flow, current*
この川は流れがゆるやかですね。
This is a gentle river, isn't it? (Literally: As for this river, the current is gentle, isn't it?)
人の流れ stream of people, flow of people
流れ星 shooting star

ながれる 流れる *1. to flow*
大きな川が町の中を流れています。
A big river flows through the town.
汗が顔を流れました。
Sweat flowed down my face.
2. to be floated, to drift, to be taken by the current

なきごえ 泣き声 *cry, crying voice (of a person)*

なきごえ 鳴き声 *(This word is generic for the vocal sounds of animals.) song (of a bird, etc.); cry (of an animal)*
六郎は鳥の鳴き声を録音するのが好きだ。
Rokuro likes to record bird songs.

なきむし 泣き虫 【COL.】*crybaby*

なく 泣く *to cry, to weep*
赤ちゃんはまだ泣いているよ。
The baby is still crying!
母は私の合格を聞いて泣きました。
My mother cried when she heard I had passed.

なく 鳴く *(This word is the generic verb for the vocal sounds of animals.) to sing; to roar; to meow*
カナリアが美しい声で鳴いています。
The canary is singing in a beautiful voice.

なぐさめ 慰め *comfort, consolation, solace*

なぐさめる 慰める *to comfort, to console*

洋子さんは悲しそうな子供を慰めた。
Yoko comforted the sad-looking child.
何とか伊藤君を慰めようとしました。
I tried to console Ito somehow.

なくす 無くす *to lose, to come to be without* [→ 失う]
父はきのう時計を無くしました。
My father lost his watch yesterday.

なくなる 無くなる *(The subject must be inanimate.) 1. to become lost*
消しゴムが無くなったよ。
The eraser's gone!
2. to run out, to be used up [→ 尽きる]
小遣いがもう無くなったよ。
My pocket money has already run out!
3. to disappear, to go away
歯の痛みが無くなりました。
My toothache has gone away.

なくなる 亡くなる 【FORMAL for 死ぬ】 *to die, to pass away*

なぐる 殴る *to hit (intentionally), to strike (intentionally) (The subject and the direct object must both be animate.)*
兄が僕の頭を殴ったよ。
My older brother hit me on the head!
犯人はその警官を殴ったそうです。
It seems that the criminal hit that police officer.

なげき 嘆き *sorrow, grief*

なげく 嘆く *to lament, to grieve over*

なげる 投げる *1. to throw, to toss, to hurl*
明ちゃんはボールを投げました。
Akira threw the ball.
遠くに石を投げました。
I threw a stone in the distance.
犬に骨を投げました。
I threw a bone to the dog.
2. to give up on and quit
試験を投げる to give up on a test

なこうど 仲人 *matchmaker, go-between*

なごやか 和やか ～な *harmonious, congenial, peaceful*
和やかな会でしたね。
It was a congenial gathering wasn't it?

なごり 名残り *1. trace, vestige, relic*
2. sadness felt on parting
名残り惜しい sad to part

なさけ 情け *sympathy, compassion, pity*
情け深い compassionate, merciful

なさけない 情けない *1. miserable, pitiable, wretched*
情けなくて泣きたかったよ。
I was so miserable I wanted to cry!
2. shameful, disgraceful
こんな試験に落ちるのは情けないよ。
Failing this kind of test is embarrassing!

なさる 【HON. for する】

なし 梨 *pear*

－なし －無し ～の *without, -less (Added to noun bases.)*
車なしの生活はアメリカでは困難です。
Life without a car is difficult in America.
－なしで／に without, in the absence of
この本は辞書なしで読めますか。
Can you read this book without a dictionary?

なしとげる 成し遂げる *to accomplish, to achieve, to carry through to completion*

なじむ 馴染む *to become familiar, to get used*
Aになじむ to become familiar with A, to get used to A

なす 茄子 *eggplant*

なぜ *why*
なぜ夏が好きなの？
Why do you like summer?
俊彦がなぜ来なかったか知っていますか。
Do you know why Toshihiko didn't come?
なぜなら the reason is
行かないほうがいいと思います。なぜなら

危ないからです。
I think it would be better not to go. The reason is because it's dangerous.

なぞ 謎 *1. riddle (involving a play on words)*

なぞを掛ける to ask a riddle, to pose a riddle

なぞを解く to solve a riddle

2. mystery, enigma

被害者の死因は警察にとってなぞです。
The reason for the victim's death is a mystery to the police.

なだめる 宥める *to soothe, to calm, to pacify*

なだらか ～な *gentle, gently-sloping* [↔ 険しい1.]

この坂はなだらかです。
This slope is gentle.

なだらかな丘 low hill, gently-sloping hill

なだれ 雪崩 *snowslide, avalanche*

なつ 夏 *summer* [↔ 冬]

夏がいちばん好きです。
I like summer best.

夏には水泳を楽しみます。
We enjoy swimming in summer.

夏休み (US) summer vacation, (UK) the summer holidays

なつかしい 懐かしい *nostalgia-inducing, longed-for, dear old*

姉は時々懐かしい学生時代を思い出す。
Sometimes my elder sister thinks about the time she was a student with fond memories.

なづける 名付ける *to name, to give a name*

Aに／をBと名付ける to name A B

なっとう 納豆 *fermented soybeans (a popular food in Japan)*

なっとく 納得 *full understanding and assent*

納得がいく one's assent is given upon full understanding

納得する to understand and give one's assent

なでる 撫でる *to stroke (gently); to pat*

少年は犬の頭をなでています。
The boy is patting his dog on the head.

など *(This particle can follow a noun or a predicate.) 1. and so on, etcetera*

その少年にケーキやパイなどをあげた。
I gave that boy cake, pie, and so on.

2. or such, the likes of (often pejorative)

兄は、来月帰るなどと言っていました。
My older brother was saying that he'll go home next month or something like that.

ナトリウム *sodium*

塩化ナトリウム sodium chloride

なな 七 *seven (see Appendix 2.)* [→ 七]

ななつ 七つ *seven (see Appendix 2.)*

ななめ 斜め ～の *slanting, diagonal*

最初に斜めの線を引きなさい。
First draw a diagonal line.

なに 何 *what*

(The alternative form 何 is also used in some combinations.)

これは何ですか。
What's this?

今何をしているのですか。
What are you doing now?

この花は英語で何と言いますか。
What do you call this flower in English?

何でも anything, everything, whatever it is

好きな物は何でも取って結構です。
You may take anything you like. (Literally: As for the things you like, you may take anything.)

息子はおもちゃなら何でも欲しがる。
If it's a toy, then my son wants it.

何でもない to be nothing, to be of no concern

パソコン入力くらい、なんでもありません。
Computer input is nothing.

「どうかしたの？」「何でもないよ」
"What's the matter?" "Nothing!"

何事 what kind of matter, what kind of affair, what kind of thing

何事にも in all matters, in everything

何色 what color

君の車は何色ですか。
What color is your car?

何か something

この袋の中に何か入っていますか。
Is there something inside this bag?

何か A some kind of A

何か飲み物をください。
Please give me something to drink.

何も nothing, (not) anything

(Always occurs in combination with a negative predicate)

何も欲しくありません。
I don't want anything.

何より(も) above all, more than anything

弟は何よりもカレーライスが好きです。
My younger brother likes curry and rice better than anything else.

何よりの better-than-anything, best

なにしろ 何しろ *anyway, at any rate* [→とにかく]

なのか 七日 *(see Appendix 2.) 1. seven days*

2. the seventh (day of a month)

なびく *to extend out and flutter, to bend over and waver (in the direction of a passing current)*

たくさんの国旗が風になびいています。
A lot of national flags are fluttering in the wind.

草が風になびいています。
The grass is blowing in the wind.

ナプキン *napkin*

ナプキンをひざにかけなさい。
Put the napkin on your lap.

ナフタリン *naphthalene*

なぶる 嬲る *to tease, to make sport of*

なべ 鍋 *pan, pot (for cooking)*

なま 生 〜の *1. raw*

野菜を生で食べるのは健康にいいですよ。
Eating vegetables raw is good for one's health!

2. live, not recorded

生ビール draft beer

生演奏 live (instrumental) musical performance

生放送 live broadcast

生卵 raw egg

なまいき 生意気 *impudence, audacity*

生意気な impudent, audacious

なまえ 名前 *name*

名前を教えてくれる？
Will you tell me your name?

ここに名前を書いてください。
Please write your name here.

Aに名前を付ける to give a name to A, to name A

その犬にリズという名前をつけました。
I named that dog Liz.

なまけもの 怠け者 *lazy person*

なまける 怠ける *1. to be lazy, to be idle*

2. to neglect, to devote insufficient effort to

仕事を怠ける to neglect one's job

なまず 鯰 *catfish*

なまり 鉛 *lead ((metal))*

なまり 訛り *accent (i.e., non-standard characteristics of pronunciation)*

メアリーさんの日本語になまりがある。
Mary speaks Japanese with an accent.

なみ 波 *wave (on the surface of a body of water)*

きょうは波が高いですね。
Today the waves are high, aren't they?

荒い〔静かな〕波 rough〔calm〕waves

なみ 並み ～の *common, ordinary, average* [→ 普通の]

なみき 並木 *row of trees*

あの通りにはポプラの並木があります。
There is a row of poplars on that street.

並木道 tree-lined street

なみだ 涙 *tear (from crying)*

お母さんの顔は涙にぬ れていました。
My mother's face was wet with tears.

緑は目に涙を浮かべてさよならを言った。
Midori said good-bye with tears in her eyes. (Literally: Midori showed tears in her eyes and said good-bye.)

涙をふく to wipe tears

涙を流す to shed tears

涙声 tearful voice

涙ぐむ to have tears well up in one's eyes

嬉し涙 tears of joy

なめくじ *slug ((animal))*

なめらか 滑らか ～な *1. smooth (-surfaced)*

赤ん坊の肌は滑らかです。
The baby's skin is smooth.

2. smooth, free from difficulties

なめる 舐める *1. to lick; to lap*

犬は私の手をなめました。
The dog licked my hand.

猫はミルクをなめてしまいました。
The cat lapped up the milk.

2. to take lightly, to look down on

あの人をなめてはいけないよ。
You mustn't take that person lightly!

なや 納屋 *barn, shed*

なやます 悩ます *to afflict, to annoy, to bother*

夏生はばかな質問をして先生を悩ませた。
Natsuo often bothers the teacher with stupid questions.

頭を悩ます to rack one's brains

なやみ 悩み *anguish, distress, worry*

なやむ 悩む *1. to become worried, to become troubled*

Aに／で悩んでいる to be worried about A, to be troubled by A

洋子さんは学校生活のことで悩んでいる。
Yoko is worried about school life.

2. to become afflicted, to suffer [→ 苦しむ]

Aに／で悩んでいる to be afflicted by A, to be suffering from A

国民は飢えに悩んでいます。
The people are suffering from hunger.

なら *1. if it is, if it were*

(This word serves as the conditional of the copula だ and follows a noun or a nominal adjective. The alternative form ならば also occurs.)

野菜なら大丈夫でしょう。
Vegetables would probably be all right.

2. if (it is really the case that) (following a predicate)

「宿題はもう終わったよ」「終わったなら、見せてちょうだい」
"I already finished my homework." "If you finished, show it to me."

ならう 習う *to study, to take lessons in* [→ 教わる] [↔ 教える]

姉は生け花を習っています。
My older sister is studying flower arranging.

健ちゃんは柔道を習っているよ。
Ken is taking lessons in judo!

習うより慣れろ。 (proverb)
Practice makes perfect. (Literally: Rather than studying (something), get used to (it).)

ならす 鳴らす *(The direct object is something that makes a sound.)*
to sound, to cause to make a sound; to ring (a bell)

管理人は火災報知器を鳴らしました。
The manager sounded the fire alarm.
警笛を鳴らしましたね。
You sounded the horn, didn't you?
指を鳴らす to snap one's fingers

ならす 慣らす, 馴らす *1. to accustom*
日本語に耳を慣らすのは時間がかかるね。
Accustoming one's ear to Japanese takes time, doesn't it?
2. to tame (an animal)
野生の動物を慣らすのはたいへんです。
Taming wild animals is difficult.

ならない *will not do*
(This word is the regular negative form of the verb 成る and has the predictable meanings as well. To have the meaning given here, it must occur in combination with a conditional clause of some kind. Translations into English ordinarily use **must not** or **may not** rather than **will not do if**, and **must** or **have to** rather than **will not do if not**.)
作業を５時までに終えなければならない。
I have to finish this work by 5:00.
父は出かけなければなりませんでした。
My father had to go out.
そんな事をしてはならない。
You mustn't do such a thing.

ならぶ 並ぶ *1. to become arranged in a line, to form a row; (US) to line up, (UK) to queue up*
食券を買うために並びました。
I lined up to buy a meal ticket.
４列に並びなさい。
Line up in four lines.
Aと並んで side by side with A, beside A
明ちゃんと並んで歩いたよ。
I walked side by side with Akira!
2. to rank, to be equal in excellence [→ 匹敵する]

ならべる 並べる *1. to put in a line, to arrange in a row*
2. to set out, to put out (a large number of items)
お皿をテーブルに並べてください。
Please set the dishes out on the table.
3. to rank, to consider equally excellent

なりきん 成金 *newly rich person, a nouveau riche (pejorative)*

なりゆき 成り行き *course of events*

なる 生る *to grow, to be produced (The subject is a fruit, nut, etc., that appears on a tree or plant.)*
あの木にたくさんのりんごがなります。
A lot of apples grow on that tree.
このみかんの木はよく実がなるね。
On this mandarin orange tree the fruit grows well.

なる 鳴る *(The subject is something that makes a sound.) to sound, to make a sound; to ring (when the subject is a bell)*
正午のサイレンが鳴っています。
The noon siren is sounding.
電話が鳴っているよ。
The telephone is ringing!

なる 成る *1. to become, to turn (into)*
非常に暑くなったね。
It's become very hot, hasn't it?
山田さんのお嬢さんは画家になりました。
Yamada's daughter became a painter.
次郎はずいぶん背が高くなったね。
Jiro has become very tall, hasn't he?
来週で15歳になります。
I will become fifteen years old next week.
秋には木の葉が赤や黄色になります。
In fall the tree leaves become red and yellow.
2. to be made up, to be composed, to consist
AがBからなる A is composed of B, A consists of B
塩はナトリウムと塩素からなります。
Salt is composed of sodium and chlorine.
AがBからなっている A is composed of

B, A consists of B

なるべく *to the extent possible* [→ できるだけ (s.v. 出来る)]

なるべく急いで歩いてください。
Please walk as fast as possible.

なるほど *1. Oh, I see (expressing a realization that something is so)*

「冗談で言ったんだよ」「なるほど」
"He said it as a joke!" "Oh, I see."

2. indeed, sure enough

なるほど、実に美しい絵ですね。
Indeed, it's a really beautiful picture, isn't it?

ナレーター *narrator*

なれる 馴れる *to become tame*

この馬はとてもなれている。
This horse is very tame.

なれる 慣れる *to get accustomed, to get used (to)*

もうこの地方の気候に慣れました。
I've already gotten used to the climate of this region.

由美さんはワープロに慣れていません。
Yumi is not used to word processing.

なわ 縄 *rope, cord (made of braided plant fibers)*

この包みを縄で縛ってください。
Please tie this package with rope.

この縄をほどいてくれる？
Will you untie these ropes for me?

なわとび 縄跳び *rope jumping*

縄跳びをする to jump rope

なん 何 [☞ 何]

何ー *1. how many (when followed by a cardinal counter; see Appendix 2.)*

田中さんは何歳ですか。
How old is Ms. Tanaka?

このクラスには生徒が何人いますか。
How many students are there in this class?

何日神戸に滞在するのですか。
How many days will you stay in Kobe?

月に何回ゴルフをしますか。
How many times a month do you play golf?

何ーAも many, any number of (A is a cardinal counter.)

伯父は何度も香港に行ったことがある。
My uncle has been to Hong Kong many times.

2. which, what (when followed by an ordinal counter; see Appendix 2.)

きょうは何日ですか。
What day of the month is it today?

この子は何年に生まれたんですか。
In what year was this child born?

何時 what time

今何時ですか。
What time is it now?

毎朝何時に起きますか。
What time do you get up every morning?

なんか 何か *1.* 【COL. for など】

2. 【COL. for 何か *(s.v.* 何*)*】

3. 【COL. for 何だか】

なんきょく 南極 *the South Pole* [↔ 北極]

南極大陸 Antarctica, the Antarctic Continent

なんこつ 軟骨 *cartilage*

なんせい 南西 *the southwest* [→ 西南]

ナンセンス 〜な *nonsensical, absurd*

なんだか 何だか *somehow, for some reason*

何だか寂しいです。
For some reason I'm lonely.

なんて 何て *1.* 【COL. for 何と】

2. 【COL. for など *2.*】

なんで 何で *why, what for* [→ なぜ]

なんと 何と *how, what*

(Used as an exclamatory modifier of an adjective, adjectival noun, or adverb in a sentence ending combination with だろう (or the semi-formal equivalent でしょう).)

何と寒いんだろう。
How cold it is!
英語を何と上手にしゃべるのだろう。
How well you speak English!
何とかわいい鳥なのでしょう。
What cute birds!

なんとう 南東 *the southeast* [→ 東南]

なんとか 何とか *(〜して) (managing) somehow (or other)*

何とか英語で手紙を書きました。
Somehow I wrote a letter in English.
何とか列車に間に合った。
I somehow managed to be on time for the train.

なんとなく 何となく *for some reason, without really knowing why*

何となくこの町が好きです。
For some reason I like this town.

なんぱ 難破 *shipwreck*

難破する to be wrecked (The subject must be a ship)
船は暗礁に乗り上げて難破した。
The ship struck a reef and was wrecked.

ナンバー *number (used as an identifier)* [→ 番号]

ナンバープレート (US) license plate, (UK) number plate
バックナンバー back number (of a periodical)

なんぶ 南部 *southern part* [↔ 北部]

なんべい 南米 *South America* [↔ 北米]

なんぼく 南北 *north and south* [↔ 東西]

南北戦争 the (American) Civil War

なんみん 難民 *1. people left destitute (by war, natural disaster, etc.)*

2. refugees [→ 避難民 (s.v. 避難)]

なんようび 何曜日 *what day of the week*

きょうは何曜日ですか。
What day of the week is it today?

に 二 *two (see Appendix 2.)*

二月 February

に *(noun-following particle) 1. at, on, in (a time)*

七月四日の午前中に出発しました。
I started out on the morning of July 4th.
いつも11時に寝ます。
I always go to bed at 11:00.
田原さんは土曜日に卓球をします。
Ms. Tahara plays table tennis on Saturdays.
母は1948年に生まれました。
My mother was born in 1948.

2. at, on, in (indicating a place where something is located)

京子さんは今公園にいます。
Kyoko is at the park now.
メキシコはアメリカ合衆国の南にある。
Mexico is south of the United States.
根室は北海道の東部にあります。
Nemuro is in the eastern part of Hokkaido.
姉は東京に住んでいます。
My older sister lives in Tokyo.

3. to, for [→ へ1.]

少年は父親の所に走っていきました。
The boy went running to his father.

4. into, onto [→ へ2.]

靴をげた箱に入れました。
I put the shoes into the shoe cupboard.

5. by (especially in combination with a passive verb)

この本はたくさんの人に読まれています。
This book is being read by a lot of people.

にあう 似合う *to become, to suit; to go well*

Aに似合う to become A, to suit A; to go well with A

この赤いセーターは彼によく似合います。
This red sweater suits my boyfriend well.

この帽子はそのドレスに似合わないよ。
This hat doesn't match that dress!

にいさん 兄さん [☞ お兄さん]

にえる 煮える *to be cooked by boiling*

じゃがいもがよく煮えました。
The potatoes have been cooked well.

におい 匂い, 臭い *odor, smell, scent*

この香水はいいにおいがします。
This perfume smells nice.

この部屋はガスのにおいがするよ。
This room smells of gas!

においをかぐ to sniff an odor

その牛乳のにおいをかいでみました。
I tried smelling the milk.

におう 臭う *to give off a smell, to smell*

この魚はにおいます。
This fish smells.

におうじて に応じて *according to, in accordance with, in proportion to (following a noun)*

能力に応じてその仕事を分担しましょう。
Let's divide up that work according to our abilities.

にがい 苦い *bitter*

この薬は苦いね。
This medicine is bitter, isn't it?

きのう苦い経験をしました。
I had a bitter experience yesterday.

苦い顔 sour face

にかかわらず *regardless of, irrespective of (following a noun)*

会合は天候にかかわらず開かれます。
The meeting will be held regardless of the weather.

にかぎって に限って *out of all the possibilities, limited to this/that particular (following a noun)*

きょうに限ってだれも来ていません。
On this particular day nobody has come.

にかけて [[→ まで1.]] *until (following a noun referring to a point in time); through (when a preceding noun refers to something longer than a point in time)*

7月から8月にかけて中国を旅行します。
I am going to travel in China from July through August.

にがす 逃がす *1. to set free, to let go* [→ 放す2.]

長田さんはこい数匹を逃がしてやった。
Mr. Nagata set several carp free.

2. to let escape, to fail to catch

チャンスを逃がす to let an opportunity get away

にがて 苦手 〜な *1. bad at, weak in (Used to describe both the people who are bad at something and the things they are bad at.)* [↔ 得意の／な]

私は料理が苦手です。
I'm no good at cooking.

2. (Used to describe both the people who find someone or something hard to deal with and the people or things they find hard to deal with.)

hard to deal with, hard to take; hard to beat (as an opponent)

大原さんは苦手です。
Ms. Ohara is hard for me to deal with.

にかんして に関して *about, concerning (following a noun)* [→ について]

にかんする に関する *about, concerning (following a noun and functioning as a noun modifier)*

動物に関する本はありますか。
Do you have any books about animals?

あの人は都市問題に関する講演をした。
That person gave a lecture about urban

problems.

にきび *pimple*

顔ににきびができたよ。
A pimple appeared on my face!

にぎやか 賑やか ～な *lively, bustling (with people)*

あの通りはにぎやかです。
That street is bustling.

これはにぎやかな場所ですね。
This is a lively place, isn't it?

にぎる 握る {5} *1. to grasp, to grip (with the hand)*

子供はお母さんの手を握りました。
The child grasped his mother's hand.

その選手はバットを握りました。
That player gripped the bat.

2. to seize, to make one's own

権力を握る to take power

にぎわう 賑わう *to become lively, to become bustling (with people)*

浜辺は若者でにぎわっていました。
The beach was bustling with young people.

にく 肉 *meat*

挽き肉 ground meat, (UK) minced meat

にくい 憎い *hateful, detestable*

あいつは憎いやつだなあ。
Man, that guy's a hateful guy!

—にくい *hard to, difficult to (Added to verb bases.)* [↔ —やすい]

このパズルは解きにくいです。
This puzzle is hard to solve.

にくしみ 憎しみ *hatred, animosity, enmity*

にくしん 肉親 *blood relative*

にくたい 肉体 *the (living) body, the flesh (as opposed to the mind or spirit)* [↔ 精神]

肉体美 physical beauty

肉体労働 physical labor

にくむ 憎む *to hate*

ライバルを憎んではいけないよ。
You must not hate your rivals!

にくらしい 憎らしい *hateful, annoying, aggravating*

そんな憎らしいことを言わないで。
Don't say such hateful things.

にげる 逃げる *to run away, to flee, to escape*

泥棒は車で逃げました。
The thief fled in a car.

熊が動物園から逃げました。
A bear escaped from the zoo.

ニコチン *nicotine*

にこにこ *(～と) smilingly, with a happy smile*

にこにこする to smile happily

にごる 濁る *1. to become muddy, to become turbid*

この川は大雨のため濁っています。
This river is muddy because of heavy rain.

2. to become spiritually impure, to become corrupt

にし 西 *the west* [↔ 東]

太陽は西に沈みます。
The sun sets in the west.

西日 afternoon sunlight

西半球 the Western Hemisphere

西ヨーロッパ Western Europe [→ 西欧]

にじ 虹 *rainbow*

にじがかかる a rainbow appears

あらしの後、空に虹がかかりました。
After the storm, a rainbow appeared in the sky.

にしたがって に従って *1. as, in accordance with, in proportion to (following a verb in the nonpast tense)* [→ につれて]

年を取るにしたがって、しわがふえます。
As one grows older, one gets more wrinkles.

2. according to, in accordance with (fol-

lowing a noun)

説明書にしたがって電話を設置しました。

I installed the telephone in accordance with the instructions.

にしては *for, with respect to being (following a noun)*

小川さんは60歳にしては若く見えます。

Mr. Ogawa looks young for sixty years old.

にじむ *to blot, to run; to spread, to ooze*

洗うと、色がにじみます。

When you wash it, the colors run.

この紙はすぐにインクがにじみます。

Ink blots easily on this paper.

にじゅう 二重 ～の *double, dual*

この部屋には二重の窓がついています。

This room has double windows.

二重顎 double chin

二重唱 (vocal) duet

二重奏 (instrumental) duet

にしん 鰊 *herring*

にすぎない に過ぎない [☞ 過ぎる2.]

にせの 偽 ～の *false, fake* [↔ 本物の]

偽物 an imitation, a fake [↔ 本物]

偽札 counterfeit bill, counterfeit banknote

にたいして に対して *(following a noun)*
1. toward, regarding

あの人は私たちに対して親切です。

He is kind toward us.

ご招待に対して心から感謝します。

I thank you from my heart for your invitation. (Literally: Regarding your invitation, I give thanks from my heart.)

2. against, in opposition to

村人はその計画に対して抗議しました。

The villagers protested against that plan.

にたいする に対する *(following a noun and functioning as a noun modifier) 1. toward, regarding*

私に対する態度はとても好意的です。

Their attitude toward me is very friendly.

2. against, in opposition to

－にち －日 *1. (counter for number of days; see Appendix 2.)*

その大会は12日続きます。

That convention will last twelve days.

2. (counter for days of the month; see Appendix 2.)

杉山さんは10月15日に来ます。

Ms. Sugiyama will come on March 15th.

にちがいない に違いない *it is certain that, there is no doubt that, it must be the case that*

(This expression generally follows an informal-style predicate, but the word preceding cannot be the copula form だ. When added to a clause that would end with だ, the だ does not appear.)

浜田さんは頭がいいに違いない。

There is no doubt that Ms. Hamada is smart.

スミスさんはイギリス人に違いないよ。

Mr. Smith must be an Englishman!

あの人は事実を知っていたに違いない。

That person must have known the truth.

にちじ 日時 *the time and date*

日時が決まったら、知らせてください。

Please notify me as soon as the time and date are set.

にちじょう 日常 ～の *everyday, daily*

日常会話 (ordinary) everyday conversation

日常生活 everyday life

電話は日常生活の一部になりました。

The telephone has become a part of everyday life.

にちぼつ 日没 *sunset, nightfall*

にちよう 日曜 [☞ 日曜日]

日曜画家 Sunday painter, week-end painter

にちようび 日曜日 *Sunday*

日曜日はたいていテニスをします。

I usually play tennis on Sunday.

次の日曜日に映画に行こう。
Let's go to the movies next Sunday.
父は毎週日曜日に車を洗います。
My father washes the car every Sunday.

にちようひん 日用品 *daily necessities, things used every day*

について *about, concerning (following a noun)*

それについて少し説明してください。
Please explain a little about that.
先生はオーストラリアについて話した。
The teacher talked about Australia.
高山植物についての本が必要です。
I need a book about alpine plants.

にっか 日課 *daily task*

にっかんの 日刊 〜の *(published) daily*

日刊紙 daily newspaper

にっき 日記 *diary*

日記を付ける to keep a diary
西田さんは5年間日記をつけています。
Ms. Nishida has been keeping a diary for five years.

ニックネーム *nickname* [→ あだ名; 愛称]

ニッケル *nickel ((metal))*

にっこう 日光 *sunlight, sunshine*

このタオルを日光で乾かしたよ。
I dried this towel in the sunshine!
日光を浴びる to sunbathe
日光浴 sunbathing
直射日光 direct sunlight

にっこり *(〜と) with a big smile, beamingly*

少女は私ににっこりとほほえみました。
The little girl smiled beamingly at me.

にっしゃびょう 日射病 *sunstroke*

にっしょく 日食 *solar eclipse*

皆既日食 total solar eclipse

にっちゅう 日中 *daytime, the daylight hours* [→ 昼間]

日中は暖かですが、朝夕は冷え込みます。
It's warm in the daytime, but cool in the morning and evening.

にってい 日程 *schedule (of what is to be done on what day)*

ニット 〜の *knitted*

ニットのスーツ knitted suit

にっぽん 日本 [☞ 日本]

につれて *as, in accordance with, in proportion to (following a verb in the nonpast tense)*

時がたつにつれて、病気はよくなった。
As time passed, the illness got better.
山を登るにつれて、空気が薄くなった。
As we climbed the mountain, the air became thinner and thinner.

にとって *for, to, from the standpoint of*

日本語を話すのは私にとっては簡単です。
Speaking Japanese is very easy for me.
その時計は弟にとって大切な物です。
That watch is important to my younger brother.

にどと 二度と *ever again (Always occurs in combination with a negative predicate.)*

二度とそこには行きたくありません。
I don't want to go there ever again.

になう 担う *to carry on one's shoulder, to shoulder* [→ 担ぐ1.]

にぶい 鈍い [[↔ 鋭い]] *1. dull, blunt, poor for cutting*

鈍い痛み dull pain

2. insensitive, not keen [→ 鈍感な]

にふだ 荷札 *baggage tag*

にほん 日本 *Japan*

あの人は日本では有名な歌手です。
That person is a famous singer in Japan.
スミスさんは日本文化に興味があります。
Mr. Smith is interested in Japanese culture.
日本語 the Japanese language

日本人 Japanese person
日本海 the Japan Sea
日本海流 the Japan Current
日本国憲法 the Constitution of Japan
日本間 Japanese-style room
日本列島 the Japanese Islands, the Japanese Archipelago
日本三景 the three most famous scenic spots in Japan (松島, 天の橋立, 厳島)
日本製の Japanese-made, made in Japan
日本酒 (Japanese) sake [→ 酒1.]

にむかって に向かって *(following a noun)*
1. toward, for, in the direction of
ヘリコプターが西に向かって飛んでいる。
A helicopter is flying west.
2. against, in opposition to
船は風に向かって進んでいます。
The boat is moving forward against the wind.

にもかかわらず 【FORMAL】 *although (following a predicate)* [→ のに1.]*; in spite of (following a noun)*
雨にもかかわらず母は出かけました。
In spite of the rain my mother went out.

にもつ 荷物 *baggage, luggage*
この荷物を運んでくださいませんか。
Won't you please carry this baggage for me?

ニュアンス *nuance*

にゅういん 入院 *going into the hospital, hospitalization*
入院する to go into the hospital, to be hospitalized
洋子ちゃんは入院しているよ。
Yoko is in the hospital!
入院患者 inpatient

にゅうかい 入会 *admission, joining (a club, association, etc.)*
入会する to join, to be admitted
入会金 admission fee, entrance fee

にゅうがく 入学 *matriculation, admission into a school*
入学する to matriculate, to be admitted, to enter
妹は来年中学校に入学します。
My younger sister will enter junior high school next year.
入学願書 application form for admission
入学試験 entrance examination [→ 入試]
入学式 matriculation ceremony

にゅうこく 入国 *entry into a country* [↔ 出国]
入国する to make an entry (into a country)

にゅうさつ 入札 *(US) bid, (UK) tender*
入札する to make a bid

にゅうし 入試 *(school) entrance examination* [→ 入学試験 (s.v. 入学)]

にゅうじょう 入場 *entrance, admission (to a sporting event, concert, etc.)*
入場する to enter
「入場お断り」 (on a sign)
No Entrance
「入場無料」 (on a sign)
Admission Free
入場券 admission ticket; platform ticket (for seeing someone off at a train station)
入場料 admission fee

ニュース *news*
これはおもしろいニュースです。
This is interesting news.
ニュース番組 news program
ニュース映画 newsreel
ニュース解説 news commentary
ニュースキャスター newscaster
ニュース速報 news flash
海外ニュース foreign news
国内ニュース domestic news

スポーツニュース sports news

にゅうりょく 入力 *input* [→ インプット] [↔ 出力]

にょうぼ 女房【COL. for 妻】*wife* [↔ 亭主]

にょうぼう 女房 [☞ 女房]

によって (following a noun) *1. by, by means of* [→ で2.]

2. by (in combination with a passive verb) [→ に5.]

新彗星がある科学者によって発見された。
A new comet has been discovered by a certain scientist.

3. depending on

それは人によって違います。
That differs depending on the person.

にらむ 睨む *to glare at, to look sharply at*

そんなふうに私をにらまないで。
Don't glare at me in that way.

にりゅう 二流 〜の *second-rate*

にる 似る *to become similar, to develop a resemblance*

似ている to be similar, to bear a resemblance
秋子さんはお母さんによく似ています。
Akiko closely resembles her mother.

にる 煮る *to cook by boiling*

母は牛肉とじゃがいもを煮ています。
My mother is boiling beef and potatoes.

にるい 二塁 *second base* [→ セカンド1.] *(in baseball)*

二塁打 two-base hit, double
二塁手 second baseman [→ セカンド2.]

にわ 庭 *garden; yard*

裏庭 back yard; back garden

にわか 〜の *sudden* [→ 突然の]

にわか雨 sudden shower

にわとり 鶏 *chicken*

鶏小屋 chicken coop

ーにん ー人 *(counter for people; see Appendix 2.)*

にんき 人気 *popularity*

Aに人気がある to be popular with A
山田先生は生徒に人気があります。
Mr. Yamada is popular with his students.
人気歌手 popular singer
人気者 a favorite, popular person
人気投票 popularity vote

にんぎょ 人魚 *mermaid, merman*

にんぎょう 人形 *doll*

人形劇 puppet show
操り人形 puppet; marionette

にんげん 人間 *human being*

人間関係 human relationships
人間性 human nature

にんじょう 人情 *human feelings, humanity*

ご主人はとても人情のある人です。
Your husband is a very warm-hearted person.

にんしん 妊娠 *pregnancy*

妊娠する to become pregnant
林さんは妊娠しています。
Ms. Hayashi is pregnant.

にんじん 人参 *carrot*

にんず 人数 *the number (of people)*

学校の生徒の人数は何人ですか。
What is the number of school students?
少人数 a small number of people
多人数 a large number of people

にんずう 人数 [☞ 人数]

にんたい 忍耐 *patience, endurance, perseverance* [→ 我慢]

忍耐する to bear, to endure, to put up with
忍耐強い very patient, persevering

ーにんまえ ー人前 *(counter for food por-*

tions; see Appendix 2.)

にんめい 任命 *appointment (to a position)*

任命する to appoint

ぬいぐるみ 縫いぐるみ *stuffed toy animal*

くまの縫いぐるみ teddy bear

ぬう 縫う *1. to sew*

母はミシンでスカートを縫っています。
My mother is making a skirt on the sewing machine.

2. to weave through, to pass through twisting and turning

ヌード *1. (portrait of) a nude*

2. the nude, nudity [→ 裸]

ぬか 糠 *rice bran*

糠味噌 salted rice-bran paste (used in pickling)

ぬかす 抜かす *to leave out, to fail to include, to skip over*

5ページの練習問題は抜かしましょう。
Let's leave out the exercises on page 5.

ぬかるみ *mire, muddy place*

ぬく 抜く *1. to pull out, to draw out*

このとげを抜いてくれる？
Will you pull out this thorn for me?

この歯を抜いたほうがいいでしょう。
It would probably be better to pull out this tooth.

2. to remove, to take out, to eliminate [→ 除く1.]

ドライクリーニングで服のしみを抜いた。
The stains on the clothes were removed by dry cleaning.

3. to omit, to leave out, to exclude [→ 省く1.]

4. to pass, to overtake, to surpass [→ 追い越す]

スポーツカーがスクールバスを抜いた。
A sports car passed the school bus.

ぬぐ 脱ぐ *to take off (clothing)* [↔ 着る; 被る; 履く]

どうぞ靴を脱いでください。
Take off your shoes, please.

健ちゃんは服を脱いで、パジャマを着た。
Ken took off his clothes and put on his pajamas.

ぬぐう 拭う *to wipe* [→ 拭く]

ぬけめない 抜け目ない *shrewd, clever*

ぬける 抜ける *1. to come out, to fall out*

きのう奥歯が抜けました。
Yesterday a molar came out.

2. to come off, to fall off

3. to be omitted, to be left out, to be excluded

この教科書は6ページ分が抜けています。
Six pages are missing from this textbook.

4. to emerge on the other side of (after passing through)

トンネルを抜ける to emerge from a tunnel

危険を抜ける to get out of danger

ぬすむ 盗む *to steal*

だれかが私の財布を盗んだよ。
Someone stole my wallet!

ぬの 布 *cloth, fabric*

ぬま 沼 *swamp, marsh*

沼地 swampy place, marshy land

ぬらす 濡らす *to make wet, to wet, to moisten*

ズボンをぬらさないようにしなさい。
Make sure not to get your pants wet.

ぬる 塗る *1. to paint, to coat with paint*

隣のおじさんは塀を茶色に塗ったね。
The man next door painted the fence brown, didn't he?

2. to apply, to spread (a liquid, paste,

etc., onto a surface)
久美さんはパンにジャムを塗りました。
Kumi spread jam on the bread.

ぬるい 温い *1. insufficiently hot, lukewarm, tepid (describing a liquid that should be hot)*

ふろがぬるい。
The bath is tepid!

この紅茶はぬるいですね。
This tea is lukewarm, isn't it?

2. insufficiently cold, warm (describing a liquid that should be cold)
ビールはぬるくなってしまいました。
The beer has gotten warm.

ぬれる 濡れる *to get wet*

ぬれたタオルは日光で乾かしましょう。
Let's dry that wet towel in the sunshine.

Aに／でぬれる to get wet from A, to get wet with A
雨にぬれました。
I got wet from the rain.
草が雨でぬれています。
The grass is wet with rain.

ね

ね 根 *1. root (of a plant)*
根を下ろす to put down roots
根が付く roots form

2. inborn characteristic, nature
江上さんは根はいい人です。
Mr. Egami is by nature a good person.

ね *(This sentence-final particle is used to elicit agreement from the listener. With falling intonation, the speaker presumes agreement; with rising intonation, the speaker requests agreement.)*

きょうは暑いですね。
It's hot today, isn't it?
息子さんは読書がお好きですね。
Your son likes reading, isn't that right?

ねあがり 値上がり *price rise*
値上がりする to go up in price

ねあげ 値上げ *price raise* [↔ 値下げ]
値上げする to raise in price
バス運賃が少し値上げされました。
The bus fare was raised a little.

ねうち 値打ち *worth, value* [→ 価値]

ねえさん 姉さん [☞ お姉さん]

ネーム *name* [→ 名前]
ネームプレート nameplate

ネオン *neon*
ネオンサイン neon sign

ネガ *(photographic) negative*

ねがい 願い *1. wish, desire*
私の願いがかなったよ。
My wish came true!

2. request, entreaty, favor (to ask) (Typically occurs in the humble form; see お願い.)

ねがう 願う *1. to wish for, to desire*
お幸せを願っています。
I am wishing for your happiness.
私たちはみんな世界平和を願っています。
We're all wishing for world peace.

2. to ask for [→ 頼む] *(Typically occurs in the humble form; see お願いする (s.v. お願い).)*

ねかす 寝かす [☞ 寝かせる]

ねかせる 寝かせる *1. to put to bed; to put to sleep*

2. to lay down, to lay horizontally

ねぎ *green onion, scallion*

ネクタイ *necktie*
ネクタイピン tiepin

ネグリジェ *negligee*

ねこ 猫 *cat*

堀川さんは猫を2匹飼っています。
Ms. Horikawa keeps two cats.
猫が外でニャーニャーと鳴いています。
A cat is meowing outside.
子猫 kitten

ねこじた 猫舌 *person whose tongue cannot stand hot food or drink*

ねごと 寝言 *talking in one's sleep*
寝言を言う to talk in one's sleep

ねころぶ 寝転ぶ *to lie down sprawlingly, to sprawl*
たくさんの人が砂浜に寝転んでいました。
A lot of people were sprawled on the sandy beach.

ねさがり 値下がり *price decline*
値下がりする to go down in price

ねさげ 値下げ *lowering prices* [↔ 値上げ]
値下げする to lower the price of
輸入品が値下げされました。
The price of imported goods has been lowered.

ねじ *1. screw ((fastener))*
ねじを締める〔緩める〕to tighten〔loosen〕a screw
2. stem (of a clock or watch)
ねじを巻く to wind the stem
ねじ回し screwdriver

ねじる 捩じる *{5} to twist, to turn (transitive)*
取っ手をねじる to turn a handle
ねじをねじる to screw a screw

ねずみ 鼠 *rat; mouse*
鼠色 gray (as a noun)
鼠取り rattrap; mousetrap

ねたむ 妬む, 嫉む *to become jealous of, to become envious of*
拓也は由美の成功をねたんでいます。
Takuya is jealous of Yumi's success.

ねだる 強請る *to press for, to importune for, to beg for*
AにBをねだる to press A for B
娘は母親に人形をねだりました。
The girl pressed her mother for a doll.
父にもっと小遣いが欲しいとねだった。
I begged Father for more pocket money. (Literally: I begged to Father that I want more pocket money.)

ねだん 値段 *price*
このTシャツの値段はいくらですか。
How much is this T-shirt? (Literally: How much is the price of this T-shirt?)
このレコードの値段は3000円です。
The price of this record is ¥3,000.
値段も手ごろです。
The price is also reasonable.
肉の値段がずいぶん上がりましたね。
Meat prices have gone up a lot, haven't they?

ねつ 熱 *1. heat, thermal energy*
熱を加える to add heat, to apply heat
2. fever, (above-normal body) temperature
けさ熱を計りましたか。
Did you take your temperature this morning?
友子さんは熱が高いよ。
Tomoko has a high temperature!

ネッカチーフ *neckerchief*

ねっきょう 熱狂 *wild enthusiasm, excitement*
熱狂する to get wildly enthusiastic, to go wild with excitement
野球部の勝利にみんな熱狂してしまった。
Everyone got excited at the baseball team's victory.
熱狂的な enthusiastic, ardent
尾崎さんはオペラの熱狂的なファンです。
Mr. Ozaki is an ardent fan of the opera.

ネックレス *necklace* [→ 首飾り]

ねっしん 熱心 *enthusiasm, zeal*

熱心な enthusiastic, fervent, devoted, zealous, ardent

明さんは熱心な学生です。

Akira is an enthusiastic student.

細川先生は植物学の研究に熱心です。

Dr. Hosokawa is devoted to botanical research.

恵さんは熱心に英語の練習をしている。

Megumi is ardently practicing English.

ねっする 熱する *{Irreg.} 1. to heat up (transitive or intransitive)*

その水をすばやく熱してください。

Please heat up that water quickly.

2. to get excited [→ 興奮する]*; to get enthusiastic, to become zealous* [→ 熱中する]

ねったい 熱帯 *the tropics* [↔ 寒帯]

熱帯魚 tropical fish

熱帯植物 tropical plant

熱帯夜 uncomfortably hot night

ねっちゅう 熱中 *enthusiastic, absorbed* [→ 夢中の]

熱中するto get enthusiastic, to become absorbed

父はゴルフに熱中しています。

My father is enthusiastic about golf.

主人は小説を読むことに熱中していた。

My husband was absorbed in reading a novel.

川本先生は歴史の研究に熱中しました。

Dr. Kawamoto became absorbed in the study of history.

ネット *net (especially in tennis, volleyball, etc.)*

ネットを張る to put up a net

バックネット backstop (on a baseball field)

ねっとう 熱湯 *boiling water*

ネットワーク *network*

テレビネットワーク television network

ねづよい 根強い *deep-rooted, unchanging, firm*

ねどこ 寝床 *bed*

ねばる 粘る *1. to be sticky; to be glutinous*

2. to persevere, to stick it out

最後まで粘らなければならないよ。

You have to stick it out to the end!

ねぶくろ 寝袋 *sleeping bag*

ねぶそく 寝不足 *lack of sleep, insufficient sleep*

ねぼう 寝坊 *1. oversleeping, getting up late*

寝坊する to oversleep

寝坊して列車に乗り遅れました。

I overslept and missed the train.

2. late riser

息子は相変らず寝坊です。

My son, as ever, is a late riser.

ねぼける 寝ぼける *to become half-asleep, to become half-awake*

兄は寝ぼけておかしいことを言いました。

My older brother was half-asleep and said something funny.

ねまき 寝巻 *traditional Japanese-style nightclothes*

ねむい 眠い *sleepy, drowsy*

眠くて本が読めないです。

I'm so sleepy I can't read the book.

ねむり 眠り *sleep*

子供は深い眠りに落ちました。

The child fell into a deep sleep.

ねむる 眠る *1. to sleep*

弟はいつも９時間眠ります。

My younger brother always sleeps for nine hours.

お父さんはまだぐっすりと眠っているよ。

Dad is still sleeping soundly!

2. to fall asleep [↔ 目覚める]

何時に眠りましたか。

What time did you go to sleep?

ねらう 狙う *to aim at, to aim for*

狩猟家はおおかみを銃でねらいました。
The hunter aimed his gun at the wolf.

このチームは優勝をねらっています。
This team is aiming for the championship.

ねる 寝る *1. to go to bed* [↔ 起きる1.]

時々夜中の12時過ぎに寝ます。
I sometimes go to bed after 12:00 at night.

もう寝る時間ですよ。
It's already time for bed!

2. to sleep [→ 眠る1.]

3. to fall asleep [→ 眠る2.]

ねる 練る *{5} 1. to knead*

2. to train, to drill, to exercise [→ 訓練する]

技を練る to exercise a skill

3. to think over and improve on

計画を練る to think over and improve on a plan

ねん 年 *1. year*

年に4回ぐらい福岡に行きます。
I go to Fukuoka about four times a year.

—年 (counter for year dates; see Appendix 2.)

太平洋戦争は1945年に終わりました。
The Pacific War ended in 1945.

池田さんは何年に生まれましたか。
In what year was Mr. Ikeda born?

—年 (counter for number of years; see Appendix 2.)

マイクさんは日本に来てちょうど1年だ。
It is exactly one year since Mike came to Japan.

その航海は3年かかりました。
That voyage took three years.

2. year in school, (US) grade [→ 学年]

年中 all year round [→ 一年中 (s.v. 一年)]

年末 end of the year

ねん 念 *1. feeling, thought*

2. [[→ 注意]] *attention, notice; care, caution*

Aに念を入れる to pay careful attention to A; to exercise care in A

念のため just in case

ねんがじょう 年賀状 *New Year's card*

ねんがっぴ 年月日 *date (i.e., year, month, and day)*

ねんかん 年鑑 *year-in-review publication, yearbook*

ねんきん 年金 *annuity, pension*

ねんげつ 年月 *many years*

ねんごう 年号 *era name (In the case of Japan, this word refers to imperial era names.)*

ねんざ 捻挫 *sprain*

ねんざする to sprain

バスケット選手は足首をねんざしました。
The basketball player sprained his ankle.

ねんじゅうぎょうじ 年中行事 *annual event*

—ねんせい —年生 *(counter for students in a given year of school; see Appendix 2.)*

1年生 first-year student

ねんだい 年代 *1. age, period, era* [→ 時代]

—年代 the decade of (Added to number bases ending in zero.)

1970年代 the 1970's

2. generation, age-group [→ 世代]

若い年代 the younger generation

ねんど 粘土 *clay*

粘土をこねる to knead clay

ねんりょう 燃料 *fuel*

燃料タンク fuel tank

ねんれい 年齢 *age (of a person or animal)* [→ 年2.]

年齢制限 age limit

平均年齢 average age
精神年齢 mental age

の *of, having to do with (noun-following particle)*
A の B B of A, B having to do with A, A's B
これは父のペンです。
This is my father's pen.
これは子供たちの部屋です。
This is the children's room.
東京は日本の首都です。
Tokyo is the capital of Japan.
久保先生は理科の先生です。
Ms. Kubo is a science teacher.
あした英語の試験があります。
There will be an English examination tomorrow.
歴史の本はあそこにあります。
The history books are over there.
姉は日比谷の映画館に行きました。
My older sister went to a movie theater in Hibiya.

の *1. one, ones (as a pronoun)*
黒いペンはあるけど、赤いのはないね。
There are black pens, but there are no red ones, are there.
先日買ったのはだめでした。
The one I bought the other day was no good.
2. -ing (Makes a preceding clause function as a noun.)
独りで行くのは危ないですよ。
Going alone is dangerous!
このラジオを組み立てるのは簡単です。
Putting this radio together is simple.

ノイローゼ *neurosis* [→ 神経症 (s.v. 神経)]

のう 能 *noh (a kind of traditional Japanese drama)*

のう 脳 *brain*
脳波 brain waves
脳溢血 cerebral hemorrhage, stroke
脳味噌 brains, gray matter
脳死 brain death

のうえん 農園 *farm (on which fruit, vegetables, etc., are raised)*

のうか 農家 *1. farmhouse*
2. farmer; farm family

のうきょう 農協 [☞ 農業協同組合 (s.v. 農業)]

のうぎょう 農業 *agriculture*
農業に従事する to engage in agriculture
農業高校 agricultural high school
農業国 agricultural nation
農業協同組合 agricultural cooperative association

のうさんぶつ 農産物 *agricultural product*

のうじょう 農場 *farm*

のうそん 農村 *farm village*
農村地帯 farm area

のうち 農地 *farmland, agricultural land*

のうみん 農民 *farmer; peasant*

のうりつ 能率 *efficiency*
能率的な efficient
英語を習得する能率的な方法は何ですか。
What is an efficient way to learn English?

のうりょく 能力 *ability, competence*
猫には暗やみの中で物を見る能力がある。
A cat has the ability to see things in the dark.

のうりんすいさんしょう 農林水産省 *the Ministry of Agriculture, Forestry and Fisheries*

ノーコメント 〜だ *to have no comment*
それについてはノーコメントです。

I have no comment about that.

ノート *1. notebook*

2. note (i.e., a brief written record)

ノートする to note down; to take notes on

テレビ講演をノートしました。

I took notes on the TV lecture.

のがす 逃す [☞ 逃がす]

のがれる 逃れる *to evade, to elude*

のき 軒 *eaves*

のこぎり 鋸 *saw ((tool))*

大工さんは板をのこぎりで切っています。

The carpenter is cutting the board with a saw.

Aをのこぎりでひく to saw A

のこす 残す *to leave, to let remain, to have remain*

その猫はえさを半分残したよ。

That cat left half its food!

山本さんは子供たちに財産を残しました。

Mr. Yamamoto left his fortune to his children.

先生は洋子ちゃんを放課後残したよ。

The teacher had Yoko remain after school!

のこり 残り *the rest, remainder*

ミルクの残りは猫にやろう。

I'll give the rest of the milk to the cat.

犬は1匹だけが雄で、残りは雌です。

Only one of the dogs is male, and the rest are female.

のこる 残る *1. to stay, to remain*

お父さんはうちに残ったよ。

Dad stayed at home!

選手たちはまだ大阪に残っています。

The players are still in Osaka.

2. to be left, to remain

宿題がたくさん残っているよ。

I have a lot of homework left!

砂糖はどのくらい残っていますか。

How much sugar is left?

のせる 乗せる *to give a ride to; to put aboard, to take aboard*

兄は私たちを車に乗せたよ。

My older brother gave us a ride in the car!

のせる 載せる *1. to put, to place (on top of something)*

テレビの上に時計を載せてはいけません。

You mustn't put your watch on the TV.

2. to put, to print, to publish, to run (in a newspaper, magazine, etc.)

この広告をあしたの新聞に載せましょう。

Let's run this ad in tomorrow's newspaper.

のぞく 除く [[↔ 含める]] *1. to remove, to eliminate*

その人の名前を名簿から除きましょう。

Let's remove that person's name from the roster.

2. to omit, to leave out, to exclude [→ 省く1.]

Aを除いて excluding A, except for A

女の子たちは恵子を除いてみんな帰った。

All the girls went home except for Keiko.

のぞく 覗く *to take a look at, to peek at, to peep at*

少年は箱の中をのぞきました。

The boy peeped into the box. (Literally: The boy peeped at the inside of the box.)

妹はカーテンの間からのぞいている。

My younger sister is peeking from between the curtains!

鏡をのぞく to look into a mirror

のぞみ 望み [[→ 希望]] *wish, desire* [→ 願い1.]*; hope, expectation*

由美さんの望みは医師になることです。

Yumi's wish is to be a doctor.

乗客が生存している望みはありません。

There is no hope that the passengers survived.

のぞむ 望む [[→ 希望する]] *to come to want, to come to desire; to hope for, to*

expect
母は僕が教師になることを望んでいます。
My mother wants me to become a teacher.
世界中の人たちが平和を望んでいます。
People all over the world desire peace.
息子が幸せに暮らすことを望んでいます。
I am hoping for my son to lead a happy life.

のち 後 *1. (~に) later, afterwards*
晴れ、後くもり。 (a weather forecast)
Fair, later cloudy.
2. time after, time later [→ 後2.]; *time in the future*
後の later, subsequent; future (as a noun modifier)
—後に later, from now (Added to number bases denoting periods of time.)
三日後にまた由美さんに会います。
I will meet Yumi again in three days.
後ほど later, after a while
では、後ほど。
See you later. (Literally: Well then, later.)
後ほどまたお電話いたします。
I'll telephone again later.

ノックアウト *knockout*
ノックアウトする to knock out

のっとる 乗っ取る *to seize, to take over; to hijack*

のっぽ 【COL.】*tall and lanky person, beanpole* [↔ ちび]

ので *because, since (clause-conjoining particle)* [→ から4.]
気分が悪いので、会社を休みます。
Since I don't feel well, I'll take time off work.
とても興奮していたので、眠れなかった。
Since I was very excited, I couldn't sleep.

のど 喉 *throat*
のどが痛い one's throat hurts, one has a sore throat
のどが渇く to get thirsty
喉仏 Adam's apple

のどか ~な *calm, peaceful* [→ 穏やかな]

のに *(clause-conjoining particle) 1. although*
風が強いのに、釣りに行きました。
Although the wind was blowing hard, they went fishing.
2. in order to [→ 為1.]
日本語を覚えるのに、時間がかかります。
It takes time in order to learn Japanese.

のばす 延ばす, 伸ばす *1. to postpone, to put off* [→ 延期する]
野球の試合を1週間延ばしました。
We postponed the baseball game one week.
あしたまで返事を延ばしました。
I put off replying until tomorrow.
2. to prolong, to extend (in time) [→ 延長する2.]
父はアメリカ滞在をもう1週間延ばした。
My father extended his stay in the United States by one week.
3. to make longer, to extend (in space) [→ 延長する1.]
その鉄道はあと10キロ延ばすそうです。
I hear they're going to extend that railroad another ten kilometers.
4. to reach out, to extend (transitive)
妹は人形を取ろうと手を伸ばしました。
My younger sister reached her hand out and tried to take the doll.
5. to let grow (longer or taller)
恵子さんは髪の毛を長く伸ばしています。
Keiko has let her hair grow long.
6. to straighten; to smooth out (a wrinkle, etc.)
背筋を伸ばす to straighten one's back

のはら 野原 *field, plain, prairie*

のび 延び, 伸び *1. growth (in length or height)*

2. increase [→ 増加]
3. stretching (one's body)
伸びをする to stretch

のびる 延びる; 伸びる *1. to be postponed*
運動会は来週の日曜日まで延びました。
The field day was postponed until next Sunday.
2. to be prolonged, to run overtime [→ 長引く]
3. to become longer, to extend, to stretch (in space)
4. to grow (longer or taller)
背が伸びるone grows taller, one's height increases

のべる 述べる *to state, to tell*
田沢さんも計画について意見を述べます。
Ms. Tazawa will also state her opinion about the plan.

のぼり 上り *1. going up, ascent* [↔ 下り1.]
2. going up (a river, etc.) [↔ 下り2.]
3. going to a capital from a provincial area [↔ 下り3.]
上り電車 inbound train
上り坂 upward slope

のぼり 登り *climb; climbing*
山登り mountain climbing

のぼり 昇り *rising (of the sun, moon, etc.)*

のぼる 上る *1. to rise, to amount, to add up (to a large total)*
赤字は100万円に上りました。
The deficit rose to one million yen.
犠牲者は5000人に上りました。
The casualties amounted to 5,000 people.
2. to go up (a river, etc.) [↔ 下る2.]
ボートで川を上っていきました。
We went up the river by boat.
3. to go (to a capital from a provincial area) [↔ 下る3.]
息子は去年東京に上りました。
My son went to Tokyo last year.

のぼる 登る *to climb up* [↔ 下りる, 降りる1.]
Aを登る to climb up A
Aに登る to climb up to the top (part) of A
うちの猫は木に登るのが好きです。
Our cat likes to climb up trees.

のぼる 昇る *to rise (when the subject is the sun, moon, etc.)*
太陽は東から昇ります。
The sun rises from the east.

のみ 蚤 *flea*

のみ 鑿 *chisel*

のみ【FORMAL】*only, just* [→ だけ1.]

のみこむ 飲み込む *1. to swallow*
2. to understand, to grasp [→ 理解する]

のみならず【FORMAL】*not only* [→ ばかりでなく (s.v. ばかり1.)]

ノミネート ～する *to nominate*

のみほうだい 飲み放題 *as much as one wants to drink*
飲み放題のバー an all-you-can-drink bar

のみみず 飲み水 *water for drinking* [→ 飲料水]

のみもの 飲み物 *drink, beverage*
何か冷たい飲み物をください。
Please give me something cold to drink.

のむ 飲む *1. to drink*
明ちゃんは毎朝牛乳を１杯飲むね。
Akira drinks a glass of milk every morning, doesn't he?
コーヒーをもう少し飲みませんか。
Won't you drink a little more coffee?
2. to take (medicine)
薬を飲むのが嫌いです。
I dislike taking medicine.

のらいぬ 野良犬 *stray dog*

のらねこ 野良猫 *stray cat*

のり 糊 *1. paste ((adhesive))*

AをBにのりではる to stick A on B with paste

2. (laundry) starch

のり 海苔 *laver (a kind of edible seaweed)*

海苔巻き sushi rolled in laver

焼き海苔 baked laver

のりおくれる 乗り遅れる *to be too late for (getting in/on a vehicle)*

Aに乗り遅れる to be too late for (and miss) A

最終列車に乗り遅れました。

I was too late for the last train.

のりかえ 乗り換え *change, transfer (from one vehicle to another)*

そんなに遠くないですけど、乗り換えは多いです。

It isn't that far, but there are a lot of changes.

のりかえる 乗り換える *to change, to transfer (from one vehicle to another)*

上野駅で青森行きの特急に乗り換えた。

At Ueno Station I changed to the express for Aomori.

名古屋で電車からバスに乗り換えます。

We will change from a train to a bus at Nagoya.

のりき 乗り気 *enthusiasm, eagerness*

Aに乗り気になる to become enthusiastic about A

のりくみいん 乗組員 *crew member (on a ship or plane)*

のりこす 乗り越す *to ride past (one's stop or destination)*

渋谷まで乗り越してしまったよ。

I rode past as far as Shibuya!

のりもの 乗り物 *vehicle, vessel, conveyance*

のる 乗る *1. to get (into/onto a means of transportation)* [↔ 降りる2.]

ここからは渋谷行きのバスに乗ります。

From here I get on a bus for Shibuya.

父の車に乗りました。

I got into my father's car.

馬に乗る to get on a horse; to ride on a horse

恵子さんは毎朝7時5分の電車に乗る。

Keiko takes the 7:05 train every morning.

太郎ちゃんは自転車に乗れるよ。

Taro can ride a bicycle!

2. to step up, to get up (onto something)

子供が父親のひざに乗りました。

The child got up onto her father's lap.

3. to take part, to get involved (in response to something)

相談に乗る to give advice

4. to be deceived, to be taken in

計略に乗る to be taken in by a scheme

のる 載る *1. to be put, to be placed (on top of something)*

その辞書は机に載っています。

That dictionary is on top of the desk.

2. to be capable of being placed (on top of something)

この箱は棚に載るでしょう。

This box will probably go on the shelf.

3. to be printed, to be published, to appear (in a newspaper, magazine, etc.)

辞書に載る to be listed in a dictionary

のれん 暖簾 *shop curtain (of the type that hangs down part way in the entry to a traditional Japanese store or restaurant)*

のろい 呪い *curse, malediction*

のろい 鈍い *slow, sluggish*

のろう 呪う *to curse (transitive)*

のろのろ *(〜と) slowly, sluggishly*

のんき 呑気 〜な *happy-go-lucky, easy-going, carefree*

福田はのんきなやつだなあ。

Boy, Fukuda's a happy-go-lucky guy.

のんびり *(〜と) in a relaxed manner; free from worry*

のんびりする to relax; to feel carefree
試験が終わってのんびりした気分です。
I can relax now that the examination is all over. (Literally: The examination is over, and I feel carefree.)

ノンフィクション *nonfiction* [↔ フィクション]

ノンプロ *a nonprofessional* [↔ プロ]

は

は *(This particle marks the preceding phrase as the topic of a sentence or as contrasting with something else. Although the phrase preceding frequently ends in a noun, there are other possibilities as well.)*
水野さんは3年生です。
Ms. Mizuno is a third-year student.
甘い物は食べません。
I don't eat sweet things.
ここにはだれもいません。
There's no one here.
趣味としてはゴルフのほうが好きです。
As a hobby, I like golf better.
あの映画を見たいとは思いません。
I don't think I want to see that movie.
安くはないけど、買いましょう。
It's not cheap, but let's buy it.
遅く寝てはいけません。
You mustn't go to bed late.

は 刃 *blade; blade edge*
この包丁の刃は鋭いよ。
The blade of this kitchen knife is sharp!

は 歯 *tooth*
大人は歯が32本あります。
Adults have 32 teeth.
きのうこの歯を治療してもらいました。
I had treatment on this tooth yesterday.
歯を一本抜いてもらいました。
I had one tooth taken out.
歯が痛い a tooth aches
歯を磨く to brush one's teeth
歯ブラシ toothbrush
歯茎 gums
歯医者 dentist
歯磨き brushing one's teeth; toothpaste
入れ歯 false tooth
前歯 front tooth
奥歯 back tooth

は 葉 [[→ 葉っぱ]] *leaf; blade (of grass)*
枯れ葉 dead leaves
落ち葉 fallen leaves
若葉 young leaves

ば 場 *1. place* [→ 場所]
2. occasion, time [→ 場合]
3. scene (in a play, etc.) [→ 場面1.]
—場 (counter for scenes; see Appendix 2)

バー *bar, barroom, (UK) pub*

ばあい 場合 *1. case, instance, occasion, time*
この場合はこれが正しい答えです。
In this case, this is the correct answer.
ふざけている場合じゃないよ。
This is no time to be joking!
2. (～に) (following a clause) when; if
雨の場合には体育館で式を行います。
If it rains, we will hold the ceremony in the sports center.
海外へ行く場合にはパスポートが必要だ。
A passport is necessary when going overseas.

パーキング *parking* [→ 駐車場]
パーキングメーター parking meter

バーゲン *bargain sale*
これをバーゲンで買ったよ。
I bought this at a bargain sale!
バーゲンセール [☞ バーゲン (above)]

パーセンテージ *percentage*

パーセント *percent, percentage* [→ パーセンテージ]

ーパーセント (counter for percent; see Appendix 2)

学生(がくせい)の53パーセントが女性(じょせい)です。
Fifty-three percent of students are women.

パーティー *party ((social gathering))*

あしたパーティーを開(ひら)きましょう。
Let's have a party tomorrow.

バーテン [☞ バーテンダー]

バーテンダー *bartender*

ハート *1. heart ((bodily organ))* [→ 心臓(しんぞう)]

2. heart, feelings [→ 心(こころ)2.]

3. hearts ((playing-card suit))

ハートのエース ace of hearts

ハート型(がた)の heart-shaped

ハード ～な *hard, severe* [→ 厳(きび)しい2.]; *hard, intense* [→ 激(はげ)しい]

パート [☞ パートタイム]

ハードウエア *(computer) hardware* [↔ ソフトウエア]

パートタイム *(working) part time, part-time work*

平野(ひらの)さんはパートタイムで働(はたら)いています。
Ms. Hirano works part-time.

パートタイムの仕事(しごと) part-time work

パートナー *partner*

ハードボイルド ～な *hard-boiled, emotionally tough*

ハードル *1. hurdle (in track events)*

ハードルを飛(と)び越(こ)える to clear a hurdle

2. hurdle race

バーナー *Bunsen burner*

ハーフ *1. person of racially mixed parentage*

2. half [→ 半分(はんぶん)]

ハープ *harp*

バーベキュー *barbecue*

パーマ *permanent (wave)*

パーマをかける to get a permanent

ハーモニー *(musical) harmony*

ハーモニカ *harmonica*

はい 灰(はい) *ash*

はい 肺(はい) *lung*

肺炎(はいえん) pneumonia

肺癌(はいがん) lung cancer

肺活量(はいかつりょう) lung capacity

はい *1.* 【FORMAL for ええ】 *yes* [↔ いいえ]

「伊藤(いとう)さんですか」「はい、そうです」
"Are you Mr. Ito?" "Yes, that's right."

「湯浅(ゆあさ)さんはサッカーはしないのですね」「はい、しません」
"Mr. Yuasa doesn't play soccer, does he?" "No, he doesn't." (In response to a question that presumes a negative answer, はい is used to mean **Yes, your presumption is correct**. A natural English translation will often have **no** rather than **yes**.)

2. I will comply, OK, all right

「気(き)をつけてください」「はい」
"Please be careful." "All right."

3. (in response to hearing one's name called) Here, Present; Yes?

「田中(たなか)さん」「はい」
"Miss Tanaka." "Here."

4 Here, Here you are (when offering something)

はい、これを食(た)べてください。
Here, please eat this.

はい 杯(はい) *sake cup*

ー杯(はい) (counter for cupfuls, glassfuls, bowlfuls, spoonfuls; see Appendix 2)

お茶(ちゃ)を一杯(いっぱい)ください。
Please give me a cup of tea.

優勝杯(ゆうしょうはい) championship cup

ばい 倍 *double, twice as much, twice as many*
弟は私の倍のお金を持っているよ。
My younger brother has twice as much money as I do!

ーばい ー倍 *(counter for multiples; see Appendix 2)*
富士山はこの山の約5倍の高さがある。
Mt. Fuji is about five times as high as this mountain. (Literally: Mt. Fuji has a height of about five times this mountain.)

パイ *pie*
アップルパイ apple pie

はいいろ 灰色 *gray (as a noun)*
きょうは灰色の空ですね。
Today the sky is gray, isn't it? (Literally: Today it's a gray sky, isn't it?)

ハイウェー *(US) expressway, (UK) motorway* [→ 高速道路 (s.v. 高速)]

はいえい 背泳 *backstroke* [→ 背泳ぎ]

ハイエナ *hyena*

バイオテクノロジー *biotechnology*

パイオニア *pioneer* [→ 開拓者 (s.v. 開拓)]

バイオリン *violin*
バイオリンを弾く to play a violin
バイオリン奏者 violinist

ハイカラ【COL.】～な *fashionable, stylish*

はいきガス 排気ガス *exhaust (gas)*

ばいきん 黴菌 *germ*

ハイキング *hiking, hike*
森へハイキングに行きましょう。
Let's go hiking in the woods.
ハイキングをする to hike

バイキング *1. smorgasbord*
2. Viking

はいく 俳句 *haiku (a kind of traditional Japanese three-line poem)*

バイク *motorbike, motorcycle*

はいけい 背景 *1. background, backdrop*
東京タワーを背景に写真を撮りましょう。
Let's take a picture with Tokyo Tower in the background.
2. backing, support
その候補者の背景に有力な政治家がいる。
That candidate has support from a powerful politician.

はいけい 拝啓【FORMAL】*(opening phrase used in formal letters)* [↔ 敬具]

はいけん 拝見 ～する【HUM. for 見る】

はいざら 灰皿 *ashtray*

はいし 廃止 *abolition, repeal*
廃止する to abolish, to repeal

はいしゃ 歯医者 *dentist*

はいしゃく 拝借 ～する【HUM. for 借りる *1.*】

ハイジャック *hijacking*
ハイジャックする to hijack

ハイジャンプ *high jump ((athletic event))* [→ 走り高跳び]

はいたつ 配達 *delivery, distribution*
配達する to deliver, to distribute
郵便は1日に2回配達されます。
Mail is delivered twice a day.
配達料 delivery charge

ばいてん 売店 *(sales) stand, (merchandise) stall*
駅の売店 station sales stand

パイナップル *pineapple*

ばいばい 売買 *buying and selling*
売買する to buy and sell, to deal in

バイパス *by-pass (road)*

ハイヒール *high-heeled shoes*

パイプ *1. (tobacco) pipe*
2. pipe, tube [→ 管]
パイプオルガン pipe organ

ハイファイ *hi-fi*

バイブル *Bible* [→ 聖書]

ハイフン *hyphen*

はいぼく 敗北 *defeat* [↔ 勝利]

敗北する to be defeated [→ 負ける1.]

ハイヤー *taxi hired for a fixed period*

はいゆう 俳優 *actor, actress* [→ 役者]

映画俳優 movie actor

ハイライト *1. highlight, outstanding part*

2. highlight, brightest part

はいる 入る *{5} 1. to enter, to go in, to come in* [↔ 出る1.]

裏口から家に入りました。
I entered the house from the back door.

入ってもよろしいですか。
May I come in?

ふろに入る to take a bath

入っている to be inside

2. to enter, to join, to become a participant [↔ 辞める]

弟は来年その中学校に入ります。
My younger brother will enter that junior high school next year.

次郎はバスケットボール部に入ったよ。
Jiro joined the basketball club!

クラブに入っていますか。
Are you in a club?

3. to fit (inside)

このホールには何人入るでしょうか。
How many people will fit in this hall?

パイロット *pilot*

パイロットランプ pilot lamp

バインダー *binder (for documents, etc.)*

はう 這う *to crawl, to creep*

赤ちゃんは隣の部屋にはっていきました。
The baby crawled into the next room.

バウンド *bound, bounce*

バウンドする to bound, to bounce

はえ 蝿 *fly ((insect))*

はえる 生える *to sprout, to appear*

雑草が花の間に生えています。
Weeds are sprouting among the flowers.

ひげが生える a beard grows

歯が生える a tooth comes in

はか 墓 *a grave*

墓参り visiting a grave

ばか 馬鹿 *1. fool*

ばかな foolish, silly [↔ 賢い]

ばかな事はよしなさい。
Stop doing foolish things.

Aをばかにする to make a fool of A, to make fun of A

2. ～になる to become nonfunctional

このねじはもうばかになったよ。
This screw doesn't hold anymore! (Literally: This screw has become nonfunctional.)

馬鹿正直 foolish honesty, naive honesty

はかい 破壊 *destruction*

破壊する to destroy

多くの家が台風で破壊されました。
Many houses were destroyed by the typhoon.

はがき 葉書 *postcard*

官製葉書 government-printed postcard

はがす 剥がす *to peel off, to tear off* [→ 剥ぐ]

ポスターを全部はがしなさい。
Take down all the posters.

はかせ 博士 *1. knowledgeable person, expert*

2. person with a doctorate

一博士 (Sometimes added to the surname of a person with a doctoral degree instead of 一先生 as a title of respect roughly equivalent to Dr.)

成田博士も出席なさいました。
Dr. Narita also attended.

博士号 doctoral degree
博士論文 doctoral thesis

ばかばかしい *absurd, ridiculous*

はかり 秤 *scale(s), weighing device*
魚屋さんはその魚をはかりにかけました。
The fish store proprietor put the fish on those scales.

ばかり *1. only, nothing but* [→ だけ1.]
太郎は猫のことばかり考えているよ。
Taro only thinks of the cat!
ばかりでなく not only
伯母は英語ばかりでなくドイツ語もできる。
My aunt can speak not only English, but also German.
2. ～だ to have just (following a past-tense verb)
私は学校に着いたばかりです。
I've just arrived at school.
3. ～に just because, simply as a result of (following a past-tense verb)
英語を知らなかったばかりに笑われた。
Just because I didn't understand English, I was laughed at.

－ばかり *about, or so (Added to number bases.)* [→－ぐらい1.]
ハワイには1週間ばかりいます。
I will be in Hawaii for about a week.

はかる 計る; 測る; 量る *to measure*
看護婦は私の体温を計りました。
The nurse took my temperature.
体育の先生は私の身長を測りました。
The physical education teacher measured my height.
姉は週に1回体重を量ります。
My older sister weighs herself once a week.

はかる 図る [[→ 企てる]] *1. to attempt*
自殺を図る to attempt suicide
2. to plan

バカンス *vacation, holiday*

はきけ 吐き気 *nausea*
吐き気がする to feel sick in one's stomach

はきもの 履物 *footwear*

はく 吐く *1. to vomit, to throw up (transitive or intransitive)*
ゆうべ少し吐きましたが、もう平気です。
Last night I vomited a little, but I'm all right now.
2. to spit out, to expel
息を吐く to breathe out

－はく －泊 *(counter for nights of a stay; see Appendix 2)*

はく 掃く *to sweep (with a broom, etc.)*

はく 履く *to put on*
(The direct object of is generally an article of clothing that goes below the waist. Compare 着る and 被る. Like other verbs for putting on clothing, in the -ている form 履く can express the meaning **be wearing, have on**.) [↔ 脱ぐ]
父は新しい靴をはきました。
My father put on his new shoes.
兄はいつもジーパンをはいているよ。
My older brother always wears jeans!

はぐ 剥ぐ *to peel off, to tear off* [→ 剥がす]

ばくげき 爆撃 *bombing attack*
爆撃する to bomb
爆撃機 bomber ((airplane))

はくさい 白菜 *Chinese cabbage, bok-choi*

はくし 白紙 *blank paper*
Aを白紙に戻す to start A afresh

はくし 博士 [☞ 博士2.]

はくしゅ 拍手 *clapping, applause*
拍手する to clap
先生の提案に生徒全員が拍手しました。
All the students clapped at their teacher's proposal.

はくしゅかっさい 拍手喝采 *clapping and cheering, a big hand*

はくじょう 白状 *confession*

白状する to confess

犯人はやっと白状しました。
The criminal finally confessed.

はくじょう 薄情 〜な *cold-hearted, cold, unkind* [→ 冷淡な]

はくじん 白人 *white person*

ばくぜん 漠然 〜と *vaguely, obscurely*

漠然としている to be vague, to be obscure

漠然とした vague, obscure [→ 曖昧な]

漠然とした回答では受け入れられません。
Vague answers will not be accepted.

ばくだい 莫大 〜な *huge, enormous*

ロケット開発にはばく大な費用がかかる。
Rocket development takes enormous expenditure.

ばくだん 爆弾 *bomb*

爆弾を都会に落しました。
They dropped bombs on cities.

原子爆弾 atomic bomb

時限爆弾 time bomb

核爆弾 nuclear bomb

水素爆弾 hydrogen bomb

はくちょう 白鳥 *swan*

バクテリア *bacteria* [→ 細菌]

ばくはつ 爆発 *explosion*

工場の地下で爆発がありました。
There was an explosion in the basement of the factory.

爆発する to explode

はくぶつかん 博物館 *museum*

はくぼく 白墨 *chalk* [→ チョーク]

はくらんかい 博覧会 *exposition, fair*

万国博覧会 world exposition, world's fair

はぐるま 歯車 *gear (-wheel), cogwheel*

はけ 刷毛 *brush ((implement))*

このはけでペンキを塗ってください。
Please apply the paint with this brush.

はげ 禿げ *baldness; bald spot*

禿げ頭 bald head

禿げ山 bare mountain

はげしい 激しい *intense, hard, heavy, violent*

風が激しく吹いているよ。
The wind is blowing hard!

激しい寒さ intense cold

激しい練習 hard training

激しい雨 heavy rain

激しいあらし violent storm

バケツ *bucket*

バケツで水を教室まで運びます。
They carry water to the classroom in a bucket.

はげます 励ます *to encourage, to cheer up*

友達がやさしい言葉で励ましてくれた。
My friend encouraged me with kind words.

はげむ 励む *to work hard, to become diligent*

妹は勉強に励んでいます。
My younger sister is working hard at her studies.

ばけもの 化け物 *ghost, goblin, monster*

はげる 剥げる *1. to peel off, to wear off (intransitive)*

塀のペンキがはげました。
The paint on the fence has peeled off.

2. to fade (when the subject is a color)

はげる 禿る *to become bald*

父はだんだん頭がはげてきました。
My father has gradually become bald. (Literally: As for my father, his head has

gradually become bald.)

はこ 箱 *box, case*

その箱の中にテニスボールが入っている。
There are tennis balls in that box.

一箱 (counter for boxes; see Appendix 2)

ぶどうを一箱買います。
I'll buy one box of grapes.

弁当箱 lunch box
絵の具箱 paintbox
本箱 bookcase
宝石箱 jewel case

はこぶ 運ぶ *1. to carry, to convey, to transport*

この荷物を部屋まで運んでください。
Please carry this baggage to the room.

お皿を台所に運びなさい。
Carry the dishes to the kitchen.

2. to progress, to continue

建設はうまく運びました。
The construction progressed well.

バザー *bazaar*

はさまる 挟まる *to get caught, to become sandwiched*

スカートがドアに挟まりました。
My skirt got caught in the door.

はさみ 鋏 *scissors*

このはさみはよく切れますね。
These scissors cut well, don't they?

1丁のはさみ one pair of scissors

はさむ 挟む *1. to insert, to sandwich (between two things)*

私は本のページの間にメモを挟んだ。
I put a note between the pages of the book.

2. to insert and have pinched

明子ちゃんは車のドアに小指を挟んだ。
Akiko got her little finger pinched in the car door.

はさん 破産 *bankruptcy*

破産する to go bankrupt

長谷川さんは事業に失敗して破産した。
Mr. Hasegawa failed in business and went bankrupt.

はし 端 *end, tip* [→ 先1.]; *edge* [→ 縁]

コップをテーブルの端に置かないで。
Don't put the glass on the edge of the table.

はし 箸 *chopsticks*

1ぜんのはし one pair of chopsticks

はし 橋 *bridge (spanning a river, etc.)*

その橋を架けるのに5年かかります。
It will take five years to build that bridge.

この川にはいくつかの橋が架かっている。
There are several bridges spanning this river.

橋を渡る to cross a bridge

はじ 恥 *shame, disgrace*

恥をかく to disgrace oneself, to be put to shame

明さんはみんなの前で恥をかきました。
Akira was put to shame in front of everyone.

恥知らず shamelessness; shameless person

はしか 麻疹 *measles*

はしかにかかる to catch measles

はしご 梯子 *ladder*

壁にはしごをかけましょう。
Let's set up a ladder against the wall.

はしごを登る to climb a ladder

はじまり 始まり *beginning, start* [→ 初め]

はじまる 始まる *to begin, to start (intransitive)*

(The time at which something begins can be marked with either に or から.)

学校は何時に始まるのですか。
What time does school begin?

テニスの試合はすぐに始まります。
The tennis match will start right away.

野球のシーズンは今月から始まります。

The baseball season begins this month.

はじめ 始め *beginning, start* [↔ 終わり]

浩は始めからその事実を知っていたよ。
Hiroshi knew that fact from the beginning!

店員は始めから終わりまで黙っていた。
The salesclerk kept silent from beginning to end.

来月の始めにベスさんが日本に来ます。
Beth will come to Japan at the beginning of next month.

初めの first; original

旅行の初めの三日間は雨でした。
It rained for the first three days of the trip.

初めは at first

由美さんは初めは恥ずかしそうでした。
Yumi looked shy at first.

はじめて 初めて *for the first time*

初めて京子さんに会ったのはいつですか。
When did you meet Kyoko for the first time?

今年初めて四国を訪れます。
I will visit Shikoku this year for the first time.

初めての first, not experienced previously

はじめまして 初めまして *How do you do? (a polite greeting used when meeting a person for the first time)*

はじめる 始める *to begin, to start (transitive) (The time at which something is begun can be marked with either に or から.)*

8時から宿題を始めます。
I'll start my homework at 8:00.

5ページから始めましょうか。
Shall we begin at page 5?

－はじめる －始める *to begin to, to start to (Added to both transitive and intransitive verb bases.)*

兄はフランス語を勉強し始めました。
My older brother began studying French.

雨が降り始めました。
It began to rain.

ばしゃ 馬車 *horse-drawn carriage; horse cart*

パジャマ *pajamas*

ばしょ 場所 *place* [→ 所1.]

お昼を食べる場所を見つけました。
I found a place to eat lunch.

場所を取りすぎる to take up too much space

はしら 柱 *post, pillar*

柱時計 wall clock

はしりさる 走り去る *to run away, to run off*

はしりたかとび 走り高跳び *(running) high jump ((athletic event))*

はしりはばとび 走り幅跳び *(running) long jump ((athletic event))*

はしりまわる 走り回る *to run around (intransitive)*

はしる 走る *{5} 1. to run (when the subject is a person or animal)* [→ 駆ける]

信次さんは走るのがとても速いね。
Shinji runs very fast, doesn't he? (Literally: As for Shinji, running is very fast, isn't it?)

弟は私のところへ走ってきました。
My younger brother came running to me.

私たちは駅までずっと走りました。
We ran all the way to the station.

2. to run (when the subject is a vehicle)

そのバスは東京・名古屋間を走ります。
That bus runs between Tokyo and Nagoya.

はじる 恥じる *be ashamed of, to feel humiliated by*

先生は自分のまちがいを恥じました。
The teacher was ashamed of her mistake.

はす 蓮 *lotus*

はず 筈 *likelihood, good reason to think*

something

はずだ it must be that, it should be the case that, I am almost sure that (following a clause)

選手たちはのどがかわいているはずだよ。
The players must be thirsty!

洋子は私の電話番号を知っているはずだ。
Yoko should know my telephone number.

妹は母といっしょに買物に行くはずです。
I am almost sure my younger sister is going shopping with my mother.

はずがない there is no reason to think that, it is very unlikely that (following a clause)

明が入試に落ちるはずがないよ。
It is very unlikely that Akira will fail on the entrance examination!

バス *bus*

博物館までバスで行きましょうか。
Shall we go to the museum by bus?

バスに乗る to get on a bus; to ride on a bus

バスを降りる to get off a bus

バスガイド guide accompanying passengers on a tourist bus

バス停 bus stop

観光バス sight-seeing bus

バス *bath* [→ 風呂]

バスタオル bath towel

バス *1. bass (voice)*

2. bass (singer)

3. bass (part)

パス *1. (free) pass; (US) commuter pass, (UK) season ticket* [→ 定期券 (s.v. 定期)]

2. pass (in basketball, football, etc.)

パスする to pass

ボールをパスする to pass the ball

3. pass (when it is one's turn in a card game, etc.)

パスする to pass

4. ～する to pass (a test, etc.)

試験にパスする to pass an examination

はずかしい 恥ずかしい *(This adjective is used to describe both people who are embarrassed or ashamed and the things they are embarrassed or ashamed about.)*

embarrassed; ashamed

美砂は恥ずかしくて、何もできなかった。
Misa was so embarrassed, she couldn't do anything.

汚れた服が恥ずかしかったよ。
I was ashamed of my dirty clothes!

バスケット *1. basket* [→ 籠]

2. [☞ バスケットボール1.]

バスケットボール *1. (the game of) basketball*

2. a basketball

はずす 外す *1. to take off, to remove; to undo, to unfasten*

母は時計を外しました。
My mother took off her watch.

ボタンを外したほうがいいでしょう。
It's probably better to undo your buttons.

2. to evade, to avoid [→ 避ける]

質問を外す to evade a question

3. to miss (what one is aiming at)

的を外す to miss a target

4. to go away from temporarily (The direct object is a place.)

席を外す to leave one's seat

パステル *pastel (crayon)*

パステル画 pastel (picture)

バスト *1. bust (measurement)*

2. bust ((sculpture))

パスポート *passport*

はずみ 弾み *1. bounce, rebound*

2. momentum; impetus, stimulus

はずみがつく momentum gathers; stimulus acts

弾み車 flywheel

はずむ 弾む *1. to bounce, to rebound*

ボールは弾んで、垣根を越えました。
The ball bounced over the fence.

2. to become lively, to become animated; to be stimulated

話が弾む talk gets lively

パズル *puzzle*

クロスワードパズル crossword puzzle

ジグソーパズル jigsaw puzzle

はずれ 外れ *1. miss, failed attempt* [↔ 当たり2.]

先週引いたくじも外れでした。
The lot I drew last week was also a miss.

2. [[→ 端]] *end; edge*

店は通りの外れにあります。
The store is at the end of the street.

湖の東の外れにホテルがあります。
There is a hotel on the eastern edge of the lake.

はずれる 外れる *1. to come off, to become detached; to come undone, to come unfastened*

ボタンが一つ外れています。
One of my buttons has come undone.

機械のベルトが外れました。
The machine belt came off.

2. to miss (a target or aim) (The subject is inanimate.) [↔ 当たる2.]

その弾は的を外れました。
That bullet missed the target.

3. to prove incorrect [↔ 当たる4.]

天気予報はよく外れます。
The weather forecast is often incorrect.

パソコン *personal computer*

はた 旗 *flag*

旗は風に翻っています。
The flag is fluttering in the wind.

旗竿 flagpole

はだ 肌 *1. (person's) skin*

京子さんは肌が白いですね。
Kyoko's skin is fair, isn't it?

浅黒い肌 dark skin

2. outer surface [→ 表面]

山肌 surface of a mountain

バター *butter*

バターを塗る to spread butter

パターン [☞ パタン]

はだか 裸 *nakedness, nudity*

裸の naked

裸になる to become naked, take off one's clothes

はたけ 畑 *(non-paddy, farm) field*

畑を耕す to plow a field

はだし 裸足 *bare feet*

はだしで with bare feet, barefoot

この子ははだしで歩くのが好きです。
This child likes to walk barefoot.

はたす 果たす *to carry out, to fulfill; to achieve, to accomplish*

聡はキャプテンとしての義務を果たした。
Satoshi carried out his duty as captain.

約束を果たす to fulfill a promise

目的を果たす to achieve a purpose

役割を果たす to play a role, to play a part

はたち 二十歳 *20 years old (see Appendix 2)*

バタフライ *butterfly ((swimming stroke))*

はたらき 働き *1. work, working*

父は会社のために目覚ましい働きをした。
Father did outstanding work for the company.

2. ability, talent [→ 才能]

働きのある人 able person

3. function [→ 機能]*; action, activity* [→ 作用]

心臓の働き the function of the heart

働き口 job, employment

働き者 hard worker

働き盛り the prime of one's working life

はたらく 働く *to work, to labor*

あの人はよく働きます。
That person works hard.

姉はパートで働いています。
My older sister works part-time.

叔父は工場で働いています。
My uncle works in a factory.

戸田さんは看護婦として働くつもりです。
Miss Toda intends to work as a nurse.

ばたん ～と *with a bang, with a thud*

ばたんと戸を閉める to shut the door with a bang

ばたんと倒れる to fall over with a thud

パタン *pattern*

はち 八 *eight (see Appendix 2)*

八月 August

はち 鉢 *1. bowl*

2. flowerpot [→ 植木鉢 (s.v. 植木)]

はち 蜂 *bee*

大きなはちがぶんぶん飛び回っているよ。
A big bee is buzzing around!

はちの巣 beehive; honeycomb

はちに刺される to be stung by a bee

蜂蜜 honey

ばち 罰 *punishment, penalty* [→ 罰]

罰が当たる to suffer punishment

はつ 初 ～の *first (-time)*

初孫 first grandchild

初耳 the first one has heard of something

初詣で first visit to a Shinto shrine after New Year's (a popular traditional activity in the first few days of a new year in Japan)

ばつ 罰 *punishment, penalty*

ばつ *an "X" mark (indicating that something is incorrect or unacceptable)*

はつおん 発音 *pronunciation*

その単語には二つの異なった発音がある。
That word has two different pronunciations.

発音する to pronounce

この単語はどう発音しますか。
How do you pronounce this word?

発音記号 pronunciation symbol

はっか 薄荷 *mint ((plant))*

はつか 二十日 *(see Appendix 2) 1. twenty days*

2. the twentieth (day of a month)

はつかねずみ 二十日鼠 *(house) mouse*

はっき 発揮 *display, exhibition, making full use (of an ability or power)*

発揮する to display, to exhibit, to make full use of

はっきり *clearly*

この眼鏡をかけると、はっきり見えます。
When I put on these glasses, I can see clearly.

はっきりする to become clear

その説明ははっきりしています。
That explanation is clear.

ばっきん 罰金 *a fine*

スピード違反で1万円の罰金を払った。
I paid a fine of ¥10,000 for a speeding violation.

罰金を課す to levy a fine

バック *1. background, backdrop* [→ 背景1.]

2. backing, support [→ 背景2.]*; backer, supporter*

3. ～する to back up, to move backwards (intransitive)

少しバックしてください。
Back up a little, please.

バッグ *bag* [→ 袋]*; satchel* [→ 鞄]

バックアップ *backing, support*

バックアップする to back up, to support

バックボーン *backbone, strength of char-*

acter

バックミラー *rearview mirror*

バックル *buckle*

ばつぐん 抜群 〜の *outstanding, excellent*

政子ちゃんの英語は抜群だよ。
Masako's English is outstanding!

パッケージ *1. packing (i.e., readying for transport)*

パッケージする to pack

2. packaging (i.e., the box, paper, etc., in which an item is packed)

3. package, parcel

パッケージツアー package tour

はっけつびょう 白血病 *leukemia*

はつげん 発言 *speaking; statement, utterance*

発言する to speak, to say something
課長は会議で一言も発言しませんでした。
The section chief didn't say a word at the meeting.
発言権 the right to speak

はっけん 発見 *discovery*

発見する to discover

だれがエックス線を発見しましたか。
Who discovered X-rays?
発見者 discoverer

はつこい 初恋 *one's first love*

はっこう 発行 *publication, issuing*

発行する to publish, to issue

この本はぜひ発行しましょう。
Let's publish this book by all means.
発行部数 the number of copies printed
発行者 publisher

バッジ *badge*

はっしゃ 発車 *departure, starting off (of a train, bus, etc.)*

発車する to depart, to start off
次の電車は10時に発車します。
The next train will depart at 10:00.
長野行きの急行は6番線から発車します。
The express for Nagano leaves from Track No. 6

はっしゃ 発射 *1. firing, shooting (of a gun)*

発射する to fire, to shoot (transitive or intransitive)

ピストルを発射する to fire a pistol

2. launch (of a rocket)

発射する to launch
発射台 launching pad

はっしん 発信 [[↔ 受信]] *transmission of a message; transmission of a broadcast*

発信する to transmit
発信機 transmitter ((machine))

ばっする 罰する *{Irreg.} to punish*

過度に罰する to punish excessively

はっせい 発生 *occurrence, outbreak; coming into existence*

地震の発生 occurrence of an earthquake

コレラの発生 outbreak of cholera

発生する to occur, to break out; to come into existence

ばった *grasshopper*

バッター *batter, hitter* [→ 打者] *(in baseball)*

バッターボックス batter's box

はったつ 発達 *development, advancement* [→ 発展]

発達する to develop, to advance (intransitive)

アメリカでは宇宙科学が発達している。
Space science is developed in the United States.
低気圧が発達して、台風になりました。
The low pressure developed into a typhoon.

ばったり *(〜と) 1. unexpectedly (modifying a verb that denotes meeting)*

ばったりAに会う to meet A unexpectedly, to run into A

音楽会でばったり古野さんに会いました。
I ran into Ms. Furuno at the concert.

2. suddenly, with a flop (modifying a verb that denotes falling over)

その老人はばったりと前に倒れました。
The elderly person suddenly fell flat on his face.

バッティング *batting, hitting (in baseball)*

バッテリー *battery (in baseball)*

バッテリーを組む to team up as the battery

バッテリー *(electric) battery* [→ 電池]

バッテリーが上がる a battery goes dead

はつでん 発電 *electricity generation*

発電する to generate electricity

発電機 generator

発電所 power plant, generating station

はってん 発展 *development, expansion* [→ 発達]

発展する to develop, to expand (intransitive)

この都市は急速に発展しました。
This city developed rapidly.

発展途上国 developing country [↔ 先進国 (s.v. 先進)]

バット *(baseball) bat*

バットを振る to swing a bat

はっぱ 葉っぱ [[→ 葉]] *leaf; blade (of grass)*

はつばい 発売 *putting on sale, putting on the market* [→ 売り出し1.]

発売する to put on sale, to put on the market [→ 売り出す]

この週刊誌は金曜日に発売されます。
This weekly magazine is put on sale on Friday.

はっぴょう 発表 *announcement; public presentation*

発表する to announce; to present publicly

はつめい 発明 *inventing, invention*

発明する to invent

だれが電信機を発明しましたか。
Who invented the telegraph?

必要は発明の母。 (proverb)
Necessity is the mother of invention.

発明品 an invention

発明家 inventor

はで 派手 〜な *gaudy, showy*

兄のネクタイは派手です。
My older brother's tie is gaudy.

歌手は派手なドレスを着ています。
The singer is wearing a showy dress.

はと 鳩 *pigeon; dove*

鳩時計 cuckoo clock

鳩小屋 pigeon house

伝書鳩 carrier pigeon

パトカー *patrol car, police car*

バドミントン *badminton*

パトロール *patrol, patrolling*

パトロールする to patrol

パトロール中の on-patrol

パトロール中の警官が犯人を逮捕した。
An on-patrol police officer arrested the criminal.

パトロールカー [☞ パトカー]

バトン *baton*

バトンガール (girl) baton twirler

はな 花 *flower, blossom*

春には多くの花が咲きます。
Many flowers bloom in spring.

毎朝花に水をやります。
I water the flowers every morning.

母は庭の花を摘みました。
My mother picked a flower from the garden.

花畑 flower field

花見 cherry-blossom viewing (a popular springtime activity in Japan)
花園 flower garden
花屋 flower shop; florist
花盛り full bloom
お花 (traditional Japanese) flower arranging (This word contains the honorific prefix お- and can also be used simply as an honorific form of 花.) [→ 生け花]

はな 鼻 *nose*
鼻の穴 nostril
鼻が高い to have a prominent nose; to be proud
鼻が低い to have a flat nose
鼻が利く to have a keen nose
鼻がつまる one's nose gets stuffed up
鼻血 nosebleed
鼻血を出す to have a nosebleed
鼻歌 humming (i.e., a kind of singing)
鼻歌を歌う to hum a tune

はな 洟 *nasal mucus, snivel*
はなが出る one's nose runs
はなをかむ to blow one's nose

はなし 話 *1. talking; conversation* [→ 会話]
話に加わりませんか。
Won't you join in the conversation?
何の話ですか。
What are you talking about?
話をする to have a talk, to talk
きのう米山さんと長い間話をしました。
Yesterday I had a long talk with Mr. Yoneyama.
話を変える to change the subject
2. story, report, account
正子さんはおもしろい話をしてくれたよ。
Masako told me an interesting story!
という話だ they say that, I hear that (following a clause) [→ そうだ]
林先生が高知にお帰りになるという話だ。
They say Mr. Hayashi will return home to Kochi.
話中の (US) busy, (UK) engaged (describing a telephone line or number)
話好きの fond of talking, talkative

はなしあう 話し合う *1. to talk with each other*
友達と将来について話し合いました。
I talked with my friend about the future.
2. to discuss
課長とその計画を話し合います。
I'll discuss that plan with the section chief.

はなしかける 話しかける *to start talking, to initiate a conversation*
知らない人が私に話しかけてきました。
A person I don't know started talking to me.

はなす 放す *1. to let go, to release one's grasp on*
主人は犬を放しました。
The master let the dog go.
Aから手を放す to release one's hold on A, to let go of A
鉄棒から手を放さないで。
Don't let go of the bar.
2. to set free, to release
母はその鳥を放してやりました。
My mother set that bird free.

はなす 話す *1. to speak, to talk*
姉はその友達とフランス語で話します。
My older sister speaks to her friend in French.
もっとゆっくり話してくださいませんか。
Won't you please speak more slowly?
あとで校長先生と話します。
I will talk with the principal later.
まずコンピューターについて話そう。
First, let's talk about the computer.
2. to talk about, to tell about
ご家族のことを少し話してください。

Please tell me a little about your family.
西岡さんに話したいことがあります。
There is something I want to tell Ms. Nishioka.

はなす 離す *to part, to separate (transitive)*
兄はけんかしている二人を離しました。
My older brother separated two people fighting.

はなたば 花束 *bouquet*

バナナ *banana*

はなび 花火 *fireworks*
花火を上げる to set off fireworks
花火大会 fireworks display

はなびら 花びら *petal*

はなむこ 花婿 *bridegroom* [↔ 花嫁]

はなやか 華やか ～な *gorgeous, brilliant, splendid*
華やかな色 brilliant colors
華やかなパーティー splendid party

はなよめ 花嫁 *bride* [↔ 花婿]
花嫁衣装 wedding dress

はなれる 離れる *to become separate; to move away, to leave (the place away from which the movement occurs can be marked either with* から *or with* を*.)*
父は朝食が終わるとすぐ食卓を離れます。
As soon as he finishes breakfast, my father leaves the table.
列を／から離れる to get out of line
離れている to be located at a distance, to be distant
小学校は駅から4キロ離れています。
The elementary school is four kilometers from the station.
この犬から離れていなさい。
Stay away from this dog.

はなわ 花輪 *flower wreath*

パニック *panic*
パニック状態 a state of panic

はね 羽 *1. feather*
2. wing [→ 翼]

ばね *(metal) spring* [→ ぜんまい]

ハネムーン *honeymoon* [→ 新婚旅行 (s.v. 新婚)]
二人はハネムーンにカナダに行きます。
The couple will go to Canada on their honeymoon.

はねる 跳ねる *1. to jump (upward)* [→ 跳び上がる]*; to bounce*
このかえるはよく跳ねるね。
This frog jumps well, doesn't it?
2. to splash, to spatter (transitive or intransitive)
エプロンに油が跳ねました。
Oil spattered on my apron.
車がドレスに泥水を跳ねたよ。
A car splashed muddy water on my dress!

パノラマ *panorama*

はは 母 *mother* [→ お母さん; ↔ 父]
母は料理が大好きです。
My mother loves cooking.
母は今忙しいのです。
My mother is busy now.
失敗は成功の母。 (proverb)
Failure teaches success. (Literally: Failure is the mother of success.)
母の日 Mother's Day
母親 mother, female parent [↔ 父親 (s.v. 父)]

はば 幅 *width*
この川の幅はどのぐらいですか。
How wide is this river?
この通りは幅が狭いです。
This street is narrow. (Literally: As for this street, the width is narrow.)
幅跳び (US) broad jump, long jump

パパ *daddy, dad*

はぶく 省く *1. to leave out, to omit, to exclude*

この文章を省きなさい。
Leave out this text.
この人の名前を名簿から省いてしまった。
I omitted this person's name from the list.

2. to curtail, to reduce, to save, to make it possible to do with less of

時間を省く to save time

ハプニング *a happening*

はま 浜 *beach*

浜を散歩しましょう。
Let's walk along the beach.
浜辺 [☞ 浜 (above)]

はまぐり 蛤 *clam*

はまる 嵌まる, 填まる *1. to fit in place (intransitive)*

戸がうまくはまりませんね。
The door doesn't close properly, does it?
型にはまる to fit a mold, to be stereotypical

2. to fall into, to get trapped

父の車が泥道にはまりました。
My father's car got stuck in the muddy road.

ハム *ham ((meat))*

ハム *ham radio operator*

ハムエッグ *ham and eggs*

はめつ 破滅 *ruin, ruination*

破滅する to be ruined

はめる 嵌める, 填める *1. to fit in place (transitive)*

大工さんは窓にステンドグラスをはめた。
The carpenter fitted stained glass into the window.

2. to put on, to slip on

(The direct object is ordinarily something that fits snugly on a hand, finger, etc. Like other verbs for putting on clothing, はめる in the -ている form can express the meaning **be wearing, have on**.)

運転手は手袋をはめました。
The driver put on gloves.
由美はいつも結婚指輪をはめています。
Yumi is always wearing a wedding ring.

3. 【CRUDE】 *to ensnare; to take in, to deceive* [→ 騙す]

ばめん 場面 *1. scene (in a play, etc.); setting*

場面が変わりました。
The scene changed.

2. situation, circumstances

危ない場面 dangerous situation

はもん 波紋 *1. concentric ripples*

2. repercussion, subsequent effect

Aに波紋を投じる to have repercussions on A

はやい 早い *early* [↔ 遅い1.]

きのうは早い昼食をとりました。
Today I took an early lunch.
きょうは早いですね。
You're early today, aren't you?
祖父はいつも早く起きます。
My grandfather always gets up early.
弟はいつもより早く学校へ出かけました。
My younger brother left for school earlier than usual.
できるだけ早く帰ってきてね。
Come home as soon you can, OK?

はやい 速い *fast, quick* [↔ 遅い2.]

山本選手は走るのが速いね。
Yamamoto runs fast, doesn't he? (Literally: As for Yamamoto, running is fast, isn't it?)
流れの速い川を渡らなければなりません。
We have to cross a fast-flowing river.
高橋君は計算が速いよ。
Takahashi is quick at calculation!
もっと速く歩いてください。
Please walk faster.

はやがてん 早合点 *hasty conclusion,*

premature conclusion
早合点する to jump to a conclusion

はやくち 早口 *rapid talking*
早口言葉 tongue twister

はやし 林 *a woods*

はやす 生やす *to let grow, to cultivate*
ひげを生やす to grow a beard

はやめに 早めに *earlier than the appointed time, ahead of schedule*

はやり [[→ 流行]] *1. fashion, vogue, popularity, popular trend*
2. going around, prevalence (of a disease)

はやる *1. to become fashionable, to become popular*
今このヘアスタイルがはやっているよ。
This hair style is in fashion now!
この歌が大学生の間ではやっています。
This song is popular among college students.
2. to go around, to become prevalent, to become widespread (when the subject is a disease)
この学校では流感がはやっています。
'Flu is going around at this school.

はら 腹 *1.* 【CRUDE for お腹】*stomach, belly*
腹が減る to get hungry
腹が痛い one's stomach aches
2. mind, heart
腹が立つ to get angry
腹を立てる to get angry

ばら 薔薇 *rose*
ばらはとてもいいにおいがしますね。
Roses smell very nice, don't they?
ばらの木 rose bush
ばら色 rose color, pale red

はらう 払う *1. to pay (The direct object is the money, charge, expense, etc.)*
きょうは私が勘定を払います。
Today I will pay the bill.
AにBを払う to pay B to A
あした大家さんに5万円払います。
I will pay ¥50,000 to the landlord tomorrow.
注意を払う to pay attention
2. to sweep away, to wipe away, to clean away
ほこりを払う to clean away dust

パラシュート parachute
パラシュートで降りる to descend by parachute

ばらす 【COL.】*1. to reveal, to divulge, to disclose*
秘密をばらす to reveal a secret
2. to take apart, to take to pieces

パラソル *parasol* [→ 日傘 (s.v. 日)]

はらばい 腹這い ～になる *to lie on one's stomach*

はらはら ～する *to become uneasy, to get anxious*
ファーストのプレーにははらはらしたよ。
I became uneasy about the first baseman's play!

ばらばら *1. ～の separate, scattered; in pieces*
私たちはばらばらに家を出ました。
We left home separately.
ばらばらになる to scatter, to disperse; to come apart
ばらばらにする to scatter, to disperse; to take apart
弟はそのおもちゃをばらばらにしました。
My younger brother took that toy apart.
2. (～と) in big drops
雨がばらばら降る rain falls in big drops

パラフィン *paraffin*
パラフィン紙 paraffin paper

バランス *balance, equilibrium* [→ 釣り合い]

バランスを失う to lose one's balance

バランスが取れる to become balanced

はり 針 *1. needle*

針に糸を通す to thread a needle

2. hand (of a clock)

時計の針が12時を指しています。
The hands of the clock are pointing to 12:00.

はりがね 針金 *(metal) wire*

バリカン *barber's clippers*

ばりき 馬力 *horsepower*

—馬力 (counter for horsepower; see Appendix 2)

この車には200馬力のエンジンがついています。
There is a 200-horsepower engine in this car.

バリケード *barricade*

バリケードを築く to set up a barricade

ハリケーン *hurricane*

バリトン *1. baritone (voice)*

2. baritone (singer)

3. baritone (part)

はる 春 *spring ((season))* [↔ 秋]

もうすぐ春です。
It will soon be spring.

春には花見に出かけます。
In the spring we go out cherry-blossom viewing.

この春家族でハイキングに行きました。
We went hiking as a family this spring.

春風 spring wind

春雨 spring rain

春休み (US) spring vacation, (UK) the spring holidays

はる 張る *1. to spread out, to stretch out (transitive or intransitive)*

その2本の木の間にロープを張ろう。
Let's stretch a rope between those two trees.

この木は枝が広く張っていますね。
The branches of this tree are spread out wide, aren't they?

テントを張る to put up a tent

帆を張る to put up a sail

胸を張る to throw out one's chest

根が張る roots spread out

値段が張る a price is expensive

2. to tauten (transitive or intransitive)

糸が張る a thread becomes taut

綱を張る to pull a rope taut

気が張る to become nervous, to become strained

気を張る to strain one's nerves

肩が張る one's shoulder becomes stiff

3. to spread over the entire surface (transitive or intransitive)

田んぼに水を張る to flood a paddy

池に氷が張る ice forms on a pond

4. to slap, to hit with an open hand

はる 貼る *to affix, to stick (on a flat surface)*

この封筒に62円切手をはってください。
Please stick a ¥62 stamp on this envelope.

掲示板にこのポスターをはりましょう。
Let's put this poster on the bulletin board.

はるか 遥か *1. ～な distant, faraway*

はるかな未来 distant future

はるかに distantly, in the distance

はるかに明かりが見えます。
A light is visible in the distance.

2. ～に by far, much [→ ずっと3.]

このギターは私のよりはるかにいいです。
This guitar is much better than mine.

バルコニー *balcony*

はるばる *(～と) all the way, covering a great distance*

その役者ははるばるモスクワからきた。

That actor came all the way from Moscow.

パルプ *(wood) pulp*

はれ 晴れ 〜の *cloudless, fair, clear*

あしたは晴れでしょう。
It will probably be fine tomorrow.

晴れのち曇り。(a weather forecast)
Fair, cloudy later.

バレー [☞バレーボール]

バレエ *ballet*

娘はバレエを習っています。
My daughter is studying ballet.

パレード *parade*

パレードする to parade

優勝チームが通りをパレードしました。
The championship team paraded along the street.

バレーボール *1. (the game of) volleyball*

バレーボールをする to play volleyball

2. a volleyball

はれつ 破裂 *bursting, rupture*

破裂する to burst, to rupture

地階のボイラーが破裂しましたよ。
The boiler in the basement burst!

パレット *(painter's) palette*

バレリーナ *ballerina*

はれる 晴れる *1. to clear up, to become cloudless*

午後には晴れるでしょう。
It will probably clear up in the afternoon.

晴れた空をひばりが飛んでいます。
Skylarks are flying in the clear sky.

気分が晴れる to feel better, to recover one's spirits

2. to clear up, to clear away (when the subject is clouds, etc.)

霧はすぐ晴れるそうです。
I hear the fog will clear up right away.

疑いが晴れる suspicion becomes cleared up

はれる 腫れる *to swell, to become swollen (The subject is part of the body.)*

けがをした指ははれるに違いないよ。
An injured finger will certainly swell!

ばれる 【COL.】 *to be revealed, to be divulged, to be disclosed*

バレンタインデー *Valentine's Day*

パロディー *parody*

バロメーター *barometer* [→ 気圧計 (s.v. 気圧)]

パワー *power*

パワフル 〜な *powerful*

はん− 半− *half- (Added to noun bases.)*

半額 half price

半世紀 half a century

半袖 short sleeves

半年 half a year

半ズボン shorts, short pants

−はん −半 *and a half (Added to number bases.)*

授業は2時間半です。
The class is two and a half hours.

今10時半です。
It's 10:30 now.

はん 判 *signature seal*

(Documents are ordinarily stamped with a seal rather than signed in Japan.) [→ 印鑑]

Aに判を押す to stamp one's seal on A, to stamp A with one's seal

この用紙に判を押してください。
Please put your seal on this form.

ばん 晩 *night, evening* [→ 夜]

私たちはいつも晩の7時に夕食を食べる。
We usually have dinner at 7:00 in the evening.

土曜日の晩に美知子さんに会います。
I'll see Michiko on Saturday night.

叔父は五月一日の晩に着きました。

My uncle arrived on the night of May 1.
健さんは朝から晩まで働いたよ。
Ken worked from morning until night!
一晩 (counter for nights; see Appendix 2)
晩ご飯 evening meal, dinner [→ 夕食]
一晩中 all night long
今晩 tonight [→ 今夜]
毎晩 every night
明晩 tomorrow night
昨晩 last night [→ 昨夜]

ばん 番 *1. one's turn*
さあ、だれの番ですか。
All right, whose turn is it?
2. keeping watch, guarding [→ 見張り 1.]
番に立つ to go on guard, to stand guard
Aの番をする to keep an eye on A, to watch over A
私はスーツケースの番をします。
I will keep an eye on the suitcase.
番人 guard, watchman; caretaker

-ばん -番 *1. (counter for numbers; see Appendix 2)*
座席は何番ですか。
What number is your seat?
2. (counter for positions in a sequence or ranking; see Appendix 2)
加藤君はクラスで3番です。
Kato is third in the class.

パン *bread*
私はご飯よりパンのほうが好きです。
I like bread better than rice.
私は朝食にバターを塗ったパンを食べた。
I had bread and butter for breakfast.
姉はよくオーブンでパンを焼きます。
My older sister often bakes bread in the oven.
パン粉 bread crumbs (used in cooking)
パン屋 bakery; baker

はんい 範囲 *range, extent, scope*
父は読書の範囲が広いです。
My father reads widely. (Literally: As for my father, the range of reading is wide.)

はんえい 繁栄 *prosperity, flourishing*
繁栄する to prosper, to flourish, to thrive

はんが 版画 *woodblock print; etching*

ハンガー *(clothes) hanger*

ハンカチ *handkerchief*
このハンカチで汗をふきなさい。
Wipe the sweat with this handkerchief.

バンガロー *bungalow*

はんきゅう 半球 *hemisphere*

バンク *bank ((financial institution))* [→ 銀行]
データバンク data bank

パンク *(tire) puncture, blowout*
パンクする to get a flat tire (when the subject is a vehicle); to be punctured, to go flat (when the subject is a tire)
父はパンクを修理してもらいました。
My father had the puncture fixed.

ハンググライダー *hang glider*

ばんぐみ 番組 *(entertainment) program*
時々子供の番組を見ます。
I sometimes watch children's programs.

はんけい 半径 *radius (of a circle or sphere)*
この地球儀の半径は25センチです。
The radius of this globe is 25 centimeters.

はんげき 反撃 *counterattack*
反撃する to counterattack

はんけつ 判決 *judicial decision, court judgment*
判決を下す to hand down a decision, to make a ruling

ばんけん 番犬 *watchdog*

はんこ 判子【COL. for 判, 印】*signature seal*

はんこう 反抗 *resistance, opposition* [↔

服従]

反抗する to resist, to oppose

ばんごう 番号 *number (used as an identifier)*

切符の番号は何番ですか。

What number is your ticket?

番号が違います。 (on the telephone)

You have the wrong number. (Literally: The number is wrong.)

番号順 numerical order

電話番号 telephone number

ばんこく 万国 *all the countries of the world*

万国博覧会 international exposition, world's fair

はんざい 犯罪 *crime*

犯罪者 a criminal

ばんざい 万歳 *hurrah, hurray*

万歳、勝ったぞ！

Hurray, we won!

ハンサム ～な *handsome*

はんじ 判事 *judge, magistrate* [→裁判官 (s.v. 裁判)]

はんしゃ 反射 *reflection (back from a surface)*

反射する to reflect (transitive or intransitive)

AがBに反射する A reflects off B

光が屋上に反射していました。

Light was reflecting off the rooftop.

はんしん 阪神 *the Osaka-Kobe area*

ハンスト *hunger strike*

パンスト [☞パンティーストッキング (s.v. パンティー)]

はんする 反する *{Irreg.} to go against, to be contrary*

その行為は法律に反しています。

That act is against the law.

はんせい 反省 *reflection, thinking back (on something one has done)*

やり直す前にもっと反省が必要です。

Before doing it over, more reflection is necessary.

反省する to reflect on, to think back on

自分の言葉を反省しました。

I thought back on my own words.

－ばんせん －番線 *(counter for railroad-station track numbers; see Appendix 2)*

名古屋行きの電車は２番線から出ます。

The train for Nagoya leaves from Track No. 2.

ばんそう 伴奏 *(musical) accompaniment*

ピアノの伴奏で歌いましょう。

Let's sing to accompaniment of the piano.

先生はピアノでバイオリンの伴奏をした。

The teacher accompanied the violin on the piano.

伴奏する to play accompaniment

ばんそうこう 絆創膏 *sticking plaster (for an injury)*

はんそく 反則 *foul (in sports)* [→ファウル2.]

反則する to commit a foul

パンダ *panda*

ハンター *hunter* [→猟師 (s.v. 猟)]

はんたい 反対 *1. the opposite, the contrary* [→逆]

「左」の反対は何ですか。

What is the opposite of "left"?

石上さんは反対の方向に歩いています。

Mr. Ishigami is walking in the opposite direction.

2. opposition, objection [↔賛成]

大統領の反対でその法案は通らなかった。

Due to the president's opposition that bill did not pass.

反対の人 a person who is opposed

反対する to be opposed, to object

この計画には強く反対します。

I am strongly opposed to this plan.

反対側 opposite side

パンタグラフ *pantograph*

はんだん 判断 *a judgment, assessment*

自分自身の判断に従って行動すべきです。
You have to act according to your own judgment.

判断する to judge, to form a judgment about

人を外見で判断してはいけないよ。
You mustn't judge a person by outward appearances!

ばんち 番地 *lot number (as part of an address)*

この手紙は番地がまちがっているよ。
This lot number on this letter is wrong!

—番地 (counter for lot numbers; see Appendix 2)

この家は何番地ですか。
What lot number is this house?

パンチ *punch, blow with the fist*

パンチ *(hole) punch*

パンチカード punch card

パンチ *punch ((beverage))*

パンツ *1. underpants*

2. exercise pants

はんてい 判定 *judgment, decision*

パンティー *panties*

1枚のパンティー one pair of panties

パンティーストッキング panty hose

ハンディキャップ *1. handicap, disadvantage*

2. handicap (in golf)

バント *bunt (in baseball)*

バントする to bunt

犠牲バント sacrifice bunt

バンド *1. belt ((clothing))* [→ ベルト1.]

2. band (on a watch, etc.)

バンド *(musical) band*

ブラスバンド brass band

ロックバンド rock band

はんとう 半島 *peninsula*

ハンドバッグ *handbag, purse*

ハンドボール *1. (the game of) handball*

2. a handball

パントマイム *pantomime*

ハンドル *1. steering wheel*

運転手はハンドルを左にきりました。
The driver cut the steering wheel to the left.

2. handlebars

左ハンドル left-side steering wheel

右ハンドル right-side steering wheel

はんにん 犯人 *criminal, culprit*

ばんねん 晩年 *one's later years*

祖父は晩年を一人で暮らしました。
My grandfather lived his later years alone.

はんのう 反応 *response, reaction*

市民は新しい計画に反応を示さなかった。
The citizens showed no reaction to the new plan.

反応する to respond, to react

化学反応 chemical reaction

連鎖反応 chain reaction

ばんのう 万能 ～の *all-around, able to do anything well; effective in all circumstances*

万能選手 all-around player

ハンバーガー *hamburger*

ハンバーグ *hamburger steak*

はんばい 販売 *selling (merchandise)*

販売する to sell, to deal in

販売部 sales department

販売員 salesperson [→ セールスマン]

自動販売機 vending machine

ばんぱく 万博 [☞ 万国博覧会 (s.v. 万国)]

はんぱつ 反発 *1. repelling, repulsion*

反発する to repel

2. rebounding, springing back

反発する to rebound, to spring back

3. resistance, opposition [→ 反抗]

反発する to resist, to oppose

パンフレット *pamphlet*

はんぶん 半分 *half*

8の半分は4です。
Half of eight is four.

私の古い切手の半分は外国のものです。
Half of my old stamps are foreign ones.

このケーキを半分に切ってください。
Cut the cake in half, please.

この仕事はもう半分終わりました。
I've already finished half this work.

ハンマー *hammer* [→ 金槌1.]

ハンマー投げ hammer throw ((athletic event))

はんらん 反乱 *revolt, rebellion*

反乱する to revolt, to rebel

反乱を起こす to revolt, to rebel

反乱軍 rebel army, rebel forces

はんらん 氾濫 *overflowing, flood*

はんらんする to overflow its banks, to flood

この川は毎年はんらんします。
The river overflows its banks every year.

はんれい 凡例 *introductory explanatory notes*

地図の凡例 map legend

ひ

ひ 火 *fire*

火のない所に煙は立たない。(proverb)
Where there's smoke there's fire. (Literally: In a place where there is no fire, smoke does not rise.)

Aに火をつける to set fire to A, to light A on fire

だれがその家に火をつけたのですか。
Who set fire to that house?

火を起こす to build a fire, to get a fire going

火を消す to put out a fire

火に当たる to warm oneself at a fire

火の用心をする to look out for fire

ひ 日 *1. the sun* [→ 太陽]; *sunshine* [→ 日光]

日が昇る the sun rises

日が沈む the sun sets

Aに日が当たる the sun shines on A, the sun shines into A

Aに日が差し込む the sun shines into A

日に焼ける to become suntanned; to become sunburned

2. day

日が短くなってきました。
The days have become shorter.

その日に映画を見に行きました。
On that day I went to see a movie.

キャンプの日を決めましょう。
Let's decide the day for camping.

日当たり the degree to which sunshine strikes

この教室は日当たりがいいですね。
This classroom is nice and sunny, isn't it?

日傘 parasol

日増しに day by day, as each day goes by

日の出 sunrise

日の入り sunset

日雇い hiring as day labor

日差し sunshine, sunlight

ひー 非ー *non-, un- (Added to noun and*

adjectival noun bases.)
非文明の uncivilized
非常識な lacking in common sense
非科学的な unscientific [↔ 科学的な (s.v. 科学)]

び 美 *beauty*
美学 (the study of) esthetics

ピアニスト *pianist*

ピアノ *piano*
ピアノを弾く to play the piano
ピアノを習う to study the piano, to take piano lessons

ビアホール *beer hall*

ピーアール *P. R.*
ピーアールする to publicize, to advertise

ビーカー *beaker*

ひいき 贔屓 *favor, partiality*
ひいきする to favor, to be partial to
母は弟をひいきしています。
My mother favors my younger brother.

ピーク *peak, maximum*

ビーズ *bead*

ヒーター *heater*

ピーティーエー *PTA*

ビート *(musical) beat*

ピーナッツ *peanut*
ピーナッツバター peanut butter

ビール *beer*
一杯のビール one glass of beer
一本のビール one bottle/can of beer
缶ビール canned beer
生ビール draft beer

ビールス *virus* [→ ウイルス]

ヒーロー *1. hero, heroic man* [→ 英雄] [↔ ヒロイン]
2. hero, protagonist (of a story) [→ 主人公 (s.v. 主人)]

ひえる 冷える *to get cold, to get chilly* [↔ 暖まる, 温まる]
夜になると、冷えますね。
It gets cold at night, doesn't it? (Literally: When it becomes night, it gets cold, doesn't it?)
ビールはまだ冷えていませんね。
The beer has not gotten cold yet, has it?

ピエロ *clown*

ひがい 被害 *damage, harm*
被害を与える to do damage, to harm
被害を受ける to suffer damage, to be harmed
台風で作物は大きな被害を受けました。
The crops suffered great damage in the typhoon.
被害者 victim

ひかく 比較 *comparison*
比較する to compare [→ 比べる]
自分の答えを正解と比較してください。
Please compare your own answers with the correct answers.
比較的(に) comparatively, relatively [→ 割合に]

ひかげ 日陰 *shade, place shaded from sunlight* [↔ 日向]
日陰で休みましょう。
Let's rest in the shade.

ひがし 東 *the east* [↔ 西]
東アジア East Asia
東風 east wind
東日本 Eastern Japan

ぴかぴか *shiningly, twinkle-twinkle*
星がぴかぴか光っています。
The stars are twinkling.
ぴかぴかの shiny
秋山さんはぴかぴかの靴をはいています。
Mr. Akiyama is wearing shiny shoes.

ひかり 光 *light, illumination*
光の速さ the speed of light
星の光 starlight

ひかる 光る *to emit light, to shine, to flash*
月が明るく光っているね。
The moon is shining brightly, isn't it?
今夜は星がいっぱい光っているよ。
A lot of stars are shining tonight!
暗い空に稲妻が光りました。
Lightning flashed in the dark sky.

ひかん 悲観 *pessimism* [↔ 楽天, 楽観]
悲観する to be pessimistic
悲観的な pessimistic
悲観的な見方 pessimistic view

ーひき ー匹 *(counter for animals; see Appendix 2)*

ひきあげる 引き上げる *1. to pull up, to raise by pulling*
沈んだ船を引き上げるのは時間がかかる。
Raising a sunken ship takes time.
2. to raise (a price)
バス会社は運賃を少し引き上げるだろう。
The bus company will probably raise fares a little.

ひきうける 引き受ける *to undertake, to take, to agree to do*
その仕事を引き受けます。
I will take on that job.

ひきおこす 引き起こす *to cause, to bring about, to give rise to*
バスの運転手は交通事故を引き起こした。
The bus driver caused a traffic accident.

ひきかえす 引き返す *to turn back; to return to where one started*
登山家は頂点に着くとすぐに引き返した。
The mountain climber turned back as soon as he reached the summit.

ひきがね 引き金 *trigger*

ひきざん 引き算 *subtraction (in arithmetic)* [↔ 足し算]
引き算する to subtract [→ 引く4.]

ひきずる 引きずる *to drag (transitive)*
子供たちは大きな箱を引きずっています。
The children are dragging a large box.

ひきだし 引き出し *drawer*
母は引き出しを開けて、靴下を出した。
My mother opened a drawer and took out some socks.

ひきだす 引き出す *1. to pull out, to draw out*
2. to withdraw (money) [→ 下ろす2.]
けさ銀行から5000円引き出しました。
This morning I withdrew ¥5,000 from the bank.

ひきつぐ 引き継ぐ *to take over, to succeed to* [→ 継ぐ]

ひきにく 挽肉 *ground meat*

ひきにげ 轢き逃げ *hit and run ((traffic accident))*
ひき逃げする to hit and run
轢き逃げ事件 hit-and-run accident

ひきのばし 引き伸ばし *enlargement ((photograph))*

ひきのばす 引き伸ばす *1. to stretch out by pulling*
2. to enlarge (a photograph)
この写真を大きく引き伸ばしてください。
Please enlarge this photograph.

ひきょう 卑怯 〜な *1. cowardly* [→ 臆病な]
逃げるのはひきょうですよ。
Running away is cowardly!
2. unfair, mean, base
それはひきょうなやり方ですよ。
That's an unfair way to do it!
卑怯者 coward

ひきわけ 引き分け *tie, draw*
試合は引き分けに終わりました。
The game ended in a tie.

ひきわける 引き分ける *1. to pull apart, to separate by pulling*

2. to tie, to draw (in a contest)

ひく 引く *1. to pull, to tug, to draw* [→ 引っ張る1.] [↔ 押す1.]

カーテンを引いてください。
Please draw the curtain.

ロープを一生懸命引きました。
I pulled the rope as hard as I could.

くじを引く to draw lots

辞書を引く to consult a dictionary

2. to draw (a line)

ペンと物差しで直線を引きます。
I draw a straight line with a pen and a ruler.

3. to attract, to draw

注意を引く to attract attention

かぜを引く to catch a cold

4. to subtract, to deduct [↔ 足す2.]

６引く２は４。
Six minus two is four. (Although odd grammatically, this kind of sentence is a typical way of stating a fact of arithmetic.)

5. 値段を～ *to lower a price*

ひく 弾く *to play (a stringed instrument); to play (music on a stringed instrument)*

バイオリンを弾くのは難しいです。
Playing the violin is difficult.

ひく 轢く *to run over (The subject can be a vehicle or a person driving.)*

その車は猫をひきました。
That car ran over a cat.

ひくい 低い *1.* [[↔ 高い1.]] *low; short (vertically)*

京子は３人のうちでいちばん背が低い。
Kyoko is the shortest of the three.

その低いいすに座ってください。
Please sit on that low chair.

低い丘 low hill

低い鼻 flat nose

2. low, not loud [↔ 高い2.]

ラジオの音を低くしましょう。
Let's turn down the sound on the radio.

もっと低い声で話してください。
Please speak in a lower voice.

声を低くする to lower one's voice

ピクニック *picnic*

ひぐれ 日暮れ *nightfall, sunset* [→ 日没]; *early evening*

日暮れに戻っていきました。
I went back at sunset.

ひげ 髭 *whiskers; beard; mustache*

ひげを伸ばす to let one's whiskers grow

ひげをそる to shave (one's whiskers)

父は毎朝ひげをそります。
My father shaves every morning.

ひげを生やす to grow a beard/mustache

その画家はひげを生やしています。
That painter has a beard.

顎髭 beard

口髭 mustache

ひげき 悲劇 *tragedy* [↔ 喜劇]

悲劇的な tragic

ひけつ 秘訣 *secret, key, trick*

ひこう 飛行 *flight*

飛行する to fly, to make a flight

飛行士 aviator, flyer

夜間飛行 night flight

ひこうき 飛行機 *airplane*

父は千歳で東京行きの飛行機に乗った。
My father boarded a plane for Tokyo at Chitose.

ソウルでこの飛行機を降ります。
We'll get off this plane at Seoul.

伯母は福岡に飛行機で行きます。
My aunt will go to Fukuoka by plane.

ひこうじょう 飛行場 *airfield; airport* [→

空港]

ひこうせん 飛行船 *airship, dirigible*

ひこく 被告 *defendant* [↔ 原告]

ひごろ 日頃 *usually, habitually, all the time* [→ 普段(に)]

日ごろの usual, habitual, everyday

ひざ 膝 *1. knee*

ボールがひざに当たりました。
A ball hit my knee.

2. lap (portion of a person's body)

子供は母親のひざの上に座っていました。
The child was sitting on her mother's lap.

膝小僧 kneecap

ビザ *visa*

ビザを取る to get a visa

観光ビザ tourist visa

ピザ *pizza*

ひさしぶり 久し振り 〜の *the first in a long while*

久しぶりのサーフィンは楽しかったよ。
It was fun surfing again after such a long time! (Literally: The first surfing in a long while was fun.)

久しぶりですね。
It's been a long time, hasn't it? (Literally: It's the first time (that I've seen you) in a long while.)

久しぶりに／で for the first time in a long while

叔父は久しぶりに帰国します。
My uncle will return to his home country for the first time in a long while.

ひざまずく 跪く *to kneel*

ひさん 悲惨 〜な *miserable, wretched, tragic*

ひじ 肘 *elbow*

肘掛け armrest

ビジネス *business ((activity))*

ビジネスホテル inexpensive hotel catering to business people

ビジネスマン businessperson [→ 実業家 (s.v. 実業)]; office worker, company employee [→ 会社員 (s.v. 会社)]

びじゅつ 美術 *art, the fine arts*

美術学校 art school

美術品 work of art

美術館 art museum

美術展覧会 art exhibition

ひしょ 秘書 *(private) secretary*

西沢さんは社長の秘書です。
Ms. Nishizawa is the company president's secretary.

ひしょ 避暑 *escaping the heat of summer (by going to a cool location)*

軽井沢へ避暑に行くつもりです。
I am planning to go to Karuizawa to avoid the heat of summer.

避暑地 summer resort area

ひじょう 非常 *1. emergency*

非常の場合はブザーを押してください。
In case of an emergency please push this buzzer.

2. 〜な extraordinary, extreme

非常に very, extremely

山口さんは非常にゆっくりと歩きました。
Ms. Yamaguchi walked very slowly.

その試合は非常におもしろかったよ。
That game was very interesting!

その知らせを聞いて非常に驚きました。
I heard that news and was really surprised.

私は音楽に非常に興味があります。
I am very interested in music.

非常ベル emergency bell

非常口 emergency exit

非常階段 emergency stairs, fire escape

ビジョン *vision, conception of the future*

ビジョンのある人 a person of vision

びじん 美人 *beautiful woman, a beauty*

お嬢さんは美人ですね。
Your daughter is a beauty, isn't she?

ビスケット *sweet cracker, (UK) biscuit*

ピストル *pistol*

ピストン *piston*

ひそか 密か ～な *secret, covert*

探偵は密かに事務所に入りました。
The detective secretly entered the office.

ひたい 額 *forehead*

広い〔狭い〕額 broad/high〔narrow/low〕forehead

ビタミン *vitamin*

ひだり 左 *the left* [↔ 右]

左に銀行が見えます。
You can see a bank on the left.

次の角を左に曲がってください。
Turn left at the next corner.

左側 left side

左側通行 left-side traffic (Typically used on signs to mean Keep left.)

左利きの left-handed

左手 left hand

ひっかく 引っ掻く *to scratch, to claw*

猫が弟の顔を引っかきました。
A cat scratched my younger brother's face.

ひっき 筆記 *1. writing down; note taking*

筆記する write down; to take notes

2. transcript; notes

筆記試験 written examination

筆記用具 writing materials

びっくり ～する *to be surprised* [→ 驚く]

高い値段にびっくりしました。
I was surprised at the high price.

びっくり箱 jack-in-the-box

ひっくりかえす ひっくり返す *1. to turn upside down (transitive)*

2. to upset, to tip over [→ 倒す1.]

コップをひっくり返して水をこぼした。
I tipped over a glass and spilled some water.

ひっくりかえる ひっくり返る *{5} 1. to turn upside down (intransitive)*

ヨットが風でひっくり返ったよ。
The sailboat turned over in the wind!

2. to fall over, to tip over [→ 倒れる1.]

ひづけ 日付 *date (written on something)*

Aに日付を書く to date A, to write the date on A

平野さんの手紙は十月十日の日付でした。
Mr. Hirano's letter was dated October 10.

日付変更線 the International Date Line

ひっこす 引っ越す *to move (to a new residence)*

広田さんは東京から京都に引っ越した。
Mr. Hirota moved from Tokyo to Kyoto.

ひっこめる 引っ込める *to put back, to return to a container*

ひつじ 羊 *sheep*

羊飼い shepherd

子羊 lamb

ひっし 必死 ～の *desperate, frantic, furious*

学生たちは必死の努力をしました。
The students made desperate efforts.

必死になって desperately, frantically, furiously

ひつじゅん 筆順 *stroke order (in Japanese writing)*

ひっしょう 必勝 *certain victory*

びっしょり *to the point of being drenched*

びっしょりぬれる to get soaking wet

びっしょりの drenched, soaked

ひつぜん 必然 ～の *inevitable, certain*

ひったくる 【COL.】 *to steal by snatching*

ぴったり *(〜と) 1. tightly, snugly; exactly, perfectly, precisely*

ぴったりの tight, snug; exact, perfect-fitting

このスニーカーは僕にぴったりだよ。
These sneakers fit me perfectly!

ピッチ *pace, rate*

ピッチを上げる to quicken the pace

急ピッチ rapid pace

ヒッチハイク *hitchhiking*

ヒッチハイクする to hitchhike

ピッチャー *(baseball) pitcher* [→ 投手]

ひってき 匹敵 〜する *to be a match, to equal*

ヒット *1. hit (in baseball)* [→ 安打]

ピッチャーはヒットを２本だけ許した。
The pitcher only allowed two hits.

ヒットを打つ to get a hit

2. hit, success [→ 当たり3.]

ヒットする to become a hit

その映画はヒットすると思います。
I think the movie will become a hit.

ヒット曲 hit song

大ヒット big hit, great success [→ 大当たり(s.v. 当たり)]

ひっぱる 引っ張る *1. to pull, to tug*

登山者は綱を引っ張っています。
The mountain climber is pulling on a rope.

馬は馬車を引っ張っていました。
The horse was pulling a carriage.

2. to take, to bring, to drag along (The direct object is a person.)

警官は犯人を警察署に引っ張っていった。
The police officer took the criminal to the police station.

ヒップ *portion of the body from hip to hip; hip circumference*

ひつよう 必要 *necessity, need*

この本を読む必要はないです。
There is no need to read this book.

大統領も行く必要があります。
It is necessary for the president to go too.

Aを必要とする to come to need A

今援助を必要としています。
I need help now.

必要な necessary

運動は健康に必要です。
Exercise is necessary for health.

ひてい 否定 *denial* [↔ 肯定]

否定する to deny

政治家はその事実を否定しました。
The politician denied that fact.

否定文 negative sentence

否定的な contradictory, negative

ビデオ *1.* [☞ ビデオテープ]

2. [☞ ビデオテープレコーダー (s.v. ビデオテープ)]

ビデオテープ *videotape*

ビデオテープに撮る to record on videotape

ビデオテープレコーダー videotape recorder, VCR

ひと 人 *1. person*

岸さんはどんな人ですか。
What kind of person is Mr. Kishi?

人は約束を守るべきです。
A person should keep promises.

あの人は寺田さんです。
That person is Ms. Terada.

そう考える人もいます。
There are also people who think so.

たくさんの人が海で泳いでいます。
A lot of people are swimming in the ocean.

2. another person, others

人には親切にしなさい。
Be kind to others.

無断で人の自転車に乗ってはいけないよ。

You mustn't ride someone else's bicycle without their permission.

人柄 personal character, personality

人並みの the same as other people

ひとー 一ー *one, a (Added to noun bases, in many cases those derived from verbs.)*

一口 one mouthful, one drink, one bite; a word, a few words

一口に言う to say in a word, to say in a few words

一仕事 a considerable task, quite a job

一泳ぎ a swim

一泳ぎする to take a swim

一眠り a nap, a sleep

一眠りする to take a nap

ひどい 酷い *terrible, awful, severe, cruel*

ひどいあらしがその地方を襲いました。
A terrible storm hit that region.

背中にひどい痛みを感じました。
I felt terrible pain in my back.

ひどい目にあう to have a terrible experience

ひとこと 一言 *a word, a few words*

一言で言う to say in a word, to say in a few words

ひとごみ 人込み *crowd of people*

ひとごろし 人殺し *1. murder* [→ 殺人]

2. murderer

ひとさしゆび 人指し指 *forefinger, index finger*

ひとしい 等しい *equal, equivalent, identical* [→ 同じ]

この縄とその竿は長さが等しいです。
This rope and that pole are equal in length. (Literally: As for this rope and that pole, the length is equal.)

ひとじち 人質 *1. hostage*

テロリストは新聞記者を人質に取った。
Terrorists took the newspaper reporter hostage.

2. hostage taking

ひとつ 一つ *one (see Appendix 2)*

サッカーは僕の好きなスポーツの一つです。
Soccer is one of the sports I like.

一つ一つ one by one

子供は箱におもちゃを一つ一つ入れた。
The child put the toys into the box one by one.

ひとで *starfish*

ひとで 人手 *workers, help*

人手不足 shortage of workers

ひとびと 人々 *people, persons*

ひとみ 瞳 *pupil (of the eye)*

ひとり 一人 *1. one (when counting people; see Appendix 2)*

健さんは私の友達の一人です。
Ken is one of my friends.

フランス語ができる人は一人もいません。
There isn't even one person who can speak French.

2. oneself alone (often written 独り)

一人にしておいてください。
Please leave me alone.

一人で, 独りで alone, by oneself

祖母は独りで住んでいます。
My grandmother lives by herself.

私は一人でその仕事をしました。
I did that work by myself.

独りの unmarried, single [→ 独身の]

独りぼっちの solitary, all alone

独りでに spontaneously, by itself

一人っ子 only child

一人息子 only son

一人娘 only daughter

ひとりごと 独り言 *talking to oneself; words directed at oneself*

独り言を言う to talk to oneself

ひな 雛 *1. newly hatched bird, chick* [→ ひよこ]

2. [☞ 雛人形(below)]

雛鳥[☞ 雛1. (above)]

雛人形 doll displayed for Hinamatsuri (the Doll Festival)

ひなぎく 雛菊 *daisy*

ひなた 日向 *place where the sun is shining* [↔ 日陰]

ひなたに出る to go out into the sun

ひなまつり 雛祭り *the Girls' Festival, the Doll Festival (March 3rd)*

ひなん 非難 *criticism, reproach*

非難する to criticize, to reproach

国民は政府の措置を非難しました。
The people criticized the steps taken by the government.

ひなん 避難 *taking refuge, taking shelter; evacuation*

避難する to take refuge, to take shelter; to evacuate

一行は小屋に避難しました。
The party took refuge in a hut.

避難訓練 evacuation practice, fire drill

避難民 refugee

ビニール *vinyl*

ビニールハウス vinyl greenhouse

ひにく 皮肉 *irony; sarcasm*

皮肉な ironic; sarcastic

先生の言葉には多少の皮肉がありました。
There was some irony in the teacher's words.

ひにち 日にち *1. date, day on which something takes place*

パーティーの日にちを決めましょう。
Let's decide the date for the party.

2. the number of days; a number of days, several days

締め切りまでまだ日にちがあります。
There are still several days until the deadline.

ひねる 捻る {5} *1. to twist, to turn (with one's fingers)*

栓をひねってガスを消しました。
I twisted the stopper and turned off the gas.

2. to turn, to twist (one's body (at the waist) or neck so as to face another direction)

体を左にひねってください。
Please twist your body to the left.

頭をひねる to think hard

ひのき 桧 *Japanese cypress*

ひのまる 日の丸 *the Japanese national flag (Literally: the Circle of the Sun)*

ひばち 火鉢 *charcoal brazier*

ひばな 火花 *spark*

火花が散る sparks fly

ひばり 雲雀 *skylark*

ひはん 批判 *criticism, critical assessment*

批判する to criticize, to assess critically

先生はその哲学者の考えを批判しました。
The teacher criticized that philosopher's ideas.

批判的な critical

ひび *crack, small fissure*

このコップにはひびが入っているよ。
There is a crack in this glass!

ひびく 響く *1. to sound, to ring out, to be widely audible*

課長の声が廊下に響きました。
The section chief's voice rang out in the hall.

2. to resound, to reverberate, to echo

3. to have an effect [→ 影響する]

飲みすぎは健康に響きます。
Drinking too much affects one's health.

ひひょう 批評 *criticism, comment, review*

批評する to criticize, to comment on, to

review
矢野教授はその本を批評しました。
Professor Yano reviewed that book.
批評家 critic, reviewer

ひふ 皮膚 *skin (of a person or animal)*
姉は皮膚が滑らかです。
My older sister's skin is smooth.
強い〔弱い〕皮膚 strong〔delicate〕skin
皮膚病 skin disease

ビフテキ *(beef-) steak* [→ ステーキ]

ひぼん 非凡 〜な *extraordinary* [↔ 平凡な]

ひま 暇 *1. (amount of) time* [→ 時間2.]
手紙を書く暇がないです。
I don't have time to write letters.
暇をつぶす to kill time
2. spare time, free time, leisure time [→ 余暇]
暇な free, not busy [↔ 忙しい]
私は暇なとき、音楽を聴きます。
I listen to music when I have spare time.
今お暇ですか。
Are you free now?
暇潰し killing time

ひまわり 向日葵 *sunflower*

ひみつ 秘密 *secret, confidential matter; secrecy, confidentiality*
これは秘密にしましょう。
Let's keep this a secret.
秘密を守る to keep a secret; to maintain secrecy
秘密を打ち明ける to confide a secret
秘密の secret, confidential
泥棒は秘密の場所にお金を隠しました。
The thief hid the money in a secret place.

びみょう 微妙 〜な *subtle, difficult to discern*

ひめい 悲鳴 *scream, cry*
悲鳴をあげる to scream, to cry out
少年は悲鳴をあげて助けを求めました。
The boy cried out for help.

ひも 紐 *string, cord, thin strap*
古雑誌をひもで縛ってください。
Please tie up the old magazines with string.
靴紐 shoelace

ひやかす 冷やかす *to make fun of, to tease* [→ からかう]

ひゃく 百 *hundred (see Appendix 2)*
百万 one million
100パーセント 100 percent

ひやけ 日焼け *suntan; sunburn*
日焼けする to become suntanned; to become sunburned
日焼け止めクリーム sunscreen

ひやす 冷やす *to cool, to chill (transitive)*
すいかを冷蔵庫で冷やしましょう。
Let's chill the watermelon in the refrigerator.
頭を冷やす to calm down, to regain one's composure

ひゃっかじてん 百科事典 *encyclopedia*

ひゃっかてん 百貨店 *department store* [→ デパート]

ひゆ 比喩 *metaphor, simile*
比喩的な metaphorical, figurative

ヒューズ *(electrical) fuse*

ヒューマニズム *humanitarianism*

ビュッフェ *buffet restaurant*

ひよう 費用 *expense, expenditure, cost*
旅行の費用は20万円くらいになります。
Travel expenses come to about ¥200,000.

ひょう 表 *chart, table; list* [→ 一覧表]
表にする to make into a table; to make into a list
先生は試験の結果を表にしました。
The teacher made the examination results into a table.

時間表 timetable
予定表 chart of one's schedule

ひょう 豹 *leopard; panther*

ひょう 票 *vote; ballot*
一票 (counter for votes; see Appendix 2)
平田さんは25票を獲得しました。
Ms. Hirata got 25 votes.

ひょう 雹 *hail ((precipitation))*
ひょうが降る hail falls

びよう 美容 *enhancing a person's beauty*
美容院 beauty parlor, beauty shop
美容師 hairdresser, beautician
美容体操 slim-down calisthenics

びょう 秒 *second (of time)*
一秒 (counter for seconds; see Appendix 2)
1分は60秒です。
One minute is 60 seconds.
秒針 second hand
秒読み countdown

びょういん 病院 *hospital, infirmary*
けが人は病院に収容されました。
The injured person was admitted to the hospital.
大学病院 university hospital
救急病院 emergency hospital
総合病院 general hospital

ひょうか 評価 *evaluation, appraisal, assessment*
評価する to evaluate, to appraise, to assess
部長は市山さんの能力を高く評価しています。
The department head evaluates Ms. Ichiyama's ability highly.
過大評価する to overestimate, to overrate
過小評価する to underestimate, to underrate

ひょうが 氷河 *glacier*
氷河時代 ice age

びょうき 病気 *sickness, illness* [↔ 健康]
祖父は目の病気にかかっています。
My grandfather is suffering from an eye disease.
妹は1週間病気で寝ています。
My younger sister has been sick in bed for a week.
重い〔軽い〕病気 serious〔slight〕illness
病気の (US) sick, ill
病気になる to become ill
病気が治る an illness gets better

ひょうきん 剽軽 ～な *funny, comical*
お兄さんはひょうきんですね。
Your older brother is funny, isn't he?

ひょうげん 表現 *expression, manifestation*
表現する to express
表現の自由 freedom of expression

ひょうさつ 表札 *nameplate (displayed near the entrance of a home in Japan)*

ひょうざん 氷山 *iceberg*
氷山の一角 the tip of an iceberg

ひょうし 表紙 *cover (i.e., the outermost part of a book, etc.)*

ひょうし 拍子 *(musical) time, (musical) rhythm*
田村さんはペンで拍子を取っています。
Mr. Tamura is keeping time with his pen.
2拍子 double time

ひょうしき 標識 *marker, sign*

びょうしつ 病室 *sickroom*

びょうしゃ 描写 *depiction, portrayal; description*
描写する to depict, to portray; to describe

ひょうじゅん 標準 *standard, norm*
この作品は標準に達していません。

This work does not come up to the standard.
標準語 standard language
標準時 standard time

ひょうしょう 表彰 *official commendation, public honoring*
表彰する to officially commend, to honor publicly
警官は人命救助で表彰されました。
The police officer was honored for saving a life.
表彰台 commendation award platform
表彰状 certificate of commendation
表彰式 commendation award ceremony

ひょうじょう 表情 *facial expression, look (on one's face)* [→ 目付き]
由美さんは悲しそうな表情でした。
Yumi had a sad look on her face.
コーチの顔には怒りの表情が浮んでいた。
An expression of anger appeared on the coach's face.

ひょうたん 瓢箪 gourd

ひょうてん 氷点 *the freezing point*
氷点下 (the temperature range) below the freezing point
今氷点下25度です。
It's 25 degrees below freezing now.

びょうどう 平等 *equality, impartiality*
平等な／の equal, even, impartial
二人は利益を平等に分けました。
The two divided the profits equally.
男女平等 equal rights for men and women

びょうにん 病人 *ill person*

ひょうばん 評判 *1. reputation*
その医者は評判がいいです。
That doctor's reputation is good.
2. fame, popularity, notoriety
評判の famous, popular, notorious
あの俳優は日本でも評判です。
That actor is popular in Japan too.

びょうぶ 屏風 *(free-standing) folding screen*

ひょうめん 表面 *surface*

ひよこ *newly hatched bird, chick (Most commonly used for chickens.)* [→ 雛1.]

ひょっと ～したら *just maybe, by some chance*
(This expression typically occurs in sentences ending with an expression of possibility (usually かもしれない). Since such a sentence has virtually the same meaning whether or not ひょっと is present, ひょっと is redundant in a sense, but it serves as a signal of how a sentence will end.)
ひょっとすると [☞ ひょっと (above)]
ひょっとして [☞ ひょっと (above)]

ビラ *handbill, leaflet, poster*

ひらおよぎ 平泳ぎ *breaststroke*

ひらがな 平仮名 *hiragana (i.e., the cursive variety of the Japanese syllabary)*

ひらく 開く *1. to open, to unclose (transitive or intransitive)* [↔ 閉じる]
戸が突然開きました。
The door opened suddenly.
庭のばらが開きました。
The roses in the yard have bloomed.
本の５ページを開きなさい。
Open the book to page 5
2. to give, to have, to hold (an event)
あしたパーティーを開きましょうか。
Shall we have a party tomorrow?

ひらける 開ける *to develop, to become developed*
この地域は徐々に開けてきました。
This area has gradually developed.

ひらたい 平たい *flat, level* [→ 平らな]

ピラミッド *pyramid*

ひらめ 平目 *(a kind of flounder)*

びり【COL.】*last place, bottom rank*

太郎はびりでゴールに入ったよ。
Taro reached the goal last!
きのうのテストでクラスのびりだったよ。
I was bottom of the class on yesterday's test!

ピリオド *period, (UK) full stop ((punctuation mark))* [→ 終止符]

ピリオド *period (in sports)*

ひりつ 比率 *ratio*

このクラスの男女の比率は 4 対 5 です。
The ratio of boys to girls in this class is four to five.

ひる 昼 *1. noon* [→ 正午]

昼までに電話してください。
Please telephone by noon.

2. daytime, the daylight hours, day [→ 日中, 昼間]

昼は暖かかったですね。
It was warm during the day, wasn't it?
夏は昼が長いです。
The days are long in summer.
父は昼も夜も忙しかったです。
My father was busy both day and night.
昼ご飯 lunch [→ 昼食]
昼寝 nap
昼休み lunch break

ビル *a building*

超高層ビル skyscraper

ひるま 昼間 *daytime, the daylight hours* [→ 日中] [↔ 夜間]

ひれ 鰭 fin

ひれい 比例 *proportion, proportionality*

比例の proportional
比例する to be proportional
A が B に比例する A is proportional to B

ひろい 広い [[↔ 狭い]] *1. wide, broad*

信濃川は川幅がとても広いです。
The Shinano River is very wide. (Literally: As for the Shinano River, the width of the river is very wide.)
トラックは広い通りに出ました。
The truck went out onto a broad street.
その画家は広く知られています。
The painter is widely known.
顔が広い one's circle of acquaintances is wide

2. large (in area), spacious

この部屋は私のより広いよ。
This room is more spacious than mine!
心が広い generous; broad-minded

ヒロイン *heroine* [→ 英雄] [↔ ヒーロー]

ひろう 疲労 *fatigue* [→ 疲れ]

ひろう 拾う *1. to pick up (something that has fallen or been scattered)*

公園のごみを拾いましょう。
Let's pick up the trash in the park.
運動場でこのボールペンを拾ったよ。
I picked up this ballpoint pen on the playground!
命を拾う to narrowly escape with one's life
タクシーを拾う to catch a taxi

2. to pick out, to select and take

ビロード *velvet*

ひろがる 広がる *1. to widen, to become more spacious*

もう少し行くと、川が広がります。
If you go a little further, the river will widen.

2. to spread, to become widespread [→ 広まる]

そのニュースは世界中に広がりました。
That news spread throughout the world.

3. to stretch out as a large expanse

目の前に青い海が広がっています。
The blue sea is stretching out before our eyes.

ひろげる 広げる *1. to widen, to make more spacious*

その道路を広げる必要があります。
It is necessary to widen that road.

2. to spread out, to lay out, to unfold (transitive)

生徒は机の上に世界地図を広げました。
The student spread out a world map on the desk.

ひろさ 広さ *1. width, breadth* [→ 幅]

2. area, spaciousness [→ 面積]

この庭の広さは20平方メートルぐらいだ。
The area of this garden is about 20 square meters.

ひろば 広場 *open space, square, plaza*

駅前の広場にみんなが集まりました。
Everyone gathered in the square in front of the station.

ひろまる 広まる *to spread, to become widespread*

その話は急速に広まりました。
That story spread quickly.

ひろめる 広める *to spread, to make widespread, to propagate*

従業員がそのうわさを広めました。
The employees spread that rumor.

びわ 枇杷 *loquat*

びん 瓶 *bottle*

瓶詰めの bottled

空き瓶 empty bottle

哺乳瓶 baby bottle

びん 便 *(airline) flight; (scheduled) ship; (scheduled) train*

次の便で行くことにしました。
I decided to go on the next flight.

ー便 (counter for number of flights or flight numbers; see Appendix 2)

ピン *pin ((fastener))*

その絵をピンで壁に留めてください。
Please pin that picture on the wall.

ネクタイピン tiepin

びんかん 敏感 〜な *sensitive, acutely-sensing* [↔ 鈍感な]

犬はにおいに敏感です。
Dogs are sensitive to smell.

ピンク *pink (as a noun)*

ひんけつ 貧血 *anemia*

ひんし 品詞 *part of speech*

ひんしつ 品質 *quality (of goods)*

品質管理 quality control

ひんじゃく 貧弱 〜な *poor, scanty, meager* [↔ 豊富な]

ヒンズーきょう ヒンズー教 *Hinduism*

ピンセット *tweezers*

一本のピンセット one pair of tweezers

びんせん 便箋 *letter-writing paper*

ピンチ *pinch, jam, fix*

ピンチを切り抜ける to get out of a pinch

ピンチに陥る to get into a pinch

ピンチヒッター pinch hitter (in baseball)

ヒント *hint, suggestion*

その問題のヒントをあげましょう。
I'll give you a hint to that question.

ピント *photographic focus, camera lens focal point*

ピントが合っている to be in focus

この写真はピントが合っていますか。
Is this picture in focus?

ピントが外れている to be out of focus

ピントを合わせる to set the focus correctly

カメラのピントを合わせて写真を撮った。
I focused the camera and took a picture.

ぴんと 〜来る *to come home to one, to ring a bell*

びんぼう 貧乏 *poverty*

貧乏な poor, indigent, destitute [↔ 金持

ちの]
この地方の人々はとても貧乏です。
The people of this region are very poor.

ピンぼけ ～の *out-of-focus, blurred*

ふ 府 *prefecture (Used to refer only to Osaka and Kyoto Prefectures.)*
京都府 Kyoto Prefecture
大阪府 Osaka Prefecture

ふー 不ー *un-, non-; bad (Added to noun and adjectival noun bases.)*
不明瞭な unclear [↔ 明瞭な]
不人気 unpopularity [↔ 人気]
不成績 bad results, poor showing

ぶ 部 *1. part, portion* [→ 部分]
一部 (counter for parts; see Appendix 2)
では、第1部から始めましょう。
Well then, let's begin with Part One.
2. department, division
部長 department head, division head
文学部 literature department
宣伝部 publicity department
野球部 baseball club, baseball team

－ぶ －部 *(counter for copies; see Appendix 2)*
そのレポートを1部送ってください。
Please send me one copy of that report.

ファースト *1. first base* [→ 一塁]
2. first baseman [→ 一塁手 (s.v. 一塁)]

ぶあいそ 無愛想 ～な *curt, unfriendly, surly*
あの店員は無愛想ですね。
That sales clerk is surly, isn't he?

ファイト *fight, fighting spirit* [→ 闘志]

ファイル *(document) file*
ファイルする to file, to put on file

ファインプレー *fine play (in sports)*

ファウル *1. foul (ball)* [↔ フェア2.]
ファウルを打つ to hit a foul
2. foul, rule violation [→ 反則]
ファウルボール [☞ ファウル1. (above)]
ファウルグラウンド foul ground, foul territory

ファクシミリ *facsimile, fax*

ファスナー *zipper* [→ ジッパー]

ファックス [☞ ファクシミリ]

ファッション *1. fashion, style, vogue* [→ 流行1.]
2. clothing fashion
ファッションモデル fashion model
ファッションショー fashion show

ふあん 不安 *unease, anxiety*
学生は試験の結果に不安を感じていた。
The student was feeling anxious about his examination results.
不安な uneasy, anxious

ファン *fan, enthusiast*
ファンクラブ fan club
ファンレター fan letter
映画ファン movie fan
野球ファン baseball fan

ファンタジー *fantasy*

ファンデーション *1. foundation ((make-up))*
2. foundation garment

ファンファーレ *(musical) fanfare*

ふい 不意 ～の *unexpected* [→ 思い掛けない]; *sudden* [→ 突然の]

ブイ *buoy*

フィート *foot (unit of measure)*
－フィート (counter for feet; see Appendix 2)

フィーバー *fever, wild enthusiasm* [→ 熱狂]
フィーバーする to become fevered

フィールド *the field (where field events are held in track and field)*
フィールド競技 field events

フィギュア [☞ フィギュアスケート]

フィギュアスケート *figure skating*

フィクション *fiction* [↔ ノンフィクション]

フィナーレ *finale*

フィルター *filter*
フィルターつきたばこ filter-tipped cigarette

フィルム *(photographic) film*
フィルムが３本必要です。
Three rolls of film are necessary.
カラーフィルム color film

ふう 風 *1. way, manner*
こんなふうに書いてください。
Please write it in this way.
2. appearance, air, manner
だらしない風をする to take on a sloppy appearance

—ふう —風 〜の／な *(Added to noun bases.) 1. -style*
細川さんは中国風の家に住んでいます。
Mr. Hosokawa lives in a Chinese-style house.
2. -like, having the air of, having the look of
お父さんは芸術家風でした。
Her father looked like an artist.

ふうけい 風景 *scenery, landscape* [→ 景色]; *view, vista* [→ 眺め]
風景画 landscape picture

ふうし 風刺 *satire*
風刺する to satirize

ふうしゃ 風車 *windmill*

ふうせん 風船 *balloon ((toy))*
風船ガム bubble gum

ふうそく 風速 *wind speed*
風速は10メートルです。
The wind speed is ten meters (per second).
風速計 wind gauge

ふうぞく 風俗 *customs, folkways, manners*
風俗習慣 manners and customs

ブーツ *boot ((footwear))*

フード *hood (on an article of clothing)*

ふうとう 封筒 *envelope*
手紙を封筒に入れて、出しました。
I put the letter in an envelope and mailed it.

ふうふ 夫婦 *married couple, husband and wife* [→ 夫妻]
あの夫婦は幸せそうですね。
That husband and wife look happy, don't they?
夫婦喧嘩 quarrel between husband and wife
新婚夫婦 newly-married couple

ブーム *boom, sudden increase in activity*
ブームになる to boom
今は高層建築がブームになっています。
Now high-rise building is booming.

ふうりん 風鈴 *wind chime*

プール *(swimming) pool*
プールで泳ぎましょう。
Let's swim in the pool.

ふうん 不運 *bad luck, misfortune* [↔ 幸運]
不運な unfortunate, unlucky
不運にも unfortunately, unluckily

ふえ 笛 *flute, pipes, woodwind instrument; whistle*

フェア *1.* 〜な *fair, equitable* [→ 公正な]
2. fair ball [↔ ファウル1.]

フェアボール [☞ フェア2. (above)]
フェアプレー fair play

フェスティバル *festival*

フェリー *ferry (-boat)*

フェリーボート [☞ フェリー]

ふえる 増える *to increase (intransitive)* [↔ 減る]

交通事故の数もだいぶ増えました。
The number of traffic accidents also increased considerably.
町の人口はこれから急に増えるでしょう。
The population of the town will probably increase rapidly from now on.
島野さんは体重が20キロ増えたよ。
Mr. Shimano's gained 20 kilograms! (Literally: As for Mr. Shimano, weight increased 20 kilograms.)

フェルト *felt*

フェンシング *fencing ((sport))*

フェンス *fence*

フォアボール *base on balls, walk* [→ 四球]

フォーク *fork ((eating utensil))*

フォークボール fork ball

フォークソング *1. (traditional) folk song* [→ 民謡]

2. American-style popular folk song

フォークダンス *folk dance*

フォーム *(athletic) form*

黒川さんのフォームはいい。
Ms. Kurokawa's form is good.

ふか 鱶 shark [→ 鮫]

ふかい 不快 ～な [[→ 不愉快な]] *1. unpleasant, distasteful*

2. displeased

ふかい 深い *deep* [↔ 浅い]

この池はどのぐらい深いですか。
About how deep is this pond?
植木屋は穴を深く掘っています。
The gardener is digging the hole deep.
市長はその問題を深く考えています。
The mayor is thinking deeply about that problem.
深い海 deep sea
深い考え deep thought
深い霧 dense fog
深い眠り deep sleep

ふかさ 深さ *depth*

この井戸の深さは何メートルですか。
How many meters deep is this well? (Literally: The depth of this well is how many meters?)

ふかのう 不可能 ～な *impossible* [↔ 可能な]

一人でそこに行くのは不可能です。
It is impossible to go there alone.

ぶき 武器 *weapon, arms* [→ 兵器]

武器を取る to take up arms

ふきけす 吹き消す *to blow out, to extinguish by blowing*

ろうそくを吹き消す to blow out a candle

ふきげん 不機嫌 ～な *in a bad mood, grouchy, displeased*

けさ先生は不機嫌ですね。
The teacher is in a bad mood this morning, isn't he?

ふきそく 不規則 ～な *irregular* [↔ 規則的な (s.v. 規則)]

ふきだす 吹き出す／噴き出す *1. to begin to blow (The subject is a wind.)*

北の風が吹き出しました。
A north wind began to blow.

2. to burst into laughter

私たちはその話を聞いて、吹き出したよ。
We heard that story and suddenly burst out laughing!

3. to spurt out, to spew out, to spout out

傷口から血が噴き出しています。
Blood is spurting out from the wound.

ふきつ 不吉 ～な *inauspicious, ominous*

ふきとばす 吹き飛ばす *to blow off (transitive) (The subject is typically a wind.)*
屋根を吹き飛ばすほど強い風です。
It's a wind strong enough to blow off roofs.

ぶきみ 不気味 ～な *eerie, weird*

ふきゅう 普及 *spread, diffusion*
知識の普及 the spread of knowledge
普及するto spread, to become more widespread
コンピューターは最近広く普及しました。
Computers have recently spread widely.

ふきょう 不況 *(economic) depression, (economic) slump* [→ 不景気]
不況の depressed, slumping

ふきん 付近 *neighborhood, vicinity* [→ 近所]
この付近には商店が多いです。
There are many stores in this neighborhood.

ふきん 布巾 *kitchen towel, dish towel*

ふく 服 *clothes, clothing*

ふく 吹く *1. to blow (intransitive) (The subject is a wind.)*
風がはげしく吹いています。
The wind is blowing hard.
2. to blow on
熱いお茶を吹いてさました。
I blew on the hot tea and cooled it down.
3. to play (a wind instrument); to play (music on a wind instrument)
野崎さんはトランペットを吹きます。
Mr. Nozaki plays the trumpet.
4 to spout out, to spew out (intransitive) [→ 吹き出す3.]
5 to spout out, to spew out (transitive)
鯨が潮を吹く a whale spouts

ふく 拭く *to wipe* [→ 拭う]
窓をきれいにふきなさい。
Wipe the windows clean.
私は皿をふいています。
I am wiping the dishes.

ふくー 副ー *vice-, assistant- (Added to noun bases.)*
副大統領 vice-president (of a country)
副会長 vice-chairperson
副校長 vice-principal
副社長 vice-president (of a company)
副支配人 assistant manager

ふぐ 河豚 *globefish, blowfish*
(This fish is considered a great delicacy in Japan, but proper preparation requires special training because its internal organs contain a deadly poison.)

ふくごうご 複合語 *compound word*

ふくざつ 複雑 ～な *complicated, complex* [↔ 単純な1.]
この複雑な機械の扱い方がわかりますか。
Do you know how to handle this complicated machine?

ふくさよう 副作用 *side-effect, harmful after-effect*

ふくさんぶつ 副産物 *by-product*

ふくし 副詞 *adverb*

ふくし 福祉 *welfare, well-being*
社会福祉 social welfare

ふくしゃ 複写 *1 copy, duplicate, reproduction* [→ コピー]
2. copying, duplicating, reproducing
複写する to copy, to duplicate, to reproduce
複写機 copying machine, duplicator

ふくしゅう 復習 *review of what one has learned* [↔ 予習]
復習する to review
もうきょうの授業を復習しました。
I have already reviewed today's classes.
さあ、6課を復習しましょう。

Now, let's review Lesson 6

ふくしゅう 復讐 *revenge*

復しゅうする to take revenge

大将は敵に復しゅうしました。

The general took revenge on the enemy.

ふくじゅう 服従 *obedience, submission* [↔ 反抗]

服従する to submit, to give obedience

ふくすう 複数 *the plural* [↔ 単数]

ふくせい 複製 *1. replica, reproduction*

2. making a replica, reproducing

複製する to make a replica of, to reproduce

ふくそう 服装 *dress, attire* [→ 身なり]

若月さんは服装に構わない人です。

Ms. Wakatsuki is a person who doesn't care about the way she dresses.

社長はいつもきちんとした服装です。

The company president always wears neat clothes. (Literally: As for the company president, it's always neat attire.)

ふくつう 腹痛 *stomachache*

ひどい腹痛がします。

I have a terrible stomachache.

ふくむ 含む *to contain, to include*

オレンジはビタミンCを多く含んでいる。

Oranges contain a lot of vitamin C.

この値段は消費税を含んでいます。

This price includes consumption tax.

ふくめる 含める *to add, to put in, to include* [↔ 除く]

Aを含めて including A

私を含めて５人が会議に出ます。

Including me, five people will attend the meeting.

ふくらはぎ 腫ら脛 *calf (of the leg)*

ふくらます 膨らます *to make swell, to inflate*

ビーチボールを膨らましました。

I inflated the beach ball.

ふくらむ 膨らむ *to swell, to bulge, to become inflated*

帆が風で膨らんでいます。

The sails are swelling in the wind.

ふくれる 膨れる *1. to swell, to expand*

パンが膨れる bread rises

2. 【COL.】 *to get sulky*

ふくろ 袋 *bag*

買い物袋 shopping bag

紙袋 paper bag

ふくろう 梟 *owl*

ふけ *dandruff*

ふけいき 不景気 *(economic) depression, bad times, hard times* [→ 不況]

今年は不景気です。

This year times are bad.

ふけつ 不潔 ～な *unclean, dirty* [→ 汚い1.] [↔ 清潔な]

ふける 更ける *to grow late, to become late (The subject is a night or a season.)*

夜が更ける to become late at night

秋が更ける to become late in autumn

ふける 老ける *to grow old*

母はもう老けてしまいました。

My mother has already grown old.

ふこう 不幸 [[↔ 幸福]] *unhappiness; misfortune*

不幸な unhappy; unfortunate

あの人は不幸な人生を送りました。

That person lived an unhappy life.

不幸にも unfortunately

ふごうかく 不合格 *failure (to meet a standard or pass a test)* [↔ 合格]

息子の不合格はまちがいないです。

My son's failure is certain.

不合格の unqualified, failed, rejected

不合格になる to fail, to be rejected

ふこうへい 不公平 *unfairness, partiality* [↔ 公平]

不公平な unfair, partial, inequitable

留学生は不公平な扱いを受けました。
The foreign student received unfair treatment.

この分け方は私にとって不公平です。
This way of dividing it is unfair for me.

ふさ 房 *1. tassel, tuft*

2. cluster, bunch (of fruit or flowers hanging from a branch)

ぶどうの房 a bunch of grapes

一房 one tuft; one bunch

ブザー *buzzer*

ブザーを鳴らす sound a buzzer

ふさい 夫妻 *husband and wife* [→ 夫婦]

—夫妻 Mr. and Mrs. (Added to a surname as a title.)

パーティーは鈴木夫妻のお宅であります。
The party will be at Mr. and Mrs. Suzuki's house.

ご夫妻【HON. for (above)】

友人夫妻 a friend and his/her spouse

ふさがる 塞がる *1. to become blocked, to become clogged*

道路は雪でふさがっていました。
The road was blocked with snow.

2. to become occupied, to become taken, to become in use

この席はふさがっていますか。
Is this seat occupied?

ふさく 不作 *bad crop* [↔ 豊作]

ふさぐ 塞ぐ *to stop up, to block*

この穴をふさいでください。
Please stop up this hole.

トラックが狭い道をふさいでいました。
A truck was blocking the narrow road.

ふざける *1. to joke, to kid around*

ふざけて言う to say in jest, to say jokingly

2. to romp, to frolic, to play around

うちの中でふざけるのはよしなさい。
Stop playing around in the house.

ふさわしい 相応しい *suitable, fitting, appropriate* [→ 適切な]

このドレスはパーティーにふさわしい。
This dress is suitable for a party.

ふし 節 *1. joint, node*

竹の節 bamboo joint

2. joint (where two bones come together) [→ 関節]

指の節 knuckle

3. knot (in wood)

4 tune, melody [→ メロディー]

ふじ 藤 *wisteria*

ぶし 武士 *samurai warrior*

武士道 the way of the samurai, the samurai code of honor

ぶじ 無事 ～な *free from mishap, safe*

兄は無事に仙台に到着しました。
My older brother arrived in Sendai safely.

ふしぎ 不思議 *marvel, wonder, strangeness*

不思議な strange, wonderful

先生がそんなことをしたとは不思議です。
It's a wonder that the teacher did such a thing.

よく不思議な夢を見ます。
I often have strange dreams.

上松さんは不思議な事件に巻き込まれた。
Mr. Uematsu got involved in a mysterious incident.

不思議なことに strangely

世界の七不思議 the Seven Wonders of the World

ふしぜん 不自然 ～な *unnatural* [↔ 自然の／な]

ぶしゅ 部首 *radical (of a Chinese character)*

ふじゆう 不自由 *inconvenience* [→ 不便]; *difficulty caused by the lack of something necessary*
不自由な inconvenient; difficult
不自由する to be inconvenienced, to have difficulty, to be in need
正美ちゃんは小遣いに不自由しています。
Masami is in need of more pocket money.

ふしょう 負傷 *getting injured, getting wounded*
負傷する to get injured, to get wounded
負傷者 injured person, wounded person

ぶしょう 無精, 不精 ～な *lazy, indolent, eager to spare oneself effort*
弟は少し無精です。
My younger brother is a little lazy.

ぶじょく 侮辱 *insult*
侮辱する to insult
人を侮辱するのはよくないですよ。
It's not good to insult people!

ふじん 夫人 *wife*
ー夫人Mrs. (Added to a family name or a given name a title.)

ふじん 婦人 *woman, lady*
婦人服 ladies' wear
婦人警官 policewoman

ふしんせつ 不親切 *unkindness* [↔ 親切]
不親切な unkind

ふすま 襖 *sliding door (of the type used between rooms in Japanese houses.)*

ふせい 不正 *injustice, unfairness* [↔ 公正]; *dishonesty; illegality*
不正を働く to do wrong
不正な unjust, unfair; dishonest; illegal

ふせぐ 防ぐ *1. to defend, to protect* [→ 守る2.]
住民は町を強盗から防ぎました。
The residents defended the town against the robbers.
2. to prevent, to protect against
事故を防ぐために規則を守りなさい。
Obey the rules to prevent accidents.
3. to keep away, to ward off
この煙は蚊を防ぐのに役立つでしょう。
This smoke will probably be useful to ward off mosquitoes.

ふせる 伏せる *1. to lay upside down, to lay face down; to turn upside down*
茶わんを食卓の上に伏せました。
I laid the bowls upside down on the table.
目を伏せる to look downward
体を伏せる to lie down face down
2. to lie down face down
少女は芝生の上に伏せています。
The girl is lying down on the grass.
3. to keep secret
私の名前を伏せてください。
Please keep my name secret.

ぶそう 武装 *arming, being armed*
武装する to arm oneself, to become armed

ふそく 不足 *insufficiency, shortage, lack*
不足する to become insufficient, to run short, to become lacking
あの島では食糧が不足しています。
Food is short on that island.
三上さんは忍耐が不足しています。
Mr. Mikami is lacking in patience.
水不足 water shortage
睡眠不足 lack of sleep, insufficient sleep
運動不足 lack of exercise, insufficient exercise

ふぞく 付属 ～の *attached, affiliated, accessory*
付属するto be attached, to belong, to be affiliated
この中学校は大学に付属しています。
This junior high school is affiliated with the university.

付属品 accessory item

ふた 蓋 *lid, cover, cap*

その箱のふたを取ってください。
Please take the lid off that box.

ふたをする to put a lid (on something)

あの瓶にふたをしましたか。
Did you put the cap on that bottle?

ふだ 札 *card, tag, label*

預り札 claim check

名札 name tag; nameplate

値札 price tag

荷札 baggage label

正札 price tag

ぶた 豚 *pig*

豚小屋 pigpen, pigsty

豚肉 pork

焼き豚 roast pork

ぶたい 舞台 *stage (for performances)*

舞台に立つ to appear on the stage

舞台俳優 stage actor

舞台照明 stage lighting

舞台装置 stage set

ふたご 双子 *twins*

あの二人は双子です。
Those two are twins.

ふたたび 再び *again, once again, once more*

花形先生は故郷を再び訪れました。
Dr. Hanagata visited her hometown again.

ふたつ 二つ *two (see Appendix 2)*

そのりんごを二つに切ってください。
Please cut that apple in two.

ふたり 二人 *two (when counting people; see Appendix 2)*

姉には息子が二人います。
My older sister has two sons.

ふたん 負担 *burden, onus*

負担する to bear, to accept (a burden, responsibility, etc.)

ふだん 普段（〜に） *usually, ordinarily* [→普通]

きょうはふだんより遅くうちを出ました。
Today I left home later than usual.

ふだんの usual, common, everyday

ふち 縁 *edge, rim*

少年はがけの縁に座っています。
The boy is sitting on the edge of the cliff.

ふちゅうい 不注意 *carelessness, inattention* [↔ 注意2.]

その事故は運転手の不注意から起こった。
That accident occurred because of the driver's carelessness.

不注意な careless, heedless [↔ 注意深い (s.v. 注意)]

不注意な発言をしないようにしなさい。
Take care not to make careless statements.

ぶつ 【COL.】 *to strike, to hit*

(The subject and the direct object must both be animate; the hitting may be intentional or accidental.)

相手の頭をぶつのはファウルだよ。
Hitting the opponent on the head is a foul!

ふつう 不通 *suspension, interruption (of transportation or communication)*

不通になる to be suspended, to stop running

新幹線は大雪のため不通になっています。
The Shinkansen is not running because of heavy snow.

ふつう 普通 *usually, commonly, ordinarily* [→普段(に)]

私は普通にうちを出ます。
I usually leave home at 7:00.

普通の／な usual, common; ordinary, unremarkable

交通渋滞は東京では普通です。
Traffic jams are common in Tokyo.
京子ちゃんは普通の女の子です。
Kyoko is an ordinary girl.
普通科 general course of study
普通郵便 ordinary mail

ふつか 二日 *(see Appendix 2) 1. two days 2. the second (day of a month)*

ぶっか 物価 *prices, the cost of things*
ハワイは物価が高いですね。
In Hawaii prices are high, aren't they?
物価が上がる〔下がる〕 prices rise〔fall〕

ふっかつ 復活 *revival, restoration, resurrection*
復活する to be revived, to be restored, to be resurrected
復活祭 Easter

ぶつかる *to hit, to run into, to collide*
その船は大きな岩にぶつかりました。
That ship hit a big rock.
困難にぶつかる to run into difficulties

ぶっきょう 仏教 *Buddhism*

ブック *book* [→ 本]
ブックエンド bookend
ブックカバー book jacket; (protective) book cover

ぶつける *1. to throw at and hit with*
犬に石をぶつけてはいけないよ。
You mustn't throw stones at dogs!
2. to hit, to bump (one thing on another)
柱に頭をぶつけました。
I hit my head on the post.

ぶっしつ 物質 *matter, material, substance*
物質文明 material civilization
物質的な material, tangible [↔ 精神的な]

プッシュホン *touch-tone telephone*

ぶつぞう 仏像 *image of Buddha*

ぶったい 物体 *physical object*

ぶつだん 仏壇 *household Buddhist altar*
(Ordinarily a wooden cabinet containing a Buddha figure and memorial tablets bearing the names of deceased family members.)

ふっとう 沸騰 *boiling*
沸騰する to come to a boil
やかんのお湯が沸騰しています。
The kettle is boiling. (Literally: The water in the kettle is boiling.)
沸騰点 boiling point

フットボール *(American) football*

フットワーク *footwork*

ぶつぶつ *murmuringly, mutteringly; complainingly*
ぶつぶつ言う to murmur, to mutter [→ 呟く]; to complain

ぶつり 物理 *1. principles of physics 2.* [☞ 物理学 (below)]
物理学 (the study of) physics
物理学者 physicist

ふで 筆 *writing brush; painting brush (for pictures)*
筆箱 pencil box
筆入れ pencil case

ブティック *boutique*

ふと *by chance; unexpectedly; suddenly*
恵子さんはふと空を見上げました。
Keiko happened to look up at the sky.
いい考えがふと頭に浮かびました。
A good idea suddenly occurred to me.

ふとい 太い *thick, large in diameter* [↔ 細い]
妹は太い木の幹によりかかっています。
My younger sister is leaning against a thick tree trunk.
ここに太い線を引いてください。
Please draw a thick line here.

父の腕は太いよ。
My father's arms are big!

太い声 big and deep voice

遠藤さんは太い声をしています。
Mr. Endo has a big, deep voice.

ぶどう 葡萄 *1. grape*
2. grapevine

葡萄畑 vineyard

葡萄酒 (grape) wine [→ ワイン]

干し葡萄 raisin

ふどうさん 不動産 *real estate*

ふところ 懐 *the inside of the part of a kimono covering the chest*

母親は赤ん坊を懐に抱いています。
The mother is holding her baby inside her kimono.

ふとさ 太さ *thickness, diameter*

この管の太さは5センチです。
The diameter of this pipe is five centimeters.

ふともも 太股 *thigh* [→ 股]

ふとる 太る *to become fatter, to gain weight* [↔ 痩せる]

赤木さんは太ってきました。
Mr. Akagi has gotten fat.

息子は1年間で20キロ太りました。
My son gained 20 kilograms in one year.

太っている to be fat

太った人 fat person

ふとん 布団 *Japanese-style bedding, futon*

(Traditional Japanese bedding is folded up and put in closets during the day and laid out on the floor at night. There are three kinds of futon: (1) the lower, mattress type; (2) the thin sheet type placed directly on the sleeping person; (3) the upper, quilt type.)

布団を敷く to lay out bedding

布団を畳む to fold up bedding

肌布団 sheet futon

掛け布団 upper futon, quilt futon

敷布団 lower futon, mattress futon

ふなびん 船便 *sea mail*

ふなよい 船酔い *seasickness*

ふね 船 *boat, ship*

竹山さんは船で四国に行きました。
Mr. Takeyama went to Shikoku by ship.

私たちは横浜行きの船に乗りました。
We boarded a ship for Yokohama.

ぶひん 部品 *part (of a machine, etc.)*

予備部品 spare part

ふぶき 吹雪 *snowstorm*

ぶぶん 部分 *part, portion* [↔ 全体]

3課の最初の部分を読んでください。
Please read the first part of Lesson 3.

部分的な partial

弟の話は部分的にはほんとうです。
My younger brother's story is partly true.

ふへい 不平 *dissatisfaction, discontent* [→ 不満]

不平を言う to express dissatisfaction, to complain

父はよく食べ物の不平を言います。
My father often complains about the food.

ふべん 不便 *inconvenience*

不便を忍ぶ to put up with an inconvenience

不便な inconvenient [↔ 便利な]

自転車のない生活はとても不便です。
Life without a bicycle is very inconvenient.

うちは買い物に不便な所にあります。
My house is in an inconvenient place for shopping.

ふぼ 父母 *father and mother, parents* [→ 両親]

ふまん 不満 *dissatisfaction, discontent* [→ 不平]

不満の dissatisfied, displeased
生徒たちの行為に不満です。
I am dissatisfied with the students' conduct.

ふみきり 踏切 *crossing (where a road crosses a railroad track)*

ふみんしょう 不眠症 *insomnia*

ふむ 踏む *to step on*
猫の足を踏んだよ。
You stepped on the cat's paw!

ふもと 麓 *foot (of a mountain)* [↔ 頂上]
山のふもとにゴルフ場があります。
There is a golf course at the foot of the mountain.

ふやす 増やす *to increase (transitive)*
母は来月から小遣いを増やしてくれます。
From next month, mother will increase my allowance.

ふゆ 冬 *winter* [↔ 夏]
去年の冬は寒かったです。
Last winter was cold.
冬は雪が多いです。
In winter there's a lot of snow.
冬服 winter clothes
冬休み (US) winter vacation, (UK) the winter holidays

ふゆかい 不愉快 ~な [[↔ 愉快な]] *1. unpleasant, distasteful*
きのう不愉快な経験をしました。
Yesterday I had an unpleasant experience.
2. displeased
あのとき私は不愉快でした。
I was displeased then.

ふよう 不要 ~の *unnecessary* [↔ 必要な]
その忠告は不要です。
That advice is unnecessary.

ふよう 不用 ~の *useless*
このカメラは私には不用です。
This camera is useless to me.

フライ *fly (ball) (in baseball)*
フライを打つ to hit a fly

フライ *deep-frying*
フライにする to deep-fry
海老フライ deep-fried shrimp

プライド *pride* [→ 自尊心]

プライバシー *privacy*
プライバシーの侵害 invasion of privacy

フライパン *frying pan*

ブラインド *(window) shade; (window) blinds*
ブラインドを上げる〔下ろす〕 to raise 〔lower〕 a shade/blinds

ブラウス *blouse*

プラカード *placard*

プラグ *(electrical) plug*

ぶらさがる ぶら下がる 【COL.】*to hang down (intransitive)*
ランプが天井からぶら下がっています。
A lamp is hanging from the ceiling.

ぶらさげる ぶら下げる 【COL. for 吊るす】 *to hang, to suspend*

ブラシ *brush ((implement))* [→ 刷毛]
Aにブラシをかける to brush A
歯ブラシ toothbrush
ヘアブラシ hairbrush

プラス [[↔ マイナス]] *1. plus (sign)*
3プラス2は5です。
Three plus two is five.
2. plus, gain, benefit

フラスコ *flask (used in chemistry, etc.)*

プラスチック *plastic*
プラスチックのおもちゃが多くなったね。
Plastic toys have increased, haven't they?
プラスチック製の manufactured out of plastic

ブラスバンド *brass band*

プラチナ *platinum*

フラッシュ *(photographic) flash*

フラッシュをたく to use a flash

フラット *(musical) flat* [↔ シャープ]

—フラット *flat (Added to numbers denoting short time periods.)*

吉田君は100メートルを11秒フラットで走ることができます。
Yoshida can run the 100 meters in 11. seconds flat!

プラットホーム [☞ ホーム]

プラネタリウム *planetarium*

ふらふら (〜と) *1. dizzily; totteringly, unsteadily*

ふらふらする to feel dizzy, feel faint; to be unsteady, to totter

きょうは熱でふらふらしています。
Today I feel dizzy with a fever.

2. aimlessly, for no particular purpose, without conscious thought

ふらふらする to waver, to be unable to decide what to do

息子は大学を出ましたが、まだふらふらして働いていません。
My son graduated from college, but still unable to decide what to do, he's not working.

ぶらぶら (〜と) *1. danglingly, swingingly*

ぶらぶらする to dangle, to swing back and forth (intransitive)

足をぶらぶらさせる to swing one's legs

2. strollingly

ぶらぶらする to take a stroll

公園をぶらぶらしましょうか。
Shall we take a stroll through the park?

3. idly, loungingly

ぶらぶらする to be idle, to loaf, to loiter

きょう父はうちでぶらぶらしています。
Today my father is loafing around at home.

プラム *plum*

プラモデル *plastic model*

プラン *1. plan (of action)* [→ 計画]

2. plan, drawing, blueprint [→ 設計図 (s.v. 設計)]

プランクトン *plankton*

ぶらんこ *swing ((toy))*

ぶらんこに乗ろうよ。
Let's go on the swings!

ふり 不利 *disadvantage*

不利な disadvantageous, unfavorable, adverse [↔ 有利な]

状況は与党に不利です。
The circumstances are unfavorable to the ruling party.

ふり 振り *pretense, false show*

振りをする to pretend, to make a pretense

池田さんは時々病気のふりをします。
Ms. Ikeda sometimes pretends to be sick.

息子は勉強している振りをしています。
My son is pretending to be studying.

ぶり 鰤 *yellowtail ((fish))*

—ぶり —振り *1. way, manner (Added to verb bases and to noun bases denoting actions.)*

あの人の話し振りが好きです。
I like that person's manner of speaking.

田村さんの勉強振りはすごいですよ。
Tamura's way of studying is amazing!

2. 〜の the first in (Added to bases denoting periods of time.)

6か月振りの演説でした。
It was the first speech in six months.

古川さんは5年ぶりにハワイへ行きます。
Ms. Furukawa will go to Hawaii for the first time in five years.

フリー 〜な／の *1. free, unconstrained* [→ 自由な]

2. freelance

フリーのジャーナリスト freelance journalist

3. free (of charge) [→ 無料の]

フリーパス free pass ((ticket))
フリースロー free throw

フリーザー *freezer*

フリースタイル *freestyle*

プリーツ *pleat*

ブリーフ *briefs ((underwear))*

ふりかえる 振り返る *{5} to look back*
忍は振り返って、さよならを言いました。
Shinobu looked back and said good-by.

ふりがな 振り仮名 *small kana printed alongside or above a Chinese character to show its pronunciation*

ブリキ *tin plate (i.e., iron or steel coated with tin)*
ブリキ缶 (US) tin can, (UK) tin

ふりこ 振り子 *pendulum*

プリズム *prism*

ブリッジ *1. bridge (spanning a river, etc.) [→ 橋]*
2. bridge (on a ship)
3. (dental) bridge
4 bridge (in wrestling)

ブリッジ *bridge ((card game))*

ふりむく 振り向く *to look back at*
母は私の方を振り向いてほほえみました。
My mother looked back at me and smiled.

ふりょう 不良 *1. delinquency, immorality*
不良の delinquent, immoral, bad
2. a delinquent, an undesirable
3. poor quality, inferiority, poor condition
不良の poor, low-quality, inferior
不良品 inferior article, defective item
不良少女 delinquent girl
不良少年 delinquent boy

フリル *frill*

プリン *pudding*

プリンス *prince [→ 王子]*

プリンセス *princess [→ 王女]*

プリンター *printer ((machine))*

プリント *1. print (from a photographic negative)*
2. printing (from a photographic negative)
プリントする to print [→ 焼く4.]
3. (mechanically) printed item
4. printing (of books, newspapers, etc.) [→ 印刷]
プリントする to print

ふる 降る *to fall (The subject must be a form of precipitation.)*
あしたは雨が降るでしょう。
It will probably rain tomorrow.
雪がはげしく降っています。
It is snowing hard.

ふる 振る *to shake, to wave, to swing, to wag*
恵子ちゃんは私に手を振っています。
Keiko is waving her hand to me.
犬はしっぽを振りました。
The dog wagged its tail.
バットを振る to swing a bat
首を横に振る to shake one's head

ふるい 古い *old, not new* [↔ 新しい]
この寺は非常に古いです。
This temple is very old.
洋子さんは古い友達です。
Yoko is an old friend.
おじいさんは古い切手を集めています。
Grandfather collects old stamps.

ふるう 振るう *1. to wield, to put to use, to exercise, to exhibit* [→ 発揮する]
腕をふるう to exhibit one's ability
暴力をふるう to use violence
2. to prosper, to thrive, to do well
今晩はあの投手は全然ふるわなかったね。
Tonight that pitcher didn't do well at all,

did he.

ブルー *blue (as a noun)*

ブルース *blues ((music))*

ブルースを歌う to sing the blues

フルーツ *fruit* [→ 果物]

フルーツケーキ fruit cake

フルーツパーラー cafe specializing in cake, drinks, etc., garnished with fruit

フルート *flute*

フルート奏者 flutist

ふるえる 震える *to tremble, to quiver*

少女は寒さで震えました。
The girl trembled from the cold.

受賞者の声は少し震えていました。
The prize winner's voice was trembling a little.

ふるくさい 古臭い *old-fashioned, outmoded*

ふるさと 古里 *place where one was born and raised, hometown* [→ 故郷]

林さんのふるさとは秋田です。
Ms. Hayashi's hometown is Akita.

ブルジョア *wealthy person who lives extravagantly*

フルスピード *full speed*

フルスピードで at full speed

ブルドーザー *bulldozer*

ブルドッグ *bulldog*

ふるほん 古本 *used book, secondhand book*

古本屋 used-book store; used-book dealer

ふるまい 振る舞い *behavior, conduct*

ふるまう 振る舞う *to behave, to conduct oneself*

その少年は行儀よくふるまいました。
That boy behaved politely.

ぶれい 無礼 *rudeness, impoliteness* [→ 失礼]

無礼な rude, impolite

プレイガイド *entertainment ticket agency*

プレー *1. play, the action (in a game or sport)*

プレーを再開する to resume play

2. a play (in a game or sport)

うまいプレー a skillful play

ファインプレー a fine play

プレーオフ *play-off*

ブレーカー *(circuit) breaker*

ブレーキ *brake*

このブレーキは利かないよ。
This brake doesn't work!

ブレーキをかける to apply the brake, to put on the brakes

プレート *1. metal plate*

2. (home) plate

3. pitching rubber

フレーム *1. frame, enclosing edge* [→ 枠]

眼鏡のフレーム eyeglasses frames

2. frame, framework, supporting part of a structure

自転車のフレーム bicycle frame

プレーヤー *1. player, athlete* [→ 選手]

2. instrument player, musical performer [→ 演奏者 (s.v. 演奏)]

3. [☞ レコードプレーヤー (s.v. レコード)]

ブレザー *blazer*

ブレザーコート [☞ブレザー (above)]

プレゼント *present, gift* [→ 贈り物]

明ちゃんへのプレゼントです。
It's a present for Akira.

村井先生にプレゼントを贈りましょう。
Let's give Ms. Murai a present.

プレゼントする to give as a present

山中さんにペンをプレゼントします。
I will give a pen to Mr. Yamanaka as a present.

プレッシャー *psychological pressure, emotional pressure*

プレッシャーに苦しむ to suffer under emotional pressure

フレッシュ ～な *fresh* [→ 新鮮な]

プレハブ *prefabricated house*

プレハブ住宅 [☞ プレハブ (above)]

ふれる 触れる *1. to bring (gently) into contact*

Aに手を触れる to touch A with one's hand

これに手を触れないでください。
Please do not touch this.

2. to come (gently) into contact

これは空気に触れるとすぐ固くなります。
This gets hard as soon as it comes into contact with the air.

目に触れる to catch one's eye

手でAに触れる to touch A with one's hand

3. to come into conflict, to infringe

法律に触れる to come into conflict with the law

4 to touch, to refer

先生はその問題に触れるでしょう。
The teacher will probably touch on that problem.

フレンド *friend* [→ 友達]

ふろ 風呂 *bath*

ふろが沸きました。
The bath has heated up.

毎日おふろに入ります。
I take a bath every day.

風呂場 bathroom (Toilets and the bathtubs are traditionally in separate rooms in Japan. This word refers to a room for taking a bath.) [→ 浴室]

風呂槽 bathtub [→ 浴槽]

風呂屋 public bathhouse [→ 銭湯]

プロ *a professional* [↔ アマチュア]

プロの professional

プロ選手 professional athlete

プロ野球 professional baseball

プロ [☞ プロダクション]

フロア *floor (i.e., bottom surface of a room)* [→ 床]

ブローチ *brooch*

ふろく 付録 *1. supplement (in a magazine, newspaper, etc.)*

2. appendix (in a book)

プログラム *1. program (list of participants, what is to be presented, etc.)*

2. (computer) program

ふろしき 風呂敷 *wrapping cloth (a square piece of cloth used to wrap items for easy carrying)*

ふろしきに包む to wrap in a wrapping cloth

風呂敷包み bundle in a wrapping cloth

プロダクション *1. production company (for movies, television programs, etc.)*

2. talent agency

プロテスタント *a Protestant*

プロデューサー *producer (in movies, television, etc.)*

プロパンガス *propane (gas)*

プロフィール [[→ 横顔]] *1. profile, side-view of a face*

2. profile, brief description

プロフェッショナル [☞ プロ1.]

プロペラ *propeller*

プロペラ機 propeller plane

プロポーズ *marriage proposal*

プロポーズする to propose marriage

ブロマイド *still (photograph) of a celebrity*

プロローグ *prologue*

フロント *1. front desk, reception desk*

2. front office (of a professional sports

team)

フロントガラス *(US) windshield, (UK) windscreen*

ふん 糞 *animal feces, manure*

ふん 分 *part, portion*

一分 (counter for parts; see Appendix 2)

一分 portion for, supply for (Added to number bases.)

救助隊は三日分の食料を持っていました。
The rescue party had a three-day food supply.

兄はカレーを３人分食べたよ。
My older brother ate enough curry for three people!

－ふん 一分 *1. (counter for minutes past the hour when telling time; see Appendix 2)*

由美さんは12時40分に家を出ます。
Yumi leaves home at 12:40.

2. (counter for minutes; see Appendix 2)

学校は駅から歩いて15分です。
The school is fifteen minutes from the station on foot.

ぶん 文 [[→ 文章]] *1. sentence*

この文の意味を説明してください。
Please explain the meaning of this sentence.

2. text, piece of writing

英語で短い文を書きました。
I wrote a short text in English.

ふんいき 雰囲気 *atmosphere, ambience*

この会合には友好的な雰囲気があります。
There is a friendly atmosphere at this meeting.

ふんか 噴火 *(volcanic) eruption*

噴火する to erupt

噴火口 (volcanic) crater

ぶんか 文化 *culture*

パテルさんは日本文化に興味があります。
Ms. Patel is interested in Japanese culture.

文化の日 Culture Day (a Japanese national holiday on November 3rd)

文化祭 cultural festival; school festival

文化的な cultural

ぶんかい 分解 *taking apart, dismantling, breaking down into components*

分解する to take apart, to break down into components

娘はそのおもちゃの自動車を分解した。
My daughter took that toy car apart.

ぶんがく 文学 *literature*

文学作品 a literary work

文学者 literary person

文学史 history of literature

英文学 English literature

日本文学 Japanese literature

ぶんかつ 分割 *division, partition*

分割する to divide, to partition

ぶんこ 文庫 *1. book storehouse*

2. series of books published in uniform pocket-size editions

文庫本 pocket-size edition of book

ぶんご 文語 *literary language, written language*

(This word denotes a variety of a language used in written texts that differs from a colloquial variety used in conversation. In the case of Japanese, it refers specifically to classical Japanese.) [↔ 口語]

文語体 literary writing style

ぶんしょう 文章 [[→ 文]] *1. text, piece of writing*

2. sentence

ふんすい 噴水 *1. spouting water, fountain*

2. fountain (device for producing spouting water)

ぶんすう 分数 *fraction (in arithmetic)*

ぶんせき 分析 *analysis*
分析する to analyze

ふんそう 紛争 *dispute, conflict* [→ 争い]

ぶんたん 分担 *apportionment, sharing (of a burden)*
分担する to divide and share, to apportion
費用をみんなで分担しましょうか。
Shall we all share the expenses between us?
その仕事を父と分担します。
I will divide that work with my father.

ぶんつう 文通 *exchanging letters, correspondence*
文通する to exchange letters, to correspond
10年前から京子さんと文通しています。
I've been corresponding with Kyoko for the past ten years.

ぶんどき 分度器 *protractor*

ぶんぷ 分布 *distribution, arrangement*
分布する to become distributed
分布図 distribution chart; distribution map

ふんべつ 分別 *discretion, good judgment, good sense*
片山さんの行動は分別が欠けています。
Mr. Katayama's actions are lacking in discretion.
分別のある人 person of good judgment, sensible person

ぶんぽう 文法 *grammar*
文法の誤りが多いですよ。
There are a lot of grammatical mistakes!
文法的な grammatical
英文法 English grammar
日本文法 Japanese grammar

ぶんぼうぐ 文房具 *stationery item*
文房具屋 stationery store; stationer

ふんまつ 粉末 *powder, dust* [→ 粉1.]

ぶんめい 文明 *civilization*
文明社会 civilized society
現代文明 modern civilization
古代文明 ancient civilization

ぶんや 分野 *field (of endeavor)*
あの学者は数学に新しい分野を開いた。
That scholar opened a new field in mathematics.

ぶんらく 文楽 *traditional Japanese puppet play*

ぶんるい 分類 *classification, division into types*
分類する to classify, to divide into types
ここの本を書名で分類しました。
I classified the books here by titles.

ぶんれつ 分裂 *division, split, fission*
分裂する to divide, to split (intransitive)
その政党は二つに分裂しました。
That political party split into two.
核分裂 nuclear fission

へ *(noun-following particle) 1. to, for, toward* [→ に3.]
父は九州へ行きました。
My father went to Kyushu.
社長は来週ニューヨークへたちます。
The company president will leave for New York next week.
飛行機は西へ飛んでいました。
The airplane was flying toward the west.
これは先生への贈り物です。
This is a present for the teacher.
2. into, onto [→ に4.]
生徒は部屋へ駆け込みました。
The student ran into the room.

人形を箱の中へ入れました。
I put the doll inside the box.

猫がテーブルへ跳び上がりました。
The cat jumped up onto the table.

ペア *pair*

ペアを組む to get together to form a pair

ヘアスタイル *hairstyle*

へい 塀 *wall, fence (surrounding a house or piece of land)*

大工さんは家の周囲に塀を建てました。
The carpenter built a fence around the house.

ブロック塀 concrete-block wall
板塀 board fence
煉瓦塀 brick wall

べいか 米価 *rice price*

へいかい 閉会 *close (of a meeting, gathering, conference, etc.)* [↔ 開会]

閉会する to close (transitive)
閉会式 closing ceremony

へいき 平気 *composure, calmness; nonchalance, indifference*

平気な composed, calm; nonchalant, indifferent, not bothered (This adjectival noun is used to describe both the people who are not bothered and the things they are not bothered by.)

雪は平気です。
I'm not bothered by snow.

雷が鳴っても平気です。
Thunder doesn't bother me. (Literally: Even if thunder sounds, I'm not bothered.)

へいき 兵器 *weapon, arms* [→ 武器]

核兵器 nuclear weapon

へいきん 平均 *1. an average*

平均の average

娘の成績はだいたい平均です。
My daughter's grades are about average.

平均する to average, to take the average
平均して on average

私は平均して1日2時間勉強します。
I study two hours a day on average.

2. balance, equilibrium [→ 釣り合い]

平均を取る to gain one's balance
平均を失う to lose one's balance
平均台 balance beam
平均以上の above-average
平均以下の below-average
平均寿命 average life span
平均年齢 average age
平均点 average score, average number of points

へいこう 平行 ~の *parallel*

平行する to become parallel

道路は鉄道に平行しています。
The road is parallel to the railroad.

平行棒 parallel bars (in gymnastics)
平行線 parallel line

へいこう 閉口 ~だ *to be at a loss, to be unable to stand*

この寒さには閉口です。
I can't stand this cold.

閉口する to be at a loss, to be unable to stand

その人には閉口します。
I can't stand that person.

べいこく 米国 *the United States* [→ アメリカ2.]

へいじつ 平日 *weekday*

べいじゅ 米寿 *88th birthday (a special birthday in Japan)*

へいせい 平成 *(Japanese imperial era name for the period beginning 1989)*

へいたい 兵隊 *soldier; sailor*

へいてん 閉店 [[↔ 開店]] *1. closing (of a store, restaurant, etc., for the business*

day)
閉店する to close (intransitive)
この店は7時に閉店します。
This store closes at 7:00.

2. closing, going out of business (of a store, restaurant, etc.)
閉店する to close, to go out of business
隣の本屋は来週閉店します。
The bookstore next-door will close down next week.

へいねん 平年 *typical year, average year*

へいほう 平方 *square (of a number)*
10の平方は100です。
The square of 10 is 100.
平方ー square (Added to bases denoting units of length.)
平方メートル square meter
ー平方メートル (counter for square meters; see Appendix 2)
この教室は120平方メートルあります。
This classroom is 120 square meters.
平方根 square root

へいぼん 平凡 ～な *ordinary, commonplace* [↔ 非凡な]
平凡な主婦にはなりたくないわ。
I don't want to become an ordinary housewife!
平凡な人々 ordinary people
平凡な出来事 an everyday event

へいめん 平面 *plane (surface)*
平面図 plane figure

へいや 平野 *a plain*

へいわ 平和 *peace, tranquility* [↔ 戦争]
みんな平和を望んでいます。
Everyone wants peace.
平和な peaceful, tranquil
私たちは平和な生活を送っています。
We are leading a peaceful life.
平和条約 peace treaty
平和運動 peace movement

へえ *No kidding!, Really?! (an interjection used to indicate that one is surprised or impressed)*
へえ、驚いた。
Really?! I'm surprised!
へえ、それはすごいね。
No kidding! That's amazing, isn't it?

ベーキングパウダー *baking powder*

ベーコン *bacon*
ベーコンエッグ bacon and eggs

ページ *page (of a book, etc.)*
ページをめくる to turn over a page
ーページ (counter for page numbers or number of pages; see Appendix 2)
その写真は15ページにあるね。
That photograph is on page 15, isn't it?
もう100ページ読んだよ。
I've already read 100 pages!

ベース *1. base (in baseball)* [→ 塁]
2. base, basis, standard
3. base (of operations) [→ 根拠地 (s.v. 根拠)]
ベースアップ increase in base wages
ベースキャンプ base camp (for an expedition, etc.)

ベース [☞ バス *(bass)*]
ベースギター bass guitar

ペーパーテスト *written test* [→ 筆記試験 (s.v. 筆記)]

ベール *veil*

ーべき ～だ *should, ought to; must*
(Added to the informal affirmative non-past-tense form of a verb (i.e., the form listed in dictionaries). Instead of する, the classical form す may appear before べき.)
すぐに医者にみてもらうべきです。
You should see a doctor immediately.
ほんとうのことを言うべきです。
You must tell the truth.

ヘクタール *hectare*

ーヘクタール (counter for hectares; see Appendix 2)

へこむ 凹む *to become dented, to become sunken, to cave in*

ベスト *vest*

ベスト *one's best (effort)* [→ 最善]

その試合に勝つためベストを尽くします。
I will do my best to win the game.

ベストー *best, top (Added to noun bases.)*

ベストセラー best seller

ベストテン the top ten

ペスト *bubonic plague*

へそ *navel, belly button*

へそくり secretly saved money

へた 下手 ～な *unskillful, poor at*

(This adjectival noun is used to describe both the people who are unskillful and the things they are unskillful at.) [↔ 上手な]

姉はスキーが下手です。
My older sister is poor at skiing.

中川さんは字が下手ですね。
Mr. Nakagawa's handwriting is poor, isn't it?

下手くそな【CRUDE for 下手な (above)】

ペダル *pedal*

べつ 別 *1.* ～の／な *another, other, different, separate* [→ 外の, 他の]

別のバッグを見せてください。
Please show me another bag.

それはまったく別の話です。
That's a completely different story.

きのう別の医者にみてもらいました。
I had a different doctor look at it yesterday.

2. ～に *particularly, in particular (in combination with a negative predicate)*

放課後別にすることがない。
I don't have anything in particular to do after school.

ーべつ ー別 ～の *classified by, according to (Added to noun bases.)*

年齢別の人口を表にしました。
I made a chart of the population classified by age.

参加者は地域別に並んでいます。
The participants are lined up according to region.

べっきょ 別居 *residing separately*

別居する to reside separately

べっそう 別荘 *summer house, country house, villa*

ベッド *(Western-style) bed*

私はいつもベッドで寝ます。
I always sleep on a bed.

出かける前にベッドを整えなさい。
Make the bed before you go out.

ベッドカバー bedspread

ベッドルーム bedroom

ベッドタウン bedroom town

ダブルベッド double bed

二段ベッド bunk bed

ペット *pet*

ペットフード pet food

ペットショップ pet shop

ヘッドライト *headlight*

べつべつ 別々 ～の *separate (from each other)*

姉と私は別々の部屋を持っています。
My older sister and I have separate rooms.

いっしょに食事したが、別々に払った。
We ate together, but paid separately.

べつめい 別名 *different name, pseudonym, alias*

ベテラン *veteran, old hand, person of long experience*

ペニシリン *penicillin*

ペニシリンの注射 penicillin injection

へび 蛇 *snake*

毒蛇 poisonous snake

へま【COL.】*blunder, goof*

へまをする to make a blunder, to make a goof

へまな bungling, stupid

へや 部屋 *a room*

これは６畳の部屋です。
This is a six-mat room.

きょう部屋を掃除するつもりです。
I'm planning to clean my room today.

広い〔狭い〕部屋 large〔small〕room

へらす 減らす *to reduce, to decrease (transitive)* [↔ 増やす]

姉は体重を減らしました。
My older sister lost weight.

ぺらぺら【COL.】*fluently (describing speaking, ordinarily in a foreign language)*

ぺらぺらの fluent [→ 流暢な]

コッホさんは日本語がぺらぺらです。
Ms. Koch's Japanese is fluent.

べらぼう【COL.】〜な *unreasonable, absurd, extreme*

べらぼうな値段 unreasonable price

ベランダ *veranda*

へりくだる 謙る *to humble oneself, to be modest*

ヘリコプター *helicopter*

へる 減る *{5} to decrease, to lessen (intransitive)* [↔ 増える]

交通事故の数が急に減りました。
The number of traffic accidents suddenly decreased.

父は体重が３キロ減りました。
My father lost three kilograms.

ベル *1. electric bell*

ベルが鳴っているよ。
The bell's ringing!

2. signaling bell (on a bicycle, etc.)

非常ベル alarm bell

ベルト *1. belt ((clothing))* [→ バンド1.]

ベルトを緩めたほうがいいです。
It would be better to loosen your belt.

座席のベルトをお締めください。
Please fasten your seat belts.

2. belt ((machine part))

安全ベルト safety belt

ベルトコンベヤー *belt conveyer*

ヘルメット *helmet, hard hat*

へん 変 〜な *strange, curious, odd*

台所で変な音がしました。
There was a strange sound in the kitchen.

変なうわさが立っています。
A strange rumor is going around.

良子さんは変なしゃべり方をします。
Yoshiko has an odd way of talking.

へん 辺 *1. area around, vicinity* [→ 辺り]

この辺に郵便局はありますか。
Is there a post office around here?

2. side (of a polygon)

三角形の辺 side of a triangle

一辺 (counter for sides; see Appendix 2)

-へん -遍 *(counter for number of times, occasions, see Appendix 2)* [→ -回2.]

べん 便 *convenience*

AはBの便がいい A is convenient to/for B

うちは地下鉄の便がいいです。
My house is convenient to the subway.

べん 弁 *valve*

ペン *pen*

住所をここにペンで書いてください。
Please write your address here with a pen.

ペンは剣より強い。(proverb)
The pen is mightier than the sword.

ペンフレンド [☞ ペンパル (below)]

ペンネーム pen name

ペンパル pen pal
サインペン felt-tip pen; roller-ball pen

へんあつき 変圧器 *(electrical) transformer*

へんか 変化 *change, alteration*
変化する to change (intransitive) [→ 変わる]
この地域では気温の変化が急です。
In this area temperature changes are sudden.
変化のある生活 a life-style with variety
変化のない仕事 monotonous job

べんかい 弁解 *excuse, exculpatory explanation* [→ 言い訳]
もう弁解の余地はないです。
There's no longer any room for excuses.
弁解する to make an excuse, to exculpate oneself

べんき 便器 *toilet fixture*

べんぎ 便宜 *convenience (for a person)*
便宜を図る to be accommodating

ペンキ *paint (for covering surfaces to improve appearance or protect)*
Aをペンキで塗る to paint A with paint
塀を白いペンキで塗りました。
I painted the fence white.
Aにペンキを塗る to apply paint to A
「ペンキ塗り立て」(on a sign)
Wet Paint
ペンキ屋 painter; paint store

べんきょう 勉強 *study, studying*
勉強する to study
真理子は熱心に日本史を勉強しています。
Mariko is studying Japanese history enthusiastically.
何を勉強したのですか。
What did you study?
勉強部屋 room for studying
勉強時間 study hours
勉強家 person who studies hard

へんきょく 編曲 *arrangement (of a musical piece)*
編曲する to arrange

ペンギン *penguin*

へんけん 偏見 *prejudice, bias*

べんご 弁護 *(verbal) defense, arguing on behalf of*
弁護する to defend, to argue on behalf of
私は自分で弁護できます。
I can defend myself.
弁護士 lawyer

へんこう 変更 *change, alteration, modification*
時間割に何か変更がありますか。
Is there some kind of change in the class schedule?
変更する to change, to alter, to modify
計画を変更しなければなりません。
We have to change our plans.

へんさい 返済 *repayment (of a loan); return (of something borrowed)*
返済する to repay; to return

へんじ 返事 *answer, reply, response (This word is not used to mean an answer to a question (cf. 答え).)*
洋子さんから返事を受け取りました。
I received an answer from Yoko.
その手紙に返事を出します。
I will send an answer to that letter.
返事する to reply, to respond
名前を呼びますので、返事してください。
I will call your names, so please respond.

へんしゅう 編集 *editing*
学校新聞の編集で忙しいです。
I'm busy with the editing the school newspaper.
編集する to edit
編集部 editorial department

編集部員 editorial staff member
編集長 chief editor
編集者 editor

べんじょ 便所 【CRUDE for トイレ】 *bathroom, lavatory*

(Toilets and bathtubs are traditionally in separate rooms in Japan. This word refers to a place containing a toilet.)
公衆便所 public lavatory

べんしょう 弁償 *compensation payment*

弁償する to pay for
割った花瓶を弁償します。
I will pay for the vase I broke.

ペンション *small home-like hotel*

ベンジン *benzene*

へんせい 編成 *formation, organization, composition*

編成する to form, to organize, to make up

へんそう 変装 *disguising oneself; disguise*

変装する to disguise oneself
犯人は老人に変装しました。
The criminal disguised himself as an elderly person.

ペンダント *pendant*

ベンチ *bench*

ペンチ *pliers*

へんでんしょ 変電所 *(electrical) transformer substation*

べんとう 弁当 *lunch (to be carried along and eaten later)*

芝生の上で弁当を食べましょうよ。
Let's eat our lunch on the grass!
弁当箱 lunch box

へんとうせん 扁桃腺 *tonsils*

べんぴ 便秘 *constipation*

便秘する to become constipated

べんり 便利 〜な *convenient, handy* [↔ 不便な]

電子レンジはとても便利です。
A microwave oven is very convenient.
バスで行くのが便利です。
Going by bus is convenient.
これは便利な道具ですね。
This is a handy tool, isn't it?

べんろん 弁論 *discussion, debate, oratory*

弁論部 debate club, debate team
弁論大会 oratory contest

ほ

ほ 帆 *sail (on a boat)*

ヨットは帆をいっぱいに張っています。
The sailboat is in full sail.
帆柱 mast

ほ 穂 *(grain) ear*

-ほ -歩 *(counter for steps, paces; see Appendix 2)*

一歩前へ進みなさい。
Move forward one step.
もう一歩も歩けないよ。
I can't walk another step!
２、３歩下がりました。
I moved back two or three steps.

ほいくえん 保育園 *nursery school*

ボイコット *boycott*

ボイコットする to boycott

ホイッスル *whistle ((device))*

ホイッスルを鳴らす to sound a whistle

ボイラー *boiler*

ぼいん 母音 *vowel* [↔ 子音]

ポイント *1. point (scored)* [→ 得点]

ポイントを稼ぐ to earn a point, to gain a point

2. (main) point, gist [→ 要点]

お話のポイントをつかみました。
I got the point of what you said.

ポイント *(US) (railroad) switch, (UK) (railroad) point*

ほう 方 *1. way, direction* [→ 方向]
こちらのほうへおいでください。
Please come this way.
警官は公園のほうへ歩いていきました。
The police officer walked in the direction of the park.
その少年は門のほうへ走りました。
That boy ran toward the gate.
2. side, type; the one (of a set of alternatives)
父は保守的なほうです。
My father is on the conservative side.
大きいほうを買いましょう。
Let's buy the big one.
3. side
(This is a figurative use in which marks which of two alternatives is more so in terms of a criterion of comparison. This can follow a noun plus の or a clause. When it follows a clause ending in an affirmative verb, the verb is typically in the past tense.)
私の部屋のほうが兄のより狭い。
My room is smaller than my older brother's.
冬より夏のほうが好きです。
I like summer better than winter.
お母さんと相談したほうがいいでしょう。
It would be better to talk it over with your mother.
一人でそこへ行かないほうがいいよ。
It would be better not to go there alone!

ほう 法 *law* [→ 法律]
法を守る to obey the law
法を破る to break the law

ーほう ー法 *way, method (Added to noun bases denoting activities.)*
治療法 medical treatment method
予防法 prevention method

ぼう 棒 *stick, rod, pole*
棒高跳び the pole vault

ぼうえい 防衛 *defense, protection* [→ 防御] [↔ 攻撃]
防衛する to defend
防衛庁 the Defense Agency (in the Japanese government)
防衛費 defense expenditures

ぼうえき 貿易 *trade, commerce*
貿易する to trade
日本は数多くの国と貿易しています。
Japan trades with numerous countries.
貿易風 trade wind
貿易会社 trading company
外国貿易 foreign trade
保護貿易 protective trade
自由貿易 free trade

ぼうえんきょう 望遠鏡 *telescope*
兄は望遠鏡で星を観察することが好きです。
My older brother likes to observe the stars with a telescope.
天体望遠鏡 astronomical telescope

ぼうおん 防音 ～の *soundproof; sound-insulated*
防音する to soundproof; to sound-insulate
防音装置 soundproofing device; anti-noise device

ほうか 放火 *arson*
放火する to deliberately set a fire
放火犯人 arsonist

ぼうがい 妨害 *obstruction, interference, disturbance* [→ 邪魔]
妨害する to obstruct, to interfere with, to disturb
交通を妨害しないでね。
Don't obstruct traffic, OK?

ほうがく 方角 *direction, way, bearings* [→ 方向]

バス停はあちらの方角です。
The bus stop is in that direction.
私たちはまちがった方角へ行きました。
We went in the wrong direction.

ほうかご 放課後 *after school*

放課後野球をしよう。
Let's play baseball after school.

ほうがんなげ 砲丸投げ *the shot put*

ほうき *broom*

ぼうぎょ 防御 *defense, protection* [→ 防衛]

防御する to defend, to protect

ほうげん 方言 *dialect*

ぼうけん 冒険 *adventure, risky undertaking*

昔は中国への航海は命がけの冒険でした。
Long ago a voyage to China was a desperate and risky undertaking.
冒険する to venture to do, to risk doing
冒険家 adventurer
冒険心 spirit of adventure
大冒険 great adventure

ほうこう 方向 *direction, way, bearings* [→ 方角]

方向音痴の having no sense of direction

ぼうこう 暴行 *act of violence, assault*

ほうこく 報告 *report, account, briefing*

私たちは先生に旅行の報告をします。
We will make a report of our trip to our teacher.
報告する to report
報告会 briefing session
報告書 (written) report

ほうさく 豊作 *good harvest, good crop* [↔ 不作]

今年は米が豊作です。
This year the rice crop is good. (Literally: This year rice is a good crop.)

ぼうし 帽子 *hat*

帽子をかぶる〔脱ぐ〕 to put on〔take off〕a hat
帽子をかぶったままで部屋に入らないで。
Don't enter the room with your hat on.
帽子屋 hat store; hatter

ほうじ 法事 *Buddhist memorial service*

ほうしゃ 放射 ～する *to emit, to radiate*

放射能 radioactivity
放射性の radioactive
放射線 radiation, rays

ほうしん 方針 *course (of action), policy, plan*

もう将来の方針を立てましたか。
Have you already made plans for the future?

ぼうず 坊主 【CRUDE】*Buddhist priest, Buddhist monk*

ぼうすい 防水 ～の *waterproof; water-resistant*

防水する to waterproof; to make water resistant

ほうせき 宝石 *jewel, gem*

宝石箱 jewel box
宝石商 jeweler

ほうそう 包装 *packing, wrapping*

包装する to wrap, to pack [→ 包む]
包装紙 wrapping paper, packing paper

ほうそう 放送 *broadcasting; broadcast*

放送する to broadcast
その事件はテレビで日本中に放送された。
That incident was broadcast on TV all over Japan.
放送局 broadcasting station
海外放送 overseas broadcasting

生放送 live broadcast
2か国語放送 bilingual broadcasting
音声多重放送 multiplex broadcasting
再放送 rerun, rebroadcast (UK) repeat
テレビ放送 television broadcast

ぼうそうぞく 暴走族 *motorcycle gang*

ほうそく 法則 *(scientific) law, principle, rule*
自然の法則 a law of nature

ほうたい 包帯 *bandage*
母は私の指に包帯をしてくれました。
My mother put a bandage on my finger.
包帯する to bandage

ほうちょう 包丁 *kitchen knife*

ぼうちょう 膨張 *swelling, expansion*
膨張する to swell, to expand
鉄は熱で膨張します。
Iron expands with heat.

ほうっておく [☞ ほっておく]

ほうてい 法廷 *court (of law)*

ほうていしき 方程式 *equation*

ほうどう 報道 *news report; reporting the news*
報道する to report
その事故は新聞で報道されています。
That accident is reported in the newspaper.
報道陣 reporters, the press
報道機関 the press, the news media

ぼうどう 暴動 *riot; rioting*

ぼうねんかい 忘年会 *year-end party*

ぼうはてい 防波堤 *breakwater*

ぼうはん 防犯 *crime prevention*

ほうび 褒美 *reward; prize* [→ 賞]
父は褒美にこのペンをくれたよ。
My father gave me this pen as a reward!
洋子ちゃんは絵で褒美をもらったよ。
Yoko got a prize for her painting!

ほうふ 豊富 ～な *abundant, plentiful* [↔ 貧弱な]
あのテレビタレントは話題の豊富な人だ。
That TV star has plenty to talk about. (Literally: That TV star is a person whose topics of conversation are plentiful.)
大橋さんの星の知識は豊富です。
Ms. Ohashi knows a great deal about the stars. (Literally: Ms. Ohashi's knowledge of the stars is abundant.)

ぼうふう 暴風 *intense wind, gale*
暴風雨 rainstorm

ほうほう 方法 *method, way*
単語を覚えるいい方法を教えてください。
Please tell me a good method for learning words.
この計画を実行する方法が知りたいです。
I want to know a way to put this plan into practice.

ほうぼう 方々 *here and there, all over* [→ あちこち]

ほうむ 法務 *judicial affairs*
法務省 the Ministry of Justice

ほうむる 葬る *to bury, to put in a grave*

ぼうめい 亡命 *defection, fleeing to another country*
亡命する to defect, to take political asylum
亡命者 defector

ほうめん 方面 *1. direction, way* [→ 方向]
－方面 the direction of (Added to bases denoting places.)
仙台方面に行くバスはどれですか。
Which one is the bus going in the Sendai direction?
2. district, area [→ 地域]
3. field (of endeavor) [→ 分野]
父はこの方面の研究では有名な科学者だ。

My father is a famous scientist in this field of research.

ほうもん 訪問 *visit, call*

訪問する to visit, to call on [→ 訪れる]

私たちは下田先生のお宅を訪問します。

We will visit Mr. Shimoda's house.

訪問客 visitor

家庭訪問 home visit (by a child's teacher)

ぼうや 坊や *little boy*

ほうりだす 放り出す *1. to throw outside*

弟は猫をドアからほうり出しました。

My younger brother threw the cat out the door.

2. (US) to fire, (UK) to sack, to dismiss [→ 首にする]

3. to give up, to quit, to abandon

仕事を途中でほうり出してはいけないよ。

You mustn't give up your work in the middle!

ほうりつ 法律 *law, statute*

その行為は法律で禁止されています。

That action is prohibited by law.

法律を守る to obey the law

法律に従う to follow the law

法律を破る to break the law

法律家 jurist

ぼうりょく 暴力 *violence, force*

暴力をふるう to use violence

ほうる 放る [[→ 投げる]] *1. to throw*

2. to give up on and quit

ぼうれい 亡霊 *dead person's spirit, ghost* [→ 幽霊]

ホウレンそう ホウレン草 *spinach*

ほえる 吠る *(a generic verb for loud cries of animals) to bark; to roar; to howl*

あの犬は由美ちゃんにほえたね。

That dog barked at Yumi, didn't it?

ライオンがおりの中でほえています。

The lion is roaring in the cage.

ほお 頬 *cheek*

京子ちゃんはばら色のほおをしています。

Kyoko has rosy cheeks.

恥ずかしくてほおが赤くなりました。

I was embarrassed and my cheeks turned red.

ボーイスカウト *1. the Boy Scouts*

2. boy scout

ボーイフレンド *casual boyfriend (as opposed to a steady boyfriend or lover)* [↔ ガールフレンド]

ホース *a hose*

ポーズ *pose*

写真のポーズを取る to pose for a photo

ボート *rowboat*

健ちゃんは湖でボートをこいでいます。

Ken is rowing a boat on the lake.

探検家はボートで川を渡っていました。

The explorers were crossing the river by rowboat.

ボートに乗る to get in a rowboat; to ride in a rowboat

貸しボート rowboats for hire

ボーナス *salary bonus*

(Japanese employees usually receive such a salary bonus twice a year in June and December)

ホープ *hope ((person))*

桜井選手はこのチームのホープです。

Sakurai is the hope of this team.

ホーム *1. home, household* [→ 家庭1.]

2. home base, home plate [→ 本塁] *(in baseball)*

ホームドラマ soap opera

ホームグラウンド home field

ホームイン scoring a run, reaching home

ホームステイ homestay

老人ホーム old people's home

ホーム *train platform*

ホームシック *homesickness*

美知子はホームシックにかかっているね。
Michiko is suffering from homesickness, isn't she?

ホームラン *home run (in baseball)*

ホームランを打つ to hit a home run

ホームラン王 home-run king

ホームルーム *homeroom*

ボーリング *bowling*

ボーリング場 bowling alley

ホール *large room, hall*

ビアホール beer hall

ホール *(golf) hole*

ホールインワン hole in one

ボール *1. ball (used in a game)* [→ 球]

野球選手はボールをバットで打ちました。
The baseball player hit the ball with the bat.

センターは簡単にボールを捕りました。
The center fielder caught the ball easily.

テニスのボール tennis ball

2. pitch out of the strike zone, ball

ボールペン *ballpoint pen*

ほか 他, 外 ～の *other, another*

ほかの生徒は帰ってよろしい。
The other students may go home.

ほかのどのスポーツよりも野球が好きだ。
I like baseball better than any other sport.

このセーターはちょっと気に入らないんです。ほかのを見せてください。
This sweater doesn't really appeal to me. Please show me another one.

ほかの人はだれもその知らせを知らない。
Nobody else knows that news.

ほかに besides, in addition, else

ほかに何かおっしゃることはありますか。
Do you have something else to say?

京子は英語のほかにフランス語も話すよ。
Kyoko can speak French in addition to English!

明のほかにはだれも欠席しなかったよ。
Nobody was absent besides Akira!

ほがらか 朗らか ～な *cheerful* [→ 明るい2.]

お嬢さんは朗らかな生徒です。
Your daughter is a cheerful student.

みんな朗らかに笑っていました。
They were all laughing cheerfully.

ほかん 保管 *safekeeping*

保管する to keep safely

ほきゅう 補給 *supply; replenishment*

補給する to supply; to replenish

難民に食糧を補給します。
We supply food to the refugees.

ぼく 僕 *I, me*

(There are several Japanese words for **I/me**. The word is ordinarily restricted to male speakers and is less formal than. Other words for **I/me** include 私, 私, あたし, and 俺.)

ぼくし 牧師 *Protestant minister, pastor*

ぼくじょう 牧場 *stock farm, (US) ranch; pasture (where farm animals graze)*

小谷さんは北海道で牧場を経営している。
Mr. Kotani is running a ranch in Hokkaido.

牧場主 rancher

ボクシング *boxing*

ボクシングをする to box

ほくせい 北西 *the northwest* [→ 西北]

北西の風 northwest wind

ぼくそう 牧草 *grass (for grazing), pasturage*

牧草地 meadow, pasture

ぼくちく 牧畜 *stock farming, stock raising*

ほくとう 北東 *the northeast* [→ 東北]

北東の風 northeast wind

ほくとしちせい 北斗七星 *the Big Dipper*

ほくぶ 北部 *northern part* [↔ 南部]

ほくべい 北米 *North America* [↔ 南米]

ほくりくちほう 北陸地方 *the Hokuriku region of Japan (Niigata, Toyama, Ishikawa, and Fukui Prefectures)*

ほくろ *mole (on the skin)*

ほげい 捕鯨 *whaling*

捕鯨船 whaling ship

ほけつ 補欠 *1. filling a vacancy, substitution*

2. person who fills a vacancy, substitute

次郎は補欠でその野球の試合に出ました。
Jiro played in that baseball game as a substitute.

補欠選挙 special election (to fill a vacancy)

補欠選手 substitute player [↔ レギュラー1.]

ポケット *pocket*

ポケットに財布を入れなさい。
Put your wallet in your pocket.

春男はポケットに両手を突っ込んでいた。
Haruo is walked with both hands in his pockets.

ズボンのポケット pants pocket

ぼける 惚ける *to become senile*

ほけん 保健 *health preservation*

保健婦 (female) public health nurse

保健所 health center, public health clinic

保健体育 health and physical education

ほけん 保険 *insurance*

Aに保険をかける to get insurance on A, to insure A

母も車に保険をかけています。
My mother also has insurance on her car.

保険に入る to get insurance, to become insured

保険会社 insurance company

保険金 insurance money

健康保険 health insurance

生命保険 life insurance

傷害保険 accident insurance

ほご 保護 *protection*

保護する to protect, to safeguard [→ 守る1.]

夏の強い日ざしから目を保護するためにサングラスをかけます。
I wear sunglasses to protect my eyes from the strong summer sun.

保護鳥 protected bird

保護者 protector, guardian

ぼこう 母校 *alma mater*

ほこうしゃ 歩行者 *pedestrian*

歩行者天国 street on which vehicular traffic has been temporarily suspended (typically on a Sunday or holiday)

ぼこく 母国 *native country*

母国語 native language

ほこり 埃 *dust (i.e., fine particles of dirt)*

時々本棚のほこりを払います。
I sometimes brush off the dust on the bookshelf.

埃だらけの covered with dust

埃っぽい dusty

ほこり 誇り *1. pride, thing to be proud of*

この博物館は市の誇りです。
This museum is the pride of the city.

2. pride, self-esteem

父は自分の仕事に誇りを持っています。
My father takes pride in his work.

ほこる 誇る *to be proud of, to take pride in*

ほし 星 *star; planet* [→ 惑星]

今夜は空に星が輝いています。
Tonight stars are shining in the sky.

今夜は星がたくさん見えるよ。
Tonight you can see a lot of stars!

星明かり starlight

星屑 stardust

星占い astrological fortune-telling

星空 starry sky

流れ星 shooting star

ほしい 欲しい *1. to want, to desire*

(This word is an adjective, and what is wanted is treated as a grammatical subject and marked with が. The word is not used to describe the wants of a third person; see 欲しがる.)

新しいドレスが欲しい。
I want a new dress.

今私は何も欲しくありません。
I don't want anything now.

これは私が長い間欲しかったステレオだ。
This is the stereo I wanted for a long time.

2. to want (someone) to (following the gerund (-て form) of a verb)

父に沖縄に連れていってほしいです。
I want my father to take me to Okinawa.

ほしがる 欲しがる *to come to want*

(Used instead of 欲しい when the person who wants is a third person.)

弟は新しい自転車を欲しがっています。
My younger brother wants a new bicycle.

ポジション *position, place, location* [→ 位置]

ほしゅ 保守 *conservatism*

保守的な conservative

ほしゅ 捕手 *(baseball) catcher* [→ キャッチャー]

ぼしゅう 募集 *1. recruitment*

募集する to recruit

理科部は部員を募集しています。
The science club is recruiting members.

「スタッフ募集」 (on a sign)
Staff Wanted

2. raising, collection, solicitation (of contributions)

募集する to raise, to collect

1億円の寄付金を募集しましたよ。
They raised donations of 100 million yen!

募集広告 want ad

ほじょ 補助 *help, assistance*

補助する to help with

恵子さんもその仕事を補助しました。
Keiko also helped with that work.

ほしょう 保証 *guarantee, warranty*

私の時計は2年間の保証がついています。
My watch has a two-year guarantee.

保証する to guarantee

運転者の安全は保証できません。
I cannot guarantee the driver's safety.

保証期間 warranty period

保証金 security money, security deposit

保証人 guarantor; sponsor

保証書 (written) guarantee

保証つきの guaranteed, with a guarantee

ほす 干す *to put out to dry*

ぬれた上着を日なたに干しました。
I put my wet jacket out to dry in the sun.

母は洗濯物を干しました。
My mother hung the washing out to dry.

ボス *boss (of henchmen)* [→ 親分]

ポスター *poster*

歌手のポスターを壁にはりました。
I put up a poster of a singer on the wall.

ポスト *(US) mailbox, (UK) postbox*

ポストに入れる to drop in a mailbox, (US) to mail, (UK) to post

途中でこの手紙をポストに入れてね。
Mail this letter on your way, won't you?

ポスト *post, position, job*

ボストンバッグ *Boston bag*

ほそい 細い *thin, slender, slim, small in diameter* [↔ 太い]; narrow [→ 狭い1.]

谷本さんの指は細いですね。
Ms. Tanimoto's fingers are slender, aren't they?

姉は細い体をしています。
My older sister is slim. (Literally: My older sister has a slim body.)
この細いひもを使ってもいいですか。
Is it all right to use this thin string?
この細い道を行けば、公園に出ます。
If you go along this narrow road, you'll come to the park.
細い声 weak voice, small voice

ほそう 舗装 *pavement; paving*
舗装する to pave
舗装道路 paved road

ほそながい 細長い *long and slender*

ほぞん 保存 *preservation; storage*
保存する to preserve; to store
このフィルムは涼しい所に保存しなさい。
Store this film in a cool place.

ほたる 蛍 *firefly*

ぼたん 牡丹 *peony*

ボタン *button*
シャツのボタンが取れました。
A shirt button came off.
ボタンをかける to button a button
ボタンを外す to unbutton a button
ボタン穴 buttonhole

ぼち 墓地 *graveyard, cemetery*
教会墓地 churchyard

ホチキス *stapler*
ホチキスで留める to fasten with a stapler
先生はコピーをホチキスで留めました。
The teacher stapled the copies together.

ほちょう 歩調 *pace, step, walking tempo*
歩調を合わせる to keep pace, to match walking tempo
ほかの人と歩調を合わせて歩きなさい。
Walk in pace with the other people.

ほっきょく 北極 *the North Pole* [↔ 南極]
北極海 the Arctic Ocean
北極星 the Polestar, the North Star

ホック *hook ((clothing fastener))*
ホックで留める to fasten with a hook
ホックをかける to hook a hook
ホックを外す to undo a hook

ボックス *box* [→ 箱]
バッターボックス batter's box
電話ボックス telephone booth

ホッケー *(field) hockey*
アイスホッケー ice hockey

ほっさ 発作 *fit, attack, spasm*

ほっそり ～した *slender, slim*

ぼっちゃん 坊ちゃん *1.* 【HON.】*(young) son; little boy*
2. spoiled and naive young man

ほっておく *1. to leave alone, to let alone*
僕のことはほっておいてください。
Please leave me alone.
2. to leave undone, to set aside
その問題をほっておきましょう。
Let's set that problem aside.

ほっと ～する *to be relieved, to feel relief* [→ 安心する]
みんなが無事だと聞いてほっとしました。
I heard that everyone is safe and felt relieved.

ポット *1. pot (for coffee, tea, etc.)*
2. thermos bottle [→ 魔法瓶 (s.v. 魔法)]

ホットケーキ *hot cake, pancake*

ホットニュース *hot news*

ホットライン *hotline*

ポップコーン *popcorn*

ほっぺた 【COL. for 頰】*cheek*

ボディーチェック *body search, frisk*

ボディーガード *bodyguard*

ボディービル *body building*

ポテト *potato* [→ じゃがいも]
ポテトチップス potato chip

ホテル *hotel*
私たちは広島のホテルに泊まりました。
We stayed at a hotel in Hiroshima.
今川さんは今ホテルに着きました。
Ms. Imagawa just now arrived at the hotel.
8時にホテルを出ます。
We will leave the hotel at 8:00.

ほど 程 *1. limit, bound* [→ 限度]
友情にも程があるよ。
There's a limit even to friendship!
程を越す to exceed the limits, to go to far
2. extent, degree (following a predicate in the nonpast tense) [→ 位1.]
この問題は信じられないほど難しいよ。
This problem is unbelievably hard! (Literally: This problem is hard to a degree that one can't believe!)
歩けないほど足が痛いです。
My leg hurts so much that I can't walk. (Literally: My leg is painful to the degree that I can't walk.)
3. the more (following a predicate first in the conditional and then in the nonpast form)
飲めば飲むほどおいしくなります。
The more you drink, the better it tastes.
早ければ早いほどいいよ。
The sooner, the better!
4 (not) as much as, (not) to the same extent as (In this use functions as a noun-following particle or follows a verb in the nonpast tense. A negative predicate must follow ほど.)
太郎は秋元さんほど英語が話せません。
Taro can't speak English as well as Ms. Akimoto.
このかばんは私のほど重くないですよ。
This bag is not as heavy as mine!
北海道ほどいい所はないです。
There's no place as nice as Hokkaido.
本は映画ほどおもしろくありません。
Books are not as interesting as movies.

—ほど —程 *about, or so (Added to number bases.)* [→ —ぐらい1.]
10分ほどして戻ってきます。
I'll come back in ten minutes or so.
20人ほどの生徒がその会に出席していた。
About twenty students were attending that party.

ほどう 歩道 *(US) sidewalk, (UK) pavement*
私たちは歩道を歩いていました。
We were walking along the sidewalk.
歩道橋 pedestrian overpass
横断歩道 crosswalk

ほどく 解く *to undo, to untie* [↔ 結ぶ1.]
この包みをほどいてくださいませんか。
Won't you please untie this package?
父はネクタイをほどきました。
My father untied his tie.

ほとけ 仏 *1. Buddha*
仏のような人 saintly person
2. deceased person
(This use is a reflection of the traditional religious belief that a person becomes an enlightened being like Buddha after death.)
仏になる to pass on, to pass away

ほととぎす 時鳥, 子規, 不如帰 *common cuckoo*

ほとんど 殆ど *1. almost, nearly, almost completely*
宿題はほとんど終わったよ。
I've almost finished my homework!
誤りはほとんどありませんでした。
There were almost no mistakes.
バケツにはほとんど水が残っていません。
In the bucket there's almost no water left.
2. almost all, the greater part
ほとんどの生徒がこの集会に参加した。
Almost all the students took part in this

meeting.
観光客のほとんどは学生です。
Almost all of the tourists are students.

ほにゅうどうぶつ 哺乳動物 *mammal*

ほね 骨 *bone*
この魚は小さな骨がたくさんあるよ。
This fish has a lot of small bones!
骨を折る to break a bone; to take pains, to make efforts
由美はスケートで右足の骨を折りました。
Yumi broke a bone in her right leg while skating.
骨を折れる a bone breaks; to be difficult, to be laborious
英語で手紙を書くのは骨を折れる仕事だ。
Writing letters in English is laborious work.
骨折り efforts, pains [→ 努力]
骨折る to make efforts, to take pains [→ 努力する]
その作品を仕上げるのに非常に骨折った。
I took great pains to finish that work.

ほのお 炎 *flame*
ガスの炎は何色ですか。
What color is a gas flame?
階段は炎に包まれていました。
The stairs were enveloped in flames.

ほのめかす 仄めかす *to hint at*
妹は留学するつもりだとほのめかした。
My younger sister hinted that she intends to study abroad.

ホバークラフト *hovercraft*

ポピュラー 〜な *popular, of wide appeal* [→ 大衆向きの (s.v. 大衆)]
ポピュラーミュージック popular music

ポプラ *poplar*

ほほ 頬 [☞ 頬]

ほぼ nearly, almost [→ 殆ど1.]

ほぼ 保母 *nursery school teacher*

ほほえましい 微笑ましい *pleasant, smile-provoking*
ほほえましい光景ですね。
It's a pleasant sight, isn't it?

ほほえみ 微笑み *smile*

ほほえむ 微笑む *to smile*
その赤ちゃんは私にほほえみました。
That baby smiled at me.
池田さんがほほえみながらこちらに来た。
Ms. Ikeda came over to us smiling.

ポマード *pomade*

ほめる 褒める *to praise, to commend* [↔ 貶す]
中野さんの勇気を褒めました。
We praised Mr. Nakano's courage.
正子は典子の新しいドレスを褒めたよ。
Masako praised Noriko's new dress!

ほら *Look!, Listen! (an interjection used to call a person's attention to something)*
ほら、電車が来たよ。
Look! The train has come!
ほら、カナリアが鳴いているよ。
Listen! A canary is singing!

ほらあな 洞穴 *cave* [→ 洞窟]

ボランティア *(community-service) volunteer*

ポリエチレン *polyethylene*

ボリューム *1. (sound) volume*
浩はテレビのボリュームを少し上げたよ。
Hiroshi turned the TV volume up a little!
2. volume, amount

ほりょ 捕虜 *prisoner of war*

ほる 掘る *to dig; to dig up, to dig for*
あそこで何を掘っているのですか。
What are they digging for over there?
このシャベルで穴を掘りました。
I dug a hole with this shovel.

ほる 彫る *to carve, to engrave* [→ 刻む2.]
AにBを彫る to carve A in/on B, to

engrave A on B

ボルト *volt*

ーボルト (counter for volts; see Appendix 2)

100ボルトの電流が流れています。
A 100-volt current is flowing.

ボルト *bolt ((fastener))*

ホルモン *1. hormone*

2. [☞ ホルモン焼き]

ホルモン焼き grilled organ meats

ぼろ *rag; ragged clothes*

ぼろ靴 worn-out shoes

ポロシャツ *polo shirt*

ほろびる 滅びる *to be destroyed, to fall, to cease to exist*

ローマ帝国がいつ滅びたかわかりますか。
Do you know when the Roman Empire fell?

ほろぼす 滅ぼす *to ruin, to destroy, to wipe out*

身を滅ぼす to ruin oneself, to bring oneself to ruin

ほん 本 *book*

兄は飛行機の本を買いたがっています。
My older brother wants to buy a book about airplanes.

本の18ページを開いてください。
Please open the book to page 18.

この図書館は本が何冊借りられますか。
How many books can one borrow from this library?

厚い〔薄い〕本 thick〔thin〕book

本箱 bookcase

本棚 bookshelf

本立て bookend

本屋 (US) bookstore, (UK) bookshop; bookseller

絵本 picture book

古本 used book, secondhand book

ーほん ー本 *(counter for long objects; see Appendix 2)*

ぼん 盆 *(serving) tray*

ぼん 盆 *the Buddhist festival of the dead*

(Celebrated on July 15 in some areas of Japan and on August 15 in other areas.) (This word is almost always used with the prefix お-: お盆.)

盆踊り Bon dance

ほんかくてき 本格的 〜な *full-scale, full-fledged, serious*

ほんき 本気 *seriousness, earnestness*

本気の serious, earnest [→ 真剣な]

本気ですか。
Are you serious?

まさか本気じゃないでしょう？
You can't possibly be serious, right?

本気で seriously, earnestly

本気にする to take seriously

そんな冗談を本気にしてはいけないよ。
You mustn't take such jokes seriously!

ぼんさい 盆栽 *bonsai, dwarf tree in a pot*

盆栽を作る to grow a bonsai

ほんしつ 本質 *essence, true nature*

ほんじつ 本日 【FORMAL for 今日】*today*

ほんしん 本心 *true feelings; real intentions*

星野君は私に本心を打ち明けてくれた。
Hoshino confided his real feelings to me.

ぼんち 盆地 *(geographical) basin*

奈良盆地 the Nara Basin

ほんてん 本店 *head office, main store* [↔ 支店]

ほんと [☞ 本当]

ボンド *bonding agent, glue* [→ 接着剤]

ポンド *pound ((unit of weight))*

ーポンド (counter for pounds; see Appendix 2)

ポンド *pound ((monetary unit))*

ーポンド (counter for pounds; see Appendix 2)

ほんとう 本当 ～の *true, real*

これはほんとうの話ですか。
Is this is a true story?

その夢はほんとうになりました。
That dream came true.

父が破産したというのはほんとうですか。
Is it true that Father has gone bankrupt?

いっしょにいてほんとうに楽しいです。
It's really fun being with you.

佐野さんはほんとうにいい人です。
Ms. Sano is a really good person.

ほんとうにそう思いますか。
Do you really think so?

「来週ハワイに行きますよ」「えっ、ほんとうですか」
"I'm going to go to Hawaii next week!" "What! Really?"

ほんとうにありがとうございます。
Thank you very much indeed. (Literally: Truly thank you.)

ほんにん 本人 *the person himself/herself, the person in question*

ほんね 本音 *true feelings, real motivation* [→ 本心] [↔ 立て前]

ほんの *only a, just a, a mere*

太郎はまだほんの子供です。
Taro is still only a child.

父はほんの少しフランス語ができます。
My father can speak French just a little.

明はほんの数日前に引っ越しました。
Akira moved out only a few days ago.

それをほんの冗談で言いました。
I said that as a mere joke.

ほんのう 本能 *instinct*

本能的な instinctive

ほんぶ 本部 *main office, headquarters; administration building*

ポンプ *pump (for liquid)*

ポンプでくみ出す to pump out

ポンプで井戸から水をくみ出しなさい。
Pump out some water from the well.

ボンベ *gas cylinder*

酸素ボンベ oxygen cylinder

ほんもの 本物 *real thing* [↔ 偽物 (s.v. 偽)]

本物の real, genuine [↔ 偽の]

これは本物のダイヤです。
This is a real diamond.

ほんやく 翻訳 *translation*

翻訳する to translate [→ 訳す]

シェークスピアを翻訳で読みました。
I read Shakespeare in translation.

翻訳者 translator

ぼんやり (～と) *1. vacantly, absentmindedly, blankly*

男の人が門のそばにぼんやりと立っている。
A man is standing by the gate vacantly.

ぼんやりする to become blank, to become vacant; to behave absentmindedly, to daydream

雅史は午前中ずっとぼんやりしています。
Masashi has been absent-minded all morning.

2. dimly, vaguely

祖父のことはぼんやり覚えているだけだ。
I only remember my grandfather vaguely.

ほんらい 本来 *originally* [→ 元来]*; by nature* [→ 生まれつき]

これは本来は中国の植物です。
This is originally a plant from China.

本来の original; inborn

ほんるい 本塁 *home base, home plate* [→ ホーム2.] *(in baseball)*

本塁打 home run [→ ホームラン]

ま 間 *1. a room* [→ 部屋]

一間 (counter for rooms; see Appendix 2)

2. space, room

間を空ける to leave space, to make room

3. time to spare; time interval

試合が始まるまで少し間があります。
There is some time to spare before the game starts.

あっという間に in an instant

まあ *1. Oh!, Oh, dear!, My!, Well! (This use, expressing surprise, is typically restricted to female speakers.)*

まあ、何ておもしろいんでしょう。
My, how interesting!

2. Come on (in a request or suggestion)

まあ、静かにしなさい。
Come on, be quiet.

3. Well (indicating partial agreement)

まあ、いいでしょう。
Well, it's probably all right.

マーガリン *margarine*

マーク *mark, label; trademark*

箱には赤い矢印のマークがついています。
On that box there's a red arrow mark.

クエスチョンマーク question mark [→ 疑問符 (s.v. 疑問)]

マーク ～する *to keep an eye on; to mark (an opposing player)*

7番をマークしてね。
Mark number 7, OK?

マーケット *market* [→ 市場]

姉はマーケットに買い物に行きました。
My older sister went to the market for shopping.

マーチ *(musical) march* [→ 行進曲 (s.v. 行進)]

マーマレード *marmalade*

－まい *(Added to the informal affirmative nonpast-tense form of a verb (i.e., the form listed in dictionaries). Alternatively, if the verb is 一段, may be added to the base (see Appendix 1). Instead of 来る and する, the forms く- and す- may occur before -まい.)*

1. probably will not, probably does not

子供だから、こんな問題はわかるまい。
He's a child, so he probably won't understand this kind of problem.

2. will not, will make sure not to (The subject must be first person.)

あの店には2度と行くまい。
I'll never go to that shop again.

－まい －枚 *(counter for flat, thin objects; see Appendix 2)*

紙が5枚必要です。
I need five sheets of paper.

パンを2枚焼いてくれる？
Will you toast two slices of bread for me?

41円の切手を10枚ください。
Please give me ten ¥41 stamps.

まい－ 毎－ *every (Added to bases denoting regularly recurring time spans.)*

毎朝 every morning

父は毎朝犬を散歩させます。
My father walks the dog every morning.

マイク *microphone*

隠しマイク hidden microphone

マイクロホン [☞マイク]

まいご 迷子 *lost child*

迷子になる to get lost (The subject is a person or animal.)

その坊やは競技場で迷子になりました。
That little boy got lost in the stadium.

マイコン *microcomputer*

まいしゅう 毎週 *every week*

父は毎週車を洗います。

My father washes the car every week.
山田さんは毎週日曜日に教会に行きます。
Mr. Yamada goes to church every Sunday.

まいそう 埋葬 *burial, interment (of a dead body or cremated ashes)*
埋葬する to bury, to inter

まいつき 毎月 *every month*
兄は毎月１回映画を見に行きます。
My older brother goes to see a movie once every month.

まいとし 毎年 *every year*
中山さんは毎年ハワイに行きます。
Ms. Nakayama goes to Hawaii every year.
日本のお盆は毎年の行事です。
Japan's Bon Festival is a yearly event.

マイナス [[↔ プラス]] *1. minus (sign)*
100マイナス30は70です。
Ten minus three is seven.
マイナスの数 negative number
2. minus, loss, detriment

まいにち 毎日 *every day*
車の事故は毎日起こります。
Car accidents happen every day.
毎日の仕事がちょうど終わったところだ。
My everyday work has just ended.

まいねん 毎年 *every year* [→ 毎年]

マイペース ～で *at one's own pace*
小林さんはマイペースでゆっくり歩いた。
Mr. Kobayashi walked slowly at his own pace.

まいる 参る *{5} 1.* 【HUM. for 行く】
2. 【HUM. for 来る*1.*】
3. 【FORMAL for 来る*2.*】

マイル *mile*
ーマイル (counter for miles; see Appendix 2)

まう 舞う *1. to dance* [→ 踊る]
2. to flutter about (in the air)

まうえ 真上 *the area directly above*
テーブルの真上にシャンデリアがある。
There is a chandelier directly above the table.

まえ 前 *1. time before, earlier in time, previous time* [↔ 後2.]
前にその絵を見たことがあるよ。
I've seen that picture before!
父はいつも朝食の前にジョギングをする。
My father always jogs before breakfast.
暗くなる前に帰りましょう。
Let's go home before it gets dark.
飲む前に電子レンジで温めました。
I heated it up in the microwave oven before drinking it. (A verb preceding is always in the nonpast tense.)
前の previous, former
この前のテストは難しかったですね。
The previous test was difficult, wasn't it?
2. the area in front, the front [↔ 後ろ]
前から３番目の席に座りました。
I sat in the third seat from the front.
駅の前に銀行があります。
There is a bank in front of the station.
明子ちゃんは私の前を歩いているよ。
Akiko is walking ahead of me!
前に立ちましょう。
Let's stand in front!
ー前 ago, before (Added to noun bases, often numbers denoting periods of time.) [↔ ー後]
それは５年前のできごとでした。
It happened five years ago. (Literally: It's an event of five years ago.)
母は10分前に買い物に出かけました。
My mother went out shopping ten minutes ago.

まえうり 前売り *advance sale, selling in advance*
前売り券 advance ticket

まえかけ 前掛け *apron* [→ エプロン]

まえがみ 前髪 *bangs, hair hanging down over the forehead*

まえきん 前金 *(full) payment in advance; down payment*

まえもって 前以て *beforehand, in advance* [→ 予め]

マガジン *magazine* [→ 雑誌]

まかす 負かす *to beat, to defeat*

兄を卓球で負かしたよ。
I beat my older brother in table tennis!

まかせる 任せる *to leave (up to someone or something else)*

全部私に任せてください。
Please leave everything to me.
両親はその決定を僕に任せました。
My parents left that decision to me.

まがりくねる 曲がりくねる *to become crooked, to become winding*

あの枝は曲がりくねっています。
That branch is crooked.

曲がりくねった道 winding road

まがる 曲がる *1. to turn, to make a turn (at a corner, etc.)*

Aを曲がる to turn at A, to make a turn along A
次の交差点を右に曲がってください。
Please turn right at the next intersection.
2. to become bent; to become curved

その曲がったくぎを使わないで。
Don't use that bent nail.
道路はそこで右に曲がっています。
The road curves to the right there.

マカロニ *macaroni*

マカロニグラタン macaroni au gratin

まき 薪 *firewood* [→ 薪]

まきこむ 巻き込む *to drag, to involve willy-nilly*

Aに巻き込まれる to get dragged into A, to get involved without wanting to in A

まきじゃく 巻き尺 *tape measure* [→ メジャー]

まきつく 巻き付く *to wind around, to coil around (intransitive)*

つたがその木に巻きついています。
Ivy has coiled itself around that tree.

まきば 牧場 *stock farm, (US) ranch ; pasture (where farm animals graze)* [→ 牧場]

まぎらわしい 紛らわしい *confusing, easily confused (with something else); easily confused (with each other)*

紛らわしい道路標識が多いですよ。
There are a lot of confusing road signs!

この2枚の写真は紛らわしいですね。
These two photos are easily confused, aren't they?

まぎれもない 紛れもない *unquestionable, beyond doubt*

まぎれる 紛れる *1. to get confused (with), to become indistinguishable (from), to be mistaken (for)*

AがBと紛れる A gets confused with B, A becomes indistinguishable from B, A is mistaken for B

2. to take advantage of by blending into

泥棒がやみに紛れて逃げました。
The thief blended into the darkness and escaped.

3. to become diverted, to become distracted, to become absorbed

Aに紛れる to become diverted by A, to become distracted by A, to become absorbed in A

気が紛れる to become diverted from one's worries

まく 幕 *1. curtain (used as a partition or on a stage)*

幕がゆっくりと上がりました。
The curtain rose slowly.

2. act (of a play)

一幕 (counter for acts; see Appendix 2)

まく 巻く *1. to wind; to roll up (transitive)*
目覚まし時計のねじをまだ巻いていない。
I haven't wound the alarm clock up yet.
じゅうたんを巻いてくれませんか。
Won't you roll up the carpet for me?
2. to tie around, to wrap around
左手に包帯を巻きました。
I wrapped a bandage on my left hand.

まく 撒く *1. to scatter; to sprinkle*
母は毎日芝生に水をまきます。
My mother waters the lawn every day.
2. to elude, to shake off (a pursuer)

まく 蒔く *to sow*
父は畑に種をまいています。
My father is sowing seeds in the field.

マグニチュード *magnitude (of an earthquake measured on the Richter scale)*
その地震はマグニチュード2でした。
That earthquake was magnitude 2.

マグネシウム *magnesium*

マグマ *magma*

まくら 枕 *pillow*
枕カバー pillowcase

まくる *to roll up (sleeves, pant legs, etc.)*
皿を洗うためにそでをまくりました。
I rolled up my sleeves to wash the dishes.

まぐれ *(lucky) fluke*
まぐれで試合に勝ったよ。
We won the game by a fluke!
まぐれのヒットでした。
It was a lucky hit.

まぐろ 鮪 *tuna*

まけ 負け *defeat, loss* [↔ 勝ち]
黒崎さんはやっと負けを認めました。
Mr. Kurosaki finally admitted his defeat.
この勝負は僕の負けです。
This game is my loss.

まけおしみ 負け惜しみ *unhappiness at losing*
負け惜しみを言う to express unhappiness at losing, to be a bad loser

まける 負ける *1. to lose, to be defeated* [↔ 勝つ]
AがBに負ける A loses B, A is defeated in B (when B denotes a contest or competition)
私たちはその試合に負けました。
We lost that game.
戦争に負ける to lose a war
AがBに負ける A loses to B, A is defeated by B (when B denotes an opponent)
5対1でそのチームに負けたよ。
We lost to that team by 5 to 1!
相手に負ける to lose to an opponent
2. to come down, to give a discount on
1000円に負けてくれませんか。
Can't you come down to ¥1,000?
このカメラを少し負けてください。
Please give me a bit of a discount on this camera.
1割負けましょう。
I'll come down ten percent.

まげる 曲げる *to bend (transitive)*
背を曲げないようにしなさい。
Make sure not to bend your back.

まご 孫 *grandchild*

まごころ 真心 *sincerity , true-heartedness* [→ 誠実]
真心を込めて with sincerity, with one's whole heart
京子さんは真心を込めてあいさつをした。
Kyoko greeted with sincerity.

まごつく *to become confused about what to do, to find oneself at a loss*
Aにまごつく to find oneself at a loss because of A, to find oneself at a loss for A
新製品の説明にまごつきました。
I was at a loss for an explanation of the

new product.

まこと 誠 *1. sincerity, true-heartedness* [→ 真心]

2. ～に【FORMAL for 本当に】*really, truly, very*

誠にありがとうございました。
Thank you very much indeed.

まさか *1. You're kidding!, That can't be true! (when used as an exclamatory response)*

「恵子は試験に落ちたよ」「まさか」
"Keiko failed on the exam!" "You're kidding!"

2. surely (not), (not) possibly (Always occurs in combination with a negative predicate.)

まさかできるとは思いませんでした。
I didn't think he could possibly do it.

まさつ 摩擦 *friction, rubbing*

摩擦する to rub (one thing with another)
貿易摩擦 trade friction

まさに 正に 【FORMAL for 確かに】*certainly, undoubtedly*

正におっしゃるとおりです。
It's just as you say.

まさる 勝る *to be/become better, to be/become superior* [↔ 劣る]

Aに／より勝る to be better than A
京子は英語では太郎よりずっと勝ります。
Kyoko is much better at English than Taro.
健康は富に勝る。(proverb)
Health is better than wealth.

まざる 混ざる *to become mixed, to mix* [→ 混じる]

まじか 間近 *1. (the area) nearby*

母も間近に住んでいます。
My mother is also living nearby.

2. (the time) near at hand

間近に迫っている to be impending, to be very near at hand

マジック *1. magic, magic spell* [→ 魔法]

2. magic trick, conjuring [→ 手品]

まじめ 真面目 ～な *serious, earnest* [→ 真剣な]

洋子ちゃんはまじめな生徒です。
Yoko is a serious student.
弟は先生の前でまじめな顔をします。
My younger brother puts on a serious face in front of the teacher.

もっとまじめに勉強しなければならない。
You have to study more seriously.

まじゅつ 魔術 *1. magic, magic spell* [→ 魔法]

2. large-scale magic trick, illusion

魔術師 magician, illusionist

まじょ 魔女 *(female) witch*

まじる 混じる *{5} to become mixed, to mix*

油と水は混じりますか。
Do oil and water mix?

まじわる 交わる *1. to associate, to keep company* [→ 交際する]

母は近所の人と交わるのが下手です。
My mother is poor at associating with the people in the neighborhood.

2. to cross, to intersect [→ 交差する]

２つの線はこの点で交わります。
The two lines cross at this point.

ます 鱒 *trout*

ます 増す *to increase (transitive or intransitive)* [→ 増える; 増やす]

２国間の緊張が増しています。
The tension between the two countries has increased.
運転手が速度を増しました。
The driver increased the speed.

まず 先ず *first, first of all*

まず原文を読みましょう。
First let's read the original text.

ますい 麻酔 *anesthesia*

麻酔薬 an anesthetic

局部麻酔 local anesthesia
全身麻酔 general anesthesia

まずい *1. bad-tasting (Can be used to describe a restaurant, cafeteria, etc., as well as food itself.)* [↔ 美味しい]

このスープはまずいよ。
This soup is bad-tasting!

このパン屋はまずいね。
This bakery is bad isn't it?

2. poor, unskilled, clumsy (describing what someone does)

あの歌手は歌がまずいね。
That singer isn't any good at singing, is she?

3. ill-advised, inappropriate; embarrassing, awkward

その秘密がばれたのはまずいなあ。
Boy, it's awkward that that secret was revealed!

マスク *1. cloth surgical mask (covering the mouth and nose to prevent dust or germs from passing through)*

かぜを引いたら、マスクをしなさい。
Since you've caught a cold, wear a cloth mask.

2. mask (of the type worn by baseball catchers and umpires)

キャッチャーはマスクを着けました。
The catcher put on the mask.

マスコット *mascot*

マスコミ *1. mass media*

その事件はマスコミでも報じられました。
That incident was also reported in the mass media.

2. mass communication

まずしい 貧しい [[↔ 豊かな]] *1. poor, indigent* [→ 貧乏な]

金田さんは貧しい家に生まれました。
Mr. Kaneda was born into a poor family.
暮らしが貧しい人もいます。
There are also people who live in poverty. (Literally: There are also people whose lives are poor.)

2. scanty, insufficient [→ 乏しい]

あの人は経験が貧しいです。
That person's experience is scanty.

マスター *1. master; employer* [→ 主人2.]

2. proprietor, shop owner [→ 主人3.]

3. master degree holder [→ 修士]

4. ～する to master

マスト *(ship's) mast* [→ 帆柱]

ますます 益々 *more and more, increasingly*

試合はますますおもしろくなりました。
The game became more and more exciting.
最近ますます寒くなってきました。
It has gotten colder and colder recently.

まぜる 混ぜる *to mix (transitive)*

牛乳に砂糖を混ぜました。
I mixed sugar into the milk.

また *1. again* [→ 再び]

来週の月曜日また会いましょう。
Let's meet again next Monday.
ではまた。
See you. (Literally: Well then, again.)

2. in addition, moreover, also

美幸は歌手で、そしてまた俳優でもある。
Miyuki is a singer, and in addition, she's also an actress.

3. similarly, in the same way (In this use, また *follows the particle* も *and is essentially redundant.)*

この契約には私の妻もまた同意している。
My wife also agrees with this contract.
雄城が行かないなら、私もまた行かない。
If Yuki is not going to go, then I'm not either.

また 股 *crotch (where the legs join)*

まだ *1. still, (not) yet* [→ 未だに]

まだ健さんから便りがありません。
There still isn't any word from Ken.

「もう済みましたか」「いいえ、まだです」
"Have you finished yet?" "No, I haven't."
島田さんはまだ若いです。
Ms. Shimada is still young.
弟はまだ4歳だよ。
My younger brother is still (only) four years old!

2. somewhat (modifying the predicate in a comparison between two unsatisfactory alternatives)

このほうがまだいいよ。
This one is somewhat better.

またぐ 跨ぐ *to step over, to straddle*
ホースをまたぎました。
I stepped over the hose.
警備員が水たまりをまたいで立っていた。
The security officer was standing straddled over a puddle.

またせる 待たせる *to keep (someone) waiting (This word is the regular causative form of* 待つ.*)*
お待たせしました。
Sorry to have kept you waiting. (Literally: I have kept you waiting. (humble))

またたく 瞬く *1. to blink (ones eye(s))*
瞬く間に in the blink of an eye, in an instant

2. (when the subject is a light source) to twinkle; to blink; to flicker
星が瞬いています。
The stars are twinkling.

または *or* [→ 或いは1.]
東京または横浜に新しいビルを建てます。
We will be constructing a new building in either Tokyo or Yokohama.

まち 町 *1. town, city*
小さな町で生まれました。
I was born in a small town.

2. district (an officially designated subdivision of a city (市) *or a ward* (区))

まち 街 *1. shopping district, bustling part of town*
母は街に買い物に行きました。
My mother went to the shopping district for shopping.

2. city street, building-lined street
街で友達に出会いました。
I ran into a friend on the street.

まちあいしつ 待合室 *waiting room*

まちあわせる 待ち合わせる *to meet (at an agreed on place and time)*
本屋の前で待ち合わせましょう。
Let's meet in front of the bookstore.

まちがい 間違い *mistake, error*
この文にはつづりのまちがいが二つある。
In this sentence there are two spelling mistakes.
その答えはまちがいです。
That answer is wrong.
間違い電話(telephoning a) wrong number
間違いないcertain, beyond doubt, indisputable
まちがいなくこの本は返します。
I will certainly return this book.

まちがえる 間違える *1. to make a mistake involving, to do incorrectly*
英語の試験で4問の解答をまちがえたよ。
I did four incorrect answers on the English test!
まちがえて弟の靴をはいて出かけました。
I made a mistake and put on my younger brother's shoes and went out.
健ちゃんは乗るバスをまちがえたよ。
Ken made a mistake about which bus to take!

2. to mistake
AをBとまちがえる to mistake A for B
美香さんは叔母を母とまちがえました。
Mika mistook my aunt for my mother.

まちかまえる 待ち構える *to be ready and wait for, to wait eagerly for*

まつ 松 *pine*
松林 pine woods
松ぼっくり pine cone
松笠 pine cone

まつ 待つ *to wait for*

だれを待っているのですか。
Who are you waiting for?

あしたまで返事を待たなければならない。
I'll have to wait until tomorrow for the answer.

ちょっと待ってください。
Please wait a little.

洋子さんからの手紙を待っています。
I am waiting for a letter from Yoko.

歳月人を待たず。 (proverb)
Time and tide wait for no man. (Literally: Time does not wait for a person.)

まっか 真っ赤 〜な *deep red, bright red, very red*

先生は怒って真っ赤になったよ。
The teacher got angry and turned bright red!

真っ赤な帽子が欲しいよ。
I want a bright red hat!

まっくら 真っ暗 〜な *very dark, pitch dark*

外は真っ暗でした。
Outside it was pitch dark.

まっくろ 真っ黒 〜な *deep black, very black; completely black*

まつげ まつ毛 *eyelash*

マリーさんは長いまつ毛をしていますね。
Marie has long eyelashes, doesn't she?

マッサージ *massage*
マッサージする to massage

まっさお 真っ青 〜な *1. deep blue, very blue*

空は真っ青ですよ。
The sky is deep blue!

2. very pale (because of illness or fear)

弘さんは良子さんの言葉を聞いて、真っ青になったよ。
Hiroshi listened to what Yoshiko said and turned very pale! (Literally: Hiroshi listened to Yoshiko's words and became very pale.)

まっしぐら *(〜に) full speed ahead, at full forward speed*

まっしろ 真っ白 〜な *snow-white; completely white*

戸田先生の髪は真っ白です。
Dr. Toda's hair is snow-white.

まっすぐ 真っすぐ *(〜に) straight ahead, without turning; directly, straight, without detours*

ここからまっすぐ行ってください。
Please go straight ahead from here.

このバスはまっすぐ新宿に行きます。
This bus goes directly to Shinjuku.

まっすぐな straight, unbent; direct, detour-free

このまっすぐな道のほうが好きです。
I prefer this straight road.

まったく 全く *quite, really, completely, absolutely; (not) at all*

それはまったく別の事だよ。
That's a completely different matter!

由美ちゃんはまったく走るのが速いね。
Yumi runs really fast, doesn't she? (Literally: As for Yumi, running really is fast, isn't it?)

まったくスキーができません。
I can't ski at all.

まつたけ 松茸 *matsutake mushroom (highly prized for its flavor)*

マッチ *match (-stick)*
マッチをする to strike a match
マッチ箱 matchbox

マット *mat (of the type used for gymnastics, etc.)*

マットレス *mattress*

マッハ *Mach, Mach number*

その飛行機はマッハ２の速度で飛びます。
The plane flies at a speed of Mach *2.*

まつばづえ 松葉杖 *crutch*

マップ *map* [→ 地図]

まつり 祭り *1. traditional Japanese festival (typically held yearly at a Shinto shrine)*

2. festival, gala event

雪祭り the Snow Festival (an annual event in Sapporo)

まで *1. until (following either a noun referring to a point in time or verb in the non-past tense); through (when a preceding noun refers to something longer than a point in time)*

私たちは５時まで図書館で勉強しました。
We studied in the library until 5:00.

雨がやむまでここにいます。
I'm going to stay here until the rain stops.

夏祭りは木曜日まで続きます。
The summer festival will continue through Thursday.

までに by, not later than

夕食までに帰ってきなさい。
Come home by supper.

火曜日までに宿題を出してください。
Hand in your homework by Tuesday!

５時までにこの仕事を終わりましょう。
Let's finish this work by 5:00.

2. as far as, to (following a noun referring to a place)

バス停まで走りましょう。
Let's run to the bus stop.

地下鉄の駅までいっしょに行きます。
I'll go with you as far as the subway station.

3. even (indicating that what precedes is extreme) [→ さえ1.]

お母さんまでそんなことを言うの？
Even your mother says that kind of thing?

まと 的 *target, mark, object*

洋子さんはクラス全員の尊敬の的です。
Yoko is the object of the entire class's respect.

まど 窓 *window*

窓を開けてください。
Please open the window.

直子さんは窓から外を見ています。
Naoko is looking out the window.

窓ガラス window pane

窓際 area right near a window

窓口 transaction window

窓枠 window frame

まとまる *1. to come together into a unit*

2. to become orderly, to become coherent, to take shape

3. to be settled, to be completed, to come to a satisfactory conclusion

まとめる *1. to bring together into a unit, to consolidate, to unify*

監督はチームをうまくまとめました。
The manager skillfully unified the team.

荷物をすぐにまとめなさい。
Get the luggage together at once.

2. to put in order, to make coherent

考えをまとめる to put one's thoughts in order

3. to settle, to complete, to bring to a satisfactory conclusion

交渉をまとめるのは時間がかかるだろう。
It will probably take time to complete the negotiations.

まどり 間取り *room layout, floor plan*

マナー *manners*

マナーのいい人 well-mannered person

テーブルマナー table manners

まないた 俎板 *cutting board (used in cooking)*

まなつ 真夏 *the midsummer* [↔ 真冬]

真夏日 very hot day

まなぶ 学ぶ *to study, to (try to) learn, to take lessons in* [→ 習う, 勉強する]

私たちは関先生から英語を学んでいます。
We are learning English from Mrs. Seki.

大学で心理学を学びたいです。
I want to study psychology at college.

マニア *enthusiast, devotee*

兄は写真のマニアです。
My older brother is a photo enthusiast.

ジャズマニア jazz devotee

切手マニア stamp enthusiast

まにあう 間に合う *1. to make it in time*

Aに間に合う to make it in time for A, to make it to A in time

急がないと、学校に間に合わないよ。
If you don't hurry, you won't make it to school in time!

2. to be able to make do, to be able to get by

このナイフで間に合います。
I can make do with this knife.

マニキュア *manicure*

指にマニキュアをする to manicure one's fingernails

まぬけ 間抜け【CRUDE】～な *stupid, foolish*

そんなことをするなんてまぬけだよ。
It's stupid to do such a thing!

まね 真似 *1. imitation, mimicry, copying*

弘さんはあの歌手のまねが上手です。
Hiroshi's imitation of that singer is skill-ful.

洋子さんは多田先生のまねをしたよ。
Yoko did an imitation of Prof. Tada!

まねする to imitate, to mimic, to copy

2. pretense, false show [→ 振り]

まねをする to pretend, to make a pre-tense

あの人は死んだまねをしました。
That person pretended to be dead.

3. behavior, action (Used to refer to behavior that is undesirable.)

ばかなまねはやめてよ。
Stop your foolish behavior!

マネージャー *manager, person in charge* [→ 支配人 (s.v. 支配)]

まねき 招き *invitation* [→ 招待]

マネキン *mannequin*

まねく 招く *1. to invite* [→ 招待する]

兄は西山夫妻を結婚式に招きました。
My older brother invited Mr. and Mrs. Nishiyama to his wedding.

誤解を招く to invite misunderstanding

2. to beckon

私を招いた店員についていくことにした。
I decided to go to the store clerk who was beckoning me.

まねる 真似る *to imitate, to mimic, to copy*

由美さんはその女優の声をまねました。
Yumi imitated that actress's voice.

まばたき 瞬き *(eye) blink*

まばたき(を)する to blink [→ 瞬く1.]

赤ちゃんはまばたきもせず私を見ていた。
The baby looked at me without even blinking.

まひ 麻痺 *paralysis; numbness*

まひする to become paralyzed; to become numb

台風で交通がまひしています。
Traffic is paralyzed by the typhoon.

寒さで指がまひしています。
My fingers are numb with the cold.

まぶしい 眩しい *blinding, dazzling, excessively bright*

太陽がまぶしくて、目がくらんだ。
The suns was blinding, and I was daz-zled.

まぶた 瞼 *eyelid*

まふゆ 真冬 *the midwinter* [↔ 真夏]

マフラー *1. muffler, scarf*

2. (US) muffler, (UK) silencer (on an automobile, etc.)

まほう 魔法 *magic, magic spell; witchcraft, sorcery* [→ 魔術1.]

魔女は魔法を使うことができます。
A witch can use witchcraft.

魔法をかける to cast a spell

悪魔は赤ん坊に魔法をかけました。
The devil cast a spell on the baby.

魔法瓶 vacuum bottle, thermos bottle

魔法使い wizard, witch, sorcerer

まぼろし 幻 *phantom, illusion*

まま *(This word is always preceded by a modifier of some kind.)*
1. unchanged state

机の上の本はそのままにしておきなさい。
Leave the books on the desk as they are.

ままだ to be in the unchanged state of

田中さんは東京に行ったままです。
Mr. Tanaka is still in Tokyo. (Literally: Mr. Tanaka is in the unchanged state of having gone to Tokyo.)

2. (〜で／に) in the unchanged state

その部屋に靴をはいたまま入りました。
I entered that room with my shoes on. (Literally: I entered that room in the unchanged state of having put on my shoes.)

ママ *mummy, mom*

ままごと *playing house*

子供たちはまだままごとをしています。
The children are still playing house.

まみず 真水 *fresh water* [→ 淡水] [↔ 塩水]

まめ 豆 *bean; pea*

まめ *blister (on the hand or foot caused by rubbing against something)*

まもなく 間も無く *soon, before long, in no time*

まもなく先生がいらっしゃるでしょう。
The teacher will probably come soon.

まもる 守る *1. to keep (a promise, etc.); to obey (a rule, etc.)*

恵子さんはいつも約束を守ります。
Keiko always keeps her promises.

校則を守らなければなりません。
We must obey the school regulations.

2. to protect, to defend [↔ 攻める]

父親は娘を危険から守りました。
The father protected his daughter from danger.

まやく 麻薬 *drug, narcotic*

まゆ 眉 *eyebrow*

眉毛 [☞ 眉 (above)]

まゆ 繭 *cocoon*

まよう 迷う *1. to become confused about which way to go*

道に迷う to lose one's way

あの小さい男の子は道に迷ったよ。
That little boy lost his way!

2. to become at a loss, to become perplexed

Aに迷う to become at a loss for A, to become perplexed about A

その時は言葉に迷っていました。
At that time I was at a loss for words.

まよなか 真夜中 *the middle of the night*

マヨネーズ *mayonnaise*

マラソン *marathon*

マラソン競走 marathon race

マラソン選手 marathon runner

マラリア *malaria*

マリファナ *marijuana*

まる 丸 *circle*

ここに丸をかいてください。
Draw a circle here, please.

丸で囲む to draw a circle around, to circle

正解を丸で囲みなさい。
Circle the correct answer.
丸顔 round face
丸— full, whole (Added to number bases periods of time.)
妹は丸三日間病気で寝ています。
My younger sister has been sick in bed for three whole days.

まるい 丸い, 円い *round*
会議室に円いテーブルがあります。
There is a round table in the conference room.
円くなって座る to sit in a circle

まるた 丸太 *log*
丸太小屋 log cabin

まるで *[[→ 全く]] quite, utterly, really; (not) at all*
まるでそれを覚えていません。
I don't remember that at all.
まるで…ような just like
京子さんはまるで病人のようです。
Kyoko looks just like a sick person.

まれ 稀 〜な *rare*
まれに rarely, seldom (Always occurs in combination with a negative predicate.)

まわす 回す *1. to turn, to spin, to rotate (transitive)*
運転手はハンドルを右に回しました。
The driver turned the steering wheel to the right.
2. to send around, to pass around; to send on, to pass on, to forward
塩を回してください。
Please pass the salt around.
この通知を支店に回します。
I'll forward this communication to the branch office.

まわり 周り [[→ 周囲]] *1. the area around, surroundings, vicinity* [→ 辺り]
周りにはだれもいませんでした。
There was no one in the vicinity.
先生の周りに座りましょう。
Let's sit around the teacher.
2. circumference, distance around

まわり 回り *1. going around, turning, spinning, rotating* [→ 回転]
2. going from place to place in succession; traveling around, touring
3. spread, spreading, circulating
火の回りが早かったです。
The fire spread quickly. (Literally: The spread of the fire was fast.)
回り道 detour [→ 迂回]; roundabout way [→ 遠回り]

—まわり —回り *by way of, via (Added to bases denoting a place where an intermediate stop is made.)* [→ —経由]
新宿回りで渋谷に行きました。
I went to Shibuya by way of Shinjuku.

まわる 回る *1. to turn, to spin, to rotate (intransitive)* [→ 回転する]
月は地球の周りを回っています。
The moon revolves around the earth.
そのこまはよく回っているね。
That top is spinning well, isn't it?
2. to go from place to place in succession; to travel around, to tour
去年は九州を回りました。
Last year I traveled around Kyushu.
3. to spread, to circulate
毒はすぐに体中に回りました。
The poison soon spread throughout his body.
4. to go via, to stop off at on the way, to make a detour through
大阪を回って帰りました。
I went home via Osaka.
5. to turn, to go past (a time on the clock)
もう9時を回りました。
It has already gone past 9:00.

ーまん ー万 *ten thousand*

父は3万円支払いました。
My father paid ¥30,000.

まんー 満ー *full (Added to number bases denoting ages or time periods.)*

あしたで満14歳になります。
I will be a full fourteen years old as of tomorrow.

まんいち 万一 *1. by some remote chance*
2. unlikely event, remote possibility

まんいん 満員 〜の *full to capacity, crowded to capacity (with people)*

教室は生徒で満員です。
The classroom is full to capacity with students.

バスはきょうも満員でした。
The bus was crowded to capacity today too.

満員電車 train crowded to capacity

まんが 漫画 *comic strip, cartoon; caricature*

姉は漫画をかくのがうまいよ。
My older sister is good at drawing cartoons!

漫画本 comic book
漫画映画 cartoon movie
漫画家 cartoonist
漫画雑誌 comic magazine

まんかい 満開 *full bloom*

チューリップが満開です。
The tulips are in full bloom.

まんがいち 万が一 [☞ 万一]

マンガン *manganese*

まんげつ 満月 *full moon* [↔ 新月]

今夜は満月です。
Tonight there is a full moon.

まんじゅう 饅頭 *steamed bun filled with sweet bean paste*

マンション *condominium*

まんぞく 満足 *satisfaction, contentment*

満足する to become satisfied

新しいステレオに満足しています。
I am satisfied with the new stereo.

満足な satisfactory, adequate

まんてん 満点 *1. (US) perfect score, (UK) full marks (on a test)*

京子さんは英語のテストで満点を取った。
Kyoko got a perfect score on the English test.

2. 〜の fully satisfactory, perfect

今晩の演奏は満点でした。
Tonight's performance was perfect.

マンドリン *mandolin*

まんなか 真ん中 *middle, center*

部屋の真ん中にテーブルがあります。
There is a table in the middle of the room.

まんねんひつ 万年筆 *fountain pen*

まんびき 万引き *1. shoplifting*

万引きする to shoplift (transitive)

2. shoplifter

まんぷく 満腹 〜の *full, satiated*

満腹する to eat until one is full

マンホール *manhole*

まんま【COL. for まま】

まんりき 万力 *vise*

まんるい 満塁 *loaded bases, full bases (in baseball)*

ツーアウト満塁です。
It's two outs, bases loaded.

満塁ホームラン grand slam (homerun)

み 身 *(This word is used mostly in fixed, often idiomatic expressions.)*

1. one's body, one's person

身をかがめる to bend over, to stoop

身も心も打ち込む to devote oneself body and soul

身につける to put on, to carry (as clothing, equipment, etc.)

2. one's self; one's heart

身を入れる to put one's heart (into something)

もっと身を入れて練習しなさい。
Put your heart into it more and practice.

身につける to learn well

3. position, status

身に余る to be more than one deserves

A の身になる to put oneself in a A's position

私の身になって考えてください。
Please put yourself in my position and think about it.

身の回り one's person; one's clothing; one's appearance

身の回りの物 one's belongings

み 実 *1. fruit; nut; berry*

このりんごの木は実がたくさんなります。
This apple tree bears a lot of fruit. (Literally: As for this apple tree, a lot of fruit grows.)

実を結ぶ to come to fruition

2. substance, real content

みー 未ー *not yet (Added to noun bases denoting actions.)*

未分析の not-yet-analyzed

未解決の not-yet-solved, unresolved

みあい 見合い *arranged first meeting between prospective marriage partners*

見合い結婚 marriage resulting from an arranged meeting

みあげる 見上げる *1. to look up at* [↔ 見下ろす]

次郎ちゃんはその背の高い人を見上げた。
Jiro looked up at that tall man.

2. to look up to, to admire [↔ 見下げる]

ミーティング *meeting* [→ 会合]

ミイラ *mummy*

みうしなう 見失う *to lose sight of*

人込みでその男の人を見失いました。
I lost sight of that man in the crowd.

みえ 見え *appearances, show, outward display, pose*

見えを張る to show off, to be ostentatious

みえる 見える *1. (What is seen is treated as a grammatical subject and marked with が rather than with を.) to be able to see; to be visible*

小さな島が見えてきました。
A small island became visible.

向こうに白い建物が見えるでしょう。
You can probably see a white building over there.

私たちの学校から海が見えます。
The ocean is visible from our school.

目が見えない to be unable to see, to be blind

2. to look, to appear (to be)

お兄さんは年より若く見えます。
Your older brother looks younger than his age.

小田さんは画家に見えるね。
Mr. Oda looks like a painter, doesn't he?

3. 【HON. for 来る *1.*】 *to come*

お客さんは6時に見えるそうです。
I understand the guests will come at 6:00.

みおくる 見送る *1. to see off* [↔ 迎える1.]

学生たちはスミス先生を空港で見送った。
The students saw Dr. Smith off at the airport.

2. to let go by, to pass up

息子は留学を見送ることにしました。
My son decided to pass up studying abroad.

みおとす 見落とす *to overlook, to fail to see*

[→ 見逃す1.]

みおろす 見下ろす *to look down at* [↔ 見上げる1.]

塔の頂上から町を見下ろしています。
We are looking down at the town from the top of the tower.

みがく 磨く *1. to polish, to shine*

僕は毎朝靴を磨くよ。
I polish my shoes every morning!

歯を磨く to brush one's teeth

2. to polish, to improve, to cultivate

才能を磨く to cultivate one's talent

腕を磨く to polish one's skill

みかた 味方 *person on one's side, ally, friend* [↔ 敵]

市長は弱い者の味方です。
The mayor is a friend of the weak.

Aに味方する to take A's side, to side with A

Aの味方をする to take A's side, to side with A

母はいつも妹の味方をします。
My mother always takes my younger sister's side.

みかづき 三日月 *crescent moon*

みかん *mandarin orange*

みかん畑 mandarin orange orchard

みかんせい 未完成 ～の *unfinished, incomplete*

みき 幹 *(tree) trunk*

この木の幹は周囲が3メートルです。
This tree trunk's diameter is three meters.

みぎ 右 *the right (as opposed to the left)* [↔ 左]

次の交差点を右に曲がってください。
Please turn right at the next intersection.

健二の右にいる女の子を知っていますか。
Do you know the girl on Kenji's right?

右側 right side

右側通行 right-side traffic (Typically used on signs to mean Keep right.)

右利きの right-handed

右手 right hand

みぐるしい 見苦しい *1. ugly, unsightly* [→ 醜い]; *shabby-looking* [→ みすぼらしい]

2. disgraceful, shameful

みこし 神輿 *portable Shinto shrine (Carried through the streets on the shoulders by a group during a festival.)*

みごと 見事 ～な *excellent, wonderful, splendid*

その試合はみごとなプレーが多かった。
A lot of excellent plays were made in that game.

みこみ 見込み *1. prospect(s), outlook, future possibility* [→ 見通し1.]

回復する見込みはほとんどありません。
There is almost no prospect of recovering.

この試合に勝つ見込みは十分あります。
There is ample prospect of winning this game.

2. (future) promise

3. expectation; estimation

これから値下がりする見込みです。
The expectation is that it will drop in price after this.

ミサ *(Catholic) mass*

ミサに参列する to attend mass

ミサイル *missile*

敵がミサイルを発射する恐れもあります。
There is also a fear that the enemy will launch missiles.

みさき 岬 *cape, promontory*

みさげる 見下げる *to look down on, to regard with disdain* [↔ 見上げる2.]

みじかい 短い *short (in length)* [↔ 長い]

洋子さんは短いスカートをはいているね。
Yoko is wearing a short skirt, isn't she?

今年の夏休みは短いですね。
This year's summer vacation is short, isn't it?

このドレスのすそを短くしました。
I shortened hem of this dress. (Literally: I made the hem of this dress short.)

みじめ 惨め ～な *miserable, pitiful, wretched*

みじゅく 未熟 ～な *1. unripe, immature*

未熟なバナナはまずいですよ。
An unripe banana is bad-tasting!

2. inexperienced; not fully developed

うちの息子は未熟なドライバーです。
My son is an inexperienced driver.

未熟児 premature baby

ミシン *sewing machine*

ミシンで何を縫っているんですか。
What are you sewing on the sewing machine?

みじん 微塵 *small particle, bit*

みじん切り cutting into tiny pieces, mincing

みじん切りにする to cut into tiny pieces, to mince

ミス *mistake* [→ まちがい]

みず 水 *1. water*

水を3杯持ってきてください。
Please bring three glasses of water.

兄は今芝生に水をまいています。
My older brother is watering the lawn now.

水を出す〔止める〕 to turn on〔off〕the water

2. cold water (in contrast to hot water) [↔ 湯]

水鉄砲 water pistol, squirt gun

水っぽい watery

水商売 the bar and entertainment business

みすい 未遂 ～の *unsuccessfully attempted (describing a crime, etc.)*

未遂に終わる to end unsuccessfully, to end abortively

暗殺未遂 attempted assassination

自殺未遂 attempted suicide

みずいろ 水色 *light blue (as a noun)*

みずうみ 湖 *lake*

僕たちは湖でボートをこいでいました。
We were rowing a boat on the lake.

子供たちは湖で泳いでいます。
The children are swimming in the lake.

みずぎ 水着 *swimsuit; swimming trunks* [→ 水泳パンツ (s.v. 水泳)]

みずたまり 水溜まり *puddle (of water)*

ミステリー *1. mystery, something unexplained* [→ 神秘]

2. mystery story [→ 推理小説 (s.v. 推理)]

みすてる 見捨てる *to desert, to abandon, to forsake*

あの人が友人を見捨てるはずはない。
There is no reason to think she would desert her friends.

みずひき 水引き *(This word refers to a kind of string made of stiff paper, which is tied in a bow around the wrapping on a formal gift. The **mizuhiki** for happy occasions is red for half its length and white for the other half. The **mizuhiki** for sad occasions is black or blue for half its length and white for the other half.)*

みずぶくれ 水膨れ *blister (on the skin)*

みずぼうそう 水疱瘡 *chicken pox*

みすぼらしい *shabby-looking, wretched-looking*

みずむし 水虫 *athlete's foot*

みせ 店 *store, shop (This word refers to restaurants, bars, etc., as well as to stores.)*

パンを買いに店に行きました。
I went to the store to buy some bread.

あの店では牛乳を売っていますか。
Do they sell milk at that store?

その店は8時に開きます。
That store opens at 8:00.

みせいねん 未成年 *1. 〜の under the legal age of adulthood, minor*

2. [☞ 未成年者 (below)]

未成年者 a minor

未成年者は酒を買えません。
Minors cannot buy liquor.

みせる 見せる *to show, to allow to see*

車掌に切符を見せました。
I showed my ticket to the conductor.

切手アルバムを見せてくれませんか。
Won't you show me your stamp album?

これは嫌いです。ほかのを見せてください。
I don't like this. Please show me another one.

みそ 味噌 *miso*

(A traditional Japanese seasoning, miso is a paste of fermented soybeans or rice bran.)

味噌汁 miso soup

みぞ 溝 *1. ditch; gutter*

2. groove

3. gap, gulf (in mutual understanding)

みぞれ 霙 *sleet*

みぞれが降る sleet falls, it sleets

みたい【COL.】〜な *to be like, to appear to be, to looks as if*

(This word follows a predicate and functions grammatically as an adjectival noun. The word preceding cannot be the copula form だ. Where だ would be the appropriate predicate, みたい follows a noun or adjectival noun directly.)

上原君は車の運転ができないみたいだね。
It looks as if Uehara can't drive, doesn't it?

部屋にはロボットみたいな物があった。
In the room there was a thing like a robot.

山田先生は母親みたいに私に話します。
Ms. Yamada speaks to me like a mother.

みだし 見出し *headline; heading; caption*

見出し語 (dictionary) entry word

みだしなみ 身だしなみ *attentiveness to one's personal appearance*

伊藤先生は身だしなみがいい。
Mr. Ito pays careful attention to his personal appearance. (Literally: As for Mr. Ito, his attentiveness to his personal appearance is good.)

みたす 満たす *1. to fill (a container with something)*

AをBで満たす to fill A with B

そのバケツを水で満たしてください。
Please fill that bucket with water.

2. to put until full (into a container)

AにBを満たす to put B into A until A is full, to fill A with B

浴槽に水を満たしました。
I filled the bathtub with cold water.

3. to satisfy (a need or desire)

一杯のコーラがのどの渇きを満たした。
One glass of cola satisfied my thirst.

みだす 乱す *to put into disorder, to disrupt*

治安を乱してはいけないよ。
You musn't disrupt the public peace!

列を乱す to break ranks, to get out of line

みだれる 乱れる *to become disordered, to become disrupted*

その国は当時非常に乱れていました。
That country was very much in disorder at that time.

列車の事故でダイヤが乱れました。
The timetable was disrupted because of a train accident.

みち 道 *1. road, street, path*

この狭い道を行けば、公園に出ますか。
If I go along this narrow road, will I arrive at the park?

このまっすぐな道を行こう。
Let's go along this straight road.

道で園田さんに会ったよ。
I met Mr. Sonoda on the street!
森を抜ける道をやっと見つけました。
We finally found a path that emerged from the woods.

2. way, route, course, path

どうも道をまちがえたらしい。
It looks very much as if I've gone the wrong way.
最も安全な道を選びましょう。
Let's choose the safest way.
優勝への道は険しいです。
The path to the championship is steep.
道端 roadside
道しるべ roadside signpost

みちくさ 道草 *fooling around on the way, wasting time on the way*
道草を食う to fool around on the way, to waste time on the way
道草を食わないで、うちに帰りなさい。
Go home without fooling around on the way.

みちびく 導く *to lead, to guide* [→ 指導する]
船長はその島に救助隊を導きました。
The captain led the rescue party to that island.

みちる 満ちる *1. to become full, to become filled*
冬の登山は危険に満ちています。
Winter mountain climbing is full of danger.
月が満ちる the moon becomes full, the moon waxes
月は満ちたり欠けたりします。
The moon waxes and wanes.

2. to go until full (into a container)

AにBが満ちる B fills A
潮が満ちる the tide comes in, the tide becomes high

みつ 蜜 *1. honey* [→ 蜂蜜 (s.v. 蜂)]

2. (flower) nectar

みっか 三日 *(See Appendix 2) 1. three days*

2. the third (day of a month)

みつかる 見つかる *to be found, to turn up*
かぎは見つかりましたか。
Did the key turn up?

ミックス *1. mix, mixture*

2. mixing

ミックスする to mix (transitive) [→ 混ぜる]
ミックスジュース mixed juice
ホットケーキミックス pancake mix

みつける 見つける *1. to find, to locate, to discover*
息子が私の指輪を見つけてくれました。
My son found my ring for me.
翻訳者は英語の誤りを見つけました。
The translator found a mistake in the English.

2. to become used to seeing [→ 見慣れる]

みつご 三つ子 *triplets*

ミッションスクール *missionary school*

みっせつ 密接 〜な *close, intimate (describing a relationship)*
密接な関係 close relationship, intimate connection

みっつ 三つ *three (see Appendix 2)*

みつど 密度 *density*
人口密度 population density

ミット *(baseball) mitt (of the type used by a catcher or first baseman)*
キャッチャーミット catcher's mitt

みっともない 【COL. for 見苦しい】

1. shameful, disgraceful

2. unsightly; shabby-looking

みつばち 蜜蜂 *honeybee*

みつめる 見つめる *to stare at*
明は忍の目をじっと見つめた。
Akira stared into Shinobu's eyes.

私たちは日の出を見つめていました。
We were gazing at the sunrise.

じっと見つめる to stare steadily at

みつゆしゅつ 密輸出 *smuggling out*

密輸出する to smuggle out

みつゆにゅう 密輸入 *smuggling in*

密輸入する to smuggle in

みてい 未定 ～の *not yet decided, not yet settled*

日時は未定です。
The date and time are not fixed yet.

計画はまだ未定ですね。
The plan is not yet settled, is it.

みとおし 見通し *1. prospect(s), outlook, future possibility*

見通しが明るい the prospects are bright

2. insight, penetration, vision

3. visibility, unobstructed view

見通しがきく visibility is good, there is an unobstructed view

みとめる 認める *1. to admit, to acknowledge*

その話はほんとうだと認めます。
I admit that that story is true.

2. to recognize (as), to regard (as) [→ 見なす]

光一は一流ピアニストとして認められた。
Koichi has been recognized as a first-rate pianist.

3. to allow, to approve [→ 許す1.]

4. to detect, to find, to notice

医者は検査で異常を認めました。
The doctor detected an abnormality in the examination.

みどり 緑 *green (as a noun)*

その緑の本を使ってください。
Please use that green book.

みどりの日 Greenery Day (a Japanese national holiday on April 29)

みな 皆[☞ みんな]

皆さん【HON.】everyone, everybody

みなおす 見直す *1. to look at again, to reexamine*

学生は答案をよく見直しました。
The student carefully reexamined the test paper.

2. to reevaluate and form a better opinion of

みなしご orphan [→ 孤児]

みなす 見なす *to regard (as), to consider (to be)*

それは反則と見なします。
I consider that a foul.

みなと 港 *harbor; port*

船が港を出ていきました。
The boat went out of the port.

港町 port town

みなみ 南 *the south* [↔ 北]

この冬は家族で南の島に行きます。
We are going to a southern island as a family this winter.

南半球 the Southern Hemisphere

南十字星 the Southern Cross

南風 south wind

みなもと 源 *1. source (of a river, etc.)*

2. source, origin [→ 起源]

みならう 見習う *to look at and follow as an example*

Aを／に見習う to follow A as an example

先生を見習って字をきれいに書きなさい。
Follow your teacher's example and write neatly.

みなり 身なり *attire, dress* [→ 格好2.]

あの子はみすぼらしい身なりをしている。
That child is wearing shabby attire.

みなれる 見慣れる *to become used to seeing, to become familiar with (from seeing frequently)*

富士山は写真で見慣れています。
I am familiar with Mt. Fuji from pictures.

ミニカー *sub-compact car*

みにくい 醜い *ugly* [↔ 美しい]

ミニスカート *miniskirt*

ミニチュア *1. miniature version (of something that is typically larger)*

2. miniature scale model

みのがす 見逃がす *1. to fail to see, to miss, to overlook* [→ 見落とす]

ゆうべ大好きなテレビ番組を見逃がした。
Last night I missed a TV program I really like.

2. to overlook, to disregard, to let go [→ 大目に見る]

今度だけはこの誤りを見逃がします。
I will overlook this mistake just this once.

みのる 実る *1. to bear fruit*

このりんごの木は毎年よく実るね。
This apple tree bears a lot of fruit every year, doesn't it?

その努力はいつかきっと実るだろう。
Those efforts will surely bear fruit someday.

2. (The subject is a fruit, nut, etc., that appears on a tree or plant.) to grow, to be produced [→ 実る]*; to become ripe* [→ 熟する]

メロンはもう実ったよ。
The melons have already ripened!

みはらし 見晴らし *view, vista* [→ 眺め]

このホテルからは琵琶湖の見晴らしがよい。
The view of Lake Biwa from this hotel is good.

みはり 見張り *1. keeping watch, being on guard*

見張りをする to keep watch, to be on guard

ガードマンは戸口で見張りをしました。
The guard kept watch at the door.

2. guard, lookout ((person))

家の外に見張りが３人います。
There are three guards outside the house.

みはる 見張る *1. to keep watch on, to keep under surveillance*

警官はあの女性を見張っています。
The policeman is keeping that woman under surveillance.

2. 目を～ *to look wide-eyed*

坊やはその模型飛行機に目を見張ったよ。
The little boy looked wide-eyed at that model plane!

みぶり 身振り *gesture*

監督は身ぶりで合図をします。
The director signals with gestures.

みぶん 身分 *status, social standing*

身分証明書 identification card

みほん 見本 *sample, specimen, model*

見本をいくつか見せてください。
Please show me some samples.

見本市 trade fair

みまい 見舞い *1. sympathetic inquiry (about a person who is sick or has suffered a loss)*

お見舞いのお手紙をどうもありがとう。
Thank you for your letter of sympathetic inquiry.

2. visit (to a person who is sick or has suffered a loss)

見舞い状 letter of sympathetic inquiry

見舞い客 visitor

みまう 見舞う *1. to inquire sympathetically about (a person who is sick or has suffered a loss)*

2. to visit (a person who is sick or has suffered a loss)

あした入院中の邦子さんを見舞います。
Tomorrow I will visit Kuniko, who is in the hospital.

みまわす 見回す *to look around at*

娘は不思議そうに辺りを見回しました。

My daughter looked around at the vicinity in wonder.

ーみまん ー未満 *under (Added to number bases.)*

18歳未満の人は参加できません。
People under 18 years old cannot participate.

みみ 耳 *ear*

この犬は耳が大きいね。
This dog's ears are big, aren't they?

耳を貸す to lend an ear, to listen (to what someone says)

弟は私の忠告に耳を貸しません。
My younger brother does not listen to my advice.

耳を傾ける to listen attentively

耳が遠い hard of hearing

耳垢 earwax

耳掻き ear pick, ear cleaner

耳朶 earlobe

みみず *earthworm*

みめい 未明 【FORMAL】 *the predawn*

みゃく 脈 *1. pulse, heartbeat*

医師は患者の脈をとりました。
The doctor took the patient's pulse.

脈が速すぎるね。
Her pulse is too fast, isn't it?

2. hope, expectation, prospect [→ 望み2.]

みやげ 土産 *souvenir; present (brought back from a trip)*

父はお土産をたくさん持って帰ったよ。
My father brought home a lot of souvenirs!

荒木さんに京都のお土産があります。
I have a souvenir from Kyoto for Mr. Araki.

土産話 story one tells about one's trip

土産物店 souvenir shop

ミュージカル *a musical*

ミュージカル映画 musical movie

みょう 妙 ～な *odd, curious, strange* [→ 奇妙な]

みょうごにち 明後日 【FORMAL for 明後日】 *the day after tomorrow*

みょうじ 名字 *family name, surname* [→ 姓]

みょうにち 明日 【FORMAL for 明日】 *tomorrow*

ミラー *mirror* [→ 鏡]

バックミラー rearview mirror

みらい 未来 *the future* [→ 将来1.]

未来の自動車に興味があります。
I am interested in cars of the future.

この国にはすばらしい未来があります。
This country has a wonderful future.

ミリ [☞ ミリメートル; ミリリットル]

ミリメートル *millimeter*

ーミリメートル (counter for millimeters; see Appendix 2)

みりょく 魅力 *charm, appeal*

あのほほえみは桂子の魅力の一つです。
That smile is one of the Keiko's charms.

魅力的な charming, attractive, appealing

お姉さんはとても魅力的ですね。
Your older sister is very attractive, isn't she?

ミリリットル *milliliter*

ーミリリットル (counter for milliliters; see Appendix 2)

みりん 味醂 *sweet sake used as a seasoning*

みる 見る *1. to look at, to watch*

さあ、このスライドを見ましょう。
All right now, let's look at these slides.

私たちはテレビでテニスの試合を見ます。
We watch a tennis match on TV.

2. to see

そんなに大きな湖は見たことがないよ。

I've never seen such a big lake!
犯人が橋を渡るのを見ました。
I saw the culprit cross the bridge.
大坪さんがプールで泳いでいるのを見た。
I saw Mr. Otsubo swimming in the pool.

3. to do and see, to try doing (following the gerund (-て form) of another verb)

そのソーダを飲んでみてください。
Please try that soda.

ミルク *milk* [→ 牛乳]

ミルクセーキ milk shake
粉ミルク powdered milk, dried milk

みわける 見分ける *to tell apart, to distinguish (by looking)*

AとBを見分ける to tell A and B apart, to distinguish A and B
たかとわしを見分けられますか。
Can you distinguish a hawk and an eagle?

みわたす 見渡す *to look out over, to survey*

ホテルから湖を見渡しました。
I looked out over the lake from the hotel.

みんかん 民間 *non-governmental circles, civilian society*

民間の non-governmental, private, civilian
民間放送 commercial broadcasting

みんげいひん 民芸品 *folk-art object*

ミンク *mink*

みんしゅう 民衆 *the people, the masses*

みんしゅしゅぎ 民主主義 *democracy*

みんしゅてき 民主的 ～な *democratic*

みんぞく 民族 *a people, ethnic group*

アジアにはたくさんの民族がいます。
There are many peoples in Asia.
民族衣装 native costume

みんな *all, each and every one; everyone involved*

従業員はみんな幸福そうです。
The employees all look happy.
みんながそのニュースを知っています。
Everyone knows that news.
ここにある物はみんな私たちの物です。
The things that are here are all our things.
みんなで all together, in all; all together, as a group
生徒はみんなで何人いますか。
How many students are there in all?
みんなで歌いましょう。
Let's sing all together.

みんよう 民謡 *(traditional) folk song*

みんわ 民話 *folktale*

むー 無ー *un-, without (Added to noun bases.)*

無条件の unconditional
無制限な／の unlimited

むいか 六日 *(see Appendix 2) 1. six days*

2. the sixth (day of a month)

むいしき 無意識 ～の *1. unconscious (i.e., having lost consciousness)*

けが人は1時間ほど無意識の状態でした。
The injured person was in an unconscious state for about an hour.

2. unconscious (i.e., not involving conscious thought)

石原さんは無意識に電車に乗りました。
Ms. Ishihara unconsciously boarded the train.

むいみ 無意味 ～な *meaningless; pointless*

その計画はまったく無意味です。
That plan is completely pointless.

ムード *mood, atmosphere* [→ 雰囲気]

そのレストランはムードがあるね。
That restaurant has atmosphere, doesn't it?

むかい 向かい *the area opposite, the area across from*
孝子さんは洋子さんの向かいに座った。
Takako sat across from Yoko.
郵便局は駅の向かいにあります。
The post office is opposite the station.
向かい側 opposite side
向かい風 head wind

むがい 無害 ～の *harmless, innocuous* [↔ 有害の]

むかう 向かう *1. to leave (for); to head (for)*
父は今晩車で大阪へ向かいます。
My father will leave for Osaka this evening by car.
船は横浜を出て、ホンコンに向かいます。
The ship will leave Yokohama, and head for Hong Kong.
台風はどこに向かっていますか。
Where is the typhoon heading for?

2. to face, to orient oneself, to direct oneself
Aに向かう to face (toward) A, to direct oneself toward A
ひまわりは太陽に向かいます。
Sunflowers face the sun.
机に向かう to sit at a desk

むかえる 迎える *1. to meet (an arriving person)* [↔ 見送る1.]
空港でいとこを迎えました。
I met my cousin at the airport.

2. to greet, to welcome, to receive (a guest)
ご両親は弟を温かく迎えてくださったよ。
Your parents welcomed my younger brother warmly!

3. to greet, to mark the coming the coming of (a new year, a season, a birthday, etc.)

むかし 昔 *long ago*
永井さんは母の昔からの友人だ。
Ms. Nagai is a friend of my mother's from long ago.
昔この大都会は農村でした。
Long ago this big city was a farming village.
昔話 tale of long ago, legend
昔々 long long ago, once upon a time

むかって 向かって [☞ に向かって]

むかで 百足 *centipede*

むき 向き *direction (of movement); facing direction (i.e., the direction something faces)*
風の向きは変わっていません。
The direction of the wind hasn't changed.
机の向きを窓のほうへ変えてください。
Please move the desk so that it faces the window. (Literally: Please change the way the desk faces to the direction of the window.)
東向きの east-facing
うちの台所は東向きです。
Our kitchen faces east.

－むき －向き ～の *intended for, suitable for (Added to noun bases.)* [→－向けの2.]

むぎ 麦 *(a generic term for wheat, barley, oats, and rye)*
麦畑 wheat/barley/oat/rye field
麦茶 barley tea
麦藁帽子 straw hat
烏麦 oats
小麦 wheat
大麦 barley
ライ麦 rye

むく 向く *1. to turn to face, to turn toward; to look toward, to turn one's head toward*
Aに／を向く to turn toward A; to look

toward A

こちらを向いてください。

Please look this way.

由美ちゃんは私のほうを向いて笑った。

Yumi turned toward me and smiled.

後ろを向く to look back

2. to face (toward) (The subject is a stationary object) [→ 面する]

Aに／を向く to face (toward) A

この家は西に向いています。

This house faces toward the west.

3. to be suited [→ 適する]

姉は教師に向いています。

My older sister is suited to being a teacher.

むく 剥く *1. to peel (something with a covering)*

京子さんは桃をむいてくれました。

Kyoko peeled a peach for me.

2. to peel off (a covering)

木の皮をむくのは難しいです。

It's hard to peel off the bark of a tree.

むくいる 報いる *to do something as appropriate reciprocation, to do something in return (for a favor, a kindness, etc.)*

明子さんの親切に報いなければならない。

I must do something in return for Akiko's kindness.

むくち 無口 〜な *taciturn, quiet, reticent* [↔ おしゃべりな2.]

姉はおしゃべりですが、妹は無口です。

My older sister is talkative, but my younger sister is taciturn.

−むけ −向け 〜の *(Added to noun bases.) 1. directed to, to be sent to*

外国向けの放送もあります。

There are also broadcasts directed to foreign countries.

2. intended for, suitable for [→−向きの]

これは中学生向けの辞書です。

This is a dictionary intended for junior-high-school students.

むける 向ける *to turn, to point, to direct (one thing toward another)*

こちらに顔を向けてください。

Please turn your face this way.

もう一つの話題に注意を向けましょう。

Let's turn our attention to the other topic.

カメラマンはカメラを私たちに向けた。

The photographer pointed the camera at us.

むげん 無限 〜の *infinite, limitless, boundless*

むこ 婿 *son-in-law* [↔ 嫁2.]

むこう 無効 〜の [[↔ 有効の]] *1. ineffective, unfruitful, futile*

2. invalid, not in effect, void

このパスポートは無効になっています。

This passport has expired.

むこう 向こう *1. the area on the opposite side, the area beyond*

私たちの学校は川の向こうにあります。

Our school is on the other side of the river.

森の向こうに別荘があります。

Beyond the woods there is a villa.

2. (the area) over there

向こうのあの窓際に座りましょう。

Let's sit by that window over there.

3. the other party (in an interaction)

今回の出張経費は向こうが払います。

The other party will pay the expenses for the business trip this time.

向こう側 the opposite side; the other party

むこうずね 向こう脛 *shin*

むざい 無罪 *innocence (of a crime)* [↔ 有罪]

無罪の innocent

無罪になる to be found innocent, to be acquitted

無罪にする to find innocent, to acquit

むし 虫 *bug; insect* [→ 昆虫]; *worm (Refers to maggots, caterpillars, etc., but not to earthworms.)*
徹さんは虫を集めているよ。
Toru collects bugs.
やぶで虫が鳴いています。
Bugs are chirping in the thicket.
虫籠 insect cage

むし 無視 ～する *to ignore, to disregard*
信号を無視してはいけないよ。
You mustn't ignore traffic lights.

むしあつい 蒸し暑い *hot and humid, sultry*
きょうは蒸し暑いですね。
Today is hot and humid, isn't it?

むしば 虫歯 *decayed tooth, tooth with a cavity*
虫歯は何本ありますか。
How many cavities do you have?
ゆうべ虫歯が痛みました。
Last night my decayed tooth ached.

むしめがね 虫眼鏡 *magnifying glass*

むじゃき 無邪気 ～な *innocent, naive, artless*
弟は赤ん坊のように無邪気だよ。
My younger brother is innocent like a baby!

むじゅん 矛盾 *contradiction, inconsistency*
矛盾する to come into contradiction, to become inconsistent
被害者の話は目撃者の証言と矛盾する。
The victim's story is inconsistent with the witness's testimony.
コーチは時々矛盾した事を言います。
The coach sometimes says contradictory things.

むしろ *rather, more accurately, preferably*
それは赤よりも、むしろピンクに近い。
That's not red; more accurately, it's close to pink.
ここにいるよりはむしろ出かけたいです。
I would rather go out than stay here.

むす 蒸す *1. to steam, to heat by steaming*
2. to be hot and muggy

むすう 無数 ～の *countless, numberless*
空には無数の星が瞬いていました。
Countless stars were twinkling in the sky.

むずかしい 難しい *difficult, hard* [↔ 易しい]
理科は私にはとても難しいよ。
Science is very difficult for me!
これは難しい問題ですね。
This is a difficult problem, isn't it?
英語を話すのは難しいです。
Speaking English is hard.

むすこ 息子 *son* [↔ 娘]
あの子はいちばん末の息子です。
That child is my youngest son.
息子さん【HON. for (above)】

むすびつく 結び付く *to become linked, to become connected*

むすびつける 結び付ける *to link, to connect (transitive)*

むすびめ 結び目 *knot (where something is tied)*

むすぶ 結ぶ *1. to tie, to bind* [↔ 解く]
宏は靴ひもを結ぶことがまだできないよ。
Hiroshi still can't tie his shoelaces!
その贈り物をリボンで結んでください。
Please tie that present with a ribbon.
2. to link, to connect
中央線は東京と松本を結んでいます。
The Chuo Line links Tokyo and Matsumoto.
3. to conclude, to finish, to close (something spoken or written)
首相はその言葉で演説を結びました。
The prime minister concluded the speech with those words.
4. to enter into (an agreement, etc.); to conclude (a treaty, etc.)

きのうその会社と契約を結びました。
Yesterday we entered into a contract with that company.

むすめ 娘 *1. daughter* [↔ 息子]
娘はまだ小学生です。
My daughter is still an elementary-school pupil.

2. girl [→ 少女]*; unmarried young woman*
娘さん【HON. for (above)】
島田先生には娘さんがいらっしゃいます。
Mr. Shimada has a daughter.

むせきにん 無責任 ～な *irresponsible*
明美さんはまったく無責任です。
Akemi is completely irresponsible.

むせん 無線 *1.* ～の *wireless (i.e., not using electrical wires for transmitting and receiving)*

2. wireless communication, radio communication
警官は無線で警察署に連絡しました。
The police officer communicated with the police station by radio.
無線電話 radiotelephone
無線技師 radio operator
無線タクシー taxi equipped with a radio
無線通信 [☞ 無線*2.* (above)]

むだ 無駄 *1. futility*
むだな futile, vain [→ 空しい]
先生の忠告はその生徒にはむだでした。
The teacher's advice was futile for that student.

2. waste, wastefulness
そんな事をするのは時間のむだですよ。
Doing such a thing is a waste of time!
むだな wasteful
むだにする to waste, to let go to waste
時間とお金をむだにしないで。
Don't waste your time and money.
無駄話 idle talk, gossip
無駄遣い waste, wasteful use

むだん 無断 ～で *without permission*
弟は無断で私の本を持っていったよ。
My younger brother took my book without permission!
明美ちゃんは無断で学校を欠席しました。
Akemi was absent from school without permission.

むち 鞭 *whip*
鞭打ち症 whiplash (injury)
鞭打つ to whip

むちゃ 無茶 【COL.】*1. absurdity, nonsense*
むちゃを言う to talk nonsense
むちゃな absurd, nonsensical

2. rashness, recklessness
むちゃな rash, reckless

むちゅう 夢中 ～の *absorbed, engrossed, carried away* [→ 熱中の]
社長はその女性に夢中です。
The company president is carried away with that woman.
夢中で absorbedly; dazedly; frantically
兄は夢中でコンピューターを使っている。
My older brother is absorbedly using the computer.

むづかしい 難しい [☞ 難しい]

むっつ 六つ *six (see Appendix 2)*

むなしい 空しい *vain, fruitless, futile*
われわれの努力はむなしかったです。
Our efforts were futile.

むね 胸 *1. chest ((body part))*
あの人は胸が広いです。
That person's chest is broad.
胸が痛くてたまりません。
My chest hurts so much that I can't stand it.
今胸がどきどきしています。
My chest is throbbing with a fast heartbeat now.

2. heart, feelings [→ 心2.]
お母さんの胸は愛でいっぱいでした。

Her mother's heart was filled with love.

むら 村 *village*

村役場 village office

むらがる 群がる *to crowd, to flock, to swarm*

少女たちが歌手の周りに群がっています。
The girls are crowding around the singer.

みつばちは花の周りに群がります。
Honeybees swarm around flowers.

むらさき 紫 *purple (as a noun)*

上田さんは紫のドレスを着ています。
Ms. Ueda is wearing a purple dress.

むり 無理 *1. unreasonableness, unjustifiability*

無理な unreasonable, unjustifiable

無理を言う to make an unreasonable request

2. ～な impossible [→ 不可能な]

８時までにそこに行くのは無理です。
It's impossible to go there by 8:00.

3. ～な forcible, against a person's will

4. excess, strain, overwork

無理な excessive, immoderate

無理をする to do too much, to strain oneself, to overwork

むりやり 無理やり *(～に) in spite of opposition, coercively*

むりょう 無料 *～の free (of charge)* [→ 唯の, 只の3.]

「入場無料」 (on a sign)
Admission Free

無料配達 free delivery

むれ 群れ *(This word is a generic term for gathered groups of people or animals) crowd, gathered group; flock; herd*

人の群れ crowd of people

羊の群れ flock of sheep

牛の群れ herd of cows

むろん 無論 *of course, certainly* [→ 勿論]

め 目 *1. eye*

小松君は目がいいよ。
Komatsu's eyes are good!

花子さんは大きな目をしていますね。
Hanako has large eyes, doesn't she?

洋子はいつも眠そうな目をしています。
Yoko always has sleepy-looking eyes!

目を開ける〔閉じる〕 to open〔close〕one's eyes

目が見えない to be unable to see, to be blind

目を伏せる to drop one's eyes

目がくらむ to become dizzy; to become dazzled

目が覚める to wake up (intransitive) [→ 目覚める]

目を覚ます to wake up (intransitive)

Aに目を通す to take a look at A, to look over A, to check A

英語で書いた手紙に目を通してください。
Please take a look at the letter written in English.

Aを見る目がある to have a good eye for A

叔父は絵を見る目があります。
My uncle has a good eye for pictures.

Aから目を離す to take one's eyes off A

目につく to catch one's eye

2. empty space between something in a crisscross pattern

この網の目は粗いです。
The mesh of this net is coarse. (Literally: The holes (between the cords) of this net are coarse.)

め 芽 *bud; sprout, shoot*
芽を出す to put out buds/shoots, to bud/sprout
ばらの花が芽を出しています。
The roses have budded.
芽が出る buds/shoots appear

ーめ ー目 *(Added to cardinal numbers to form ordinal numbers; see Appendix 2.)*

めあて 目当て *1. purpose, objective, aim* [→ 目的]
ここに来た目当ては何ですか。
What was your purpose in coming here?
2. guide (i.e., a thing to keep one's eyes on)
漁師は灯台を目当てに船を走らせた。
The fisherman sailed the boat with the lighthouse as a guide.

めい 姪 *niece* [↔ 甥]
姪御さん【HON. for (above)】

ーめい ー名【FORMAL for ー人】*(counter for persons; see Appendix 2)*

めいあん 名案 *excellent idea*

めいおうせい 冥王星 *(the planet) Pluto*

めいかく 明確 ～な *clear, precise, definite*

めいさん 名産 *well-known product*
桃は岡山の名産です。
Peaches are a well-known product of Okayama.

めいし 名刺 *business card, calling card, (UK) visiting card*
名刺を出す to present one's card
名刺を交換する to exchange cards

めいし 名詞 *noun*

めいじ 明治 *(Japanese imperial era name for the period 1868-1912)*
明治維新 the Meiji Restoration
明治時代 the Meiji Era
明治天皇 the Meiji Emperor

めいしょ 名所 *famous place, sight*
ロンドン塔はロンドンの名所の一つです。
The Tower of London is one of the sights of London.
パリの名所を見物したいと思います。
I want to see the sights of Paris.
その庭園は桜の名所です。
That garden is famous for its cherry blossoms. (Literally: That garden is a famous place of cherry blossoms.)

めいじる 命じる *to give an order for, to give a command for* [→ 命令する]
AにBを命じる to give an order for B to A , to order A to do B
社長は川崎さんに転勤を命じた。
The company president ordered Mr. Kawasaki to change jobs.
先生は生徒たちに静かにするよう命じた。
The teacher ordered the students to be quiet.

めいしん 迷信 *superstition*
僕は迷信を信じないよ。
I don't believe in superstitions!

めいじん 名人 *master, skilled expert*
奥村さんは将棋の名人です。
Mr. Okumura is a master of shogi.

めいせい 名声 *good reputation, renown, illustriousness*

めいちゅう 命中 *hit, on-target impact*
命中する to hit, to make an on-target impact
犯人が投げた石が警官の頭に命中した。
The stone that the criminal threw hit the police officer on the head.

めいにち 命日 *anniversary of a person's death*

めいはく 明白 ～な *clear, plain, evident* [→ 明らかな]

めいぶつ 名物 *1. well-known product* [→ 名産]
2. well-known feature, well-known attrac-

tion

めいぼ 名簿 *name list, name register*

私の名前は名簿に載っています。
My name appears on the name list.
部員の名簿を作りましょう。
Let's make a name list of the club members.

めいめい 銘々 *1. each, each respectively* [→ それぞれ]

生徒はめいめい違った意見を持っている。
The students each have a different opinion.

2. each respective one

めいめいの each, each respective

めいよ 名誉 *honor, credit, glory*

石川さんの昇進は私にとっても名誉です。
Ms. Ishikawa's promotion was a credit for me as well.
名誉な／の honorable, meritorious, glorious
Aの名誉を汚す to stain A's honor, to bring dishonor on A
名誉教授 emeritus professor; honorary professor

めいりょう 明瞭 ～な *clear, plain, evident* [→ 明らかな]

めいれい 命令 *command, order*

私は社長の命令に従います。
I follow the company president's orders.
命令する to give an order for [→ 命じる]
AにBを命令する to give an order for B to A , to order A to do B
先生は私たちに出発を命令しました。
Our teacher ordered us to depart.
命令文 imperative sentence

めいろ 迷路 *maze*

青年は数時間迷路で迷っていました。
The young man was lost in the maze for several hours.

めいわく 迷惑 *trouble, annoyance, inconvenience* [→ 面倒]

Aに迷惑をかける to trouble A, to bother A, to put A to trouble
その友達にはたいへん迷惑をかけました。
I really troubled that friend.
ご迷惑をおかけして申し訳ございません。
I am sorry for troubling you.

メインイベント *main event*

メインスタンド *main stands (in a stadium, etc.)*

メインストリート *main street, major street* [→ 大通り]

めうえ 目上 *one's superior (in status)* [↔ 目下]

メーカー *manufacturer, maker*

メーキャップ *makeup (especially that worn by actors)*

メーキャップする to put on makeup

メーター *meter ((device))*

電気のメーター electric meter
タクシーのメーター taxi meter

メーター *meter ((unit of measure))* [→ メートル]

ーメーター (counter for meters; see Appendix 2)

メーデー *May Day*

メートル *meter ((unit of measure))*

ーメートル (counter for meters; see Appendix 2)
この橋の長さは50メートルです。
The length of this bridge is 50 meters.
メートル法 the metric system
平方メートル square meter
ー平方メートル (counter for square meters; see Appendix 2)
立方メートル cubic meter
ー立方メートル (counter for cubic meters; see Appendix 2)

めかた 目方 *weight*

この丸太は100キロの目方があります。
This log weighs 100 kilograms.

このハムは目方で売ります。
This ham is sold by weight.

Aの目方を計る to measure the weight of A, to weigh A

メカニズム *mechanism*

めがね 眼鏡 *(eye-) glasses*

父は読書するとき眼鏡をかけます。
My father wears glasses when he reads.

メガホン *megaphone*

めがみ 女神 *goddess*

めぐすり 目薬 *eye lotion, eye drops, eye medicine*

母は時々目薬を差します。
My mother sometimes applies eye drops.

めくばせ 目配せ ～する *to signal with one's eyes; to signal with a wink*

何も言わないで友達に目くばせしました。
I didn't say anything and signaled my friend with my eyes.

めぐまれる 恵まれる *to come to be blessed, to come to be favored*

祖父は健康に恵まれています。
My grandfather is blessed with good health.

めくる *1. to turn (a page)*

恵美は辞書をめくって単語を調べました。
Emi turned the pages of the dictionary, looking for a word.

2. to roll up (sleeves, pant legs, etc.) [→ まくる]

3. to peel off

めざす 目指す *to make one's goal, to aim at, to set one's mind on*

花村君はパイロットを目指しています。
Hanamura is aiming to become a pilot. (Literally: Hanamura is aiming at a pilot.)

めざましい 目覚ましい *remarkable, wonderful* [→ すばらしい]

岡田さんの英語は目覚ましく進歩した。
Mr. Okada's English improved remarkably.

めざめる 目覚める *to wake up (intransitive)*

毎朝５時に目覚めます。
Every morning I wake up at 5:00.

めし 飯 【CRUDE for ご飯】 *1. boiled rice* *2. meal*

めしあがる 召し上がる 【HON. for 食べる; 飲む *1.*】 *to eat; to drink*

めした 目下 *one's inferior (in status)* [↔ 目上]

メジャー *tape measure* [→ 巻き尺]

めじるし 目印 *(identification) mark*

ガイドさんは地図に目印をつけました。
The guide put a mark on the map.

めす 雌 *a female (animal)* [↔ 雄]

この猫は雄ですか、雌ですか。
Is this cat male or female?

メス *scalpel*

めずらしい 珍しい *1. rare, unusual, uncommon, novel*

息子は珍しい小鳥を飼っています。
My son is keeping an unusual bird.

きのう珍しい光景に出会いました。
Yesterday I came across a novel sight.

めだつ 目立つ *to be conspicuous, to stand out*

きょうのバレーボールの試合では浜田選手の活躍が目立ちました。
Hamada stood out in today's volleyball game. (Literally: In today's volleyball game, Hamada's activeness stood out.)

このポスターを目立つ場所にはりなさい。
Put up this poster in a conspicuous place.

めだま 目玉 *eyeball*

目玉焼き egg fried sunny side up

メダリスト *medalist*

メダル *medal, medallion*
銅メダル bronze medal
銀メダル silver medal
金メダル gold medal

めちゃくちゃ 滅茶苦茶【COL.】～な *1. absurd, nonsensical* [→ 無茶な1.]
めちゃくちゃな事を言う to talk nonsense
2. rash, reckless [→ 無茶な2.]
3. very messy, in great disorder
遠藤さんの部屋はめちゃくちゃです。
Mr. Endo's room is very messy.

めつき 目つき *look (on one's face)*
看護婦さんは優しい目つきをしています。
The nurse has a gentle look.

めっき 鍍金 *plating (i.e., a coating of one metal on another)*
めっきする to apply as plating

メッセージ *message (that someone asks one person to give to another person)*

めったに 滅多に *seldom, rarely (Always occurs in combination with a negative predicate.)*
信枝ちゃんはめったに遅刻しないよ。
Nobue is seldom late!
この子はめったに泣きません。
This child rarely cries.

めでたい *auspicious, joyous, worthy of congratulations*
それはめでたい事ですね。
That's an auspicious event, isn't it?

めど 目処 *prospect(s), hope* [→ 見通し1.]
めどがつく the prospects become hopeful, light appears at the end of the tunnel

メドレー *1. (musical) medley*
2. medley (race)
個人メドレー individual medley

メトロノーム *metronome*

メニュー *menu*
メニューを見せてください。
Please let me see a menu.

めまい 眩暈 *dizziness, giddiness*
目まいがする to feel giddy

メモ *memo, note*
メモする to note down, to make a note of
その電話番号をメモしました。
I made a note of that telephone number.
メモ帳 memo pad, scratch pad
メモ用紙 memo paper, note paper, scratch paper

めもり 目盛り *division, graduation (on a measuring device)*
この物差しにはミリの目盛りがあります。
This ruler is marked with millimeter divisions.

メモリー *memory (especially in a computer)*

メリーゴーラウンド *merry-go-round* [→ 回転木馬 (s.v. 回転)]

メリット *merit, strong point* [→ 長所]

メルヘン *fairy tale* [→ 童話]

メロディー *melody* [→ 節4.]

メロン *melon*
マスクメロン muskmelon

めん 面 *1. surface* [→ 表面]
2. facet, side, face (of a polyhedron)
一面 (counter for facets; see Appendix 2)
3. aspect, phase, respect
4. page (of a newspaper)
一面 (counter for pages; see Appendix 2)

めん 面 *1. face (of a person or animal)* [→ 顔]
面と向かって face to face
2. mask, false face [→ 仮面]
3. protective mask, face guard

めん 綿 *cotton (fabric)* [→ 木綿]
綿花 raw cotton

綿シャツ cotton shirt

めんえき 免疫 *immunity*

めんかい 面会 *face-to-face meeting, seeing; interview* [→ 面接]

面会する to see, to meet; to have an interview

Aに／と面会する to see A, to meet (with) A, to have an interview with A

入院中の森さんにあした面会します。
I will see Miss Mori, who is in the hospital tomorrow.

面会時間 visiting hours

めんきょ 免許 *1. licensing, official permission*

2. [☞ 免許証 *(below)*]

免許証 license, permit

メンス *menstruation* [→ 月経, 生理2.]

めんする 面する {*Irreg.*} *to face (The subject is a stationary object)*

Aに面する to face (toward) A

この窓は南に面しています。
This window faces south.

めんぜい 免税 ～の *tax-free, tax-exempt, duty-free*

免税する to exempt from tax

免税店 duty-free shop

めんせき 面積 *area, amount of surface*

この土地の面積は500平方メートルだ。
The area of this land is 500 square meters.

めんせつ 面接 *interview*

面接する to interview (transitive)

面接試験 oral interview examination

メンツ *face, honor*

メンツを保つ to save face

メンツを失う to lose face

めんどう 面倒 *trouble, annoyance, complication* [→ 迷惑]

Aに面倒をかける to bother A, to put A to trouble

ご両親にあまり面倒をかけないで。
Don't put your parents to too much trouble.

面倒な troublesome, complicated, annoying

浩はいつも面倒な仕事を私に押しつける。
Hiroshi always forces the troublesome work on to me.

Aの面倒を見る to look after A, to take care of A

だれが赤ちゃんの面倒を見るんですか。
Who is looking after the baby?

めんどうくさい 面倒臭い 【COL. for 面倒な】 *troublesome, annoying, bothersome*

メンバー *(group) member*

も *1. (noun-following particle) too, also; either (in combination with a negative predicate)*

野球も好きです。
I like baseball, too.

あなたが行かないなら、私も行かないよ。
If you're not going, then I won't either!

外国からも手紙が来ました。
Letters also came from foreign countries.

AもBも both A and B; either A or B (in combination with a negative predicate)

健さんも洋子さんも英語が話せます。
Both Ken and Yoko can speak English.

僕は肉も魚も食べません。
I don't eat either meat or fish.

2. (noun-following particle) even [→ さえ1.]

生徒たちは放課後も教室で勉強している。
The students are studying in the classroom even after school.

3. (Following a number, indicates that the speaker considers that number inordinately large.)
友達は漫画本を10冊も買ったよ。
My friend bought TEN comic books!

4. (in combination with the gerund (-て form) of a predicate) even if, even though
雨が降っても行きましょう。
Let's go even if it rains.
安くても買わないほうがいいでしょう。
Even if it's inexpensive, it would probably be better not to buy it.

もう *1. already* [→ 既に1.]
もう宿題は終わったよ。
I've already finished my homework!
お母さんはもう出かけたの？
Has Mother already gone out?
もう砂糖を使いきってしまいました。
I've already used up all the sugar.
2. any more, any longer (in combination with a negative predicate) [→ 既に2.]
テニスはもうできません。
I cannot play tennis any more.
3. any time now, soon [→ 間も無く]
父はもう帰ってくるでしょう。
My father will probably come home soon.

もう *another, an additional (Always precedes a word referring to a relatively small quantity.)*
もう一度奈良へ行きたいです。
I want to go to Nara one more time.
牛乳をもう一杯ください。
Please give me one more glass of milk.
もう少し飲みませんか。
Won't you drink a little more?

もうかる 儲かる *1. to make money, to make a profit (when the subject is a person)*
田口さんは株でもうかりました。
Mr. Taguchi made money in stocks.
2. to be lucrative, to make a profit, to pay (when the subject is an activity)
このパートはもうからないね。
This part-time job doesn't pay, does it.
父の商売はとてももうかっています。
My father's business is really making a profit.

もうけ 儲け *(monetary) profit*
農業は儲けが少ないそうです。
In agriculture the profits are small.
大儲け big profit

もうける 設ける *1. to provide; to prepare* [→ 用意する]
この大学に体育館を設けることになった。
It's been decided to provide a gym for this college.
2. to establish, to set up
市長は新しい学校を設けました。
The mayor established a new school.
規則を設ける to establish a rule

もうける 儲ける (金を〜) *to make money, to make a profit (The subject must be a person.)* [→ 儲かる1.]

もうしあげる 申し上げる【HUM. for 言う】

もうしこみ 申し込み *1. request, proposal*
結婚の申し込み marriage proposal
2. applying, application (for something)
申し込みの受け付け期間は1週間です。
The acceptance period for applications is one week.
申し込みの締め切りは六月三日です。
The deadline for applying is June 3rd.
申し込み書 written application
申し込み用紙 application form

もうしこむ 申し込む *1. to make a request for, to propose*
清は和子に結婚を申し込みました。
Kiyoshi proposed marriage to Kazuko.
Aに試合を申し込む to propose a game to A, to challenge A to a game
2. to apply for

その大学に入学を申し込みます。
I'm going to apply for admission to that college.

Aに参加を申し込む to apply for participation in A, to enter A

もうしぶん 申し分 ～がない *to be faultless, to be perfect; to be ideal*

もうじゅう 猛獣 *fierce animal*

もうしわけ 申し訳 *excuse, exculpatory explanation* [→ 言い訳]

申し訳ない inexcusable

申し訳ない事をしてしまいました。
I did an inexcusable thing.

遅くなって申し訳ありません。
I'm very sorry I'm late. (Literally: I'm late, and it's inexcusable.)

もうす 申す【HUM. for 言う】

もうちょう 盲腸 *(veriform) appendix*

盲腸炎 appendicitis

もうふ 毛布 *blanket*

もうれつ 猛烈 ～な *intense, severe, furious* [→ 激しい]

猛烈なあらしが関東地方を襲いました。
A severe storm hit the Kanto region.

もえる 燃える *to catch fire; to burn*

駅前のスーパーが燃えていますよ。
The supermarket in front of the station is on fire!

モーター *motor; engine* [→ エンジン]

モーターボート *motorboat*

モード *1. fashion (in clothing)*

これがパリの最新のモードです。
This is the latest fashion in Paris.

2. mode, style, form [→ 様式]

もがく *to struggle, to writhe, to wriggle*

逮捕された犯人はまだもがいています。
The arrested criminal is still struggling.

もぎしけん 模擬試験 *practice examination*

もくげき 目撃 ～する *to witness*

歩行者がその事故を目撃しました。
A pedestrian witnessed that accident.

目撃者 (eye-) witness

もくざい 木材 *(US) lumber, (UK) timber* [→ 材木]

もくじ 目次 *table of contents*

まず目次を見てください。
Please look at the table of contents first.

もくせい 木星 *(the planet) Jupiter*

もくぞう 木造 ～の *made-of-wood, wooden*

木造の家 wooden house

もくてき 目的 *purpose, aim, goal*

実業家はついに目的を果たしました。
The businessman finally achieved his aim.

目的地 destination

目的語 object (in grammar)

もくひょう 目標 *1. aim, goal, purpose* [→ 目的]

目標を突破する to surpass a goal

2. landmark; guide; sign [→ 目印]

3. target [→ 的]

もくよう 木曜 [☞ 木曜日]

もくようび 木曜日 *Thursday*

もぐら *mole ((animal))*

もぐる 潜る *1. to dive (starting in the water)*

山中さんはプールの底にもぐりました。
Ms. Yamanaka dived to the bottom of the pool.

2. to burrow, to slip (inside or under something)

地震のときはベッドの下にもぐりなさい。
When there's an earthquake burrow under your bed.

もくろく 目録 *list, catalog*

もけい 模型 *model (of the real thing)*

模型飛行機 model plane

モザイク *mosaic*

もし *if (Introduces a conditional clause.)*

もしあした天気がよければ、出かけます。
If the weather is good tomorrow, I'll go out.

もし届かなかったら、知らせてください。
If it doesn't arrive, please let me know.

もじ 文字 *letter, character (in a writing system)*

文字放送 teletext

小文字 small letter, lower-case letter

大文字 capital letter, upper-case letter

もしかしたら【COL. for 或いは*2.*】*perhaps*

(This expression typically occurs in sentences ending with an expression of possibility (usually かもしれない). Since such a sentence has virtually the same meaning whether or not もしかしたら is present, もしかしたら is redundant in a sense, but it serves as a signal of how a sentence will end.)

もしかしたらもう終わったかもしれない。
It may, perhaps, have ended already.

もしかすると [☞ もしかしたら]

もしもし *1. Hello (on the telephone)*

もしもし、田辺さんですか。
Hello, is that Ms. Tanabe?

2. Excuse me, Say (Used to get a person's attention.)

もしもし、これはあなたのボールペンではありませんか。
Say, isn't this your ballpen?

もず 百舌 shrike

もたらす 齎す *to bring, to bring about, to produce*

モダン ～な *modern, up-to-date* [→ 現代的な(s.v. 現代)]

モダンダンス modern dance

もち 餅 *rice cake*
(Traditionally made by pounding cooked rice in a mortar.)

もちをつく to make rice cakes (by pounding)

餅搗き rice-cake making

もちあげる 持ち上げる *1. to lift, to raise*

その箱を持ち上げてください。
Please lift that box.

2. to flatter

もちあわせ 持ち合わせ *something on one, something on hand*

Aの持ち合わせがある to have A with one, to have A on hand

もちあわせる 持ち合わせる *to come to have on one, to come to have with one, to come to have on hand*

もちいる 用いる *1. to use* [→ 使う]

2. to adopt, to accept [→ 採用する1.]

3. to hire, to employ [→ 雇う]

もちだす 持ち出す *1. to take out, to carry outside*

重要書類を持ち出すのはやめてください。
Refrain from taking out important documents.

2. to bring up, to propose, to offer

もちぬし 持ち主 *owner* [→ 所有者 (s.v. 所有)]

この店の持ち主はだれですか。
Who is the owner of this shop?

もちはこぶ 持ち運ぶ *to carry, to convey, to transport* [→ 運ぶ]

もちろん 勿論 *of course, certainly*

「私といっしょに行ってくれる？」「もちろん、行くよ」
"Will you go with me?" "Certainly, I'll go!"

もちろん見たいけれど、きょうは無理だ。
Of course I'd like to see it, but today it's impossible.

もつ 持つ *1. to hold, to take hold of; to carry*

手に何を持っているの。
What are you holding in your hand?

ロープをしっかり持ってください。
Please hold the rope tightly.

おばあちゃんの荷物を持ってあげなさい。
Carry Grandma's baggage for her.

持っていく to take (from one place to another) (The direct object is ordinarily an inanimate object.)

きょうは傘を持っていきなさい。
Today take your umbrella.

それを部長に持っていってください。
Please take that to the department head.

持ってくる to bring, to fetch (The direct object is ordinarily an inanimate object.)

新聞を持ってきてくれる？
Will you bring me the newspaper?

2. to come to have, to come to possess; to come to own

父は車を3台持っています。
My father has three cars.

この土地はだれが持っているんですか。
Who owns this land?

3. to last, to remain intact

この傘はあと1年ぐらい持つでしょう。
This umbrella will probably last about one more year.

もっきん 木琴 *xylophone*

もったいない *wasted, regrettable (because of a more appropriate alternative)*

こんないいペンは子供にはもったいない。
Such a fine pen would be wasted on a child.

もっていく 持っていく [☞ 持つ1.]

もってくる 持ってくる [☞ 持つ1.]

もっと *more, to a greater degree*

もっとお茶はいかがですか。
How about some more tea?

もっと本を読みなさい。
Read more books.

旅行のことをもっと聞かせてください。
Please tell me more about your trip.

もっと注意深く運転してください。
Please drive more carefully.

映画はその原作よりもっとおもしろい。
The movie is much more interesting than the book.

もっと安いのがありますか。
Do you have a cheaper one?

モットー *motto*

もっとも 尤も *1. ～な natural, not surprising [→ 当然の]; reasonable, sensible, rational*

お客さんがそう考えるのはもっともです。
It is natural for the customer to think so.

ごもっともです。
You are quite right. (Literally: It is reasonable. (honorific))

2. of course (however)

卒業生は大学に入ります。もっとも、例外もあります。
The graduates enter college. Of course, there are also exceptions.

もっとも 最も *the most (indicating a superlative)* [→ 一番]

水泳は最もおもしろいスポーツだと思う。
I think swimming is the most interesting sport.

エベレストは世界で最も高い山です。
Everest is the highest mountain in the world.

もっぱら 専ら *(describing the degree of involvement in an activity) mainly, chiefly; exclusively, entirely, wholeheartedly*

モップ *mop*

Aにモップをかける to mop A

もてなし 持て成し *hospitable treatment,*

hospitable reception

もてなす 持て成す *to treat hospitably, to entertain (a guest)*

奥さんは私たちを温かくもてなしてくれた。

The wife entertained us warmly.

もてる 持てる *to be made much of, to be popular*

(This word is the potential form of 持つ *and has the predictable meanings as well.)*

健ちゃんは女の子にもてるね。

Ken is popular with the girls, isn't he?

モデル *1. model, type* [→ 型1.]

2. model (of the real thing) [→ 模型]

3. model, sample, prototype [→ 模範]

4. (artist's) model

5. (fashion) model [→ ファッションモデル (s.v. ファッション)]

モデルチェンジ model change

モデルガン model gun

モデルカー model car

もと 元, 本 *1. cause* [→ 原因]*; origin, source* [→ 起源]

失敗の元は何でしたか。

What was the cause of the failure?

2. foundation, basis [→ 基礎]

3. materials, ingredients [→ 材料]

4. once, formerly, previously [→ 以前1.]

木田さんは元は大阪に住んでいました。

Mr. Kida once lived in Osaka.

元の former; original

ハリス氏は元の首相です。

Mr. Harris is a former prime minister.

5. capital, funds (for starting an enterprise)

元手 [☞ 元*5.* (above)]

もと 下, 許 *1. the area under, the area below* [→ 下2.]

2. same place of residence, same roof

あの大学生は親のもとで暮らしています。

That college student lives with his parents.

3. position of compliance

Aの下で under A

橋本さんは丸山先生の下で研究している。

Mr. Hashimoto is doing research under Prof. Maruyama.

もどす 戻す *to return, to put back, to give back* [→ 返す]

かぎを戻すのを忘れないでください。

Please don't forget to return the key.

その辞書を机の上に戻しなさい。

Put the dictionary back on the desk.

もとづく 基づく *to be based (on)*

小説は作家自身の経験に基づいています。

The novel is based on the author's own experiences.

もとめる 求める *1. to ask for, to request* [→ 要求する]

友達に助けを求めました。

I asked my friend for help.

2. to look for, to seek [→ 捜す, 探す]

姉は今職を求めています。

My older sister is now looking for a job.

3. to buy, to purchase [→ 買う]

もともと 元々 *from the beginning, originally* [→ 元来]*; by nature, as an inborn characteristic* [→ 生まれつき]

僕はもともとその計画に反対でした。

I was against the plan from the beginning.

市川君はもともとテニスがうまいよ。

Ichikawa is naturally good at tennis!

もどる 戻る *to return (intransitive)*

ちょっと待ってね。すぐ戻ってくるよ。

Wait a little while, OK? I'll come back right away!

自分の席へ戻りなさい。

Return to your own seat.

もの 物 *thing, object*

手品師は袋からたくさんの物を出した。
The magician took many things out of the bag.

別の物を見せてください。
Please show me a different one.

どんな物でもいいです。
Any kind of thing is all right.

これは私の物です。
This is mine.

もの 者 *1.* 【HUM. for 人】*person*

イタリア語の話せる者もおります。
There is also someone who can speak Italian.

2. 【FORMAL for 人】*person*
(Always preceded by a modifier of some kind and not used to refer to a specific, known individual.)

新大統領は弱い者の味方です。
The new president is a friend of the weak.

ものおき 物置 *closet, storeroom; storage shed*

ものがたり 物語 *tale, story, narrative*

『平家物語』 "The Tale of the Heike"

『イソップ物語』 "Aesop's Fables"

ものごと 物事 *things, everything*

さまざまな角度から物事を検討しなさい。
Examine things from different angles.

ものさし 物差し *ruler ((measuring device))*

物差しで線の長さを計りなさい。
Measure the line with a ruler.

ものずき 物好き *1. overly strong curiosity; eccentric interest*

物好きな overly curious; interested in eccentric things

2. overly curious person; person with eccentric interests

ものすごい 物凄い *amazing, tremendous, astounding, startling* [→ 凄い]

ものすごい光景だったよ。
It was an amazing sight.

ものたりない 物足りない *unsatisfactory, not good enough*

ものまね 物真似 *mimicking, doing an impression (of people or animals)*

あのテレビタレントは物まねがうまいね。
That TV star is good at doing impressions, isn't she?

Aの物まねをする to mimic A, to do an impression of A

モノレール *monorail*

もはや 最早 *[[→ 既に]] 1. already*

2. (no) longer, (not) any more (in combination with a negative predicate)

宇宙旅行はもはや夢ではありません。
Space travel is no longer a dream.

もはん 模範 *example, model, pattern* [→ 手本]

妹さんたちの模範になりなさい。
Be an example to your younger sisters. (Literally: Become your younger sisters' example.)

もみじ 紅葉 *1. autumn leaves* [→ 紅葉]

2. maple [→ 楓]

もむ 揉む *1. to rub between one's hands*

2. to knead; to massage [→ マッサージする]

肩をもんでくれる？
Will you massage my shoulders?

3. to debate thoroughly

4. 気を〜 *to get worried, to get anxious* [→ 心配する]

試験のことで気をもんでいます。
I'm worried about the exams.

もめん 木綿 *cotton (fabric)* [→ 綿]

木綿糸 cotton thread

もも 桃 *peach*

もも 股 *thigh*

もやす 燃やす *to set on fire; to burn*

この手紙を燃やしてください。
Please burn this letter.

もよう 模様 *1. (decorative) pattern, (decorative) design*

2. look, appearance [→ 様子2.]

縞模様 striped pattern

空模様 the look of the sky, the weather

もよおし 催し *1. gathering, meeting, social function* [→ 会1.]

2. auspices, sponsorship [→ 主催]

大学の催しで音楽会が開かれます。
A concert will be held under the auspices of the college.

もよおす 催す *1. to hold (an event)* [→ 開催する]

2. to feel (an emotional or physical reaction)

涙を催す to be moved to tears

もらう 貰う *(In either use of this word the giver cannot be the speaker, the speaker's group, or a person or group with whom the speaker is identifying.)*
1. to receive, to get

Aから／にBをもらう to receive B from A

玲子さんから手紙をもらったよ。
I received a letter from Reiko!

兄は奨学金をもらっています。
My older brother is receiving a scholarship.

2. to receive the favor of (following the gerund (-て form) of another verb)

いとこに写真を撮ってもらいました。
My cousin took a photograph for me. (Literally: I received the favor of taking a photograph from my cousin.)

もらす 漏らす *to let leak, to let out*

だれが秘密を漏らしたのかしら。
I wonder who let the secret out.

モラル *morals, sense of morality* [→ 道徳]

あの政治家はモラルに欠けている。
That politician lacks a sense of morality.

もり 森 *woods, forest*

森の中で道に迷いました。
I lost my way in the forest.

もる 盛る *1. to pile up (transitive)*

庭師は庭に土を盛りました。
The gardener piled up earth in the garden.

2. to serve (food onto a dish)

お母さんが皿に肉を盛ってくれました。
His mother served the meat onto my plate.

モルタル *mortar (for holding bricks, etc., together)*

モルモット *guinea pig*

もれる 漏れる *to leak out, to escape*

ガスが漏れているよ。
The gas is leaking!

もろい 脆い *easily broken, fragile, brittle*

このれんがはもろくて使いにくい。
These bricks are brittle and hard to use.

もん 門 *gate; gateway*

校門 school gate

もん 紋 *family crest, family insignia*

もんく 文句 *1. (connected) words, phrase, expression*

英語の歌の文句が聞き取れません。
I can't catch the words of English songs.

2. complaint

文句を言う to complain

小遣いのことで文句を言ってはいけない。
You mustn't complain about your allowance.

もんしょう 紋章 *family crest, family insignia* [→ 紋]

モンスーン *monsoon*

モンスーン気候 monsoon climate

モンタージュ *montage*

もんだい 問題 *1. question (on a test, etc.), problem (in arithmetic, etc.)*
この問題は解けるでしょう？
You can solve this problem, right?
森先生は難しい問題を出します。
Dr. Mori sets difficult questions.
2. problem, difficult matter, issue
失業も最近問題になってきました。
Unemployment, too, has recently become a problem.
3. matter, question, topic
それは時間の問題です。
That's a matter of time.
問題児 problem child
問題集 collection of (sample examination) questions

もんぶしょう 文部省 *the Ministry of Education*

もんもう 文盲 *1. illiteracy*
2. an illiterate

や 矢 *arrow (used with a bow)*
光陰矢のごとし。(proverb)
Time flies. (Literally: Time is like an arrow.)
矢を放つ to shoot an arrow
猟師はその鹿をねらって、矢を放ったよ。
The hunter took aim at that deer and fired an arrow!
矢印 arrow (-shaped indicator)

や *and*
(Unlike と, the noun-conjoining や particle implies that there are items in addition to those actually mentioned.)
僕はスパゲッティやピザが好きです。
I like (things such as) spaghetti and pizza.

やあ【COL.】*Hi!*
(This greeting is ordinarily restricted to male speakers and is not appropriate for addressing a social superior.)
やあ、元気？
Hi! How are you?

ヤード *yard ((unit of measure))*
ーヤード (counter for yards; see Appendix 2)

やおちょう 八百長【COL.】 *fixed game, fixed contest*
あの試合は八百長だったよ。
That game was fixed!

やおや 八百屋 *1. (US) vegetable store, (UK) greengrocer's*
2. (US)vegetable store proprietor, (UK) greengrocer

やがて *soon, before long, by and by* [→ そのうち]
父もやがてわかってくれるでしょう。
My father will probably understand me soon.
やがて日が暮れました。
Before long it got dark.
やがて春がやってくるね。
Spring will come before long, won't it?
あの人がここに来てやがて1年になる。
It'll soon be a year since that person came here.

やかましい *1. noisy* [→ 煩い1.]
2. given to nagging, given to complaining [→ 煩い2.]
3. particular, fussy [→ 煩い3.]

やかん 夜間 *nighttime, the night hours* [↔ 昼間]
夜間飛行 night (plane) flight

やかん 薬罐 *tea kettle*

やぎ 山羊 *goat*

やきとり 焼き鳥 *small pieces of chicken grilled on bamboo skewers*

やきもの 焼き物 *pottery, ceramic ware*

やきゅう 野球 *(the game of) baseball*

僕は野球のチームに入っているよ。
I'm on the baseball team!

野球をする to play baseball

野球部 baseball club, baseball team

野球ファン baseball fan

野球場 baseball stadium, ball park

野球選手 baseball player

やく 役 *1. post, office, position, job*

役に就く to take up a post, to assume a position

石井さんは支配人の役に就きました。
Mr. Ishii took up the post of manager.

2. role, function [→ 役割]

役を勤める to play a role, to serve a function

役に立つ to be useful, to be helpful, to serve a purpose

この本は役に立つし、おもしろいよ。
This book is useful and also interesting!

この箱は役に立たないね。
This box is no use, is it.

3. part, role (in a play, etc.)

姉はジュリエットの役を演じました。
My older sister played the part of Juliet.

役立つ [☞ 役に立つ (above)]

やく 約 *approximately, about* [→ およそ]

ここから駅まで約1キロあります。
It's approximately one kilometer from here to the station.

やく 訳 *translation* [→ 翻訳]

やく 焼く *1. to burn (transitive)* [→ 燃やす]

お父さんは落ち葉を焼いたよ。
Dad burned the fallen leaves!

2. to roast, to broil (transitive); to bake (transitive)

母は牛肉を焼いています。
My mother is roasting beef.

恵子さんはアップルパイを焼きました。
Keiko baked an apple pie.

夕食に魚を焼きましょう。
Let's broil some fish for supper.

3. to tan (one's skin)

肌を焼く to tan one's skin

4. to print (from a photographic negative)

やくいん 役員 *officer, director, executive*

やくざ *(Japanese) gangster, yakuza*

やくざいし 薬剤師 *pharmacist*

やくしゃ 役者 *actor, actress* [→ 俳優]

人気役者 popular actor

やくしょ 役所 *public office (building), government office (building)*

区役所 ward office

市役所 city office

やくす 訳す *to translate* [→ 翻訳する]

それを日本語に訳してください。
Please translate that into Japanese.

やくそく 約束 *1. promise*

北野さんはいつも約束を守ります。
Mr. Kitano always keeps his promises.

前田さんは約束を破ることはありません。
Ms. Maeda never breaks a promise.

約束する to promise, to give one's word

登ちゃんは早く起きると約束したね。
Noboru promised that he would get up early, didn't he?

2. appointment, engagement, promise to meet

すみませんが、ほかに約束があります。
I'm sorry, but I have another engagement.

3時の約束だったが、由美は来なかった。
It was a 3:00 date, but Yumi didn't come.

約束する to make an appointment

やくにん 役人 *(government) official*

やくば 役場 *public office (building) (in a small town or village)*

町役場 town office

村役場 village office

やくひん 薬品 *1. medicine, drug* [→ 薬]

この実験には5種類の薬品を使います。
We will use five kinds of drugs in this experiment.

2. chemical (agent)

やくめ 役目 *job, role, function* [→ 役割]

皿洗いは君の役目だよ。
Washing the dishes is your job!

役目を果たす to carry out a job, to play a role, to serve a function

進は学校の代表としての役目を果たした。
Susumu fulfilled his duties as a school representative.

やくわり 役割 *role, part, function* [→ 役目]

役割を果たす to play a role, to play a part, to serve a function

秋元君は生徒会で重要な役割を果たした。
Akimoto played an important role in the student council.

やけ *desperation, despair*

やけになる to despair, to fall into despair

浩はやけになって本を床にたたきつけた。
Hiroshi fell into despair and threw the book on the floor.

やけど 火傷 *burn; scald*

やけどする to get burned/scalded; to burn/scald (The direct object is part of the subject's body.)

ストーブに近づきすぎるとやけどするよ。
If you go too near the heater, you'll get burned.

お湯で手をやけどしました。
I scalded my hand with hot water.

やけどをする to get a burn/scald

また指にやけどをしたよ。
I burned my finger again!

やける 焼ける *1. to burn (intransitive)* [→ 燃える]

隣の家はゆうべ火事で焼けました。
The house next door burned down last night.

2. to roast, to broil (intransitive); to bake (intransitive)

その魚が焼けるまで待ってください。
Please wait until that fish is broiled.

3. to become suntanned; to become sunburned

スキーでそんなに焼けたの？
Did you get so suntanned from skiing?

日に焼ける to get tanned in the sun; to get burned in the sun

やこう 夜行 *overnight train*

僕は10時発、熊本行きの夜行に乗った。
I took the 10:00 night train for Kumamoto.

やさい 野菜 *vegetable*

父は庭で野菜を作っています。
My father grows vegetables in the garden.

野菜サラダ vegetable salad

野菜スープ vegetable soup

やさしい 優しい *kind, nice* [→ 親切な]; *gentle, mild*

この犬はとても優しい目をしています。
This dog has very gentle eyes.

おばあさんは少女にとても優しく話した。
That old woman spoke to the little girl very kindly.

やさしい 易しい *easy, simple* [→ 簡単な1.] [↔ 難しい]

テキストは易しい英語で書いてあります。
The textbook is written in simple English.

その宿題は思ったより易しかったよ。
The homework was easier than I thought!

やし *palm ((tree))*

やしの木 palm tree

やしの実 coconut

やじ 野次 *jeering, heckling*

野次馬 curiosity seeker (who rushes to see fires, accidents, etc.)

やしなう 養う *1. to support, to provide a living for (a family, etc.)*

森さんは少ない収入で家族を養っている。
Mr. Mori supports his family on a small income.

2. to bring up, to rear, to raise [→ 育てる2.]

武田さんは３人の孤児を養いました。
Ms. Takeda brought up three orphans.

3. to train, to cultivate (an ability, capacity, etc.)

習慣を養う to cultivate a habit

やじる 野次る *{5} to jeer, to heckle*

やしん 野心 *ambition, aspiration*

あの若者は野心に燃えています。
That young person is burning with ambition.

野心作 an ambitious work

やすい 安い *inexpensive, cheap* [↔ 高い3.]

この時計は安いですね。
This watch is cheap, isn't it?

もっと安いのを見せてください。
Please show me a cheaper one.

あの店ではカメラが安く買えるよ。
You can buy cameras cheap at that store!

ーやすい *easy to (Added to verb bases.)* [↔ ーにくい]

この本は読みやすいよ。
This book is easy to read!

弟はかぜをひきやすい体質です。
My younger brother easily catches cold.

やすうり 安売り *(bargain) sale* [→ バーゲン]

安売りをする to have a sale

あの店では家具の安売りがあります。
At that store they're having a furniture sale.

毎週土曜日に安売りがあります。
They have a sale every Saturday.

安売りする to sell at a reduced price

やすみ 休み *1. rest, break, recess* [→ 休息]

授業と授業の間に10分間の休みがある。
There is a ten-minute break between classes.

2. holiday, day off [→ 休日]*; vacation* [→ 休暇]

きょうは学校は休みです。
There's no school today. (Literally: Today, as for school, it's a day off.)

3. absence (from school, work, etc.) [→ 欠席]

洋子さんはきょうは休みです。
Yoko is absent today.

やすむ 休む *1. to rest, to take a break* [→ 休息する]*; to take a break from*

少しの間休みましょう。
Let's rest for a while.

少し勉強を休もうよ。
Let's take a break from studying for a little while!

2. to be absent from, to stay home from [→ 欠席する]

きのうは学校を休んだよ。
Yesterday I was absent from school!

3. to go to bed [→ 寝る1.]*; to sleep* [→ 寝る2.]

きょうは早く休みましょう。
Let's go to bed early tonight.

林さんはまだ休んでいます。
Mr. Hayashi is still sleeping.

やすらか 安らか 〜な *peaceful, tranquil*

やすり 鑢 *file ((tool))*

Aにやすりをかける to use a file on A

紙やすり sandpaper

やせい 野生 〜の *wild, untamed (describing an animal); wild, uncultivated (describing a plant)*

山道で野生の猿を見ました。
I saw a wild monkey on the mountain path.

やせる 痩せる *to lose weight, to become*

thinner [↔ 太る]

母は２か月で５キロやせました。
My mother lost five kilograms in two months.

やせている to be slender, to be thin

京子さんはやせているね。
Kyoko is slim, isn't she?

やせた人 slender person, thin person

やたい 屋台 *1. roofed street stall*
(Food vendors prepare and serve simple dishes in these stalls, usually on roadsides. The stalls are often on wheels for easy transport.)

2. outdoor dance platform (sometimes on a parade float)

屋台店 [☞ 屋台 *1.* (above)]

やちょう 野鳥 *wild bird*

やちん 家賃 *rent (payment)*

東京の叔父は高い家賃を払っています。
My uncle in Tokyo is paying high rent.

やつ 奴【CRUDE for 人】 *guy, gal*

明はいいやつだよ。
Akira's a nice guy!

やっかい 厄介 *trouble, annoyance* [→ 面倒]

Ａのやっかいになる to become reliant on A (for care, support, etc.)

やっかいな troublesome, bothersome

やっきょく 薬局 *pharmacy, (US) drugstore, (UK) chemist's*

やっつ 八つ *eight (see Appendix 2)*

やっつける【COL.】*to successfully attack, to get; to finish off, to take care of*

やってくる *to come, to come along, to turn up*

激しいあらしがやってきたよ。
A violent storm came along!

また梅雨がやってきたね。
The rainy season has come again, hasn't it?

やっと *1. at last, finally* [→ 遂に1.]

やっと山小屋に到着しました。
At last we arrived at the mountain hut.

2. just barely [→ 辛うじて]

やっと授業に間に合いました。
I was just barely in time for class.

やっとこ *pincers, pliers*

やっぱり【COL. for やはり】

やとう 野党 *opposition party, party out of power* [↔ 与党]

やとう 雇う *to hire, to employ*

その会社では警備員を８人雇っています。
At that company they employ eight security guards.

やなぎ 柳 *willow*

やに 脂 *1. resin (from a tree)*

2. tar (from burned tobacco)

やね 屋根 *roof*

屋根に上がってはいけないよ。
You mustn't go up on the roof!

屋根裏部屋 attic, loft

やはり *as one might expect; just as I thought, sure enough*

私もやはりクラシックが好きです。
As you might expect, I also like classical music.

近藤さんは今もやはり甲府に住んでいる。
Just as I thought, Mr. Kondo is still living in Kofu.

一生懸命練習したが、やはりだめだった。
I practiced as hard as I could, but sure enough it was no good.

やばん 野蛮 〜な *savage, barbarous*

野蛮人 a savage, a barbarian

やぶ 藪 *thicket*

やぶく 破く *to tear* [→ 破る1.] *(transitive)*

やぶける 破ける *to tear (intransitive)* [→ 破れる1.]

やぶる 破る *1. to tear (transitive)* [→ 裂く]
次郎はあの手紙を破ったよ。
Jiro tore that letter!
2. to break, to damage [→ 壊す1.]
犬が垣根を破って入ったよ。
A dog broke the fence and went in!
3. to break (a previous record)
関口選手はマラソンで世界記録を破った。
Sekiguchi broke the world record in the marathon.
4. to break, to violate
約束を破る to break a promise
5. to defeat, to beat [→ 負かす]
西武は３対１で近鉄を破りました。
Seibu beat Kintetsu 3 *to* 1

やぶれる 敗れる *to be defeated, to lose* [→ 負ける1.]
僕たちのチームは決勝で敗れました。
Our team was defeated in the final.

やぶれる 破れる *1. to tear (intransitive)* [→ 裂ける]
かがんだときにズボンが破れました。
When I bent down my pants tore.
そのカーテンは破れているよ。
That curtain is torn!
2. to break, to get damaged [→ 壊れる]

やま 山 *1. mountain*
今年の夏は山へ行きましょう。
This summer let's go to the mountains.
私たちは高い山に登りました。
We climbed a high mountain.
2. speculation, venture
山をかける to take a calculated risk
山小屋 mountain hut
山ほど as much as a mountain, amounting to a great deal
する事が山ほどあるんです。
I have a mountain of things to do.
山火事 mountain forest fire
山くずれ mountain landslide
山道 mountain path
山盛り large serving
山登り mountain climbing

やまのて 山の手 *hillier residential sections of a city, uptown* [↔ 下町]
(The desirable residential neighborhoods of a Japanese city are typically in hilly areas away from a low-lying downtown area.)

やまびこ *echo* [→ こだま]

やみ 闇 *darkness, the dark* [→ 暗闇]
やみの中を手探りで進みました。
I went forward through the dark by groping.
闇夜 dark night

やむ 止む *to stop, to cease, to end, to die down*
雪がやみました。
The snow stopped.
激しい雨ですが、まもなくやむでしょう。
It is violent rain, but it will probably die down soon.
雨が降ったりやんだりしています。
It's raining on and off. (Literally: Rain is alternately falling and stopping.)

やむをえない やむを得ない *cannot be helped, to be unavoidable*
多少の混乱はやむをえないだろう。
A certain amount of confusion can't be avoided.
やむをえない事情で浩二は会社を休んだ。
Koji was absent from work due to unavoidable circumstances.

やめる 止める *1. to stop (doing)*
けんかをやめてください。
Please stop quarreling.
夜遅く寝るのをやめなさい。
Stop going to bed late at night.
2. to give up, to stop indulging in
父はたばこをやめました。

My father gave up smoking.

3. to give up on, to abandon (a planned activity)
突然寒くなったから、遠足をやめました。
It suddenly got cold, so we gave up the excursion.

やめる 辞める *to resign from, to quit*
来月テニス部を辞めるつもりです。
I'm planning to quit the tennis club next month.
上原さんはもうすぐ議長を辞めます。
Mr. Uehara will resign from the chair soon.

やもり *gecko*

やや *a little, somewhat, slightly*
相手はやや疲れたようです。
My opponent seems to have gotten somewhat tired.
それはややりんごに似ています。
That looks a little like an apple.

ややこしい *complicated* [→ 複雑な]; *troublesome* [→ 面倒な]
これはたいへんややこしい問題です。
This is a very complicated problem.

やり 槍 *spear; javelin*
槍投げ the javelin throw

やりかた やり方 *way of doing* [→ 仕方]
将棋のやり方を教えてください。
Please teach me how to play shogi.
島田さんは何でも自分のやり方でやる。
Mr. Shimada does everything in his own way.

やりとげる やり遂げる *to accomplish, to complete, to carry through*
会長はその計画を一人でやり遂げました。
The chairperson carried through that plan by himself.

やりとり やり取り *giving and taking, reciprocal exchange*

やりなおす やり直す *to do over, to redo*
社長はもう一度やり直すように言った。
The company president said to do it over again.

やる 遣る *(In either use of this word the recipient must not be the speaker, the speaker's group, or a person or group with whom the speaker is identifying. In contrast to* 上げる*, the use of* やる *implies that the recipient is inferior in status to or on very intimate terms with the giver.)*

1. to give (to a recipient)
犬に水をやるのを忘れないでね。
Don't forget to give water to the dog, OK?

2. to do the favor of (following the gerund (-て form) of another verb)
息子に車を買ってやりました。
I bought a car for my son.

やる 遣る【COL. for する*1.*】 *to do, to engage in*
今宿題をやっているところだよ。
I'm in the middle of doing my homework now!
夕方までにこれをやってしまいましょう。
Let's finish this by late afternoon.
やって行く to get along, to live
大谷さんなら部長とうまくやっていける。
If it's Mr. Otani, he can get along well with the department head.

やれやれ *whew (an interjection expressing relief, fatigue, or disappointment)*

やわらかい 柔らかい, 軟らかい *1.* [[↔ 堅い, 固い, 硬い1.]] *soft; flexible, pliant; tender (describing meat, etc.)*
このクッションはとてもやわらかいよ。
This cushion is very soft!
秋のやわらかい日ざしが大好きです。
I love the soft sunshine of autumn.
このステーキはやわらかいですね。
This steak is tender, isn't it?

2. gentle, mild

やわらかい声 gentle voice

やわらげる 和らげる *to soften, to moderate, to ease*

この薬は痛みを和らげます。
This medicine will ease the pain.

声を和らげる to soften one's voice

ヤング *young person* [→ 若者]

ゆ

ゆ 湯 *hot water, warm water* [↔ 水2.]

お湯で手を洗いなさい。
Wash your hands with warm water.

母は紅茶を入れるためにお湯を沸かした。
My mother boiled water to make tea.

ふろに湯を入れてくれますか？
Will you put hot water in the bath for me?

湯船 bathtub [→ 浴槽]

湯豆腐 tofu boiled in water

湯飲み teacup

湯沸かし器 water heater

ゆいいつ 唯一 ～の *the (one and) only*

これは阪神にとって唯一のチャンスです。
This is the only chance for Hanshin.

ゆいごん 遺言 *last words, dying wishes, will*

遺言状 (written) will [→ 遺書]

ゆういぎ 有意義 ～な *significant, worthwhile, valuable*

この失敗は有意義な経験になるでしょう。
This failure will probably be a valuable experience.

ゆううつ 憂鬱 ～な *gloomy* [↔ 快活な]

来週は試験なので、憂うつです。
I'm depressed because we have exams next week.

このごろ憂うつな天気が続いています。
These days gloomy weather continues.

ゆうえき 有益 ～な *rewarding, instructive, useful*

ゆうえつかん 優越感 *superiority complex* [↔ 劣等感]

ゆうえんち 遊園地 *amusement park*

ゆうが 優雅 ～な *elegant, refined*

茶道や生け花は優雅な趣味ですね。
The tea ceremony and flower arrangement are elegant pursuits, aren't they?

ゆうかい 誘拐 *kidnapping, abduction*

誘拐する to kidnap, to abduct

ゆうがい 有害 ～の *harmful, injurious* [↔ 無害の]

たばこは健康に有害です。
Tobacco is harmful to one's health.

ゆうがた 夕方 *late afternoon, early evening*

(Typically understood to mean the period from an hour or two before sunset until the end of twilight.)

姉はたいてい夕方には帰宅します。
My older sister usually comes home in the early evening.

兄は夕方6時ごろに外出しました。
My older brother went out at about 6:00 in the evening.

父はきのうの夕方旅行に出かけました。
My father left on a trip late yesterday afternoon.

ゆうかん 夕刊 evening edition of a newspaper [↔ 朝刊]

ゆうかん 勇敢 ～な *brave* [→ 勇ましい]

あの探検家は勇敢な男だね。
That explorer is a brave man, isn't he?

兵隊は国のために勇敢に戦いました。
The soldier fought bravely for his country.

ゆうき 勇気 *courage*

石川さんは勇気のある人ですね。
Ms. Ishikawa is a courageous woman, isn't she?
僕にはそれをする勇気がないよ。
I don't have the courage to do that!
勇気を出す to muster one's courage
勇気を失う to lose one's courage
勇気づける to encourage
友達の言葉に勇気づけられました。
I was encouraged by my friend's words.

ゆうぎ 遊戯 *1. playing, game, recreation* [→ 遊び]
2. directed group play (combining exercise and recreation for young children at a day-care center or school)
幼稚園の子供たちは遊戯をしています。
The children in the kindergarten are doing group play.
遊戯場 playground [→ 運動場 (s.v. 運動)]; recreation center

ゆうぐれ 夕暮れ *the time of evening around sunset, dusk*

ゆうげきしゅ 遊撃手 *shortstop* [→ ショート] *(in baseball)*

ゆうけんしゃ 有権者 *person with the right to vote, voter*

ゆうこう 有効 〜な [[↔ 無効]] *1. effective, fruitful*
洪水を防ぐ有効な手段を教えてください。
Teach us effective measures to prevent floods.
夏休みを有効に使いなさい。
Use of your summer vacation fruitfully.
2. valid, in effect
この往復切符は 6 日間有効です。
This round-trip ticket is valid for six days.

ゆうこう 友好 friendship, amity
友好的な friendly, amicable
今の友好的な関係を続けることが重要だ。
It is important that we continue the present friendly relations.

ゆうざい 有罪 *(criminal) guilt* [↔ 無罪]
有罪の guilty

ゆうしゅう 優秀 〜な *excellent, superior*
京子ちゃんはとても優秀な中学生でした。
Kyoko was an excellent junior high school student.
兄は優秀な成績で高校を卒業しました。
My older brother graduated from high school with excellent grades.
最優秀選手 most valuable player

ゆうしょう 優勝 *winning the championship*
優勝する to win the championship
私たちのクラスは卓球の試合で優勝した。
Our class won the table tennis championship.
優勝チーム champion team
優勝カップ championship trophy, championship cup
優勝旗 championship flag, championship pennant
優勝者 champion

ゆうじょう 友情 *friendship, fellowship*
皆さんの温かい友情を決して忘れません。
I will never forget everyone's warm friendship.
友情に厚い friendly

ゆうしょく 夕食 *evening meal, supper, dinner* [→ 夜ご飯 (s.v. 夜), 晩ご飯 (s.v. 晩)]
きのう私は夕食を作りました。
Yesterday I made supper.
夕食の前に 2 時間勉強します。
I study for two hours before supper.
うちでは夕食は 7 時です。
At our house dinner is at 7:00.

ゆうじん 友人 *friend* [→ 友達]

ユースホステル *youth hostel*

ゆうせいしょう 郵政省 *the Ministry of Postal Service and Telecommunications*

ゆうせん 優先 *priority, preference*

優先する to have priority, to take precedence

優先順位 order of priority

ゆうそう 郵送 *(US) mailing, (UK) posting*

郵送する to send by mail, to mail

その本をあした郵送します。

I will mail that book tomorrow.

郵送料 postage (charge)

ユーターン *U-turn*

ゆうだい 雄大 〜な *grand, majestic, magnificent*

頂上からの雄大な眺めを楽しみました。

We enjoyed the magnificent view from the summit.

ゆうだち 夕立 *sudden evening shower*

きのう夕立が降りました。

There was a sudden evening shower yesterday.

夕立にあう to get caught in a sudden evening shower

ゆうとうせい 優等生 *honor student*

ゆうどく 有毒 〜な *poisonous*

有毒ガス poisonous gas

ユートピア *utopia*

ゆうのう 有能 〜な *able, capable, competent*

森田さんは有能な記者です。

Ms. Morita is a capable reporter.

ゆうはん 夕飯 *evening meal* [→ 夕食]

ゆうひ 夕日 *evening sun, setting sun* [↔ 朝日]

夕日がその部屋に差し込んでいます。

The setting sun is shining into that room.

ゆうびん 郵便 *1. (US) mail (service), postal service*

けさの郵便でこの手紙が来ました。

This letter came in the morning mail.

この荷物を郵便で送ってください。

Please send this package by mail.

ロンドンまで郵便は何日かかりますか。

How many days does mail take to London?

2. (US) (item sent in the) mail, (UK) (item sent in the) post

きょうは郵便がたくさん届いています。

A lot of mail has come today.

郵便番号 (US)zip code, (UK) postcode

郵便物 [☞ 郵便*2.* (above)]

郵便葉書 postcard

郵便配達人 (US) mail carrier, postman

郵便切手 postage stamp [→ 切手]

郵便局 post office

郵便局員 post-office clerk

郵便料金 postage (charge)

郵便受け (US) mailbox, (UK) letter box (in which mail is received)

ユーフォー *UFO*

ゆうふく 裕福 〜な *rich, wealthy* [→ 金持ちの]

萩原さんは裕福な家に生まれました。

Mr. Hagiwara was born into a wealthy family.

ゆうべ 夕べ *evening*

僕たちは音楽の夕べを催しました。

We held a musical evening.

叔父のうちで楽しい夕べを過ごしました。

We spent a pleasant evening at my uncle's home.

ゆうべ 昨夜 *last night, yesterday night* [→ 昨夜]

ゆうべはよく眠れましたか。

Did you sleep well last night?

ゆうぼう 有望 〜な *promising, likely to turn out well*

有望な前途 a promising future

ゆうめい 有名 ～な *famous, well-known*

早田さんは将来有名な作家になるだろう。
Ms. Hayata will probably become a famous writer in the future.

有森さんは世界的に有名な科学者です。
Mr. Arimori is a world-famous scientist.

この寺は庭園で有名です。
This temple is famous for its garden.

有名人 famous person, celebrity

有名校 big-name school

ユーモア *humor, wit*

谷村さんはユーモアがわからないね。
Mr. Tanimura doesn't understand humor, does he.

ユーモラス ～な *humorous*

小田さんはユーモラスな話をしてくれた。
Mr. Oda told us a humorous story.

ゆうやけ 夕焼け *sunset (colors)*

僕と忍は美しい夕焼けを眺めていました。
Shinobu and I were looking at the beautiful sunset.

ゆうらん 遊覧 *excursion, going around to see the sights*

遊覧する to go around and see the sights of, to make an excursion through

遊覧バス sight-seeing bus

遊覧船 excursion ship, pleasure boat

ゆうり 有利 ～な *advantageous, favorable, profitable* [↔ 不利な]

今なら生命保険に加入するのが有利です。
If it's now, taking out life insurance would be advantageous.

その決定は私たちに有利なものでした。
That decision was favorable to us.

ゆうりょう 有料 ～の *requiring payment, involving a fee, not free* [↔ 無料の]

その競技会は有料です。
That athletic meet isn't free.

有料駐車場 pay parking lot

有料道路 toll road

有料トイレ pay toilet

ゆうりょく 有力 ～な *1. strong, powerful, influential*

お父さんは有力な政治家です。
His father is an influential politician.

2. strong, convincing, compelling

有力な証拠は何もありません。
There is no strong evidence. (Literally: As for strong evidence, there is nothing.)

有力者 influential person, powerful person

ゆうれい 幽霊 *dead person's spirit, ghost* [→ 亡霊]

幽霊なんて信じないよ。
I don't believe in such things as ghosts!

ゆうわく 誘惑 *temptation, enticement; seduction*

誘惑に勝つ to overcome a temptation

誘惑に負ける to give in to temptation

誘惑と戦う to fight temptation

誘惑する to tempt, to entice; to seduce

やくざはお金でその青年を誘惑しました。
The gangster enticed that young man with money.

ゆか 床 *floor (i.e., bottom surface of a room)*

床運動 floor exercise (in gymnastics)

ゆかい 愉快 ～な [[↔ 不愉快な]] *1. pleasant, delightful, merry*

先生とおしゃべりするのは実に愉快です。
Chatting with the teacher is really pleasant.

きょうはとても愉快だったね。
Today was really delightful, wasn't it?

2. cheerful, pleased

ゆかた 浴衣 *informal cotton kimono*

(A ゆかた is usually worn in summer as a bathrobe and for sleeping. Hotels generally provide them for guests.)

ゆがむ 歪む *to become distorted, to become twisted, to become crooked*

キャッチャーの顔は苦痛でゆがんでいた。
The catcher's face was twisted with pain.

テレビの画面がゆがんでいるよ。
The (picture on the) TV screen is distorted!

ゆがめる 歪める *to distort, to twist, to make crooked*

通訳は大統領の言葉をゆがめました。
The interpreter distorted the president's words.

ゆき 雪 *snow*

雨が雪に変わりました。
The rain has changed to snow.

今年は雪が多い。
There's a lot of snow this year.

山には雪が10センチ積もっています。
On the mountain ten centimeters of snow have accumulated.

雪が降る snow falls

雪が降りそうですね。
It looks as if it's going to snow, doesn't it?

雪が激しく降っているよ。
It's snowing hard!

雪がやむ snow stops falling

雪だるま snowman

雪解け snow thaw

雪合戦 snowball fight

雪国 snowy region

初雪 the first snow of the season

大雪 heavy snowfall

きのう大雪が降りましたよ。
There was a heavy snowfall yesterday!

ーゆき ー行き ～の *bound for, going to (Added to nouns denoting places.)*

松本で新宿行きの列車に乗り換えました。
In Matsumoto I transferred to a train bound for Shinjuku.

このバスは三島行きです。
This bus is going to Mishima.

ゆきさき 行き先 *destination*

ゆく 行く {*Irreg.*} [☞ 行く]

ゆくえ 行方 *whereabouts, where one has gone*

大使の行方がわかりません。
They don't know the ambassador's whereabouts.

行方のわからなかった少女は無事でした。
The girl who had been missing was safe.

行方不明のwhereabouts unknown, missing

うちの犬はまだ行方不明です。
Our dog is still missing.

ゆげ 湯気 *(visible) steam, vapor*

ゆけつ 輸血 *blood transfusion*

輸血する to give a blood transfusion

医者はその患者に輸血しました。
The doctor gave that patient a blood transfusion.

ゆしゅつ 輸出 *exportation* [↔ 輸入]

輸出する to export

アメリカは日本へ小麦を輸出しています。
The United States exports wheat to Japan.

輸出品 export, exported item

ゆず 柚 *citron*

ゆすぐ 濯ぐ *to rinse* [→ 濯ぐ]

食後は口をよくゆすぎなさい。
After meals rinse your mouth well.

ゆする 揺する *to shake (transitive); to rock (transitive)*

木を揺すってくりの実を落としました。
We shook the tree and made the chestnuts fall.

ゆずる 譲る *to yield, to let have*

AにBを譲る to yield B to A, to let A have B

電車でおばあさんに席を譲りました。
I let an old woman have my seat on the train.

父は右折する車に道を譲りました。
My father yielded the roads to the car turning right.
井沢さんは娘さんに全財産を譲りました。
Mr. Izawa let his daughter have his whole fortune.
友達にピアノを6万円で譲ったよ。
I let my friend have the piano for ¥60,000!

ゆそう 輸送 *transporting*
輸送する to transport
その島に週に一度食糧を船で輸送します。
They transport food to that island by boat once a week.

ゆたか 豊か ～な [[↔ 貧しい]] *1. abundant, ample, rich* [➞ 豊富な] [↔ 乏しい]
その国は石油が豊かです。
In that country oil is abundant.
この子は想像力が豊かです。
This child has a rich imagination.
2. rich, wealthy [➞ 裕福な] [↔ 貧乏な]
カナダは豊かな国です。
Canada is a wealthy country.

ゆだん 油断 *carelessness, negligence*
油断する to be careless, to let one's guard down
油断すると、けがをするよ。
If you're careless, you'll get injured!

ゆっくり (～と) *slowly, in a leisurely manner, without hurrying*
もう少しゆっくり話していただけますか。
Could we have you speak a little more slowly?
あわてないで、ゆっくりやってください。
Don't rush, please take your time doing it.
ゆっくり眠る to sleep well
ゆっくり間に合う to be in plenty of time
ゆっくりする to take one's time; to stay a long time
どうぞごゆっくり。
Please stay as long as you like.

ゆでる *to boil (in plain water) (transitive)*
母は卵を固くゆでました。
My mother boiled the eggs hard.

ゆでん 油田 *oil field*

ユニーク ～な *unique; unusual*
橋本さんの考え方はとてもユニークです。
Ms. Hashimoto's way of thinking is very unusual.

ユニホーム *a uniform*
運転手はユニホームを着ていました。
The chauffeur was wearing his uniform.

ゆにゅう 輸入 *importation* [↔ 輸出]
輸入する to import
日本はアメリカから小麦を輸入しています。
Japan imports wheat from America.
輸入品 import, imported item

ゆび 指 *finger; toe*
姉はほっそりした指をしているよ。
My older sister has slender fingers!
子供は1から5まで指で数えました。
The child counted from one to five on his fingers.
指折の leading, prominent
指先 fingertip; toe tip
人差し指 index finger
小指 little finger; little toe
薬指 ring finger
中指 middle finger
親指 thumb; big toe

ゆびわ 指輪 *(finger) ring*
赤塚さんはルビーの指輪をしています。
Ms. Akatsuka is wearing a ruby ring.
結婚指輪 wedding ring
婚約指輪 engagement ring [➞ エンゲージリング]

ゆみ 弓 *bow (used to shoot arrows)*
アーチェリーの選手は弓に矢をつがえた。
The archery competitor fitted an arrow to

the bow.
猟師は弓を引いて矢を放った。
The hunter drew the bow and shot the arrow.

ゆめ 夢 *dream*
役者になるのが私の夢です。
Becoming an actor is my dream.
夢が現実になりました。
The dream became reality.
夢を見る to dream, to have a dream
亡くなった母の夢を見たよ。
I dreamed about my deceased mother!
夢にも思わない to never dream
勝つとは夢にも思わなかったよ。
I never dreamed that I would win!

ゆらい 由来 *origin, derivation, past history*
由来する to originate, to derive, to date back

ゆり 百合 *lily*

ゆりかご 揺り籠 *cradle*
揺りかごから墓場まで from the cradle to the grave

ゆるい 緩い *1. loose, slack; loose-fitting* [↔ きつい1.]
このズボンは僕には緩いよ。
These pants are loose on me!
2. lax, lenient (describing a restriction, regulation, etc.)
この学校は校則が緩い。
This school's rules are lax.

ゆるし 許し *1. permission* [→ 許可]
店員は許しを得ずに外出しました。
The store clerk went out without getting permission.
2. forgiveness, pardon

ゆるす 許す *1. to allow, to permit* [→ 許可する]
父は釣りに行くのを許してくれたよ。
My father let me go fishing!
2. to forgive, to pardon
兄は私のまちがいを許してくれました。
My older brother forgave my mistake.
私の不注意を許してください。
Please forgive my carelessness.

ゆるむ 緩む *1. to become loose, to slacken*
歩いているうちに靴のひもが緩みました。
While I was walking my shoelaces became loose.
2. to abate
傷の痛みがだんだん緩みました。
The pain of the wound gradually abated.

ゆるめる 緩める *to loosen, to slacken (transitive)*
大工はまずねじを緩めました。
The carpenter first loosened the screw.
気を緩める to relax one's attention

ゆるやか 緩やか ～な *1.* [[↔ 急な3.]] *gentle (describing a slope); gentle (describing a curve)*
ここからは緩やかな坂を上ります。
From here we're going to go up a gentle slope.
2. slow, gentle (describing a flow) [↔ 急な4.]
ボートは緩やかな流れを下りました。
The boat went down a slow stream.

ゆれる 揺れる *to shake (intransitive); to sway (intransitive); to rock (intransitive)*
地震で家が揺れるのを感じました。
I felt the house sway in the earthquake.
船が激しく揺れました。
The ship rocked terribly.

よ *(sentence-final particle indicating exclamation)*
一人で行きましたよ。

I went alone!

よ 世 *1. the world, the way the world is, society* [→ 世間]

この世 this world, this life

あの世 the next world, life after death

僕はあの世を信じないよ。
I don't believe in the next world!

世を去る to leave this world, to die

その詩人は若いときに世を去りました。
That poet died when he was young.

2. [[→ 時代]] *era; the times*

よ 夜 *night* [→ 夜]

夜が明ける day breaks (Literally: Night brightens.)

もうすぐ夜が明けるでしょう。
It will be probably be daybreak soon.

夜通し all night long

田中さんは夜通し起きていました。
Ms. Tanaka was up all night long.

よあけ 夜明け *dawn, daybreak*

私たちは夜明けに出発しました。
We started out at dawn.

よい 良い [☞ いい]

よう 用 *matter to attend to, business, errand* [→ 用事]

今晩は用があります。
I have a matter to attend to this evening.

父は会社の用で大阪へ行きます。
My father is going to go to Osaka on company business.

よう 酔う *1. to get drunk*

父は酔うと、口数が多くなります。
When my father gets drunk, he becomes talkative.

2. to get motion sickness

僕は飛行機では酔いませんよ。
I don't get motion sickness on planes!

船に酔う to get seasick

車に酔う to get carsick

よう 様 *1. 〜な (The word follows a predicate and functions grammatically as an adjectival noun. The word preceding cannot be the copula form だ. Where だ would be the appropriate predicate, の (following a noun) or な (following an adjectival noun) appears instead. It is also possible to use the demonstratives この, その, あの, and どの before .) like, seeming, apparent, as if [→ らしい 1.]*

AのようなB a B like A

鳥のように空を飛ぶのは楽しいでしょう。
Flying through the sky like a bird is probably fun.

このような紙が折り紙には最適です。
Paper like this is the most suitable for origami.

父はいつものように7時に帰宅した。
My father returned home at 7:00 as usual.

次郎は兄さんのように一生懸命勉強した。
Jiro studied hard like his older brother.

石川さんは何もできないような人ですね。
Mr. Ishikawa is a person who appears unable to do anything.

エレベーターが壊れているようです。
It seems that the elevator is broken.

雨が降るようだね。
It looks as if it's going to rain, doesn't it?

2. 〜に so that, in order to (following a verb in the nonpast tense) [→ 為1.]

急行に間に合うように早くうちを出た。
I left home early so that I would be in time for the express.

ようにする to make sure that, to bring it about that (following a verb in the nonpast tense)

全部使うようにしましょう。
Let's make sure that we use it all.

ようになる to come about that, to get to the point that (following a verb in the nonpast tense)

緑はやっと自転車に乗れるようになった。
Midori was finally able to ride a bicycle.

3. (〜に) (Following a verb in the nonpast tense and preceding a verb of requesting, ように *is used to report a request.)*
父は弟に気をつけるように注意しました。
My father warned my younger brother to be careful.

ーよう ー様 *way of doing, way to do (Added to verb bases.)* [→ ー方]
古い自転車はもう直しようがありません。
There is no longer any way to fix the old bicycle.

ーよう ー用 〜の *for use in; for use by (Added to noun bases.)*
家の前に工事用のトラックが止っていた。
A truck for construction-use was parked in front of the house.
男性用の化粧品もあります。
There are also cosmetics for men.

ようい 用意 *preparation* [→ 準備]
用意をする to make preparations, to get ready
母は夕食の用意をしています。
My mother is making the preparations for supper.
用意ができる preparations become completed
朝食の用意ができました。
Breakfast is ready. (Literally: Breakfast preparations have been completed.)
出発の用意はできましたか。
Are you ready to start out? (Literally: Have the preparations for starting out been completed?)
用意、どん。
Ready, go! (when starting a race)
用意する to prepare, to get ready (transitive or intransitive)

ようい 容易 〜な *easy, not difficult* [→ 易しい]

ようか 八日 *(see Appendix 2) 1. eight days*
2. the eighth (day of a month)

ようがん 溶岩 *lava*

ようき 陽気 *1. 〜な cheerful, merry* [↔ 陰気な]
陽気な歌を歌おうよ。
Let's sing cheerful songs!
恵子ちゃんはとても陽気な子です。
Keiko is a very cheerful child.
洋子さんは陽気に笑っていました。
Yoko was laughing merrily.
2. seasonal weather, (short-term) weather pattern [→ 天候]

ようぎ 容疑 *suspicion of having committed a crime*
あの人は殺人の容疑で逮捕されました。
That person was arrested on suspicion of murder.
容疑者 (crime) suspect

ようきゅう 要求 [[→ 請求]] *demand; request*
要求する to demand; to request
AにBを要求する to demand B from/of A to request B from/of A
被害者はバス会社にお金を要求しました。
The victim demanded money from the bus company.
市長に約束を守るよう要求しました。
We requested that the mayor keep his promise.

ようご 用語 *term, terminology*
専門用語 technical term, technical terminology

ようこそ *welcome (as a greeting)*
ようこそ日本へ。
Welcome to Japan.
ようこそいらっしゃいました。
I'm glad you came. (Literally: Welcome you came.)

ようさい 洋裁 *dressmaking, sewing Western-style clothes*

ようさん 養蚕 *sericulture*

ようし 陽子 *proton* [↔ 電子; 中性子]

ようし 用紙 *paper (for a specific use); form (to fill in)*

この用紙に記入してください。
Please fill in this form.

解答用紙 answer sheet

試験用紙 examination paper

ようし 養子 *adopted child*

ようじ 用事 *matter to attend to, business, errand* [→ 用]

ようじ 幼児 *young child, preschool child*

ようじ 楊枝 *toothpick* [→ 爪楊枝]

ようしき 様式 *style, form, mode*

この寺院はロマネスク様式で建てられた。
This temple has been built in Roman style.

生活様式 lifestyle

ようしつ 洋室 *Western-style room* [↔ 和室]

ようしょく 洋食 *Western-style food* [↔ 和食]

ようしょく 養殖 *raising, culture, farming (in the sense of increasing the yield of a marine product by artificial means)*

養殖する to raise, to culture, to farm

真珠の養殖 pearl culture

養殖場 (fish)farm, (oyster)bed

ようじん 用心 *heed, caution, prudence* [→ 注意2.]

用心する to take care, to be careful; to take care with, to be careful of

食べすぎないように用心しなさい。
Be careful not to eat too much.

用心深い very careful, very cautious

ガードマンは用心深く辺りを見回した。
The guard looked around very carefully.

ようす 様子 *1. state of affairs, situation, condition* [→ 状態]

特派員が戦争の様子を報告しました。
The correspondent reported the war situation.

2. appearance; air, manner; sign, indication

スチュワーデスはひどく疲れた様子です。
The stewardess appears to be terribly tired.

あの人の様子はおかしいね。
That person's manner is strange, isn't it?

この空の様子では、あしたは雨でしょう。
By the appearance of this sky, tomorrow it will probably rain.

雪が降りそうな様子です。
It looks likes snow. (Literally: It's an appearance that it looks as if snow will fall.)

ようするに 要するに *in short, to sum up* [→ つまり2.]

要するに、その考えは誤りだったのだ。
In short, that idea was mistaken.

ようせい 妖精 *fairy*

ようせき 容積 *capacity, volume (of a container)*

ようそ 要素 *element, factor*

ようだい 容体, 容態 *condition (of one who is ill)*

祖父の容体が悪化しました。
My grandfather's condition got worse.

ようち 幼稚 ～な *childish, infantile*

それは幼稚な意見ですね。
That is a childish opinion, isn't it?

ようちえん 幼稚園 *preschool, kindergarten*

ようてん 要点 *the point, the gist*

お話の要点がわかりません。
I don't understand the point of what you are saying.

ようふく 洋服 *1. clothes* [→ 服]

川田さんの洋服はぬれています。
Mr. Kawada's clothes are wet.

2. Western-style clothes [↔ 和服]
洋服だんす (clothes-storage) wardrobe
洋服屋 tailor; tailor shop

ようもう 羊毛 *wool*
羊毛製品 woolen manufactured article

ようやく 漸く *1. at last, finally* [→ 遂に]
2. just barely [→ 辛うじて]
3. gradually [→ 次第に]

ようりょう 要領 *1. the point, the gist* [→ 要点]
要領を得る to become to the point
大蔵大臣の答えは要領を得ていた。
The Finance Minister's answers were to the point.
2. knack [→ こつ]
要領がいい efficient (describing a person); shrewd

ようれい 用例 *usage example*
先生はいくつかの用例をあげて説明した。
The teacher explained it by giving several usage examples.

ヨーグルト *yogurt*

ヨーロッパ *Europe*
ヨーロッパ人 a European

よか 余暇 *leisure time, spare time* [→ 暇2.]
父は余暇に絵をかくのが趣味です。
My father's hobby is painting in his leisure time.

よぎない 余儀ない *unavoidable*

よきん 預金 *1. depositing money (in a bank, etc.)*
預金する to deposit money; to deposit (money)
母は銀行に5万円預金しました。
My mother deposited ¥50,000 in the bank.
2. money on deposit
郵便局に預金が2万円あります。
I have ¥20,000 on deposit in the post office.
銀行から預金を1万円引き出しました。
I withdrew ¥10,000 from the bank.
預金通帳 bankbook, passbook
普通預金 ordinary deposit
定期預金 fixed-time deposit

よく 欲 *desire, want*
由美さんは欲のない人です。
Yumi is a person of no wants.
知識欲 desire for knowledge
食欲 appetite

よく 良く *1. well*
(This word is the regular adverbial form of 良い, but it is also used as the (irregular) adverbial form of いい)
ゆうべはよく眠れましたか。
Were you able to sleep well last night?
藤森さんのことはよく知っています。
I know Mr. Fujimori well.
この写真をよく見てください。
Please look at this picture carefully.
よくやったよ。
Well done! (Literally: You did it well!)
よく来ましたね。
How nice of you to come. (Literally: You came well, didn't you?)
2. often [→ 度々]
秀子ちゃんはよく遅刻するね。
Hideko is often late, isn't she?
兄とよく釣りに行くよ。
I often go fishing with my older brother!

よく— 翌— *the next, the following (Added to bases denoting regularly recurring time spans.)*
翌朝 the next morning, the following morning
翌日 the next day, the following day
翌年 the next year, the following year

よくしつ 浴室 *bathroom*

(Toilets and the bathtubs are traditionally in separate rooms in Japan. This word refers to a room for taking a bath.) [→ 風呂場 (s.v. 風呂)]

よくそう 浴槽 *bathtub* [→ 湯船]

よくばり 欲張り *1. greed*
欲張りな greedy
2. greedy person

よくぼう 欲望 *desire, want* [→ 欲]

よけい 余計 *1. (〜に) more than ordinarily; even more* [→ 一層]
暗いから、よけい怖いんです。
Because it's dark, it's even more frightening.
2. 〜な excess, surplus, extra [→ 余分の]
よけいなお金は全然ないよ。
I don't have any extra money!
電話代を50円よけいに払ってしまった。
I paid ¥50 too much for the telephone bill.
3. 〜な unnecessary, uncalled-for
よけいな事は言わないほうがいいよ。
It's better not to say uncalled-for things!

よける 避ける *to avoid* [→ 避ける]; *to make way for*
歩道に立って、車をよけなさい。
Stand on the sidewalk and make way for the car.

よげん 予言 *prophecy, prediction*
経済学者の予言が当たりました。
The economist's prediction proved true.
予言する to foretell, to predict
選挙の結果はだれも予言できません。
No one can foretell the results of the election.
予言者 prophet

よこ 横 *1. side (part); the area beside*
ママの横に座りたいよ。
I want to sit beside Mama!
横の入口から建物に入りました。
I entered the building from the side entrance.
横を向く to turn one's face to the side
2. width (as opposed to height or length) [↔ 縦1.]
この箱は横が56センチあります。
The width of this box is 56 centimeters.
3. 〜の [→ 縦の2.] *horizontal; side-by-side*
横の線 horizontal line
横になる to lie down [→ 横たわる]

よこがお 横顔 *1. profile, side-view of a face*
2. profile, brief description

よこぎる 横切る *{5} to cross, to go across (the short way from one side to the other of something long and narrow)*
ここで道路を横切ってはいけません。
You must not cross the street here.

よこく 予告 *advance notice*
予告する to give advance notice of, to announce in advance
予告編 preview (of a movie, television program, etc.)

よごす 汚す *to make dirty, to stain*
服を汚してはだめよ。
You mustn't get your clothes dirty!
順子ちゃんはこの紙をインクで汚したよ。
Junko stained this paper with ink!

よこたえる 横たえる *to lay down, to put down horizontally*
病人はベッドに体を横たえました。
The ill person laid himself on the bed.

よこたわる 横たわる *to lie down*
父はソファーに横たわりました。
My father lay down on the sofa.

よごれ 汚れ *dirt, grime; stain* [→ 染み]
汚れを落とす to wash off dirt; to get out a stain
兄は自転車の汚れを落としました。
My older brother washed the dirt off his bicycle.

汚れ物 dirty things; dirty clothes

よごれる 汚れる *to become dirty, to become stained*

そのハンカチは汚れています。
That handkerchief is dirty.
白い車は雨の日にはすぐ汚れます。
A white car soon gets dirty on a rainy day.
汚れた手で触らないで。
Don't touch it with dirty hands.
この辺りの空気は汚れているね。
The air around here is dirty, isn't it?

よさん 予算 *budget, estimate of expenditures*

予算を立てる to prepare a budget
母は旅行の予算を立てました。
My mother prepared a budget for the trip.

よし *All right, OK (an interjection expressing resolve, agreement, or solace)*

よしゅう 予習 *preparing what is to be learned, studying beforehand* [↔ 復習]

予習する to prepare, to study beforehand
あしたの予習をしましょう。
Let's prepare for tomorrow's lesson. (Literally: Let's do tomorrow's preparation.)

よす 止す [[→ 止める]] *1. to stop (doing)*

そんなことはよしなさい。
Stop doing that kind of thing.

2. to give up, to stop indulging in
父は酒をよしました。
My father gave up liquor.

3. to give up on, to abandon (a planned activity)
きょうの登山はよします。
We will abandon today's mountain climb.

よせる 寄せる [[→ 近付ける1.]] *to bring near, to put close; to let come near, to let approach*

生徒たちは机を窓ぎわに寄せました。
The students put their desks close to the windows.
Aに心を寄せる to feel for A; to take to A (A is ordinarily a person.)

よせん 予選 *preliminary (competition); primary (election)*

佐藤選手は100メートルの予選を通過した。
Sato got through the 100-meter preliminary.

よそ 余所 *another place, somewhere else*

ペンをどこかよそに忘れたに違いない。
I must have forgotten the pen somewhere else.
たばこはどこかよそで吸ってください。
Please smoke somewhere else.
よその人 stranger, outsider

よそう 予想 *expectation, anticipation, supposition*

私の予想に反して吉岡君は試験に落ちた。
Contrary to my expectations, Yoshioka failed on the examination.
予想する to expect, to anticipate
予想通り as expected

よそみ 余所見 *looking away*

よそ見する to look away

よだれ *drool*

よだれが出る drool comes out

よち 余地 *(available) room, margin, leeway* [→ 余裕]

そこにもう1台自転車を置く余地がある。
There's room to put one more bicycle there.

よっか 四日 *(see Appendix 2) 1. four days*

2. the fourth (day of a month)

よつかど 四つ角 *intersection where two roads cross at right angles*

よっつ 四つ *four (see Appendix 2)*

よって [☞ によって]

ヨット *sailboat, sailing yacht*

伯父は琵琶湖でヨットを走らせます。
My uncle sails his sailboat on Lake Biwa.
新聞記者は太平洋をヨットで横断した。
The newspaper reporter crossed the Pacific in a sailboat.
ヨットハーバー yacht harbor
ヨットレース (sailing) yacht race

よっぱらい 酔っぱらい【COL.】*drunken person*
酔っぱらい運転 drunken driving
酔っぱらい運転者 drunken driver

よっぱらう 酔っ払う 【COL. for 酔う *1.*】 *to get drunk*
広川さんはそのとき酔っぱらっていたよ。
Ms. Hirokawa was drunk then!

よっぽど【COL. for 余程】

よてい 予定 *plan(s), arrangement, schedule*
今度の日曜日は何か予定がありますか。
Do you have any plans this coming Sunday?
社長は予定を変更しました。
The company president changed his plans.
飛行機は予定より30分遅れて着きます。
The plane will arrive thirty minutes behind schedule.
予定を立てる to make plans, to make a schedule
夏休みの予定はもう立てましたか。
Have you already made plans for the summer vacation?
駅前に集まる予定です。
The arrangement is to gather in front of the station.
予定する to arrange, to plan, to schedule
試合は土曜日の午後に予定されています。
The match is scheduled for Saturday afternoon.
予定どおり on schedule, as planned
予定表 (written) schedule

よとう 与党 *ruling party, party in power* [↔ 野党]

よなか 夜中 *the late night hours*

よのなか 世の中 *the world, the way the world is, society* [→ 世間]
世の中は狭いものですね。
It's a small world, isn't it?
世の中が変わりました。
The world has changed.

よび 予備 *reserve, extra supply*
予備の spare, extra
予備のタイヤはないよ。
There's no spare tire!
予備知識 background knowledge, preliminary knowledge
予備校 cram school (to prepare students for college entrance examinations)
予備選挙 primary election

よびかける 呼び掛ける *1. to call out (to a person)*
校長先生が2階から私に呼びかけました。
The headmaster called out to me from the second floor.
2. to appeal for [→ 訴える1.]
大統領は国民に支持を呼びかけました。
The president appealed to the people for support.

よびだす 呼び出す *to call over, to summon over; to page*
星野さんを電話口に呼び出してください。
Please call Ms. Hoshino over to the phone.
お呼び出しいたします。鈴木様。(public address announcement)
Paging Mr. Suzuki. (Literally: I summon. Mr. Suzuki.)

よぶ 呼ぶ *1. to call, to hail*
タクシーを呼んだが止まらなかった。
I hailed the taxi but it didn't stop.
2. to call for, to summon, to send for

すぐお医者さんを呼んでください。
Please send for the doctor at once!
電話でタクシーを呼んでください。
Please telephone for a taxi.
柳沢君、加藤先生が呼んでいるよ。
Yanagisawa, Ms. Kato is calling for you!

3. to invite [→ 招待する]
宇野さんを食事に呼びました。
I invited Ms. Uno to dinner.

4. to call out, to say out loud
先生は生徒の名前を呼びました。
The teacher called out the student's name.

5. to call, to name
マサと呼んでください。
Please call me Masa.

よぶん 余分 *an excess, a surplus*
余分の extra, spare, surplus [→ 余計な2.]
いくらか余分のお金を持っていますか？
Do you have any extra money?

よほう 予報 *forecast*
天気予報 weather forecast

よぼう 予防 *prevention*
かぜの予防にビタミンCをとりなさい。
Take vitamin C for prevention of colds.
予防する to prevent
予防注射 preventive injection, inoculation
火災予防週間 Fire Prevention Week

よほど 余程 *1. very, extremely* [→ 非常に]
あの歌手はよほど金持ちに違いない。
That singer must be very rich.

2. by far, much [→ ずっと3.]
この部屋のほうがよほど涼しいですね。
This room is much cooler, isn't it?

よみかた 読み方 *1. way of reading*

2. reading, pronunciation (of a Chinese character)

よむ 読む *to read*
時々ベッドで本を読みます。
I sometimes read a book in bed.
兄は漫画の本を読んでいます。
My older brother is reading a comic book.
声を出して読んでください。
Please read aloud.
妹は子供たちに本を読んでいます。
My younger sister is reading a book to the children.
イギリスの小説を読んだことがありますか。
Have you ever read an English novel?

よめ 嫁 *1. bride* [→ 花嫁]*; wife* [→ 妻]

2. daughter-in-law [↔ 婿]
お嫁さん【HON. for (above)】

よやく 予約 *1. reservation (at a hotel, restaurant, etc.)*
京都のホテルの予約をしましたか。
Did you make reservations at the hotel in Kyoto?
予約を受け付ける to take a reservation
予約を取り消す to cancel a reservation
予約する to reserve
会議にその部屋を予約しました。
I reserved that room for the meeting.

2. subscription (to a magazine, newspaper, etc.)
予約する to subscribe to
3. appointment (with a doctor, dentist, etc.)
お医者さんに電話して、午後4時の予約をとりました。
I phoned the doctor and got a 4:00 PM. appointment.
予約席 reserved seat

よゆう 余裕 *(available) room, margin, leeway* [→ 余地]
車に私が乗る余裕がありますか。
Is there room for me in the car?
時間の余裕がありますか。
Is there any leeway in the time?

買う余裕 leeway to buy, ability to afford
新車を買う余裕はないよ。
I can't afford to buy a new car!

より *1. than (This word is used in comparisons and can follow either a noun or a verb.)*
父は母より年下です。
My father is younger than my mother.
この本はあの本よりおもしろいよ。
This book is more interesting than that one!
英語より数学が好きです。
I like mathematics better than English.
小説は読むより書くほうが楽しいよ。
Writing novels is more fun than reading them! (Literally: As for novels, writing is more enjoyable than reading!)

2. 【FORMAL for から*1.*】*from, out of, off of (noun-following particle)*

3. 【FORMAL for から*2.*】*from, since, (beginning)at, (beginning)on (noun-following particle)*

よりかかる 寄り掛かる *to lean (for support) (intransitive)*
探偵は木に寄りかかっていました。
The detective was leaning against the tree.
手すりに寄りかからないでください。
Please don't lean on the handrail.

よりどり 選り取り *choosing and taking what one likes*
「選り取り1000円」(on a sign in a store)
Your choice, ¥1,000

よりみち 寄り道 *stopping off on the way*
寄り道する to stop off on the way
寄り道しないでまっすぐ帰りなさい。
Come straight home without stopping off on the way.

よる 夜 *night, nighttime* [→ 晩] [↔ 昼2.]
夜遅くまで勉強していました。
I was studying until late at night.
兄は金曜の夜に飛行機でパリに向かった。
My older brother will go to Paris by plane on Friday night.
きのうの夜は10時に寝ました。
Last night I went to bed at 10:00.
夜８時までに戻りなさい。
Come back by 8:00 PM.
夜ご飯 evening meal, dinner, supper [→ 夕食]

よる 因る, 拠る *1. to be due, to be caused*
事故は運転手の不注意によるものでした。
The accident was due to the driver's carelessness.

2. to be based [→ 基づく]
この計画は課長の考えによるものです。
This plan is based on the section chief's idea.
Aによると according to A
きょうの新聞によると、名古屋で大火があったそうです。
According to today's paper, there was a big fire in Nagoya.
Aによれば according to A

3. to depend, to be contingent
試合が行われるかどうかは天候による。
Whether the game will be played or not depends on the weather.

よる 寄る *1. to get near, to approach close* [→ 近付く]
もっと火に寄りなさい。
Get nearer to the fire.

2. to drop in, to stop by [→ 立ち寄る]
きょう帰りにあの店へ寄るよ。
I'll stop by at that store today on my way home!

3. to gather, to get together (intransitive) (The subject must be animate.)

よろい 鎧 *armor*

よろこばせる 喜ばせる *to please, to make happy (This word is the regular causative form of* 喜ぶ*.)*

その赤ちゃんを喜ばせるのは簡単です。
Pleasing that baby is easy.

よろこび 喜び *joy, pleasure, delight*
ご両親は喜びでいっぱいでした。
The parents were filled with joy.
音楽を聴くことが姉の何よりの喜びです。
Listening to music is my older sister's greatest pleasure.

よろこぶ 喜ぶ *to become glad, to become pleased; to become glad about, to become pleased at*
恵子も雄二の成功をとても喜んでいます。
Keiko is also very pleased with Yuji's success.
喜美はその知らせを聞いて喜んだよ。
Kimi heard that news and was glad!
喜んで with pleasure, gladly
(This form is the gerund (-て form) of 喜ぶ, and it has the predictable range of meanings as well.)
喜んで教えてあげるよ。
I'll gladly teach you!

よろしい 宜しい 【FORMAL for いい*2.*】 *all right, very well*
よろしい、もう一度見ましょう。
Very well, I will look one more time.
これでよろしいですか。
Is this all right?

よろしく 宜しく *(This word is the regular adverbial form of* 宜しい *and has the predictable range of meanings as well.) 1.* ～お願いします *I humbly beg you, I ask you kindly*
(This statement is a polite way of asking for a favor when it is clear what that favor is. When addressed to a person one has just met, the favor is understood to be something like **treating me well in the future**. The statement is often preceded by どうぞ, and it is frequently abbreviated by omitting お願いします.)
始めまして。鈴木です。どうぞよろしく。
How do you do? I'm Suzuki. Glad to meet you.
2. ～伝えてください *Please say hello, Please give my best*
(This request is frequently abbreviated by omitting 伝えて下さい*.)*
洋子さんによろしく伝えてください。
Please say hello to Yoko.

よろん 世論 *public opinion* [→ 世論]
世論調査 public opinion poll

よわい 弱い *weak* [↔ 強い]
この子は生まれつき体が弱いのです。
This child is weak by nature. (Literally: As for this child, the body is weak by nature.)
Aに弱い weak in A, bad at A; easily affected adversely by A
僕は数学に弱い。
I'm weak in math.
うちの娘は乗り物に弱いのが悩みです。
The fact our daughter gets motion sickness in vehicles is a worry. (Literally: The fact that our daughter is easily affected adversely by vehicles is a worry.)
気が弱い to be timid
意志が弱い to be weak-willed

よわまる 弱まる *to become weaker* [↔ 強まる]

よわみ 弱み *weakness, weak point* [→ 弱点]
親分は決して弱みを見せないよ。
The boss never shows his weaknesses!

よわむし 弱虫 【COL.】 *coward*

よわめる 弱める *to make weaker* [↔ 強める]

よわる 弱る *1. to lose vigor, to get weaker*
重病の父は日増しに弱っています。
My critically-ill father is getting weaker day by day.

2. to get into difficulty, to get into a quandary, to become troubled [→ 困る]

よん 四 *four* [→ 四] *(see Appendix 2)*

ら

ラーメン *Chinese noodles (ordinarily served in broth)*

らいう 雷雨 *thunderstorm*

きのうは雷雨がありました。
Yesterday there was a thunderstorm.

ライオン *lion*

らいげつ 来月 *next month*

トムさんは来月の六日に帰ります。
Tom will go home on the sixth of next month.

来月京都に行きます。
I'm going to Kyoto next month.

らいしゅう 来週 *next week*

来週の金曜日に神戸に行きます。
I'm going to Kobe on next Friday.

兄は来週ロンドンにいるでしょう。
My older brother will probably be in London next week.

来週のきょう a week from today

ライセンス [[→ 免許]] *1. licensing, official permission*

2. license, permit

ライター *(cigarette) lighter*

父はライターでたばこに火をつけました。
My father lit the cigarette with a lighter.

ライター *(professional) writer* [→ 作家]

シナリオライター scenarist

らいちょう 雷鳥 *ptarmigan ((bird))*

ライト *lights, lighting, illumination* [→ 照明]

ライトをつける〔消す〕to turn on〔off〕the lights

ライト *1. right field* [→ 右翼2.]

2. right fielder [→ 右翼手 (s.v. 右翼)] *(in baseball)*

ライトバン *(US) station wagon; (UK) estate car*

ライナー *line drive, liner (in baseball)*

田辺選手はサードへライナーを打った。
Tanabe hit a liner to third.

らいにち 来日 *coming to Japan (on a visit)*

来日する to come to Japan

らいねん 来年 *next year*

その歌手は来年日本に来ます。
That singer will come to Japan next year.

父は来年の3月に中国から帰国します。
My father will come home from China next March.

ライバル *a rival*

工藤君と僕はスケートのいいライバルだ。
Kudo and I are friendly rivals in skating.

ライブラリー *library* [→ 図書館 (s.v. 図書)]

ライフル *rifle*

ライフル銃 [☞ ライフル (above)]

ライフワーク *one's lifework*

ライン *1. line (mark on a surface)* [→ 線1.]

2. (transportation) line, route [→ 線2.]

3. row, (US) line, (UK) queue (i.e., entities arranged in a row or line) [→ 列]

スタートライン starting line

ラウンド *1. round (in boxing)*

ーラウンド (counter for rounds; see Appendix 2)

2. round (of golf)

らく 楽 〜な *1. easy, simple* [→ 易しい]

それは楽な仕事です。
That is easy work.

きょうの宿題は楽にできたよ。
I was able to do today's homework easily!

2. comfortable, easy, at ease [→ 安楽な]

どうぞお楽になさってください。
Please make yourself comfortable.
気を楽に持つ to take it easy

らくえん 楽園 *paradise*

らくがき 落書き *graffiti, prank scribbling*
落書きする to write graffiti, to do scribbling as a prank
黒板に落書きしないで。
Don't scribble on the blackboard.
「落書き禁止」 (on a sign)
No Graffiti

らくご 落語 *traditional Japanese comic storytelling*
落語家 comic storyteller

らくだ 駱駝 *camel*

らくだい 落第 *1. failure (on an test)*
落第する to fail
石原君はその試験に落第したよ。
Ishihara failed on that test!
2. being held back, failure to be promoted (to the next grade in school)
落第する to be held back
落第生 student who has been held back
落第点 failing score, failing grade
兄は２科目で落第点を取ったよ。
My older brother got failing grades in two subjects!

らくてん 楽天 *optimism* [→ 楽観] [↔ 悲観]
楽天家 optimist
楽天的な optimistic

ラグビー *rugby*

ラケット *racket (for tennis, badminton, etc.); paddle (for Ping-pong)*

らしい *(This word follows a predicate and functions grammatically as an adjective. The word preceding cannot be the copula form だ. Where だ would be the appropriate predicate, らしい follows a noun or adjectival noun directly.)*
1. it seems that, it appears as if [→ ような1.]
金田さんは勉強にあきたらしい。
It seems that Ms. Kaneda has gotten tired of studying.
坂本さんはどうも病気らしい。
It really appears that Ms. Sakamoto is ill.
2. I hear that, people say that [→ そうだ]
太郎さんはアメリカへ行くらしいよ。
I hear Taro will go to the United States!

—らしい *appropriate for, typical of, in accord with the true character of (Added to noun bases.)*
きょうは春らしい天気ですね。
Today's weather is typical of spring, isn't it?
うそをつくのは君らしくないよ。
Telling lies isn't like you!

ラジウム *radium*

ラジエーター *radiator*

ラジオ *1. radio (broadcasting) (providing programs to the general public)*
2. radio (receiver) (for listening to programs broadcast to the general public)
母はラジオをよく聴きます。
My mother often listens to the radio.
大橋さんはラジオで音楽を聴いています。
Ms. Ohashi is listening to music on the radio.
ラジオの音を小さくしてください。
Please turn down the sound on the radio.
ラジオ番組 radio program
ラジオ放送 radio broadcasting, radio broadcast
ラジオ体操 radio calisthenics

ラストシーン *last scene*

ラストスパート *last spurt*
マラソン選手はラストスパートをかけた。
The marathon runner made her last spurt.

らっかん 楽観 *optimism* [→ 楽天] [↔ 悲観]
楽観する to be optimistic

楽観的な optimistic

ラッキー ～な *lucky* [→ 幸運な]

ラッキーセブン the lucky seventh (inning)

ラッコ *sea otter*

ラッシュアワー *rush hour*

兄は朝のラッシュアワーを避けて、6時半にうちを出ます。
My older brother leaves home at 6:30 to avoid the morning rush hour.

らっぱ 喇叭 *bugle*

ラテン－ *Latin- (Added to noun bases.)*

ラテンアメリカ Latin America

ラテン語 the Latin language

ラテン音楽 Latin music

ラブレター *love letter*

ラベル *label* [→ レッテル]

その箱に赤いラベルをはりました。
I put a red label on the box.

らん 欄 *column (in a newspaper, etc.)*

スポーツ欄 sports column

らん 蘭 *orchid*

ランキング *ranking, standing (usually in sports)*

ランク *rank* [→ 順位]

ランクする to rank

あの人は新人歌手の中で第1位にランクされています。
That person is ranked first among the new singers.

らんし 乱視 *(eye) astigmatism*

ランチ *lunch* [→ 昼食]

ランチタイム lunchtime

お子様ランチ special restaurant lunch for children

ランデブー *1. date (with a person)* [→ デート]

2. (spacecraft) rendezvous

ランドセル *knapsack*

(This word refers specifically to a sturdy leather knapsack used by Japanese elementary-school children to carry books and supplies to and from school.)

ランドリー *laundry, cleaner's (shop)* [→ クリーニング屋 (s.v. クリーニング)]

コインランドリー laundromat

ランナー *runner* [→ 走者]

長距離ランナー long-distance runner

短距離ランナーsprinter

ランニング *running (in competition or for exercise)*

ランニングする to run

ランニングホーマー inside-the-park home run (in baseball)

ランニングシャツ sleeveless T-shirt

ランプ *lamp, lantern (usually of the type that uses oil or batteries)*

らんぼう 乱暴 *violence, roughness; unruliness; rudeness*

乱暴はよしたほうがいいよ。
It's better to not to use violence!

乱暴な violent, rough; unruly; rude

あの人はレコードを乱暴に扱います。
That person handles records roughly.

乱暴する to use violence; to behave wildly; to behave rudely

り

リーグ *(sports) league*

リーグ戦 league game, league match

パシフィック・リーグ the Pacific League (in Japanese professional baseball)

セントラル・リーグ the Central League (in Japanese professional baseball)

リーダー *leader* [→ 指導者 (s.v. 指導)]

リード *1. lead (in a competition)*

リードする to take the lead

僕たちのチームは2点リードしています。
Our team is leading by two points.

2. leading the way, guiding along

林さんのリードで無事に着きました。
With Mr. Hayashi leading the way, we arrived safely.

リードする to lead on the way, to guide along

りえき 利益 *profit, gain*

りか 理科 *(the study of) science*

りかい 理解 *understanding, comprehension*

Aに理解がある to have an understanding of A; to have an appreciation of A; to be understanding toward A, to be sympathetic to A

知事は文化交流に理解がある人物です。
The governor is a figure who has an understanding of cultural exchange.

理解する to understand, to comprehend

この文章を理解しましたか。
Did you understand this text?.

委員長の言う事が理解できますか。
Can you understand what the committee chairperson is saying?

りく 陸 *(dry) land* [↔ 海]

船はだんだん陸に近づきました。
The ship gradually approached the land.

リクエスト *request* [→ 要求]

リクエストする to request

FM局に大好きな曲をリクエストした。
I requested on FM station to play my favorite song.

リクエスト番組 request program

リクエスト曲 requested song, request

歌手は私のリクエスト曲を歌いました。
The singer sang my requests.

りくぐん 陸軍 *army*

りくじょうきょうぎ 陸上競技 *track and field events*

りくつ 理屈 *logic, reasoning* [→ 道理]

Aに理屈を言う to reason with A

理屈に合う to be reasonable, to make sense

堤さんが言うことは理屈に合っています。
What Mr. Tsutsumi says is reasonable.

りこう 利口 ～な *clever, bright, smart* [→ 賢い]

小田君は利口な青年ですね。
Oda is a clever young man, isn't he.

バスで行くのが利口だと思うよ。
I think going by bus is smart!

りこん 離婚 *divorce*

離婚する to get divorced

リサイタル *(musical) recital*

姉は先月、初めてのリサイタルを開いた。
My older sister gave her first recital last month.

りし 利子 *interest (paid on borrowed money)*

この預金は5パーセントの利子がつく。
This deposit gets 5% interest.

りじ 理事 *director, trustee*

理事会 board of directors, board of trustees

りす 栗鼠 *squirrel*

リスト *list* [→ 一覧表]

この名はリストに載っていますか。
Is this name on the list?

リズム *rhythm* [→ 拍子1.]

私たちは太鼓のリズムに合わせて踊った。
We danced to the rhythm of the drums.

りせい 理性 *reasoning ability, rationality*

理性的な rational

りそう 理想 *an ideal*

洋子さんは理想を実現しました。
Yoko realized her ideal.

理想主義 idealism

理想主義者 idealist

理想的な ideal

江崎先生は理想的な先生です。
Ms. Ezaki is an ideal teacher.

ここはキャンプには理想的な場所です。
This is an ideal place for camping.

リゾート *(vacation) resort*

りつ 率 *rate, proportion, percentage*

試験に合格する率はいつも7割ぐらいだ。
The passing rate of the examination is always about 70%. (Literally: The rate of passing on the examination is always about 70%.)

打率 batting average
犯罪率 crime rate
投票率 voting rate
割引率 discount rate

りっこうほ 立候補 *candidacy*

立候補する to become a candidate, to run

うちの宏は生徒会長に立候補しました。
Our Hiroshi ran for student council president.

立候補者 candidate

りったい 立体 *(geometrical) solid, three-dimensional figure*

立体交差 two-level road intersection

リットル *liter*

ーリットル (counter for liters; see Appendix 2)

りっぱ 立派 ～な *fine, excellent, praiseworthy*

内田さんは立派な家に住んでいます。
Ms. Uchida lives in a fine house.

お兄さんは立派な医者になりました。
Her older brother became a fine doctor.

明は数学で立派な成績を収めました。
Akira got excellent grades in math.

田崎さんは立派に仕事を成し遂げました。
Mr. Tazaki accomplished the task very well.

りっぽう 立方 *cube (of a number)*

立方根 cube root
立方メートル cubic meter

りっぽうたい 立方体 *cube ((geometrical figure))*

リハーサル *rehearsal*

その劇のリハーサルはあしたから始まる。
The rehearsals for that play will begin tomorrow.

リハーサルをする to rehearse

リバイバル *revival (of an old movie, play, etc.)*

リバイバル映画 revival film

りはつ 理髪 *haircutting, barbering*

理髪店 barber shop [→ 床屋]

リハビリ [☞ リハビリテーション]

リハビリテーション *rehabilitation*

リフト *ski lift*

リベート *1. rebate*

2. commission (payment); kickback

リポート *(written) report* [→レポート1., 報告書 (s.v. 報告)]

リボン *ribbon*

リモートコントロール [☞ リモコン]

リモコン *remote control*

りゃく 略 [[→ 省略]] *1. abbreviation; abridgement*

2. omission, leaving out

りゃくす 略す *1. to abbreviate; to abridge*

2. to omit, to leave out

後は略して結構です。
You may omit the rest.

りゆう 理由 *reason, grounds*

失敗の理由はわかりません。
I don't understand the reason for the failure.

病気が理由で山崎さんは欠席しました。

Illness was the reason why Mr. Yamazaki was absent.

りゅう 竜 *dragon*

りゅうがく 留学 *study abroad*

僕たちの英語の先生は留学の経験がある。
Our English teacher has overseas study experience.

留学する to study abroad; to go abroad to study

去年、千香子はイギリスに留学しました。
Last year, Chikako went to England to study English.

留学生 student studying abroad; foreign student (in Japan)

りゅうきゅうしょとう 琉球諸島 *the Ryukyu Islands*

りゅうこう 流行 [[→ はやり]] *1. fashion, vogue, popular trend, popularity*

流行する to come into fashion, to become popular [→ はやる]

そのヘアスタイルが今流行しています。
That hairstyle is in fashion now.

このスタイルが今年は流行するでしょう。
This style will probably come into fashion this year.

2. going around, prevalence (of a disease)

流行する to go around, to become prevalent, to become widespread

今インフルエンザが流行しています。
The flu is going around now.

流行病 epidemic disease

流行歌 popular song

流行遅れの out of fashion

大流行 great popularity

最新流行 the latest fashion

りゅうざん 流産 *miscarriage*

流産する to have a miscarriage

りゅうせい 流星 *shooting star* [→ 流れ星 (s.v. 流れ)]

りゅうちょう 流暢 〜な *fluent*

エリックさんは流暢に日本語を話します。
Eric speaks Japanese fluently.

りゅうつう 流通 *circulation, flow; distribution (of products)*

流通する to circulate, to flow; to be distributed

りゅうは 流派 *school, body of followers (of a traditional art form)*

リューマチ *rheumatism*

リュックサック *rucksack, knapsack*

りよう 利用 *use, utilization*

利用する to use, to make use of

今後は太陽熱を大いに利用します。
From now on we will make use of solar heat a great deal.

利用者 user

りょう 猟 *hunting* [→ 狩, 狩猟]

猟犬 hunting dog

猟師 hunter

りょう 量 *quantity, amount* [↔ 質]

長雨で湖の水の量がだいぶ増えました。
The quantity of water in the lake greatly increased from the long rain.

量的な quantitative

りょう 寮 *dormitory*

寮生 student living in a dormitory

りょう 漁 *(large-scale) fishing*

漁をする to fish

漁師 fisherman

大漁 a big catch

りょうかい 了解 *(considered) consent* [→ 承諾]

了解する to consent to

藤本君もついにその計画を了解した。
Fujimoto also finally consented to that plan.

了解！ (typically part of a conversation

by two-way radio, etc.)
OK!, Roger!

りょうがえ 両替 *1. changing (money from large denominations to small)*
両替する to change [→ 崩す2.]
千円札を百円玉に両替してくれますか。
Will you change a ¥1000 bill into ¥100 coins for me?
2. (foreign) exchange [→ 外国為替 (s.v. 為替)]
両替する to change
アメリカに行く人は円をドルに両替する。
People going to the United States change yen into dollars.

りょうがわ 両側 *both sides (i.e., the area to the right and to the left)*
道路の両側に並木があります。
There are rows of trees on both sides of the road.

りょうきん 料金 *charge, fee, fare, toll*
兄はホテルの料金を支払いました。
My older brother paid the hotel charges.
料金は１時間いくらですか。
What is the charge for one hour?
料金表 price list
料金所 tollgate
バス料金bus fare
駐車料金 parking fee
入場料金 admission fee

りょうじかん 領事館 *consulate* [→ 総領事館 (s.v. 総領事)]

りょうしゅうしょ 領収書 *(written) receipt*

りょうしん 両親 *(both) parents* [→ 親]

りょうしん 良心 *conscience*
良心に恥じない行動をすることが大切だ。
It's important to act according to one's conscience. (Literally: Acting so not to be ashamed in one's conscience is important.)
良心がとがめる one's conscience troubles one
良心的な conscientious

りょうど 領土 *territory (under a country's jurisdiction)*

りょうほう 両方 *both; neither (in combination with a negative predicate)*
父は英語もフランス語も両方とも話せる。
My father can speak both English and French.
私の母はピアノもギターも両方弾けない。
My mother can play neither the piano nor the guitar.

りょうめん 両面 *both sides, front and back*
両面コピー two-sided copy

りょうり 料理 *1. cooking, preparing food*
姉は料理が好きです。
My older sister likes cooking.
父は料理が下手です。
My father is poor at cooking.
料理する to cook
2. cuisine, dish(es)
いちばん好きな料理は何ですか
What is your favorite dish?
おいしい料理 delicious dish, delicious cuisine
あっさりした料理 simple cuisine
料理番組 cooking program
中国料理 Chinese cuisine, Chinese dishes
フランス料理French cuisine, French dishes

りょうりつ 両立 ～する *to be compatible; to be combined harmoniously*
兵器産業と世界平和は両立しません。
The armaments industry and world peace are not compatible.
両立させる to combine harmoniously, to do both well
勇は勉強とアルバイトを両立させている。
Isamu is doing both his studies and a part-time job well.

りょかん 旅館 *inn*

りょこう 旅行 *travel; trip, journey, tour*

沖縄への旅行はどうだった？
How was your trip to Okinawa?
旅行する to take a trip; to travel
旅行に行く to go on a trip
旅行案内 travel information; guidebook
旅行会社 travel agency
旅行者 traveler
団体旅行 group tour
海外旅行 traveling abroad
パック旅行 package tour
世界一周旅行 around the world trip
新婚旅行 honeymoon
修学旅行 school excursion
宇宙旅行 space travel

リラックス ～する *to relax*

尾形さんはとてもリラックスしているように見えました。
Ms. Ogata looked as if she were very relaxed.

リリーフ *relief (pitching) (in baseball)*

リリーフする to relieve
鈴木は8回に田中をリリーフしました。
Suzuki relieved Tanaka in the eighth inning.

りりく 離陸 *take-off (of an airplane, etc.)* [↔ 着陸]

離陸する to take off
父の乗った飛行機は10時に離陸した。
The plane my father was on took off at 10:00.

リレー *relay (race)*

800メートルリレー 800-meter relay
メドレーリレー medley relay

りれきしょ 履歴書 *resume, curriculum vitae*

りろん 理論 *theory*

理論と実践 theory and practice
理論家 theorist, theoretician
理論的な theoretical

―りん ―輪 *(counter for flowers; see Appendix 2)*

りんかいがっこう 臨海学校 *seaside summer-school*

りんかく 輪郭 *outline*

りんかんがっこう 林間学校 *open-air summer-school*

りんぎょう 林業 *forestry*

リング *1. (finger) ring* [→ 指輪]
2. ring (for boxing, wrestling, etc.)

チャンピオンがリングに上がりました。
The champion entered the ring.
エンゲージリング engagement ring

りんご *apple*

このりんごは酸っぱくて食べられないよ。
This apple is so sour I can't eat it!
林檎ジャム apple jam

りんじ 臨時 ～の *special, added out of unanticipated necessity*

臨時国会 special session of the Diet
臨時ニュース special newscast
臨時列車 special train

リンパせん リンパ腺 *lymph gland*

りんり 倫理 *ethics*

るい 塁 *base (in baseball)*

本塁 home (base)
一塁 first base
二塁 second base

三塁 third base

るい 類 *kind, sort, class* [→ 種類]

類は友を呼ぶ。(proverb)
Birds of a feather flock together. (Literally: A class invites its friends.)

るいじ 類似 *resemblance*

類似する to become similar [→ 似る]

アメリカンフットボールはラグビーに類似しています。
American football is similar to rugby.

類似品 an imitation; similar item

類似点 point of similarity

ルーキー *rookie*

ルーズ ～な *careless, inattentive, sloppy, lax* [→ だらしない]

母は時間にルーズです。
My mother is lax about time.

福井さんはお金にルーズです。
Mr. Fukui is careless about money.

ルーズリーフ *loose-leaf notebook*

ルーツ *ancestry, roots*

ルート *route; channel*

僕たちは別のルートで山頂に達しました。
We reached the summit by another route.

社長はアジアでの販売ルートを開拓した。
The company president developed a sales route in Asia.

ルート *(mathematical) root (Ordinarily understood to mean square root unless otherwise specified.)*

ルート9は3です。
The square root of nine is three. (Although odd grammatically, this kind of sentence is a typical way of stating a fact of arithmetic.)

ルーム *a room* [→ 部屋]

ルームクーラー room air conditioner

ルームサービス room service

ルール *rule, regulation* [→ 規則]

ルールを守らなければなりません。
One must obey the rules.

るす 留守 *being out, being away (i.e., not at home or not at one's workplace)*

姉は今留守です。
My older sister is out now.

うちを留守にする to go away from home

Aの留守に来る to come while A is out

高野さんは課長の留守に来ました。
Mr. Takano came while the section chief was out.

るすばん 留守番 *1. taking care of a house (while others are away)*

留守番をする to take care of a house

2. person taking care of a house (while others are away)

留守番電話 telephone with an answering machine

ルビ *1. small kana printed alongside or above a Chinese character to show its pronunciation* [→ 振り仮名]

2. the small-size type used to print such small kana

ルビー *ruby*

ルポ [☞ ルポルタージュ]

ルポライター on-the-scene reporter

ルポルタージュ *on-the-scene reporting; on-the scene report*

れい 礼 *1. bow (of respect)* [→ お辞儀]

起立！礼！
Stand up! Bow! (Typically used as instructions to a group by a person in charge, especially at schools to a body of students.)

礼をする to bow

2. (expression of) thanks; token of gratitude, reward

お礼の言葉もありません。
I don't know how to thank you. (Literally: I don't have even words of thanks.)
お礼には及びません。
It's not necessary to thank me.
手伝ったお礼に2000円もらったよ。
I got two ¥2,000 as a reward for having helped!
礼状 thank-you letter

れい 例 *1. example, instance*
例をあげる to give an example
2. habit, custom, usual practice
例の the usual, the customary; the much-talked-about
例のレストランでお昼を食べましょう。
Let's eat lunch at the usual restaurant.
例によって as usual, as always
坂田君は例によって遅刻しました。
Sakata was late as usual.
例文 example sentence

れい 零 *zero* [→ゼロ]
その試験で0点だったよ。
I got zero on that exam! (Literally: On that exam I was zero!)
5対0で私たちのチームが試合に勝った。
Our team won the game five to zero.

レイアウト *layout (on a printed page, etc.)*
レイアウトする to lay out

れいか 零下 *(the temperature range) below zero* [→氷点下 (s.v. 氷点)]
けさは零下2度だったよ。
It was two degrees below zero this morning!
零下の気温 sub-zero temperature

れいがい 例外 *exception, unusual case*
この規則にはいくつかの例外があります。
There are several exceptions to this rule.

れいぎ 礼儀 *etiquette, manners* [→作法]
そうするのが礼儀です。
It is etiquette to do so.
あの子は礼儀を知らないね。
That child doesn't know her manners, does she.
礼儀正しい polite, well-mannered [↔無礼な]
戸田さんは礼儀正しい人です。
Ms. Toda is a well-mannered woman.

れいきん 礼金 *money given as an expression of gratitude*

れいせい 冷静 ～な *calm, cool, composed*
興奮しないで、冷静に考えてください。
Don't get excited; think about it calmly.

れいぞうこ 冷蔵庫 *refrigerator*

れいだい 例題 *example problem, exercise* [→練習問題 (s.v. 練習)]

れいたん 冷淡 ～な *cold (-hearted), unfriendly* [→冷たい2.]
野崎さんは私に冷淡です。
Mr. Nozaki is cold to me.

れいとう 冷凍 ～する *to freeze (in order to preserve)*
この肉は冷凍しましょう。
Let's freeze this meat.
冷凍庫 freezer
冷凍食品 frozen food

れいはい 礼拝 *worship (of a deity); worship service*
あしたの礼拝に出ます。
I will attend tomorrow's worship service.
江崎さんたちは教会へ礼拝に行きます。
Mr. Ezaki and the others will go to church to worship.
礼拝する to worship
礼拝堂 chapel

れいぼう 冷房 *air conditioning* [↔暖房]
「冷房完備」 (on a sign)
Air-conditioned

冷房車 air-conditioned (train) car
冷房装置 air conditioner [→ エアコン]

レインコート *raincoat*

レーサー *racing driver*

レーザー *laser*
レーザーディスク laser disk
レーザー光線 laser beam

レース *lace*
レースの手袋 lace gloves
レース編み lacework

レース *race*
太郎はそのレースに勝つだろう。
Taro will probably win that race.
ヨットレース sailboat race

レーダー *radar*

レール *(metal) rail*
レールを敷く to lay rails
カーテンレール curtain rail

れきし 歴史 *history*
私たちの学校は40年の歴史があります。
Our school has a history of forty years.
日本の歴史 the history of Japan
歴史家 historian
歴史的な historic
これは歴史的に有名な建物です。
This is a historically famous building.

レギュラー *1. regular (player)* [↔ 補欠選手 (s.v. 補欠2.)]
2. regular (on a radio or TV program)

レクリエーション *recreation, recreational activity*
レクリエーションにハイキングに行った。
We went hiking for recreation.

レコード *1. (phonograph) record*
そのレコードをかけてください。
Please play that record.
2. (world) record [→ 記録2.]
レコードプレーヤー record player
レコード店 record shop
ＬＰレコード an LP

レジ *1. cash register*
2. checkout counter
レジで払ってください。
Please pay at the checkout counter.
3. [☞ レジ係 *(below)*]
レジ係 (register) cashier

レシート *(written) receipt* [→ 領収書]

レシーバー *receiver (i.e., the part of a telephone or other device held to the ear to hear a transmission)* [→ 受話器]

レシーバー *person who receives serve (in tennis, volleyball, etc.)*

レシーブ *receiving serve (in tennis, volleyball, etc.)*
レシーブする to receive serve

レジャー *1. leisure time* [→ 余暇]
2. leisure-time activity

レストラン *restaurant*
ここはパスタで有名なレストランです。
This is a restaurant famous for pasta.

レスリング *wrestling*

れつ 列 *row, (US) line, (UK) queue (i.e., entities arranged in a row or line)*
明美ちゃんは４番目の列にいます。
Akemi is in the fourth row.
列に割り込む to cut in line
列を作る to form a line [→ 並ぶ]
切符を買うために列を作って待っていた。
We formed and waited in a line in order to buy tickets.

れっしゃ 列車 *(railroad) train*
原田さんは列車に乗り遅れました。
Mr. Harada missed the train.
恵子さんは列車に間に合いました。
Keiko was in time for the train.
午後５時半の列車で行きましょう。

Let's go on the 5:30 PM train.
列車時刻表 train timetable
普通列車 local train
急行列車 express train
特急列車 limited express train

レッスン *lesson, instruction*
恵子さんは英語のレッスンを受けている。
Keiko is taking English lessons.

レッテル *label*
レッテルをはる to affix a label

れっとう 列島 *island chain, archipelago*
日本列島 the Japanese Islands, the Japanese Archipelago

れっとうかん 劣等感 *inferiority complex* [↔ 優越感]

レバー *lever* [→ 挺子]

レバー *liver ((food))*

レパートリー *repertory, repertoire*
このピアニストはレパートリーが広い。
That pianist's repertory is wide.

レフェリー *referee*

レフト *1. left field* [→ 左翼2.] *(in baseball)*
2. left fielder [→ 左翼手 (s.v. 左翼)]

レベル *level, degree* [→ 水準]
その国の文化のレベルは高いらしい。
The level of culture in that country seems to be high.

レポート *1. (written) report* [→ リポート, 報告書 (s.v. 報告)]
2. (school) report, (term) paper
レポートを提出しましたか。
Did you hand in your paper?

レモン *lemon*
レモンスカッシュ lemon squash (an iced drink consisting of lemon juice mixed with soda water)
レモンティー tea with a slice of lemon

れんあい 恋愛 *love, romantic attachment, being in love* [→ 愛, 恋]
真知子との恋愛はいつまでも続きそうだ。
It looks as if his romance with Machiko will continue forever, doesn't it.
恋愛結婚 love marriage [↔ 見合い結婚 (s.v. 見合い)]
恋愛小説 love story

れんが 煉瓦 *brick*
煉瓦造りの built of bricks

れんきゅう 連休 *two or more holidays in succession*

れんこう 連行 ～する *to transport under custody (The direct object is ordinarily a criminal, prisoner, etc.)*

れんごう 連合 *alliance, coalition*
連合する to form an alliance
連合国 the Allied Powers

れんこん 蓮根 *lotus root*

れんさはんのう 連鎖反応 *chain reaction*

レンジ *(kitchen) range*
電子レンジ microwave oven
ガスレンジ gas range

れんしゅう 練習 *practice, training*
練習する to practice
妹は毎日3時間ピアノを練習します。
My younger sister practices the piano three hours every day.
練習問題 example problem, exercise [→ 例題]
練習試合 practice game

レンズ *lens*
望遠レンズ telephoto lens
標準レンズ standard lens
広角レンズ wide-angle lens
コンタクトレンズ contact lens

れんそう 連想 *association (of ideas)*
連想する to think of by association, to be

reminded of
サイレンの音を聞くと、空襲を連想します。Whenever I hear the sound of a siren, I am reminded of air raids.

れんぞく 連続 *uninterrupted continuity; succession, series*
連続するto continue uninterrupted; to happen in succession, to happen consecutively
連続して continuously; in succession, consecutively
事故が連続して起こりました。
The accidents occurred in succession.
連続テレビ番組television series

レンタカー *rent-a-car, rental car*
良男はレンタカーで湖までドライブした。
Yoshio drove to the lake in a rental car.

レンタル *renting (to others)*
レンタルスキーrental skis

れんちゅう 連中 【CRUDE】 *group of people, bunch*

レントゲン *1. x-ray (radiation)* [→ エックス線]
2. [☞ レントゲン写真(below)]
レントゲン写真x-ray (photograph)
レントゲン写真を撮る to take an x-ray

れんぽう 連邦 *federation*
連邦政府 federal government

れんめい 連盟 *league, union, federation*
日本学生野球連盟 the Students' Baseball League of Japan

れんらく 連絡 *1. contact, communication, touch*
連絡する to communicate, to let know
AにBを連絡する to communicate B to A, to let A know B
新しい住所を電話で連絡してください。
Please let me know your new address by telephone.
Aと連絡を取る to get in touch with A
洋子さんと連絡を取りましたか。
Did you get in touch with Yoko?
2. (transportation) connection [→ 接続2.]
連絡する to connect
この電車は仙台駅で特急と連絡している。
This train connects with the express at Sendai station.
3. connection, affiliation [→ 関係]
連絡船 connecting ferryboat

ろ

ロイヤルボックス *royal box*

ろう 蝋 *wax*
蝋人形 wax doll
蝋細工 waxwork, wax craft

ろうか 廊下 *hallway, corridor*

ろうがん 老眼 *presbyopia*

ろうじん 老人 *old person*
老人ホーム old people's home
老人クラブ old people's club

ろうそく 蝋燭 *candle*
ろうそくの明かりcandlelight
ろうそくをつける to light a candle
ろうそくを吹き消すto blow out a candle
蝋燭立て candlestick, candle holder

ろうどう 労働 *labor, work*
労働する to labor, to work
労働時間 working hours
労働組合 (US) labor union, (UK) trade union
労働者 worker, laborer
労働省 the Ministry of Labor
重労働 heavy labor

ろうどく 朗読 *reading aloud*

朗読する to read aloud

ろうにん 浪人 *1. masterless samurai*

2. person who has failed college entrance examinations and is studying to try again the following year

浪人する to study for the following year's college entrance examinations after having failed

ろうひ 浪費 *waste, wasteful use*

それは時間の浪費です。
That's a waste of time.

浪費する to waste

そんな物にお金を浪費しないで。
Don't waste your money on such a thing.

浪費家 wasteful person

ろうりょく 労力 *hard work, effort, pains* [→ 骨折り(s.v. 骨)]

あの大工さんは労力を惜しまないね。
That carpenter doesn't spare any effort, does he.

ローカル ～な *local; provincial* [→ 地方の]

ローカルニュース local news

ローカル線 local (transportation) line

ロース *sirloin; pork loin*

ロータリー *traffic circle, (UK) roundabout*

ローテーション *rotation, regularly recurring succession*

ローテーションで in rotation

ロードショー (a movie's) first run in selected theaters

ロープ *rope, cable* [→ 綱, 縄]

ロープウェー *ropeway, aerial cableway*

ローマじ ローマ字 *Roman letters, romanization*

ローラースケート *1. roller skating*

ローラースケートをする to roller-skate

2. roller skate

ローラースケート場 roller skating rink

ロールパン *(bread) roll*

ローン *(monetary) loan*

銀行ローン bank loan

住宅ローン home loan

ろく 六 *six (see Appendix 2)*

六月 June

ろくおん 録音 *audio recording*

録音する to record, to tape

そのラジオ番組を録音しました。
I taped that radio program.

録音室 recording room, studio

録音テープ magnetic tape, recording tape

ろくが 録画 *video recording*

録画する to videotape, to record

野球の試合を録画しましょう。
Let's videotape the baseball game.

ろくまくえん 肋膜炎 *pleurisy*

ロケーション *(filming) location*

ロケット *rocket*

先月ロケットを打ち上げました。
They launched a rocket last month.

月ロケット moon rocket

ロス *loss, disadvantageous outcome* [→ 損失]

ピッチャーのけがはチームにとってたいへんなロスです。
The pitcher's injury is a terrible loss to the team.

ロスする to suffer the loss of

ろせん 路線 *1. route (of a bus, train, etc.)*

2. course (of action) [→ 方針]

ロッカー *locker*

ロッカールーム locker room

コインロッカー coin-operated locker

ロック *rock (music)*

ロックンロール *rock'n'roll (music)*

ロッジ *mountain lodge*

ろば 驢馬 *donkey*

ロビー *lobby (of a building)*

ロボット *robot*

産業用ロボット industrial robot

ロマンス *romance, love affair*

ロマンチック ～な *romantic*

ろんぎ 論議 [[→ 議論]] *argument, debate; discussion*

論議する to have an argument, to have a debate; to have a discussion

ろんじる 論じる *to discuss; to debate*

私たちはその問題を論じました。
We discussed that problem.

ろんそう 論争 *verbal dispute, argument*

論争する to dispute, to argue

社長は賃金について組合幹部と論争した。
The company president argued with the union leader about wages.

ろんぶん 論文 *(scholarly) paper, essay, article; thesis, dissertation*

ろんり 論理 *logic*

論理学 (the study of) logic

論理的な logical

先生は論理的な説明をしました。
The teacher gave a logical explanation.

わ 輪 *circle, ring*

子供たちは手をつないで輪になりました。
The children joined hands and formed a circle.

わ *(This sentence-final particle is spoken with rising intonation and expresses mild exclamation. It is generally used only by female speakers, and it often occurs in combination with a following* よ *or* ね.*)*

これはできないわ。
I can't do this!

わ 和 *peace, harmony (between people)*

－わ －羽 *(counter for birds; see Appendix 2)*

わあ *(an interjection expressing surprise, hearty approval, or dismay) Oh!, Gee!, Heavens!, Gosh!; Yay!, Hurray!*

わあ、臭い！
Gosh, it's smelly!

わあ、うれしい！
Oh, I'm happy!

ワードプロセッサー *word processor*

ワープロ [☞ ワードプロセッサー]

ワイシャツ *dress shirt (the type typically worn with a suit)*

ワイドスクリーン *wide (movie) screen*

ワイパー *windshield wiper*

わいろ 賄賂 *bribe*

わいろを贈る to give a bribe

わいろを受け取る to take a bribe

ワイン *wine* [→ 葡萄酒 (s.v. 葡萄)]

ワイングラス wineglass

赤ワイン red wine

ロゼワイン rose wine

白ワイン white wine

わえいじてん 和英辞典 *Japanese-English dictionary*

わかい 若い *young* [↔ 年取った (s.v. 年)]

あの歌手は若い人たちの間に人気がある。
That singer is popular among young people.

安部さんは年の割には若く見えます。
Mr. Abe looks young for his age.

祖父は若いころジャズが好きでした。
My grandfather liked jazz when he was young.

わかさ 若さ *youth, youthfulness*

この世の中で若さに勝る物はありません。
In this world there is nothing better than

youth.

わかす 沸かす *1. to bring to a boil, to heat until boiling (The direct object must be a liquid.)*

お湯を沸かしてください。
Please boil some water.

2. to heat (a bath to the appropriate temperature)

おふろを沸かすのを忘れないで。
Don't forget to heat the bath.

わかば 若葉 *young leaves, new leaves*

わがまま *selfishness*

わがままな selfish
山川君は実にわがままだよ。
Yamakawa is really selfish!

わかめ 若布 *wakame (a kind of edible seaweed)*

わかもの 若者 *young person*

わかる 分かる *1. to understand (What is understood is treated as a grammatical subject and marked with が rather than with を.)*

日本語がわかりますか。
Do you understand Japanese?
浜田さんはこの文の意味がわかるだろう。
Ms. Hamada probably understands the meaning of this sentence.

あの人の言ってることがわかりますか。
Do you understand what that person is saying?

2. to come to know, to find out; to realize, to know (What is known or realized is treated as a grammatical subject and marked with が rather than with を.)

山田さんが辞めた理由がわかりました。
I found out the reason why Mr. Yamada resigned.

どうすればいいかわかりません。
I don't know what I should do.

分かりにくい hard to understand

この本はわかりにくいよ。
This book is hard to understand!

分かり易い easy to understand

この説明はわかりやすい。
This explanation is easy to understand.

わかれ 別れ *parting, farewell, good-by*

英子さんは友達に別れを告げました。
Eiko said good-by to her friends.

お別れパーティー farewell party

わかれめ 分かれ目 *turning point*

それが大統領の人生の分かれ目でした。
That was the turning point in the president's life.

わかれる 分かれる *to become divided; to branch*

その本は3部に分かれています。
That book is divided into three parts.

クラスの意見はこの点で分かれています。
Class opinion is divided on this point.

わかれる 別れる *1. to part, to say good-by*

駅で京子さんと別れました。
I parted from Kyoko at the station.

ここで別れましょう。
Let's say good-by here.

2. to get divorced [→ 離婚する]

わき 脇 *1. the area beside* [→ 横1.]

相手は僕のわきに立っていました。
My opponent was standing beside me.

次郎は太郎のわきに座りました。
Jiro sat down beside Taro.

2. armpit, underarm [→ 脇の下]

緑さんはラケットをわきに抱えています。
Midori is holding a racket under her arm.

わきのした 脇の下 *armpit, underarm* [→ 脇2.]

わきみ 脇見 *looking aside*

わき見をする to look aside

わきでる 湧き出る *to gush out, to spurt out, to flow out*

ここに温泉がわき出ています。

A hot spring flows out here.

わく 枠 *frame, enclosing edge*

枠組み framework

窓枠 window frame

わく 沸く *1. to come to a boil (The subject must be a liquid.)*

お湯が沸いています。
The water is boiling.

2. to become heated (to the appropriate temperature when the subject is a bath)

おふろが沸いていますよ。
The bath is heated!

わくせい 惑星 *planet*

ワクチン *vaccine*

インフルエンザのワクチン influenza vaccine

わけ 訳 *1. reason* [→ 理由]*; cause* [→ 原因]

休んだ訳を言いなさい。
Tell me the reason you stayed home.

どういう訳でそこへ行ったのですか。
Why did you go there? (Literally: For what reason did you go there?)

2. meaning, sense [→ 意味]

この英文は訳がわかりません。
I don't understand the meaning of this English sentence.

3. the case (that something is true)

忘れた訳じゃないよ。
It's not (the case) that I forgot!

4. 〜にはいかない *cannot very well (following a verb in the nonpast tense)*

途中であきらめる訳にはいかないだろう？
I can't very well give up in the middle, right?

わける 分ける *to divide (something into parts)* [→ 分割する]*; to share*

母はそのケーキを８つに分けました。
My mother divided the cake into eight pieces.

美佐子はチョコレートを順子と分けた。
Misako shared the chocolate with Junko.

わご 和語 *native Japanese word* [↔ 外来語; 漢語]

わゴム 輪ゴム *rubber band*

わざ 技 *skill, art, technique* [→ 技術]

大内さんは柔道ですばらしい技を見せた。
Mr. Ouchi showed us wonderful judo techniques.

わざ 業 *1. deed, act* [→ 行為]

2. task [→ 仕事]

わざと *on purpose*

わざとそう言ったのですか。
Did you say so on purpose?

わざとらしい forced, unnatural

俳優の笑いはわざとらしかったですね。
The actor's smile was unnatural, wasn't it?

わさび 山葵 *Japanese horseradish, wasabi*

わざわざ *to go to all the trouble of (in combination with a verb)*

伯父は神戸からわざわざ父に会いに来た。
My uncle went to all the trouble of coming from Kobe to see my father.

わし 鷲 *eagle*

わしつ 和室 *Japanese-style room* [↔ 洋室]

わしょく 和食 *Japanese cuisine* [↔ 洋食]

わずか 僅か *1. a few, a little* [→ 少し]

お金はわずかしか持っていません。
I have only a little money.
2. merely, only

駅から歩いてわずか５分です。
It's only five minutes on foot from the station.

わずかな paltry, scanty, meager, slight

わずかに覚えています。
I remember slightly.

わずかな給料 meager salary

わずかな違い slight difference

わすれっぽい 忘れっぽい *forgetful*
祖父は年を取って忘れっぽくなった。
My grandfather has grown old and become very forgetful.

わすれもの 忘れ物 *thing forgotten and left behind*
忘れ物をする to forget something and leave it behind

わすれる 忘れる *1. to forget, to cease to remember*
橋本さんの電話番号を忘れてしまった。
I forgot Mr. Hashimoto's telephone number.

あしたメモ帳を忘れないでください。
Please don't forget your notebooks tomorrow.

2. to leave behind, to forget (to take) [→ 置き忘れる]
バスの中にカメラを忘れました。
I forgot my camera in the bus.

だれかが傘を忘れていきました。
Somebody left an umbrella behind.

わた 綿 *1. cotton (plant), raw cotton*
2. cotton wadding
綿菓子 cotton candy

わだい 話題 *topic, subject*
話題を変えましょう。
Let's change the subject.

わたくし 私 【FORMAL for 私】

わたし 私 *I, me*

(There are several Japanese words for **I/me**, and this is the most commonly used in translation from English. Particularly for male speakers, it is rather formal. Other words for **I/me** include 私, あたし, 僕, and 俺.)
私は中学生です。
I am a junior-high-school student.

これは私のペンじゃないわ。
This isn't my pen!

父は私をしかったよ。
My father scolded me!

由美子さんの時計は私のよりいいね。
Yumiko's watch is better than mine, isn't it.

私たち we, us
小島先生は私たちの英語の先生です。
Ms. Kojima is our English teacher.

わたす 渡す *1. to hand, to pass* [→ 手渡す]
京子さんは先生に手紙を渡しました。
Kyoko handed the teacher a letter.

2. to ferry across

3. to place across, to position so as to span
あのおじさんが溝に板を渡してくれた。
That man put a board across the ditch for us.

わたりどり 渡り鳥 *migratory bird*

わたる 渡る *to cross, to go over, to go across*
中西さんは太平洋をヨットで渡りました。
Ms. Nakanishi crossed the Pacific in a sailboat.

ここで道路を渡りましょう。
Let's cross the road here.

Aの手に渡る to pass into A's possession

わたる 亘る *to extend, to range, to spread* [→ 及ぶ]
その研究は30年にわたりました。
That research extended over thirty years.

ワックス *wax (used to make a surface shiny and smooth)*

わっと *1. with a sudden burst of noise*
勝った人はわっと泣き出しました。
The person who won burst out crying.

2. as a throng, in a crowd
特売が始まると、客がわっと集まった。
When the sale starts, the customers will gather in a crowd.

ワット *watt*

ーワット (counter for watts; see Appendix 2)

100ワットの電球もありますか。
Do you also have a 100-watt light bulb?

わな 罠 *trap, snare*

わなにかかる to become caught in a trap

わなを仕掛ける to set a trap

すずめを捕るためにわなをしかけよう。
Let's set a trap to catch sparrows.

わに 鰐 *crocodile; alligator*

わび 詫び *apology*

わびしい 侘びしい *1. lonely, lonesome* [→ 寂しい]

2. wretched-looking [→ みすぼらしい]

わびる 詫びる *to apologize for* [→ 謝る]

わふう 和風 *Japanese style, Japanese type*

和風の家 Japanese-style house

わふく 和服 *traditional Japanese clothes* [↔ 洋服2.]

わめく 喚く *to yell, to scream* [→ 叫ぶ]

わやく 和訳 *translation into Japanese*

和訳する to translate into Japanese

この英文を和訳してください。
Please translate these English sentences into Japanese.

英文和訳 translation from English into Japanese

わら 藁 *straw (plant stem)*

藁葺き straw thatching

わらい 笑い *1. laugh, laughter*

おかしくて笑いが止りません。
It's so funny I can't stop laughing. (Literally: It's funny, and my laughter won't stop.)

2. smile [→ 微笑み]

笑いを浮かべる to wear a smile

笑い話 joke, funny story [→ 冗談]

笑い声 laughing voice

大笑い big laugh, good laugh

大笑いする to have a good laugh

わらう 笑う *1. to laugh*

委員はみんな大声で笑いました。
The committee members all laughed loudly.

くすくす笑う to chuckle

けらけら笑う to chortle

げらげら笑う to guffaw

2. to smile [→ 微笑む]

にこにこ笑う to smile beamingly, to beam

赤ちゃんは私を見てにこにこ笑っていた。
The baby was looking at me and beaming.

にっこり笑う to smile broadly

にたにた笑う to grin

わらび 蕨 *bracken*

わり 割 *rate; proportion, ratio* [→ 比率]

1時間500円の割で払いましょう。
I'll pay at the rate of ¥500 an hour.

Aの割に in proportion to A, for A

父は年の割には若く見えます。
My father looks young for his age.

割に relatively, rather [→ 比較的(に) (s.v. 比較)]

ーわり ー割 *(counter for tenths; see Appendix 2)*

生徒の2割がインフルエンザにかかった。
Two tenths of the students have influenza.

わりあい 割合 *1.* [[→ 割]] *rate; proportion, ratio* [→ 比率]

1週間に2冊の割合で本を読んでいます。
I'm reading at the rate of two books a week.

5対3の割合で酢と砂糖を混ぜなさい。
Please mix vinegar and sugar in a pro-

portion of 5 to 3.

2. (～に) relatively, rather [→ 割に]

わりあて 割り当て *allotment, quota*

わりあてる 割り当てる *to assign, to allot, to apportion*

母は私にお皿を洗う役を割り当てました。
My mother assigned the role of washing the dishes to me.

わりかん 割り勘 【COL.】*splitting the cost*

割り勘にする to split the cost of

ピクニックの費用を割り勘にしましょう。
Let's split the picnic expenses.

わりこむ 割り込む *to cut (in line) ; to break (into a conversation)*

列に割り込まないでください。
Please don't cut in line.

わりざん 割り算 *division (in arithmetic)* [↔ 掛け算]

割り算をする *to divide* [→ 割る3.]*; to do division*

わりばし 割り箸 *disposable wooden chopsticks*

(Provided for customers in most restaurants and for guests at a home meal, these chopsticks are wrapped in paper and must be split apart for use.)

わりびき 割引 *discount*

割引する to discount, to give a discount on

—割引 (counter for discounts in steps of 10%; see Appendix 2)

この時計を1割引で買いました。
I bought this watch at a 10 percent discount.

この品は2割引です。
There is a 20 percent discount on this item. (Literally: This item is a 20 percent discount.)

割引券 discount ticket

わる 割る *1. to break into pieces (transitive); to crack open (transitive); to chop, to split*

だれがこのコップを割ったのですか。
Who broke this glass?

卵を割る to crack open an egg

2. to divide (something into parts) [→ 分ける]*; to apportion* [→ 割り当てる]

3. to divide (in arithmetic)

9割る3は3。
Nine divided by three is three.
(Although odd grammatically, this kind of sentence is a typical way of stating a fact of arithmetic.)

わるい 悪い *1. bad* [↔ いい1.]

きょうは天気が悪いですね。
Today the weather is bad, isn't it.

たばこは健康に悪いですよ。
Tobacco is bad for your health!

うそをつくのは悪いことだ。
Telling lies is a bad thing.

2. at fault, to blame

そのときは僕が悪かったのです。
That time I was to blame.

わるぎ 悪気 *malice, ill will*

悪気があって out of malice, with ill will

悪気があってしたわけじゃないよ。
It's not that I did it out of malice.

わるくち 悪口 *bad-mouthing, speaking ill*

Aの悪口を言う to speak ill of A, to bad-mouth A

他人の悪口を言ってはいけない。
You mustn't speak ill of others.

わるぐち 悪口[☞ 悪口]

ワルツ *waltz*

ワルツを踊る to dance a waltz

わるもの 悪者 *villain, rascal*

われ 我 *oneself*

我に返る to come to, to regain consciousness

我に返ると私は病室のベッドに寝ていた。

When I came to, I was lying in a hospital bed.

我(われ)を忘(わす)れる to forget oneself

我(われ)を忘(わす)れて読書(どくしょ)にふけっていました。
I was so absorbed in reading that I forgot myself.

われる 割(わ)れる *1. to break into pieces (intransitive); to crack open (intransitive); to split (intransitive)*

その古(ふる)い茶(ちゃ)わんが割(わ)れました。
That old teacup broke.

2. to become divided

われもの 割(わ)れ物(もの) *fragile item*

われわれ 我々(われわれ) *we, us* [→ 私(わたし)たち (s.v. 私(わたし))]

わん 湾(わん) *bay; gulf*

東京湾(とうきょうわん) Tokyo Bay

メキシコ湾(わん) the Gulf of Mexico

わんしょう 腕章(わんしょう) *arm-band (worn as a badge)*

わんぱく 腕白(わんぱく) 【COL.】*naughtiness, brattiness, unruliness (of a child)*

わんぱくな naughty, bratty, mischievous, unruly

腕白坊主(わんぱくぼうず) naughty boy

ワンピース *one-piece dress*

ワンマンショー *one-man show, solo performance*

わんりょく 腕力(わんりょく) *1. arm strength*

腕力(わんりょく)の強(つよ)い人(ひと) person with strong arms

2. force, violence [→ 暴力(ぼうりょく)]

強盗(ごうとう)は腕力(わんりょく)で健(けん)からかばんを奪(うば)いとった。
The thief took the bag away from Ken by force!

わんわん *1. bow-wow, woof-woof*

その犬(いぬ)は私(わたし)に向(む)かってわんわんとほえた。
That dog barked at me.

2. doggie

を *1. (noun-following particle marking the direct object of a clause)*

だれが日本語(にほんご)を勉強(べんきょう)していますか。
Who is studying Japanese?

2. (noun-following particle marking the path of motion)

このバスはトンネルを通(とお)ります。
This bus passes through a tunnel.

Appendices

1. Conjugation

Japanese predicate words can be divided into three types: verb, adjective, and copula. There are, of course, many different verbs and many different adjectives, but there is only one copula. Each predicate word has a variety of different forms, and this set of forms is sometimes called a conjugation. This appendix provides a brief description of the conjugations of each type of predicate word.

1. Regular Verbs

Most Japanese verbs have conjugations that can be classified as one of two traditionally recognized regular types.

a. **Ichidan** Verbs

A verb of the first regular type has an informal nonpast affirmative form (the form listed in dictionaries) that ends in the sequence **-iru** or **-eru**. The verbs 落ちる and 食べる are typical examples, and several forms of each are listed below. Notice that the portions **ochi-** and **tabe-** are common to every form.

ochi-ru	informal nonpast affirmative
ochi-nai	informal nonpast negative
ochi-masu	semi-formal nonpast affirmative
ochi-tai	informal nonpast affirmative desiderative
ochi-ta	informal past affirmative
ochi-tara	**-tara** conditional
ochi-tari	alternative
ochi-te	gerund
ochi-reba	**-ba** conditional
ochi-ro	imperative
ochi-yoo	informal volitional

tabe-ru	informal nonpast affirmative
tabe-nai	informal nonpast negative
tabe-masu	semi-formal nonpast affirmative
tabe-tai	informal nonpast affirmative desiderative
tabe-ta	informal past affirmative
tabe-tara	**-tara** conditional
tabe-tari	alternative
tabe-te	gerund
tabe-reba	**-ba** conditional
tabe-ro	imperative
tabe-yoo	informal volitional

The traditional name **ichidan** 一段 means one-row and comes from the fact that in kana spelling, the same letter occurs before the ending in every form of a given verb (ち in the case of 落ちる and べ in the case of 食べる). In the traditional 10-

column 5-row arrangement of the kana syllabary, the letters for syllables containing the same vowel are in the same row, so the letter before the endings in the forms of an **ichidan** verb represents only one row of the syllabary.

As noted above, the form of an **ichidan** verb that is listed in a dictionary ends in **-iru** or **-eru**. Unless there is an explicit notation to the contrary, any verb listed in this dictionary with final -**iru** or -**eru** is **ichidan** and has a conjugation like 落ちる and 食べる.

b. Godan Verbs
A verb of the second regular type has an informal nonpast affirmative form (the form listed in dictionaries) that ends in one of the following syllables: **-u, -ku, -gu, -su, -tsu, -nu, -bu, -mu, -ru**. The traditional name **godan** 五段 means five-row and comes from the fact that the stem is followed by each of the five vowels in at least one form. Thus, in the kana spelling of the forms of a **godan** verb, at least five different letters occur to represent the final consonant of the stem (if any) and the initial vowel of an ending. In the traditional 10-column 5-row arrangement of the kana syllabary, the letters for syllables containing the same vowel are in the same row, so the relevant letters in the forms of a **godan** verb represent all five rows of the syllabary.

Although all **godan** verbs share certain obvious similarities in their conjugations, it is convenient to describe each of the nine subtypes separately.

i. Final **-u** Subtype
Any verb listed in this dictionary with final **-u** following a vowel has a conjugation like 洗う.

ara-u	informal nonpast affirmative
araw-a-nai	informal nonpast negative
ara-i-masu	semi-formal nonpast affirmative
ara-i-tai	informal nonpast affirmative desiderative
arat-ta	informal past affirmative
arat-tara	**-tara** conditional
arat-tari	alternative
arat-te	gerund
ara-eba	**-ba** conditional
ara-e	imperative
ara-oo	informal volitional

ii. Final **-ku** Subtype
Unless there is an explicit notation to the contrary, any verb listed in this dictionary

with final **-ku** has a conjugation like 歩く.

aruk-u	informal nonpast affirmative
aruk-a-nai	informal nonpast negative
aruk-i-masu	semi-formal nonpast affirmative
aruk-i-tai	informal nonpast affirmative desiderative
aru-i-ta	informal past affirmative
aru-i-tara	**-tara** conditional
aru-i-tari	alternative
aru-i-te	gerund
aruk-eba	**-ba** conditional
aruk-e	imperative
aruk-oo	informal volitional

iii. Final **-gu** Subtype
Any verb listed in this dictionary with final **-gu** has a conjugation like 急ぐ.

isog-u	informal nonpast affirmative
isog-a-nai	informal nonpast negative
isog-i-masu	semi-formal nonpast affirmative
isog-i-tai	informal nonpast affirmative desiderative
iso-i-da	informal past affirmative
iso-i-dara	**-tara** conditional
iso-i-dari	alternative
iso-i-de	gerund
isog-eba	**-ba** conditional
isog-e	imperative
isog-oo	informal volitional

iv. Final **-su** Subtype
Any verb listed in this dictionary with final **-su** has a conjugation like 話す.

hanas-u	informal nonpast affirmative
hanas-a-nai	informal nonpast negative
hanash-i-masu	semi-formal nonpast affirmative
hanash-i-tai	informal nonpast affirmative desiderative
hanash-i-ta	informal past affirmative
hanash-i-tara	**-tara** conditional
hanash-i-tari	alternative
hanash-i-te	gerund
hanas-eba	**-ba** conditional
hanas-e	imperative
hanas-oo	informal volitional

v. Final **-tsu** Subtype
Any verb listed in this dictionary with final **-tsu** has a conjugation like 保(たも)つ.

tamots-u	informal nonpast affirmative
tamot-a-nai	informal nonpast negative
tamoch-i-masu	semi-formal nonpast affirmative
tamoch-i-tai	informal nonpast affirmative desiderative
tamot-ta	informal past affirmative
tamot-tara	**-tara** conditional
tamot-tari	alternative
tamot-te	gerund
tamot-eba	**-ba** conditional
tamot-e	imperative
tamot-oo	informal volitional

vi. Final **-nu** Subtype
The only Japanese verb that ends with **-nu** is 死(し)ぬ.

shin-u	informal nonpast affirmative
shin-a-nai	informal nonpast negative
shin-i-masu	semi-formal nonpast affirmative
shin-i-tai	informal nonpast affirmative desiderative
shin-da	informal past affirmative
shin-dara	**-tara** conditional
shin-dari	alternative
shin-de	gerund
shin-eba	**-ba** conditional
shin-e	imperative
shin-oo	informal volitional

vii. Final **-bu** Subtype
Any verb listed in this dictionary with final **-bu** has a conjugation like 遊(あそ)ぶ.

asob-u	informal nonpast affirmative
asob-a-nai	informal nonpast negative
asob-i-masu	semi-formal nonpast affirmative
asob-i-tai	informal nonpast affirmative desiderative
ason-da	informal past affirmative
ason-dara	**-tara** conditional
ason-dari	alternative
ason-de	gerund
asob-eba	**-ba** conditional
asob-e	imperative
asob-oo	informal volitional

viii. Final **-mu** Subtype

Any verb listed in this dictionary with final **-mu** has a conjugation like 頼む.

tanom-u	informal nonpast affirmative
tanom-a-nai	informal nonpast negative
tanom-i-masu	semi-formal nonpast affirmative
tanom-i-tai	informal nonpast affirmative desiderative
tanon-da	informal past affirmative
tanon-dara	**-tara** conditional
tanon-dari	alternative
tanon-de	gerund
tanom-eba	**-ba** conditional
tanom-e	imperative
tanom-oo	informal volitional

ix. Final **-ru** Subtype

Any verb listed in this dictionary with final **-uru**, or -**oru** has a conjugation like 守る (see below).

Unless there is an explicit notation to the contrary, any verb listed in this dictionary with final **-aru** has a conjugation like 守る (see below).

As noted above in Section 1.a, unless there is an explicit notation to the contrary, any verb listed in this dictionary with final **-iru** or **-eru** is **ichidan.** If a verb ending in **-iru** or **-eru** is **godan** (and therefore has a conjugation like 守る below), its entry in this dictionary contains the notation *{5}* immediately after the ordinary Japanese writing of the entry word. For example, the verb 走る is **godan**, and its entry in this dictionary begins: 走る *{5}*.

mamor-u	informal nonpast affirmative
mamor-a-nai	informal nonpast negative
mamor-i-masu	semi-formal nonpast affirmative
mamor-i-tai	informal nonpast affirmative desiderative
mamot-ta	**-tara** conditional
mamot-tari	alternative
mamot-te	gerund
mamor-eba	**-ba** conditional
mamor-e	imperative
mamor-oo	informal volitional

2. Irregular Verbs

Any verb listed in this dictionary which is neither **ichidan** nor **godan** is marked with the notation *{Irreg.}* to indicate that it is irregular.

a. ある

The verb ある has a conjugation like that of a final **-ru** subtype **godan** verb (see Section 1.b.ix above) in most respects, but the informal negative forms lack the expected initial **ara-** . For example, the informal nonpast negative is **nai** (instead of the expected but nonexistent **ar-a-nai**), the informal past negative is **na-katta** (instead of the expected but nonexistent **ar-a-nakatta**), etc.

b. Irregular Verbs Ending in **-aru**
There are five verbs ending in **-aru** which have conjugations similar to those of final **-ru** subtype **godan** verbs (see Section 1.b.ix above). These five irregular verbs are all honorific or formal in terms of speech level, and each has some forms that deviate from the regular **godan** pattern.

i. くださる, なさる, おっしゃる
These three verbs are all honorific and share the same conjugation pattern. The forms of くださる are given below as illustrations.

kudasar-u	informal nonpast affirmative
kudasar-a-nai	informal nonpast negative
kudasa-i-masu	semi-formal nonpast affirmative
kudasar-i-tai	informal nonpast affirmative desiderative
kudasat-ta	informal past affirmative
kudasat-tara	**-tara** conditional
kudasat-tari	alternative
kudasat-te	gerund
kudasar-eba	**-ba** conditional
kudasa-i	imperative
[not used]	informal volitional

ii. いらっしゃる
This honorific verb has forms parallel to those of the three verbs just above in Section 1.b.i, with additional alternative forms for the informal past affirmative and for the forms that are historically related to the informal past affirmative (i.e., the **-tara** conditional, the alternative, and the gerund).

irasshar-u	informal nonpast affirmative
irasshar-a-nai	informal nonpast negative
irassha-i-masu	semi-formal nonpast affirmative
irasshar-i-tai	informal nonpast affirmative desiderative

irasshat-ta ~ irash-i-ta	informal past affirmative
irasshat-tara ~ irash-i-tara	**-tara** conditional
irasshat-tari ~ irash-i-tari	alternative
irasshat-te ~ irash-i-te	gerund
irasshar-eba	**-ba** conditional
irassha-i	imperative
[not used]	informal volitional

iii. ござる

The formal verb ござる has a conjugation pattern parallel to that of the three verbs above in Section 1.b.i, but ござる is now archaic except in forms with semi-formal endings (i.e., **-masu, -mashita, -masen, -masho**, etc.). The semi-formal nonpast affirmative, for example , is **goza-i-masu**.

c. 行(い)く and 行(ゆ)く

The verb 行(い)く and its somewhat archaic equivalent 行(ゆ)く have a conjugation pattern like that of final **-ku** subtype **godan** verbs (see Section 1.b.ii above) except for the informal past affirmative and the forms that are historically related to the informal past affirmative (i.e., the **-tara** conditional, the alternative, and the gerund). Illustrative forms of 行(い)く and 行(ゆ)く are given below.

ik-u	informal nonpast affirmative
ik-a-nai	informal nonpast negative
ik-i-masu	semi-formal nonpast affirmative
ik-i-tai	informal nonpast affirmative desiderative
it-ta	informal past affirmative
it-tara	**-tara** conditional
it-tari	alternative
it-te	gerund
ik-eba	**-ba** conditional
ik-e	imperative
ik-oo	informal volitional

d. くれる

The verb くれる has a conjugation pattern like that of an **ichidan** verb (see Section 1.a above) except for the imperative form, which is **kure** (instead of the expected but nonexistent **kure-ro**).

e. 来(く)る and する

These two verbs are, for practical purposes, completely irregular. Each has a unique conjugation pattern.

ku-ru	informal nonpast affirmative
ko-nai	informal nonpast negative
ki-masu	semi-formal nonpast affirmative
ki-tai	informal nonpast affirmative desiderative
ki-ta	informal past affirmative
ki-tara	**-tara** conditional
ki-tari	alternative
ki-te	gerund
ku-reba	**-ba** conditional
ko-i	imperative
ko-yoo	informal volitional

su-ru	informal nonpast affirmative
shi-nai	informal nonpast negative
shi-masu	semi-formal nonpast affirmative
shi-tai	informal nonpast affirmative desiderative
shi-ta	informal past affirmative
shi-tara	**-tara** conditional
shi-tari	alternative
shi-te	gerund
su-reba	**-ba** conditional
shi-ro	imperative
shi-yoo	informal volitional

f. Verbs Ending in **-suru**

A number of Japanese verbs can be analyzed as a single element of Chinese origin (written with a single Chinese character) combined into a compound with する. However, there are differences of opinion among native Japanese speakers about the conjugations of these verbs, and an individual speaker's opinion will not be consistent from verb to verb. The verb 罰(ばっ)する is a typical example, and several forms are listed below. The differences of opinion involve the alternative forms for the informal nonpast affirmative and the informal nonpast negative (and other forms based on it). For the informal nonpast affirmative, a speaker may or may not accept the shorter alternative (**bassu** for this verb). For the informal nonpast negative, a speaker may accept one or both of the two alternative forms (**basshinai** and **bassanai** for this verb).

bassu-ru ～ bass-u	informal nonpast affirmative
basshi-nai ～ bass-a-nai	informal nonpast negative
basshi-masu	semi-formal nonpast affirmative
basshi-tai	informal nonpast affirmative desiderative
basshi-ta	informal past affirmative
basshi-tara	**-tara** conditional

basshi-tari	alternative
basshi-te	gerund
bassu-reba	**-ba** conditional
basshi-ro	imperative
basshi-yoo	informal volitional

3. Verb Bases

In this dictionary, the term verb base refers to what precedes the informal nonpast affirmative desiderative ending **-tai**. For example, the base of 食(た)べる (see Section A.1.a above) is 食(た)べ, and the base of 話(はな)す (see Section A.1.b.iv above) is 話(はな)し.

4. Adjectives

Every Japanese adjective has an informal nonpast affirmative form (the form listed in dictionaries) that ends in **-i**.

a. Regular Adjectives
All Japanese adjectives except いい (see Section B.2 below) have the same conjugation pattern. The adjective 高(たか)い is a typical example, and several forms are listed below.

taka-i	informal nonpast affirmative
taka-ku	adverbial
taka-kute	gerund
taka-kereba	**-ba** conditional
taka-katta	informal past affirmative
taka-kattara	**-tara** conditional
taka-kattari	alternative

b. いい
The adjective いい is derived historically from よい, which is still used as a somewhat more formal alternative. The conjugations of the two words differ only in the informal nonpast affirmative form. For all other forms, the regular forms of よい are used. Several forms of いい are listed below to illustrate.

i-i	informal nonpast affirmative
yo-ku	adverbial
yo-kute	gerund
yo-kereba	**-ba** conditional
yo-katta	informal past affirmative
yo-kattara	**-tara** conditional
yo-kattari	alternative

c. Negative Forms

The negative forms of an adjective are made by combining the adverbial form with forms of the separate word ない, and ない itself has the conjugation of an adjective. For example, the informal nonpast negative of 高い is **takaku na-i**, the informal past negative is **takaku na-katta**, etc.

d. Adjective Bases

In this dictionary, the term adjective base refers to what precedes the endings other than the informal nonpast affirmative ending **-i**. For example, the base of 高い (see Section B.1. above) is 高, and the base of いい (see Section B.2 above) is よ.

5. The Copula

a. Affirmative Forms

When a noun or adjectival noun is used as a predicate, it is followed by a form of the copula. The Japanese copula thus has a function analogous to some uses of the English verb *to be*. Several forms of the copula are listed below.

da	informal nonpast affirmative
desu	semi-formal nonpast affirmative
datta	informal past affirmative
deshita	semi-formal past affirmative
dat-tara	**-tara** conditional
dattari	alternative
de	gerund
nara(-ba)	**-ba** conditional
daro	informal tentative
desho	semi-formal tentative

b. Negative Forms

The negative forms of the copula are made by combining the gerund with forms of the separate word ない, usually with the particle は in between. The word ない itself has the conjugation of an adjective. For example the informal nonpast negative of the copula is で（は）ない, the informal past negative is で（は）なかった, etc. In conversation, では typically contracts to じゃ.

2. Numerals, Counters, and Numbers

1. Numerals

A number in Japanese ordinarily consists of a numeral followed by a counter. Two sets of numerals are in use, one native and one borrowed from Chinese. The only native numerals still used in modern Japanese are those denoting 1–10, and with the exception of なな (7) and the variant forms よん (4) and とう (10), they do not occur as independent words. Still other variant forms appear in certain numeral+counter combinations, but the basic native numerals are:

ひと	一	one
ふた	二	two
み	三	three
よ	四	four
いつ	五	five
む	六	six
なな	七	seven
や	八	eight
ここの	九	nine
とう	十	ten

The borrowed numerals can generally occur as independent words. (Those denoting very large quantities—万, 億, 兆—occur only in combinations with another numeral preceding, but these combinations can function as independent words; see below.) They are used independently in activities such as counting to ten or doing arithmetic. A number of variant forms appear in certain numeral+counter combinations, but the basic borrowed numerals are:

いち	一	one
に	二	two
さん	三	three
し	四	four
ご	五	five
ろく	六	six
しち	七	seven
はち	八	eight
く／きゅう	九	nine
じゅう	十	ten
ひゃく	百	hundred
まん	万	ten thousand
おく	億	hundred million
ちょう	兆	trillion

Large numerals are made by combining these elements. Many combinations involving large numerals show variations in a form like those found in numeral+counter combinations. These combinations are listed below.

ひゃく	百	one hundred
にひゃく	二百	two hundred
さんびゃく	三百	three hundred
よんひゃく	四百	four hundred
ごひゃく	五百	five hundred
ろっぴゃく	六百	six hundred
ななひゃく	七百	seven hundred
はっぴゃく	八百	eight hundred
きゅうひゃく	九百	nine hundred
せん／いっせん	千／一千	one thousand
にせん	二千	two thousand
さんぜん	三千	three thousand
よんせん	四千	four thousand
ごせん	五千	five thousand
ろくせん	六千	six thousand
ななせん	七千	seven thousand
はっせん	八千	eight thousand
きゅうせん	九千	nine thousand
いちまん	一万	ten thousand
にまん	二万	twenty thousand
さんまん	三万	thirty thousand
よんまん	四万	forty thousand
ごまん	五万	fifty thousand
ろくまん	六万	sixty thousand
ななまん	七万	seventy thousand
はちまん	八万	eighty thousand
きゅうまん	九万	ninety thousand
じゅうまん	十万	one hundred thousand
ひゃくまん	百万	one million
せんまん／いっせんまん	千万／一千万	ten million
いちおく	一億	one hundred million
いっちょう	一兆	one trillion
ひゃくちょう	百兆	one hundred trillion

2. Counters

When actually counting something rather than using numbers as abstract quantities, numbers consisting of numeral+counter are generally required. Choosing the appropriate counters for different situations is not a simple matter in Japanese. There is a degree of arbitrariness in the conventions for counting certain things with certain counters, and in many cases there is more than one acceptable choice of counter.

When no specific counter is available (or when a specific counter is possible but not chosen), the counter つ is used. This counter combines with native numerals, but if the number is greater than 9, つ does not appear. The variant native form とう is used for 10, and the numerals borrowed from Chinese, with no counter attached, are pressed into service for numbers greater than 10. The numbers in this series are listed below.

ひとつ	一つ	one
ふたつ	二つ	two
みっつ	三つ	three
よっつ	四つ	four
いつつ	五つ	five
むっつ	六つ	six
ななつ	七つ	seven
やっつ	八つ	eight
ここのつ	九つ	nine
とう	十	ten
じゅういち	十一	eleven
じゅうに	十二	twelve
いくつ	幾つ	how many

Years of age can also be counted with this series of numbers, but the special irregular form はたち is used for twenty years old, whereas the regular form にじゅう is used for twenty of anything else counted with this series.

In addition to the problem of choosing appropriate counters, numeral+counter combinations show a surprising variety in their forms. The catalog below contains an entry for each counter listed in the body of this dictionary. The first entry, for アール lists the regular numeral+counter combinations; thereafter only the irregular combinations are provided.

Each catalog entry begins with a counter in its basic form (the form in which it is listed in the body of this dictionary) and a brief indication of the kinds of things it is typically used to count. When a single counter has two clearly distinct uses, each use is numbered.

Each use is marked as cardinal (C), ordinal (O), or both (C/O). A cardinal counter forms cardinal numbers, that is, numbers specifying quantities. For example, the counter ーメートル is cardinal, so the combination 一メートル means **one meter** (not **meter one**). An ordinal counter forms ordinal numbers, that is, numbers naming something at a given position in a series. For example, the counter ー番線(ばんせん) is ordinal, so the combination 一番線(いちばんせん) means **track one** (not **one track**). An example of a counter that can be either cardinal or ordinal is ーページ. The combination

一ページ can mean either **one page** or **page one**. More general ordinal numbers can be formed by adding the suffix 一目 to cardinal numbers. For example, 一ページ目 means **first page** (which may or may not be page one). The prefix 第一 can also combine with many cardinal numbers to form ordinals. For example, 第一歩 means **first step**.

In the first catalog entry, the combinations for 1–10, 100, and 1,000 are given. In addition, this entry provides the word for **how many** (marked with the notation [?]). Thereafter only irregular combinations are listed under each entry.

For counters introduced in Jorden & Noda, the numeral+counter combinations listed in the catalog generally follow the forms given there (Eleanor Harz Jorden & Mari Noda, *Japanese: The Spoken Language*, 3 vols. Yale University Press, 1987–1990.). Otherwise, the combinations generally follow the commentary by Sakurai & Akinaga in the NHK accent and pronunciation dictionary (桜井茂治, 秋永一枝「数詞・助数詞の発音とアクセント」『日本語発音アクセント辞典』日本放送出版協会). In all cases, however, native speakers have been consulted for judgments, and these judgments have served as the final authority. Alternative forms are listed for many combinations, and in real-life situations, forms that do not appear below often occur.

3. Catalog of Counters and Numeral+ Counter Combinations

一アール *ares (C)*
[1] 一アール [2] 二アール [3] 三アール [4] 四アール [5] 五アール [6] 六アール [7] 七／七アール [8] 八アール [9] 九アール [10] 十アール [100] 百アール [1,000] 千アール [?] 何アール

一アンペア *amperes (C)*

一インチ *inches (C)*

一円 *yen (C)*
[4] 四／四円

一日 See 一日 below

一回 *1. times, occurences (C) 2. innings (C/O)*
[1] 一回 [6] 六回 [8] 八回／八回 [10] 十回／十回 [100] 百回

一階(かい) *building stories (C/O)*
[1] 一階(いっかい) [3] 三階(さんかい) [6] 六階(ろっかい) [8] 八階(はっかい)／八階(はちかい) [10] 十階(じゅっかい)／十階(じっかい) [100] 百階(ひゃっかい) [?] 何階(なんがい)

一海里(かいり) *nautical miles (C)*
[6] 六海里(かいり) [8] 八海里(はっかいり)／八海里(はちかいり) [10] 十海里(じゅっかいり)／十海里(じっかいり) [100] 百海里(ひゃっかいり)

一か月(げつ) *months (C)*
[6] 六(ろっ)か月(げつ) [8] 八(はっ)か月(げつ)／八(はち)か月(げつ) [10] 十(じゅっ)か月(げつ)／十(じっ)か月(げつ) [100] 百(ひゃっ)か月(げつ)

一ヵ国(こく) *countries (C)*
[1] 一(いっ)ヵ国(こく) [6] 六(ろっ)ヵ国(こく) [8] 八(はっ)ヵ国(こく)／八(はち)ヵ国(こく) [10] 十(じゅっ)ヵ国(こく)／十(じっ)ヵ国(こく) [100] 百(ひゃっ)ヵ国(こく)

一ヵ国語(こくご) *languages (C)*
[1]一(いっ)ヵ国語(こくご) [6] 六(ろっ)ヵ国語(こくご) [8] 八(はっ)ヵ国語(こくご)／八(はち)ヵ国語(こくご) [10] 十(じゅっ)ヵ国語(こくご)／十(じっ)ヵ国語(こくご)
[100] 百(ひゃっ)ヵ国語(こくご)

一箇所(かしょ) *places (C)*
[1] 一箇所(いっかしょ) [6] 六箇所(ろっかしょ) [8] 八箇所(はっかしょ)／八箇所(はちかしょ) [10] 十箇所(じゅっかしょ)／十箇所(じっかしょ) [100] 百箇所(ひゃっかしょ)

一月(がつ) *months of the calendar* (O)
[1(January)] 一月(いちがつ) [2(February)] 二月(にがつ) [3(March)] 三月(さんがつ) [4(April)] 四月(しがつ)
[5(May)] 五月(ごがつ) [6(June)] 六月(ろくがつ) [7(July)] 七月(しちがつ) [8(August)] 八月(はちがつ) [9(September)] 九月(くがつ)
[10(October)] 十月(じゅうがつ) [11(Novermber)] 十一月(じゅういちがつ) [12(December)] 十二月(じゅうにがつ) [?] 何月(なんがつ)

一株(かぶ) *shares of stock (C)*
[1] 一株(ひとかぶ) [2] 二株(ふたかぶ) [3] 三株(みかぶ)／三株(さんかぶ) [4] 四株(よかぶ)／四株(よんかぶ) [6] 六株(ろっかぶ) [8] 八株(はっかぶ)／八株(はちかぶ)
[10] 十株(じゅっかぶ)／十株(じっかぶ) [100] 百株(ひゃっかぶ)

一カラット *carats (C)*
[10] 十(じゅっ)カラット／十(じっ)カラット [100] 百(ひゃっ)カラット／百(ひゃく)カラット

一カロリー *calories (C)*
[6] 六(ろっ)カロリー／六(ろく)カロリー [10] 十(じゅっ)カロリー／十(じっ)カロリー
[100] 百(ひゃっ)カロリー／百(ひゃく)カロリー

一ガロン *gallons (C)*

一巻(かん) *volumes (in a set of books) (C)*
[6] 六巻(ろっかん) [10] 十巻(じゅっかん)／十巻(じっかん) [100] 百巻(ひゃっかん)

—級(きゅう) *classes, grades, ranks (C/O)*
[1] 一級(いっきゅう) [6] 六級(ろっきゅう) [8] 八級(はっきゅう)／八級(はちきゅう) [10] 十級(じゅっきゅう)／十級(じっきゅう) [100] 百級(ひゃっきゅう)

—行(ぎょう) *lines of text (C)*

—曲(きょく) *musical pieces (C)*
[1] 一曲(いっきょく) [6] 六曲(ろっきょく) [8] 八曲(はっきょく)／八曲(はちきょく) [10] 十曲(じゅっきょく)／十曲(じっきょく) [100] 百曲(ひゃっきょく)

—切れ(き) *slices, cut pieces (C)*
[1] 一切れ(ひときれ) [2] 二切れ(ふたきれ) [3] 三切れ(みきれ)／三切れ(さんきれ) [4] 四切れ(よんきれ)／四切れ(よきれ) [6] 六切れ(ろっきれ)／六切れ(ろくきれ)
[8] 八切れ(はっきれ)／八切れ(はちきれ) [10] 十切れ(じゅっきれ)／十切れ(じっきれ) [100] 百切れ(ひゃっきれ)／百切れ(ひゃくきれ)

—キロ *1. kilograms (C) 2. kilometers (C)*
[6] 六(ろっ)キロ [8] 八(はっ)キロ／八(はち)キロ [10] 十(じゅっ)キロ／十(じっ)キロ [100] 百(ひゃっ)キロ

—キログラム *kilograms (C)*
See キロ above.

—キロメートル *kilometers (C)*
See キロ above.

—キロワット *kilowatts (C)*
[6] 六(ろっ)キロワット [10] 十(じゅっ)キロワット／十(じっ)キロワット [100] 百(ひゃっ)キロワット

—組(くみ) *sets, pairs (C)*
[1] 一組(ひとくみ) [2] 二組(ふたくみ) [3] 三組(さんくみ)／三組(みくみ) [6] 六組(ろっくみ) [8] 八組(はっくみ)／八組(はちくみ) [10] 十組(じゅっくみ)／十組(じっくみ) [100] 百組(ひゃっくみ)

—グラム *grams (C)*

—桁(けた) *digit, figure (in an Arabic numeral) (C)*
[1] 一桁(ひとけた) [2] 二桁(ふたけた)／二桁(にけた) [3] 三桁(みけた)／三桁(さんけた) [4] 四桁(よんけた)／四桁(よけた) [6] 六桁(ろっけた) [8] 八桁(はっけた)／八桁(はちけた)
[10] 十桁(じゅっけた)／十桁(じっけた) [100] 百桁(ひゃっけた)／百桁(ひゃくけた)

—件(けん) *incidents (C)*
[1] 一件(いっけん) [3]三件(さんけん)／三件(さんげん) [6] 六件(ろっけん) [8] 八件(はっけん)／八件(はちけん) [10] 十件(じゅっけん)／十件(じっけん) [100] 百件(ひゃっけん)

—軒(けん) *houses, small buildings (C)*
[1] 一軒(いっけん) [3] 三軒(さんげん)／三軒(さんけん) [6] 六軒(ろっけん) [8] 八軒(はっけん)／八軒(はちけん) [10] 十軒(じゅっけん)／十軒(じっけん) [100] 百軒(ひゃっけん)
[1,000] 千軒(せんげん) [?] 何軒(なんげん)

—個(こ) *objects (especially spherical or cube-shaped) (C)*
[1] 一個(いっこ) [6] 六個(ろっこ) [8] 八個(はっこ) [10] 十個(じゅっこ)／十個(じっこ) [100] 百個(ひゃっこ)

－語(ご) *words (C)*

－号(ごう) *train numbers, magazine issues (O)*

－光年(こうねん) *light years (C)*
[6] 六光年(ろっこうねん)／六光年(ろくこうねん) [10] 十光年(じゅっこうねん)／十光年(じっこうねん) [100] 百光年(ひゃっこうねん)

－歳(さい) *years of age (C)*
[1] 一歳(いっさい) [8] 八歳(はっさい) [10] 十歳(じゅっさい)／十歳(じっさい)

－サイクル *cycles per second (C)*
[8] 八(はっ)サイクル／八(はち)サイクル [10] 十(じゅっ)サイクル／十(じっ)サイクル

－冊(さつ) *books, magazines (C)*
[1] 一冊(いっさつ) [8] 八冊(はっさつ) [10] 十冊(じゅっさつ)／十冊(じっさつ)

－皿(さら) *helpings, courses (of food) (C)*
[1] 一皿(ひとさら) [2] 二皿(ふたさら) [3] 三皿(みさら) [4] 四皿(よんさら)／四皿(よさら) [8] 八皿(はっさら)／八皿(はちさら) [10] 十皿(じゅっさら)／十皿(じっさら)

－時(じ) *hours on the clock, o'clock (O)*
[4] 四時(よじ)

－字(じ) *letters, characters (C)*
[4] 四字(よじ)／四字(よんじ)

－シート *sheets (of stamps, etc.) (C)*
[10] 十(じゅう)シート／十(じっ)シート

－時間(じかん) *hours (C)*
[4] 四時間(よじかん)

－週間(しゅうかん) *weeks (C)*
[1] 一週間(いっしゅうかん) [7] 七週間(ななしゅうかん) [8] 八週間(はっしゅうかん) [10] 十週間(じゅっしゅうかん)／十週間(じっしゅうかん)

－種類(しゅるい) *kinds, sorts, types (C)*
[1] 一種類(いっしゅるい)／一種類(ひとしゅるい) [2] 二種類(にしゅるい)／二種類(ふたしゅるい) [8] 八種類(はっしゅるい)／八種類(はちしゅるい) [10] 十種類(じゅっしゅるい)／十種類(じっしゅるい)

－章(しょう) *book chapters (C)*
[1] 一章(いっしょう) [7] 七章(ななしょう) [8] 八章(はっしょう) [10] 十章(じゅっしょう)／十章(じっしょう)

ー畳(じょう) *tatami mats (traditional unit of measure for room size) (C)*
[4] 四畳(よじょう)／四畳(よんじょう)

ー世紀 *1. centuries (C) 2. centuries of an era (ad unless otherwise specified) (O)*
[1] 一世紀(いっせいき) [8] 八世紀(はっせいき)／八世紀(はちせいき) [10] 十世紀(じゅっせいき)／十世紀(じっせいき)

ーセット *sets (in sports) (C)*
[1] 一(いっ)セット／一(いち)セット [8] 八(はっ)セット／八(はち)セット [10] 十(じゅっ)セット／十(じっ)セット

ー膳(ぜん) *1. pairs of chopsticks (C) 2. bowls of rice (C)*
[7] 七膳(ななぜん)

ーセンチ *centimeters (C)*
[1] 一(いっ)センチ [8] 八(はっ)センチ／八(はち)センチ [10] 十(じゅっ)センチ／十(じっ)センチ

ーセンチメートル *centimeters (C)*
See ーセンチ above.

ーセント *cents (C)*
[1] 一(いっ)セント [8] 八(はっ)セント [10] 十(じゅっ)セント／十(じっ)セント

ー足(そく) *pairs of footwear (C)*
[1] 一足(いっそく) [3] 三足(さんぞく) [8] 八足(はっそく)[10]十足(じゅっそく)／十足(じっそく) [1,000] 千足(せんぞく) [?] 何足(なんぞく)

ーダース *dozens (C)*

ー台(だい) *vehicles, machines (C)*

ー代(だい) *people in succession to a headship (C)*

ー束(たば) *bundles, bunches (C)*
[1] 一束(ひとたば) [2] 二束(ふたたば) [3] 三束(みたば)／三束(さんたば) [8] 八束(はったば)／八束(はちたば) [10] 十束(じゅったば)／十束(じったば)

ー単位(たんい) *units of academic work (C)*
[1] 一単位(いちたんい)／一単位(いったんい) [8] 八単位(はったんい)／八単位(はちたんい) [10] 十単位(じゅったんい)／十単位(じったんい)

ーチャンネル *broadcast channels (C/O)*
[1] 一(いっ)チャンネル [8] 八(はっ)／八(はち)チャンネル [10] 十(じゅっ)チャンネル

ー対(つい) *pairs (C)*
[1] 一対(いっつい) [7] 七対(ななつい) [8] 八対(はっつい) [10] 十対(じゅっつい)／十対(じっつい)

－通(つう) *letters (of correspondence) (C)*
[1] 一通(いっつう) [8] 八通(はっつう) [10] 十通(じゅっつう)／十通(じっつう)

－粒(つぶ) *grains, drops (C)*
[1] 一粒(ひとつぶ) [2] 二粒(ふたつぶ) [3] 三粒(みつぶ)／三粒(さんつぶ) [4] 四粒(よつぶ)／四粒(よんつぶ) [5] 五粒(いつつぶ)／五粒(ごつぶ) [8] 八粒(はっつぶ)／八粒(はちつぶ) [10] 十粒(じゅっつぶ)／十粒(じっつぶ)

－坪(つぼ) *tsubo (units of area of approximately 3.3 m2) (C)*
[1] 一坪(ひとつぼ) [2] 二坪(ふたつぼ) [3] 三坪(みつぼ)／三坪(さんつぼ) [4] 四坪(よつぼ)／四坪(よんつぼ) [5] 五坪(いつつぼ)／五坪(ごつぼ) [7] 七坪(ななつぼ) [8] 八坪(はっつぼ) [10] 十坪(とつぼ)

－点(てん) *1. scored points (C) 2. items (C)*
[1] 一点(いってん) [8] 八点(はってん)／八点(はちてん) [10] 十点(じゅってん)／十点(じってん)

－度(ど) *1. times, occurrences (C) 2. degrees (of temperature or arc) (C)*
[9] 九(きゅう)／九度(くど)

－頭(とう) *large animals (C)*
[1] 一頭(いっとう) [8] 八頭(はっとう)／八頭(はちとう) [10] 十頭(じゅっとう)／十頭(じっとう)

－等(とう) *classes, rankings (O)*
[1] 一等(いっとう) [8] 八等(はっとう)／八等(はちとう) [10] 十等(じゅっとう)／十等(じっとう)

－ドル *dollars (C)*

－トン *(metric) tons (C)*
[1] 一(いっ)トン [8] 八(はっ)トン／八(はち)トン [10] 十(じゅっ)トン／十(じっ)トン

－日(にち) *1. days (C) 2. days of a month (O)*
[1(cardinal)] 一日(ついたち) [1(ordinal)] 一日(いちにち) [2] 二日(ふつか) [3] 三日(みっか) [4] 四日(よっか) [5] 五日(いつか) [6] 六日(むいか) [7] 七日(なのか) [8] 八日(ようか) [9] 九日(ここのか) [10] 十日(とうか) [14] 十四日(じゅうよっか) [20] 二十日(はつか)

－人(にん) *people (C)*
[1] 一人(ひとり) [2] 二人(ふたり) [4] 四人(よにん) [9] 九人(きゅうにん)／九人(くにん)

－人前(にんまえ) *portions of food for people (C)*
[4] 四人前(よにんまえ) [9] 九人前(きゅうにんまえ)／九人前(くにんまえ)

－年(ねん) *1. years (C) 2. years of an era (ad unless otherwise specified) (O)*
[4] 四年(よねん) [9] 九年(きゅうねん)／九年(くねん)

—パーセント *percent (C)*
[1] 一(いち)パーセント／一(いっ)パーセント [6] 六(ろく)パーセント／六(ろっ)パーセント [8] 八(はち)パーセント／八(はっ)パーセント [10] 十(じゅっ)パーセント／十(じっ)パーセント

—杯(はい) *cupfuls, glassfuls, bowlfuls, spoonfuls (C)*
[1] 一杯(いっぱい) [3] 三杯(さんばい) [6] 六杯(ろっぱい) [8] 八杯(はっぱい)／八杯(はちはい) [10]十杯(じゅっぱい)／十杯(じっぱい) [100] 百杯(ひゃっぱい) [1,000] 千杯(せんばい) [?] 何杯(なんばい)

—倍(ばい) *multiples (i.e.,* ***n*** *times as much/many) (C)*

—泊(はく) *nights of a stayover (C)*
[1] 一泊(いっぱく) [3]三泊(さんぱく) [4] 四泊(よんぱく) [6] 六泊(ろっぱく) [8] 八泊(はっぱく)／八泊(はちはく) [10] 十泊(じゅっぱく)／十泊(じっぱく) [?] 何泊(なんぱく)

—箱(はこ) *boxes, boxfuls (C)*
[1] 一箱(ひとはこ) [2] 二箱(ふたはこ) [3] 三箱(みはこ)／三箱(さんぱこ) [6] 六箱(ろっぱこ) [8] 八箱(はちはこ)／八箱(はっぱこ) [10] 十箱(じゅっぱこ)／十箱(じっぱこ) [100] 百箱(ひゃっぱこ) [1,000] 千箱(せんばこ) [?] 何箱(なんばこ)

—番(ばん) *numbers in a series (O)*
[4] 四(よん)／四番(よばん) [9] 九(きゅう)／九番(くばん)

—馬力(ばりき) *horsepower (C)*

—晩(ばん) *nights (C)*
[1] 一晩(ひとばん) [2] 二晩(ふたばん) [3] 三晩(みばん) [4] 四晩(よばん) [?] いく晩(ばん)

— 番地(ばんち) *lot numbers (used in addresses) (O)*
[9] 九(きゅう)／九番地(くばんち)

—番線(ばんせん) *railroad station track numbers (O)*

—匹(ひき) *animals (C)*
[1] 一匹(いっぴき) [3] 三匹(さんびき) [4] 四匹(よんひき)／四匹(しひき) [6] 六匹(ろっぴき)／六匹(ろくひき) [8] 八匹(はっぴき)／八匹(はちひき) [10] 十匹(じゅっぴき)／十匹(じっぴき) [100] 百匹(ひゃっぴき) [1,000] 千匹(せんびき) [?] 何匹(なんびき)

—票(ひょう) *votes (C)*
[1] 一票(いっぴょう) [3] 三票(さんびょう) [6] 六票(ろっぴょう)／六票(ろくひょう) [8] 八票(はっぴょう)／八票(はちひょう) [10] 十票(じゅっぴょう)／十票(じっぴょう) [100] 百票(ひゃっぴょう) [1,000] 千票(せんびょう) [?] 何票(なんびょう)

—秒(びょう) *seconds (C)*

—便(びん) *airline flights (C/O)*

－部(ぶ) *parts (C)*

－部(ぶ) *copies (of documents, books, etc.) (C)*
See －部(ぶ) above.

－フィート *feet (i.e., units of linear measure) (C)*
[10] 十(じゅう)／十(じゅ)／十(じっ)フィート

－分(ふん) *1. minutes (C) 2. minutes past the hour (when telling time) (O)*
[1] 一分(いっぷん) [3] 三分(さんぷん) [4] 四分(よんぷん) [6] 六分(ろっぷん) [8] 八分(はっぷん)／八分(はちふん) [10] 十分(じゅっぷん)／十分(じっぷん) [100] 百分(ひゃっぷん) [?] 何分(なんぷん)

－分(ぶん) *parts, portions (C)*

－平方(へいほう)メートル *square meters (C)*

－ページ *pages (C/O)*
[1] 一(いち)ページ ／一(いっ)ページ [10] 十(じゅっ)ページ／十(じっ)ページ

－ヘクタール *hectares (C)*

－辺(へん) *polygon sides (C)*
[1] 一辺(いっぺん) [3]三辺(さんべん)／三辺(さんへん) [6] 六辺(ろっぺん)／六辺(ろくへん) [8] 八辺(はっぺん)／八辺(はちへん) [10] 十辺(じゅっぺん)／十辺(じっぺん) [100] 百辺(ひゃっぺん) [?] 何辺(なんべん)

－遍(へん) *times, occurrences (C)*
[1] 一遍(いっぺん) [3] 三遍(さんべん) [6] 六遍(ろっぺん)／六遍(ろくへん) [8] 八遍(はっぺん)／八遍(はちへん) [10] 十遍(じゅっぺん)／十遍(じっぺん) [100] 百遍(ひゃっぺん) [?] 何遍(なんべん)

－歩(ほ) *steps, paces (C)*
[1] 一歩(いっぽ) [3] 三歩(さんぽ)／三歩(さんぼ) [4] 四歩(よんぽ) [6] 六歩(ろっぽ) [8] 八歩(はっぽ)／八歩(はちほ) [10] 十歩(じゅっぽ)／十歩(じっぽ) [100] 百歩(ひゃっぽ) [1,000] 千歩(せんぽ) [?] 何歩(なんぽ)

－ボルト *volts (C)*

－本(ほん) *long objects (C)*
[1] 一本(いっぽん) [3] 三本(さんぼん) [6] 六本(ろっぽん) [8] 八本(はっぽん)／八本(はちほん) [10] 十本(じゅっぽん)／十本(じっぽん) [100] 百本(ひゃっぽん) [1,000] 千本(せんぼん) [?] 何本(なんぼん)

－ポンド *pounds (i.e., units of weight) (C)*
[1] 一(いち)ポンド ／一(いっ)ポンド [10] 十(じゅっ)ポンド／十(じっ)ポンド

ーポンド *pounds (i.e., monetary units) (C)*
See ーポンド above.

ー間(ま) *rooms (C)*
[1] 一間(ひとま) [2] 二間(ふたま) [3] 三間(みま) [4] 四間(よんま)／四間(よま)

ー枚(まい) *flat objects (C)*

ーマイル *miles (C)*

ー幕(まく) *acts of a play (C)*
[1] 一幕(ひとまく) [2] 二幕(ふたまく) [3] 三幕(みまく)／三幕(さんまく)

ーミリ *1. millimeters (C) 2. milliliters (C)*

ーミリメートル *millimeters (C)*

ーミリリットル *milliliters (C)*

ー名(めい) *people (C)*

ーメーター *meters (i.e., units of linear measure) (C)*
See ーメートル below.

ーメートル *meters (i.e., units of linear measure) (C)*

ー面(めん) *polyhedron facets (C)*
[4] 四面(よんめん)／四面(しめん) [9] 九面(きゅうめん)／九面(くめん)

ーヤード *yards (i.e., units of linear measure) (C)*

ーラウンド *boxing rounds (C)*

ーリットル *liters (C)*

ー立方(りっぽう)メートル *cubic meters (C)*

ー羽(わ) *birds, rabbits (C)*
[3] 三羽(さんば)／三羽(さんわ) [4]四羽(よんわ)／四羽(よんば)／四羽(しわ) [6] 六羽(ろっぱ)／六羽(ろくわ) [10] 十羽(じゅっぱ)／十羽(じっぱ) [100] 百羽(ひゃくわ) [1,000] 千羽(せんば) [?] 何羽(なんわ)

ーワット *watts (C)*

ー割(わり) *tenths (C)*
[9] 九割(きゅうわり)／九割(くわり)

ー割引(わりびき) *discounts in steps of 10% (C)*

3. Place Names

1. Japanese Prefectures

愛知 (県) Aichi
青森 (県) Aomori
秋田 (県) Akita
石川 (県) Ishikawa
茨城 (県) Ibaragi
岩手 (県) Iwate
愛媛 (県) Ehime
大分 (県) Oita
大阪 (府) Osaka
岡山 (県) Okayama
沖縄 (県) Okinawa

香川 (県) Kagawa
鹿児島 (県) Kagoshima
神奈川 (県) Kanagawa
岐阜 (県) Gifu
京都 (府) Kyoto
熊本 (県) Kumamoto
群馬 (県) Gunma
高知 (県) Kochi

埼玉 (県) Saitama
佐賀 (県) Saga
滋賀 (県) Shiga
静岡 (県) Shizuoka
島根 (県) Shimane

千葉 (県) Chiba

東京 (都) Tokyo
徳島 (県) Tokushima
栃木 (県) Tochigi
鳥取 (県) Tottori
富山 (県) Toyama

長崎 (県) Nagasaki
長野 (県) Nagano
奈良 (県) Nara
新潟 (県) Niigata

兵庫 (県) Hyogo
広島 (県) Hiroshima
福井 (県) Fukui
福岡 (県) Fukuoka
福島 (県) Fukushima
北海道 Hokkaido

三重 (県) Mie
宮城 (県) Miyagi
宮崎 (県) Miyazaki

山形 (県) Yamagata
山口 (県) Yamaguchi
山梨 (県) Yamanashi

和歌山 (県) Wakayama

2. Selected Japanese Cities

青森[あおもり] (市[し]) Aomori
秋田[あきた] (市[し]) Akita
宇都宮[うつのみや] (市[し]) Utsunomiya
浦和[うらわ] (市[し]) Urawa
大分[おおいた] (市[し]) Oita
大阪[おおさか] (市[し]) Osaka
岡山[おかやま] (市[し]) Okayama

鹿児島[かごしま] (市[し]) Kagoshima
金沢[かなざわ] (市[し]) Kanazawa
北九州[きたきゅうしゅう] (市[し]) Kita-Kyushu
岐阜[ぎふ] (市[し]) Gifu
京都[きょうと] (市[し]) Kyoto
熊本[くまもと] (市[し]) Kumamoto
高知[こうち] (市[し]) Kochi
神戸[こうべ] (市[し]) Kobe
甲府[こうふ] (市[し]) Kofu

佐賀[さが] (市[し]) Saga
札幌[さっぽろ] (市[し]) Sapporo
静岡[しずおか] (市[し]) Shizuoka
下関[しものせき] (市[し]) Shimonoseki
仙台[せんだい] (市[し]) Sendai

高松[たかまつ] (市[し]) Takamatsu
千葉[ちば] (市[し]) Chiba
津[つ] (市[し]) Tsu
東京[とうきょう] (都[と]) Tokyo
徳島[とくしま] (市[し]) Tokushima

鳥取[とっとり] (市[し]) Tottori
富山[とやま] (市[し]) Toyama

長崎[ながさき] (市[し]) Nagasaki
長野[ながの] (市[し]) Nagano
名古屋[なごや] (市[し]) Nagoya
那覇[なは] (市[し]) Naha
奈良[なら] (市[し]) Nara
新潟[にいがた] (市[し]) Niigata

函館[はこだて] (市[し]) Hakodate
広島[ひろしま] (市[し]) Hiroshima
福井[ふくい] (市[し]) Fukui
福岡[ふくおか] (市[し]) Fukuoka
福島[ふくしま] (市[し]) Fukushima

前橋[まえばし] (市[し]) Maebashi
松江[まつえ] (市[し]) Matsue
松山[まつやま] (市[し]) Matsuyama
水戸[みと] (市[し]) Mito
宮崎[みやざき] (市[し]) Miyazaki
盛岡[もりおか] (市[し]) Morioka

山形[やまがた] (市[し]) Yamagata
山口[やまぐち] (市[し]) Yamaguchi
横浜[よこはま] (市[し]) Yokohama

和歌山[わかやま] (市[し]) Wakayama

3. Selected Foreign Countries

アイルランド Ireland
アイスランド Iceland
アフガニスタン Afghanistan
アメリカ America
アラブ首長国連邦(しゅちょうこくれんぽう) United Arab Emirates
アルジェリア Algeria
アルゼンチン Argentina
アルバニア Albania
アンゴラ Angola
イエメン Yemen
イギリス Great Britain
イスラエル Israel
イタリア Italy
イラク Iraq
イラン Iran
インド India
インドネシア Indonesia
ウェールズ Wales
ウガンダ Uganda
ウクライナ Ukraine
ウルグアイ Uruguay
英国(えいこく) Great Britain
エクアドル Ecuador
エジプト Egypt
エチオピア Ethiopia
エルサルバドル El Salvador
オーストラリア Australia
オーストリア Austria
オーマン Oman
オランダ Holland
ガーナ Ghana
ガイアナ Guyana
カタール Qatar
カナダ Canada
カメルーン Cameroon
ガンビア Gambia
カンボジア Cambodia
ギニア Guinea
キプロス Cyprus
キューバ Cuba
ギリシャ Greece
グアテマラ Guatemala
クウェート Kuwait
グリーンランド Greenland
グレナダ Grenada
ケニア Kenya
コートジボアール Ivory Coast
コスタリカ Costa Rica
コロンビア Colombia
コンゴ Congo
サウジアラビア Saudi Arabia
ザイール Zaire
ザンビア Zambia
シエラレオネ Sierra Leone
ジャマイカ Jamaica
シリア Syria
シンガポール Singapore
ジンバブエ Zimbabwe
スーダン Sudan
スイス Switzerland
スウェーデン Sweden
スコットランド Scotland
スペイン Spain
スリランカ Sri Lanka
セイシェル Seychelles
赤道(せきどう)ギニア Equatorial Guinea
ソマリア Somalia
ソロモン諸島(しょとう) Solomon Islands
タイ Thailand
大韓民国(だいかんみんこく) (韓国(かんこく))
Republic of Korea (South Korea)
タイワン Taiwan
タヒチ Tahiti
タンザニア Tanzania

チャド Chad
中央アフリカ共和国 Central African Republic
中華人民共和国 (中国) People's Republic of China (China)
チュニジア Tunisia
朝鮮民主主義人民共和国 (北朝鮮) People's Republic of Korea (North Korea)
チリ Chile
デンマーク Denmark
ドイツ Germany
ドミニカ(共和国) Dominican Republic
トリニダード・トバゴ Trinidad and Tobago
トルコ Turkey
ナイジェリア Nigeria
ニカラグア Nicaragua
ニジェール Niger
西サモア Western Samoa
ニューギニア New Guinea
ニュージーランド New Zealand
ネパール Nepal
ノルウェー Norway
バーレーン Bahrain
ハイチ Haiti
パキスタン Pakistan
バチカン the Vatican
パナマ Panama
バハマ the Bahamas
パラグアイ Paraguay
バルバドス Barbados
パレスチナ Palestine
ハンガリー Hungary
バングラデシュ Bangladesh
フィジー Fiji
フィリピン the Philippines
フィンランド Finland
ブラジル Brazil
フランス France
ブルガリア Bulgaria
ブルキナファソ Burkina-Faso
ブルネイ Brunei
ベトナム Vietnam
ベネズエラ Venezuela
ベリーズ Belize
ペルー Peru
ベルギー Belgium
ポーランド Poland
ボツワナ Botswana
ボリビア Bolivia
ポルトガル Portugal
香港 Hong Kong
ホンジュラス Honduras
マーシャル諸島 Marshall Islands
マカオ Macao
マダガスカル Madagascar
マラウィ Malawi
マレーシア Malaysia
マルタ Malta
ミクロネシア Micronesia
南アフリカ South Africa
ミャンマー Myanmar
メキシコ Mexico
モーリシャス Mauritius
モーリタニア Mauritania
蒙古 Mongolia
モザンビーク Mozambique
モナコ Monaco
モルジブ Maldives
モロッコ Morocco
モンゴル Mongolia
ヨルダン Jordan
ラオス Laos
ラトビア Latvia
リトアニア Lithuania
リビア Libya
リヒテンシュタイン Liechtenstein
リベリア Liberia
ルーマニア Rumania
ルクセンブルク Luxembourg
ルワンダ Rwanda
レバノン Lebanon
ロシア Russia

ふりがな和英辞典

1995年3月15日　第1刷発行
2000年1月20日　第5刷発行

編　者　吉田正俊・中村義勝
発行者　野間佐和子
発行所　講談社インターナショナル株式会社
〒112-8652 東京都文京区音羽 1-17-14
電話：03-3944-6493

印刷所　大日本印刷株式会社
製本所　牧製本印刷株式会社

定価はケースに表示してあります。

Printed in Japan
ISBN 4-7700-1983-1